D1271971

Machiavelli
Volume II

GREAT POLITICAL THINKERS

Editors: **John Dunn**

Fellow of King's College and Professor of Political Theory,
University of Cambridge, UK

Ian Harris

Department of Politics, University of Leicester, UK

This important new series presents critical appraisals of great political thinkers from the Greeks to the present day. It focuses on those thinkers who are generally recognized as being central to the development of political thought. The series will be valuable for a clear understanding of the origin and development of political ideas and the role played by the leading thinkers of the past.

1. Plato (two volume set)
2. Aristotle (two volume set)
3. Augustine (two volume set)
4. Aquinas (two volume set)
5. Machiavelli (two volume set)
6. More (two volume set)
7. Grotius (two volume set)
8. Hobbes (three volume set)
9. Locke (two volume set)
10. Hume (two volume set)

Wherever possible, the articles in these volumes have been reproduced as originally published using facsimile reproduction, inclusive of footnotes and pagination to facilitate ease of reference.

For a list of all Edward Elgar published titles visit our site on the World Wide Web at
http://www.e-elgar.co.uk

Machiavelli
Volume II

Edited by

John Dunn

Fellow of King's College and Professor of Political Theory,
University of Cambridge, UK

and

Ian Harris

Department of Politics, University of Leicester, UK

GREAT POLITICAL THINKERS 5

An Elgar Reference Collection
Cheltenham, UK • Lyme, US

Published by
Edward Elgar Publishing Limited
8 Lansdown Place
Cheltenham
Glos GL50 2HU
UK

Edward Elgar Publishing, Inc.
1 Pinnacle Hill Road
Lyme
NH 03768
US

A catalogue record for this book is available from the British Library

Library of Congress Cataloguing in Publication Data
Machiavelli / edited by J.M. Dunn and Ian Harris.
        (Great Political Thinkers ; 5) (An Elgar reference
collection)
      Includes bibliographical references.
      1. Machiavelli, Niccolò, 1469–1527—Contributions in political
science. I. Dunn, John, 1940–   . II. Harris, Ian. III. Series.
IV. Series: An Elgar reference collection.
JC143.M4M315   1997
320.1—dc21   97–8552
                                                                          CIP

Printed and bound in Great Britain by Bookcraft (Bath) Ltd

ISBN 1 85898 101 8 (two volume set)
      1 85898 096 8 (10 title set)

Contents

Acknowledgements

The editors and publishers wish to thank the authors and the following publishers who have kindly given permission for the use of copyright material.

American Political Science Association for article: Harvey C. Mansfield, Jr (1983), 'On the Impersonality of the Modern State: A Comment on Machiavelli's Use of *Stato*', *American Political Science Review*, **77** (4), December, 849–57.

Cambridge University Press for excerpt: Quentin Skinner (1989), 'The State', in Terence Ball, James Farr and Russell L. Hanson (eds), *Political Innovation and Conceptual Change*, Chapter 5, 90–131; Nicolai Rubinstein (1990), 'Machiavelli and Florentine Republican Experience', in Gisela Bock, Quentin Skinner and Maurizio Viroli (eds), *Machiavelli and Republicanism*, Chapter 1, 3–16.

Canadian Journal of Political and Social Theory for article: J.G.A. Pocock (1978), 'Machiavelli and Guicciardini: Ancients and Moderns', *Canadian Journal of Political and Social Theory*, **2** (3), Autumn, 93–109.

Curtis Brown Ltd and Viking Penguin, a division of Penguin Books USA, Inc. for excerpt: Isaiah Berlin (1979), 'The Originality of Machiavelli', *Against the Current: Essays in the History of Ideas*, 25–79.

Duke University Press for articles: Victoria Kahn (1988), 'Reduction and the Praise of Disunion in Machiavelli's *Discourses*', *Journal of Medieval and Renaissance Studies*, **18**, 1–19; Hans Baron (1991), 'The *Principe* and the Puzzle of the Date of Chapter 26', *Journal of Medieval and Renaissance Studies*, **21**, 83–102; Patricia J. Osmond (1993), 'Sallust and Machiavelli: From Civic Humanism to Political Prudence', *Journal of Medieval and Renaissance Studies*, **23**, 407–38.

J.H. Hexter for his own article: (1964), 'The Loom of Language and the Fabric of Imperatives: The Case of *Il Principe* and *Utopia*', *American Historical Review*, **LXIX** (4), July, 945–68.

Johns Hopkins University Press for excerpt: Marcia L. Colish (1993), 'The Idea of Liberty in Machiavelli', in William J. Connell (ed.), *Renaissance Essays*, Volume II, Chapter IX, 180–207.

Longman Group UK Ltd for articles and excerpt: Hans Baron (1961), 'Machiavelli: The Republican Citizen and the Author of "The Prince"', *English Historical Review*, **LXXVI** (299), April, 217–53; J.N. Stephens and H.C. Butters (1982), 'New Light on Machiavelli',

English Historical Review, **XCVII** (382), January, 54–69; Richard Tuck (1990), 'Humanism and Political Thought', in Anthony Goodman and Angus MacKay (eds), *The Impact of Humanism on Western Europe*, Chapter Three, 43–65.

New Left Review for article: Lev Kamenev (1962), 'Preface to Machiavelli', *New Left Review*, **15**, May/June, 39–42.

Northwestern University Press and Editions Gallimard for excerpt: Maurice Merleau-Ponty (1964), 'A Note on Machiavelli', in *Signs*, Chapter 10, 211–23.

Princeton University Press for excerpt: Paul Oskar Kristeller (1980), 'The Moral Thought of Renaissance Humanism', in *Renaissance Thought and the Arts: Collected Essays*, Chapter II, 20–68.

Regents of the University of California and the University of California Press for article: Victoria Kahn (1986), '*Virtù* and the Example of Agathocles in Machiavelli's *Prince*', *Representations*, **13**, Winter, 63–83.

Renaissance Society of America for articles: Caroline Robbins (1961), 'Influence or Coincidence – A Question for Students of Machiavelli?', *Renaissance News*, **XIV** (4), Winter, 243–8; Russell Price (1977), 'The Theme of *Gloria* in Machiavelli', *Renaissance Quarterly*, **XXX**, 588–631.

Routledge for excerpt: J.H. Whitfield (1971), 'Machiavelli's Use of Livy', in T.A. Dorey (ed.), *Livy*, Chapter IV, 73–96.

Sage Publications, Inc. for article: J.G.A. Pocock (1985), 'Machiavelli in the Liberal Cosmos', *Political Theory*, **13** (4), November, 559–74.

Sixteenth Century Journal for article: Marcia L. Colish (1978), 'Cicero's *De Officiis* and Machiavelli's *Prince*', *Sixteenth Century Journal*, **IX** (4), 81–93.

University of Toronto Press, Inc. for excerpts: Thomas Flanagan (1972), 'The Concept of *Fortuna* in Machiavelli', in Anthony Parel (ed.), *The Political Calculus: Essays on Machiavelli's Philosophy*, Chapter 6, 127–56; John Plamenatz (1972), 'In Search of Machiavellian *Virtù*, in Anthony Parel (ed.), *The Political Calculus: Essays on Machiavelli's Philosophy*, Chapter Seven, 157–78.

University of Utah Press for article: Quentin Skinner (1986), 'The Paradoxes of Political Liberty', in Sterling McMurrin (ed.), *The Tanner Lectures on Human Values*, Volume VII, Chapter 1, 227–50.

Westfield Publications in Medieval Studies for excerpt: Alison Brown (1988), 'Savonarola, Machiavelli and Moses: A Changing Model', in Peter Denley and Caroline Elam (eds), *Florence and Italy: Renaissance Studies in Honour of Nicolai Rubinstein*, 57–72.

Every effort has been made to trace all the copyright holders but if any have been inadvertently overlooked the publishers will be pleased to make the necessary arrangement at the first opportunity.

In addition the publishers wish to thank the Library of the London School of Economics and Political Science, the Marshall Library and the University Library, Cambridge University and B & N Microfilm, London, for their assistance in obtaining these articles.

[1]

Machiavelli: the Republican Citizen and the Author of 'The Prince'

FEW subjects exist which humble and caution the historical student so much as does the history of the interpretation of Machiavelli's works. It would be complacent to judge that our understanding has simply been increasing. The truth is that there have been losses as well as gains; as some facets caught the light, others passed into darkness. To Florentines still near to Machiavelli personally, his life and work had seemed to have two faces. According to Giovanni Battista Busini, an anti-Medici republican, writing about the middle of the sixteenth century, Machiavelli 'was a most extraordinary lover of liberty', but wrote the *Prince* to teach Duke Lorenzo de' Medici how to rob the rich of their wealth and the ordinary citizens of their freedom, and later in his life accepted a pension from the head of the Medici family, Pope Clement VII, for writing his *Florentine History*. So here already, in the language of the party passions of Machiavelli's time, appears the puzzle of his later readers: how could the faithful secretary of the Florentine republic, the author of the *Discourses on the First Ten Books of Titus Livy*, also be the author of the *Prince*? [1]

[1] Some of the investigations on which the answer proposed in the present paper relies, were first published in 1956 under the title 'The *Principe* and the Puzzle of the Date of the *Discorsi*', *Bibliothèque d'Humanisme et Renaiss.*, xviii (1956), 405–28. A number of objections were raised by G. Sasso in *Giornale Stor. della Lett. Italiana*, cxxxiv (1957), esp. 500 ff., cxxxv (1958), 251 f., and by J. H. Whitfield, in *Italian Studies*, xiii (1958), esp. 38 ff. Whitfield, subsequently, in *Le Parole e le Idee*, i (1959), 81 ff., indicated strong disagreement with Sasso's arguments while seemingly assenting to the chronology proposed in my paper of 1956. The reader of the present paper who consults those controversies will find that none of the doubts of my critics, even if any were accepted, would destroy the substance of the proposed theory. In restating it here on a much enlarged basis and adding a glimpse of its consequences for the appraisal of Machiavelli, I have considered Sasso's and Whitfield's objections implicitly, making few direct or polemical references. The chief objective of the present paper (read before the American Historical Association in Chicago, 29 Dec. 1959, in a somewhat shorter form) is to concentrate on the vital points. In doing so, I have this time avoided reliance on the studies of the genesis of the *Discourses* by Felix Gilbert ('The Composition and Structure of Machiavelli's *Discorsi*', *Jour. Hist. Ideas*, xiv [1953], 136–56) and J. H. Hexter ('Seyssel, Machiavelli, and Polybius VI: the Mystery of the Missing Translation', *Studies in the Renaissance*, iii [1956], 75–96) which in my article of 1956 were used as platforms from which to start. Since Gilbert's and Hexter's theories have been shown by critics to be not fully demonstrable and partly incorrect, while my own different thesis is independent of the validity of their conclusions and can perfectly stand on its own, I now use Gilbert's discussion only to draw one inference from his observations (see *infra*, p. 237), while keeping entirely aloof from Hexter's argument (see *infra*, p. 248, n. 3).

Until the end of the seventeenth century, the view that Machiavelli had worn two faces developed no further, overshadowed as it was by the deep impression made by the teachings of the *Prince*—to the sixteenth and seventeenth centuries a diabolical guide for princes, prescribing lies, treachery, and cruelty. The use that a few great intellects like Bacon and Bodin made of the *Discourses* did not change the fact that Machiavelli was usually known only as the author of the *Prince*. Awareness that he had also been a Florentine republican citizen became, however, general with the Enlightenment. This was an event of lasting significance, even though the arguments on which the eighteenth century relied are to us unacceptable. It was now reasoned that, since Machiavelli in the *Discourses* shows himself an adherent and great teacher of political freedom, and since he suffered loss of his position and punishment when the Medici rose to power, he cannot have wished to help the same Medici with the advice given in the *Prince*. The *Prince* must have been misunderstood by its readers. Either the pamphlet wished to expose the need for brutal ruthlessness on the part of an absolute prince in order to warn the people against tyrants; or Machiavelli wanted to tempt the Medici on to a career of crimes, foreseeing that this would recoil eventually on the malefactors.

We meet these arguments from the time of the first heralds of the Enlightenment, like Spinoza, to Rousseau and to the late eighteenth century when the introduction to Machiavelli's complete works published in Florence in 1782 stated that these reinterpretations of the author of the *Prince* from the perspective of the republican *Discourses* had dislodged the notion of the diabolical counsellor of despots.[1] Indeed, the author of the *Discourses* had for the first time come into his own. He was not merely celebrated as a virtuous republican by political doctrinaires, but in a writer like Montesquieu one notes that the politico-historical ideas of the *Discourses* were now exerting a genuine influence. From their echo in Montesquieu's *Considérations sur les causes de la grandeur des Romains* one might reconstruct the key-ideas of the *Discourses*. One finds there all the tenets dear to the politico-historical philosopher of the *Discourses*, little modified by the Frenchman of the eighteenth century. For instance: while states must be founded by great individuals, it is the energy of the people, shown in their civic and military devotion to the commonwealth, that maintains them; this energy grows best in small states, and only where there is no feudal inequality between a few great lords and a dependent mass; and the Roman Republic flowered just as long as not only patricians but also plebeians, even at the cost of occasional civil strife, maintained their status in the

---

[1] The passage quoted from Busini is in his *Lettere a Benedetto Varchi* (Florence, 1861), pp. 84-5. For eighteenth century interpretations of Machiavelli, cf. A. Sorrentino, *Storia dell' Antimachiavellismo Europeo* (Naples, 1936), and Ernst Cassirer, *The Myth of the State* (Yale Univ. Press, 1946), pp. 119 ff.

community, and as long as the expanse of the Empire had not become oppressive.[1]

It is strange to think that after so much study and absorption of the ideas of the *Discourses*, the historical notion of Machiavelli could once again be reduced primarily to that of the author of the *Prince*. But this is what occurred at the turn of the eighteenth century. While to Montesquieu the Machiavellian teachings of the *Prince* had continued to be offensive, the tables were turned when about 1800 there arose a more relativistic historical attitude, which was prepared to base judgment on the specific circumstances of a past period. Now the *Prince* began to seem the most intelligible and even the most precious part of Machiavelli's works. This happened first in Germany. From Herder to Hegel, Fichte and Ranke the reasoning ran that the *Prince* was written at a moment when only power and cool 'reason of state' could save Italy from foreign domination; that the key to the work was the impassioned appeal, in the last chapter, for national liberation through the 'new prince'; and that the pamphlet was not intended to lay down rules valid for all ages, but to prescribe poison for the invigoration of a desperately sick body—setting a possible example for the Germany of about 1800, similarly divided into small states, invaded by foreigners, and waiting for a strong unifier. So, at least in Germany, Machiavelli again became the author of principally one book, the *Prince*, although now he was praised instead of cursed for the ruthless teachings given to a saviour-prince.[2] In Italy, the other country still waiting for national unification, there was the same shift of perspective and emphasis. Only here it took a considerably longer time—until the triumph of the *Risorgimento* at the middle of the nineteenth century—before the eighteenth-century inclination to look upon the author of the *Discourses* as a defender of freedom against tyranny finally faded out.[3]

In England, Macaulay protested against interest being exclusively fixed on the *Prince* as early as 1827. Yet his more balanced approach was almost as far removed from the Machiavelli of the eighteenth century as was the narrowing of the focus to the *Prince* in Germany and Italy. Macaulay, too, no longer attempted to detect a secret meaning in the pamphlet. From the perspective of the historical relativism of the new century he realized that the 'Machiavellian' traits stemmed from the conditions of Machiavelli's

---

[1] E. Levi-Malvano, *Montesquieu et Machiavelli* (Paris, 1912), esp. pp. 46, 51 ff., 63 f., 74ff.; F. Meinecke, *Die Entstehung des Historismus* (Munich, 1936), esp. i. 130 ff., 148, 155 f.

[2] A. Elkan, 'Die Entdeckung Machiavellis in Deutschland zu Beginn des 19. Jahrhunderts', *Historische Zeitschrift*, cxix (1919), 427–58; F. Meinecke, *Die Idee der Staatsräson* (Munich, 1924), pp. 445 ff., 460 ff.; in the English trans. by D. Scott, *Machiavellism: The Doctrine of Raison d'État* (Yale Univ. Press, 1957), pp. 357 ff., 369 ff.

[3] C. Curcio, *Machiavelli nel Risorgimento* (Milan, 1953).

age. The same traits, he pointed out, are also present in the *Discourses*, with the one difference that there they are applied not merely to the ambitions of an individual ruler but to the complex interests of a society. In neither work, says Macaulay, do the Machiavellian maxims, though great blemishes in many respects, prevent their author from revealing ' so pure and warm a zeal for the public good ' as is rarely found in political writings. That the goals change—republican freedom in the *Discourses* and independence of the Italian states from the foreigners in the *Prince*—this need not astonish us, given the political situation in Machiavelli's time. ' The fact seems to have been that Machiavelli, despairing of the liberty of Florence, was inclined to support any government which might preserve her independence.'[1]

The discovery and vindication of the national passion of the *Prince* had been the one great innovation in the interpretation of Machiavelli, but Macaulay's penetrating essay points forward to other major changes which were to happen to the memory of Machiavelli during the nineteenth and early twentieth centuries. The ' Machiavellianism ' of his teachings was to be better understood historically, and was soon to be traced in all his works, not only in the *Prince*; Machiavelli's conception of politics and of the relations between politics and ethical values was to be scrutinized without bias. But at the same time there would almost fade away the memory of what had been the strongest impression for eighteenth-century readers: that the *Discourses* were different in spirit from the *Prince* and, as an epitome of the political ideals and experiences in the Italian city-state republics, represented a precious Renaissance legacy in their own right. As the nineteenth century advanced, serious differences in political outlook and conviction between the *Prince* and the *Discourses* were more and more denied. In the light of the nineteenth-century ideal of the nation-state, it seemed most natural that Machiavelli, though brought up and sentimentally remaining a Florentine republican, should decide that national independence and monarchical unification of Italy were the goals of the hour. He was thought to have felt—like the Italian republicans of the early nineteenth century who accepted the final triumph of a unified Italian monarchy, or like the *Nationalliberalen* in Germany who submitted to Bismarck's solution of the German question— that in his own day republican nostalgia had to give way to princely *Realpolitik*. Machiavelli thus appeared as the father of a cool historical and scientific relativism, and in this seemed to lie his greatness and modernity.

The final definition of this presumed relativism came from Friedrich Meinecke when, during the nineteen-twenties, he recast the historical appraisal of the Machiavellian method from the viewpoint

---

[1] Macaulay, *Machiavelli*, in *Works* (London, 1879), esp. v. 48, 75 f.

of *Staatsräson*. According to Machiavelli (so Meinecke argued) all states are founded by the *virtù* of some lonely great individual, while the *virtù* of the citizens develops in the frame of institutions created by the original lawgiver, and after him slowly degenerates until a new lawgiver starts a fresh cycle. Machiavelli, therefore, must have looked upon the principate as a recurrent and indispensable phase in the life of states, and his descriptions of the cycle of forms of government in the *Discourses*, and of the task of the *principe nuovo* in the pamphlet, neatly interlock. 'Though a republican by ideal and inclination', Machiavelli was 'an adherent of monarchy by reason and resignation', and 'consequently the contrast between the monarchical attitude of the *Prince* and the republican inclination of the *Discourses* is merely a specious one (*ist nur scheinbar*)'. 'Only later centuries', Meinecke remarked, 'have evaluated the differences between forms of government in terms of a quarrel between basic truths, almost between *Weltanschauungen*'.[1] In Gerhard Ritter's well known continuation and modification of Meinecke's views, we are told still more pointedly that the once fashionable confrontation 'between the [republican] *Discourses* and the "absolutistic" *Prince* was caused by a wrong question'. 'It is the universally accepted result of all modern Machiavelli research that the *Discourses* and the *Prince* are derived from one uniform conception.' So little did Machiavelli's crucial ideas change, Ritter affirms, 'that one need not hesitate to elucidate the meaning of the *Discourses* through the *Prince* and *vice versa*'.[2]

The sincerity of Machiavelli's call, in the epilogue of the *Prince*, for a deliverer of Italy from foreign domination has remained a matter of debate until today. But most of those who have questioned the genuineness of Machiavelli's national passion in its odd company with the coldest, most 'Machiavellian' teachings in the guide-book for the prince, have been only the more inclined to believe in his personal disengagement and relativism. They have increasingly aimed at an analysis of Machiavelli's thought which fuses the teachings of all his works in a harmonious, static system. Seen through the eyes of the internationally best-known available synthesis of Machiavelli's ideas, the French *Machiavel* by A. Renaudet, Machiavelli worked alternately as *un théoricien de la République*

---

[1] Meinecke, *Idee*, pp. 40 f., 54 (English trans., pp. 32 f., 43); and his 'Einführung' to *Machiavelli: Der Fürst und kleinere Schriften*. Übersetzt von E. Merian-Genast ('Klassiker der Politik', viii; Berlin, 1923), pp. 14 f., 31 f.

[2] G. Ritter, *Die Dämonie der Macht* (6th edn., Munich, 1948), p. 186 (not in the English trans., *The Corrupting Influence of Power*, Hadleigh, 1952) ; 'Machiavelli und der Ursprung des modernen Nationalismus', in Ritter's *Vom sittlichen Problem der Macht* (Bern, 1948), pp. 40 ff., esp., 44, 55 f. ('Machiavelli's basic ideas', Ritter says here, p. 44, 'hardly changed any more after they had been first penned in 1512/13.') An authoritative, widely consulted summary actually composed, like a mosaic, of pieces taken indiscriminately from all writings of Machiavelli is Francesco Ercole's *La Politica di Machiavelli* (Roma, 1926).

and as *un théoricien de la Monarchie*, advancing easily from his work on the *Discourses* to that on the *Prince*, and again back to the *Discourses*; for the essential feature of his work was the creation of a *méthode strictement positive*, one equally applicable to either part of his *science de la politique*.[1] Thus, ever since the early nineteenth century it has been and still is the consensus of the majority of students that the choice between republican liberty and the principate of the Renaissance, whose fierce struggle formed the centre of Florentine and Italian history in Machiavelli's lifetime, was not among the fundamental inspirations and moulding forces of Machiavelli's thought, and must remain of secondary importance in its interpretation. Indeed, with few exceptions, for a century and more the study of Machiavelli's works has been rather narrowly directed to his views on the nature of political action, on the autonomy of politics, and on its conflicts with morality. Even in Italy, which for some decades has already seen the beginnings of a changed approach, today's most influential account of Machiavelli's ideas by a leading literary historian, Luigi Russo, still avers that ' Machiavelli was interested not in monarchy or republic, in liberty or authority, but merely in the technique of politics; he wants to be and always is *lo scienziato . . . dell' arte di governo*. . . . Liberty or authority, republic or principate are the *subject*, but not, in the Kantian sense, the *form* of Machiavelli's thinking '.[2]

It is at this point that the impression becomes inescapable that modern efforts to overcome eighteenth-century partisanship by a cool, objective appraisal of Machiavelli's method have in some respects exchanged one blind spot in our vision for another. When after so much plausible reconstruction of the alleged harmonious relationship between Machiavelli's two major political works we return to a reading of the *Discourses*, we still find ourselves face to face with the undisguised scale of values of a Florentine citizen, who is just as far as eighteenth-century readers had believed him to be from being indifferent to, or merely secondarily interested in, the political and historical role of freedom. Although it is true that the extension of the rules and maxims of the *Prince* to the life

[1] A. Renaudet, *Machiavel* (Paris 1942; Éd. revue et augmentée 1955), pp. 117 f.; cf. also 119 ff., 218 f., 289 ff. A number of other writers have also lately tried to give a more proportionate share to the *Discourses*; but, with the exception of the Swiss group referred to *infra*, p. 228, n. 2, and of G. Sasso in his recent book (see *infra*, p. 230), this has, as with Renaudet, in practice only meant that Machiavelli's ' Machiavellianism ' was to be studied from the *Discourses* as well as from the *Prince*. A striking English example is Harold J. Laski, ' Machiavelli and the Present Time ', *The Danger of Obedience and Other Essays* (New York, 1930), pp. 238–63.

[2] L. Russo, *Machiavelli* (3rd edn., Bari, 1949), p. 214. In the background of all Italian interpretations of this type is Benedetto Croce's influential thesis, propounded since the nineteen-twenties, that Machiavelli's had been the discovery of ' the necessity and autonomy of politics, of politics which are beyond good and evil '. Cf. A. P. D'Entrèves in his introduction (pp. xii f.) to Chabod's *Machiavelli and the Renaissance*, quoted *infra*, p. 229, n. 1.

of republics is one of the basic features of the *Discourses* (these are to deal with both republic and monarchy despite the fact that the republic attracts the major interest), it is a different world of values to which the teaching of 'Machiavellianism' is here applied—a world that often looks as though devised by another author. For instance, in the third book of the *Discourses*, we find in chapters 41–2 a direct reference to the eighteenth chapter of the *Prince* in which the *principe nuovo*, who must know human nature and cannot expect anybody to keep faith, is taught to be himself unfaithful, disguise his true character, and learn to be a master in feigning and dissembling. In the *Discourses*, the subject matter discussed under the chapter heading 'Promises exacted by force should not be kept' is the behaviour of the Roman consul Spurius Posthumius who during the defeat of his troops in the Caudine Forks showed himself ready to accept any condition in order to save the Roman army, but afterwards persuaded the Senate to break the faith and send him as the one responsible for the repudiated treaty back to the enemy in chains. On this occasion the author of the *Discourses* notes that here there was a model case to be remembered by every citizen because, where the common weal is at stake, ' no consideration of justice or injustice, of humanity or cruelty, of what brings praise or infamy should be allowed to prevail, but putting every other thought aside, that action should be taken which might save the *patria* and maintain her liberty '. Outside the area of the ' Machiavellian ' teaching, the author of the *Discourses* boldly upholds the claim, in opposition to some of his favourite ancient writers, that a multitude of citizens, disciplined by good laws, has better judgment than a prince.[1] He thinks that republics are more reliable and grateful than princes and that the major forward strides of nations have been made in republics, as in Athens and Rome after the expulsion of their kings, while princes, in the long run, can only prolong the life of a stagnant society.[2] Once decadence has gone far, as it has in his own time, even the principate will hardly bring salvation because heredity on the throne does not make available the variety of talents required in different emergencies, nor does it produce the long succession of outstanding men needed to reform a degenerate people.[3] Garrett Mattingly has recently said, not without good reasons, that instead

[1] *Disc.* I 58.

[2] *Disc.* I 29, I 58, I 59, II 2. *Cf.* also III 9 : ' A republic has more vitality and enjoys good fortune for a longer time than a principate since, owing to the diversity found amongst its citizens, it is better able than a prince to adapt itself to varying circumstances '. Here, and throughout this paper, quotations in English from the *Discourses* follow as far as possible the translation by Leslie J. Walker, *The Discourses of Niccolò Machiavelli* (translated . . . with an introduction and notes. 2 vols., London and New Haven, 1950). I diverge from Walker's text, substituting a translation of my own, wherever this seems to be desirable for a more exact understanding of Machiavelli's thought or terminology. I am indebted also to Walker's not always exhaustive, but immensely helpful, commentary.

[3] *Disc.* I 11, I 20, III 9.

of closing our eyes to the profound differences between such convictions and the counsels for a despotic ruler in the *Prince*, it would be better to return to the eighteenth-century suspicion that some of the prescriptions in the *Prince* were not meant seriously, but were intended to satirize the life of princes.[1]

It seems to me that clearly definable differences can be found in the very area which is most basic to the thesis of a harmony between the *Prince* and the *Discourses*. The *Discourses* are a complex work. By choosing, in accord with Livy, the history of early republican Rome as an ideal centre, they have, from the first page, one major theme and standard: the moral health and political vigour of a free nation as the ultimate source of power. This standard is so basic to the book that the perspective on the period of the Roman kings as well as that on Caesar and the emperors is at all crucial points drawn from the needs of republican freedom. Yet the practical goal of the book—resuscitation of the wisdom of ancient politics for use in the present—is in the preface defined in the broader sense that everyone, kings as well as republican leaders, generals as well as individual citizens, should be able to find ancient examples to follow. The wisdom thus gained from antiquity suggests that the principles of ‘ Machiavellianism ’ apply to the policies of principates and republics alike and stimulates Machiavelli to provide special advice to all those types of political leaders—at times in evident conflict with the republican groundwork of the book. For instance, in the famous chapter on conspiracies (III 6), we find discussed how conspirators must behave in order to succeed, as well as how princes and other rulers must behave in order to successfully suppress conspirators. At several points the author says that if the reformer of a state, in spite of all that is put forward about the enduring need in monarchies as well as republics of loyal respect for institutions and laws, nevertheless wishes to establish autocratic and tyrannical rule, he must act in ways which, as here described, are virtually identical with those of the pamphlet on the *Prince*. But in the *Discourses* these are digressions, sometimes characterized as such, sometimes splitting up a continuing discussion.[2]

[1] G. Mattingly, ‘ Machiavelli’s *Prince:* Political Science or Political Satire? ’, *The American Scholar*, xxvii (1958), 489 ff.

[2] This is usually not sufficiently realized. I can illustrate this point here only with two examples, which will prove useful again later in our discussion. *Disc.* I 16 and I 17 deal with the difficulties that must be overcome by a newly founded republic replacing a former monarchy; this theme runs through both chapters, starting with a consideration of the regicide Brutus’s condemnation of his own sons to death when these became traitors of the young republic. Within this discussion on ‘ the sons of Brutus ’, we find (from the words ‘ E chi prende a governare una moltitudine o per via di libertà or per via di principato ’) an excursus teaching that neither a new republic nor a new principate can endure unless all political foes are destroyed in the. beginning. Or rather, these ruthless teachings, most similar to those given in the 8th chapter of the *Prince*, are (after the initial statement that every new state, whether principate or republic, ought to heed them) actually applied only to the policy of a new prince.

We may speak of digressions, because the major line of the argument maintains that the founder or restorer of a state will become a political saviour only if he gives vigour to the institutions and laws that are the matrix of a people's political health and ethos; and thus there runs through the *Discourses* a continuous concern about how to prevent the rule of a reformer or ' new prince ' from developing into absolutism and tyranny. While the founders of states with good institutions are praiseworthy (so we read in the first book, chapters 9 and 10), those of tyrannies are reprehensible: this applies in Roman history to Caesar, because he strove, and paved the way, for absolute power. The unique greatness of Romulus, on the other hand, rests on the fact that, in founding the Roman state, he reserved to himself only the command of the army and the right of convoking the Senate. As a consequence, since Rome's constitution (*ordini*) under her kings was to all intents and purposes a *vivere civile e libero* and in no respect an *assoluto e tirannico* regime, there was after the expulsion of her kings no need for any other change but that annual consuls replace the hereditary kings. Relying on the same criterion, the author of the *Discourses* sees in the French monarchy the happiest hereditary kingdom of his time

Thus they have nothing whatever to do with the theme with which chapter I 16 had started: the founding of a *republic*. This is noted by the author himself, who remarks: ' and although this argument does not fit the one discussed before, because we are now going to talk about a prince, whereas we had been talking about a republic [e benché questo discorso sia disforme dal soprascritto, parlando qui d'uno principe e quivi d'una republica], nevertheless I will say a few words about it, so as not to be compelled to return once more to this matter '. After the end of the ' Machiavellian ' intermezzo, the subject of ' the sons of Brutus ' is taken up again (from the words ' Sendo pertanto il popolo romano ancora . . .') and carried to completion.

As for the origin of this excursus, one might recall a somewhat obscure note in the same chapter VIII of the *Prince* which shows so much similarity with chapter 16 of *Disc.* I. In the *Prince*, Machiavelli says that the rise of a private citizen to the position of a prince could be discussed with more particulars ' in a context where one dealt with republics ' (' dove si trattassi delle republiche '). This seems to suggest that Machiavelli at that time had in his desk materials or notes which did not fit the frame of his book on the *Prince* and were put aside for possible later use in connection with republics. They were eventually used in the 16th (perhaps also in the 26th) chapter of *Disc.* I, even though the treatment of the problem in the *Discourses* was so profoundly different that the integration did not succeed too well.

In *Disc.* I 25-7, there is a related discussion, based on the following argument: whoever in a republic (in *uno vivere politico*) wishes to introduce *uno vivere nuovo e libero*, whether in a republican or monarchical form (*o per via di republica o di regno*; for the terminology here used, *cf. infra* p. 226, n. 1), should preserve as many of the preceding institutions and traditions as possible. This discussion of chapter 25 is, in chapter 26, followed by one considering the exact opposite, namely that a ' new prince ' who does not want to keep within the legal limits of a republic or a monarchy, ' but wants to set up an absolute power, also called by writers " tyranny " ' (' vuole fare una potestà assoluta, la quale dagli autori è chiamata tirannide '), ought to act contrarily, namely change everything in the state, tolerate only new creatures dependent on himself, shrinking from no cruelty, but only from indecision and compromise. This alternative discussion is entirely out of tune with the often repeated condemnation in the *Discourses* of any *potestà assoluta*; *cf.* the examples in the next two notes.

The present paper is not the place for an historical appraisal of the complex structure of the *Discourses*, but some conclusions will be drawn *infra*, pp. 248-50.

because the kings (as he believes) had absolute power only in military and financial matters, but were otherwise pledged to observe the laws of the state. The great ability of the French monarchy to regenerate its internal strength is attributed to the right of the *Parlements*, especially the *Parlement* of Paris, not only to take action against princes, but even to condemn the king. To principates as well as republics it is ' equally essential to be regulated by laws. For a prince who knows no other control but his own will is like a madman. . . .' 'Princes should learn that they begin to lose their state the moment they begin to break the laws.' According to the *Art of War*, written soon after the completion of the *Discourses*, well-constituted monarchies ' do not grant absolute rule to their kings except for the command over the army '.[1]

One way of taking the measure of the *Prince*, is to find out whether any similar concern appears in the advice given to the *principe nuovo*. There have been students who think it does; for does not the *Prince*, too, refer to Romulus as a noble example, while considering the establishment of *nuovi ordini* as a principal task of the new ruler, and does it not praise the role of *Parlement* for the French monarchy?[2] The author of the *Prince* does all this; but what in practice are the *ordini* for which, in the *Prince*, Romulus, along with Moses, Cyrus, and Theseus, stands as a patron-saint? The *principe nuovo* is asked to imitate ' the new institutions and forms of government which

[1] *Disc.* I 16, I 58, III 1, III 5 ; *Art of War*, in *Tutte le Opere*, ed. Mazzoni e Casella, p. 272. Machiavelli's constitutional terminology, to which usually little attention is paid, is still waiting for an exact examination. H. De Vries's dissertation, *Essai sur la terminologie constitutionelle chez Machiavel* (' Il Principe '), Univ. d'Amsterdam, 1957, makes only a slight start, and that merely for the *Prince* ; but one may take it for certain that as a rule (Machiavelli is never wholly consistent) *il vivere politico*—almost identical with *una republica*—means what we call a republic, while *il vivere libero, il vivere civile, la vita civile* may be found in monarchies as well as republics. If these terms apply to *un regno*, they mean that there exist laws and institutions preventing the ruler from arrogating *una potestà assoluta* or *tirannide*. *Cf.* the passages from *Disc.* I 25, quoted on the preceding page, as well as Disc. I 26 (If a *principe* in *una città* ' non si volga o per via di regno o di republica alla vita civile '); furthermore I 18 (' . . . E perché il riordinare una città al vivere politico presuppone uno uomo buono '); I 2 (' Perché Romolo e tutti gli altri Re fecero molte e buone leggi, conformi ancora al vivere libero; ma perché il fine loro fu fondare un regno e non una republica, quando quella città rimase libera vi mancavano molte cose che era necessario ordinare in favore della libertà . . .'); I 9 (on the other hand, under the kings, ' gli ordini ' of Rome—as distinct from single laws—had been ' più conformi a uno vivere civile e libero che ad uno assoluto e tirannico ', so that ' quando Roma divenne libera, . . . non fu innovato alcun ordine dello antico, se non che in luogo d'uno Re perpetuo fossero due Consoli annuali '); I 55 (' . . . quelle republiche dove si è mantenuto il vivere politico ed incorrotto, non sopportono che alcuno loro cittadino né sia né viva a uso di gentiluomo ').

[2] This is what J. H. Whitfield maintains in his papers, ' On Machiavelli's use of *Ordini* ', *Italian Studies*, x (1955), 33–9, and ' Machiavelli e il Problema del Principe ', in *I Problemi della Pedagogia*, iv, no. 1 (1958). The same identification is found in the chapter on Machiavelli in R. von Albertini's *Das Florentinische Staatsbewusstsein im Übergang von der Republik zum Prinzipat* (Bern, 1955), where the hope that a *riordinatore* would establish a *vivere politico* and *libero* through ' restoration of the *ordini antichi* ' is said to be the practical programme of the *Prince* and to find a 'theoretische Fundierung' in the *Discourses* (pp. 69 f.).

men [who like those legendary heroes rose to princely power by their *virtù*] have been forced to introduce in order to establish their regime and their security '.[1] Subsequently, the nature of the *ordini* giving 'security' is explained by more ordinary and palpable examples. Hiero, tyrant of Syracuse, after dissolving the old citizen army and creating new troops, changed all alliances of the city and made everything in the state depend only on himself. Other models of founders of new *ordini* are found in Francesco Sforza, the *condottiere* who destroyed the republic in Milan and made himself duke; in Cesare Borgia; and in a modern counterpart to the great malefactor Agathocles of Sicily, the tyrant Oliverotto da Fermo, who rose to power by murdering the leading citizens after he had invited them to a banquet. 'When in this fashion all had died who could offend him, Oliverotto da Fermo strengthened his position with *nuovi ordini civili e militari* ', with the effect that within one year he had established security for his regime.[2] One wonders how anyone, hearing of these *nuovi ordini civili* for the rule of tyrants, can find in them a counterpart in spirit to the *ordini* of the nascent Roman commonwealth for which Romulus is praised in the *Discourses*.

The fact that there is a chapter on the *principatus civilis* in the *Prince* (chap. IX) does not mean that in this context we at last find a parallel to Romulus's *vivere civile e libero*. *Principatus civilis* here means one-man rule established with the consent of the citizens in a former republic, and the chapter presents a discussion not of the harmfulness, but of the suitable moment for the introduction, of absolute rule. There will be trouble (so we read) when a prince in such an environment wishes to advance from an *ordine civile* to *autorità assoluta* and tries to do so at a moment of emergency in order to fortify himself, instead of doing so at a time when every citizen is dependent on the new regime. And what about the reference to the *Parlement* of Paris? The author of the *Discourses* praises the French monarchy for the right of *Parlement* to condemn in its judgments even the king. The author of the *Prince* also praises the existence of 'countless good ordinances' in the kingdom of France, the first of which is the great authority of the *Parlement*. But *libertà e sicurità*, as seen in the *Prince*, are promoted by *Parlement* not for the subjects but for the king. In any kingdom or principate, the great nobles must be restrained, the people befriended and both balanced against each other; so the wise lawgiver of France established *Parlement* as a judge and buffer 'to relieve the king of the dissatisfaction that he might incur among the nobles by favoring the people, and among the people by favoring the nobles '. This was the most prudent measure ever devised, teaching the lesson

[1] *Prince*, chap. VI ('. . . da' nuovi ordini e modi che sono forzati introdurre per fondare lo stato loro e la loro securtà ').

[2] *Ibid.* chap. VI–VIII.

Machiavelli II

' that princes should let the carrying out of unpopular duties devolve on others, and bestow favors themselves '.[1]

The closer the comparison of the two works, the more absurd seems the idea that these should be two harmonious parts of one and the same political philosophy.[2] The author of the *Prince* does not care for restrictions on the ruler in the name of liberty; he does not think of the people as an active force nor of its future, which is the central concern of the author of the *Discourses* in discussing leadership. So the puzzle of the relationship between Machiavelli's two works remains what it has been; and unless we are ready to return to the eighteenth-century suspicion that the *Prince* must hide a different meaning from what it seems to say, there is only one alternative: the conclusion that between the creation of two so deeply divergent views of the political world some crisis or development must have occurred in the author's mind. It appears, therefore, that the tables must again be turned: instead of so many efforts to harmonize Machiavelli's thought, we ought to face the obvious differences and explore whether their secret may, after all, yield to a genetic approach.

It is one of the most interesting features of present Machiavelli scholarship that this logically needed next step has already been

---

[1] *Disc.* II 1 ; *Prince*, chap. XIX.

[2] Perhaps this is being felt by a growing number of students. In addition to Garrett Mattingly (see *supra* p. 224, n. 1), one may refer to J. H. Hexter, whose paper ' *Il principe* and *lo stato* ', *Studies in the Renaissance*, iv (1957), esp. 133 f., has drawn attention to an unnoticed difference in language and terminology between the two works: while the conception of the State as ' a political body transcending the individuals who compose it ' is central to the *Discourses*, it does not exist in the *Prince*; terms that are frequent in the *Discourses*, like *il vivere civile* or *politico*, or like *il bene commune*, have no equivalent in the *Prince*. Again, Ernst Cassirer, in his *The Myth of the State*, pp. 145–8, has spoken of a ' bewildering ' contrast in the political attitude of the two works; but Cassirer's comment, that in Machiavelli's opinion a chance for republican life had existed only in antiquity, but did not exist in his own time, is the old, perilous over-simplification of a much more complicated situation. Among Italian writers, helpful protests against the traditional tendency to harmonize the views of the *Discourses* and the *Prince* have come (besides from Chabod and his school, about whom we shall have more to say presently) from Carmelo Caristia: *cf.* his strongly polemical *Il Pensiero Politico di Niccolò Machiavelli* (2nd edn., Naples, 1951), pp. 57 ff. Similar protests have lately come from a group of Swiss scholars, who gave added significance to the noted difference by proposing that the true and lasting convictions of Machiavelli, the Florentine citizen, must be sought in the republican *Discourses*, his ' life-work ', while the *Prince* had been ' written for a special occasion ' (' Gelegenheitsschriftchen ') and was the ' fruit of a few summer weeks ': *cf.* W. Kaegi, *Historische Meditationen*, i. 107–9; a mere episode thrown in between the writing of the *Discourses*: *cf.* L. v. Muralt, *Machiavellis Staatsgedanke*, pp. 103 f., 162. Essentially the same arguments reappear in A. Renaudet's *Machiavel*, where (pp. 175 f.) we read that, whereas ' les *Discours* . . . expriment la pensée qu'il a véritablement soutenu jusqu'à la mort ', ' le *Prince* . . . ne représente que l'occupation de quelques mois, consacrés à l'étude d'une hypothèse illusoire '. The contrast thus suggested does not stand the test, as we shall soon find out: the ideas of the *Prince* did have an incubation period of many years, and they were not preceded by any of the republican considerations found in the *Discourses*. But whatever the validity of the attempted solutions, the emergence of so many scattered dissents from the long established tendency to minimize or smooth over the apparent rifts in Machiavelli's thought indicates the actuality of the problem.

taken in one school of studies. In Italy, where scholars have always been more inclined than in other countries to pay biographical attention to Machiavelli's relations to his Italian and Florentine environment, Federico Chabod wrote as early as 1926: ' At one time the Machiavelli of *The Prince* was placed in grotesque opposition to the Machiavelli of the *Discourses*. Today . . . critics are too often led to minimize the differences that arise from his varying emotional outlook.' ' Machiavelli was not an abstract theoretician who developed, first in one sense, then in another, a concept that had been completely assimilated from the start; he was a politician and a man of passion, who gradually unfolded and defined his ideas. . . .'[1]

The heart of Chabod's thesis and that of a large Italian school under his leadership is the proposition that the *Discourses* should be used as a biographical document—like a diary that reflects successive changes in a writer's outlook and evaluations. In the first half of the first book, so Chabod argues, we meet a strong republican confidence, the conviction that a vigorous state must be built on collective action by all its citizens; here we find the theory of the healthy effects of the civil strife between patricians and plebeians in ancient Rome, evidence that every class was free and held its own in the Roman state. Going on, however, we encounter some chapters (I 16–18 and 26–7) where the interest in the people, who had been ' the animating spirit' in the previous discussions, is replaced by that in the personal success of a prince. We now read —we have already come upon these passages [2]—that if a ' new prince' should not wish to found a legally ordered state, but should aspire to the kind of *potestà assoluta* called ' tyranny', he must change every institution and authority in his new state, make the former rich, poor, and the former poor, rich, shrinking from no cruelty, because a new tyrant can hope for survival only when every subject, by patronage or out of fear, has become his creature. Chapters like these, according to Chabod, suggest that, while they were being written, the republican confidence of the preceding chapters gave way to the mood in which the *Prince* was composed.

It is possible, thought Chabod, to recognize the cause of this transition. After discussing Rome's foundation and the rise and fall of her civic energies, Machiavelli, when reaching the seventeenth and eighteenth chapters, remembers the conditions of his own day and states that in a phase of full corruption of civic virtue it would be very difficult, perhaps impossible, to ' maintain or restore' any republic. Whoever in such a phase wants to rebuild the state ' must by necessity resort to extraordinary methods, such as the use

---

[1] F. Chabod, *Machiavelli and the Renaissance* (London, 1958), pp. 41, 117; Ital. edn., *Del 'Principe' di Niccolò Machiavelli* (' Biblioteca della *Nuova Rivista Storica* ', no. 8; Milan, 1926), pp. 8 f., 67.

[2] *Supra* p. 225.

of force and an appeal to arms; before he can achieve anything, he must become a prince in the state'. 'And so', Chabod comments, 'we have *The Prince*'; that is, at this point of his experience Machiavelli must have interrupted work on the *Discourses* and set out to write the *Prince*, until, frustrated and disillusioned, he later on returned to the *Discourses*, to complete them in accord with the original character of the work.[1]

One might, perhaps, object to this ingenious construction by saying that Machiavelli in the eighteenth chapter eventually reaches the conclusion that, for many reasons, the founding of such a princely position would be an enterprise of the utmost difficulty, and perhaps impossible; but a recent book from Chabod's school, by Gennaro Sasso, has skilfully shown that the theory can be adapted to this objection: although the scepticism of the eighteenth chapter is not identical with the standpoint of the *Prince*, argues Sasso, it shows the writer in the immediately preceding phase; the chapter allows us a glimpse of the doubt and the despair which caused Machiavelli to excogitate the ruthless means which yet might make it possible for someone not shrinking back from crime to achieve the almost impossible.[2]

Do these speculations suggest more than plausible possibilities? That they were immediately accepted by a large number of Italian students [3] and since then have found ever-widening assent also in other countries [4] had, it seems, several reasons. Above all, here for the first time was an open acknowledgment of the deep difference in spirit between Machiavelli's two works and an effort to discover its cause in a change of the author's experiences and evaluations. This method was bound to appeal to those who were afraid that scholars were losing touch with Machiavelli as a man of politics with changing values and passions, and who could not close their eyes to the actual, shrill dissonances between the two treatises.

Furthermore, how could one question this argument since it seemed to be borne out by some incontestable textual observations. At the beginning of the second chapter of the *Prince*, there is a note saying that the author would omit the discussion of republics in this work 'since on another occasion I have reasoned about them at length'. ('... perchè altra volta ne ragionai a lungo'). We do

---

[1] Chabod, *op. cit.* pp. 21 and 36–41 (Ital. edn., pp. 4–9): 'The Republic yielded place to the Principate; ... the vision of past glory—a vision clouded by nostalgic regret—was replaced by the theoretical prospect of Italy's political recovery'.

[2] G. Sasso, *Niccolò Machiavelli: Storia del suo pensiero politico* (Naples, 1958), pp. 213 ff., 357 ff., esp. 218 f.

[3] Three representative examples: V. Branca, 'Rileggendo il *Principe* e i *Discorsi*', *La Nuova Italia*, viii (1937), 107 f.; G. Prezzolini, *Machiavelli Anticristo* (Rome, 1954), p. 171; R. Ridolfi, *Vita di Niccolò Machiavelli* (Rome, 1954), pp. 223 ff., 254.

[4] According to Felix Gilbert's judgment in *Renaissance News*, xii (1959), 95, 'it will be very difficult to disprove the validity of the analysis by which Sasso shows the close connection of the first eighteen chapters of the *Discorsi* with the *Prince*'.

not know of any other work of Machiavelli's of which it could be said that he had there ' reasoned about republics at length ' but the *Discourses*; [1] and this characterization would be particularly to the point when applied to the introductory part where types of republics are distinguished according to their origin and subsequently Roman liberty is traced from the times of the Roman kings. Since, on the other hand, in later parts of the *Discourses* (in the second and third book) we find three or four cross-references to the *Prince*,[2] we seem to have a situation of mathematical lucidity: whereas the second and third book must have followed the composition of the *Prince*, the first book, or at least its initial portion, must have been older than the *Prince* because it is referred to in the *Prince's* second chapter. And since Chabod could prove that the *Prince*, though not dedicated to Lorenzo di Piero de' Medici before 1515–16, was, as far as we can check its knowledge of the contemporary political scene, written and completed in the autumn of 1513, the outcome appears to be this: after having written a substantial section of the first book of the *Discourses* by the summer of 1513, Machiavelli composed the *Prince* during the autumn and, possibly, the winter, while, soon afterwards or a few years later, he continued the *Discourses*, eventually dedicating them to Cosimo Rucellai who died in 1519.

Most of the adherents of this theory have also been guided by a more profound reflection. The presumed development of Machiavelli seems to crown a widely accepted notion of the political course of Renaissance Italy. By the time of Machiavelli, so the argument runs, the city-state republic born of the Italian commune had been hopelessly outdated by the efficiency of princely absolutism. Is it not natural, and a testimony to Machiavelli's perspicacity, that his way led him from humanistic admiration of the Roman Republic to the insight that, under the conditions of his own age, rational expediency in politics, and perhaps national unification, were to come from the absolutism of princes? Even though Machiavelli's hope that a 'new prince' would restore Italy's national strength was Utopian on the level of practical politics, said Chabod, yet the

---

[1] Therefore the only way to escape from the conclusions which follow is to make the hypothesis that the reference to ' altra volta ' had been aiming at a lost work, one of which no other trace or reference has survived. This is the thesis suggested, though hesitatingly, by Felix Gilbert in 1953, ' The Structure and Composition of Machiavelli's *Discorsi* ', *Jour. Hist. Ideas*, xiv, 150 ff. But this conjecture, daring under all circumstances, could qualify for consideration only if we had information that Machiavelli, before or during 1513, was indeed occupied with the problems discussed in *Disc.* I 1–18. However, the opposite is the case: we can establish with assurance that Machiavelli did not occupy himself with those problems by 1513; see *infra*, p. 243. Furthermore, whatever we shall argue against the possibility of Machiavelli referring in 1513, in the *Prince*, to an *unpublished* fragment of the text of the *Discourses* (see *infra*, p. 241), will implicitly also disprove the assumption of Machiavelli referring to the draft of a hypothetic work unpublished and later lost.

[2] *Disc.* II 1, II 20 (indubitably referring to *Prince* chaps. XII and XIII, not to the *Art of War*), III 19, III 42.

notion that a 'vigorous unitarian policy' was to come from a
government with 'absolute supremacy' represented the quintessence of the political experience of Renaissance Italy. It was
'unique good fortune' that Machiavelli's pamphlet, while Renaissance Italy suffered its tragic break-down, 'epitomized' the results
of the Italian development, handing them down to the age of
absolutism.[1]

Here we see not only the ultimate reason for the long, un-
challenged dominance of the approach ushered in by Chabod's
essay of 1926, but also its vulnerable point: as soon as we begin to
doubt the validity of an historical conception in which the political
thought of the Italian Renaissance appears essentially as a contribution to absolutism, we shall be inclined to question and re-examine
a reconstruction of Machiavelli's development so closely bound to
one specific notion of the Renaissance. We will wonder especially
about the plausibility of two major premises of this theory: whether
the *Discourses*, in spite of the deeply divergent outlook of Machiavelli's two works, can really be thought to envisage the very solutions to some of Machiavelli's basic problems that are spelled out in
the *Prince*; and whether we are indeed allowed to make the assumptions that the *Discourses*, chapter by chapter, originated in the order
in which we have them, and that the author's work, after the 18th
chapter or somewhat later, suffered an interruption of several years.

In order to determine if Machiavelli, when asking in the first
book of the *Discourses* how the political health of a republic might be
restored in a time of decadence, can have had in mind the monarchical solution offered in the *Prince*, we must pay attention to his
subtle reasoning in the 18th chapter of *Discourses I*. There, to be
sure, it is argued that in a period of corruption of the civic spirit
any possible regeneration requires recourse to force and violence;
a potential reformer, therefore, before anything else, would have to
make himself a *principe* in his republic. Yet, the aim of the chapter
is definitely not to present the rise of a usurper prince as a necessary
and saving remedy in any phase of the history of a republic. The
author of the 18th chapter of the *Discourses* is too deeply convinced
that anyone who at such a moment is ready to make himself a prince
will not be the man to act for his people's good. 'It presupposes
a good man', he ponders, 'to reorganize the constitutional life of
a republic; but to have recourse to violence, in order to make
oneself prince in a republic, presupposes a bad man. Hence very
rarely will there be found a good man ready to use bad methods in
order to make himself prince though with a good end in view, nor
yet a bad man who, having become a prince, . . . will use well that
authority which he had acquired by bad means.' This, of course,
is the very consideration never entered into in the pamphlet on the

---

[1] Chabod, *op. cit.* pp. 41, 98 ff., 104 f., 121 ff.

Prince, in which the *principe nuovo* is taught to ' use the beast ' in man whenever it is needed.[1]

For the author of the 18th chapter, the psychological doubt comes on top of the observation (made at the end of chapter 17) that the life of an individual, or of two of them if a ruler should be followed by an equally efficient successor, is too short to effect anything permanent after the *virtù* of a people has become corrupt. So the argument faces in a different direction from that of the replacement of a republic by a *principe nuovo*, and the 18th chapter ends with the counsel that those who in the face of all these almost unsurmountable difficulties ' are called upon to create or maintain a republic ' in a period of corruption, should strengthen the author-itative-monarchical element within the constitution by modifying the existing laws ' in the direction of a regal rather than a demo-cratic order ',[2] so that citizens unrestrained by law might be ' curbed in some measure by an almost regal power ' (' da una podestà quasi [!] regia '). ' To try to restore men to good conduct in any other way ', adds Machiavelli, ' would be either a most cruel or an impossible undertaking.'[3]

This clearly repudiates a programme of salvation through the ruthless actions of a princely usurper in the manner recommended in the *Prince*. Resignation and relativism, but in a sense very

---

[1] '. . . è necessario venire allo straordinario, come è alla violenza cd all'armi, *e diventare innanzi a ogni cosa principe di quella città e poterne disporre a suo modo*. E perché il riordinare una città al vivere politico presuppone uno uomo buono, e il diventare per violenza principe di una republica presuppone uno uomo cattivo, per questo si troverrà che radissime volte accaggia che uno buono, per vie cattive, ancora che il fine suo fusse buono, voglia diventare principe; e che uno reo, divenuto principe, voglia operare bene' (*Disc.* I 18). As for the striking formulation, that the reformer must ' diventare innanzi a ogni cosa *principe*' in his ' città ', in order to be able to ' poterne disporre a suo modo ', it would be quite erroneous to interpret this as meaning that he must destroy the republic and found a *principato*. It hardly means more than that he must make himself a dictator by force, and Machiavelli's problem is precisely whether a dictator who has used force will ever be ready to become a reformer of constitutional life, instead of an absolute prince. According to *Disc.* I 26, anyone who becomes a ' principe d'una città o d'uno stato ' can follow three different paths: he can maintain ' quel principato ' as a ' nuovo principe ' by reversing every particle of the former order of the state, but he can also turn either ' per via di regno ' or ' per via di republica ' ' alla vita civile '. Here the term *principe* is applied to someone who might employ his power for establishing constitutional government in the form of a legally limited monarchy (' regno ') or even a ' republica '. This use of the term must be borne in mind in any explanation of what Machiavelli, in I 18, wished and did not wish to say with the statement that it was necessary to ' diventare innanzi a ogni cosa *principe* di quella città'. For the terminology of *vivere politico* and *vita civile*, *cf. supra* p. 226, n. 1.

[2] This is the meaning of the advice, ' sarebbe necessario ridurla [*i.e.*, una republica] più verso lo stato regio, che verso lo stato popolare '.

[3] 'Da tutte le soprascritte cose nasce la difficultà o impossibilità, che è nelle città corrotte, a mantenervi una republica o a crearvela di nuovo. E quando pure la vi si avesse a creare o a mantenere, sarebbe necessario ridurla più verso lo stato regio che verso lo stato popolare, acciocché quegli uomini i quali dalle leggi per la loro insolenzia non possono essere corretti, fussero da una podestà quasi regia in qualche modo frenati. E a volergli fare per altre vie diventare buoni, sarebbe o crudelissima impresa o al tutto impossibile '. (*Disc.* I 18).

different from what Meinecke and his school have in mind, appears to be the gist of the 17th and 18th chapters: although theoretically a great monarch might rejuvenate a decadent state, given the nature of man one cannot hope for so much, but may learn from history that when things have come to such a pass, institution of a ' quasi-regal power ' within a republic is relatively the best remedy. Nor can there be any doubt that this discussion applies to the conditions of Machiavelli's own age.   In the 17th chapter (with which the 18th is formally interrelated),[1] after pointing out that Rome, when uncorrupted, had remained free after the expulsion of her kings, whereas corrupted Rome could not preserve her liberty after Caesar's murder, Machiavelli defines his understanding of ' corruption ' and ' ineptitude for a free mode of life ' with a view to modern Italy.   The cause of such an ineptitude, chapter 17 suggests, lies in the ' inequality ' produced by feudal conditions, as confirmed by the examples of present-day peoples ('. popoli conosciuti ne' nostri tempi ').   The peoples are those of Milan and Naples; nothing, we are told, could ever introduce a viable republic in countries like these.   There is no mention of Florence here, but a reference points to a later chapter—*Discourses* I 55[2]—where the meaning of this omission becomes clear: the presence of *gentiluomini* (' gentlemen ')—defined as lords who do not work, but ' live in idleness on the revenue derived from their estates ' and own castles and subject people—makes any form of free political life impossible in Lombardy and Naples, throughout the Romagna, and in the Papal State.   However in Tuscany, where feudal lords are only few and far between, Florence, Siena, and Lucca have always been republics, every small country town strives to be free, and here ' a wise man familiar with the ancient forms of civic government should easily be able to introduce a civic way of life '.   But ' so great has been Tuscany's misfortune that up to the present nothing has been attempted by any man with the requisite ability and knowledge '.[3]

[1] Chapter 18 begins : ' Io credo che non sia fuora di proposito, né disforme dal soprascritto discorso [that is, chapter 17] considerare se in una città corrotta si può mantenere lo stato libero, sendovi; o quando e' non vi fusse, se vi si può ordinare.'
[2] The reference does not identify the chapter—' come *in altro luogo* più particularmente si dirà '—but says that at that later point it would be shown that inequality can be changed into equality (the condition of republican freedom) only by such ' extraordinary devices as few would know how to employ, or would be ready to employ '. Precisely this is the object of *Disc.* I 55, where transformation of a country of equality into one of inequality, and *vice versa*, is said to be so difficult that there are ' but few who have had the ability to carry it through, . . . partly because men get terrified and partly owing to the obstacles encountered '; wherefore the fitness for monarchy of Naples, the Papal States, Romagna, and Lombardy, as well as the fitness for republican life of Tuscany and Venice, must be looked upon as practically unchangeable.
[3] ' . . . ma esservi [*i.e.* in Tuscany] tanta equalità.che facilmente da uno uomo prudente, e che delle antiche civiltà avesse cognizione, vi s'introdurebbe uno vivere civile. Ma lo infortunio suo è stato tanto grande che infino a questi tempi non si è abattuta a alcuno uomo che lo abbia possuto o saputo fare.'   It might seem strange at first

Machiavelli, in writing the 17th, 18th, and 55th chapters of the *Discourses*, was focusing, as we can now see, not upon the founder of a new *principatus* in the anarchic region of the Papal State (as envisaged in the *Prince*), but on a lawgiver who would maintain or restore some republican or civil form of life in Tuscany. And indeed, shortly after the completion of the *Discourses*, he proved that he took this contention of the continuing fitness of Tuscany and Florence for republican institutions seriously. When Pope Leo and the Cardinal Medici (later Clement VII) in 1519–20 asked a number of Florentine citizens for counsel on Florence's government in the years to come, Machiavelli dared to propose, in his *Discorso delle cose fiorentine dopo la morte di Lorenzo*,[1] the vision of the first book of the *Discourses*. He then again argued, and this time as practical political advice, that, since Florentine society was free of *gentiluomini*, the only workable and far-seeing plan was to rebuild the Florentine constitution under the overlordship of those two high-placed members of the Medici family in such a way that after their deaths the Florentine republic would be able to resume her normal functions. And so the gulf between the philosopher of *uno vivere politico e civile* in the *Discourses*, and the analyst and advocate of absolute rule in the *Prince*, remains as wide as ever—too wide to admit the bridge between Machiavelli's two works so ingeniously constructed by Chabod and his school.[2]

sight to read that ' uno uomo prudente ' should introduce, in Tuscany, ' uno vivere *civile* ', and not ' uno vivere *politico* ' as one would expect according to Machiavelli's normal usage (see *supra* p. 226, n. 1). This is particularly surprising in view of the fact that the problem, in the same chapter, had been previously stated in the normal fashion, namely that ' repubbliche dove si è mantenuto il vivere politico ed incorrotto ' do not admit ' gentiluomini ', whereas in those Italian regions that have feudal lords ' non è mai surta alcuna republica né alcuno vivere politico; perché tali generazioni di uomini sono al tutto inimici d'ogni civiltà ', and that in order to restrain (' frenare ') such lords ' vi bisogna ordinare . . . maggior forza, la quale è una mano regia che con la potenza assoluta ed eccessiva ponga freno alla eccessiva ambizione e corruttela de' potenti '. Although the phrases ' inimici d'ogni *civiltà* ' and ' delle antiche *civiltà* ' form a connecting link between the terminologies of the two parts of the chapter, the use of ' uno vivere civile ' instead of ' uno vivere politico ' in the application to the conditions of Tuscany remains an inconsistency, but is, perhaps, not impossible to explain. Only a few years later, in his *Discorso* of 1519–20 on the Florentine constitution, Machiavelli was to suggest for Florence for the time being a quasi-monarchical government under Pope Leo X and Cardinal Giulio de' Medici, with so many features of civic participation in the offices and city-councils—*i.e.* a ' vivere civile '—built in, that after the death of Leo and Giulio de' Medici Florence would automatically return to its republican way of life. *Cf.* text *supra*, on this page.

  [1] Called ' Discorso sopra il riformare lo Stato di Firenze ' until R. Ridolfi in his *Vita di Niccolò Machiavelli*, pp. 275, 450 f., adopted the above title from an early manuscript. There, pp. 450 f., also persuasive reasons for the date 1519–20.

  [2] As for Chabod's related argument (see *supra*, p. 229), that in *Disc.* I 16–18 and 26–7 counsel for an absolute prince replaces the usual concern of the *Discourses* for a government built on the *virtù* and active participation of the people in the state, it has been shown (*supra* p. 225) that the pertinent sections of those chapters are deviations from the main argument and lack perfect fusion with the context. The phrases Chabod has in mind, therefore, may have been written and given their place in the text at practically any time; they need not necessarily have been part of the first draft of the chapters in which they occur.

We can show the extreme improbability also of the assumption
that portions of the first book of the *Discourses* may have been
written years ahead of the remainder of the work. Indeed, the
more one tries to visualize the consequences of this hypothesis, the
more one gets caught in a maize of contradictions. Two well
informed contemporaries—Filippo de' Nerli and Jacopo Nardi—
tell us that the *Discourses* were written at the request of the group of
older and younger cultured citizens who met in the Oricellari
Gardens;[1] but Machiavelli can hardly have been a visitor there
before 1515, certainly not in 1513.[2] He himself, in the preface to the
Discourses, thanks Zanobi Buondelmonti and Cosimo Rucellai, two
principal members of that group, precisely ' for having impelled me
to write down what I would never have written of my own accord '.[3]
To be sure, this does not make it inconceivable that a portion of the
work composed for the Oricellari friends had been prepared at an
earlier time. Still, Nerli and Nardi knew nothing of it; so Machiavelli must have made a secret of the fact—if it was a fact—that a
weighty and essential part of his book had lain in his desk for a
number of years. And why, in his preface, did he not thank
Buondelmonti and Rucellai for having roused him to resume and
save an interrupted work, instead of thanking them for the inducement to ' write ' it?

More doubts arise when one realizes that Machiavelli in the
synthetic chapters at the beginning of the *Discourses* displays a
breadth and profoundness in historical vision and a penetration in
the analysis of social forces that, in comparison, makes the mere
interest in governmental action characteristic of the *Prince* look
superficial and less mature. Chabod and other students of his
group have felt this to be puzzling. In advancing from the *Discourses* to the *Prince*, Sasso has commented recently, one does not
observe an expansion of Machiavelli's horizon but rather sees a
process of ' impoverishment ', by which ' the power of historical
comprehension ' found in the *Discourses* is ' reduced ' to ' one
isolated element '—attention paid to power built on indigenous
troops and the ruler's diplomacy. Thus Sasso feels compelled to
speak of the ' lesser profundity of the *Prince* in comparison to the
Discourses '; he says that the *Prince* ' remains without doubt considerably below the far-reaching analyses in the *Discourses* '.[4] Those
who adhere to the sequence: *Discourses-Prince*, account for this
anomalous development by pointing to the need in the practical
guide for princes to focus upon a few concrete and malleable factors.

---

[1] For particulars, I may refer to my discussion of the chronology of the *Discourses*
in *Bib. d' Hum. et Ren.*, xviii, quoted *supra* p. 217, n. 1; *cf.* esp. pp. 420 f.

[2] See *infra*, pp. 239 f., n. 2.

[3] '. . . che mi avete forzato a scrivere quello ch'io mai per me medesimo non arei
scritto '.

[4] Chabod, *op. cit.* pp. 79 f., 86, 96 f.; Sasso, *op. cit.* pp. 119, 223 f., 227, 303.

Still, where else have the changes in the minds of great political and historical thinkers from one major work to another amounted to a process of narrowing of interests and to a loss of profundity?

Even greater puzzles await us. In 1953, Felix Gilbert drew attention to the fact that, while the introductory parts of each of the three books of the *Discourses* have been worked up into a rounded treatise on politics (and into a rounded picture of ancient Rome, one should add), there follow sections in the latter parts of all three books that look like a simple commentary, with each chapter centred on the discussion of one or a few important passages from Livy. Here, the succession of the chapters is not according to the problems with which they deal, but parallels the sequence of the selected passages in Livy's narrative. It would be very hard to think of any other genesis of this unusual arrangement but that Machiavelli originally had worked out comments following Livy's order, and that he subsequently broke down this commentary into three books according to contents, expanding some—especially the introductory—chapters of each book into treatises no longer closely connected with Livy, while the unchanged, or little changed, pieces of the commentary were left together in subsequent portions of each book, often in their original order.

One need not see eye to eye with Gilbert regarding the boundaries between the transformed sections and the chapters still representing the initial commentary (perhaps the individual chapters were modified to different degrees); and one may disagree with him regarding most of his conclusions about the early history and the date of the completion of the *Discourses*. All this will matter little as long as we assume—as obviously we must—that Machiavelli's labours developed from a running commentary to a semi-systematic work. No doubt, he first had to acquire his knowledge of Rome's religion, constitution, military order, and foreign politics through a pedestrian study of Livy's history, before, thus prepared, he could eventually construct the great synthetic pictures at the beginnings of the three books.[1]

If this was the course of Machiavelli's labours, the first eighteen chapters of the *Discourses* cannot possibly belong to an early phase of the work, and least of all can they have been the part of the

---

[1] *Cf.* Gilbert's 'Composition', *ubi supra*, esp. pp. 147 ff. It should be noted, however, that Gilbert did not admit the validity of the above conclusions for the all-important first eighteen chapters, but, instead, proposed what he called a 'speculative' theory, namely that Machiavelli, when breaking down and transforming his Livy commentary into the present three books, used in the composition of *Disc.* I 1–18 a lost work on republics which he had drafted before the composition of the *Prince* and, consequently, several years before the beginning of his labours on the Livy commentary (Gilbert, pp. 150, 152). For the fallacies inherent in this inacceptable hypothesis, *cf. supra* p. 231, n. 1, and *infra* pp. 241, 245. In Gilbert's eyes, therefore, *Disc.* I 1–18, far from representing Machiavelli's thought during a phase subsequent to the *Prince*, shows an 'approach' which—in contrast to the rest of the *Discourses*—'is very similar to that in the *Prince*' (p. 149).

Discourses first written. Therefore, the eighteen chapters could have existed in 1513 only if most of the labour on the *Discourses* had already been done by the autumn of 1513. This, however, would be so fantastic that nothing more has ever been suggested than that at best the first book was composed by the autumn of 1513. But if the *Discourses* started as a running commentary, this cannot have happened.

Are we approaching the point where we can recognize that the thesis of a development of Machiavelli from parts of the *Discourses* to the *Prince* has mocked us by leading us in a wrong direction? It would seem so were it not for the stumbling-block presented by the statement in the second chapter of the *Prince* that the author would not discuss republics, 'since on another occasion I have reasoned about them at length '.[1]   Yet, is this passage really the documentary evidence which it has been supposed to be—definite proof that a part of the *Discourses* existed when the *Prince* was being written?   If we had a manuscript of the *Prince* from the year 1513 and the text contained a cross-reference to a former work dealing with republics, this would, no doubt, be conclusive proof.   But all extant early manuscripts of the *Prince* include the dedication to Lorenzo de' Medici,[2] which for compelling reasons must have been written between the autumn of 1515 and the autumn of 1516, most probably between March and October 1516.[3]   The lack of earlier manuscripts suggests that Machiavelli in 1513 had not allowed his work to be circulated, and so in 1515–16 he was still at liberty to adapt the text to changed conditions.   Chabod's important demonstration that no political experiences or events later than 1513 have left their marks on the text of the *Prince* and that, consequently, from the angle of Machiavelli's development as a political thinker the *Prince* is basically a document of the year 1513,[4] is not identical with the conclusion that nothing was changed in the wording of the text at the time when the preface to Lorenzo was added.   On

---

[1] ' Io lascerò indrieto el ragionare delle republiche, perché altra volta ne ragionai a lungo.   Volterommi solo al principato. . . .'

[2] A. Gerber, *Niccolò Machiavelli: Die Handschriften, Ausgaben und Übersetzungen* . . . (Gotha, 1912), i. 82.

[3] Before 8 Oct., 1516, when Lorenzo was made duke of Urbino, because, as R. Ridolfi, *La Vita*, pp. 439 f., has pointed out conclusively, Machiavelli after that event would have addressed Lorenzo in his preface as 'magnificus' and *Duke*, and not as 'eccellenza'.   As for the *terminus a quo*, Ridolfi argues that Machiavelli could hardly have put so much hope in Lorenzo before Lorenzo's election as Florentine *capitano generale* in Sept. 1515.   While this, too, is convincing as far as it goes, one should also consider the following facts: that Machiavelli's original intention had been to dedicate the *Prince* to Giuliano de' Medici; that this plan cannot have remained secret after his letter to Vettori on 10 Dec., 1513; and that Giuliano died in Mar. 1516.   So most likely the dedication of the *Prince* to Lorenzo was made after Giuliano had died and Lorenzo had taken Giuliano's place as Medicean pretender to a princely position in the Papal State—that is, during or after Mar. 1516.

[4] *Cf.* Chabod's recent statement in *Machiavelli and the Renaissance*, p. 36, with a reference to the observations he had made in a paper in *Archivum Romanicum*, 1927

the contrary, from a textual viewpoint, the *Prince* as handed down
to posterity is a publication of about 1516 in which no *visible* entries
or changes of a later date than 1513 have been found, except for
the preface, but many *invisible* changes may well have been made in
1514, 1515, and 1516. In fact, our greatest critical problem is not
whether, in a publication of the year 1516, we may ascribe a passage
fitting conditions of about 1516 to that very year, but whether in
trying to reconstruct the mind of Machiavelli in 1513 from a text
released about 1516, we do not unwittingly attribute some opinions
or phrasings of the Machiavelli of 1516 to the Machiavelli of 1513.

The cross-reference in the *Prince* to ' another occasion ' is made
on the first page; it virtually belongs to the introductory matter,
following the brief opening definition (chapter I) of ' how many kinds
of principates exist and how they are acquired '. The context does
not become incomplete—it rather becomes more logical—when the
cross-reference is omitted.[1] It would be perfectly possible, therefore, that the author, before sending his book away with an added
dedication, inserted also the note of reference in order to establish
some kind of link with the very different kind of work in which he
had become engaged by 1516. Neither can we exclude the possibility that there still was an opportunity for an insertion as late as
1517 or early in 1518. For after sending off the dedication copy
to Lorenzo, Machiavelli may easily have waited for Lorenzo's
reaction before allowing other copies to be made. By 1517/18 the
Discourses had been finished, but even in the spring or summer
of 1516 work on the *Discourses* was probably far advanced and
Machiavelli's engagement in this task was sufficiently known to
his friends, to permit a vague reference like ' on *another occasion*
[*altra volta*] I have reasoned at length '.[2]

To be sure, all these observations do not give us any *certitude*,

[1] *Cf.* my detailed demonstration in *Bib. d' Hum. et Ren., ubi supra*, pp. 409 f.

[2] I think I was able to demonstrate these facts in the paper just cited, pp. 411-19.
The following three comments should further help to clarify the crucial point that
Machiavelli could very well have joined the Oricellari circle and have finished the major
part of his work on the *Discourses* by the time the *Prince* was dedicated to Lorenzo. In
the first place, the period in which the dedication occurred can almost certainly be
shortened from Oct. 1515—Oct. 1516 to Mar. 1516—Oct. 1516, as pointed out, *supra*
p. 238, n. 3. Secondly, Machiavelli's attendance at the Oricellari meetings early in 1516
is suggested by the conversation described in his *Art of War*. The debate there
presented is supposed to have taken place in the Oricellari Gardens in Machiavelli's
presence (' essendo con alcuni altri nostri amici stato presente ', lib. I, beginning),
and although the setting of a Renaissance dialogue can only in rare cases be used as a
testimony to biographical facts, Machiavelli's *Art of War* seems to be among the
exceptions. The conversation, which according to the preface shows Cosimo Rucellai's
excellence in debate, is identified with an historical event: the visit of the *condottiere*
Fabrizio Colonna to Florence and to Cosimo in the early part of 1516. The book—
written four years later, after Cosimo's death—claims that it is meant to keep Cosimo's
memory fresh among all those who had been eye-witnesses to that event, and to show
his great qualities to others. This does not necessarily mean that a great deal of the
conversation as presented must have had any counterpart in Cosimo's and Colonna's
actual encounter, but it is very unlikely that Machiavelli would have written that he

they only prove the *possibility* that the reference in the *Prince* to the *Discourses* was written between late 1515 and early 1518 (most probably about the middle of 1516), instead of in 1513. But knowledge that the disturbing citation in the *Prince* is chronologically neutral and by itself cannot decide anything about the sequence of Machiavelli's two works, has almost the same effect as would the final identification of the date. For since this passage has long operated like a switch by which the attention of students was automatically turned away from ever examining the possibilities of the *Discourses* having been begun later than 1513, recognition of the *neutrality* of the passage means that, no longer bound by old prejudices, we can make a new start. We now may freely make up our minds as to whether the idea of a meandering journey from the first eighteen chapters (or a larger part) of the first book of the *Discourses* to the *Prince*, and back to the rest of the *Discourses*, preserves any appearance of plausibility once we are at liberty to consider, as an alternative, a natural succession from the one work to the other.

drew upon his own observations in making the event of 1516 a memorial for Cosimo had he not attended the meetings in the Gardens together with the ' altri nostri amici during Colonna's visit. This should allay Ridolfi's doubts (*Vita*, pp. 252, 441) regard' ing Machiavelli's presence in the Gardens before the summer of 1517.

Third and finally, in spite of Sasso's and Whitfield's scepticism, the seven or eight-visible hints to the year 1517 (or possibly 1518) in the text of the *Discourses* do reveal themselves as likely revisions of a text already written. To recognize this, we must remove from our examination three of them that do not really refer to 1517 events. In *Disc.* II 17 and III 27, two earlier events are said to have happened 15 and 24 years ago, which, it is true, takes us to 1517: But this does not mean that the passages in question were written in 1517; it would be quite natural that any notes in the text saying that certain events had happened so and so many years ago were brought up to date during a last revision before dedication and publication. A similar brief correction during that revision, one should think, was due in *Disc.* I 1 where we read that the Mameluk militia in Egypt could have served as a good example until its recent destruction by the Turks early in 1517. In these three cases, no textual analysis can reconstruct with certainty what changes the author actually made during the year 1517. But the remaining five examples testify to rather clumsy, and therefore detectable, insertions in an already finished and coherent text. Twice a somewhat incongruous supplement appears to have been added to an original triad of references, complete without the supplement. (In particular, in I 19 we find a comparison of three kings in Rome, in Israel, and among the Turks, and this comparison becomes complete with the sentence: ' Ma se il figliuolo suo Salì [Selim I], presente signore, fusse stato simile al padre e non all' avolo, quel regno rovinava '. Yet this ' but ' sentence is supplemented by another one with ' but ', appended, one would think, under the fresh impression of Selim's victory over the Mameluks early in 1517: ' Ma . . . rovinava; ma c' si vede costui essere per superare la gloria dell' avolo '. In II 10, on the other hand, we meet a sequence of one example taken from Greek history, one from Roman history, and one that had occurred ' ne' nostri tempi '; but this last is followed by one that happened ' a few days ago ' [' pochi giorni sono '], which is clearly an oddly appended event also from ' ne' nostri tempi '). In the last three phrases indicative of 1517, the references occur in places where they do not fit logically, or where an argument, later continued, is suddenly split up. (This happens in II 17, II 22, and II 24. I believe the results of my detailed analyses in *Bib. d'Hum. et Ren.*, xviii, 415–19, are convincing on this score.) Even the most insistent sceptic could not contend on the basis of five such suspiciously phrased hints at 1517, quite possibly if not probably mere changes in the text, that Machiavelli's work *cannot* in substance have been composed before 1517.

We have already seen that the hypothesis that the initial portion of the *Discourses* was composed a few years ahead of the rest of the work is contradicted by direct and indirect information on its genesis. The contradictions multiply when, with this hypothesis in mind, we examine Machiavelli's literary occupations in 1513 and during the preceding years of his life. Indeed, the further we proceed the more do we run into a whole string of implausibilities. We must consider all of them before we can decide whether or not we may dare to close our eyes to the consequences of the belief in the composition of a part of the *Discourses* in 1513.

In the first place, the very phrasing of the reference to the *Discourses* in the *Prince* would give cause for wonder if it came from the year 1513. Provided that the initial eighteen chapters of the *Discourses* existed in that summer, they would at that moment not have been more than a draft hidden in the author's desk; a draft still far from the state in which a work nearing completion might have been known to his friends or even talked about in public. So if we insist on 1513 as the year of origin, we must be ready to believe that Machiavelli, when telling his readers not that he was to talk about republics elsewhere but that he had sufficiently reasoned about them ' on another occasion ' and need not repeat himself, thought of a discontinued draft in his desk, known only to himself —unknown even to one of his most intimate friends as is apparent from his correspondence with Francesco Vettori.

In December 1513, after completion of the draft of the *Prince*, Machiavelli wrote a letter to Vettori, then Florentine ambassador in Rome, to tell him of his recent labours, their purpose, and their origin. The two friends had been in frequent correspondence about the international political situation during the month of August, but there had been a pause afterwards until late in November when Vettori sent a detailed report on his life during the interval. On 10 December, Machiavelli reciprocated with an equally full account on how he had spent his time since September (' dirvi in questa mia lettera . . . qual sia la vita mia '). He starts with the famous description of his miserable life among rude lumbermen and country people, neighbours on his tiny estate near S. Casciano—a life which is however changed at nightfall when, donning dignified clothes, he retires to his rural study where for four hours each night he forgets the misery of his life while inquiring into the teachings and deeds of the great men of antiquity ' who out of their humanity ' receive him well and answer his inquisitive questions. In those hours of close spiritual intercourse with the ancient writers, he says, ' I completely give myself over to the ancients '. Then he adds: ' And because Dante says that there is no knowledge unless one retains what one has read, I have written down the profit I have gained from this conversation, and composed a little book *De*

Principatibus. . . . If ever any of my trifles can please you, this one should not displease you.' [1]

This is a report on the genesis of the *Prince* and on Machiavelli's life during the pause in his correspondence from September to November 1513. But we would be poor critics if we failed to make this clear and elaborate account throw some light upon a wider area of his occupations. From the report we may learn that the intimate friend who was more interested than any other in Machiavelli's political ideas and writings knew at the time of the composition of the *Prince* nothing of the *Discourses*. For if Vettori had known that Machiavelli had been occupied with a work on republics earlier in the year, Machiavelli could not have told him, in December, of the composition of a work *De Principatibus* without any hint as to what had happened to the preparation of the work on *republics* which Vettori, in that case, must have expected to emerge from Machiavelli's studies, instead of the *Prince*. Moreover, Machiavelli's report excludes by implication the possibility that he had pursued studies of the sort he describes before the autumn. The purpose and the basic mood of his letter is the communication of something new and wonderful that had entered his life during the recent time of silence. If the spiritual communion with the great ancients, which necessarily must have preceded the *Discourses* as well as the *Prince*, had already been going on during the spring or summer and in September or October earlier experience was only renewed, the phrasing and intonation of the letter to Vettori would in all likelihood be very different. As for the autumn, one could hardly be more precise than Machiavelli in saying that ' the little book *De Principatibus* ' was *the*—not *a*—record of his new experience. So the letter leads us much further than to a mere, inconclusive *argumentum ex silentio*; [2] its wording seems explicit enough to tell us that neither the writer nor the recipient of the letter can have known of the preparation of a work on *republics* during the autumn or the earlier part of 1513. We are hardly at liberty to neglect these implications of Machiavelli's own report.

Also, if we were to adhere to the hypothesis of the composition of the first part of the *Discourses* in 1513, we should have to assume that Machiavelli wrote their republican-minded opening in the very phase of his life in which he was most eagerly craving for a career in the service of the Medici. As his letters show, he was (rightly or wrongly) convinced that he had owed his delivery from imprisonment and torture in February to Giuliano de' Medici. After his

---

[1] ' E perché Dante dice che non fa scienza senza ritener lo havere inteso, io ho notato quello di che per la loro conversazione ho fatto capitale, e composto uno opusculo *De principatibus* [the oldest form of the title, also found in manuscripts], dove io mi profondo quanto io posso nelle cogitazioni di questo subietto, disputando che cosa è principato. . . .' For this letter as an historical source, *cf.* also the article just referred to, pp. 424 ff.

[2] As G. Sasso, *Giornale Stor. della Lett. Ital.* cxxxiv (1957), 509, has charged.

dismissal from prison, through several months, we see him besieging all his friends to use their influence in his favour with Giuliano and Cardinal Giovanni de' Medici. In March, he celebrated the cardinal's elevation to the papal see as Leo X with a poem,[1] and in April he sighed, writing to Vettori: if only Leo would use him in some office, in Rome or in the Papal State, if not in Florence. In June he tried 'to think myself into the pope's place' and work out an analysis of Leo's political interests in Italy and in Europe.[2] About five months later, he decided to offer his services to Giuliano by dedicating the *Prince* to him. These anxious efforts clearly suggest Machiavelli's state of mind during the period in which the *Discourses* must have been conceived if started in 1513.[3]

Finally, we would have to believe that the *Discourses* originated not only when Machiavelli's faith in the cause of the Florentine Republic was lowest, but also at a time when, as far as we know, none of the basic ideas of the *Discourses* had yet been prepared. From his letters, political, and historical writings we know about his interests during the years 1498 to 1512.[4] It would be a fair summary to say that these years had seen an uninterrupted exercise in the thought of which the *Prince* was to become an epitome; nowhere do we find the slightest anticipation of the attention paid by the *Discourses* to the forces that moulded the social and constitutional life of the *Respublica Romana* and of other republics. Indeed, students have noted with surprise that Machiavelli in the writings which accompanied the creation of a Florentine militia in 1506, did not yet give any thought to the conditions in the Roman Republic as a model or counterpart.[5] Again, when as late as about the middle of 1512 he worked out the final versions of the *Portraits* (*Ritratti*) of Germany and France[6] and noted, in contrast to conditions

[1] As R. Ridolfi, *Vita*, pp. 210, 431, has demonstrated.
[2] Letters to Vettori of 16 Apr. and 20 June, 1513.
[3] Neither can one overlook the fact that the dominant note in all of Machiavelli's letters from Mar. to June 1513 is the utter personal despair of the writer; I have become useless to my friends, my family, myself, he laments again and again. The puzzle which must be faced by those who believe in the composition of parts of the *Discourses* during those months has been put aptly and honestly by Sasso, *Niccolò Machiavelli*, p. 196: 'It is indeed singular [è veramente singolare] that Machiavelli during the preparation . . . of his *magnum opus* . . . should have been able to express such limitless discouragement in his letters to Vettori and, above all, never hint at the great work in which he was engaged.'
[4] Three excellent and comprehensive analyses allow us to judge this point with great assurance: Federico Chabod, *Niccolò Machiavelli, Parte I: Il segretario fiorentino* (Rome, 1953); Raffaello Ramat, 'Vigilia Machiavellica', *Studi Letterari: Miscellanea in onore di Emilio Santini* (Palermo, 1956), pp. 197-213; Gennaro Sasso, *op. cit.* pp. 7-181. Additional confirmation may now be found in J. R. Hale's *Machiavelli and Renaissance Italy* (London, 1961), pp. 28-140—the first biography of Machiavelli which, after tracing his experiences and writings during his youth, adopts the view that, while the *Prince* originated in 1513, no part of the *Discourses* was written until several years later.
[5] *Cf.* F. Chabod, *Niccolò Machiavelli, Parte I*, pp. 154 f.
[6] For the dates, see Ridolfi, *Vita*, pp. 420 f., and Sasso, *Giornale Stor. della Lett. al.*, cxxxiv (1957), 510.

in the German cities, the exclusion of the feudal nobility from
the Swiss cities, he did not give any indication that he was already
looking upon this sort of civic equality as a decisive element in the
fabric of republican life.[1] And in portraying the French monarchy
and mentioning the *Parlement* of Paris, he showed himself solely
interested in the growing power of the Crown; he failed to give
the slightest hint that he already paid attention to the institutions
which guaranteed the rule of law over the king—the central
point in the portraiture of the French kingdom in the *Discourses*.

Not that Machiavelli at that time was still unfamiliar with at
least some of the ancient sources that were to play so decisive a part
for the historical vision embodied in the *Discourses*. Livy at least
appears to have been his frequent reading since, when he was
seventeen, his father had compiled the index of the first printed
edition of Livy in Florence and a copy, fetched by Niccolò from
the binder, found its place in the family library. But this early
occupation with Livy was no preparation for the views which were
later to make the *Discourses* largely a treatise on republics. In the
several places where Livy's influence is perceptible in Machiavelli's
writings during the years of his secretaryship, the Livian narrative
is used not as a guide to the spirit and to the constitutional fabric of
the *Respublica Romana*, but as a stimulus for themes of Machiavellian
politics that reappear in the *Prince* and in related ' Machiavellian '
chapters of the *Discourses*. The first teaching drawn from Livy's
history is encountered on the occasion of Machiavelli's first legation to France in 1500, when Florence attempted to restrain the
French ally from compromises with Spain. France, in her north-
Italian politics, was to ' follow the procedure of those who in the
past had aimed at the possession of foreign provinces '. The
Roman method had been, ' to humiliate all those who had power,
fondle the subject people, give help to friends, and be wary of
those who strive for equal authority in the same place '.[2] A
warning against half-measures and indecision is also the theme on
the next occasion where Machiavelli's preoccupation with Livy
becomes manifest. After a brief defection of Arezzo in 1502,
Machiavelli's advice in one of his best-known early writings was
that Florence should respond either with deliberately cruel punishment or with such great clemency that she could expect to make
friends. The Romans, he contended, had always judged the

---

[1] Sasso, *Niccolò Machiavelli*, pp. 169 f.

[2] '. . . che questa Maestà doveva . . . seguire l'ordine di coloro che hanno per lo
addrieto volsuto possedere una provincia esterna, che è diminuire e' potenti, vezeggiare
li sudditi, mantenere li amici, e guardarsi de' compagni, cioè da coloro che vogliono in
tale luogo avere equale autorità '. From the letter of 21. XI. 1500, in Machiavelli's
Legazioni, to Cardinal d'Amboise. The same ideas on the treatment of a new province
were later resumed in the *Prince* chap. III.

' middle way' injurious in their dealings with their subjects.[1] After the fall of the Florentine Republic in 1512, Machiavelli again had recourse to Livy when reflecting that the Gonfaloniere, Piero Soderini, honest and well-meaning statesman that he was, after having maintained himself and the republic through many years, perished and ruined his state when he refused—or was unable—to turn to cunning and cruelty in a time of emergency that demanded those qualities from the men in power. For the solution of this typically ' Machiavellian' problem inspiration was sought in Livy's account of how Hannibal and Scipio, the one by cruelty and perfidy, the other by compassion and faithfulness, through many years achieved equal success.[2]

Down to the year 1513, no political or historical viewpoints other than those connected with such ' Machiavellian' problems ever seem to appear. Perhaps one could not expect anything else in view of Machiavelli's occupations and experiences from the day of his entrance into the Florentine chancery to the fall of the republic. With hardly any pause his diplomatic missions had taken him, besides to France and Germany and to the Papal See, to the countless cities and small lords in the almost lawless region of the Romagna and the State of the Church, and back to missions within the Florentine territorial state: suppression of revolts, conflicts with neighbouring Tuscan city-states, difficult negotiations with treacherous mercenary *condottieri*, the institution of a Florentine militia in the territory. Thus he had watched the superior power of the large nation-states and their oppressive impact on weak Italy, as well as the efforts of tyrannical rulers in central Italy to build, by shrewdness, ruthlessness and crime, in a region of constant change, lacking any tradition, a ' new principate', from Alexander VI and his *nepote* Cesare Borgia, to Julius II and his *nepote* Francesco Maria della Rovere, to Leo X and his *nepote* Giuliano de' Medici. At home, he had been in close contact with the problems of Florence's military defence and her difficult rule over often unwilling subjects in her Tuscan territories. In brief, the Florentine secretary had served his republic through fourteen years, to the last shred of his immense devotion, almost without ever stepping, in action or thought, outside the endless stream of power politics.[3]

[1] ' Puossi per questa deliberazione considerare come i Romani nel giudicare di queste loro terre ribellate pensarono che bisognasse o guadagnare la fede loro con i benefizi o trattarli in modo che mai più ne potessero dubitare: e per questo giudicarono dannosa ogni altra via di mezzo che si pigliasse '. ' I Romani pensarono una volta che i popoli ribellati si debbano o beneficare o spegnere e che ogni altra via sia pericolosissima '. From the pamphlet, *Del Modo di trattare i popoli della Valdichiana ribellati*, 1503.
[2] In the letter (so-called *Ghiribizzi scritti in Raugia*) to Piero Soderini, late 1512. The same comparison between Hannibal and Scipio was later resumed in *Disc.* III 21.
[3] That Machiavelli, in additon to being ' second chancellor' of the chancery, also ranked as ' secretary' (the term we have been using throughout this paper) and in this capacity was used outside his chancery office, including as a member of missions to foreign powers, has been shown in N. Rubinstein's ' The Beginnings of Niccolò Machiavelli's Career in the Florentine Chancery ', *Italian Studies*, xi (1956), 76, 78, 85.

Such was the only life Machiavelli had known before the winter of 1512–13, when suddenly he found himself condemned to live in solitude, leisure and penury. The letters of the year 1513 allow us to observe the influence of this change on the state of his mind. For several months, until in the autumn he discovered a new life in his studies of the ancients, his every thought was bent on regaining a place in the world of action, and his attention focused on the news about the rapid changes of the contemporary scene. Gradually, by application of his knowledge of the nature of the power struggle to the events before his eyes, the problems of the *Prince* emerged. As early as April, in discussing with Vettori the annexation of the Duchy of Milan by France or Spain, he talked of the ' ways by which new states are retained '; in mapping an unscrupulous course for the policy of the king of Spain, he remarked that ' good faith and obligations are not taken into consideration today '.[1] But even if the psychological and factual evidence from documents were lacking, it would be fantastic to conjecture that Machiavelli, almost immediately, between March and August, sat down to write a book centred in ideas and built on studies that lacked any contact with the former direction of his life and interests. Yet we would have to make this very assumption, in defiance of all rules of historical plausibility, if we were to cling to the hypothesis of the origin of the *Discourses* in 1513; and we would have to place this assumption on top of all those others, each of them an offence to probability: that Machiavelli, in 1513, in a work intended (according to the letter to Vettori) to be dedicated and therewith published, referred to a discussion which at that time could have existed only in an unfinished and unpublished draft in his desk; that his own report on his reading and writing in 1513 must be deemed gravely inaccurate and misleading; and that he wrote the republican-minded chapters of the first book of the *Discourses* in a time of daily efforts to reconcile himself with the overthrow of the Florentine Republic and win a place in the service of her new rulers. It seems to me that no critical reader will easily be persuaded to acquiesce in such improbable assumptions.

Moreover, we would have to disregard the fact that our examination of the structure and genesis of the *Discourses* has called in question the two major premises underlying the theory that parts

---

[1] ' Et uno de' modi con che li stati nuovi si tengono . . .'; ' . . . et della fede et delli obblighi non si tiene hoggi conto '. We are assured of the date of this letter—29 Apr. 1513—by manuscript findings already known to P. Villari, *Niccolò Machiavelli e i suoi tempi* [2nd edn., Milan 1897], iii. 416, and O. Tommasini, *La vita e gli scritti di Niccolò Machiavelli* (Rome, 1911), II. i. 86. The latter already called the interest shown by the letter in the ' modi ' of preserving ' stati nuovi ' a testimony ' that the substance of the pamphlet on the *Prince* was developing in Machiavelli's mind as early as at that time '. Sasso, *op. cit.* pp. 208–10, fully and interestingly discusses the appearance of basic ideas of the *Prince* early in 1513, but does so without drawing the proper consequences from his observations.

of the *Discourses* originated shortly before the *Prince* was written. As we have seen, it proves impossible to construct bridges between the ideal of a *principe nuovo*, saviour of the state, as pictured in the *Prince*, and the intentions of the 17th and 18th chapters of the *Discourses*; the latter (like Machiavelli's memorandum of 1519-20 on the Florentine constitution) take their orientation from the belief that Tuscany, a country without feudal lords, is suited only for the republican way of life. We have further been forced to conclude that the introductory chapters of the *Discourses* cannot have been composed in the same year as the *Prince* for the reason that they are certain to be the product of a late phase of Machiavelli's work on the *Discourses*. So all indications, without exception, point in one direction; all concur in establishing a very definite, though negative result: no part of the *Discourses* was written as early as 1513.

This, however, is actually all we need for solving the old riddle of the course of Machiavelli's labours. For since the composition of the *Prince* in the autumn of 1513 is a certainty, proof that work on the *Discourses* cannot have started as early as that year amounts to demonstration that the *Discourses* were written later than the *Prince* and, consequently, that the reference to the *Discourses* in the *Prince* was inserted after 1513. If this is a reliable conclusion—and there is no escape from it—the old, unhappy notion of the *Prince* and the *Discourses*, as indissolubly joined as a pair of Siamese twins, can be at last dismissed, to give way to the idea of a natural succession and a development of the author's mind from the one work to the other.

Instead of looking at the *Prince* and the *Discourses* as two complementary parts of one harmonious whole, we would, indeed, do better to reconsider what to earlier generations had seemed to be so manifest: that Machiavelli's two major works are in basic aspects different and that the *Discourses* have a message of their own. This, of course, does not suggest a return to the unhistorical judgments of the eighteenth century. The evolutionary understanding at which we seem to have arrived will, by necessity, remain very close to the genetic approach first proposed by Italian scholars since Chabod. Yet the long period in which awareness of the individual character of the *Discourses* was being dimmed may at last come to an end, now that we have proof that the *Prince* and the *Discourses* were composed in different phases of Machiavelli's life. What the changed picture will eventually be, is, to be sure, hardly yet foreseeable in detail, but along at least three new avenues we should be able to reach vantage-points from which fundamental aspects of the growth of Machiavelli's mind will present themselves in a fresh light.

In the first place, it becomes possible to reconstruct a more intelligible pattern of Machiavelli's personal development. Work on the *Prince*, we can now see, did not compel the author to swerve from any path he had previously trodden; nor was the composition of the pamphlet a mere episode or fruit of a few summer weeks. Neither was it accompanied by a contraction of broader historical or philosophical horizons previously spanned.[1] What Machiavelli intended to offer to a Medici prince late in 1513 was a synthesis of his experiences and reflections during the fourteen years in which his world had been that of the power struggle for Italy and of the fight for survival of the weak Florentine dominion in northern Tuscany. In this sphere of diplomatic technique and administrative efficiency, whatever he had learned in the service of the republic could also help in building up the rule of a new prince. He used this expertness and knowledge when, after the frustration of his former loyalties, both his burning desire for a place of action in the world of politics and his wounded Italian feelings caused him to nurture a fresh hope for a powerful founder of a new state.

But though the views and counsels given in pamphlet form in the *Prince* were the fruit of many years of Machiavelli's life, they merely stand for its first phase. We could hardly imagine a greater contrast in a writer's life than that between Machiavelli's active existence prior to 1513 and the period roughly from 1515 to 1520 when for a long while he lived a life of literary leisure in a circle of educated citizens, the group meeting in the Oricellari Gardens. Here he must have formed closer contacts with the traditions of civic Humanism than he had ever been able to during the busy years of his absorption in political and military affairs.[2] These traditions included an historical outlook which for several generations of humanistic students had centred in the admiration of antiquity as an era of city-states and institutions built on the life of a free society. Even though Machiavelli had previously studied Livy and other Latin and Greek authors (the latter in translation), it is clear that in the changed climate of his intellectual interests the ancient world was now to reveal to him a different dimension.[3]

---

[1] See the assumptions mentioned *supra* p. 228, n.2 and pp. 229 f., 236.

[2] On the re-emergence in the Oricellari circle of some of the central concerns of civic Humanism (although the answers given to the old problems after a hundred years were, of course, not always identical), *cf.* D. Cantimori, 'Rhetoric and Politics in Italian Humanism', *Jour. of the Warburg Institute*, i (1937-8), esp. 94 ff., and R. von Albertini, *Das Florentinische Staatsbewusstsein*, passim, esp. pp. 76 ff.

[3] If J. H. Hexter's reasoning in his study on 'Seyssel, Machiavelli, and Polybius VI: the Mystery of the Missing Translation', *Studies in the Renaissance*, iii (1956), 75-96, is correct, we may even assume that one of the chief inspirations for the introductory part of the *Discourses*—the fragments of the sixth book of Polybius—did not become available to Machiavelli in Latin until the time of his contacts with the circle in the Oricellari Gardens. In that case his inability to read Polybius VI before 1515 because of his ignorance of Greek would give us a further weighty argument against the composition of *Disc.* I 1-18 before 1515. However, Sasso (*Giornale Stor. della Letteratura Ital.*, cxxxv. 242 ff.) and Whitfield (*Italian Studies*, xiii. 31 ff.) have suggested that there had been chances for Machiavelli to procure a Latin version of Polybius VI other than that by Janus Lascaris (to which Hexter has pointed) as early as 1513 or even earlier, although we do not know whether Machiavelli took advantage of these opportunities.

This is not to suggest that the *Discourses* could or should be appraised one-sidedly on the strength of their relations to a republican-minded Humanism. In many chapters, as noted, this work intends to apply to republics the methods and conceptions of 'Machiavellianism', and, on that basis, to deal with both principates and republics. Yet the *Discourses* as we know them developed only because the comments on the rule of republics already planned at the time of the *Prince*[1] were subsequently joined by a politico-historical philosophy firmly based on a new vision of the life of nations and the rise and fall of their freedom and vigour—the legacy of fifteenth-century Humanism. Although the central problem for Machiavelli remained that of the winning and defence of political power, the sources were no longer sought in diplomatic craftsmanship exclusively, but in the first place in a social and constitutional fabric that allowed the civic energies and a spirit of political devotion and sacrifice to develop in all classes of a people. A revived and strengthened republicanism was helping Machiavelli to arrive at a more profound answer to the question which he had been so passionately asking since his early years.

Not that Machiavelli ever became a steadfast republican with regard to the practical problems of Florence's future. He always remained wavering between his awareness of the need, under the Tuscan conditions of civic equality, for a republic and his lingering hope that some new *principatus* in the provinces of the Papal State might create a power nucleus strong enough to make possible successful Italian resistance to the foreign invaders of the peninsula. When after Giuliano de' Medici's death Lorenzo de' Medici seemed to be on the threshold of erecting in the tyrant-prone territory of the Papal State the principality vainly aspired to by the *nepoti* of Alexander VI and Julius II, we see Machiavelli in the midst of his preparations for the *Discourses* take from his desk his old guide for the prince and dedicate it to Lorenzo. When this hope, too, had failed, he inscribed his *Discourses*, a few years later, to Buondelmonti and Rucellai, two Florentine citizens from the circle of the Oricellari Gardens, thereby, as he said, 'departing from the usual practice of authors . . . to dedicate their works to some prince, and . . . to praise him for all his virtuous qualities when they ought to have blamed him for all manner of shameless deeds'. In 1519-20, he dared to recommend to Leo X as practical advice the teaching of the *Discourses* that only republican forms of life could have duration in

As a consequence, we had better not try to use Hexter's discovery of a plausible late channel of Machiavelli's knowledge of Polybius VI as *proof* of a late composition of *Disc.* I 1-18 (as I did in 1956, *Bib. d'Hum. et Ren.*, xviii. 408). On the other hand, since the present paper establishes by other means that the section of the *Discourses* which depends on knowledge of Polybius VI was not written before 1516, the probability that Polybius VI did not become known to Machiavelli until 1515 is now increasing.

[1] This seems to follow from the phrase 'dove si trattassi delle republiche' at the beginning of chap. VIII of the *Prince*, discussed *supra* p. 225.

Florence under the Tuscan conditions of civic equality. Yet afterwards his restless mind began to explore still another approach to the past and present. During the fifteen-twenties, in his *Florentine History*, there appeared a third Machiavelli—the earliest Florentine writer to see Florence's development in the melancholy light in which it was to appear as the sixteenth century advanced, and to judge that, throughout Florentine history, the energies of freedom had continually consumed themselves until the end could only be extinction of all party passion and the establishment of a stable order under the Medici.

From the viewpoint of Florentine republicanism, therefore, Machiavelli was certainly, despite his great love and inspiring teaching of civic liberty, not a good and faithful citizen—as we have heard Giovanni Battista Busini say. The story of his life will always have to be presented as a delicate texture of sometimes contrasting motivations, not simply as a neat succession of a few, clean phases. Yet for all these fluctuations, the history of the growth and of the moulding forces of Machiavelli's thought looks profoundly different once we have recognized that on the way from the *Prince* to the *Discourses* new experiences entered his life—that the horizon of his mind *expanded* with the years, as that of every great, creative thinker.

Moreover—and here the second new avenue opens up—since this expansion, from another point of view, was a development from realistic positivism to humanistic classicism, the problems of Machiavelli's 'Realism' and 'Humanism', hotly debated in recent years,[1] can now also be viewed from a fresh perspective. If we accept that all three books of the *Discourses* were subsequent to the *Prince*, the political realism of the pamphlet, far from being the second step or even the climax in Machiavelli's development, actually represents an earlier phase. On the other hand, what followed was by no means merely a return to classicist belief in the imitation of antiquity but included the *historical* 'realism' of which we find the most mature expression in the synthetic chapters introducing the three books of the *Discourses*.

These introductions, continuing a line started by Leonardo Bruni and Flavio Biondo a century before, stress the point that the ancient world had been full of independent states, most of them freedom-loving city-states, before Rome's conquest of the world extinguished

---

[1] According to Chabod, *Machiavelli and the Renaissance*, pp. 37 f., 'the ancient world was gradually obliged [that is, during Machiavelli's presumed development from the first book of the *Discourses* to the *Prince*] to retreat before the modern world'; 'the classical examples are replaced by men and events taken from contemporary history', and Machiavelli's 'receptivity and imagination, having been moulded and developed by the civilization of the Ancients, were being applied once more to present-day life . . .'. According to F. Gilbert (*Jour. Hist. Ideas*, xiv. 148 f., 153 ff., 156) and G. Sasso (*Niccolò Machiavelli*, pp. 374 ff., 401 f., 410 ff.), the *Prince* and the opening part of the *Discourses* had been 'realistic', but Machiavelli's alleged subsequent return to the last two books of the *Discourses* reveals to a degree a backward trend, a return to 'a traditional literary genre' and to classicist bias and imitation of antiquity.

much of the early vitality. The Roman Empire is no longer viewed as a divine foundation, destined to last to the Judgment Day, but is an historical phenomenon with a natural growth and decline, followed by the emergence of new cities and states. And just as interstate struggle and change is never to come to rest, so—in the view of these introductions—there does not exist in social and constitutional life any perfect pattern that could endure without change and adaptation. Political *virtù*, in all groups and classes of a healthy people, must be continuously reproduced. Even the political and military greatness of Rome did not derive from Rome's endowment with an ideal, perfect constitution, but rested on an order that allowed the civic energies to be constantly regenerated by free rivalry and even by civil strife between all Roman classes and estates.[1]

Clearly, this vision of Rome and the ancient world is not 'classicist' in the sense of a contrast to 'realism'. It rather provided an opportune frame in which the sovereignty of each individual state, taken for granted in the *Prince*, could be perceived as an innate quality of the body politic which through the ages strives anew for its independence after every bondage to empire or foreign rule. In other words, through intensified contact with antiquity as viewed through humanists' eyes, some of the implied premises of the *Prince* grew into an ever more distinctly modern approach to the political and historical world.[2]

The last, but not the least consequence of our changed understanding of the growth of Machiavelli's thought concerns the balance in Renaissance Italy between the principate and the city-state republic. Thirty years ago, as we have noted, the great persuasiveness of the thesis that the *Prince* followed and superseded some basic ideas of the *Discourses* had much to do with the then prevailing opinion that the inherent trend of the Italian Renaissance was everywhere one from the commune and republic to the principate, and that by Machiavelli's time the perspicacity of a political

---

[1] *Disc.* I 1–1 6; II Introd. and II 1–11 4; III 1.

[2] It should be noted that Machiavelli's relationship to Humanism was, of course, not altogether positive. His pessimistic view of man and explicit subordination of the pursuits of culture to those of power and military efficiency make him in some respects one of the first great antipodes of the humanistic attitude in Italy, as has been convincingly pointed out by August Buck, 'Die Krise des humanistischen Menschenbildes bei Machiavelli', *Archiv für das Studium der neueren Sprachen*, clxxxix (1953), 304–17. But this need not prevent us from recognizing that certain other humanistic tendencies are basic to Machiavelli's thought and that he is one of their most important representatives. This is not only true of his classicist belief that contemporary Italy could be regenerated through a 'rebirth' of the political wisdom and the military organization of ancient Rome, but applies also to his relationship to the historical—and even the political—outlook of Florentine civic Humanism in pre-Medici Florence, in particular to that of Leonardo Bruni. *Cf.* my *The Crisis of the Early Italian Renaissance: Civic Humanism and Republican Liberty in an Age of Classicism and Tyranny* (Princeton Univ. Press, 1955), pp. 56, 371 f., 374, 443, 468, and Sasso, *Niccolò Machiavelli*, pp. 285 ff., 316 ff., 333 ff.

thinker would show itself in his ability to understand that the principate was the modern and progressive element, whereas the day of the city-state republic had passed. During the last twenty years, however, this picture of a one-track road has been increasingly replaced by an awareness that the transition from the republic to the principate was less ubiquitous and uniform. The civilization of the Quattrocento had depended on interaction of both elements, and one may question which was the more creative of the two.[1] Similar questions have recently been asked concerning the Florence of Machiavelli's generation. Thanks to the rediscovery and reinterpretation of a great number of vital testimonies on Florentine political ideas during the fifteen-tens and fifteen-twenties [2] we have become aware that, while some members of the Florentine nobility at that time finally decided for the principate, in other Florentine groups of all social classes republican ideals gained new momentum, drawing partly upon fifteenth-century Humanism and partly upon the constitutional thought of the period of Savonarola. Eventually, this strong current was to play its part in the last Florentine Republic of 1527–30.

Today we are beginning to realize that, indeed, throughout the entire late Italian Renaissance there were at work vigorous forces, eager to bring to maturity in the realm of thought and sometimes even in actual life, before the final triumph of absolutism, some of the elements of freedom on which life in Renaissance Italy had largely rested to the end of the fifteenth century. Not only in Florence, although she was and remained the focus, but also elsewhere on the Italian peninsula more and more instances of such reactions to princely absolutism have come to light. They form an indispensable part of the picture—and of the legacy—of the late Italian Renaissance.[3]

[1] For the new vista of the political balance in the Quattrocento—initiated especially by Nino Valeri—*cf.* the appendix ' Interpretations of the Political Background of the Early Renaissance' to *The Crisis of the Early Italian Renaissance*, pp. 379–90, and the summary in the writer's chapter ' Fifteenth Century Civilisation and the Renaissance' in *The New Cambridge Modern History*, i (Cambridge, 1957), 71 ff. For recent views of the cultural balance, *cf.* W. J. Bouwsma's *The Interpretation of Renaissance Humanism* (Amer. Hist. Ass., 1959), pp. 14 ff., and the discussion of the role of civic Humanism for the intellectual history of the fifteenth and sixteenth centuries in the writer's ' Secularization of Wisdom and Political Humanism in the Renaissance', *Jour. Hist. Ideas*, xxi (1960), 138 ff.

[2] In particular, through the reconstruction of the political ideas discussed in the meetings in the Oricellari Gardens, by Felix Gilbert ('Bernardo Rucellai and the Orti Oricellari ', *Jour. of the Warburg Institute*, xii [1949], 101–31) and by the authors quoted *supra* p. 248, n. 2. Much of the earlier picture has been replaced by the fundamental synthesis in Rudolf von Albertini's *Das Florentinische Staatsbewusstsein im Übergang von der Republik zum Prinzipat* (Bern, 1955), which traces the political and historical thought of the various Florentine groups and parties from *c.* 1500 to 1550. *Cf.* the writer's note on von Albertini's work in *Amer. Hist. Rev.*, lxii (1957), 909–11.

[3] To mention only the most obvious one from the area with which Machiavelli students are immediately concerned, one cannot fully weigh the growth of Machiavelli's mind in its twofold response to his Florentine environment and to the impact of the

It is against this expanding horizon of our knowledge of Machiavelli's age that we shall have to appraise the fact that the course of his development was not one from the *Discourses* to the *Prince*, but from the *Prince* to the *Discourses*—from a treatise on the Renaissance principate to the most penetrating Renaissance treatise dealing with the republic.

Newberry Library, Chicago   HANS BARON

contemporaneous events in Rome and the State of the Church, without remembering the reflection of the experiences of the same years in the mind of the Roman jurist and statesman, Mario Salamonio degli Alberteschi. This Roman contemporary, who had served as *capitano del popolo* in Florence under the Savonarolan republic in the year in which Machiavelli entered the Florentine chancery, inscribed to Leo X, almost simultaneously with Machiavelli's *Prince*, a Latin treatise *De Principatu*. Beside a preference, reminiscent of Machiavelli, for a native militia (' arme proprie ') over mercenary troops, we here encounter an historical interpretation of the ancient Roman imperial monarchy that endeavours to present the Roman *princeps*, viewed in the light of Augustus's *principatus*, as a contractual representative of the Roman people. This is another example from Machiavelli's age of the uses of history against rising absolutism—an attack against the notion of ' princeps legibus solutus '—in a work still read by late sixteenth-century *monarchomachi*. *Cf.* Marius Salamonius de Alberteschis, *De Principatu Libri Septem, nec non Orationes ad Priores Florentinos*, ed. M. d'Addio (Milan, 1955); and M. d'Addio, *L'Idea del contratto sociale dai sofisti alla riforma, e il ' De Principatu' di Mario Salamonio* (Milan, 1954).

[2]

Influence or Coincidence—a Question for Students of Machiavelli?

by CAROLINE ROBBINS

THE historian, most especially the historian of ideas, since he cannot undo the processes of time, is always in difficulties over problems of causation, transmission, and migration. Hume determined to leave speculation aside and observe only sequence. We cannot decide what the intellectual climate of Stuart England would have been like without the *Advancement of Learning* or the Authorized Version, or of Western Europe without *The Discourse on Method*. Yet certain coincidences tempt investigation. Machiavelli, for two or three centuries a familiar name of both authority and reproach, was very widely read, if even more widely misrepresented and oversimplified. Scholarship has been occupied with his legend. Yet little attention has been focused on the identity of many of the ideas of the *Discorsi* with the commonplaces of political writers between the Renaissance and the French Revolution in England and France.

Was the influence of the Florentine even greater than we have supposed? Does the coincidence of thought suggested by the most cursory rereading of Machiavelli's work after a course of study in the books of the Enlightenment reveal an even larger following, or does it rather suggest common circumstance, common classical authorities, a temper or fashion of thought which may be found throughout the period? Research by experts might be worth while. In most periods intellectual presuppositions and dogmas owe some considerable part of their content to influences other than the works of the favored prophet, whose power indeed may derive as much from the familiarity of his doctrine as from its novelty.

There is no need in this note to recur to the idea of polity, of the priority of the necessities of statecraft over considerations of morality. If anything, Machiavelli's role in the developing secularization of the state has been overstressed; rulers with power never, one imagines, lacked the argument for actions outside the canons of virtue. Here a few ideas not as familiar will be listed: uniformity among men and the institutions developed by man;[1] renewal of first principles, that is, a concern for stocktaking at intervals in the development of a people and a state;[2] emphasis not only on renewal but on the stimulus of contest and party within the state;[3] the importance of warlike activity without its boundaries;[4] the advantage of a citizen militia over a standing and mercenary army;[5] an admiration for the mixed government rather than for pure monarchy, aristocracy, or democracy;[6] a determinedly secular attitude towards the church and the clergy;[7] a wish for a numerous population, increased where necessary by general naturalization;[8] a firmly if not fully developed mercantilist attitude towards colonies, provinces, and plantations;[9] all these may be regarded as the assumptions of thoughtful politicians among the classical republicans of seventeenth-century England as well as among many of the *philosophes* associated with the *Encyclopédie* of eighteenth-century France.

The principle of uniformity enunciated by David Hume is not different from that which appears in the *Discorsi*. 'There is a great uniformity among the actions of men, in all nations and ages . . . human nature remains the same in its principles and operations, the same motives always produce the same actions, the same events follow the same causes.' The eagerness with which men studied history—'an inexhaustible well' out of which eternal verities must inevitably be drawn up—was due to the belief that useful deductions from the course of nations would be made and would enable wise men to better their condition, to avert or temper disaster. Neither Machiavelli nor Edward Gibbon was as optimistic as Bacon or Condorcet but all were equally convinced of a certain immutability in the laws regulating human conduct and believed that a science of politics could and should be based on as wide a knowledge of these as possible. Montesquieu, Vico, Adam Ferguson, each in very different ways, studied ancient history convinced that men under similar circumstances behaved in similar fashion and that their mistakes could assist contemporaries to avoid the decline which had overcome earlier empires and peoples.[10]

[1] Niccolo Machiavelli, *The Prince and the Discourses*, with an introduction by Max Lerner (Modern Library, New York, 1940), p. 216.

[2] *Ibid.*, p. 397.

[3] *Ibid.*, pp. 118–121.

[4] *Ibid.*, pp. 83, 371.

[5] *Ibid.*, pp. 44, 175–176.

[6] *Ibid.*, pp. 115–116.

[7] *Ibid.*, pp. 149–153, 284–285.

[8] *Ibid.*, pp. 288.

[9] *Ibid.*, pp. 9, 10.

[10] David Hume, *Essays*, edited by T. H. Green (2 vols., London, 1875), II, 68. Giam-

Machiavelli's attempt to analyze and understand the nature of an enduring polity was early in a long line of similar efforts. Montesquieu praised the English constitution when describing the Roman, which at its optimum he probably admired more. But among the English he detected a flexibility in action and a skill in renewing first principles which at a critical period the Romans lacked. Walter Moyle and Algernon Sidney emphasized the lessons of Roman history and the neglect, as decline was manifested in the imperial age, of earlier and better ways. Andrew Marvell, observing that all societies wear away much of their primitive institution, said that the true wisdom of all ages had been 'to review at fit periods those errours, defects, or excesses, that have insensibly crept in'. Ferguson a century later lamented the failure of the Romans to arrest the progress of decadence but pointed out that, granted virtue, valor, knowledge, and able men, nations that had learned the lessons of history might always hope for salvation.[11]

Even when effecting alterations or renewal, Machiavelli had urged the retaining of old forms and in nothing did Englishmen of most political persuasions agree with him more warmly. 'Green wood', too much innovation, ruined the experiments of the Commonwealth; what assured the success of the 'Glorious Revolution' was an adherence within necessary limits to the form and the first principles of the old constitution. This was the conviction of Burke and the theme of his *Appeal from the New to the Old Whigs*, but underneath the belief in the advantage of going slowly lay the sense, which he shared with the revolutionaries like Sidney, Harrington, and Neville, that renewal, flexibility, and even a measure of change was advantageous and indeed essential to national survival.[12]

---

battista Vico, *The New Science*, tr. T. G. Bergin & M. H. Fisch (Cornell Univ. Press, Ithaca, 1948), pp. 4, 92. C. K. de S. Montesquieu, *Grandeur and Decadence*, tr. J. Baker (New York, 1882), p. 23. Adam Ferguson, *Institutes of Moral Philosophy* (Edinburgh, 1769), p. 313.

[11] Montesquieu, *op. cit.*, p. 173. Algernon Sidney, *Works* (London, 1772), p. 406. Walter Moyle, *Works* (London, 1726, 2 vols.), I, 1–148, 'An Essay on the Roman Government', the whole of which is interesting in the present context. Though Moyle (1672–1721) as a disciple of Henry Neville (1620–94) might be thought an example of direct influence by Machiavelli, a study of the notes of his essays reveals that he got most of his excellent if biased history directly from the classical authorities. Andrew Marvell, 'The Rehearsal Transpros'd', *Works* (edited Alex. B. Grosart, 4 vols., 1875), III, 381. Adam Ferguson, *An Essay on the History of Civil Society* (Philadelphia, 1819), p. 506.

[12] Edmund Burke, *An Appeal* in *Works* (London, 1887), III, 1–115. Thomas Burton's

Some rectification might be brought about by competition, in the service of the state by groups within it, like the aristocracy and the plebeians in ancient Rome or men of different parties or factions in more modern states whose dissensions helped to promote the all-essential vigor and interest of an alert citizenry. Some fermentation was necessary and 'discordent parties' could be the salvation of states. Without this liveliness, indifference might undermine public spirit.[13]

Another stimulus to valor was warlike activity 'to take down our grease and luxury', as Marvell put it. Sidney argued, in support of republican institutions, the moral of the victories of both ancient Rome and puritan England. That state was best which was most prepared for the exigencies of war. Gibbon like Machiavelli before him blamed Christianity for having infected the Romans with a desire for peace and for the pursuits of nonbelligerency.[14] Service for the state was still largely military and that service for the best improvement of internal morale and external prestige should consist in a personal participation in a national militia. The vices of a standing mercenary army and its inferiority to bands of citizen soldiery were described, without, it must be admitted, the slightest influence on the growing military establishments of contemporary rulers. In Britain, Andrew Fletcher, Sidney, John Trenchard, and a host of others wrote classic expositions of the theories also put forward in the *Discorsi*, and this theory passed into American thought in the formative years of the United States. Prejudice on the matter in both Britain and America was to outline the period described here. In France the different development of government was attributed by some critics of the *ancien régime* in part to the use of mercenaries from the fifteenth century on by French monarchs.[15]

Diary, ed. J. T. Rutt in 4 vols. (London, 1828), III, 557 (a long speech by Col. Gibbons urging the men of the Cromwellian Parliament not to build with green timber). Machiavelli, pp. 182–183.

[13] See article by present writer, 'Discordant Parties', *PSQ*, LXXXIII, No. 4, 505–529, where a number of examples of a defense and acceptance of party may be found. For another see H. Wansey, *Journal of an Excursion* (Salisbury, 1796), p. 91.

[14] Marvell, *op. cit.*, p. 89; Sidney, *op. cit.*, II, XXII; Edward Gibbon, *The Decline and Fall*, ed. J. B. Bury (7 vols., 6th ed., London, 1925), II, chapters 15 and 16 (1–70, 71–139). For Gibbon's optimism see IV, 166–169.

[15] Examples of the standing army versus militia controversy are John Trenchard (1662–1723), *A History of Standing armies* (1698), and *An Argument showing that a standing army is inconsistent with a Free Government* (1697); Andrew Fletcher (1655–1716), *A Discourse concerning Militias and Standing Armies* (1697); Edward Wortley Montagu (1713–76), *Re-*

Another theme of these years concerned the virtue of mixed government, though the most superficial study of its proponents will reveal considerable variety in definitions of that constitutional mode. Machiavelli had pronounced in its favor. Nearly all Englishmen thought of their government as the best example of mixture. For preserving the balance of power between the various parts of the body politic, Sidney, Fletcher, and Moyle stressed the role of the aristocratic order in a somewhat different vein but with the same vehemence as that so often indulged in by French writers of the eighteenth century. Aristocracy as the guardian of liberty—a certain kind of liberty—against tyranny was regarded as admirable by revolutionaries in England and by conservatives in France. The mixed government emphasized the importance of each element in it, monarchical, noble, and popular.

Growing diminution of the authority of the church was characteristic of the age, and Machiavelli's ideas found echoes or companions from his own day to those in which Voltaire was uttering anathemas on clerical influence and interference. The Reformation hardly settled the question. Anticlericalism continued to manifest itself. The ever memorable John Hales blamed on the ambitions of the clergy half the schisms of the time. Bishops were the 'first deluders of mankind'. The evils of churchmen were continually pointed out and culminated not only in the excesses of the French Revolution but in the separation of church and state in America.[16]

A less important but interesting item in the present context is the persistent discussion of the role of population in the prosperity of a state and in the recurrence of schemes for general naturalization which spring from this. Rome was supreme when her population enlarged itself by numerous families and by liberal treatment of immigrants. Countries should profit by encouraging the settlement of industrious and sober men. Brandenburg Prussia followed such a policy, and the matter was mooted many times in the English parliaments under the later Stuarts and in literature in the eighteenth century. Interest waned only as popu-

---

flection on the Rise and Fall of the Ancient Republics (1759). All these were reprinted and reached a wide public on both sides of the Atlantic. The same moral is given by Charles Forman, the Translator to Boulainvilliers *Ancient Parliament of France*, particularly to XII.

[16] Marvel, *Works*, III and IV, 'The Rehearsal Transpros'd', 'A Short Historical Essay', all anticlerical. Cf. John Hales, 'Of Schism', *Tracts*, 1677, and Voltaire, *Philosophical Dictionary* (tr. Boston, 1836), pp. 41, 281–282, and throughout. Moyle as above, p. 87, on 'Diviners' and Romans. Gibbon as above, n. 14.

lation pressures began to be felt in Europe. Only as the New World filled up a good deal later did the fairly general assumption that immigration should not be limited begin to be assailed, and the door stand less widely open.[17]

In the period considered here colonies and provinces were neither asylums nor even relief centers for surplus people; they were areas which might, if properly regulated in subservience to the mother state, become as Roman and Venetian provinces had been, sources of wealth, power, and empire. The theory of mercantilism in this respect is too well known to need annotation or elaboration, but it was in some particular aspects anticipated by Machiavelli and represents the development into logical politics of widely held theories. Even 'liberals' like Henry Neville, both a revolutionary and a Machiavellian, pointed with pride to the policy of using only English in the government of the Irish dependency and expatiated on the advantages of that kind of colonial rule. Once more the Florentine and the attitude of western Europeans in succeeding centuries were in accord.[18]

Old Nick had a bad name; his reputation for the advocacy of improper and unscrupulous statecraft was widespread. Detractors were many, but there were probably many more who openly or without acknowledgment or even consciousness of sympathy, put forward theories often identical with those found in the *Discorsi* and the *Prince*. Some of them studied, translated, and analyzed the works of Machiavelli; others may never have connected his pronouncements with the policies they advocated. Most, like him, had studied Livy, Tacitus, and Polybius, in whose works might also be found statements about all the topics mentioned here. The coincidence is remarkable; whether due more to direct influence or to similar social circumstance and a common core of reading might be worth some further consideration.

---

[17] Moyle cites liberal naturalization policy at Rome in the essay noted above, note 11. Roger Coke, *A Detection of Church and State* (3rd ed., 1697), pp. 556, 607–608; J. R. McCulloch, *Early English Tracts* (reissue Cambridge, 1952), in works by William Petyt (1626–1702) and others, pp. 219–224, 251–274, 358.

[18] Henry Neville, *Plato Redivivus* (1681, 2nd ed.), pp. 50–51.

[3]

Preface to Machiavelli

Lev Kamenev

The inclusion of the works of Niccolo Machiavelli in the series of volumes published by 'Academia' needs no justification. The episodes which inspired Machiavelli's works, the works themselves (propagandist, historical, fictional), the bitter disputes which raged around his name for centuries afterwards—all these are major events in the cultural history of Europe. The Soviet reader who comes across, as he is bound to do, references to Machiavelli in historical studies, in current editorials in the press ('Machiavellism', 'Machiavellian politics' etc.), and in literary works, rightly wants an opportunity to read the actual, original texts of the secretary of the Florentine Republic in the sixteenth century. The 'Academia' edition is intended to meet this need.

In an excellent study specially written for this volume, A. K. Dzhivelegov outlines Machiavelli's life and the historical circumstances which influenced his work. The fate of Machiavelli's ideas and works after his death falls outside the scope of his study. In fact, their destiny was remarkable and revealing. A study of the attitudes displayed by different groups in European society towards Machiavelli over a period of four centuries (sixteenth to the nineteenth centuries), in the course of which his work was the object of constant attention on the part of politicians, propagandists and historians, would provide the richest and most varied material for a history of the ideological terms of the class struggle, from the overthrow of feudalism to the era of the proletarian revolution. We can only venture a few remarks in this connection here.

In spite of accepted terminology, the importance of Machiavelli does not lie in his 'theory' or 'political system'. He has in fact no

40

'theory' nor 'system', in the sense of a deeply considered and fully developed doctrine of society, or even of the state. He had no gift for profound philosophical enquiry, nor yet for broad sociological generalisations. His real talent is that of the political publicist, writing on urgent contemporary issues, or on past events as recorded by historians of the ancient world. In either case his aim is to have direct, immediate influence on the political events of his time. In either case his 'theoretical judgments' and his professional reports really amount to the same thing—a record of the first-hand observations of one whose position was close to the real centre of the struggle for power.

The social content of power, its social determinations, interested him very little. Whether power was in the hands of Alexander VI or Cesar Borgia, Cesar Borgia or Prince Orsini, Prince Orsini or the Duke of Urbino, in the final analysis its content remained virtually unchanged. Machiavelli's primary concern is with the actual process of the struggle for power. His most famous work, 'The Prince', is not a study of the changing social groups which have won power, and the conditions and significance of these changes: it is concerned with the *mechanism* of the struggle for power within one narrow social group, in the period of transition from feudalism to capitalism.

Of course, Machiavelli's work bears the impress of a major historical force: the drive to create a powerful, national and essentially bourgeois state in Italy, by the systematic destruction of the complex of independent feudal, semi-feudal and commercial communes, republics and dukedoms. But in Italy at the end of the fifteenth and the beginning of the sixteenth century this idea had to fight its way (and at the time it was unsuccessful) through the inextricable confusion of countless myriads of powerful and petty Italian rulers incessantly warring against each other. It is the political *practice* made up of these innumerable clashes which receives open formulation in Machiavelli's treatise.

He was a master of political aphorism and a dialectician of brilliance, who from his observations had come to the firm conclusion that all concepts and all criteria of good and evil, of the permissible and the impermissible, of the lawful and the criminal, were relative. Machiavelli made his book an astonishingly acute and expressive catalogue of the rules which a prince of that period had to follow in order to win power and to retain it victoriously in the face of all attempts to wrest it from him. This was far from being a sociology of power, but from his recommendations there emerges a magnificent picture of the zoological features of the struggle for power in a slave society, in which a rich minority ruled over a toiling majority. Thus by accident or design the secretary to the Florentine bankers, their ambassador at the Papal court, set off a shell of such tremendous explosive force that it disturbed the peace of mind of rulers for centuries afterwards.

In Machiavelli's work there is not the slightest mention of a religious or metaphysical 'essence' of the state, not a word about the 'divinely chosen' ruler—even of the Papal domain, not one reference

Preface to Machiavelli

to the 'will of the people', to the 'laws of history', to the 'interests
of humanity'. This servant of the Florentine oligarchy was not
afraid to look at the political reality of his time and to reveal behind
the broad banners and paltry finery its true countenance: an oppressive class of masters struggling amongst themselves for power over
the labouring masses. In one small book he put to scorn the most
learned scholars, the authors of innumerable theological, moral and
political treatises on the nature of political power, full of references
to the philosophy of Aristotle, the tablets of Moses and the precepts
of St. Paul.

This was magnificent in its naked truthfulness—and therefore
frightening. Popes, courtiers, statesman, kings rushed to attack the
secretary of the Florentine oligarchs. The nearer their actions came
in practice to his observations, the more determined were their
attempts to refute his maxims. The secretary of the Order of the
Jesuits called him the 'devil's partner in crime', a 'dishonest writer and
an unbeliever'. Apologists for absolute monarchy found his views too
strong meat for them, and hastened to announce that 'there never
was a man so devoid of moral scruple as this Florentine'. That typical
example of unbridled despotism, the Prussian king Frederick, called
the Great, wrote a book whose title was 'Anti-Machiavelli'.
Machiavelli's name came to be used as an epitome of political cynicism by those bent on concealing the real nature of power in feudal
and bourgeois society.

In fact, the cynicism is not in the words of Machiavelli, but in
what they describe. Machiavelli's book is unprincipled, criminal and
harsh only because he resolved, to use Lassalle's words, 'aussprechen
was ist': to express what is. If Machiavelli's picture of the ruler's
conduct in feudal and bourgeois society could not but provoke
consternation and outrage among the rulers, it inevitably also
attracted the attention of those who in some way or another shared
his critical outlook. 'We should be grateful to Machiavelli and others
like him who openly and without concealing anything described how
people normally behaved, and not how they were supposed to
behave' wrote Francis Bacon, the 'true originator of English materialism and in general of the experimental sciences of our time', as Marx
described him. Hegel had the same opinion of the secretary to the
Council of Ten: he categorically refused to render a moralising
judgment on Machiavelli, and saw in his 'lack of principles' and
'anti-religious' propaganda only a transcription of the methods of
political struggle which inevitably prevailed in that epoch of human
history. 'Machiavelli' wrote Hegel, 'established the truly necessary
basic principles for the formation of states, principles imposed by the
conditions of that period.'

The young Marx wrote down aphorisms from the 'Examination of
Titus Livius' in the notebooks in which he developed some of the
ideas for the 'Communist Manifesto'; as a result he repeatedly reread the works of Machiavelli and pronounced at least some of
them 'magisterial', 'genuine masterpieces'. Engels included this
'devil's partner in crime' in his gallery of the 'giants' of the Enlighten-

42

ment, the great destroyers of feudal culture whom the founders of scientific socialism held in such great esteem, because in the fulfilment of their historical task, the creation of the new bourgeois state, they 'were not limited in a petty bourgeois way.' (Dialectics of Nature).

The acute perception of the authors of the 'Communist Manifesto' detected in the writings of the Florentine secretary the beginnings of the theory of the class struggle, and a lucid vision, free from all mysticism or idealism, of the nature of the state and the struggle for power. His was a superbly realistic portrait of the political reality of his day. In the works of Machiavelli emperors, popes, kings, lords, bankers and merchants walk without masks, and by their actions confirm the truth of the historical views of the founders of dialectical materialism.

The writings of this publicist of the sixteenth century were an outstanding contribution to the work of discovering the real nature of power in class society, consummated in our own time in the writings of Marx, Engels, Lenin and Stalin. For this Machiavelli has a right to the attention of the reader of today.

[4]

The

AMERICAN
HISTORICAL
REVIEW

VOLUME LXIX, NUMBER 4   JULY 1964

The Loom of Language and the Fabric of Imperatives:

The Case of *Il Principe* and *Utopia*

J. H. HEXTER*

THIS essay concerns the way two men, Niccolò Machiavelli and Thomas More, in two books, *Il Principe* and *Utopia,* used a few words. It argues in effect that the peculiar ways in which these men worked at the loom of language indicates that they stood in a peculiar relation to the fabric of imperatives of their own time.

The loom of language provides men with the words and word patterns by means of which they communicate with one another. By processes so complex as to require a separate branch of the science of linguistics for their explication, words and patterns of words undergo a great variety of changes under a wide variety of circumstances with the passage of time. By glacially slow modifications of an ancient tongue whole new language families evolve. Words come to point to things they did not formerly designate, or cease to point to things they did designate. New words are created

* Mr. Hexter, formerly of Washington University, now of Yale University, is the author of *Reappraisals in History* (London and Evanston, Ill., 1961; New York, 1963). His major field of interest is early modern Europe.

J. H. Hexter

to designate new-found things, or old ones are put to new uses in the process of discovery. And, massively, words and word sequences drop out of use and become archaic or obsolete, which is to say unintelligible or nearly so. The changes even in a language relatively as stable as English during the past four hundred years have been such that in teaching Shakespeare or expounding Scripture from the King James Version, the expositor finds himself becoming more and more the translator in the technical sense—the person engaged in finding equivalents of the words of his text that will be intelligible to his audience.

This essay proposes to deal with a small sample of a particular kind of change in language, and that kind itself amounts to only a tiny fraction of the changes that language constantly undergoes. The few changes to be investigated here, however, may have a particular interest for historians, especially for historians of ideas, of moral sentiments, of political institutions, and of social structures, which means for a great many historians today. They may have this interest because of the peculiar circumstances in which they took place. For one thing they did not emerge anonymously from the folk; they were the work of readily identifiable individuals—More and Machiavelli —each of whom made a strong and indelible mark on the history of his times. In the second place the changes were not casual word coinages. The words that will concern us concerned More and Machiavelli; in effect they are not words merely *dropped* by their authors but words *placed* (or in one instance not placed) by them. Finally when Machiavelli and More tampered with the sense of the words that will concern us, they cared not at all or not solely for the aesthetic impact or the logical efficiency of what they were doing. They were concerned with the relation of those words and their meanings to the men and communities of men that they knew best. They were in effect concerned with the product of the loom of language in the area where it weaves the fabric of imperatives.

In contrast to the region of "I want," the fabric of imperatives occupies the whole region of "Thou shalt," of "You ought," of "I ought."[1] Between these two regions there is for each of us a greater or lesser measure of congru-

---

[1] To pile yet one more metaphorical phrase on an area already blanketed by "patterns of culture" and "webs of values" may seem a contribution only to a confusion of tongues already quite sufficient. But although what the phrase "fabric of imperatives" refers to in this essay certainly lies in the blanketed area, the part it covers, while overlapping the parts covered by the other phrases, is not identical with either of them. "Patterns of culture" refers to the things the people of a culture normally do. Thus in the adolescent male American subculture of my day, boasting—sometimes quite remarkable in its inaccuracy—about one's amorous achievements was a standard pattern. It was not, however, part of the fabric of imperatives; there was no explicit rule to the effect that wholesome American boys ought to lie like Ananias about their priapic exploits. The notion of "web of values" will not do because the term "value" appears to have become highly ambiguous, and in the process of aggravated bifurcation it has left uncovered

ence, but whatever the correspondence may be, the regions are functionally distinct. The one concerns the satisfaction of human desires, the other the rules of human conduct. The function of any fabric of imperatives is so to regulate the satisfaction of human desires as to make the living together of men at least possible, and at most to make it good. The fabric of imperatives regulates the satisfaction of human desires by sanctions ranging from the overtly coercive ones of law enforced by public power, through the pressure of community opinion working by means of gossip and social acceptance or rejection, to the still small voice within.

Because the fabric of imperatives determines the ordinary day-to-day expectations of men with respect to the actions of their fellows, it is resistant to drastic and sudden change. It is also of varying density at a given time and over spans of time. Thus in the Middle Ages it lay relatively thick with respect to matters of male attire and relatively thin with respect to acts of physical violence, whereas today it lies thin with respect to the former and thick with respect to the latter. And this is as much as to say that despite its resistance to alteration, the fabric has in fact undergone alteration. Thirdly, it is subject to stress from a variety of sources: changes in technology, in the range and depth of human understanding, in the direction of human aspirations and desires, in the forms of social and political institutions, in the relative power and the demands of interest groups, in the character of men's faith and hope. Finally, to cope with the tensions generated by such changes, and to prevent them from fatally rending the fabric of imperatives, all but very primitive societies support a specialized maintenance force to keep it in repair. In most societies we find among these specialists the doom deemers or law givers, the judges, the priests or holy men, and the pedagogues. Moreover, in particular ages and particular cultures the maintenance work is undertaken by different kinds of men—in ancient Greece, for example, successively by epic poets, lyric poets, dramatists, and philosophers; in the West by theologians, humanists, philosophes, and today by sociologists, psychoanalysts, novelists, and editorial writers. What these men have in common is an expertise at the loom of language that enables them to produce

---

an important area lying between its two segments. In one sense it seems to mean the highest goals that individuals and communities set for themselves; in the other sense it means whatever men and groups of men want, as revealed by their actual choices and stated preferences. It has long been used in approximately this sense in economics and is occasionally so used in sociology, e.g., in Bernard Berelson, *Content Analysis in Communication Research* (Glencoe, Ill., 1952). The notion of a "fabric of imperatives" covers but also extends far beyond the web of values in the first sense, and it occupies a different cultural region altogether from the web of values in the second sense.

the material they deem necessary to reinforce or patch or rebuild or modify the fabric of imperatives in accord with their often varying estimate of the need.

Most specialists at the loom of language are satisfied most of the time to work to preserve the fabric of imperatives pretty much as they find it. This is why what they produce is often insufferably monotonous and repetitive. But all the specialists are not always satisfied. Most of the subversive initial and direct onslaughts on the fabric of imperatives have been delivered by men who come out of the milieus of the maintenance specialists. Their divine or daemonic discontent is not a rarity to wonder at; it is a common and repeated fact of history.

Since the work of registering or initiating the transformation of imperatives falls to maintenance specialists who are word weavers, in the course of drastic changes, attempted or achieved, in the fabric of imperatives, something odd usually happens at the loom of language. This fact may provide us with a useful tactical resource for the investigation of the history of ideas at a point where, to borrow the title of a very poor book, "ideas have consequences." A careful study of activity at the loom of language may render possible the close identification of points of stress in the fabric of imperatives at a particular moment.

The stress or breakdown in the fabric of imperatives does not always register in the sort of change at the loom of language that so sharply calls attention to itself when one word wholly replaces another in an area of human discourse. Sometimes the change is not a change *of* words but a change *in* words, an alteration of meaning that leaves the verbal shell intact. When such a change takes place in words widely current prior to the change and still widely current today, he who attempts to understand the fabric of imperatives by studying the loom of language needs to proceed with considerable caution. In the first place it is easy to miss such a change altogether. Having descried the change, however, the investigator may unwarily assume that the word has shifted all the way from its previous sense to its present range of connotation. This is by no means always the case.

The above monition about changes in words is necessary because the examination of several such changes will be our concern in what follows. The changes occur in two works on politics written in the years just prior to the Reformation: Machiavelli's *Il Principe* (1513) and More's *Utopia* (1515–16). From the time they reached the public to the present those two slim books have exercised a powerful and continuous fascination over men's minds, a

The Loom of Language   949

fascination more powerful than that of any works contemporary with them. Yet, is it useful to attempt to understand what More and Machiavelli were doing to the fabric of imperatives by an investigation of the language of *Utopia* and *Il Principe* only? To do so raises serious and difficult questions. Is the More of *Utopia* the *real* More? Did More *really* believe what what he wrote in *Utopia*? Did Machiavelli *really* believe what he wrote in *Il Principe*? Is the Machiavelli of *Il Principe,* that hasty chance tract, the *real* Machiavelli? Is not the real Machiavelli rather the author of the *Discorsi,* the work that represents the meditation of a lifetime? [2]

If by the real Machiavelli one means that aspect of the man which expressed itself in his most durable concerns, convictions, habits of thought, and patterns of action, then probably the *Discorsi* better than *Il Principe* reflects the real Machiavelli. But this identification of the real Machiavelli is a dangerous game; it has led to the dubious inference that only those elements in *Il Principe* duplicated in or reconcilable with the *Discorsi* represent the real Machiavelli, and that what is left over is to be disregarded or explained away. Yet so to treat *Il Principe* is to miss perhaps the most important point about it. What gives *Il Principe* its remarkable power and its perennial liveliness is that in it Machiavelli's imagination takes wings and his vision soars above his ordinary perceptions and conceptions to a new height.

And so it is with Thomas More in *Utopia.* If the Machiavelli of the *Discorsi* rather than of *Il Principe* is the real Machiavelli, the More of the letter to Martin Dorp in defense of Erasmus and Christian humanism,[3] the More of the *Dialogue concerning Heresies* supporting Christian unity against its enemies,[4] rather than the author of *Utopia,* is the real More. The unique heights they attain above their own times put *Il Principe* and *Utopia* beyond the ordinary reach of the contemporaries of Machiavelli and More—beyond the reach of *all* their contemporaries, and therefore beyond the reach of More and Machiavelli, too. For it is not necessary to believe that almost two

---

[2] This issue is frequently raised with respect to both these books and a considerable number of other great books, Plato's *Republic,* for example. It was raised, in fact, by one of the readers to whom the editor of the *AHR* sent this study. The following section first written to meet the issue with respect to *Utopia* alone as part of the introduction to *Utopia* (New Haven, Conn., 1964), Volume IV of the Yale edition of *The Complete Works of St. Thomas More,* is included here in slight paraphrase at the suggestion of the editor of the *AHR* and with the kind permission of the executive editor of the Yale edition, Professor Richard Sylvester.

[3] Thomas More, *Correspondence of Sir Thomas More,* ed. E. F. Rogers (Princeton, N. J., 1947–   ), no. 15; Thomas More, *Selected Letters,* ed. E. F. Rogers (New Haven, Conn., 1961), no. 4.

[4] Thomas More, *A Dialogue concernynge heresyes and matters of religion,* in *Works of Sir Thomas More, Knyght, sometyme Lorde Chancellor of England, wrytten by him in the Englysh tonge* (London, 1557), cols. 103–104, pp. 105–288.

decades or even two years later Machiavelli and More saw all things precisely as they saw them in the moments of acute perception that possessed them when they wrote *Il Principe* and *Utopia*. Sustained imaginative vision is indeed like being possessed; it is not necessarily progressive or cumulative or even readily preserved intact. It is a dizzy height that a very few men scale once or twice in a lifetime and fewer still attain more often. When such vision is turned on the ways men live together, it may bring some facets of human affairs into focus with a fierce brilliance, but in so doing it is almost bound to throw whole spans of men's experience, the visionary's as well as others', into the shadow. The greatness of a book that does this lies not in its harmony but in its intensity. And after he has attained this height the writer of such a book may seem not to advance from it but to recede from it. In regaining his balance he loses some of his impetus. This happened to Machiavelli after he wrote *Il Principe;* it happened to More after he wrote *Utopia*. In both cases the convictions the books express are not so much repudiated as drawn back into the setting from which something like poetic inspiration had momentarily freed them. They are not consciously rejected but integrated with their writer's previous habit of thought and thereby transmuted and toned down.

Although in *Utopia* and *Il Principe* More and Machiavelli rise above their milieus, it is their own milieus they rise above and therefore have in view as they write. This much relation at least each man's book bears to his own time and place, and although the times of More and Machiavelli were closely contemporaneous, their places were different in ways most significant for what they wrote in their great little books.

The place of Machiavelli was Italy; the rest of Europe and the rest of the world he saw only with fragmented, unfocused, peripheral vision.[5] To him as to his contemporary fellow Florentine and fellow student of the past, Francesco Guicciardini, the Italy of his day was the scene of massive and utterly appalling political disarray, of *calamità,* following with catastrophic suddenness an era of order, prosperity, and peace.[6] This view is at odds with that of a number of historians who have seen and see the entire age of the Renaissance in Italy as one of political confusion, violence, and decay. It is nevertheless confirmed by a reasonable consideration of the evi-

---

[5] This is evident enough even in Machiavelli's descriptions of France and Germany written after he had been engaged in legations to both those lands. (Niccolò Machiavelli, "Ritratto delle cose di Francia," in Machiavelli, *Tutte le opere di Niccolò Machiavelli,* ed. Francesco Flora and Carlo Cordiè [2 vols., n.p., 1949], I, 677–90; "Ritratto delle cose della Magna," *ibid.,* 697–702.)

[6] Francesco Guicciardini, *Opere,* ed. Vittorio de Caprariis (La Letterature Italiana, Storia e Testi, XXX [Milan, n.d.], 373).

The Loom of Language   951

dence. From the death of Giangalleazzo Visconti in 1403 to the incursion of Charles VIII of France in 1494 Italy enjoyed a level of tranquillity among its centers of political power and even within its political units that to contemporary Frenchmen, Englishmen, Spaniards, and Germans could only have seemed Elysian. If everything was not well—and of course during those ninety years everything was not always well anywhere in Italy and was about as bad as ever in Naples—still it was better than the hideous turmoil that plagued the transmontane monarchies for decades on end.[7]

Machiavelli had lived out his youth in the last golden days of a near century of political stability. In that happy autumn of illusion the brutal interventions of barbarians from across the mountains were but a memory of dark days past. In his young manhood Machiavelli saw the bitter end of Italy's autumnal dream. The barbarians came again. In 1494 the French host of Charles VIII swept, irresistible as a winter storm, from the Alps to Naples. That storm of armed force left the old political lines of order among the Italian powers and of rule within them in blasted disarray. And this was but the beginning of a series of political disasters for the Italians that reached a climax but did not end in Machiavelli's lifetime. He not only lived in the midst of these disasters; in his most active years he wholly gave himself to an attempt to stave them off or temper their effects in his native Florence.[8] In this he failed wretchedly and utterly, and his failure captured him. He spent the rest of his life in an almost obsessed contemplation of the apparatus—the levers and gears—of political power.

With the passion of the failure who seeks his own justification, Machiavelli tried to find in political action some sort of meaning not canceled by each random gesture of that fickle bitch Fortuna. Never was Machiavelli more fully obsessed by politics than in 1513, the year when with an aimless hand Chance swept away at once his means of livelihood and his way of life. With the Medicis in tow, a Spanish force had thrust aside as if it were not there the Florentine militia on which Machiavelli had lavished his pains, effortlessly turning into a nightmare joke the fifteen years he had given to the work of maintaining the political viability of the republic. The restored Medici deprived Machiavelli of his office, tortured him on suspicion of complicity in a plot against them, and exiled him from the city.[9] The fate of Italy and his own fate had become inextricably intermeshed, and he

[7] Garrett Mattingly, *Renaissance Diplomacy* (London, 1955), 83–100, has pointed out how precarious and imperfect the order of Italy was from 1403 to 1494. The contrast between Italy and the great transmontane realms remains nonetheless remarkable.

[8] Roberto Ridolfi, *Vita di Niccolò Machiavelli* (Rome, 1954), 22–197; John Hale, *Machiavelli and Renaissance Italy* (London, 1961), 31–131.

[9] Ridolfi, *Vita di Machiavelli*, 197–214; Hale, *Machiavelli and Renaissance Italy*, 131–41.

needed above all to know how it had come about that in his day Italy was "overrun by Charles, sacked by Louis, outraged by Ferdinand, and disgraced by the Swiss,"[10] while he had to spin out his life on a wretched farm in the hills of Tuscany. And so in 1513 he channeled but scarcely controlled his passion for politics, pouring his frustrated urge for deeds into a spate of words, somehow compounded of ice and fire, which became *Il Principe*.

Others might talk sensibly about silks and woolens, about profit and loss, but, he wrote, "for me it is fitting to talk sensibly about *lo stato,* and I must do so or take the vow of silence."[11] Machiavelli took no such vow. Whether sensibly or not, during the next few months in *Il Principe* he talked much about *stato,*[12] and readers of that work have long recognized that Machiavelli had done something to *stato* that wrenched it out of its medieval matrix of connotation.[13] The men who made this discovery were themselves heavily committed to political nationalism. The consequence was almost inevitable: they took Machiavelli's *stato* and decked it out in all the finery of the modern national state, passionately and romantically conceived as the politically unitary expression of the will of the nation's people.[14] For a number of reasons this view of the matter just will not do. The most obvious difficulty is that in Chapter XXVI of *Il Principe,* where somewhat belatedly Machiavelli assumes the stance of an Italian patriot (belatedly since Chapter XXVI is also the last), the word *stato* does not appear at all, although it occurs in all but three preceding chapters;[15] in effect where Machiavelli starts talking about Italian patriotism is where he stops talking about *lo stato.*

The problem then comes to this: in *Il Principe* Machiavelli imparts a peculiar twist to the term *stato* which might indicate that when he wrote the book he was doing something odd to the current fabric of imperatives. But what is the peculiar twist? And precisely what, if anything, does it do to the fabric of imperatives? In the first place *stato* appears in *Il Principe* only rarely in the senses in which it appeared very frequently in medieval political writing and in the writing of such a contemporary of Machiavelli's as Claude Seyssel. Machiavelli scarcely ever used it to mean "condition in general" as in "solid state," "state of war," "state of mind." Nor did he use *stato* much more often in the sense of "social condition" or "order of society," as the "estate of the nobility" or "estates of the realm." The word occurs 115 times

10 Niccolò Machiavelli, *Il Principe,* Chap. XII.

11 *Id., Lettere* (2 vols., Lanciano, 1915), I, 127. The letter is dated April 1513.

12 His letter to Francesco Vettori of December 10, 1513, suggested that he had nearly finished *Il Principe.* (*Ibid.,* II, 24–27.)

13 For a full elaboration of most of what follows about *stato,* see my "*Il principe* and *lo stato*," *Studies in the Renaissance,* IV (1957), 113–38.

14 See, e.g., Francesco Ercole, *La Politica di Machiavelli* (Rome, 1925), 65–196.

15 All except Machiavelli, *Il Principe,* Chaps. XIII, XVI, XXV.

The Loom of Language   953

in *Il Principe*. In 110 times it does not have either of the common medieval denotations just described. All those 110 times it denotes something that we would call political, not something we would call either social or general.

But what exactly does it denote those 110 times? To this question the embarrassing answer is, "We cannot say," or more justly, "*Il Principe* does not tell." One Italian student of linguistics, Fredi Chiapelli, thought it did tell,[16] and proceeded to classify the denotations of *stato* he believed he had found in the book. He came up with 75 per cent of the occurrences denoting "state in its full maturity with its fundamental political, territorial, and national implications," and a scatter of other occurrences with four or five other denotations.[17] Unfortunately Chiapelli's method vitiated his own argument. He started by substituting "state in its full maturity" wherever *stato* occurred. Where it happened to fit, he accepted it as the denotation Machiavelli intended; he did not try any of his other denotations of *stato* to see if they fit. Then he divided the *stati* he had left over, the ones that "state in its full maturity" did not fit, among those other denotations. The trouble is that in almost every case where "state in its full maturity" fits in the immediate context, one or more of the other untried denotations of *stato* also fit quite as well, because the context is just not full enough to provide an univocal denotation.[18]

The failure of an examination of denotation of *stato* in *Il Principe* to reveal what Machiavelli was doing to the word suggests that we next search syntax for a clue. In effect there are about seven occurrences of *stato* as the subject of an active verb in *Il Principe*. Eleven times as often as this—about 70 per cent of all its appearances in a political context—it is either the object of an active verb or the subject of a passive one. Syntactically, therefore, *stato* is not up to much in *Il Principe*. If *lo stato* is not doing much, what is being done to it? It is not being worked for, or helped, or served, or revered, or admired, or feared, or loved, as Chiapelli's *stato* "in its full maturity" would be worked for, helped, served, revered, admired, feared, and loved in the twentieth century—not once, not ever. Time after time it is being added to, assaulted, disarmed, won, injured, occupied, possessed, conceded, seized, taken, regained, had, and most often of all acquired, held, kept, lost, and taken away. Indeed, *lo stato* never acquires, holds, keeps, loses, or takes anything from anyone, but on a reasonable rather than a strictly grammatical construction of its situation, in about half its occurrences someone is acquir-

[16] Fredi Chiapelli, *Studi sul linguagio del Machiavelli* (Florence, 1952). For a fuller discussion of Chiapelli's method, see Hexter, *"Il principe,"* 135–37.
[17] Chiapelli, *Studi,* 59–73, esp. 68.
[18] See examples in Hexter, *"Il principe,"* 137.

J. H. Hexter

ing, holding, keeping, and losing *lo stato* or having it taken away from him. If we go further and examine the occurrences of *stato* where it is in less immediate syntactical relation to a verb, nothing happens to alter the impression left by the peculiar verbs with which it ordinarily keeps company and the peculiar way in which that company is kept. Whatever Machiavelli meant to denote by *stato* (on this point the evidence is most ambiguous), in *Il Principe, lo stato* is what is politically up for grabs. And it is nothing more than what is up for grabs. It therefore lacks at least one important dimension of what Chiapelli calls "the state in its full maturity with its fundamental political, territorial, and national implications." *Lo stato* is no body politic; it is not the people politically organized, the political expression of their nature and character and aspirations, their virtues and their defects. Rather it is an inert lump, and whatever vicarious vitality it displays is infused into it not by the people, but by the prince who gets it, holds it, keeps it, and aims not to lose it or have it taken away. Our investigation has led us to a curious conclusion. In *Il Principe* Machiavelli has not stretched *stato;* he has shrunk it. He has drained away most of its medieval social meanings and has not given it its modern political amplitude.

What implications this devitalization of *stato* has for the fabric of imperatives we will try to discern shortly. At the moment we want to explore another linguistic corridor: what might be called motif-word magnetism. Common sense suggests that when a sense shift like the one in *stato* occurs it ought to pull the sense of other words with it. In the case of *Il Principe* the word that immediately recommends itself for a test of *lo stato*'s magnetism is *virtù*. Machiavelli's use of the term *virtù* exercised a kind of fascination for a considerable number of persons in the twentieth century interested in politics as idea or act. Before the First World War a number of Germans wrote extensively about Machiavelli's concept *virtù*,[19] and between the wars Italians whose stomachs or whose eyes to the main chance were stronger than their political prescience saw the modern embodiment of Machiavelli's *virtù* in the posturing lantern-jawed bully and charlatan who unfortunately for them ended dangling head down from the end of a rope in Milan.[20]

Nevertheless *virtù* is not what *Il Principe* is mainly about. As the alternative titles, *Il Principe* and *De Principatibus, De Principati* or *De Principe*,[21] that he gave his little book indicate, Machiavelli thought it was about princes

---

[19] Friedrich Meinecke, *Machiavellism,* tr. Douglas Scott (New Haven, Conn., 1957), 31–44; E. W. Mayer, *Machiavellis Geschichtsauffassung und sein Begriff "Virtù"* (Munich, 1912).
[20] Ercole, *La Politica,* 5–64.
[21] Machiavelli, *Discorsi sopra la prima deca di Tito Livio,* Bk. II, Chap. 1: reference to *nostro trattato de principati;* Bk. II, Chap. XLII: reference to *nostro trattato de Principe.*

The Loom of Language   955

and *principati*. And a *principato* is a species of *stato;* about *stato* we already know something. On a gross count *virtù* occurs about two-thirds as often as *stato* in *Il Principe*.[22] And while *stato* or *principato* fail to show up in only one chapter of *Il Principe*,[23] on the other hand *virtù* is missing from over a quarter of the chapters.[24] More than this, *virtù* is not always necessary to a prince for getting or even keeping a *stato,* while qualities intentionally distinguished from *virtù—industria, prudenzia, astuzia, scelleratezza;* industry, prudence, craft, even orneriness[25]—also come in handy. And when one subjects the denotations of *virtù* and its derivatives in *Il Principe* to the dreary rigors of linguistic analysis, they turn out to be as perplexing as the denotations of *stato,* but in a different way. In most cases they are not particularly ambiguous or hard to ascertain. But they are rich in variety and very poor in novelty. Machiavelli does not use the term with any signification different from those of *virtus* in classical Latin. More than this, in the half century before Machiavelli wrote *Il Principe* the English used their cognate term "virtue," and the French used theirs, *virtu,* with every denotation *virtù* has in *Il Principe*.[26] This does not mean that there is nothing especially worthy of note about the way Machiavelli used the term. It does mean that once again the mere listing of denotation is a dead end.

The first useful thing to note about *virtù* in *Il Principe* is that it tends to occur in thick clots: of its seventy occurrences, forty-five (a little short of two-thirds) appear in less than one-fourth of the chapters of the book. Moreover, the chapters in which *virtù* shows up with high frequency themselves form a couple of clusters: Chapters VI–VIII, Chapters XII and XIII, and off alone at the very end, Chapter XXVI. We start with that last chapter and its famous appeal for union among Italians to end the barbarian domination, which "stinks in the nostrils of every man." In that chapter half the time *virtù* is not the *virtù* of the prince but that of the Italian soldiers. It refers unmistakably to their fighting quality, their valor. The whole point of the chapter is that all Italy needs is a military leader as valiant—with as much *virtù*—as its soldiery, and that the time is propitious for such a leader to come forward. The next cluster to consider is the ten occurrences in Chapters XII and XIII. But those chapters deal with military problems specifically and exclusively. Probably

---

[22] *Stato* appears 115 times, *virtù* and its adjectival and adverbial forms 70. The discrepancy is the more marked since, for Machiavelli, *stato* had no adjectival or adverbial forms.

[23] Machiavelli, *Il Principe,* Chap. XXV.

[24] *Ibid.,* Chaps. II, V, X, XVIII, XX, XXII, XXIII.

[25] *Ibid.,* Chaps. II, III (*industria*), Chap. III (*prudenzia*), Chap. IX (*astuzia*), Chap. VIII (*scelleratezza*).

[26] For Latin, see Forcellini's *Lexicon* and Du Cange's *Glossarium;* for English, the *Oxford English Dictionary;* for French, the dictionaries of Godefroy and La Curne de St. Palaye.

J. H. Hexter

in all ten occurrences, certainly in nine out of ten, *virtù* refers to soldierly qualities, sometimes of kinds of soldiers (auxiliaries), sometimes of peoples (the Venetians, the Romans, the Goths), and sometimes of military commanders.

And now as to the largest cluster of all: nearly two-fifths of the *virtùs* in *Il Principe* show up in Chapters VI–VIII,[27] that is, in about one-eighth of the chapters and one-sixth of the book. It is this section above all that has provided the material for the more elaborate fantasies that have enveloped *Il Principe*. To put these chapters in perspective, they treat of new principalities, one of the five types into which Machiavelli divides *principati*: hereditary, mixed, new, ecclesiastical, civil. To get hold of *lo stato*, of what was politically up for grabs in a country, a new prince had to have an army of his own or someone else's, or craft, or villainy, or luck (*fortuna*), or *virtù*, or some combination of these. But once having acquired a *stato* the only secure way to keep it was with an army of one's own and with *virtù*, that is the capacities and qualities, the valor or prowess, needed to keep the *stato* and command the army. If a prince had "lucked" into rule or got there by using someone else's army, then he had particular need of *virtù* to hack through the difficulties of holding onto a *stato* so acquired. Thus with Savonarola in mind, who had the *stato* of Florence in hand but for lack of prowess and an army lost it, Machiavelli says contemptuously "profeti disarmati ruinorno" (prophets without arms go down in ruin).[28] This seems to be about the residue of the *mystique* of *virtù* so dear to the heart of Machiavelli worshipers of a later day. Virtù usually refers to that cluster of qualities which makes a military commander successful, whether on the offensive—taking—or on the defensive—keeping. This is not, however, quite all that needs to be said about *virtù* in *Il Principe*.

Whatever else it may be, *Il Principe* is a book written early in the sixteenth century about ruling. In that age men who wrote such books always instructed the ruler on the *virtus* or *virtutes,* or the *vertu* or *vertus,* or the virtue or virtues, or the *virtù* he ought to have. In these treatises there is no disharmony between the significances of *virtù*. In a military or political context *virtù* is still suffused with the aura of moral qualities or goodness, and it recurs again and again in a clearly moral sense in the wearisome lists of virtues that the prince is admonished to possess himself of. In *Il Principe*, however, *virtù* appears unmistakably and unambiguously in the sense of the moral qualities and personal goodness of the ruler only thrice,[29] that is, once

[27] Twenty-seven occurrences equaling 38 per cent.
[28] Machiavelli, *Il Principe*, Chap. VII.
[29] Once *ibid.*, Chap. XV, twice *ibid.*, Chap. XVI.

The Loom of Language   957

out of every twenty-three times that Machiavelli uses the term. The disjunction of *virtù* in the sense of moral qualities from *virtù* in its other senses is sharp and decisive; there is no continuity or overlay between the former sense and the others. The way in which Machiavelli marks the disjunction is especially significant. In effect when he talks of the *virtù* that a prince needs if he is to hold onto a *stato*, or get more of it, or not lose it, he is never talking about moral virtues or goodness. And this is evident from the fact that on each of *virtù*'s rare appearances in this very common sense of moral qualities, it is accompanied by an admonition to the prince that for his own good he had better avoid it or by the observation that only a lucky prince can get away with it, while without *virtù* in the other sense a prince cannot hold a new *stato*, no matter how he acquires it. In thus driving a wedge between the *virtù* the prince could not get along without and the *virtù* he could not get along with, Machiavelli did more than strain the contemporary fabric of political imperatives; he contemptuously swept much of it aside as useless for the guidance of human action.

And now we can answer our question about the magnetic pull of *lo stato*. In *Il Principe*, Machiavelli's preoccupation with how to acquire *lo stato*, how to keep it, hold it, and avoid losing it has violently modified the accustomed orbit of *virtù* in the political universe. Not only has half that orbit disappeared, but it is the half that then lay and still lies in the realm of universal ethical imperatives. The impulsions to which *virtù* responds in *Il Principe* emanate from *lo stato* and the military and political means necessary to its appropriation and exploitation.

Of all value-bearing modifiers the most general and all-encompassing are the family, good-well, bad-ill, or in Italian, *buono-bene, malo-male*. One would expect the sort of magnetic force that *stato* exercised on *virtù* also to affect this wide-span group of words in *Il Principe*. Again a mere listing of denotation proves useless. The whole gamut of denotations is there from the neutral emphatic function of denoting "really" or "indeed" [30] to the notion of a universal good, *bene alla università delle uomini*.[31] It is when we try to find out who the good in *Il Principe* is good for and who the ill is ill for that we note a replication of that somewhat terrifying shift in the object of words of ethical specification which we have already found in *virtù*. The good refers to the common good or general welfare twice and to what we might call civic goodness or merit five times. In contrast forty-three times what is good or bad is simply good or bad for the prince, to his advantage

---

[30] *Ibid.*, Chap. xvi.
[31] *Ibid.*, Chap. xxvi.

J. H. Hexter

or to his disadvantage. What was to his advantage and therefore good was to be able to acquire a *stato,* or more *stato* (*più stato*), to build it, to keep it, to defend it, to occupy it, possess it, seize it, take it. What was disadvantageous and therefore bad was to lose *stato,* have it taken away. In these instances to ask whether what the prince did was good or bad for anyone else—the people, say, or even the state in its present-day sense—is a mere irrelevance. When Machiavelli capitulated to his own need to *ragionare dello stato* in *Il Principe,* he was not concerned to "talk sensibly" about what was good or bad for anyone but the prince.

Buono-bene-malo-male also appear in the sense of "morally right" or "morally wrong" in *Il Principe.* And here their verbal orbit is precisely symmetrical with that of *virtù.* In almost every instance they appear in this sense only when Machiavelli is taking pains to point out that to get *stato* and keep or increase it a prince must look as good as he can and be as bad as he needs. By its magnetic force *stato* has here altered the orbit of the most ordinary of all words used for discriminating between right and wrong.

In the light of the foregoing examination of some of the operations Machiavelli performed on the loom of language in *Il Principe,* it seems to me that the conclusion I arrived at some years ago when I merely considered *lo stato* holds up fairly well. "In *Il Principe* there is no justification for the relation of the prince to *lo stato.* There can be none because *lo stato* is not a matrix of values, a body politic; it is an instrument of exploitation, the mechanism the prince uses to get what he wants. . . . If the prince exploits *lo stato* with astuteness he will keep his grip on *lo stato* and even tighten it, and will be glorified as a man of honor and praised by everyone, for, as Machiavelli says in the climactic sentences of *Il Principe,* the mob is always gulled by appearances and by the way things work out, and the mob is all there is in the world. So *si guarda al fino,* take heed of the result. The result is political success or failure. It is not right to succeed, it is not wrong to fail. It is merely success to succeed, and failure to fail. Right is not might, might is not right; might is might, and that is what *Il Principe* is about. As to right—any kind of right of the individual or of the state—that is not really what *Il Principe* is about."[32]

The relation of *Il Principe* to the fabric of political imperatives of Machiavelli's own day should by now be evident enough: it makes a shambles of it.

In England, shortly after Machiavelli wrote *Il Principe,* another worker

[32] Hexter, "*Il principe,*" 134.

The Loom of Language   959

at the loom of language, Thomas More, dealt in a very peculiar way with the fabric of imperatives of his day in his greatest book, *Utopia*. His native land, which stood at the focus of More's vision and experience when he wrote *Utopia*, was one of those *stati hereditari*[33] that did not evoke Machiavelli's interest because by a rapid but inaccurate reading of the past in the light of the present he had concluded that they were easy to hold. Since in about 1514 he was getting ready to write his history of the reign of Richard III,[34] and since like most of his contemporaries in his native land he saw his own times against the background of the bloody chronicle of English kings in the fifteenth century, More knew better than that. Nevertheless he wrote *Utopia* with his mind fixed on his own land in his own time, and in the second decade of the sixteenth century England was not disturbed by the sort of political upheaval that was the milieu of *Il Principe* and that confirmed and strengthened Machiavelli's obsession with *lo stato*. What concerned More was not *lo stato* but, as the full title of *Utopia* indicated, the *status reipublicae*.[35] Between Machiavelli's *stato* and More's *status* the connection is wholly etymological. More was impelled to write *Utopia* by "the state of the nation," as we might say, or perhaps better, by the "condition of the commonweal" of England and Christendom. When he wrote of the traits that in the minds of ordinary men constituted the true worth of commonweals, he produced curious effects on the loom of language. He did so again by his way of using some of the terms ordinarily used to designate the masters of the commonwealth of England and of Christendom. Indeed because of an oddity of language, which reflects an oddity of contemporary thought, those latter terms are not, as we shall see, readily separable from the then current common notion of true worth.

These traces in words of the relation between *Utopia* and the fabric of imperatives in More's milieu when he wrote his work are easier to make out than those which Machiavelli left in the language of *Il Principe*. More did not cut away a large part of the range that a motif word had in his own day and then omit to extend that word to the range which it has today, as Machiavelli did with *lo stato*. What he did was take a cluster of words that gave a particular character to an important sector of the fabric of imperatives in his day and reverse the signs on them. From pluses he turned them into minuses; from honorific terms he transformed them into pejorative

---

[33] Machiavelli, *Il Principe*, Chap. II.
[34] *The History of King Richard III* (New Haven, Conn., 1963), Volume II of *The Complete Works of St. Thomas More*, ed. Sylvester, lxiii–lxv.
[35] Thomas More, *Utopia*, ed. J. H. Lupton (Oxford, Eng., 1895), facing page lxxvi, *De Optimo Reip. Statu deque nova insula Utopia libellus vero aureus* . . . .

ones. Thus, there is no more honorable (*magis honorificum*) source of profit to the king, according to More, than penalties for disobeying laws long unenforced and forgotten "since they have the look of justice about them."[36] When it is offended, the brightest manifestation of earthly power, majesty (*majestas*), even the majesty of the highest temporal dignitary, the Holy Roman Emperor, can be salved with gold.[37] Elegance and splendor are disgraceful, the vain show of a set of foolish popinjays.[38] *Gloria* is *ostentatio*, ostentation.[39] At worst, when it is the satisfaction a ruler derives from acquiring and holding a land other than his own, it is *gloriola*,[40] petty self-satisfaction. Majesty, splendor, glory, honor—these are attributes of God or what men owe Him. But in *Utopia* they are what men with power and riches seek and demand for themselves merely as their due for possessing power and riches. They are the things of God that a host of petty Caesars claim and force men to render unto them. And in demanding such things the rulers of the earth subvert their meaning, making them literally preposterous.

More striking than the foregoing is the treatment *nobilis* and *generosus* received in *Utopia*. These two words were tightly keyed into the whole image of the cosmos by means of which for centuries most men who thought about such matters at all arrayed and ordered vast tracts of their experience and provided them with ostensibly rational meaning. That image had two dimensions. The first dimension was the "great chain of being," the conception that in His outflow of creative love God left uncreated no kind of thing from the insensate gross earth at the bottom to the highest rational spirits, the angels, at the top.[41] The cosmos then was scaled from top to bottom, from highest to lowest, from best to least good; it was shot through with a conception of graded worth. The other dimension was the conception of correspondences.[42] The best-known correspondences perhaps are those among the human body, the body of the family, the body politic, and the body, so to speak, of the cosmos itself, with the head, the father, the king, and the sun paramount in each. Parallels ran horizontally between corresponding levels of each genus of entities. The effect, it would seem, of this mode of perception would be to diminish precision and clarity of specific observation, at once to enrich and becloud the imagination, and to impart

[36] *Ibid.* (References hereafter are to Lupton's edition. Except when otherwise indicated, however, translations are modified in the light of the forthcoming Yale edition of *Utopia* referred to above.)

[37] *Ibid.*, 82.

[38] *Ibid.*, 196, 178–79.

[39] *Ibid.*, 157.

[40] *Ibid.*, 86.

[41] Arthur Lovejoy, *The Great Chain of Being* (Cambridge, Mass., 1936), esp. 45–51, 67–80.

[42] E. M. W. Tillyard, *The Elizabethan World Picture* (London, 1952), 77–93.

The Loom of Language   961

to certain words a massiveness of connotation and of implication of worth or merit that we can only with difficulty grasp.

Nobilis, generosus, and their equivalents in the various languages of Europe were words possessing this massive quality in a pre-eminent degree. They were indicators of high status in a world where status was a fundamental assumption rather than a recent discovery of sociologists. They were also symbols of merit, and through the process of correspondences the notion of merit was firmly fixed to the notion of status. There were noble men and base men as there were noble metals and base metals. Scarcely a half year before Thomas More began to write *Utopia,* a French contemporary gave perfect and naïve expression to this cultural stereotype, expression the more notable because the author was not otherwise a particularly naïve man. In *La Monarchie de France* Claude Seyssel discusses the favor the crown owed to the noblesse over the other orders of society. Other things being equal or perhaps just a trifle less than equal, Seyssel justifies that favor because the nobility is more *digne,* more worthy than the well-to-do or the common people and because "ils sont de meilleur étoffe" (they are made of better stuff).[43] This, he says, is as reason would have it. Obviously he identifies reason with the whole climate of opinion or spiritual syndrome created by the juncture of the great chain of being with the parallel ladders of correspondence. Under such circumstances to change the signs on *generosus* and *nobilis* implies more than a downgrading of a segment of the social hierarchy; it means the displacement of a whole sector of the fabric of imperatives.

Men who were charged with or had assumed responsibility for the care of the fabric of imperatives in the late Middle Ages and the Renaissance made much of the noble and the gentle in their word spinning. The older tradition excoriated the lives lived by nobles and gentlemen in the degenerate days of the current excoriator. This denunciation was a prelude to an appeal to the noble and gentle to return to the ancient or original or natural virtues of their order, forgotten or abandoned in the present degenerate age. The more recent literary ploy, a favorite of the humanist, was to raise the question of what constituted true nobility. With a degree of consensus unusual among them the humanists tended to agree that being noble was not a matter of long lineage, wealth, or great ancestry; it was rather a matter of being a man of true excellence. On examination it turns out, not too surprisingly, that the humanists' man of true excellence bears a marked likeness to the humanist ego ideal. If More had used *nobilis* or *generosus* in either of these

[43] Claude Seyssel, *La Monarchie de France,* ed. Jacques Poujol (Paris, 1961), 122–23.

     J. H. Hexter

ways in *Utopia,* he would have fallen into one of two well-known literary stereotypes: that of the "defections of the estates,"[44] standard in medieval social polemics, or that of the "debate on true nobility,"[45] standard in the self-serving effusions of humanists.

In fact he did neither. In the first place *generosus* and *nobilis* never appear in a favorable context when More is referring to the cosmopolitan military elite, the aristocracy of his own day. They occur seventeen times with pejorative overtones, thrice with doubtful connotation, and just once with honorific implications.[46] And that once, *generosus* is used to describe the stoutheartedness of the citizen militia of Utopia in language that would have given joy to Machiavelli.[47]

What More was up to is clear from his speech; it is yet clearer from his silence, especially his silence in the second part of *Utopia* where he describes the best ordering of a commonweal or civil society. For in that society there are no "true" nobles or "true" gentlemen; there are no *nobiles* or *generosi* at all; there are only citizens. This is curious enough, most eccentric indeed with respect to that large sector of the current fabric of imperatives which assimilated excellence to status by blanketing both with the terms *nobilis* and *generosus*. Yet the language of Part II of *Utopia* is even more revealing and more curious if one looks at it from the vantage point provided by the English translation of the book that Ralph Robinson made in the 1550's.

Robinson lightly sprinkled Part II of that translation with the adjectives "gentle" and its cognates used in an honorific sense comportable with the contemporary fabric of imperatives. When one looks at the identical places in More's Latin original for the equivalent word *generosus* and its cognates, however, one does not find them. More had used entirely different words to designate the qualities he was praising. Thus Robinson says that King Utopus brought his new subjects to "humanity and civil gentleness," where

---

[44] Ruth Mohl, *The Three Estates in Medieval and Renaissance Literature* (New York, 1933), 341–66.

[45] Sir Thomas Elyot, *The Boke named the Governour,* ed. H. H. S. Crofts (2 vols., London, 1880), II, 26–38, and references in footnotes there.

[46] More, *Utopia,* ed. Lupton, *passim.*

	Nobilis	*Generosus*
honorific		page 258
doubtful	pages 178, 181	page 37
pejorative	pages 45, 52, 56, 146, 196, 197 (2), 251, 308	pages 47 (2), 50 (2), 52, 56, 146, 302
neutral		page 300

[47] *Ibid.,* 258.

The Loom of Language   963

More had written *cultus humanitatisque perduxit*.[48] He described clemency as "the gentlest affection of our nature," but More had called it *humanissimum naturae nostrae affectum*.[49] Where Robinson translates, "Nature biddeth thee to be good and gentle to other[s but] she commandeth thee not to be cruel and ungentle to thyself," we find *bonus* and *inclementem* in More's Latin, but we find no equivalent at all for "gentle" and "ungentle."[50] A little later Robinson simply put "gently" where More put *clementer*,[51] and then wrote "gently and favorably" where More only had *indulgenter*.[52] Again where More writes of a *humanitatis ac benignitatis officium,* Robinson translates "a point of humanity and gentleness."[53] Thus one way or another Robinson equated gentility with humanity, goodness, clemency, kindliness, and benignity. More, however, had done nothing of the sort. There were abundant humanity, goodness, clemency, kindliness, and benignity in the utopian commonwealth, but More never linked any of these traits with gentility or nobility, with gentlemen or noblemen. The ascription of these qualities to ordinary men who worked with their hands in town and country ran counter to one of the most persistent of all linguistic phenomena of the English language, the movement of terms from the point where they simply designated low status or mere youth to the point where they designated some sort of moral depravity or viciousness. The carl, or "ordinary guy," became a churl, while unpleasant conduct became "churlish"; the knave, started as a young boy (a *knabe*), became a servant, and thence a rascal; the boor began as a farmer and became a gross lout; the villain came to a worse ending still, just because he stayed down on the farm working for the owner of the villa.

In one place Robinson took action the reverse of that which we have caught him in above. More had charged *nobilis, aurifex,* and *foenerator,* who did nothing or did ill to the commonwealth, with the injustice of living idly while the true supporters of society—laborers, carters, carpenters, and farmers—worked like beasts of burden. Robinson carries the charge home to the "rich goldsmith" and the "usurer," but he leaves the nobleman out.[54] The asynchronous silence of More's Latin and Robinson's English in these instances is perhaps even more significant than the tone of contempt with which the words *nobilis* and *generosus* so often ring when they do appear in

---

[48] *Ibid.,* 118.
[49] *Ibid.,* 158
[50] *Ibid.,* 192.
[51] *Ibid.,* 222.
[52] *Ibid.,* 232.
[53] *Ibid.,* 193. For further examples, see pages 168, 212, 220.
[54] *Ibid.,* 301. There is another possible instance of the same thing, only involving *generosus* on page 47.

J. H. Hexter

the Latin original. A view of the world that rejected the assimilation of the good to the noble and the gentle was alien to Robinson, as it was to most articulate men in the sixteenth century. He translated Part II of *Utopia*, but the idea behind it did not fully penetrate his consciousness. In his translation, quite unconsciously one suspects, he set the loom of language to work to repair the holes More had torn into the current fabric of imperatives. What was the import of that rending?

When I consider . . . the condition of all commonwealths flourishing anywhere in the world today so help me God, I can see nothing but a kind of conspiracy of the rich aiming at their own interests under the name of the commonwealth. They devise every available way first to keep without fear whatever they have amassed . . . and second to buy as cheap as possible and exploit the labor of the poor. These become law just as soon as the rich have decreed their observance in the name of the public—that is in the name of the poor, too! [55]

In the eyes of Thomas More, who had envisaged, he believed, the conditions for the right ordering of a commonwealth the very structure of the princely commonwealths of Europe is an enormous fraud perpetrated by the rich and powerful on the poor and weak. In saying this in *Utopia*, More was impelled to set on some quite common words values opposite to those they bore among most of his contemporaries.

The immediate implication of our examination of the loom of language as it appeared in Machiavelli's *Il Principe* and More's *Utopia* is that in the years just before the Reformation Machiavelli in *Il Principe* and More in *Utopia* did indeed wreak strange havoc on the fabric of imperatives. Moreover, although they were men whose temperaments and convictions stood far apart, they wrought a similar sort of havoc in overlapping though not identical areas of the fabric. In effect they treated the language of politics each in a different way, yet each in such a way as to make clear their view that the current imperatives of politics were an exploitative swindle by means of which the possessors of power grabbed chunks of it from one another and withheld it and its advantages from those who did not possess it. No more for the English writer than for the Italian was the existing order of the human community a true *vinculum juris,* a bond of rightful law, and as long as that order remained what it was, talk about political obligation, which has been described as the central problem of politics,[56] could have very little meaning.

[55] *Ibid.*, 303–304.
[56] Alessandro Passerin d'Entrèves, *Medieval Contributions to Political Thought* (Oxford, Eng., 1939), 3.

The Loom of Language   965

Our detailed inquiry into the way Machiavelli and More used a few words in *Il Principe* and *Utopia* may permit the following tentative and general conclusions about the possibilities latent in this kind of investigation.

A careful examination of the loom of language can provide solid evidence about shifts in the fabric of imperatives at least in the minds of particular writers at certain points in their lives.

The changes in words that provide this evidence vary in kind. They may be grossly conspicuous word substitutions. They may be curtailments in the current senses of a word or reversals in its value. Or they may show themselves in a word's syntactical posture and in the company it keeps with other words.

This is a monitory point, and one only hinted at in the preceding paper. The kind of probing here illustrated should not lead to indulgence in precipitate statements about changes in the entire climate of opinion of a society, statements made in haste to be repented at leisure. The relation between the sort of language shifts we have described and changes in the climate of opinion are the appropriate subject not for assumption but for painstaking investigation.[57]

Most historians tend to be impatient, perhaps too quickly impatient, with discussions of the general methodological implications and possibilities of a mode of historical investigation. They prefer to hear in detail what follows in a particular case. What follows in the particular case of the foregoing study of the language of *Il Principe* and *Utopia*? In relation to the fabric of imperatives both Machiavelli and More were of the group of men we have described as maintenance specialists. The effect of their books, however, was

---

[57] How these very tentative remarks will strike investigators working in relevant and related areas of the linguistic sciences and how this investigation relates to those conducted in those sciences, I do not know. I was warned by the reader of an early draft of this paper that it would appear naïve if it made no reference to parallel studies by students of historical linguistics. Because, however, I had read no such works, nor indeed any work at all on linguistics, when I wrote the paper, the warning has not been heeded. Since then, I have studied the subject a bit, but a little knowledge is a dangerous thing, especially dangerous to him who is rash enough to display it before those who possess a great deal of it; thus my recently acquired dim light will remain judiciously hidden under a bushel. One particular point about method, however, may appropriately be made. The metaphor of the loom of language and the fabric of imperatives is strictly *ad hoc*, for the particular task to which this paper addresses itself, and it is not fully elaborated. It may or may not be worth such elaboration, and it may overlap or even duplicate kinds of concepts or imagery already used in linguistics. In the various areas of human inquiry there are times for conceptual rigor and times for a certain imaginative looseness, times when premature precision may reduce a whole area to sterility. My little reading has persuaded me that the area of linguistics on which this paper touches is of the latter kind. An undue zeal for scientific rigor in hypothesizing in that area at this point might seriously hamper investigation, as the attempt to subject them to the rigor of Galilean mechanics hampered the life sciences in the seventeenth century. This of course in no way should license any but the most meticulous accuracy in the testing and use of *historical* data.

not to reinforce, to mend, or to adjust that part of the fabric which was their immediate concern; it was to destroy it. In very different ways the language of *Il Principe* and that of *Utopia* express a common sense of the condition of things and a common spiritual malaise. They express alienation. This alienation is of course in some measure personal to Machiavelli and More, but in their view their personal alienation was but an image of alienation, cleavage, disjunction in the world they lived in. For Machiavelli that disjunction lay between the fabric of political imperatives and the conditions of effective political action. For fools who took them seriously such imperatives lit the way to death or defeat. For the shrewd and bold, who used them to gull the mob, they were means to get, hold, or increase *stato*—whatever prizes were about for the taking in the region of politics.[58] They certainly did not provide a viable set of rules to give legitimate order to and guide men in their doings in that region. In sum they were a swindle; the language of *Il Principe* makes it clear enough that Machiavelli considered them a swindle. In the same way the language of *Utopia* makes it clear that More regarded the imperatives supposed to legitimate the position of those who dominated the social order in his world a swindle. It might be argued that the language of More and Machiavelli betrays an alienation from the areas of the contemporary fabric of imperatives to which it relates more radical than that of Luther to the religious imperatives of the same age.

A year after the publication of *Utopia*, however, Luther's alienation set in train the events that shortly wrought a violent, long, and shattering upheaval —a great revolution—in the Western world. What did the alienations of Machiavelli and More wreak? What followed directly from their onslaughts on the fabric of imperatives? Nothing or almost nothing. And for this there was good reason. To believe *Il Principe*, men must believe that the repository of the ultimate earthly power to which they are subject is merely the passive prize of a game in which they may take part or not as they will. They must also believe that unless they are willing to carry a frightful handicap they can only play the game by cutting clear away from the fabric of imperatives. Such a view was too radical, the alienation it embodied too absolute to be acceptable to Machiavelli's contemporaries; indeed as is evident in certain chapters of the *Discorsi*, it was too radical for Machiavelli himself.[59] More's alienation as expressed and discussed in *Utopia* was even larger in its scope than Machiavelli's, involving a greater area of the fabric of imperatives, encompassing the whole *status reipublicae*, or, as we would say, the entire

[58] Machiavelli, *Il Principe*, Chap. xviii.
[59] Esp. *id.*, *Discorsi*, Bk. I, Chaps. ix, x.

The Loom of Language   967

political, economic, and social order. Nor was More ready to let it go at that, and like Machiavelli simply to investigate the qualities and stratagems useful for the exploitation of the chances for aggrandizement which that order and its fraudulent fabric of imperatives made available. Instead More presented an alternative fabric of imperatives, an *optimus status reipublicae,* in which the means of alienation in his own society—money, private property, inequality, and the fabric of imperatives that support them and that they support—would not exist. In such a commonweal his own alienation—he calls it a prison[60]—would end, and so would the alienation—he calls it worse than bondage[61]—of almost all humankind. But how are men to pass from this world of alienation and bondage to that world of reconciliation and freedom? To this question More gives no answer, but only tells a tale of Utopus, a king who never was, who seventeen hundred years ago brought this blessed consummation to Utopia, a land that never was. *Utopia* is literally nowhere.[62]

For more than three hundred years *Il Principe* and *Utopia,* two of the most radical repudiations and two of the most drastic onslaughts on the fabric of imperatives of Western men, two of the most powerful images of the alienation which that fabric engendered, stood isolated and separated at the threshold of the modern age. Separated because no imagination emerged powerful enough to bind together and reduce to a mutual coherence the nightmare of the Florentine official and the daydream of the English humanist.

Only in the 1830's and 1840's did some Europeans, new prophets of a new age, grasp the possibilities latent in the visions of Machiavelli and More. Property was theft; the state was the supreme instrument of exploitation. Together they brought about that alienation of man from his true nature which was the sum of human history. But if the state was merely a means of exploitation, a weapon in the warfare which those who had forever waged against those who had not, then it was for the exploited and alienated to seize the weapon and destroy it or use it to destroy the means of their alienation: private ownership and the system of buying and selling for money which maintained it. By means appropriate to that totally alienated man, Machiavelli's prince, the totally alienated class, the exploited and dispossessed, were to grasp *lo stato,* and through the exploitation of the exploiter, uproot alienation itself, thereby clearing the way for the restoration of men to the

---

[60] Desiderius Erasmus, *Opus Epistolarum,* ed. P. A. Allen *et al.* (12 vols., Oxford, Eng., 1906–58), II, no. 499, line 60.

[61] More, *Utopia,* ed. Lupton, 141.

[62] "Nowhere" (Lat. *Nusquama*) is, of course, the meaning of the Greek name for the island—Utopia.

J. H. Hexter

family of man, the classless society, utopia. The link between the Machiavellian actuality and the utopian dream was not a mythical King Utopus; it was
class war, seizure of power, revolution.[63] But in the second decade of the
sixteenth century, the secular *kairos,* the ripeness of time, which was to bring
into the arena of action the alienation for which Machiavelli and More in
their divergent ways found words, was hundreds of years off. In the meantime *Il Principe* and *Utopia* retained a high level of intellectual visibility;
people did not forget them. But men have ways of dealing with inconvenient,
wide-eyed, small boys who shout in the street, "The Emperor is wearing no
clothes!" They called *Il Principe* wicked and *Utopia* a mere fantasy. And
this may have been as sensible a way of dealing with them as any. At least,
since men a hundred-odd years ago discovered means of fusing the visions
these little books contained, nothing has happened that demands that we
believe otherwise.

[63] This potpourri of conceptions, intentionally not sorted out or made precise here, was
concocted in the milieu of Paris between 1840, the publication date of Pierre Proudhon's *What
Is Property?* and 1848, that of the *Communist Manifesto* of Karl Marx and Friedrich Engels.
For brief but excellent accounts, see Isaiah Berlin, *Karl Marx* (London, 1939), 80–120, and
Robert Tucker, *Philosophy and Myth in Karl Marx* (Cambridge, Eng., 1961), 95–161.

[5]

10 / A Note on Machiavelli[1]

How could he have been understood? He writes against good feelings in politics, but he is also against violence. Since he has the nerve to speak of *virtue* at the very moment he is sorely wounding ordinary morality, he disconcerts the believers in Law as he does those who believe that the State is the Law. For he describes that knot of collective life in which pure morality can be cruel and pure politics requires something like a morality. We would put up with a cynic who denies values or an innocent who sacrifices action. We do not like this difficult thinker without idols.

He was certainly tempted by cynicism: he had, he says, "much difficulty in shielding himself" from the opinion of those who believe the world is "ruled by chance." [2] Now if humanity is an accident, it is not immediately evident what would uphold collective life if it were not the sheer coercion of political power. Thus the entire role of a government is to hold its subjects in check.[3] The whole art of governing is reduced to the art of war,[4] and "good troops make good laws." [5] Between those in power and their subjects, between the self and the other person, there is no area where rivalry ceases. We must either undergo or exercise coercion. At each instant Machiavelli speaks of oppression and aggression. Collective life is hell.

But what is original about Machiavelli is that, having laid down the source of struggle, he goes beyond it without ever forgetting it. He finds something other than antagonism in struggle itself. "While men are

1. A paper sent to the Umanesimo e scienza politica Congress, Rome-Florence, September, 1949.
2. *The Prince*, Chap. XXV.
3. *Discourses*, II, 23, quoted by A. Renaudet, *Machiavel*, p. 305.
4. *The Prince*, Chap. XIV.
5. Chap. XVII.

trying not to be afraid, they begin to make themselves feared by others; and they transfer to others the aggression that they push back from themselves, as if it were absolutely necessary to offend or be offended." It is in the same moment that I am about to be afraid that I make others afraid; it is the same aggression that I repel and send back upon others; it is the same terror which threatens me that I spread abroad—I live my fear in the fear I inspire. But by a counter-shock, the suffering that I cause rends me along with my victim; and so cruelty is no solution but must always be begun again. There is a circuit between the self and others, a Communion of Black Saints. The evil that I do I do to myself, and in struggling against others I struggle equally against myself. After all, a face is only shadows, lights, and colors; yet suddenly the executioner, because this face has grimaced in a certain way, mysteriously experiences a slackening—*another anguish* has relayed his own. A sentence is never anything but a statement, a collection of significations which as a matter of principle could not possibly be equivalent to the unique savor that each person has for himself. And yet when the victim admits defeat, the cruel man perceives another life beating through those words; he finds himself before *another himself*. We are far from the relationships of sheer force that hold between objects. To use Machiavelli's words, we have gone from "beasts" to "man." [6]

More exactly, we have gone from one way of fighting to another, from "fighting with force" to "fighting with laws." [7] Human combat is different from animal combat, but it is a fight. Power is not naked force, but neither is it the honest delegation of individual wills, as if the latter were able to set aside their differences. Whether new or hereditary, power is always described in *The Prince* as questionable and threatened. One of the duties of the prince is to settle questions before they have *become insoluble* as a result of the subjects' emotion. [8] It would seem to be a matter of keeping the citizens from becoming aroused. There is no power which has an absolute basis. There is only a crystallization of opinion, which tolerates power, accepting it as acquired. The problem is to avoid the dissolution of this consensus, which can occur in no time at all, no matter what the means of coercion, once a certain point of crisis has been passed. Power is of the order of the tacit. Men let themselves live within the horizon of the State and the Law as long as injustice does not make them conscious of what is unjustifiable in the two. The power which is called legitimate is

6. Chap. XVIII.
7. *Ibid.*
8. Chap. III.

that which succeeds in avoiding *contempt* and *hatred*.⁹ "The prince must make himself feared in such a way that, if he is not loved, he is at least not hated." ¹⁰ It makes little difference that those in power are blamed in a particular instance; they are established in the interval which separates criticism from repudiation, discussion from disrepute. Relationships between the subject and those in power, like those between the self and others, are cemented at a level deeper than judgment. As long as it is not a matter of contempt's radical challenge, they survive challenge.

Neither pure fact nor absolute right, power does not coerce or persuade; it thwarts—and we are better able to thwart by appealing to freedom than by terrorizing. Machiavelli formulates with precision that alternation of tension and relaxation, of repression and legality, whose secret is held by authoritarian régimes, but which is a sugar-coated form constitutes the essence of all diplomacy. We sometimes *prize* more highly those to whom we give credit: "A new prince has never disarmed his subjects; far from it, he hastens to arm them if he finds them without arms; and nothing is shrewder, for henceforth the arms are his. . . . But a prince who disarms his subjects offends them by leading them to believe that he mistrusts them, and nothing is more likely to arouse their hatred." ¹¹ "A city accustomed to freedom is more easily preserved by being governed through its own citizens." ¹² In a society in which each man mysteriously resembles every other, mistrusting if he is mistrustful and trusting if he is trustful, there is no pure coercion. Despotism calls forth scorn; oppression would call forth rebellion. The best upholders of authority are not even those who created it; they believe they have a right to it, or at least feel secure in their power. A new power will make an appeal to its adversaries, provided that they rally around it.¹³ If they are not retrievable, then authority will lose half its force: "Men must either be won over or gotten rid of; they can avenge themselves for slight offenses, but not for serious ones." ¹⁴ Thus the conqueror may hesitate between seducing and annihilating the vanquished, and sometimes Machiavelli is cruel: "the only way to preserve is to lay waste. Whoever becomes master of a town which has begun to enjoy freedom and does not destroy it should expect to be destroyed by it." ¹⁵ Yet pure violence can only be episodic.

9. Chap. XVI.
10. Chap. XVII.
11. Chap. XIV.
12. Chap. V.
13. Chap. XV.
14. Chap. V.
15. Chap. III.

214 / SIGNS

It could not possibly procure the deep-seated agreement which constitutes power, and it does not replace it. "If [the prince] finds it necessary to punish by death, he should make his motives clear." [16] This comes down to saying that there is no absolute authority.

Thus he was the first to form the theory of "collaboration" and rallying the opposition (as he was the first, moreover, to form that of the "fifth column"), which are to political terror what the Cold War is to war. But where, it will be asked, is the profit for humanism? It lies first of all in the fact that Machiavelli introduces us to the milieu proper to politics and allows us to estimate the task we are faced with if we want to bring some truth to it. It also lies in the fact that we are shown a beginning of a human community emerging from collective life as if those in power were unaware of it, and by the sole fact that they seek to seduce consciousnesses. The trap of collective life springs in both directions: liberal régimes are always a little less so than is believed; others are a little more so. So Machiavelli's pessimism is not *closed.* He has even indicated the conditions for a politics which is not unjust: it will be the one which satisfies the people. Not that the people know everything, but because if anyone is innocent they are. "The people can be satisfied without injustice, not the mighty: these seek to practice tyranny; the people seek only to avoid it. . . . The people ask nothing except not to be oppressed." [17]

In *The Prince,* Machiavelli says no more than this about the relationships between those in power and the people. But we know that in the *Discourses on Titus Livy* he is a republican. So perhaps we may extend to the relationships between those in power and the people what he says about the relationships between the prince and his advisors. He describes, then, under the name of *virtue,* a means of living with others. The prince should not decide according to others; he would be despised. Nor should he govern in isolation, for isolation is not authority. But there is a possible way of behaving which lies between these two failures. "The priest Luke said of the emperor Maxmilian, his master, who was reigning at the time, that he took counsel from no one and yet never acted according to his own opinions. In this respect he follows a course diametrically opposed to the one I have just sketched out. For since this prince does not reveal his projects to any of his ministers, observations come at the very moment these projects must be carried out, so that, pressed for time and overcome by conflicts

16. Chap. XVII.
17. Chap. IX. We are not far from the definition of the State in Thomas More's *Utopia:* "quaedam conspiratio divitum de suis commodis reipublicae nomine titulogue tractantium."

which he had not foreseen, he gives way to the *opinions* others give him." [18] There is a way of affirming oneself which aims to suppress the other person—and which makes him a slave. And there is a relationship of consultation and exchange with others which is not the death but the very act of the self. The fundamental and original struggle always threatens to reappear: it must be the prince who asks the questions; and he must not, under pain of being despised, grant anyone a permanent authorization to speak frankly. But at least during the moments when he is deliberating, he communicates with others; and others can rally around the decision he makes, because it is in some respects their decision.

The ferocity of origins is dissipated when the bond of common works and destiny is established between the prince and his ministers. Then the individual grows through the very gifts he makes to those in power; there is exchange between them. When the enemy ravages their territory, and the subjects, sheltered with the prince inside the town, see their possessions lost and pillaged, it is then that they devote themselves unreservedly to him: "for who does not know that men are attached as much by the good they do as by that which they receive?" [19] What difference does it make, it will be said, if it is still only a matter of deception, if the chief ruse of those in power is to persuade men that they are winning when they lose? But Machiavelli nowhere says that the subjects are being deceived. He describes the birth of a common life which does not know the barriers of self-love. Speaking to the Medici, he proves to them that power cannot be maintained without an appeal to freedom. In this reversal, it is perhaps the prince who is deceived. Machiavelli was a republican because he had found a principle of communion. By putting conflict and struggle at the origins of social power, he did not mean to say that agreement was impossible; he meant to underline the condition for a power which does not mystify, that is, participation in a common situation.

Machiavelli's "immoralism" thereby takes on its true meaning. We are always quoting maxims from him which restrict honesty to private life and make the interest of those in power the only rule in politics. But let us see his reason for withdrawing politics from purely moral judgment; he gives two of them. The first is that "a man who wants to be perfectly honest among dishonest people can not fail to perish sooner or later." [20] A weak argument, since it could be applied equally well to private life, where Machiavelli nevertheless remains "moral."

18. Chap. XXIII.
19. Chap. V.
20. Chap. XV.

216 / SIGNS

The second reason goes much further: it is that in historical action, goodness is sometimes catastrophic and cruelty less cruel than the easygoing mood. "Cesare Borgia was considered cruel; but it was to his cruelty he owed the advantage of reuniting Romagna and its States, and reestablishing in this province the peace and tranquillity it had so long been deprived of. And all things considered, it will be admitted that this prince was more humane than the people of Florence who, to avoid seeming cruel, let Pistoia be destroyed.[21] When it is a question of holding one's subjects to their duty, one should never be worried about being reproached for cruelty, especially since in the end the Prince will be found to have been more humane in making a small number of necessary examples than those who, through too much indulgence, encourage disorders and finally provoke murder and brigandage. For these tumults overturn the State, whereas the punishments inflicted by the Prince bear on only a few private individuals."[22]

What sometimes transforms softness into cruelty and harshness into value, and overturns the precepts of private life, is that acts of authority intervene in a certain state of opinion which changes their meaning. They awake an echo which is at times immeasurable. They open or close hidden fissures in the block of general consent, and trigger a molecular process which may modify the whole course of events. Or as mirrors set around in a circle transform a slender flame into a fairyland, acts of authority reflected in the constellation of consciousnesses are transfigured, and the reflections of these reflections create an appearance which is the proper place—the truth, in short—of historical action. Power bears a halo about it, and its curse (like that of the people, by the way, who have no better understanding of themselves) is to fail to see the image of itself it shows to others.[23] So it is a fundamental condition of politics to unfold in the realm of appearance: "Men in general judge more by their eyes than their hands. Every man can see, but very few know how to touch. Each man easily sees what he seems to be, but almost no one identifies what he is; and this small number of perceptive spirits does not dare contradict the multitude, which has the majesty of the State to shield it. Now when it is a matter of judging the inner nature of men, above all of princes, since we cannot have recourse to courts we must stick only to consequences. The main thing is to keep oneself in power; the means, whatever they may be, will always seem honorable, and will be praised by everyone."[24]

21. By failing to wipe out the families which divided Pistoia into factions.
22. *Ibid.*, Chap. XVII.
23. ". . . I think that one must be a prince to know the people's nature well, and a man of the people to know that of the prince." Dedication to *The Prince*.
24. Chap. XVIII.

A Note on Machiavelli / **217**

This does not mean that it is necessary or even preferable to deceive. It means that at the distance and the degree of generality at which political relations are established, a legendary character composed of a few words and gestures is sketched out; and that men honor or detest blindly. The prince is not an impostor. Machiavelli writes expressly: "A prince should try to fashion for himself a reputation for goodness, clemency, piety, loyalty, and justice; *furthermore, he should have all these good qualities. . . .*" [25] What he means is that even if the leader's qualities are true ones, they are always prey to legend, because they are not *touched* but *seen*—because they are not known in the movement of the life which bears them, but frozen into historical attitudes. So the prince must have a feeling for these echoes that his words and deeds arouse. He must keep in touch with these witnesses from whom all his power is derived. He must not govern as a visionary. He must remain free even in respect to his virtues. Machiavelli says the prince should have the qualities he seems to have but, he concludes, "remain sufficiently master of himself to show their contraries when it is expedient to do so." [26] A political precept, but one which could well be the rule for a true morality as well. For public judgment in terms of appearances, which converts the prince's goodness into weakness, is perhaps not so false. What is a goodness incapable of harshness? What is a goodness which wants to be goodness? A meek way of ignoring others and ultimately despising them.

Machiavelli does not ask that one govern through vices—lies, terror, trickery; he tries to define a political *virtue*, which for the prince is to speak to these mute spectators gathered around him and caught up in the dizziness of communal life. This is real spiritual strength, since it is a question of steering a way between the will to please and defiance, between self-satisfied goodness and cruelty, and conceiving of an historical undertaking all may adhere to. This virtue is not exposed to the reversals known to moralizing politics, because from the start it establishes a relationship to others which is unknown to the latter. It is this virtue and not success which Machiavelli takes as a sign of political worth, since he holds up Cesare Borgia (who did not succeed but had *virtù*) as an example and ranks Francesco Sforza (who succeeded, but by good fortune) far behind him. [27] As sometimes happens, tough politics loves men and freedom more truly than the professed humanist: it is Machiavelli who praises Brutus, and Dante who damns him. Through mastery of his relationships with others, the man in power clears away obstacles between man and man and puts a little daylight in our

25. Chap. XVII. My italics.
26. *Ibid.*
27. Chap. VII.

relationships—as if men could be close to one another only at a sort of distance.

The reason why Machiavelli is not understood is that he combines the most acute feeling for the contingency or irrationality in the world with a taste for the consciousness or freedom in man. Considering this history in which there are so many disorders, so many oppressions, so many unexpected things and turnings-back, he sees nothing which predestines it for a final harmony. He evokes the idea of a fundamental element of chance in history, an adversity which hides it from the grasp of the strongest and the most intelligent of men. And if he finally exorcises this evil spirit, it is through no transcendent principle but simply through recourse to the givens of our condition. With the same gesture he brushes aside hope and despair. If there is an adversity, it is nameless, unintentional. Nowhere can we find an obstacle we have not helped create through our errors or our faults. Nowhere can we set a limit to our power. No matter what surprises the event may bring, we can no more rid ourselves of expectations and of consciousness than we can of our body. "As we have a free will, it seems to me that we must recognize that chance rules half, or a little more than half, our actions, and that we govern the rest." [28] Even if we come to assume a hostile element in things, it is as nothing for us since we do not know its plans: "men ought never give way to despair; since they do not know their end and it comes through indirect and unknown ways, they always have reason to hope, and hoping, ought never give way to despair, no matter what bad luck and danger they are in." [29] Chance takes shape only when we give up understanding and willing. Fortune "exercises her power when no barriers are erected against her; she brings her efforts to bear upon the ill-defended points." [30] If there seems to be an inflexible course of events, it is only in past events. If fortune seems now favorable, now unfavorable, it is because man sometimes understands and sometimes misunderstands his age; and according to the case, his success or ruin is created by the same qualities—but not by chance. [31]

Machiavelli defines a virtue in our relationships with fortune which (like the virtue in our relationships with others) is equally remote from solitude and docility. He points out as our sole recourse that presence to others and our times which makes us find others at the moment we give up oppressing them—that is, find success at the moment we give up chance, escape destiny at the moment we under-

28. Chap. XXV.
29. *Discourses*, II, 29, quoted by A. Renaudet, *Machiavel*, p. 132.
30. *The Prince*, Chap. XXV.
31. *Ibid.*

A Note on Machiavelli / 219

stand our times. Even adversity takes on a human form for us: fortune is a woman. "I think it is better to be too bold than too circumspect, because fortune is a woman; she gives in only to violence and boldness; experience shows she gives herself to fierce men rather than to cold ones." [32] For a man it matters absolutely not who is wholly against humanity, for humanity is alone in its order. The idea of a fortuitous humanity which has no cause already won is what gives absolute value to our *virtue*. When we have understood what is humanly valuable within the possibilities of the moment, signs and portents never lack. "Must heaven speak? It has already manifested its will by striking signs. Men have seen the sea half open up its depths, a cloud mark out the path to follow, water spring forth from the rock, and manna fall from heaven. It is up to us to do the rest; since God, by doing everything without us, would strip us of the action of our free will, and at the same time of that portion of choice reserved for us." [33]

What humanism is more radical than this one? Machiavelli was not unaware of values. He saw them living, humming like a shipyard, bound to certain historical actions—barbarians to be booted out, an Italy to create. For the man who carries out such undertakings, his terrestrial religion finds the words of that other religion: *"Esurientes implevit bonis, et divites dimisit inanes."* [34] As Renaudet puts it: "This student of Rome's prudent boldness never intended to deny the role played in universal history by inspiration, genius, and that action of some unknown daemon which Plato and Goethe discerned. . . . But in order for passion, aided by force, to have the property of renewing a world, it must be nourished just as much by dialectical certainty as by feeling. If Machiavelli does not set poetry and intuition apart from the practical realm, it is because this poetry is truth, this intuition is made of theory and calculation." [35]

*   *   *

What he is reproached for is the idea that history is a struggle and politics a relationship to men rather than principles. Yet is anything more certain? Has not history shown even more clearly after Machiavelli than before him that principles commit us to nothing, and that they may be adapted to any end? Let us leave contemporary history aside. The progressive abolition of slavery had been proposed by Abbé Gregory in 1789. It is passed by the Convention in 1794, at the moment

32. *Ibid.*
33. Chap. XXVI.
34. *Discourses*, 1, 26, quoted by A. Renaudet, *Machiavel*, p. 231.
35. *Ibid.*, p. 301.

when, in the words of a colonist, "domestic servants, peasants, workers, and day-laborers are manifesting against the appointive aristocracy," [36] and the provincial bourgeoisie, which drew its revenues from San Domingo, is no longer in power. Liberals know the art of holding up principles on the slope of inopportune consequences.

Furthermore, principles applied in a suitable situation are instruments of oppression. Pitt discovers that fifty per cent of the slaves brought into the British Islands are being resold to French colonies. English Negroes are creating San Domingo's prosperity and giving France the European market. So he takes a stand against slavery. "He asked Wilberforce," James writes, "to join the campaign. Wilberforce represented the influential Yorkshire region. He was a man of great reputation. Expressions such as humanity, justice, national shame, etc. pealed from his mouth. . . . Clarkson came to Paris to stir the torpid energies [of the *Société des Amis des Noirs*], to subsidize them, and to inundate France with British propaganda." [37] There can be no illusions about the fate this propaganda had in store for the slaves of San Domingo. At war with France a few years later, Pitt signs an agreement with four French colonists which places the colony under English protection until peacetime, and re-establishes slavery and discrimination against mulattoes. Clearly, it is important to know not only *what principles* we are choosing but also what forces, which men, are going to apply them.

There is something still more clear: The same principles can be used by two adversaries. When Bonaparte sent troops against San Domingo who were to perish there, "many officers and all the men believed they were fighting for the Revolution; they saw in Toussaint a traitor sold to the priests, the émigrés, and the English . . . the men still thought they belonged to a revolutionary army. Yet certain nights they heard the Blacks within the fortress sing *La Marseillaise,* the *Ça ira,* and other revolutionary songs. Lacroix tells how the deluded soldiers, hearing these songs, raised up and looked at their officers as if to say: 'Could justice be on the side of our barbaric enemies? Are we no longer soldiers of republican France? Could it be that we have become vulgar political tools?' " [38] But how could this be? France was the fatherland of the Revolution. Bonaparte, who had consecrated a few of its acquisitions, was marching against Toussaint-L'Ouverture. So it was evident that Toussaint was a counter-revolutionary in the service of the enemy.

Here, as is often the case, everyone is fighting in the name of the same values—freedom and justice. What distinguishes them is the

36. James, *Les Jacobins noirs,* p. 127.
37. *Ibid.,* p. 49.
38. *Ibid.,* p. 295.

kind of men for whom liberty or justice is demanded, and with whom
society is to be made—slaves or masters. Machiavelli was right: values
are necessary but not sufficient; and it is even dangerous to stop with
values, for as long as we have not chosen those whose mission it is to
uphold these values in the historical struggle, we have done nothing.
Now it is not just in the past we see republics refuse citizenship to their
colonies, kill in the name of freedom, and take the offensive in the
name of law. Of course Machiavelli's toughminded wisdom will not
reproach them for it. History is a struggle, and if republics did not
struggle they would disappear. We should at least realize that the
means remain bloody, merciless, and sordid. The supreme deception of
the Crusades is not to admit it. The circle should be broken.

It is evidently on these grounds that a criticism of Machiavelli is
possible and necessary. He was not wrong to insist upon the problem of
power. But he was satisfied with briefly evoking a power which would
not be unjust; he did not seek very energetically to define it. What
discourages him from doing so is that he believes men are immutable,
and that régimes follow one another in cycles.[39] There will always be
two kinds of men, those who live through history and those who make
it. There are the miller, the baker, and the innkeeper with whom the
exiled Machiavelli spends his day, chatters, and plays backgammon.
("Then," he says, "disputes, vexatious words, insults arise; they argue
at the drop of a hat and utter cries that carry all the way to San
Casciano. Closed up in this lousy hole, I drain the cup of my malignant
destiny down to the lees.") And there are the great men whom he reads
history with and questions in the evening, clothed in court dress, and
who always *answer him.* ("And during four long hours," he says, "I no
longer feel any boredom; I forget all misery; I no longer fear poverty;
death no longer terrifies me. I pass completely into them.") [40] No doubt
he never resigned himself to parting company with spontaneous men.
He would not spend days contemplating them if they were not like a
mystery for him. Is it true that these men *could* love and understand
the same things he understands and loves? Seeing so much blindness
on one side, and such a natural art of commanding on the other, he is
tempted to think that there is not one mankind, but historic men and
enduring men—and to range himself on the side of the former. It is
then that, no longer having any reason to prefer one "armed prophet"
to another, he no longer acts except at random. He bases rash hopes
upon Lorenzo di Medici's son; and the Medici, following their own
rules, compromise him without employing him. A republican, he repudiates in the preface to the *History of Florence* the judgment the

39. *Discourses,* I, quoted by A. Renaudet, *Machiavel,* p. 71.
40. Letter to Francesco Vettori, quoted by A. Renaudet, *Machiavel,* p. 72.

republicans had brought against the Medici; and the republicans, who do not forgive him for it, will not employ him either. Machiavelli's conduct accentuates what was lacking in his politics: a guideline allowing him to recognize among different powers the one from which something good could be hoped for, and to elevate *virtue* above opportunism in a decisive way.

To be just we must also add that the task was a difficult one. For Machiavelli's contemporaries the political problem was first of all one of knowing if Italians would long be prevented from farming and living by French and Spanish incursions, when they were not those of the Papacy. What could he reasonably hope for, if not for an Italian nation and soldiers to create it? It was necessary to begin by creating this bit of human life in order to create the human community. Where in the discordancy of a Europe unaware of itself, of a world which had not taken stock of itself and in which the eyes of scattered lands and men had not yet met, was the universal people which could be made the accomplice of an Italian city-state? How could the peoples of all lands have recognized, acted in concert with, and rejoined each other? There is no serious humanism except the one which looks for man's effective recognition by his fellow man throughout the world. Consequently, it could not possibly precede the moment when humanity gives itself its means of communication and communion.

Today these means exist, and the problem of a real humanism that Machiavelli set was taken up again by Marx a hundred years ago. Can we say the problem is solved? What Marx intended to do to create a human community was precisely to find a different base than the always equivocal one of principles. In the situation and vital movement of the most exploited, oppressed, and powerless of men he sought the basis for a revolutionary power, that is, a power capable of suppressing exploitation and oppression. But it became apparent that the whole problem was to constitute a power of the powerless. For those in power either had to follow the fluctuations of mass consciousness in order to remain a proletarian power, and then they would be brought down swiftly; or, if they wanted to avoid this consequence, they had to make themselves the judge of proletarian interests, and then they were setting themselves up in power in the traditional sense—they were the outline of a new ruling class. The solution could be found only in an absolutely new relationship between those in power and those subject to it. It was necessary to invent political forms capable of holding power in check without annulling it. It was necessary to have leaders capable of explaining the reasons for their politics to those subject to power, and to obtain from themselves, if necessary, the sacrifices power ordinarily imposes upon subjects.

A Note on Machiavelli / 223

These political forms were roughed out and these leaders appeared in the revolution of 1917; but from the time of the Commune of Kronstadt on, the revolutionary power lost contact with a fraction of the proletariat (which was nevertheless tried and true), and in order to conceal the conflict, it begins to lie. It proclaims that the insurgents' headquarters is in the hands of the White Guards, as Bonaparte's troops treat Toussaint-L'Ouverture as a foreign agent. Already difference of opinion is faked up as sabotage, opposition as espionage. We see reappearing within the revolution the very struggles it was supposed to move beyond. And as if to prove Machiavelli right, while the revolutionary government resorts to the classic tricks of power, the opposition does not even lack sympathizers among the enemies of the Revolution. Does all power tend to "autonomize" itself, and is this tendency an inevitable destiny in all human society? Or is it a matter of a contingent development which was tied to the particular conditions of the Russian Revolution (the clandestine nature of the revolutionary movement prior to 1917, the weakness of the Russian proletariat) and which would not have occurred in a Western revolution? This is clearly the essential problem. In any case, now that the expedient of Kronstadt has become a system and the revolutionary power has definitely been substituted for the proletariat as the ruling class, with the attributes of power of an unchecked élite, we can conclude that, one hundred years after Marx, the problem of a real humanism remains intact—and so we can show indulgence toward Machiavelli, who could only glimpse the problem.

If by humanism we mean a philosophy of the inner man which finds no difficulty in principle in his relationships with others, no opacity whatsoever in the functioning of society, and which replaces political cultivation by moral exhortation, Machiavelli is not a humanist. But if by humanism we mean a philosophy which confronts the relationship of man to man and the constitution of a common situation and a common history between men as a problem, then we have to say that Machiavelli formulated some of the conditions of any serious humanism. And in this perspective the repudiation of Machiavelli which is so common today takes on a disturbing significance: it is the decision not to know the tasks of a true humanism. There is a way of repudiating Machiavelli which is Machiavellian; it is the pious dodge of those who turn their eyes and ours toward the heaven of principles in order to turn them away from what they are doing. And there is a way of praising Machiavelli which is just the opposite of Machiavellianism, since it honors in his works a contribution to political clarity.

[6]

IV

Machiavelli's Use of Livy

J. H. WHITFIELD

IN the beginning there is Dante's word for it, 'Come scrive Livio che non erra' ('As Livy writes who cannot err'), and then there is Petrarch, whose work on the text of Livy, unadvertised by himself, has only recently been brought to light, 'Quid enim est omnis historia, nisi Romana laus?' ('What is any history but the praise of Rome?'). But for Machiavelli we have a closer case than this general matter of the regard for Livy in the stream of Italian humanism. It begins with his father, Bernardo, in 1475, when Niccolò is six. Until the publication of his *Ricordi* in 1954 Bernardo had been a name; but since then there has come enhancement of his status by the fact that Bartolomeo Scala, Chancellor for the Medici of the Florentine Republic, called him 'amicus et familiaris meus' in a Dialogue of 1483—which gives him some substantial quality. It was this Bernardo who in 1475 entered into a contract with a Florentine printer to supply an index of place-names to the text of Livy. In return, Bernardo received a copy of *Le Deche tutte di Livio in forma* (all the decades of Livy printed)—an edition which must have been one of the three so far printed at Rome—and this was to become his property upon completion of his index. The printer, Niccolò di Lorenzo della Magna, started to publish at Florence in 1477, but the intended edition of Livy does not seem to have appeared. However, after over eight months' work, on 5 July 1476, Bernardo handed over his index of 120 pages quarto, with the names of all the towns, countries, rivers, islands, hills attributed to their place in the three decades of Livy; and as reward for his labour the copy he had worked with was made over to him. To which there is an epilogue: for in 1486 Bernardo sent two books to the binder, one of them a printed folio

73

LIVY

Livy; and ten days later, with as intermediary 'my young son Nicolò', he paid the binder with a barrel of red wine.[1]

We may presume this was the same copy or we may think, in view of the ten years' gap, that it was a new one. But what is evident is that we have Livy as a household name for Niccolò. And to the new evidence for Bernardo we may add its parallel for Niccolò's teacher of Latin, Ser Pagolo da Ronciglione, whose mere name Bernardo recorded in 1481, when at the age of twelve Niccolò began to study under him. For he also was a scholar of standing in Florence, who taught such eminent pupils as Pietro Crinito and Michele Verino.[2] We still know next to nothing of the first half of Machiavelli's life— that is, from 1469 to 1498, when he also entered the Florentine Chancery; but now there is the presumption that from home influence and school training he will be at ease with the Latin classics, starting with Livy. And indeed he is already bursting with the confidence that knowledge gives when he puts pen to paper. Amongst the first short treatises a special place belongs to *Del modo di trattare i popoli della valdichiana ribellati* ('The way to treat the rebellious populations of the Valdichiana'), written in the second half of 1503. His experience in the service of Florence is still, mostly, before him: his reading of Livy is obviously already strong enough for the example to leap into his mind, and dictate the answer. It is of Lucius Furius Camillus faced with rebellious Latium, and, oblivious of the fact that the circumstances were entirely different, Machiavelli set down *ad verbum* (as he says himself) some forty lines of Livy, in his Italian, as the key to action. Since the treatise is only five pages long, it is clear that this is its kernel, and that Livy has hold of Machiavelli's imagination. Nor is the general statement wanting:

> I have heard say that history is the schoolmistress to our actions, and especially of princes, and the world was always lived in in one way, by men who have always had the same passions, and always there were those who serve and those who command; and those who serve unwillingly and who serve willingly; those who rebel and are rebuked.[3]

There is in this a sharp idealism, in the sense that Machiavelli looks to literature for the solution to the problems of life; sharp, in the sense that he looks to a world of black and white in clear outlines, where one must seize the white and reject not only the black, but also the grey which lies implicitly between. Here we may take the

74

MACHIAVELLI'S USE OF LIVY

lesson from another text of Livy, where Herennius gives his advice upon the treatment of the Roman army captured in the Caudine Forks:

> Quum filius aliique principes percunctando exsequerentur, 'Quid si media via consilii caperetur; ut et dimitterentur incolumes, et leges iis iure belli victis imponerentur?' 'Ista quidem sententia,' inquit, 'ea est, quae neque amicos parat, neque inimicos tollit.' (IX.3).

> When his son and other leading men kept asking him, 'What if some compromise were adopted such as letting them go unharmed but imposing terms on them, since they have been defeated according to the rules of war?' he replied: 'Your proposal is the kind that neither wins friends nor destroys enemies.'

In a celebrated phrase of Machiavelli's, the *via di mezzo* ((the middle way, i.e. compromise) becomes what the Romans shunned, their method being, with their rebels, 'illorum animos, dum exspectatione stupent, seu poena, seu beneficio praeoccupari' ('their feelings should be overwhelmed, while they are still numb with anticipation, either by punishment or by kindness'). And for this also Machiavelli found a sharp, and celebrated, phrase, 'o beneficare o spegnere e che ogni altra via sia pericolosissima' ('either to benefit or else to extinguish (them), and that any other course was perilous'). It does not matter that the Florence to which he proffered this advice was weakly dependent on French arms for the recovery of rebellious Arezzo. What matters is a *forma mentis* for Machiavelli which some have taken as being his essential characteristic; one, at the least, to which he clings in his own imagination even when he has made his own discovery that there are no pure blacks and whites, but only greys, in life. But for those who like, economically, to see Machiavelli remaining true to himself, the Livian phrase returns more sharply in the *Prince*: 'li uomini si debbono o vezzeggiare o spegnere' ('men must be either caressed or else extinguished').

We cannot follow the course of Machiavelli's reading in the years in which he served in public office (1498-1512). There is nothing in the *Legations*, three full volumes out of the eight of his works, which seems to echo Livy. But in the *Ritratto di cose di Francia* (end 1512?, beginning 1513?) he quotes Caesar on the French as more than men when they begin to fight, and less than women afterwards; and means not Caesar, but Livy (as he will later specify in *D.*, III.xxxvi).* And

* I refer to Machiavelli's works in the Feltrinelli edition for convenience, quoting the *Prince* as *P.*, the *Discorsi* as *D.*, and the *Istorie fiorentine* as *I.f.*

LIVY

two years before, in 1510, his friend and colleague, Biagio Buonaccorsi, had quoted to him in a letter another of the sharp Livian
phrases (on neutrality, to be shunned), 'Sine gratia, sine honore,
premium victoris erimus' ('without influence, without honour, we
shall be spoils for the victor'). It echoes Livy, XXXV.49, and stuck
in Machiavelli's mind too, so that it returns in a letter of Machiavelli
of 1514 and in the *Prince*, XXI. Meanwhile, to remind us that it is
obviously not a taste for Livy only, Vettori writes to him from Rome
in November 1513, that he has assembled many historians, Livy
with Florus, Sallust, Plutarch, Appian, Tacitus, Suetonius, Lamprid-
ius and Spartianus, with Herodian, Ammianus Marcellinus and
Procopius. This list comes at a significant moment, for in December
of that year, only a month afterwards, Machiavelli wrote him back
the most famous letter written in Italian. It is the one in which he
tells Vettori of his life at San Casciano, the pettiness of day, and
then at night the putting on of nobler clothes, the entry into the
court of ancient men, the feeding on that food, 'che *solum* è mio, et
che io nacqui per lui' ('which alone is mine, and I was born for it').
And though he adds no list of his own, there is no doubt that
Vettori's one will do for Machiavelli; to prove it, there is the phrase
in the Dedication of the *Prince* (to which the letter to Vettori was the
birth-certificate) on the knowledge of the actions of great men,
'learnt by a long experience of modern things and a continual reading
of the ancient ones'. Nor should we expect after that the simple
annexation of an ancient text, such as we found in starting with
L. F. Camillus as example in 1503.

The *Prince*, that is to say, will mirror largely the problems of 1513,
in the light of Machiavelli's experience. But we can be sure that Livy,
inter alios, will contribute to the texture. For that matter, the patron
saints of the Prince (very different in reality from Caesar Borgia, who
is more normally cast for the role) are Moses, Cyrus, Romulus and
Theseus; and Romulus comes, of course, from Livy, I. But it will
have been seen already that Machiavelli is not limited in his sweep
through Livy. And here he instances (*P.*, III) the Romans in Greece,
and means to refer to Livy, XXVI; or Nabis, tyrant of Sparta (Livy,
XXXIV); he traces at some length the habits of Philopoemen, trying
out his companions on the military aspects of the countryside, and
keeps the surface of the dialogue very near the passage in Livy,
XXXV; twice an odd phrase echoes in Italian two words of Livy,
one of these places on the *inumana crudeltà* (*inhumana crudelitas—*

MACHIAVELLI'S USE OF LIVY

inhuman cruelty) of Hannibal, from Livy, XXI; then the rebellion of Scipio's army in Spain (Livy, XXVIII) and Fabius' accusation against Scipio as the corrupter of military discipline, with that other judgment on him ('of some men born rather not to err, than to correct error'), from Livy, XXIX. It will be seen, and has not always been realized, that Machiavelli is quoting from a full stomach, and that he has the first three decades at command. And, in fact, there is one case where Machiavelli may be thought to have a quite ana-chronistic dependence on his Livy. It is in *Prince*, III, where he repeatedly urges the example of the Romans, in sending *colonies*; and then, in summing up, puts the five errors of the King of France in Italy, amongst which there is 'non vi messo colonie' ('he had not sent colonies there'). The form of words echoes, for instance, Livy, I.11 ('utroque coloniae missae'—colonies were founded in both places), and *messo* is a Latinism, more connected with *mittere* than with its derivative *mettere* (which means *to put*): it corresponds to the *mandare* which Machiavelli used in the earlier references. This is as inapplicable as the advice to Florence of 1503.

To the general instances we can add three which have, perhaps, more bite. At the beginning of *P.*, XV, there is a famous scornful phrase on Machiavelli's going for reality, and not for its shadow: the *verità effettuale* (things as they really are) and not the imagination of what things are. 'And many', adds Machiavelli immediately, 'have imagined republics and principalities never seen or known in fact.' Now this has seemed the essentially revolutionary spirit of the Machiavellian gospel—things and not shows; nor has it been at all customary to write the name of Livy in the notes. Lisio, in fact, wrote Plato's name, took this as a tilt against his imaginary Republic. It is an odd coincidence that an old commentator also wrote Plato's name against a passage in Livy: 'Eludant nunc antiqua mirantes. Non equidem, si qua sit sapientium civitas, quam docti fingunt magis, quam norunt, aut principes graviores temperantioresque a cupidine imperii, aut multitudinem melius moratam censeam fieri posse' ('Now let men cease to marvel at things of old. If there were any city of philosophers—such as learned men create on the basis of imagination rather than knowledge—I do not think there could be leading men more responsible and free from ambition or a populace of more sterling character') (XXVI.22). First, for Sigonius's note: 'Platonem intelligit in libris de Republica'—he means Plato in the *Republic*. And then, apart from the correspondence, the implication.

LIVY

For Livy, the reality of the Roman people outdoes the imaginations of the philosophers; and this view we have found, and shall find more, is sober truth for Machiavelli. But what then of the *verità effettuale*? For here we can not forget that we live in the post-Taine era, and see Livy's Rome more of his construction, and less of stark reality. We cannot suggest the connection here without diminishing the value of that talisman of Machiavelli, brandished as *their* passport so often by his critics. Machiavelli may be less close to the *verità effettuale* than he imagined.

The other two passages are also notable. First, there is the statement (*P.*, XXII) of the three types of brain: the first which understands by itself, the second which can discern what others understand, the third which understands neither by itself, nor others. . . . It is a notorious passage, swift and scornful in its dismissal of the useless (larger) sort of men. It could have come from Hesiod, via the fifteenth-century Florentine Matteo Palmieri; but Lisio put in his notes what is after all sufficient as a source: 'Saepe ego, inquit, audivi, milites, eum primum esse virum, qui ipse consulat, quid in rem sit; secundum eum qui bene monenti obediat: qui nec ipse consulere, nec alteri parere sciat, eum extremum ingenii esse' ('I have often heard, soldiers, that man is pre-eminent who himself knows what to do: second is the man who follows good advice; but the person who cannot either decide for himself or obey another is last in intelligence') (XXII.29). And, finally, after the two suggestive passages, which chime, but might just possibly be independent, comes the triumphant one, where the last chapter of the *Prince* bursts into fire, and the flame is Livy, because here Machiavelli puts his message in a Latin text, not copied from the book in hand, but remembered (and so, as often, just a little crinkled in the handling): 'Qui è iustizia grande' ('Here there is great justice') 'iustum enim est bellum quibus necessarium, et pia arma ubi nulla nisi in armis spes est' ('War is just where it cannot be avoided, and arms are righteous where arms are the only hope'). For which, see Livy, IX.1: but also, so easily does it spring to Machiavelli's lips, so deeply is it imprinted in his memory, see *Discorsi*, III.12, and *Istorie fiorentine*, V. For this is the nub of Machiavelli's writing: the plight of Italy, caught unprotected by the ultramontane wars.

When he wrote the *Prince* in 1513, then, Machiavelli had Livy at his fingertips, and his quotations, though relatively few, range over the first three decades: only Books XLI-XLV, we may say, remain

78

MACHIAVELLI'S USE OF LIVY

outside his knowledge. He could therefore have embarked on his *Discourses upon Livy* at the same time, or before. But did he? Now this is a notorious problem which has much exercised the critics of Machiavelli recently. For there is a sentence in *P.* II, referring to a long discussion of republics, already made: this has left a vague, but persistent, impression that *Discorsi*, I, were started, then abandoned for the urgent writing of the *Prince*. And, naturally, as the pace of Machiavelli scholarship has quickened, scholars have claimed to detect the break. So they have identified *Discorsi*, I.1-18, first as the original nucleus. Then, faced with the problem of Machiavelli's borrowing from Polybius (of the concept of the cycle of the six sorts of government), *D.*, I.1-18 became a sort of general post-preface to the rest: written afterwards, since Machiavelli, knowing no Greek, had to wait for news out of Polybius, then put as an introduction to what had begun as a straightforward commentary to Livy, decade 1. Now it is true that there is a question-mark over that sentence of *P.*, II, but nothing very useful, or even very true, has yet come out as answer. And, as Hans Baron saw, the letter to Vettori of December 1513 is bursting with the information of the nascent *Prince* but there is no trace in the same correspondence of the genesis of the *Discorsi*. And in dedicating them later to two friends Machiavelli wrote that they had forced him to write what he would never have set down by himself. It is plain, if he was speaking the truth, and not just penning a compliment, that they could not start him writing before they knew him. And these two, Zanobi Buondelmonti and Cosimo Rucellai, belong to the group who met in the gardens of the latter, and who exercised themselves in the reading of history. At their instance, a contemporary said, Machiavelli wrote his *Discorsi*. But this association with the Orti Oricellari (the Rucellai Gardens) begins for Machiavelli not earlier than 1515.[4]

Now, there is a little evidence that the *Discorsi* (of which no autograph text remains) received some re-arrangement. For Guicciardini wrote some *considerations* critical of certain passages in what was still only circulating in manuscript, and his numeration varies, though only slightly, from the edition of 1531. In addition, there is a reference to something said before about the Venetians, in *D.*, I.53, which in appearance refers forward to something only said at last in *D.*, III.11.[5] It is easy to build on this a picture of Machiavelli shuffling at will the loose structure of his *Discourses upon Livy*. But it is neither realistic nor rewarding. In particular, those who have

79

LIVY

tried to isolate *D.*, I.1-18, either as the original germ or as a later adjunct, have failed to point out that there is no break between 18 and 19, and that the earlier section contains Machiavelli's basic discussion of the Roman kings. Since *D.*, I.19-60 (claimed as a straightforward commentary to Livy, *Dec.*, I) does not come back to that fundamental material, it is clear that Machiavelli composed his work more or less as we have it; and will remain so until we have irrefragable proof, out of newly discovered autographs, of the processes of composition and revision. But we shall lose nothing, and gain much (the power, that is, to see the *Discorsi* whole and by themselves, without the magnetic influence of the *Prince*) if we accept provisionally a date post-1515 for the actual composition of the work. To which we may set as pendant, since Cosimo Rucellai, to whom with Buondelmonti it is dedicated, died in 1519, this latter year as a rough *terminus ad quem*: remembering also that there is a certain convergence of many contemporary happenings related on the intermediary year 1517. And certainly after this period Machiavelli, as we shall see, did something else: the *Art of War* (printed in 1521), the *Florentine Histories* (commissioned in 1520, and written between then and 1525), are no longer centred on Livy.

The problem of the *Discorsi* is not (for us, at any rate) their date, nor yet their relationship to the *Prince*: it is primarily that of Machiavelli's relationship to Livy, and, secondarily, the relationship of either with reality. Now, I mentioned before Vettori's list of historians as valid, more or less, also for Machiavelli; and I might have said that in the *Prince* Machiavelli quoted directly in the Latin text Virgil (*Aeneid*, I.562-3) and Tacitus (from whom he probably took the phrase *novus principatus*, *Principato nuovo*). Once again, Tacitus is quoted with the ease of someone who does not need to look up the text, so slightly altered verbally. And Tacitus, with whom Machiavelli thus reveals a similar familiarity, is an author who has long been thought, both stylistically and temperamentally, as close to Machiavelli. Yet he does not think of writing—as people at the end of the sixteenth century will do abundantly—a commentary to Tacitus? Of course not: this is an elementary fact about his attitude to Roman history. Here we may take one name, that of the Gracchi, as a watershed. In all the *Discorsi* there are three references to the Gracchi, and they all make the same point: 'from the Tarquins to the Gracchi, more than three hundred years, the disturbances in Rome rarely give rise to exile, and very rarely to bloodshed' (*D.*,

MACHIAVELLI'S USE OF LIVY

I.4); the Agrarian Law, awakened from its sleep by the Gracchi, 'ruined entirely the liberty of Rome' (*D.*, I.36). On the next page, and in the same chapter, Machiavelli adds, after Marius and Sulla, the rise of Caesar, 'who was the first tyrant in Rome, so that city was never free again'. To which we may add the convergent remarks on Caesar in *D.*, I.10: more detestable than Catiline, as one who did than one who wished to do a wrong, so that those who read history, and make their capital out of the knowledge of antiquity, will wish to live rather as Scipios than Caesars; or will desire to possess a corrupt city, 'not to spoil it utterly as Caesar did, but to reorder it like Romulus'. By these tokens it becomes abundantly clear what are the reasons for Machiavelli's concern with Roman history, and what the vital area, and that it must be Livy from whom he draws his nourishment.

In the margin of one of his own minor works Machiavelli scrawled 'post res perditas' ('after the disaster'). It is perhaps a reference only to his extrusion from office in 1512; but we should not be doing wrong if we extend its implications to the Italy of his time. Here the clue is already in the *Prince*, on mercenary soldiery: 'tanto che li hanno condotta Italia stiava e vituperata' ('so much so that they have reduced Italy to servitude and ignominy') (*P.*, XII). It is a phrase that echoes through Machiavelli's writing, and echoes his concern. Obviously, the remedies for 'questo guasto mondo' ('this ruined world') (*I.f.*, V) must be sought in the incorrupt area of Roman history. The rest will serve at times to illustrate a case (as did the account of Roman emperors, out of Herodian, in *P.*, XIX), but it is not the fount of healing, the pattern of conduct. Now it may well be that the phrase *res perditae* is itself a textual quotation from Livy, who uses it, naturally about various losers, not infrequently. But it is equally clear that Machiavelli comes to Livy as the one author who deals with the span of history in which all—for the Romans—went right; from which, therefore, since as we saw in starting the elements of the world remain the same, the lessons of rightness can be drawn. Nor is it irrelevant to this state of mind that Livy himself writes from a similar presumption. We are, of course, at the Preface to Livy's *History*:

Ad illa mihi pro se quisque acriter intendat animum, quae vita, qui mores fuerint: per quos viros, quibusque artibus, domi militiaeque, et partum et auctum imperium sit. Labente deinde paullatim disciplina, velut desidentes primo mores sequatur animo; deinde ut magis

LIVY

magisque lapsi sint; tum ire coeperint praecipites: donec ad haec tempora, quibus nec vitia nostra, nec remedia pati possumus, perventum
est. Hoc illud est praecipue in cognitione rerum salubre ac frugiferum, omnis te exempli documenta in illustri posita monumento
intueri: inde tibi tuaeque reipublicae, quod imitere, capias: inde,
foedum inceptu, foedum exitu, quod vites. Ceterum aut me amor
negotii suscepti fallit, aut nulla unquam respublica nec maior, nec
sanctior, nec bonis exemplis ditior fuit: nec in quam civitatem tam
serae avaritia luxuriaque immigraverint: nec ubi tantus ac tam diu
paupertati ac parsimoniae honos fuerit: adeo, quanto rerum minus,
tanto minus cupiditatis erat. Nuper divitiae atque libidinem pereundi
perdendique omnia invexere.

These are the points that I would like my reader to consider carefully: the life and character of the people of old; the men and the
accomplishments at home and in the field that won and enlarged their
power. Then, with the gradual weakening of moral training, let the
reader follow the character of the Romans as it began to topple; next,
as it slid more and more; as it began to go headlong; until he comes to
the present times, when we find insufferable not only our vices but
the methods of curing them. This is what is particularly beneficial
and fruitful in a knowledge of history: to contemplate examples of
every pattern set out in a clear record; from them you can choose what
to imitate, for yourself and your country; from them you can see
what to avoid, as being foul at the start and foul in the outcome. But
unless I am deceived by my love for my task, there has never been a
country so great, so devout, and so rich in noble examples, nor any
community into which greed and lust were so late in entering or
where for so long poverty and thrift were accorded such high respect.
So true it was that the less men's material wealth, the smaller their
desire for it. In recent times, however, affluence has introduced
greed, and an excess of physical pleasure has brought about a
morbid longing utterly to destroy and be destroyed in an orgy
of lust.

Who more than Livy, in this text, betrays himself as a moralist,
laudator temporis acti? This praising of the past is something Machiavelli
discusses in the Proem to Book II. It is a general tendency, and so it
may be right, or wrong, according to the actual slope of time. But
in his own case, it is clearer than the day, for now there is nothing
to redeem from 'ogni estrema miseria, infamia e vituperio' ('no
observance of religion, of laws, of militia. . . . The present is *corrupt*':

I do not know then if I shall be accounted one of those mistaken ones,
if in these my discourses I praise too much the times of the ancient

MACHIAVELLI'S USE OF LIVY

Romans, and blame our own. And truly if the virtue that reigned then and the vice which reigns now were not clearer than the sun, I should go slower in my speech, fearing to incur that error which I blame in some. But since this is so obvious that all can see it. . . . Because it is the office of a good man, to teach to others that good which through the malignity of the times you have not been able to effect yourself. . . .

There is nothing usually his readers are more reluctant to learn than that Machiavelli writes as a moralist, with the intentions of a good man; and were it not, to use his language, clearer than the sun, I would hesitate to affirm it. But what, then, of the *verità effettuale*? It is plain we tread on slippery ground. Not, of course, that Machiavelli has Dante's naïve faith in Livy ('Livy, who never errs'). Indeed, Machiavelli allows himself the luxury of doubting Livy's word. The first case is *D.*, I.58, where he begins by alleging the authority of Livy, backed up by all the other historians, all united in affirming the inconstancy of the multitude. And to strengthen their hand, he quotes two texts from Livy. Then, in defiance of them all, he puts their united authority upon one side, not counting it a defect to defend opinion by reason, without recurrence to authority or force. And so he adds immediately that what the writers say about the multitude is true of all men, and especially of princes: 'for all who are not regulated by law will incur the errors of an unrestrained multitude'. And, of course, also Machiavelli has the trump-card in his hand, and plays it straight from Livy—not Livy in particular judgment, but Livy *in general*: the great exemplar is the Roman people, who proved in their (in Livy's, that is) long history what goodness can be in the people:

> and one will find there was in Rome that same goodness that we see in them, and we shall see that Rome neither ruled proudly nor served humbly: such was the Roman people, while the Republic lasted incorrupt, it never served humbly, and never ruled proudly; rather with its laws and magistrates it kept its rank honourably.

So what Livy said about the multitude, he said about one not ruled by law (as that of Syracuse), not of the Roman people. And on the other hand, there are very many examples both among the Roman emperors and among other tyrants and princes, where one sees such inconstancy and such variation of life, as never could be found in any multitude.

83

LIVY

The case is clear and interesting. What Machiavelli has done is to refute Livy, out of Livy: to put the spirit of the history of the Roman people, as seen by Livy, against the stereotypical judgment on the people. Nor is his procedure different in the other main case where he contradicts his author. Did the Romans gain their empire by *virtus* or *fortuna*? Livy seems to go for fortune: 'which I will not admit in any way, nor do I think that it can be upheld' (*D.*, II.1). The answer is, again, the *virtus* which shines out in Livy's pages. And the *verità effettuale*? Now once more it is clear why Machiavelli looks this way, and not that: to the Roman people, not to the Roman emperors, who are here swept again, as formerly was Caesar only, on one side, as no pattern for example. But, of course, Machiavelli's choice is critical, and uncritical. He has taken for sober truth the colours of Livy's history, ready to use them as material for construction in his own time. This is a natural process, but I fear it may be as far from reality as was that first appropriation of Lucius Furius Camillus in 1503. The first remove from reality is in the colours of Livy's narrative, which lends already an idealistic flavour to the history of early Rome. The second remove (which is what Guicciardini implied in his *Considerations*) is in taking all this as the basis for action in the sixteenth century. We are as far as may be from that old bogy of a Machiavelli, who accepts what is because it is, and admires it if it is ruthless and successful. What he wants, instead, is what you might do with what is, in the way things had been done right once. The *verità effettuale* is further from his grasp than Machiavelli, or most of his readers, realized. What Guicciardini saw was that you could not imitate the Romans unless the elements were all the same, and so, as in his *Storia d'Italia*, he dissolved the picture because the elements do not indeed cohere. For Guicciardini is the anticipation of Pirandello, with whom the elements of life do not *consist*. But Pirandello realized that we must try, for our own benefit, to make them consist. We must strive to give them the meaning that they do not possess in themselves. The one way, chaos and madness lie; the other is the only hope. And hence the dual function of Livy and of Machiavelli; the first constructs the past, makes it consist; the second seizes what is relevant, in the effort to construct the present, and to make the future consist. How better should mankind progress, out of the natural chaos of human events, towards order?

If we have this approach in mind we shall be less surprised by the

MACHIAVELLI'S USE OF LIVY

terms of Machiavelli's Proem to the *Discorsi* than if we come straight
from what everyone thinks they know about the Machiavelli of the
Prince. He writes 'urged on by that natural desire which I have always
had to do without regard those things which seem to me to be for
the general benefit of all'. It is this which has set him on a path not
so far trodden. Seeing what history relates, the things done by kings,
captains, legislators, and others who strove for their birthplace, and
nothing of their virtue now remaining. . . .

> Nevertheless, in ordering republics, in maintaining states, in ruling
> kingdoms, in ordering the militia and administering war, in judging
> subjects, in increasing rule, there is no prince or republic has recourse
> to the examples of the ancients.

It is because men have no real knowledge of history, to draw out by
reading both the savour and the lesson. And Machiavelli exclaims
again, as if the sky, the sun, the elements, and men, were different
in motion, order, power, from what they were *antiquamente*! Therefore he is impelled to write a commentary to all the books of Livy
not cut off from us by time. Into it he will put 'all that I know and
all that I have learnt, through long experience and continual reading,
of human affairs': so that we need not be surprised if this is both more
than a commentary to Livy, and less. More, in that Machiavelli is
not limited to one author, or the printed page as a source for wisdom;
less, in that the urgency of his concern is with the lesson and the
wisdom, so that he does not ever feel the need to be systematic and
orderly in the presentation of his author; or even (obviously) to
complete his task. But meanwhile it is clear that this Proem rewrites,
in a very personal style, Livy's own Preface:

> Hoc illud est praecipue in cognitione rerum salubre ac frugiferum,
> omnis te exempli documenta in illustri posita monumento intueri:
> inde tibi tuaeque reipublicae, quod imitere capias.
>   . . . non si truova principe né republica che agli esempli delli antiqui
> ricorra . . . [there is no prince or republic has recourse to the example
> of the ancients].
>   . . . quanto dal non avere vera cognizione delle storie . . . [so much
> as from not having real knowledge of history].

An idealist is one, by definition, who looks for perfection; nor is it
surprising, after what we have found thus far, that Machiavelli sees

G   85

LIVY

it, on the basis of Livy's account, in ancient Rome. We may legitimately ignore here the contribution of Polybius, and the problems it gives rise to (of whence Machiavelli's knowledge of the untranslated fragments of Polybius, VI, in his apparent lack of Greek): because what matters is not the general cycle of the six sorts of rule, but the formula which arrests rotation, and which kept Rome safeguarded by the laws of Romulus, Numa and their heirs, so that the fertility of the site, the commodity of the sea, the frequency of victory, the greatness of their sway could not corrupt for many centuries. The conclusion of the second chapter of Book I (which is normally thought of as the chapter of Polybius) is on the perfection of the Roman balance between the three elements, *principato*, *ottimati*, *popolare* (princely, aristocratic, and popular). With the institution of consuls, Senate, and tribunes of the people, they halted the movement of human affairs, and achieved the *perfect* state. Now in the past there has been attempted some spying out of Machiavellian vocabulary, but no one has emphasized the insistent beat of these blameless words. From the first *perfetto e vero fine* (true and perfect aim) to the heading of the next chapter iii, eight times Machiavelli reverts to this idea of *perfection* in Rome. And out of the laws which *prudently* obviated the defect of the good type of rule slipping always into its pejorative—to make Polybius' circle—he adds that by mixing the sorts of rule they made one which was *più fermo e più stabile* (more firm and stable).

A compromise implies a contrast. Nor does Machiavelli miss the implication. Indeed, it is a problem which he had already stated in the *Prince*: 'for in all cities there are these two different humours; and it springs from this, that the people wish not to be commanded or oppressed by the great, and the great wish to command and oppress the people: and from these two different appetites comes in cities one of the three effects, either principality or liberty or licence' (*P.*, IX). To the repetition of the statement of the *two humours* Machiavelli now adds (*D.*, I.4) that all the laws (in Rome) in favour of the public liberty sprang from their disunion. *Leggi e ordini in beneficio della publica libertà* (laws and institutions for the benefit of public liberty): this is the primary lesson to be learnt from Rome, and it leads Machiavelli to a phrase which, in the general manner of his vocabulary, will recur as an insistent beat—*the guard on Roman liberty*. 'La guardia della libertà': it is a phrase that springs straight from Livy's lips:

MACHIAVELLI'S USE OF LIVY

. . . se, quod intra muros agendum esset, libertati populi Romani consulturum. Maximam autem eius custodiam esse, si magna imperia diuturna non essent (VI.xxiv).

As regards what had to be done within the walls, he would pay regard to the liberty of the Romans. But the best protection of liberty would be to ensure that great power was not held for too long.

For the last theme, see *D.*, III.24, 'La prolungazione degl'imperii fece serva Roma' ('The lengthening of the periods of command reduced Rome to servitude'.) The danger from the nobles is what Machiavelli calls *insolence*, and Livy *superbia* or *arrogantia*; that from the people is licence. The genuine *vivere libero* lies in between, and needs a constant guard: which, for Machiavelli, since the humour of the people (not to be oppressed) is more honest than that of the nobles (to oppress), is better placed with the people. And already we have anticipated the concluding chapters of *D.*I, that the governments of peoples are better than the governments of princes: a conclusion which is itself the commentary to what we saw on the lessons of the long history of Rome.

'Ceterum et mihi, vetustas res scribenti, nescio quo pacto, antiquus fit animus' ('But as I write of things of old, somehow my feelings take on an old-fashioned tinge'), wrote Livy nostalgically. And it is more than natural that Machiavelli should be similarly inspired. And yet he cannot help there being a mental reservation, which leaves him in effect less heroic, and more Florentine. Would it have been possible to avoid the strife between patricians and plebs? It might have been; Venice and Sparta managed with less turbulence than Rome: but if the people are tamer, then you cannot use them for bold purposes. If you are going to expand, like Rome, you must give the people their head, like Rome. But do you want to expand? It is here that Machiavelli posits his true political ideal, a city strong enough to inspire respect, prohibited by its own constitution from the course towards expansion:

E sanza dubbio credo che potendosi tenere la cosa bilanciata in questo modo, che e'sarebbe il vero vivere politico e la vera quiete d'una città (*D.*, I.6).

And without doubt I believe, if matters could be kept balanced in this way, that it would be the true body politic, the real peace of a city.

MACHIAVELLI'S USE OF LIVY

What he aspires to privately is Florence, but Florence safe, and the tone of that sentence betrays sufficiently how strong, how intimate, is the desire. But the world that he has seen does not allow such a haven of modest security. The affairs of men are always in movement, they will not stay firm, so must go up or else go down.

That private wish for the modesty of Florence is latent, and permanent, in Machiavelli. Meantime, although the terms he uses are notoriously his own, Livy is not out of sight, or mind. With Livy, this statement of the basic human dilemma is still concerned with the watch on liberty, the rivalry of classes, and comes in the passage where the modesty of one side begets, by a strange fatality, the insolence of the other:

> Adeo moderatio tuendae libertatis, dum aequari velle simulando ita se quisque extollit, ut deprimat alium, in difficili est; cavendoque ne metuant homines, metuendos ultro se efficiunt: et iniuriam a nobis repulsam, tanquam aut facere aut pati necesse sit, iniungimus aliis (III.65).[6]

> So difficult it is to protect liberty, with each man, under the pretext of equality, struggling to pull himself up and push his neighbour down; by guarding against fear, men make themselves feared; and the injustice we have kept away from ourselves we impose on others, as if there was no alternative between doing and suffering wrong.

This we shall find, in Machiavelli's Italian, in *D.*, I.46. But whatever may be of the private wish, the open conclusion is that one must imitate, not Venice or Sparta, but Rome, and be prepared to expand and not to shrink. But that is why it is important that, in the whole period from the Tarquins' exit to the Gracchi, the struggle between plebs and patricians is one that keeps liberty alive. Nothing in that struggle excites the attention of Machiavelli as much as the episode of Appius Claudius and the Decemvirs. And here, as long as we have forgotten the vulgar prejudices about the *Prince*, and remembered the verdict on Caesar and Catiline, we know instinctively the upshot. For tyranny arises in cities from too great a desire for liberty in the people, and too great a desire to command among the nobles. And if they cannot compromise for liberty, if one side plumps for a single man, then tyranny is the result. And the judgment on Appius Claudius? It will be found in the swift Chapter xlii of *D.* I: the Decemvirate shows how easily men are corrupted, how Quintus Fabius (Vibulanus), 'blinded by a little ambition', from being good

MACHIAVELLI'S USE OF LIVY

changed to grow like Appius. 'And this examined well, will make the legislators of republics and kingdoms all the more ready to check human appetites, and to take from them all hope of being able to err with impunity.' There is nothing more immutably constant in the text of the *Discorsi* than what we saw on princes and peoples erring when freed from the restraint of law. And if we turn back to the beginning of the episode of the Decemviri (the comment runs from *D.*, I.35 to *D.*, I.42) we shall find how uncompromising Machiavelli is, and how he repudiates the possibility of a good absolute ruler: 'Nor does it help in this case that the matter be not corrupt; because an absolute authority in a very short time corrupts the matter and makes for itself friends and partisans' (*D.*, I.35). It would be convenient for Machiavelli criticism if those who are anxious to make pronouncements on Machiavelli's admiration for absolute despots (on the basis of a presumed acquaintance with the *Prince*) were obliged to weigh the consistent statements of the *Discorsi* first.

Livy and Machiavelli are both, as we have seen, with eyes turned the same way; and since the one derives many of his ideas from his perusal of the other, it follows naturally that they tend to speak the same language. The first key-words were in Livy's Preface: *disciplina, remedia, avaritia, luxuria, paupertas et parsimonia*. Others follow in the text: *avida novarum rerum, ambitio, superbia, negligentia, licentia, modestia, concordia, nimia potestas, necessitas, ferroque non auro, caritas patriae*. So consonant are the two that, without warning, even without reference to a specific Livian situation, a phrase may transliterate from Livy: 'foeda cupiditas regni' ('an evil lust for power') (VI.20), 'una brutta cupidità di regnare' (*D.*, III.8); 'giudicandolo piú fermo e piú stabile' (*D.*, I.2, on the balance of the Roman constitution, but the pair of adjectives, which represent a basic concern for Machiavelli, recur), 'regnum adeo stabile ac firmum reliquit' ('he bequeathed a kingdom so stable and firm') (XXXIII.21, on the virtues of Attalus). Sometimes also their vocabulary, though convergent in direction, springs from a different idiom. *Ordini*, than which no word is more characteristic for Machiavelli, and especially for the Machiavelli of the *Discourses on Livy*, comes from the politics of Florence, and means the constitutional provisions of a state. *Ordines*, than which nothing is more regular in Livy, means one of two things: either the ranks of society or the ranks of an army in ordered military discipline. But hence *ordinatus*, and hence also *extra ordinem*, as of that blindly

89

LIVY

obedient soldier who would never fight, even to win, if it was *extra ordinem*; and hence also *consilia ordinaria* and *extraordinaria*, the latter ones which are outside the normal scheme provided for by law and custom. And here Machiavelli's idiom links up with Livy's, for his *straordinario* is by definition what lies outside the *leggi e ordini* which form the normal structure of the State: outside which there lies the recourse to violence. One other instance of the casual chiming of Machiavelli's with Livy's language: I quoted above the conclusion of Machiavelli on the two humours, that of the people more honest than that of the nobles. And look how the page of Livy answers back: 'Quum haesitaret Hegesianax, nec infitiari posset, honestiorem causam libertatis, quam servitutis' ('When Hegesianax was caught in a dilemma and could not deny that the cause of liberty was more honourable than that of slavery') (XXXIV.59). In which, of course, the sense that I have given to *more honest* may be illuminated. To the above we may add some technical terms, as *ossidione*, *espugnare*, *deletto* (*delectus*), *detrettare la zuffa* (*detrectare pugnam*), which Machiavelli appropriates without assuring them a permanent entry into Italian; and some others, as *sedizione*, which could be the establishment in Italian of a word only sporadic before.

In the book I wrote in 1947 on Machiavelli I dropped the name of Sir William Beveridge to illustrate the notion, stated firmly in the *Discorsi*, that a single legislator is best (it is the excuse for Romulus in *D.*, I.9), and was reproved by a sharp critic for frivolously dragging in irrelevant material. But the *Discorsi* are not an archaeological inquiry, or even a critical discussion of Livy, seen in historical perspective. In his Dedication of them to his friends Buondelmonti and Rucellai, Machiavelli wrote, as we have seen, that he had expressed in them all that he knew, from long experience and continual reading, of the things of the world. He had no embarrassment in throwing in the affairs of the present, alongside those of the past, because the whole purpose of the *Discorsi* is to find out how to deal with the otherwise intractable present. To put it still in Livian terms, what Machiavelli hopes for 'inter corrupta omnia' ('amidst general corruption') (XXIII.2) is 'priscos revocare mores posse' ('to be able to restore old-fashioned morality') (XXXIX.41). So answering to that cry of his of Italy, *stiava e vituperata*, there is the constant hope, 'Requiescat aliquando vexata tam diu Italia' ('May Italy gain respite at last after her long torments') (XXVIII.44). The *Discorsi* are not written *by* Livy, nor, though it might perhaps seem so from this

MACHIAVELLI'S USE OF LIVY

account, or in this context, are they written *for* Livy. They are written because history, as we saw Machiavelli claiming on humanist advice in 1503, is the schoolmistress to human actions. It was Burd, that diligent Victorian annotator of the *Prince*, who marked a dozen (was it?) pages of the *Discorsi* as revealing the same unscrupulous doctrines as in the *Prince* itself. He implied, if he did not state, that this dose of Machiavellian sin tainted the whole; though, if he had had any wits about him, he would have reflected that a score of 12 pages out of 450 in the edition which he used (and this score often unaccountably contrived) left room for something else than wickedness. And it will be apparent to anyone who comes to the *Discorsi* with an open and inquiring mind that they represent the first great attempt at an *esprit des lois* in the course of European literature.

'Itaque corpus duntaxat suum ad id tempus apud eos fuisse; animum iam pridem ibi esse, ubi ius ac fas crederent coli '(XXVII.17) ('their bodies at any rate had till then been on the enemy side, but their spirits had long been where they believed right and justice were observed'). It is notoriously in the *Arte della guerra* (printed in 1521) that Machiavelli displays this nostalgia most. 'I will never depart, in the example of anything, from my Romans,' says his mouthpiece in the dialogue at the outset of Book I. And at the end of the final Book VII, 'I say then that there is no action done now by men so easy to be brought back to ancient ways than the militia, but by those alone who are rulers of a state big enough for them to raise at least fifteen to twenty thousand young men out of their subjects.' Then, to show we are not on a different track from that of the *Discorsi*, soon after the first of those remarks there is a repetition: 'I miei Romani, come ho detto, mentre che furono savi e buoni' ('My Romans, as I said, while they were still wise and good'). It is still the same period, which sees the Romans conquer the known world, with which Machiavelli is concerned. The theme of *armi proprie* (forces of one's own) is one of perpetual concern to Machiavelli: he began with a battle for establishing a militia (*ordinanza*) in Florence, well before the *Prince* and his other works, each of which repeats the lesson against mercenaries and auxiliaries. In *D.*, III.36 he had quoted in the Latin text one of those Livian passages which castigate the absence of military discipline ('polluta semel militari disciplina'):

> nemo hominum, nemo deorum verecundiam habeat; non edicta imperatorum, non auspicia observentur; sine commeatu vagi milites

in pacato, in hostico errent, immemores sacramenti, licentia sola se,
ubi velint, exauctorent; infrequentia deserantur signa; neque conveni-
atur ad edictum, nec discernatur, interdiu, nocte, aequo, iniquo loco,
iussu, iniussu imperatoris pugnent; et non signa, non ordines servent;
latrocinii modo caeca et fortuita, pro sollenni et sacrata militia sit
(VIII.34).

No one would have respect for God or men; they would pay no regard
to their general's orders or to the auspices; the troops would roam at
will, without leave of absence, in peaceful territory and in enemy
country; heedless of their oath, they would take their own discharge
at their own whim; the ranks, now thinned, would be deserted; they
would not mobilize at the proclamation; they would fight without
caring if it be night or day, favourable or unfavourable ground, at
their general's orders or without them, they would not keep rank or
formation; military service, instead of being something regular and
hallowed, would be unseeing and haphazard, like banditry.

This is the burden of Machiavelli's lament, and the theme of the
Arte della guerra is the imitation of antiquity, a renascence which is
possible in this as it has been in other fields, but this time in the
things that are *forti e aspre* (strong and sharp), not just in those that
are *delicate e molli* (delicate and soft): and, of course, 'pigliare i modi
della antichità vera e perfetta, non quelli della falsa e corrotta' ('to
imitate the ways of the ancients when antiquity was true and
perfect, not those when it was false and corrupt'). The military
apparatus which conquered the world is a beacon from which
Machiavelli cannot take his eyes. Naturally, it will play him false:
and it is well known that he makes such elementary blunders as
underrating the new weapon of artillery. And naturally, too,
Machiavelli has other authors than Livy from whom to deduce the
military usages of the Romans, as, for instance, Vegetius or Frontinus;
and this, together with the mistaken deduction, lessens our interest
in this context for Livy. Indeed, it is sad to say that perhaps the
most prominent connection with Livy in the *Art of War* occurs at a
point where both Livy and Machiavelli came a cropper. It arises
from a famous, and over-detailed, account in Livy, VIII.8 on the
drawing up of a Roman battlefront, a three-tier affair, in which the
successive ranks were sparsely set, so that the light-armed com-
batants in the front could fall back without upsetting the second
rank if they were discomfited. And if this process was again repeated,
the main body fell back into the reserves: 'inde "rem ad triarios

MACHIAVELLI'S USE OF LIVY

redisse", quum laboratur, proverbio increbuit' ('as a result, the well-known proverb has arisen "the fighting reached the reserves", to denote serious trouble'). It seems here that Livy may have been as much deceived as Machiavelli in this matter of tactics, and what remained for many centuries a *locus classicus* on what to do to ensure success in battle only a non-soldier's dream. Certainly, this tripartite division never entered the military history of the Renascence. We may take this as a symbol of the fact that the true vitality of the *Arte della guerra* lies, not in its technical contribution to the theory of war, but in the general ideas of Machiavelli, characteristically expressed in the opening book and in the close to the whole work. Here also he may be found to be less Roman, and more Florentine, than we had thought.

'I will never depart from the example of my Romans', said Machiavelli in the *Art of War*; and might seem, though flatteringly, yet tamely, subservient. But there is nothing which can demonstrate the inherent strength and independence of Machiavelli so much as his last great undertaking, the *Istorie fiorentine*. There was a nineteenth-century notion on the servile and imitative qualities of Renascence writing, a continual aping of antiquity. But if you look through the Index to the *Istorie fiorentine* you will not find the name of Livy mentioned. And if you read, you will not find that there is anything in the idiom, or the method of narration, which betrays a consciousness of Livy's *History*; or of any other classical model. At the most, what we may say is that there is a general similarity in the fact that both Livy and Machiavelli tend to follow, for some particular period, a written source. But that is, of course, a casual and external coincidence which, since the periods are naturally as different as the sources, does not draw them together as writers, or even as historians. Once, perhaps, we should suspect an echo out of Livy, and at a point where Machiavelli has been often praised for his imaginative insight. It is the sentence where he enumerates the changes in the Roman provinces, on the gradual dissolution of Roman rule: 'which varied not only in government and princes, but in laws, customs, way of life, religion, tongue, dress, and name' (*I.f.*, I.5). It is the gradation which has struck his readers. But what of the inhabitants of Croton? 'Morituros se affirmabant citius quam, immixti Bruttiis, in alienos ritus, mores, legesque, ac mox linguam etiam verterentur' ('They declared that they would rather die than join with the people of Bruttium and adopt different rites, customs and laws, and soon even

LIVY

a different language') (XXIV.3). It will be seen that this is not
offered as an obligatory connection; and even if we accept it as a
derivation, we must take it, in the 500 pages of the *Istorie fiorentine*,
as even less prominent than Burd's twelve 'wicked' pages in the 450
of the *Discorsi*. The *Istorie fiorentine* are written without any thought
of classical historiography as a model: they deal with something
entirely different, and in a different way.

Then we have forgotten Livy? Not at all, but the lesson is implicit,
and not superimposed. Let us look at one of the places where
Machiavelli pauses from the narration of events to reflect upon
their meaning. The opening of Book IV presents his basic ideas: cities,
especially those which are not *bene ordinate*, do not vary between
freedom and servitude, as many think, but between servitude and
licence. It is only when there arises by good fortune of the city a
wise, good and powerful citizen, who ordains laws by which the
humours of nobles and people are quieted, that the city can be
called free, 'e quello stato si può stabile e fermo giudicare' ('and that
State can be judged stable and firm'): it was the judgment on the
balance of the Roman Constitution at the opening of the *Discorsi*,
and, as I have suggested, the adjectives echo the text of Livy
('regnum adeo stabile ac firmum'). We know beforehand what the
comment of Machiavelli will be: that in antiquity there were such
states which had such *leggi e ordini* and enjoyed long life. It is the
defect of the modern age to have no *stability*, to vary between
tyranny and licence. From this we may turn to the opening of Book
V, which underwrites the lesson. For here is the Florentine equivalent
for Livy's *corrupta omnia: in questo guasto mondo* (in this corrupted
world) there is no valour of soldiers, no capacity of captains, no
amore verso la patria (caritas patriae . . . love of one's country) in
citizens, only the tricks by which princes, soldiers, leaders of republics
seek to maintain a reputation they do not deserve. But to know this
may be no less useful than the knowledge of antiquity, for the one
kindles in liberal minds the desire to follow it, the other to shun the
wrong example:

> Il che sarà forse non meno utile che si sieno le antiche cose a cogno-
> scere, perché, se quelle i liberali animi a seguitarle accendono, queste
> a fuggirle e spegnerle gli accenderanno (*I.f.*, V.1).

> Which will be perchance no less useful than to know ancient history,
> because, if the latter excites liberal minds to follow their example,
> these things will excite them to shun and cancel them.

MACHIAVELLI'S USE OF LIVY

In that passage it is the recurrent verb *accendere* which is noteworthy, and it echoes a famous passage in the *Discorsi* from which I have deliberately steered clear previously. For to those who held to well established views on the coldness and unscrupulous nature of Machiavelli's talent it was a chapter to be dismissed as *irony*. This is the tenth chapter of *D.*, I, the praise for those who found, the condemnation for those who destroy, states; the choice to be Scipios, not Caesars; to be Agesilaus, Timoleon, Dion, not Nabis, Phalaris or Dionysius; the good emperors cast against the bad ones; on the one side *gloria* and *sicurtà*, on the other *biasimo* and *timore*, eternal *infamy*. And there also the eager temperament of Machiavelli burst out with the sanguine conclusion on the teachability of man:

> E sanza dubbio se e'sarà nato d'uomo, si sbigottirà da ogni imitazione de'tempi cattivi, ed accenderassi d'uno immenso desiderio di seguire i buoni.

> And without doubt if he is born of man, he will shrink from any imitation of the bad times, and will burn with an immense desire to imitate the good.

To which there followed the sentence, which I have already quoted, on the path to glory, to have a city which is corrupt, *not to ruin it entirely, as Caesar did, but to reorder it, as Romulus*. The constancy of this language, of himself and even others (all who are born of man!) burning to right the world, is not to be lightly overlooked in any estimate of Machiavelli which is based on the reading of his works, and the estimate of his models, and not on rash thoughts about the title of the *Prince*. And in the *Istorie fiorentine* it means, of course, the implication (at these points brought to the surface) that the history of Rome is example, and the history of Florence warning. There is nothing to surprise in this: after all, it is exactly what he had said on a particular point in the opening of the *Discorsi*: 'This was well ordered in Rome, and has always been ordered ill in the city of Florence' (*D.*, I.8, on accusations and calumnies). The opening of Book III makes the general point, picks up what we have seen in *Prince* and *Discorsi* on the two humours in all cities, and notes that disunion in Rome was tolerable, and led to compromise: whereas in Florence it led, via deaths and exiles, to the partisan rule of one side, with all the laws not for the common good, 'ma tutte in favore del vincitore si ordinavano' ('but all were passed to suit the

LIVY

conqueror') (*I.f.*, III.1). The upshot in Florence, for in Florence nevertheless the Florentine Machiavelli finds much good (and were it the context here it could be shown that the ultimate ideals of *Istorie fiorentine* are modest ones, Florentine rather than Roman), is an equality of condition which could be moulded properly were there to arise a wise legislator. But the backward view implies the need of this, as much as it implies the corrective of the example of Rome, set forth from Livy in the *Discorsi*. The *Istorie fiorentine* and the *Discorsi*, so different in their surface, are two halves of the same whole.

NOTES

1 Bernardo Machiavelli, *Libro di ricordi* (Firenze, 1954), 11, 35, p. 223.

2 Cf., for instance, F. Gilbert, *Machiavelli and Guicciardini*, pp. 318-22.

3 In the volume *Arte della guerra*, etc., p. 73.

4 The discussion on the dating of the *Discorsi*, not strictly relevant here, can be followed up in my article, 'Gilbert, Hexter and Baron' (in *Discourses on Machiavelli*, Heffer, 1969, 10, 181).

5 v. Carlo Pincin, 'I Discorsi sopra la prima deca di Tito Livio', in *Atti della Accademia della Scienze di Torino*, vol. 96 (1961-2), p. 88, and, for Guicciardini's *Considerations*, p. 94.

6 There are two other suggestively Machiavellian passages in Livy on this fluidity of human society: 'Nulla magna civitas diu quiescere potest. Si foris hostem non habet, domi invenit: ut praevalida corpora ab externis causis tuta videntur, sed suis ipsa viribus onerantur' (XXX.44). (No great country can remain inactive for long. If it has no enemy without it will find one within: just as over-powerful physiques seem to be proof against dangers from outside, but are weighed down by their own strength.') 'Ipse, ut est humanus animus insatiabilis eo, quod fortuna spondet, ad altiora et non concessa tendere: et quoniam consulatus quoque eripiendus invitis Patribus esset, de regno agitare (IV.xiii). ('But he—for the human heart can never be satisfied by Fortune's promise— aimed at a higher—and forbidden—goal; since even the consulship would have to be torn from the hands of the reluctant patricians, he began to think of king-ship.') The second passage is echoed verbally by Machiavelli in *D.*, II, Proem: 'Sendo, oltra di questo, gli appetiti insaziabili, perché avendo dalla natura di potere e volere desiderare ogni cosa, e dalla natura di potere conseguitarne poche, ne risulta continuamente una mala contentezza nelle menti umane, ed uno fastidio delle cose che si posseggono.' ('Since, moreover, the appetites are in-satiable, because we have by nature the power and the wish to desire all things, and by nature also the ability to attain to few, it follows that men's minds are always dissatisfied, and wearied with the things they have.')

[7]

SIX

The Concept of *Fortuna* in Machiavelli

THOMAS FLANAGAN

THE HISTORY OF THE GODDESS FORTUNA[1]

Fortune is only one of a large number of the powers and deities who have been imagined to control human affairs. Within the history of the west, we could distinguish at least the following forces, which have been widely supposed to control our destiny.

Fortune	Fortuna	Tyche
Fate(s)	Fatum(a)	Moirai, Heimarmene
Necessity	Necessitas	Ananke
Providence	Providentia	Pronoia

To separate one from the other is practically impossible, for the lines between all of them were blurred even in antiquity. All of these con-

---

1 In this paper I have dealt solely with *fortuna* as it is opposed to *virtus*, which is indeed the most common usage in the history of western thought. However *fortuna* or *tyche* has also been contrasted to *natura* or *physis*, in which case the meaning of fortune approaches that of 'accident.' Although I have not treated this topic, it is a theme which should be pursued; for Machiavelli speaks in several places of a relation between *virtù* and *natura*, and hence implicitly of a relation between *natura* and *fortuna*. Cf. the references in A. Parel, 'Machiavelli Minore.'

128 The Political Calculus

ceptions, however, refer to different aspects or moments of the fundamental experience that man does not totally control his destiny on the earth. Sometimes we feel that our lives are ruled from without, that we are in the grip of a force which guides our actions; while at other times our doings appear almost as random events, not caused by anything at all. Sometimes we seem to perceive a benevolent plan which shapes our lives, while at other moments there may seem to be no plan at all, or even a malicious one. These and other experiences can be represented in complex and shifting ways by the symbols of fortune, fate, necessity, and providence – singly or in combination.

One set of symbols, those associated with the goddess Fortuna, was particularly important to Machiavelli.[2] Now he did not speak solely of fortune; particularly in his poetic works, he often used other terms. I have found instances where he speaks of providence, the heavens, fate and the fates, the stars, grace, and the times.[3] Of these terms only 'the times' is used rather frequently in Machiavelli's treatises on politics; and when it appears, as I will show below, it is of one piece with the conception of fortune. The other terms are all

2 Most authors who have written on Machiavelli have devoted at least a page or two to *fortuna*, but there is no wholly satisfactory specialized treatment. The three essays cited below are particularly deficient in that they treat Machiavelli's *fortuna* without sufficient reference to its widespread popular usage before, during, and after Machiavelli's era.

Burleigh T. Wilkins, 'Machiavelli on History and Fortune,' *Bucknell Review*, 8 (1959), 225-45; Charles D. Tarlton, 'The Symbolism of Redemption and the Exorcism of Fortune in Machiavelli's *Prince*,' *Review of Politics*, 30 (1968), 332-48; Vincenzo Cioffari, 'The Function of Fortune in Dante, Boccaccio, and Machiavelli,' *Italica* 24 (1947), 1-13

3 The following references are not meant to be complete but merely indicative. The text used is Allan H. Gilbert, ed., *Machiavelli: The Chief Works and Others*, 3 vols (Durham NC 1965).
a/providence: *L'Asino d'Oro*, II; Gilbert, II, 758
b/the heavens: *Discourses*, II, 29; Gilbert, 406-7
c/fate: Letter 137; Gilbert, II, 929
d/the fates: Letter 116; Gilbert, II, 896-7
e/the stars: Letter 116; Gilbert, II, 897
f/grace: 'On Ambition'; Gilbert, II, 739
g/the times: *The Prince*, 25; Gilbert, I, 90

129 Concept of *Fortuna* in Machiavelli

much less frequently employed, and again I have not been able to find occasions where *fortuna* could not just as well have been substituted. On the basis of frequency of occurrence, then, I would conclude that *fortuna* is Machiavelli's major term for designating the uncertainty and dependency of human affairs. The other words appear to be merely literary variations which do not involve a substantial change in meaning. In the following pages, therefore, I will briefly discuss the origin and development of the symbolism of fortune, not to provide a complete history but only to suggest the richness of the tradition upon which Machiavelli drew.[4]

The word *fortuna* is formed adjectivally from the Latin *fors* (luck), which is ultimately derived from the root of *ferre* (to bring). Thus the core of meaning of *fors* is 'that which is brought'; and Fortuna is she who brings it. Similarly the Greek equivalent, Tyche, is derived

4 On *fortuna* in the classical world, see the relevant articles in J. Hastings, ed., *Encyclopaedia of Religion and Ethics* (New York 1914); and in Pauly-Wissowa, *Real-Encyclopädie der Classischen Altertumswissenschaft*. On the development of the idea after the end of the Roman empire, the recognized authorities are A. Doren, 'Fortuna im Mittelalter und in der Renaissance,' *Vorträge der Bibliothek Warburg* II (1922-3), 71-151; and H.R. Patch, *The Goddess Fortuna in Medieval Literature* (Cambridge, Mass. 1927); 'The Tradition of the Goddess Fortuna in Roman Literature and in the Transitional Period,' *Smith College Studies in Modern Languages* III3 (1922); 'The Tradition of the Goddess Fortuna in Medieval Philosophy and Literature,' ibid., III4 (1922). Two other monographs deal with special questions: Ida Wyss, *Virtus and Fortuna bei Boiardo und Ariost* (Leipzig 1931); Klaus Heitmann, *Fortuna and Virtus – Eine Studie zu Petrarchas Lebensweisheit* (Cologne 1958). Finally there are a number of articles of value: D.C. Allen, 'Renaissance Remedies for Fortune,' *Studies in Philology*, 38 (1941), 188-97; K. Hampe, 'Zur Auffassung der Fortuna im Mittelalter,' *Archiv für Kulturgeschichte*, 17 (1926); Aby Warburg, 'Francesco Sassettis letztwillige Verfügung,' *Kunstwissenschaftliche Beiträge, August Schmarsow gewidmet* (Leipzig 1907); Rexmond C. Cochrane, 'Francis Bacon and the Architect of Fortune,' *Studies in the Renaissance*, 5 (1958). This list omits certain titles by nineteenth-century scholars, but these are easily obtained from the bibliographies in the above works, particularly by Patch, Doren, Heitmann, and Wyss. I have not seen the privately printed monograph of Vincenzo Cioffari, *Fortune and Fate from Democritus to St Thomas Aquinas* (New York 1935).

130 The Political Calculus

from a root meaning 'to succeed' or 'to attain.' The basic meaning in both cases is not what we moderns term 'chance,' that is, events which seem to occur randomly. Rather the connotation is that of success, which is brought about by an unseen person or power who works in ways inscrutable to us. Thus there is never a clear distinction between fortune and fate. Both conceptions refer to the order of the gods which can never be fully understood by men. If there is a difference, it is one of emphasis. Fate represents the divine will as something fixed and inflexible, while fortune represents it as elastic, unpredictable, and open to influence by human supplication. According to the authorities, therefore, the worship of Fortuna was not a surrender to chance or randomness in which individual effort was abandoned; it was much more an attempt to propitiate the goddess so that she would smile on an undertaking. Fortuna may be capricious, but her behaviour is not random.

It would be difficult to overestimate the importance of Fortuna in the religious life of ancient Rome. Even before the syncretistic period of the Empire, she was worshipped under a variety of cult names. The fortune of the harvest, the fortune of the sea, the fortune of mothers – whenever life becomes uncertain fortune was worshipped. The symbols denoted success and uncertainty together. She was ordinarily depicted in one of three ways – with a horn of plenty, holding the rudder of a ship, or rotating a ball or a wheel. Always a popular and colourful goddess, fortune's role expanded impressively under the Empire. Pliny the Elder has given us a classic description of how widespread her worship became:

> Everywhere in the whole world at every hour by all men's voices fortune alone is invoked and named, alone accused, alone impeached, alone pondered, alone applauded, alone rebuked and visited with reproaches; deemed volatile and indeed by most men blind as well, wayward, inconstant, uncertain, fickle in her favors and favoring the unworthy. To her is debited all that is spent and credited all that is received, she alone fills both pages in the whole of mortals' account; and we are so much at the mercy of chance that chance herself, by whom God is proved uncertain, takes the place of God.[5]

5 Gaius Plinius Secundus, *Natural History* (Loeb Classical Library 1957), II, 22

131 Concept of *Fortuna* in Machiavelli

She became one of those universal deities who gradually replaced the old Roman contingent of gods. Names like Isis-Fortuna, Fortuna Panthea, and Fortuna Populi Romani suggest the wide scope to which her worship attained. She endured to become, as Patch remarks, 'the last of the gods.'[6]

In the higher culture of antiquity – in philosophy, literature, history, and art – fortune occupied a position fully as prominent as in popular worship and superstition. There is no space here to catalogue all the usages; suffice it to say that almost no important writer was free from her influence. In particular it became a part of the conventional wisdom of antiquity to debate the respective contributions to success of *virtus*, or human ability, and *fortuna*, or divine favour. Considerations on the subject were seldom lacking from any work devoted to analyzing human activity. As one writer has put it, 'the contrast between *virtù* and *fortuna* must have been so current in Rome even before the time of Cicero, indeed even so banal, that it could sink to the level of a pedagogical device for rhetorical exercises.'[7]

It is not surprising, then, that Fortuna, both as a popular goddess and a topic of debate for learned men, lived on after the collapse of the Roman Empire. In spite of the polemics of Augustine, who quite logically argued that a notion of fortune is hardly compatible with the Christian faith in an all-wise providence, Fortuna found a secure place in the Christian imagination. In particular, Boethius' work on the *Consolation of Philosophy* provided the mould for much of the speculation on fortune, at least in the early Middle Ages before the recovery of the classics. It is instructive to observe how the image of Fortuna changed as she was adopted by a civilization with a different spirit. In Rome she had been a beguiling figure whose cornucopia was a promise of abundance. *Bona Dea* she was called – the 'good goddess.' But after Boethius she is a much more sombre figure; almost all of her colourful imagery has been lost. Only the wheel remains, which Fortuna grimly turns.[8] Men rise and fall inexorably in the

6 Patch, 'The Tradition of the Goddess Fortuna in Roman Literature and in the Transitional Period,' 158

7 Heitmann, *Fortuna and Virtus: Eine Studie zu Petrarcas Lebensweisheit*, 18-19

8 Doren, 'Fortuna in Mittelalter und in der Renaissance,' 145-51; the article contains an excellent series of reproductions of *fortuna*, as she was variously conceived in the Middle Ages and Renaissance.

132 The Political Calculus

medieval conception; there is little if any room for maneuver against her. In this fashion, as a symbol of the transitoriness of earthly glory, Fortuna and the wheel appear throughout Europe during the Middle Ages.

It has been held that the symbolism of Fortuna became particularly widespread during the Renaissance; but this is an oversimplification, since as we have seen, wide interest in the goddess was also present in the medieval era. What began to change in the Renaissance was the spirit in which Fortuna was regarded. After the time of Dante and Petrarch, whose opinions on fortune were still distinctively medieval, she gradually evolved from the grim woman turning her relentless wheel into a much friendlier power who could be a distinct help in human affairs. It is fascinating to see how the symbolism of the wheel was increasingly supplemented by the revived symbols of antiquity, particularly the sailing ship. There are even portraits extant in which Fortuna, although she is still a passenger in the ship, no longer controls the rudder; that is left to the individual himself.[9]

In her revived antique trappings, Fortuna permeated the consciousness of the Renaissance. Just as in antiquity, she was a standard part of literature, philosophy, history and the arts. And, also as in the classical world, she not only appeared in higher culture but in popular life. A complete survey is beyond the scope of this paper, but a few examples will indicate the wide extension of the symbolism of fortune in the era in which Machiavelli grew up. Jacob Burckhardt, for instance, relates the story of a ruler of Bologna who carved the following inscription in Latin on the newly built tower of his palace: 'This monument was built by Giovanni Bentivoglio, the gracious ruler of his land, whose virtue [*virtus*] and fortune [*fortuna*] have led to all the good things which a man could want.'[10] Other anecdotes supplied by Burckhardt also demonstrate how the cult of Fortuna extended to the popular festivals. When Alfonso the Great entered Naples in 1443, an important part of the procession was a chariot in which rode a figure of Fortuna. Similarly, when Massimiliano Sforza entered Milan in 1512, Fortuna was the chief figure on the triumphal

9 Warburg, 'Francesco Sassettis letztwillige Verfügung'
10 Jacob Burckhardt, *The Civilization of the Renaissance in Italy*, tr. S.G.C. Middlemore (New York 1958), II, 482

arch, elevated over Fama, Speranza, Audacia, and Penitenza.[11] Finally Machiavelli himself, in the *History of Florence*, tells an interesting story about one of the leading citizens of Florence (ca. 1380), Piero degli Albizzi:

> Once when he was giving a banquet to many citizens, somebody ... sent him a silver cup full of sweet meats with a nail hidden among them. When the nail was found and seen by all the guests they interpreted it as a suggestion that he nail fortune's wheel in its present place; since she had brought him to the top of it, it could do nothing else, if it kept turning, than carry him to the bottom.[12]

The preceding paragraphs are far too short to do justice to the history of Fortuna; but they do show how influential she was from antiquity through the Renaissance. Though she appeared in different guises, there was never a time when her presence was not felt in the discussions of intellectuals as well as in the daily doings of popular life.

THE 'SOURCES' OF MACHIAVELLI'S FORTUNA

Even this cursory sketch of the history of Fortuna has important implications for understanding Machiavelli's use of the symbol. In particular, it seems unlikely there is a single 'source' for Machiavelli's ideas on fortune, even though some writers have attempted to discover one. Joseph Mazzeo, for example, has suggested that Machiavelli drew his notion of Fortuna from Polybius.[13] J.H. Whitfield maintains that Machiavelli 'obviously' learned to discuss events in terms of *virtù* and *fortuna* 'from the Latin historians';[14] and he devotes some space to pointing out similarities with Quintus Curtius'

11 Ibid., I, 417

12 *History of Florence*, III, 19; Gilbert, III, 1170-1

13 Joseph Mazzeo, *Renaissance and Seventeenth-Century Studies* (New York 1964), 154

14 J.H. Whitfield, *Machiavelli* (New York 1965), 95

134 The Political Calculus

life of Alexander the Great, though he does not say explicitly that
the latter book should be considered a direct source of Machiavelli's
ideas. There are undoubtedly similarities between Machiavelli's *fortuna* and those of Polybius and Quintus Curtius, but to interpret
these as evidence that those writers are in a real sense the sources of
Machiavelli usage would be an unwarranted exaggeration. For as we
have seen, the notions of *virtù* and *fortuna* were the common property of an entire civilization; and Machiavelli would have been exposed to them at every turn, in daily conversation as well as in his
study of the classic authors.

We can illustrate the complexity of the problem by referring to the
Discourses, where Walker has done a thorough job of uncovering the
sources which Machiavelli employed in composition. First of all, Machiavelli specifically refers in two places to other authors' notions of
Fortuna. In chapter 1 of the second book, where he discusses the
role of fortune in the rise of Rome, he mentions Plutarch and Livy
as having believed that Rome owed more to fortune than to the ability of her citizens. Machiavelli's interpretation of Plutarch and Livy
may be one-sided; we are only interested here in the fact that he was
aware of the importance of *fortuna* in their works.[15] The other reference in the *Discourses* is also to Livy. In book II, chapter 29, Machiavelli uses a quotation from Livy as his chapter heading: 'Fortune
blinds the intellects of men when she does not wish them to oppose
her plans.'[16] Yet, although these are the only passages in the *Discourses* known to me where Machiavelli refers to another author's
conception of fortune, it would hardly be safe to conclude that these
authors are the only sources. Livy and Plutarch are only two of the
seventeen writers[17] whose names or works are explicitly mentioned
in the *Discourses*; and of these seventeen, several have contributed
notably to the development of the symbolism of Fortuna. Aristotle,
Cicero, Quintus Curtius, Sallust, Thucydides, Virgil, and Dante would

15 The reference to Plutarch is to *De fortuna romanorum*. The allusion to Livy
   cannot be specified; Machiavelli writes only that Livy 'seldom has any Roman
   make a speech in which he refers to ability without adding fortune.' *Discourses*,
   II, 1, Gilbert, I, 324
16 Livy, *Histories*, V, 37
17 L.J. Walker, *The Discourses of Niccolò Machiavelli* (London 1950), II, 271

135 Concept of *Fortuna* in Machiavelli

all be mentioned in any reasonably complete account of the history of Fortuna. Polybius, too, whom Machiavelli does not mention by name but whose works (or parts of them) he certainly knew, extensively used the idea of fortune in his writing. Thus even within the pages of the *Discourses*, we can see that Machiavelli drew upon the works of a number of authors who were accustomed to thinking in terms of fortune.

With the exception of Dante, the names above are all of classical writers. Machiavelli was not inclined to cite his contemporaries as authorities, so we do not know exactly whom he read. Yet let us assume for the moment merely that he was familiar with the works of his great Florentine humanistic predecessors: Dante, Petrarch, Boccaccio, Poggio. Here again we find that each of these men was deeply concerned with the impact of fortune on human affairs. To give one final example of another possible 'source': in a letter to Vettori[18] Machiavelli quotes from his Neapolitan contemporary Pontano, who had written a widely circulated tract *De fortuna*. I am not suggesting that the list of sources for Machiavelli's notion of *fortuna* should be extended to include all of these individuals; the point is rather that a definitive list would be rather difficult to compile. Fortune was not only a universal concept in literature and history from antiquity to the Renaissance, but also a widespread part of popular culture. When Machiavelli spoke of *fortuna*, he was using a term which he must have absorbed as a child and which would have come naturally, almost spontaneously to his lips.

MACHIAVELLI'S DOCTRINE OF FORTUNA

The term *fortuna* runs like a refrain throughout Machiavelli's works. Though it might be useful to do a numerical survey of all its uses as Hexter has done for the concept of *lo stato*, I have attempted to establish the meaning of *fortuna* by referring to Machiavelli's major utterances on the subject. Certainly the most famous passage is the twenty-fifth chapter of *The Prince*, where Machiavelli is preparing to exhort the future prince of Italy to action. This chapter is a conveni-

18 Letter 156, 20 Dec. 1514; Gilbert, II, 960

136 The Political Calculus

ent starting point, for it contains in one way or another all the major themes connected with Machiavelli's use of *fortuna*. 'As I am well aware,' this chapter opens, 'many have believed and now believe human affairs so controlled by Fortune and by God that men with their prudence cannot manage them – yes, more, that men have no recourse against the world's variations.'[19] These words express very well what concerned Machiavelli – the riddle of the success or failure of human action. Men attempt 'with their prudence' to carry out some plan, to fulfill some project; but it often appears that their prudence is of no avail against the 'world's variations.' Yet characteristically Machiavelli refuses to endorse the pessimistic opinion that man's strength and cleverness can never prevail against fortune's constant change. 'Thinking on these variations,' he tells us, 'I myself now and then incline in some respects to their belief.'[20] But this is only an occasional inclination, not his real conviction. His true opinion is more complex: 'Fortune may be mistress of one half our actions but ... even she leaves the other half, or almost, under our control.'[21] There follows that famous metaphor, in which Machiavelli tries to illustrate the role which fortune plays in our lives:

> I compare Fortune with one of our destructive rivers which, when it is angry, turns the plains into lakes, throws down the trees and the buildings, takes earth from one spot, puts it in another; everyone flees before the flood; everyone yields to its fury and nowhere can repel it. Yet though such it is, we need not therefore conclude that when the weather is quiet, men cannot take precautions with both embankments and dykes, so that when the waters rise, either they go off by a canal or their fury is neither so wild nor so damaging. The same things happen about Fortune. She shows her power where strength and wisdom do not prepare to resist her, and directs her fury where she knows that no dykes or embankments are ready to hold her. If you consider Italy – the scene of these variations and their first mover – you see that she is a plain without dykes and without any embankment; but

19 Gilbert, I, 89
20 Ibid., 90
21 Ibid.

if she were embanked with adequate strength and wisdom, like Germany, Spain, and France, this flood either would not make the great variations it does or would not come upon us. I think this is all I need to say in general on resisting Fortune.[22]

This I take to be Machiavelli's real opinion of our ability to resist fortune, that there are always precautions we can take which will improve our possibilities of success. It is true that at times Machiavelli sounds a good deal more pessimistic than this. In the *Life of Castruccio Castracani,* for example, he introduces his narrative by remarking on the childhood of many eminent men, whose birth was often marked by marvels and wonders; and then he adds 'I well believe that this comes about because fortune, wishing to show the world that she – and not prudence – makes men great, first shows her forces at a time when prudence can have no share in the matter ...'[23] And again in the *Discourses,* Machiavelli appears to reverse his earlier judgment that the rise of Rome was due more to *virtù* than *fortuna*. He seemingly credits fortune with the power to intervene directly in our affairs to accomplish his goals, regardless of our plans:

> Skillfully Fortune does this, since she chooses a man, when she plans to bring to pass great things, who is of so much perception and so much ability that he recognizes the opportunities she puts before him. So in the same way when she intends to bring to pass great failures, she puts there men to promote such failure. And if somebody there is able to oppose her, she either kills him or deprives him of all means for doing anything good.[24]

Yet even in such a pessimistic mood, Machiavelli never counsels us to give up the conduct of our affairs to fortune. Remember the death of Castruccio. After fortune has raised him to glory and then struck him down, he still reflects on what he would have done differently, had he known of his impending death. He would not, he tells his heir, have accumulated so much territory and with it so many ene-

22 Ibid.
23 Ibid., II, 534
24 *Discourses,* II, 29; Gilbert, I, 407-8

138 The Political Calculus

mies. He would have left behind him a smaller but more secure holding. He advises his adopted son, therefore, to pursue the arts of peace
rather than of war. The point of the tale is, I take it, that even in disaster human reason can devise ways of working with fortune and
hence of mitigating the loss. Machiavelli's advice in the *Discourses*
confirms this interpretation. In connection with the passage above,
he tells us:

> I assert, indeed, once more that it is very true, according to what
> we see in all the histories, that men are able to assist Fortune but
> not to thwart her. They can weave her designs but cannot destroy
> them. They ought, then, never to give up as beaten, because, since
> they do not know her purpose and she goes through crooked and
> unknown roads, they can always hope, and hoping is not to give
> up, in whatever fortune and whatever affliction they may be.[25]

Even at the darkest hour, then, Machiavelli counsels never to give
up our aspirations; for we may be able after all to place ourselves in
alignment with her plans. And in fact, in the midst of our uncertainty,
it may be best to pursue an active, aggressive course; for 'Fortune is a
woman and it is necessary, in order to keep her under, to cuff and
maul her.'[26] Yet this element of impetuousness should not be overestimated; Machiavelli would never argue that rashness is a virtue.
Boldness may be effective, but only when it is in basic agreement
with Fortune's plans. The core of Machiavelli's teaching on Fortune
I take to be this, that man 'can weave her designs but cannot destroy
them.' This is a theme which Machiavelli has articulated several times
in his writings in almost the same words. To show how uniform Machiavelli's teaching is, it is worth-while to quote the relevant passages
at some length. One very clear statement is found in the twenty-fifth
chapter of *The Prince*:

> any prince who relies exclusively on Fortune falls when she varies.
> I believe also that a prince succeeds who adapts his way of pro-

25 *Discourses*, II, 291; Gilbert, I, 408
26 *The Prince*, 25; Gilbert, I, 92

139 Concept of *Fortuna* in Machiavelli

ceeding to the nature of the times, and conversely one does not succeed whose procedure is out of harmony with the times. In the things that lead them to the end they seek, that is, glory and riches, men act in different ways: one with caution, another impetuously; one by force, the other with skill; one by patience, the other with its contrary; and all of them with these differing methods attain their ends. We find also that of two cautious men, one carries out his purpose, the other does not. Likewise, we find two men with two differing temperaments equally successful, one being cautious and the other impetuous. This results from nothing else than the nature of the times, which is harmonious or not with their procedure.[27]

Equally clear are the comments in book III of the *Discourses*, where Machiavelli discusses the personal factors which enter into success:

Many times I have observed that the cause of the bad and of the good fortune of men is the way in which their method of working fits the times, since in their actions some men proceed with haste, some with heed and caution. Because in both of these methods men cross the proper boundaries, since they cannot follow the true road, in both of them they make errors. Yet a man succeeds in erring less and in having prosperous fortune if time fits his ways, for you always act as Nature inclines you.

We are unable to change for two reasons: one, that we cannot counteract that to which Nature inclines us; the other, that when with one way of doing a man has prospered greatly, he cannot be persuaded that he can profit by doing otherwise. That is why Fortune varies for the same men; she varies the times, but he does not vary his ways.[28]

Again, we find the same sentiments expressed in Machiavelli's letter of early 1513 to Piero Soderini, his patron who had recently been driven from Florence by the Medici. It is significant that this letter, written at a time when Machiavelli himself had sorely suffered the

27 *The Prince*, 25; Gilbert, I, 90-1
28 *Discourses*, III, 9; Gilbert, I, 452-3

140 The Political Calculus

blows of fortune, contains opinions identical to those we have seen
above:

> I believe that as Nature has given each man an individual face, so
> she has given him an individual disposition and an individual im-
> agination. From this it results that each man conducts himself
> according to his disposition and his imagination. On the other
> hand, because times vary and affairs are of varied types, one
> man's desires come out as he had prayed they would; he is fortu-
> nate who harmonizes his procedure with his time, but on the con-
> trary he is not fortunate who in his actions is out of harmony
> with his time and with the type of its affairs. Hence it can well
> happen that two men working differently come to the same end,
> because each of them adapts himself to what he encounters, for
> affairs are of as many types as there are provinces and states.
> Thus, because times and affairs in general and individually change
> often, and men do not change their imaginings and their proce-
> dures, it happens that a man at one time has good fortune and at
> another time bad.
>   And certainly anybody wise enough to understand the times
> and the types of affairs and to adapt himself to them would have
> always good fortune, or he would protect himself always from
> bad, and it would come to be true that the wise man would rule
> the stars and the fates. But because there never are such wise
> men, since men in the first place are shortsighted and in the sec-
> ond place cannot command their natures, it follows that Fortune
> varies and commands men and holds them under her yoke.[29]

All of the passages exhibit the identical teaching. We live in an unpredictable world, and so our actions often do not turn out as we
planned. If we were clever enough to understand the times in which
we live, and if we were flexible enough to adjust our tactics accordingly, we might always be successful. But this is a practical impossi-
bility; for, as Machiavelli tells us, there never are men so wise nor
men with such perfect control over their own character. We act, instead, as nature inclines us. Hence man will never be entirely deliv-

29 Letter 116; Gilbert, II, 896-7

141　Concept of *Fortuna* in Machiavelli

ered from the power of fortune; even plans well laid and brilliantly executed may fail due to unforeseen contingencies. I must disagree with a recent critic who has maintained that for Machiavelli fortune can be 'completely overcome.'[30] It is true that Machiavelli speaks of overcoming fortune; but ordinarily he adds in the same breath that such efforts are eventually bound to fail. Machiavelli in effect promises only that we can increase our chances against Fortune, not that we can eliminate her effects entirely. Where he describes how a man could always have good fortune, this is only to point out the ideal condition which nature will never let us achieve. In Machiavelli one finds, perhaps, a certain enthusiasm for his own ideas, but not a messianic promise that he has the solution to all problems.

The various themes connected with fortune are all woven into Machiavelli's *Capitolo* on the subject. The poem may be divided roughly into three sections. In the first, the author dedicates his lines to the recipient, Giovan Battista Soderini, and then asks that the goddess Fortuna might deign to look favourably on him as well: 'she yet may look on him who has courage to sing of her dominion.' After this plea, Machiavelli begins to describe the dread goddess and to enumerate the things she does to the human race. She 'turns states and kingdoms upside down'; she 'times events as suits her'; and 'Over a palace open on every side she reigns and she deprives no one of entering, but the getting out is not sure.' In general, Fortune presides over our lives and makes it impossible for us to reckon with any assurance of success. Yet as in his prose works, Machiavelli is not content to leave things there. He is driven to seek some way of overcoming bad luck, of making the universe a little more predictable. In this quest he makes a fascinating change in the traditional imagery associated with Fortune. Since the time of Boethius, she had been represented with a single, inexorably turning wheel, on which men could ascend for a while but which would eventually throw them off. Machiavelli, however, writes: 'Within her palace, as many wheels are turning as there are varied ways of climbing to those things which every living man strives to attain.' These many wheels offer new possibilities for outwitting Fortune; for at any one time there is more than one course of action:

30　Charles Tarlton, 'The Symbolism of Redemption and the Exorcism of Fortune in Machiavelli's *Prince,' Review of Politics*, 30 (1968), 342

142 The Political Calculus

That man most luckily forms his plan, among all the persons in
Fortune's palace, who chooses a wheel befitting her wish,

since the inclinations that make you act, so far as they conform
with her doings, are the causes of your good and your ill.

Yet you cannot therefore trust yourself to her nor hope to escape her hard bite, her hard blows, violent and cruel,

because while you are whirled about by the rim of a wheel that
for the moment is lucky and good, she is wont to reverse its
course midcircle.

And since you cannot change your character nor give up the disposition that Heaven endows you with, in the midst of your journey she abandons you.

Therefore, if this he understood and fixed in his mind, a man
who could leap from wheel to wheel would always be happy and
fortunate,

but because to attain this is denied by the occult force that rules
us, our condition changes with her course.

Yet Machiavelli is not deceived by his own remarkable image of the
adventurer scrambling from wheel to wheel. *If* we could read Fortune's plan, and *if* we could change our own character and disposition, there might be some hope of keeping up the game indefinitely;
but since this is impossible, eventually we will be doomed to fail. This
is the same complex teaching that we have found in Machiavelli's
other major works: theoretically, continued success might be attainable, if a man could always suit his behaviour to the situation; but it
seems to be impossible that any man could be so astute. Hence we
must always act in uncertainty. Prudence and audacity will be of assistance in recognizing and seizing the opportunity that offers itself;
but in the last analysis, there remains an unpredictability to success
and failure that we cannot expect to banish.

FORTUNE AND TRANSCENDENCE

What is the significance of Machiavelli's opinions on fortune? One
point needs to be emphasized at the outset: What is most important

143 Concept of *Fortuna* in Machiavelli

in Machiavelli's understanding of fortune is precisely that which he never bothered to express in writing. What he left unsaid speaks volumes; for it serves to place his interpretation of fortune in the context of two thousand years of history.

There are, reaching back to antiquity, two great conceptions of fortune, which we might label the immanent and the transcendent. In the immanent conception, the human contest with Fortuna is a closed field of action. It is assumed without question that each man would like to possess the *bona fortunae*, the 'goods of fortune,' however variously they may be imagined – health, wealth, friendship, etc. All men play by fortune's rules, so to speak; they are winners or losers insofar as they achieve those rewards which fortune can bestow. *Virtus* – the ability pertaining to a man – is the counterweight to *fortuna*; a man's own strength and shrewdness can improve his chances in the struggle for the *bona fortunae*, although it can never guarantee success. But it never occurs to the contestant to ask why he should compete for Fortune's favours in the first place. As soon as this question is asked, the spell is broken, and a new conception of Fortune arises. For there is no compelling reason why one has to strive for the prizes which Fortune can distribute. There are other goods, goods of the mind and soul, which do not lie within the power of Fortune to confer or to remove. This insight is at the core of the Socratic teaching that it is better to suffer injustice than to commit it. If a man refrains from evil, he will be happy even if he suffers the worst blows of fortune. In a sense, he can transcend Fortune through refusing to play her game; this is why I have chosen to speak of a transcendental conception.

It is, of course, well known, that the words *virtus* and *arete* became ambiguous during antiquity due to the rise of philosophy. Originally connected with a man's power to achieve something, they later acquired a moral meaning as the perfection of the soul. It is perhaps less well known that, as I have pointed out above, the connotations of *fortuna* developed in precisely the same way, from immanence to transcendence. Hence there is no universal doctrine of antiquity concerning *virtus* and *fortuna*, but rather two distinct conceptions. When we read in Livy that 'fortune favours the bold,' we are confronted with the mood of immanence, where fortune's rewards appear worth seeking. Yet when we read in the *Consolation of Philosophy* that all fortune is good fortune because it can never rob the soul of virtue,

144 The Political Calculus

the concern is with transcendence over fortune by directing one's attention to the divine good.

As far as the evidence of written documents is concerned, the immanent conception of fortune practically perished during the Middle Ages. It is unlikely that all men gave up their hopes of success in this world; but those who expressed themselves in writing were more concerned about the world to come. The solution of Boethius, which is really the method of transcendence developed by classical philosophy, persisted; but there was also developed a more distinctively Christian formulation of the problem. According to Boethius, all fortune was good because it could not touch the virtue of the inner man; but this notion still leaves logical problems for the Christian. Why does evil happen? The answer of a consistent faith is to see in the perturbations of fortune the workings of divine providence. Bad fortune is not only something to be transcended; it is part of God's plan to lead us to perfection. This identification of *fortuna* with providence is the solution adopted by Dante in the famous seventh canto of the *Inferno*.[31] It is also the attitude indicated by an interesting seal found in Hungary, on which the design consists of a wheel with the head of Christ in the centre. Around the outside is the inscription *Et Deus in rota:*[32] 'God in the wheel.' The implication is clear: in the centre of our shifting fortunes, we can find the divine plan of salvation.

It is informative to compare this thirteenth-century representation of Fortune's wheel with Machiavelli's image of the multiple wheels. In less than three hundred years the transcendent response to fortune has given way to the immanent – Machiavelli's adventurer, who skips from wheel to wheel, never stops to consider what the purpose of his striving is. His plans and desires are confined within the rules prescribed by Fortuna. He will achieve success if he can stay in harmony with her plans, that is, by selecting the correct wheel; if not, he is

31 Cf. also Chaucer's *Balade of Fortune*, II, 65-8:
   Lo, th'execucion of the magestee
   That al purveyeth of his rightwisnesse,
   That same thing 'Fortune' clepen ye,
   Ye blinde bestes, ful of lewednesse!

32 Doren, 'Fortuna im Mittelalter und in der Renaissance,' 147, contains an illustration.

145 Concept of *Fortuna* in Machiavelli

doomed to failure. Nowhere in this imagery is there the slightest hint
that bad fortune is not able to harm the soul, or that ill luck might
be part of an overall design to lead man to redemption. Machiavelli
does not even attack these considerations of transcendence; they are
simply foreign to him, and he does not bother to mention them.

Throughout Machiavelli's works we find the triumph of the immanent conception of Fortuna. She is always the opponent, success is
always the goal. Previously this had not always been so. In the thirteenth century, it was necessary to consider not only the means of
achieving success but also the possible ill effect on the soul. Petrarch's
famous discourse on fortune, for example, is entitled *De Remediis
utriusque fortunae*: 'Remedies for both kinds of fortune.' The book
is written in the form of two conversations; in the first, Reason debates with Joy, in the second with Sorrow. The point of both dialogues is the same, namely that both joy over success and sorrow
over failure are immanent, transitory emotions. The correct response
to both is to turn to God. Reason quotes with approval the advice of
Lactantius: 'They that know God, are not only safe from incursions
of Devyls, but also ... are not tyed by destinie.'[33] This is the epitome
of the medieval transcendence over fortune – liberation from both
good and bad luck. In comparison, it is worthwhile to read what Machiavelli says about the proper response to good fortune; for his
words clearly illustrate the gap that separates his view from the medieval one. In the third book of the *Discourses*, Machiavelli comments
on the words of Camillus who was once made dictator of Rome and
then fell into disfavour: 'As for me, the dictatorship did not exalt my
spirits nor exile depress them.'[34] Machiavelli continues:

> From this we learn that great men are always in every sort of for-
> tune just the same; if that varies, now raising them now putting
> them down, they do not vary, but always keep their courage firm
> and so closely united with their way of life that we easily see that
> Fortune does not have power over a single one of them. Quite
> different is the conduct of weak men, because they grow vain and

33 Petrarch, *Phisicke against Fortune, as well Prosperous as Adverse*, tr. Thomas
   Twyne (London 1579), 14
34 Livy, *Histories*, II, 7

146 The Political Calculus

are made drunk with good fortune, assigning all their prosperity
to an ability which they have not displayed at any time. As a
result, they become unbearable and hateful to all around them.
From this situation, then, issues some sudden change in their lot,
and when they look that in the face, they fall at once into the
other defect and become despicable and abject. Consequently
princes of that sort, when in adversity, think more about running
away than about defending themselves, since, having used good
fortune badly, they are unprepared for any defense.[35]

In his own way, Machiavelli is suggesting that there is a danger attached to good fortune; but his interpretation is totally immanent.
Good fortune may be bad for a weak man because he will become
insolent and not take sufficient precautions for the future. Hence a
lucky success may lead directly to a later downfall. But there is no
implication here that success in itself is a questionable thing; it is
only dangerous if it does not perpetuate itself. The ultimate standard of judgment is thus clearly the *bona fortunae*; no transcendent
considerations are present at all. The 'remedy' for good and bad fortune is not to turn to God but to use success wisely so that it will
not slip from one's grasp.

If the response to success is to strive for still more, the loss of the
transcendent dimension is equally visible in the reaction to failure.
Here again, Machiavelli does not seek consolation in thoughts of eter-
nity. He offers rather a type of resigned stoicism which accepts what
cannot be altered but which does not turn from earthly to other-
worldly considerations. Witness his own case. After his fall from his
position, after his imprisonment and sufferings, Machiavelli can do
nothing but salvage a little pride in the fortitude with which he endured his unhappiness. 'As to turning my face to resist Fortune,' he
wrote to Vettori shortly after his release from prison, 'I want you to
get this pleasure from my distresses, namely that I have borne them
so bravely that I love myself for it and feel that I am stronger than
you believed.'[36] He must have had the same unhappy experiences in
mind when he wrote in *The Ass of Gold*:

35 *Discourses*, III, 31; Gilbert, I, 498
36 Letter 119; Gilbert, II, 899

147 Concept of *Fortuna* in Machiavelli

Ma perche il pianto a l'uom fu sempre brutto,
sie debbe al volto della sua fortuna
voltare il viso di lacrime asciutto.

'But because weeping has always been shameful to a man, he should turn to the blows of Fortune a face unstained with tears.'[37]

Similar considerations apply to Machiavelli's humorous little poem *Dell'occasione* ('On Opportunity'). In it the poet meets Opportunity, who explains to him how hard she is to catch: her hair falls forward over her face, so she cannot be recognized, while in back she is bald, so she cannot be seized while she runs. The poet asks her who her companion is, and she replies that it is Penitence; and 'whoever does not know how to capture me will get her.'[38] In this dialogue there is no hint that Penitence refers to anything other than simple regret at having let opportunity slip by. There is no suggestion at all of the medieval repentance which guides the soul to thoughts of immortality. Admittedly one should not make too much of this one short poem; Machiavelli consciously modelled it on an epigram of Ausonius, and the thought expressed is his. Yet Machiavelli felt the poem worth imitating, so he probably found nothing amiss in the contents. Furthermore, this is not an isolated instance; it is only one of a series of cases where Machiavelli speaks of fortune and kindred themes without ever mentioning that transcendence over fortune is at least a conceivable option. Such repeated silence forces us to conclude that such possibilities of transcendence must have been absent from Machiavelli's mind when he used the symbolism of fortune.

This analysis of Machiavelli's use of *fortuna* is largely independent of the vexed question of his religious convictions. I have only suggested that when he spoke of *fortuna*, he did so exclusively in an immanent context. This does not mean that in other situations Machiavelli did not reflect on the transitory nature of the *bona fortunae*. If, for example, we take the 'Exhortation to Penitence' at face value, its implication is that we should become conscious of our entanglements

---

37 *The Ass of Gold*, III, 11.85-7; Gilbert, II, 757

38 L.18: 'chi non sa prender me, costei ritiene.' Machiavelli, *Opere* (Milano 1965), VIII, 325. The poem is not contained in the Gilbert edition.

148 The Political Calculus

in the world 'And repent and understand clearly/that as much as pleases the world is a short dream.'[39] Yet regardless of how genuine Machiavelli's emotions of penitence were, it is clear that, in this case, he did not choose to express them with the symbolism of *fortuna*. We also find a similar situation in the *Capitolo* 'On Ambition.' Here Machiavelli gives us a very powerful description of the bad effects of ambition:

> Pass over Siena's fraternal contests; turn your eyes, Luigi, to this region, upon these people thunderstruck and bewildered,
>
> you will see how Ambition results in two kinds of action: one party robs and the other weeps for its wealth ravaged and scattered.
>
> Let him turn his eyes here who wishes to behold the sorrows of others, and let him consider if ever before now the sun has looked upon such savagery.
>
> A man is weeping for his father dead and a woman for her husband; another man, beaten and naked, you see driven in sadness from his own dwelling.
>
> Oh how many times, when the father has held his son tight in his arms, a single thrust has pierced the breasts of them both![40]

It is significant that this moving description is quite divorced from any reference to fortune. Though Machiavelli is capable of pity, he does not express it with references to fortune. Where *fortuna* does appear in the poem, it is toward the end, where the frame of reference has shifted considerably – Machiavelli has concluded that ambition can never be exorcised from the heart, and that therefore the only remedy is to bring it under control through forceful government. It is at this point, when musing on the difficulty of creating a government which can curb ambition, that he remarks that 'in the world most men let themselves be mastered by fortune' (11.176-7). Thus we must conclude that, even though Machiavelli was conscious at times of the desire for transcendence over the limitation of politics,

---

39 Petrarch, Sonnet 1; quoted by Machiavelli at the end of the 'Exhortation to Penitence,' Gilbert, I, 174

40 Gilbert, II, 738; 11.124-38

149 Concept of *Fortuna* in Machiavelli

this desire was expressed in other ways than by the symbolism of *fortuna*.

Although, as I shall point out in the next section, there are certain inconsistencies in Machiavelli's use of *fortuna*, there is this one regularity, that the dimension of transcendence over the struggle with fortune is never present. In this respect, Machiavelli represents the culmination of two centuries of development since Dante and Petrarch. In this period, as I have remarked, the immanent conception of fortune modelled on that of antiquity had increasingly appeared alongside the other-worldly, medieval notion. The result was the extraordinary confusion in the identity of *fortuna* which many historians have perceived in the Renaissance. Chabod, for example, writes that:

> "Fortune" is very hard to define – At one moment in conformity with the Christian adaptation of the ancient concept, it appears in the guise of an *ancilla Dei* – At another it resumes its ancient character of a blind, uncontrollable fate.[41]

Felix Gilbert has observed the same phenomenon in his study of the protocols of the Florentine *pratiche*:

> Thus to the Florentine Fortuna had preserved many of the characteristics of a pagan goddess ... Yet at the same time this pagan goddess exerts her power in a Christian world and has to be integrated in it ... thus it is not possible clearly to distinguish between what is done by God and what is done by Fortuna.[42]

With Machiavelli, however, this tension between the differing ideas of fortune is resolved in favour of the immanent conception. Although Machiavelli occasionally refers to God instead of fortune, these tend to be stylized references which do not exhibit any deep feeling.[43]

---

41 Federico Chabod, *Machiavelli and the Renaissance*, tr. David Moore (New York 1965), 189
42 Felix Gilbert, *Machiavelli and Guicciardini* (Princeton NJ 1965), 41
43 E.g., in the *History of Florence*, VII, 21, Machiavelli speaks of certain citizens 'conducting themselves as though God and Fortune had given them the city to be plundered.' Gilbert, III, 1364. In the *Second Decennale* he writes of the

150 The Political Calculus

They are not joined to any profound reflections on the transitoriness
of earthly pursuits. In all the cases where Machiavelli speaks at any
length about Fortune and with any great emotion, his frame of reference is clearly the closed world of immanent political action, where
all men by definition strive for the *bona fortunae*.

THE PLACE OF FORTUNE IN MACHIAVELLI'S THOUGHT

Students of Machiavelli have differed widely in assessing the role of
fortuna in his thought. One position, advanced by several eminent
scholars, is that generally speaking, *fortuna* represents the breakdown
of reason in Machiavelli's thinking. Where he could not go any farther
in explaining a phenomenon, he would attribute it in quasi-superstiti-
ous fashion to the workings of fortune. Burd, for example, says with
respect to fortune that 'whenever Machiavelli – and Guicciardini too –
were taken off the lines familiar to them, their natural acumen appears to desert them and they share the superstition of the age.'[44]
Burd implies, although without adducing any weighty textual evidence, that Machiavelli's notion of fortune was astrological in character. Ernst Cassirer seems to have come to similar conclusions, although he grants Machiavelli perhaps a bit more rationality. In *The
Myth of the State*, he writes that Machiavelli knew that even the best
political advice was sometimes ineffective.

> His logical and rational method deserted him at this point. He
> had to admit that human things are not governed by reason, and
> that, therefore, they are not entirely describable in terms of rea-
> son. We must have recourse to another – to a half-mythical power.
> "Fortune" seems to be the ruler of things.[45]

tribulations of Italy 'by divine wisdom foreordained.' Gilbert, III, 1457. In *The
Prince*, ch.11, he declares that ecclesiastical principalities are 'maintained by
God,' Gilbert, I, 44. This last statement I would interpret ironically; the first
two appear to be stylized references only.

44 Burd, *Il Principe* (1891), 355
45 Ernst Cassirer, *The Myth of the State* (New Haven 1963), 157

151 Concept of *Fortuna* in Machiavelli

By and large, Chabod also shares this opinion, that *fortuna* is at least half-mythical. He declares that Machiavelli sometimes regarded *fortuna* 'as the force and logic of history,' but more often 'as a mysterious, transcendent grouping of events, whose incoherence is unintelligible to the human mind.'[46]

An almost antithetical interpretation has, however, been developed by Leonardo Olschki. According to Olschki, Machiavelli produced in *The Prince* a 'new science' of man and society in much the same way as Galileo created a new science of matter. The fundamental concepts of this science were *fortuna* and *virtù*. Whatever may be the connotations of *fortuna* in Machiavelli's literary works, in *The Prince*

> fortune is neither a goddess nor a personification, neither an allegory nor a metaphor, as it has been in poetry, in Machiavelli's own Capitolo on Fortune, or in moral philosophy ... it is ... an abstract and secular concept ... In other words: fortune represents the passive condition of political success in conquests or internal administration. *Virtù* is its active counterpart.[47]

Thus fortune and virtue are 'technical terms of a rational system of political thought';[48] they are the building blocks of a scientific analysis of political behaviour. It would be hard to imagine a position more contrary to that of Burd, Cassirer, and Chabod, who see in *fortuna* not an advance in rational thought but a survival of a pre-logical description of the world.

I find it impossible to accept the full burden of Olschki's argument. It is not enough that scientific concepts be abstract and general, so that they can refer to a multitude of phenomena. They must also be relatable in such a way that the result is a testable proposition. In other words, there must be associated with the pure concepts operational definitions which permit empirical verification. In this respect Machiavelli's notions of *fortuna* and *virtù* are utterly deficient. He gives no rules, either explicit or implicit, by which each can be defined. In practice, therefore, their use is tautological. If a man's at-

46 Federico Chabod, *Machiavelli and the Renaissance*, 69-70

47 Leonardo Olschki, *Machiavelli the Scientist* (Berkeley 1945), 37-8

48 Ibid., 39

152 The Political Calculus

tempts, like those of Cesare Borgia, fail in spite of impressive efforts, the result must be due to the malice of fortune. The logical problem involved is rather similar to that of the modern dilemma of environment and heredity. The concepts appear to be reasonable, and yet the lack of unimpeachable operational definitions makes it impossible ever to decide between them.

Yet even if Olschki's controversial thesis cannot be accepted entirely, it suggests the problem facing Machiavelli's reader. The term *fortuna* is used so often and in so many different connections that it is easy for confusion to arise over its precise meaning. I suggest, furthermore, that there is good reason for this confusion and for the disagreement between Olschki and other students of Machiavelli. There is in fact a fundamental ambiguity in Machiavelli's *fortuna* which makes it appear to be now a mythical image, now a rational concept. Without ever acknowledging that he is speaking of two different things, Machiavelli employs *fortuna* to designate not only the unexpected occurrence of an unique and contingent event, but also the whole constellation of social forces in which the event transpires. This is a problem of which the modern development of statistical theory has made social scientists acutely aware. It is becoming obvious that one can describe the macro-structure of society (or at least certain aspects of it) in terms of probability, but that this yields no information about the occurrence of a single event. To give an example, one can make estimates of social mobility within a class system, and thus make predictions about the levels to which certain percentages of a social stratum will probably rise; but this does not enable us to say anything about a specific individual. With respect to the behaviour of the system, his behaviour must be taken as random or fortuitous.

Similar epistemological questions arise not only in statistical models but also in the genetic explanations of the historian. One can trace the antecedents of a social event, and suggest why it 'had to happen'; but it is impossible to explain why it happened on a particular day and involved the people it did. At this point the historian usually points to the role of personality or the individual; but this is a thinly disguised appeal to the principle of chance, which merely transfers the problem to the psychologist.

I would argue, then, that it is perfectly in accord with the common principles of modern social science to distinguish between the macro-level of causation and the micro-level of fortuitousness. Now this is a distinction which Machiavelli did not draw. Obviously he cannot be blamed for not doing so; it is only in this century that we have become aware of the critical and ineradicable role of chance in scientific explanation. But even though we can hardly reproach Machiavelli for not being aware of the difficulty, the fact remains that his failure to do so renders his conception of *fortuna* ambiguous and mystified. For under *fortuna* he includes not only the truly fortuitous and contingent single event, but also the entire context in which such events occur; and while the individual event must remain mysterious, the large-scale constellation of social forces is in principle explicable.

It is noteworthy that when Machiavelli is speaking of *fortuna* in this second sense, he frequently substitutes the totally secularized concept of 'the times' (*i tempi*). This happens in several of his most important discussions of fortune. Yet it would not be accurate to state that he replaces *fortuna* with *i tempi*. It is rather the case that he uses the two terms interchangeably at certain points. Although the germ of the notion is there in his work, he is not ready to say with Montesquieu that:

> it is not fortune who governs the world, as we see from the history of the Romans. There are general causes, moral or physical, which operate in every monarchy, raise it, maintain it, or overthrow it; all that occurs is subject to these causes; and if a particular cause, like the accidental result of a battle, has ruined a state, there was a general cause which made the downfall of this state ensue from a single battle. In a word, the principal movement draws with it all the particular occurrences.[49]

It is only with the benefit of hindsight that we can say that Machiavelli's use of *fortuna* to describe large-scale constellations of circumstances is a mystification.

Yet even though Machiavelli was not conscious of epistemological problems in the fashion of modern investigators, he was an extraordinarily acute student of politics. Hence, when he uses *fortuna* to describe a potentially intelligible concatenation of factors, this does not

49 Montesquieu, *Considerations on the Greatness and Decadence of the Romans* (1734), cited in J.B. Bury, *The Idea of Progress* (London 1920), 145-6

154 The Political Calculus

remain a total mystification. We can see at work the analytical powers of a man whose credo it was that it is well to reason upon all
things. Thus even though *fortuna* is fundamentally a symbol of a
power or force which is beyond fathoming, Machiavelli's conception
of it contains a striking amount of rationalism.

The first point to consider is his relation to astrology. The Renaissance was indeed a superstitious era, even more so than the Middle
Ages, now that certain of the restraints of the orthodox faith in divine Reason had been weakened. Most men believed in omens and
magic of some type, and Machiavelli was no exception, if we are to
take at face value *Discourses*, I, 56: 'Before great events occur in a
city or a region, there are signs that presage them or men who predict them.' And yet I must disagree with Burd that Machiavelli's notion of *fortuna* is an astrological one. On the contrary, wherever Machiavelli attributes events to the workings of fortune, astrology and
superstition of any sort are noticeably absent. Although it seems true
that he believed in the existence of omens, Machiavelli did not use
astrology as an operating approach to political analysis. Instead he
preferred to work out rational explanations based on personal motives or impersonal forces. Hence, in spite of the chapter on omens
in the *Discourses*, what is remarkable in Machiavelli's use of *fortuna*
is precisely the absence of superstitious associations. I would conclude that *Discourses*, I, 56 is due to Machiavelli's desire to write a
complete treatise, taking into account the day's conventional wisdom; that chapter most decidedly does not represent his typical approach to politics.

If occult forces do not play any noteworthy role in Machiavelli's
thinking on politics, neither does the more respectable practice of
prayer. In *L'Asino d'Oro* he specifically rules out divine favour or intervention in favour of reliance on more immediate means of action:

> To believe that without effort on your part God fights for you,
> while you are idle and on your knees, has ruined many kingdoms
> and many states.

> But there should be no one with so small a brain that he will be-
> lieve that, if his house is falling, God will save it without any
> other prop, because he will die beneath that ruin.[50]

50 *The Ass of Gold*, V; Gilbert, II, 764

155 Concept of *Fortuna* in Machiavelli

Characteristically, Machiavelli adds that prayer is of some value – because it promotes 'union and good order' among those participating, and on the solidarity of the group 'rests good and happy fortune'! He could hardly say more clearly that man must rely on his own efforts if he is to achieve his goals, and that he cannot expect any supernatural benefits. It is highly instructive, too, to look more closely at the one time when Machiavelli appears to say that God intervenes in human affairs. In the eleventh chapter of *The Prince*, he takes up the topic of ecclesiastical principalities, only to say that it would be presumptuous of him to discuss them, since they are 'set on high and maintained by God.'[51] Yet how much credence can be placed in such an assertion, when Machiavelli is discussing the papal states in a book dedicated to win the favour of a close relative of the pope? Furthermore, immediately after humbly refusing to discuss the politics of the papacy, Machiavelli starts a new sentence with 'nevertheless' and goes on to deliver a number of comments about the success of the papacy under Alexander VI and Julius II. I, for one, would seriously question whether Machiavelli thought the papal states were particularly protected by God in their political dealings.[52]

Yet just as we cannot ignore the rationalistic elements in Machiavelli's conception of fortune, so we cannot wish away the very real irrational components. This is the truth contained in Cassirer's dictum that Machiavelli's *fortuna* is 'half-mythical.' Particularly when he is referring to the unique and contingent event, he does so in words which suggest that fortune possesses consciousness, personality, and intention.

I am not referring so much to obvious literary devices, such as that in the twenty-fifth chapter of *The Prince*, where Machiavelli refers to Fortuna as a woman who has to be handled with authority, as to other places where he seems to say in a straightforward way that Fortuna consciously plans our lot. In the *Discourses*, for example, he quotes with approval Livy's saying that 'Fortune thus blinds the minds of men when she does not wish them to resist her power,' and then continues in a similar vein:

51 Gilbert, I, 44

52 I am afraid that the assumption of Father Walker that these words of Machiavelli were sincerely meant and demonstrate his religious faith, is a piece of wishful thinking. Cf. Walker, *Discourses*, I, 80

156 The Political Calculus

Skillfully Fortune does this, since she chooses a man, when she
plans to bring to pass great things, who is of so much perception
and so much ability that he recognizes the opportunities she puts
before him. So in the same way when she intends to bring to pass
great failures, she puts there men to promote such failure. And if
somebody there is able to oppose her, she either kills him or deprives him of all means for doing anything good.[53]

The rest of the paragraph is an impressive enumeration of the things
which Fortuna accomplishes when she is in the mood. Similarly the
whole story of Castruccio Castracani is meant to illustrate how Fortune intervenes in human affairs because she wishes 'to show the
world that she – and not prudence – makes men great.'[54] There is perhaps a tendency for modern readers to skip lightly over passages like
these or to rationalize them as pieces of allegory. Yet they occur so
frequently in Machiavelli's works that we should be careful not to
underrate their importance. It is safer to assume that, even if Machiavelli did not think of Fortuna as a specific woman in a specific place,
he must have conceived of her in a way we would today call mythical, which does not strictly differentiate abstract concepts from the
human emotions bound up with them.
    It would be convenient if one could say that Machiavelli had two
distinct conceptions of *fortuna,* a rational one referring to large social
causes and synonymous with *i tempi,* and a non-rational one referring to the fortuitous crystallization of these causes in a single event.
But matters are not so simple. Machiavelli himself was not aware of
the distinction we have made. He did not distinguish between that
which is unknown, but potentially intelligible, and that which is on
principle unknowable. The most that can be done is to draw the distinction in hindsight and to suggest that it grows naturally out of
Machiavelli's use of *fortuna* and *i tempi,* even if it did not occur to
Machiavelli himself.

53 *Discourses,* II, 29; Gilbert, I, 407-8
54 Gilbert, II, 534

[8]

SEVEN

In Search of Machiavellian *Virtù*

JOHN PLAMENATZ

The most vilified of political thinkers is also the one of whom it has been said that he 'concentrated all his real and supreme values in what he called *virtù*.'[1] There is nothing here to be surprised at; for those who have been shocked by Machiavelli have been so, not only by his seeming to justify murder, cruelty, and treachery, but by his way of speaking about virtue.

Machiavelli is no longer shocking, and it is widely agreed that those who were shocked by him in the past misunderstood him. But he is still a subject of controversy. In particular, there are differences of opinion about what he called *virtù*. These differences are, I think, less about what is to be understood by the term, what qualities it refers to, than about the place of *virtù* in Machiavelli's political thought generally and his conception of man. Some ninety years ago Villari said that Machiavelli 'always used the word *virtue* in the sense of courage and energy both for good and evil. To Christian virtue in its more general meaning, he rather applied the term *goodness,* and felt much less admiration for it than for the pagan virtue that was always fruitful of glory.'[2] Later scholars, though they have qualified this ver-

1 F. Meinecke, *Machiavellism: The Doctrine of Raison d'Etat and Its Place in Modern History*, tr. Douglas Scott (London & New Haven 1957), 31

2 P. Villari, *Life and Times of Machiavelli*, tr. Linda Villari, 4 vols (London, n.d.), II, 92

158 The Political Calculus

dict, have not disagreed with it substantially – though they have sometimes believed that they were doing so. It is not true that Machiavelli
always used the word *virtù* in this general sense, or in narrower senses
that fall within its scope. He sometimes used it in quite other senses.
It has been questioned whether he admired *virtù* more than he did
goodness, and it is doubtful whether what he understood by goodness
(*bontà*) has much that is peculiarly Christian about it. Still, though
writers since Villari's time have gone further than he did in distinguishing the various senses that Machiavelli gave to *virtù*, they have
not seriously challenged his account of it. They have tried rather to
improve on it.

No one has gone further than Meinecke in treating the idea of *virtù*
as the key to understanding Machiavelli's conceptions of man and of
the state. Meinecke distinguishes two important senses in which Machiavelli uses the term. Sometimes he has in mind what is nowadays
called *civic virtue*, and sometimes something altogether more rare
and excellent – a virtue peculiar to rulers and leaders of men, and especially to founders of states and religions. This second virtue, to distinguish it from the first, we might call *heroic* – though Meinecke
does not give it that name. Heroic and civic virtue are not mutually
exclusive; indeed, they are closely related in the sense that each sustains the other or gives scope to it, but they are different.

If, among Machiavelli's twentieth-century interpreters, Meinecke
makes the most of *virtù*, Professor Whitfield seems to make the least.
'There is,' he says, 'no doctrine of *virtù* in Machiavelli. If there were
it would be easy to discover in his works, but Machiavelli was not
given to such theorizing, and he himself would be the first to be surprised at the stir the word has caused.'[3] Whitfield, in his English way,
felt perhaps a certain impatience with other scholars 'theorizing'
about a writer who, in his eyes, has the merit of not being 'given to
theorizing.'

Professor Whitfield is right; there is no doctrine of *virtù* in Machiavelli. Machiavelli does not define the word, even in the most general
way, let alone distinguish different senses in which he uses it. Nor is
it part of a systematic theory about man and the state, for Machiavelli has no such theory. There is no more a doctrine of *virtù* in Ma-

3 J.H. Whitfield, *Machiavelli* (Blackwell 1947), 95

159 In Search of Machiavellian *Virtù*

chiavelli than there is a doctrine of *vertu* in the plays of Corneille. Still, what each expresses by the word is worth, and has received, close scrutiny; for this scrutiny is one way, and a good way, of getting at how they think and feel about man.

Neither Meinecke, who says that Machiavelli 'concentrates his real and supreme values in *virtù*,' nor Whitfield, who denies that he has a doctrine of it, disagrees with Villari that part of what Machiavelli understands by *virtù* is energy or strength of will. No moderately attentive reader of *The Prince* and the *Discourses* can help but notice that Machiavelli finds *virtù* both in the Roman citizen devoted to the republic and in such men as Romulus, Lycurgus, Moses, and Numa Pompilius, the 'founders' of states or religions. Though Machiavelli does not define either the virtue of the citizen or that of the maker or restorer of a state or religion, though he does not point to the differences between them, there can really be no doubting that he does not attribute the same range of qualities to the citizen and to the heroic creator or preserver of what brings order to men.

Thus, though there is no doctrine of *virtù* in Machiavelli, there is no denying that he uses the word in related and yet different senses, and that the attempt to explain how they differ and how they are connected with his other ideas about man, the human condition and the state, is an attempt to interpret what can properly be called a philosophy. Because a writer produces no systematic theory, it does not follow that he has nothing that deserves to be called philosophy – for his ideas may be coherent and may have implicit in them a comprehensive attitude or way of looking at the human condition, either at all times and everywhere or within broad limits of time and territory. Of course, there are inconsistencies and obscurities in Machiavelli; but then there are also in the much more systematic Hobbes, who loved to define and to distinguish. And it may be that Machiavelli was not the less consistent and lucid of the two.

Though Machiavelli did not 'theorize' about *virtù*, Whitfield does so for some thirteen pages and to good purpose. Machiavelli, he says, sometimes contrasts *virtù* with *viltà*, and at least once with *ozio*, but more often with *fortuna*.[4] Now, *viltà* is cowardice, or faint-heartedness, and sometimes baseness or meanness, and *ozio* is idleness. So

4 Ibid., 97

160 The Political Calculus

that Whitfield agrees with Villari that *virtù* is, first and foremost, courage and energy; for courage is the opposite of cowardice, and energy of idleness. And though courage and energy are not properly the *opposites* of fortune, they can be *opposed* to it. Machiavelli speaks of fortune, sometimes, as if it were a person, as if it had purposes of its own, benevolent or malevolent, and at other times as if it were opportunity that a man may take or not take; and he speaks of it also as whatever in human affairs is unforeseen and must be faced when it comes. He speaks of it as sailors, in the old sailing days, spoke of the sea, as if it were both friend and enemy, propitious and threatening, itself unconquerable but the occasion of human defeats and victories. Fortune is what man is 'up against'; and *virtù* is opposed to it in the sense that it makes the best of it, either by taking advantage of what it brings or by bearing up under it. Here again *virtù* is courage and energy, and something more besides; it is fortitude, or courage in adversity, and also intelligence and resourcefulness, the ability to recognize how you are placed and to act in time and effectively. There is nothing that Whitfield says or implies about *virtù* to which either Villari or Meinecke need disagree.

This is not to suggest that he only repeats what they, who wrote before he did, said. For example, he shows how close Machiavelli stands to other writers, earlier or later, who never, as he did, shocked posterity. He quotes from Cicero's *De Officiis* (II, X, 320): 'For they [men] do not despise everyone of whom they think ill. They think ill of those who are wicked, slanderous, fraudulent, ready to commit injustices, without indeed despising them. Wherefore, as I said, those are despised who, as the saying goes, are of no use either to themselves or others, in whom there is no exertion, no care for anything.'[5] This is good, and to the point. At least since Villari's time, Machiavelli's 'pagan' idea of *virtù* has been contrasted with the 'Christian' idea of *bontà*. Yet even the best of Christians does not despise all that he blames; he does not despise, any more than Machiavelli did, courage and energy, fortitude and resourcefulness – even in the wicked, even when he blames what they could not have done had they not had these qualities. Actions that require *virtù*, though sometimes evil, are never despicable. Cicero said it, or rather implied it, long before Machiavelli did.

5 Ibid., 100

161 In Search of Machiavellian *Virtù*

Excellent, too, and to the point, are Whitfield's quotations from La Rochefoucauld: 'Weakness is more opposed to virtue than is vice,' or 'No one deserves the name of good unless he has strength and boldness enough to be wicked – all other goodness is most often a form of idleness or of impotence of the will,' or 'There are evil heroes as well as good ones.'[6] The virtue that La Rochefoucauld speaks of is not Machiavelli's *virtù*, but the two ideas have a good deal in common. Where there is virtue, for La Rochefoucauld as for Machiavelli, there is strength of will. But Professor Whitfield goes too far when he suggests that what passes uncondemned in Cicero and La Rochefoucauld (and in others) is found shocking in Machiavelli. The Frenchman never said, and Whitfield does not show that the Roman did either, that actions ordinarily held to be wicked are justified when they are committed for the founding or preserving of the state. This doctrine – whatever is to be said for or against it – is not to be found in La Rochefoucauld and is not implied by the passage that Whitfield quotes from Cicero. But it is to be found in Machiavelli or at least it has seemed so to those who have accused him of condoning wickedness. To quote from some of the great 'moralists' to make clearer what Machiavelli meant by *virtù* is an excellent idea but to use the quotations to suggest that he is no more open than they are to the accusation that he justifies immorality is to misuse them.

I have touched briefly on the views of three writers, Villari, Meinecke, and Whitfield, who have all in their different ways thrown light upon what Machiavelli meant by *virtù*. They do not all three say the same things. Neither Villari nor Whitfield distinguishes, as Meinecke does, *civic* from what might (for want of a better word) be called *heroic* virtue. Indeed, Meinecke himself does not go far in making this distinction; he rather suggests that it ought to be made than puts himself to the trouble of making it, for he does not explain in detail how the two sorts of virtue differ. He goes no further in this direction than to say: 'it [*virtù*] therefore embraced the civic virtues and those of the ruling class; it embraced a readiness to devote oneself to the common good, as well as the wisdom, energy and ambition of the great founders and rulers of states.'[7] But 'common good'

6 Ibid., 100-1. Whitfield quotes from La Rochefoucauld in French, but I give these quotations, as all others in this article, in English.
7 Meinecke, *Machiavellism*, 32

162 The Political Calculus

is a vague term, and the founder and the ruler may be as ready as the ordinary citizen to promote it. Civic virtue is perhaps better described as a readiness to perform the duties of one's office or role in the state than as devotion to a common good. The citizen, and not only the ruler, needs 'energy' if he is to be a good citizen, and even some measure of wisdom. As for ambition, I doubt, for reasons that I shall give later, whether it is to be included in Machiavellian *virtù*.

We may regret that Meinecke did not explain more adequately and fully the difference between these two kinds of 'virtue,' but we cannot deny that they differ considerably and are closely related, and that both are important in the thought of Machiavelli. Nor can we go far in disagreeing with Meinecke's account of what they consist in, for he says too little about them to allow us to do that. He neither repeats what Villari said nor contradicts him, and is not contradicted by Whitfield. Where he goes wrong – so at least it seems to me – is not so much in his meagre account of what Machiavelli meant by *virtù*; it is rather in some of the conclusions he draws from it. The distinction he makes between *civic* and what I have called *heroic* virtue is one that needs to be made, though it ought to be made more clearly than he makes it. But to say, as he does, that 'the ethical sphere of his (Machiavelli's) *virtù* lay in juxtaposition to the usual moral sphere like a kind of world on its own'[8] which was, for Machiavelli, a 'higher world' is to misinterpret Machiavelli, attributing to him beliefs and attitudes which there is no good reason to believe were his. And it is just as misleading to say that 'the development and creation of *virtù* was for Machiavelli the ideal, and completely self-evident, purpose of the state.'[9] There are no better scholars in the world than the Germans. Yet the weight of German scholarship sometimes lies heavy on what it studies, pushing it out of shape. How it does so in this case I shall try to show later. But first let us look at some examples of how Machiavelli speaks of *virtù* in the two most often read of his books, *The Prince* and the *Discourses*.

If we read only English translations of Machiavelli, we are hard put to it to discover what he meant by *virtù*. For his translators, more often than not, do not render *virtù* by 'virtue.' They have an excel-

8 Ibid., 33
9 Ibid., 34

163 In Search of Machiavellian *Virtù*

lent excuse for not doing so; for *virtù*, as Machiavelli uses it, often does not mean what 'virtue' means in the English of our day. So they render *virtù* by some other word, such as valour, ability, merit, courage, or genius, or by some combination of words. Take for example the nineteenth chapter of the first book of the *Discourses*, which in most editions, both Italian and English, is from two to three pages long. In it Machiavelli speaks of *virtù* ten times; Detmold, in one of the most widely used of English translations, renders *virtù* by 'virtue' only twice, and on both occasions adds the word 'valour,' presumably in the hope of coming closer to the original; while Allan Gilbert, the most recent and perhaps the most accurate of Machiavelli's translators into English, abstains altogether from the word 'virtue' in his version of this chapter.[10] On all ten occasions he renders *virtù* by ability, leaving it to the reader to judge from the context what kind of ability is in question. Detmold renders *virtù* by 'character,' 'virtue and valour,' 'vigour and ability,' 'genius and courage,' 'good qualities and courage,' 'great abilities and courage,' 'military ability,' 'merits.' If we take only this chapter, Gilbert is the more prudent translator of the two, and also the more faithful to the original. Yet *virtù*, as Machiavelli uses the word, has not quite the same meaning, or range of meanings, as the broader and more colourless English word 'ability.' Which is not to suggest that Gilbert was wrong to prefer it to the more varied expressions to which Detmold resorted.

In the third chapter of *The Prince*, Machiavelli praises the Romans for their foresight. He says of them that 'seeing their troubles far ahead, [they] always provided against them, and never let them continue in order to avoid war, because they knew that such a war is not averted but is deferred to the other's advantage ... Nor did they approve what all day is in the mouths of the wise men of our age: to profit from the help of time; but they did profit from that of their own vigor [*virtù*] and prudence.'[11] Here *virtù* is associated with prudence. The Romans looked far ahead, taking resolute and timely ac-

---

10 For Detmold's rendering see his translation of the *Discourses* in the Modern Library College edition of *The Prince* and the *Discourses*, 172-4; for Gilbert's see *Machiavelli: The Chief Works and Others*, tr. Allan H. Gilbert, I, 244-5.

11 Gilbert, *Chief Works*, I, 17. I shall quote only from Allan Gilbert's translation of Machiavelli, putting the word *virtù* or other Italian words or phrases in brackets next to Gilbert's renderings of them.

tion. What, according to Machiavelli, do the wise – the falsely-wise – mean by 'the help of time'? They mean that we can see only a little way ahead, and that therefore difficult decisions are best left un-taken. This is the excuse of the pusillanimous. True, we cannot be sure of the future, but we must look ahead as far as we can, seeing what is to be done for the best, and doing it in good time. With the old Romans, at least in the eyes of Machiavelli, foresight, energy, and courage went naturally together.

In the sixth chapter of *The Prince*, speaking of men who have be-come rulers, Machiavelli says: 'they had from Fortune nothing more than opportunity, which gave them matter into which they could introduce whatever form they chose; and without opportunity, their strength of will [*la virtù dello animo loro*] would have been wasted, and without such strength, the opportunity would have been use-less';[12] and then, a little further on, he continues: 'Their opportuni-ties then made these men prosper, since their surpassing abilities [*la eccelenza virtù loro*] enabled them to recognize their opportunities. As a result, their countries were exalted and became very prosper-ous.'[13] Here *virtù* consists, in the first place, of strength of will or mind, and in the second, of insight. The possessor of *virtù* sees his chance to mould something to his own design, not some inert or physical thing, but something human, some community or some as-pect of communal life; he has imagination and intelligence enough to see what can be done, to see what is invisible to others, and strength of purpose enough to do it. He is strong, bold, and of good judgment, to his own great advantage and to the advantage of his people or community.

This is not to say that, in the opinion of Machiavelli, these qualities fail to qualify as *virtù* unless their possessor actually gets what he wants for himself or his people. Courage, energy, and intelligence do not cease to be what they are when they fail of their purpose. Small men have small purposes and are often successful, but their success is no evidence of *virtù* in them, and great men – who are great be-cause their courage, energy, and intelligence are out of the ordinary – sometimes fail. One of the meanings that Machiavelli gives to *virtù* is

12 Ibid., 25
13 Ibid., 26

165 In Search of Machiavellian *Virtù*

the capacity to form large and difficult purposes, and to act resource-fully and resolutely in pursuit of them. *Virtù*, in this (the heroic) sense, is imagination and resilience as well as courage and intelligence. There is no scope for it except where there are difficulties, where there are risks to be taken; and where risks are taken, there is a chance of failure. Machiavelli's feelings towards the most notorious, and (in some eyes) the most oddly chosen, of his heroes varied con-siderably. There was a time when he came close to despising Cesare Borgia – not because Borgia failed of his purpose but because he lost his nerve and his dignity when things went against him.

Villari is right when he says that Machiavellian *virtù* is 'fruitful of glory.' The actions it inspires are of the kind that bring fame or repu-tation: fame where *virtù* is heroic and reputation where it is civic. But it is a mistake to include, as Meinecke does, ambition among the qualities that make up *virtù*. I have found no example of Machiavelli using the word in such a way as to suggest that ambition is itself a part of *virtù*. True, he thought well of ambition, and was himself am-bitious. The desire for glory promotes *virtù*; it is the strongest of the forces that move men to display it, especially the heroic kind. And even the citizen who displays only civic *virtù* is concerned for his good name; and this concern, though it is not what is ordinarily call-ed ambition, is akin to it. But to hold that ambition is a prime mover of *virtù* is still not to treat ambition as a part of *virtù*.

In some of the most discussed pages he wrote, in the eighth chap-ter of *The Prince*, Machiavelli denies that a really wicked man who achieves a great ambition can be said to be virtuous, even though he displays great strength of mind and courage. This denial has been called half-hearted, and is certainly ambiguous. Speaking of Agatho-cles, a potter's son who by ruthless means became tyrant of Syracuse, Machiavelli says: 'It cannot, however, be called virtue [*virtù*] to kill one's fellow-citizens, to betray friends, to be without fidelity, with-out mercy, without religion; such proceedings enable one to gain sovereignty but not fame. If we consider Agathocles' ability [*se si considerassi la virtù di Agatocle*] in entering into and getting out of dangers, and his greatness of mind in enduring and overcoming adver-sities, we cannot see why he should be judged inferior to any of the most excellent generals [*a qualunque eccelentissimo capitano*]. Nev-ertheless, his outrageous cruelty and inhumanity ... do not permit

him to be honoured among the noblest men [*che sia infra li eccelen-
tissimi uomini celebrato*].'[14] The translator, in a footnote to the passage I have quoted, suggests that the first *virtù* means moral excellence, and the second, the kind attributed to Agathocles, courage and
prudence. This, no doubt, is why he renders only the first as 'virtue.'

Now, the other great 'captains' – for example, Romulus or Cesare
Borgia – to whom Machiavelli attributes *virtù* were not morally excellent. Or at least, he was not pointing to their moral excellence when
he spoke of their *virtù*. He was pointing to much the same qualities
in them as he found in Agathocles – to their courage, energy, fortitude, and ability to see and to seize opportunities. These qualities are,
of course, compatible with moral excellence just as they are with cruelty, murder, and perfidy. They are qualities that men, wherever they
recognize them for what they are, are disposed to admire. It is not
peculiar to Machiavelli that he admired them. They are also, so Machiavelli tells us (and surely he is right?), qualities that men are the
readier to recognize and to admire, the better they like, or the more
they come to accept, their effects. That is why the crimes of the man
of heroic *virtù* are so often excused when his achievement is recognized, and why he is admired in spite of them. He is not admired for
being murderous, perfidious, and cruel. For the cowardly, the irreso-
lute, and the stupid, and those who lose their heads in the face of
danger or unexpected difficulties, may also kill, betray, and be cruel.
He is admired for the largeness and boldness of his purpose, for his
resolution, courage, and skill in carrying it out, for daring to do what
has to be done to achieve it. Yet there are limits to this admiration;
it is sometimes given grudgingly or even withheld from someone of
whom it cannot be denied that he possesses these rare qualities. Not
because he lacks moral excellence; for the others, the honoured, the
celebrati, may do so too. Borgia, as Machiavelli describes him, is not
less selfish than Agathocles. But because his purpose, when achieved
– no matter what his motives in pursuing it – is not accepted by others, is not found good by them or does not attract their sympathy,
or else because, in pursuing it, he commits unnecessary crimes. If he
is wantonly cruel or treacherous, or if his purpose or achievement
is unintelligible to others or awakens no response in them, then his

14 Ibid., 36

167 In Search of Machiavellian *Virtù*

qualities are not admired or perhaps even recognized, or are so grudgingly, even though they are of a kind ordinarily much admired. *Virtù*,
wherever it is recognized, is apt to be admired because it consists of
qualities that most men understand and wish they had. Why then was
it not admired in Agathocles? Why the reluctance to admit that he
had it? Was it because he lacked moral excellence? Or because he was
entirely selfish? I doubt whether Machiavelli had such reasons as these
in mind when he wrote the eighth chapter of *The Prince*. Not that he
cared nothing for moral excellence or unselfishness. But these things,
I suggest, seemed irrelevant to him when he was asking how it came
about that Agathocles was less admired than other men of no greater
strength of purpose, resourcefulness and courage than himself.

The *virtù* that Machiavelli speaks of in *The Prince* is for the most
part not civic but heroic. In the *Discourses* he has more to say about
the *virtù* of the citizen, and what he says there allows us to draw
some conclusions about how the two kinds of *virtù* are connected.
In the eleventh chapter of book I he says: 'Kingdoms depending on
the vigor [*virtù*] of one man alone are not very lasting because that
vigor departs with the life of that man ... It is not, then, the salvation
of a republic or kingdom to have a prince who will rule prudently
while he lives but to have one who will so organize it that even after
he dies it can be maintained.'[15] And in the first chapter of the same
book he says: 'Those who read in what way the city of Rome began,
and by what lawgivers and how she was organized, will not marvel
that so much vigor was kept up in that city for so many centuries
[*che tanta virtù si sia per più secoli mantenuta in quella città*] and
that finally it made possible the dominant position to which that republic rose.'[16]

The *virtù* 'of one man alone' is the *virtù* of the ruler or of the
founder of a state or religion, whereas the *virtù* that survived in Rome
for centuries was widespread among the citizens. Clearly, there are
here two kinds of *virtù* in question; they may have something in
common but they also differ. If a state is to be well organized or reformed, it must have a founder or restorer who has the first and rarer
kind of *virtù*. But, unless it is well organized or reformed, its citizens

15 Ibid., 226
16 Ibid., 192

168 The Political Calculus

are unlikely for long to have much of the second kind, the kind that many can share. So much is, I think, clearly implied by Machiavelli in these and other chapters of the *Discourses*, even though he never distinguishes between two kinds of *virtù*.

Speaking in the *Discourses* (book I, chapter 4) of the dissensions between patricians and plebeians in the Roman republic, he says that a republic cannot 'in any way be called unregulated [*inordinata*] where there are so many instances of honorable conduct [*dove sieno tanti esempli di virtù*]; for these good instances have their origin in good education; good education in good laws; good laws in those dissensions that many thoughtlessly condemn. For anyone who will properly examine their outcome will not find that they produce any exile or violence damaging to the common good, but laws and institutions conducive to public liberty.'[17] The examples of *virtù* are examples of devotion to the republic and respect for her laws, of civic virtue, and we are told that they abounded in Rome, not only in spite of dissensions, but indeed – though indirectly, no doubt – because of them. Dissension sometimes enhances respect for law, and therefore civic virtue, since this respect is part of that virtue; and sometimes has the opposite effect. In the *History of Florence* (book III, chapter 1), Machiavelli enquires why discord between the nobles and the people strengthened the republic in ancient Rome and weakened it in Florence. It was, he thinks, because the Roman people, unlike the Florentines, were moderate and content to share power with the nobles. Thus 'through the people's victories the city of Rome became more excellent [*virtuosa*] ... and ... as she increased in excellence [*virtù*], increased in power.' Whereas in Florence, the nobles, deprived of office by the people, when they tried to regain it 'were forced in their conduct, their spirit, and their way of living not merely to be like the men of the people [*popolani*] but to seem so ... [so much so that] the ability in arms [*virtù dell'armi*] and the boldness of spirit [*generosità di animo*] possessed by the nobility were destroyed, and these qualities could not be rekindled in the people,

17 Ibid., 203 – I do not know why Gilbert has translated *esempli* by *instances* rather than *examples*, for Machiavelli is speaking here of conduct which he thinks is exemplary.

169 In Search of Machiavellian *Virtù*

where they did not exist, so that Florence grew always weaker and more despicable.'[18]

It would seem, then, that even civic virtue is, or may be, aristocratic in origin, and later acquired by the people from the nobles, provided that the people are moderate. The *virtù* of the citizen is more than just respect for the laws and institutions, and more than courage and devotion to the community; it is also a kind of wisdom or self-restraint which it would be misleading to call *prudence*, as that word is now used in English.

The *virtù* of the citizen does not consist of all the qualities in him that help to make the state strong; it consists only of qualities that he exhibits when he acts as a citizen. The Romans, at least in the days of the republic, were (so thought Machiavelli) a religious people, and Rome was the stronger for their being so. Yet being religious is no part of *virtù*, as Machiavelli conceives of it. For religion sustains both goodness (*bontà*), or what might be called private morals, and civic virtue. We are told in the *Discourses* (I, 55) that: 'Where this goodness [*bontà*] does not exist, nothing good can be expected, as nothing good can be expected in regions that in our time are evidently corrupt, as is Italy above all, though in such corruption France and Spain have their share. If in those countries fewer disorders appear than we see daily in Italy, the cause is not so much the goodness of the people – which for the most part no longer exists – as that they have a king who keeps them united, not merely through his ability [*virtù*] but also through the still unruined organization of these kingdoms. In Germany this goodness and this religion are still important among the people. These qualities enable many republics to exist there in freedom and to observe their laws so well that nobody outside or inside the cities dares to try to master them.'[19] It is the *virtù* of its citizens that makes a state formidable, and this *virtù* is sustained by religion and good morals. It is sustained also by good laws and institutions, for if a state were not well organized (*ordinata*) *virtù* could not survive for long inside it. Thus good laws and civic virtue support one another, and both are supported by religion and morals.

18 Ibid., III, 1141
19 Ibid., I, 307

170 The Political Calculus

The well-ordered state is not – so Machiavelli implies – the slow work of time, the undesigned effect of human endeavour that men learn to value as they come to appreciate its benefits. It is the achievement of one, or of at most a few, clear-sighted and bold men who see further and dare more than other men do. These men, the founders and restorers of states and religion, possess a *virtù* far rarer than that of the ordinary citizen, even at his Roman best. They have greater foresight and insight, more firmness of purpose, more ruthlessness (*ferocia*), and a courage that most men – even the brave – lack. They can set aside scruples to achieve some large aim. They may not be good men, but it is good that there should be such men; for if there were not, there would exist no well-ordered states, and therefore little scope for either the more ordinary virtue of the citizen or for the goodness that Machiavelli always praises except when it endangers the state. This goodness, which he attributes to the old Roman and to the German of his own day, is not quite goodness as the Christian understands it, or as many who are not Christians have understood it, whether in our times or in others. He says so little about it that we cannot be sure quite what it consists of. He says much less about it than about *virtù* – which does not in the least mean that he holds it of little account. On the contrary; for he tells us that no community can do without it – can for long have either internal security or be formidable to other communities. All this he tells us, though he also tells us that sometimes it takes a man willing to set this goodness aside to establish or to save a community.

If we do Machiavelli the simple justice of attributing to him only opinions that he expressed or clearly implied, we must not even say that he valued goodness, as distinct from *virtù*, merely for its political effects. We must say only that he had more to say about its political effects than about its nature – which is perhaps not surprising in a historian and a writer on politics.

It is a pity that Meinecke should say that, for Machiavelli, the 'ethical sphere of *virtù*' is 'higher' than the 'usual moral sphere' because it is 'the vital source of the state,' or that 'the development and creation of *virtù* is for him the 'self-evident purpose of the state.'[20] In

20 Meinecke, *Machiavellism*, 33-4

171 In Search of Machiavellian *Virtù*

spite of this and other attempts to make a German philosopher of him, Machiavelli remains obstinately an Italian of the Renaissance.

Certainly, he tells us that it takes a man of rare *virtù* to found, preserve, or restore a state, and that such a man, to achieve his purpose, may have to do what is ordinarily condemned as an atrocious crime. But to say this is not to imply that there is an 'ethical sphere' higher than ordinary morality. Nothing that Machiavelli says about *virtù*, so far as I can see, justifies Meinecke's attributing this belief to him. No doubt, Machiavelli does imply that there is a sphere of action in which ordinary moral rules do not always apply. He implies also that, unless the men who act in this sphere disregard these rules when they have to, the other sphere, in which the rules do always apply, cannot be established or preserved. That, more or less, is his position as it is usually, and no doubt correctly, interpreted.[21] There are two spheres, and they are, as Meinecke says, 'juxtaposed' – for neither can exist without the other. In a world without scope for heroic virtue, there would be no scope for civic virtue either. Though Machiavelli does not say this in so many words, it is a fair inference from what he does say, especially in the *Discourses.* But it is not a fair inference that he considered one of these spheres 'higher' than the other.

Indeed, we might well ask, higher in what sense? For Meinecke does not tell us. He points to nothing in Machiavelli's argument that could justify our concluding that, in his eyes, one sphere – the one that allows of 'necessary crimes' – is higher (or for that matter lower) than the other. The belief imputed to him by Meinecke follows from nothing he said. Among the many respectable defenders of Machiavelli quoted by Lord Acton in his introduction to Burd's edition of *The Prince* is Fichte, the champion of another kind of virtue. 'Questions of political power are never,' says Fichte, 'least of all among a corrupt people, to be solved by moral means, so that it is stupid [*unverständig*] to cry down *The Prince. Machiavelli had a ruler to describe and not a monk.'[22] Must we say, then, that Fichte also believed in a

21 The sociologist might argue that, even in the case of the most ordinary of mortals, life consists of several interdependent spheres, and that rules that apply to one sphere often do not apply to another.

22 *Il Principe*, ed. L. Arthur Burd (Oxford 1891), xxxvii. Surely, Fichte ought not to have said that such questions are *never* solved by moral means. Machia-

172 The Political Calculus

'politico-ethical' sphere *higher* than the sphere of ordinary morality? Or if we refuse to say so, must we then conclude that he wrote these sentences in a moment of aberration?

There is no warrant, either, for saying that, for Machiavelli, 'the development and creation of *virtù*' is 'the self-evident purpose of the state.' Nowhere does he speak of any such purpose. There is to be found in his writings no conception of a good or a best life for man, and therefore no attempt to justify the state on the ground that it makes possible that kind of life. What is the *virtù* that Meinecke has in mind when he attributes this belief to Machiavelli? Is it what he calls civic virtue? Or is it the *virtù* that he says is of a higher order, the kind that I have called heroic? On the face of it, it would seem to make better sense to treat civic virtue, rather than the other, as the purpose of the state; for it is the virtue that flourishes in the state. It can exist only in a political community; and so we can speak of it without absurdity as an end to which the political community, the state, is a means. We need not speak of it in this way, not even if, following Aristotle, we speak of the state as a means to 'the good life'; for our conception of that life may include much more than civic virtue. Still, we can so speak of it. But how does the state stand to the *virtù* which is – as Meinecke interprets Machiavelli – of a higher order? This is the *virtù* that establishes or restores the state, and so the state is its product. How then can this *virtù* be the purpose or end of the state? Does the worth of the state consist above all in the fact that the making and preserving of it are occasions for certain kinds of excellence? Is the state to be valued wholly – or at least primarily – as a work of art? Or rather (which is not quite the same thing) as an effect of *virtù*; of rare courage, strength of mind, insight and foresight?

There is no shred of evidence that Machiavelli thought of *virtù*, whether civic or heroic or both together, as the end of the state. On the contrary, there is evidence in plenty that he valued the *virtù* of the ruler or leader largely because it establishes or preserves the state. Only the creation or preservation of the state excuses actions that would otherwise be inexcusable. In the *Discourses* (I, 10) he says:

velli did not say it. How these German philosophers, even the best of them, exaggerate!

173 In Search of Machiavellian *Virtù*

'those men are infamous and detestable who have been destroyers of
religions, squanderers of kingdoms and republics, enemies of virtue
[*delle virtù*] ,[23] of letters, and of every art that brings gain and honor
to the human race ... And no one will ever be so foolish or so wise,
so bad or so good, that ... he will not praise what is to be praised and
blame what is to be blamed.'[24] If the 'purpose' of the state were only
to give occasion for displays of *virtù*, this purpose might sometimes
be achieved in destroying it and not in establishing or restoring it;
for the business of destruction can require as much *virtù*, especially
of the heroic kind that Meinecke says is the higher in the Machiavellian scale, as the business of construction: as much and as rare courage, tenacity of purpose, foresight and skill. It all depends on what
is being destroyed or created. Though it takes a Titian to paint a picture by Titian but not to destroy one, it may take a Caesar to destroy
a Roman republic.

Though Machiavelli never enquires what is the purpose of the state,
he does in the *Discourses* (I, 3) say that the lawgiver must assume
that all men are evil. He then quotes the saying 'that hunger and poverty make men industrious, and the laws make them good.'[25] But in
the next sentence he qualifies what he has said by suggesting that
where there is a good custom, there is no need of law. In the idiom
of a later age, we can attribute to him the belief that good laws and
good customs make men good – that is to say, disposed so to behave
that they do not harm but benefit others and themselves. If he had
been asked what the state should do for men, he would probably
have answered that it should give them security, and perhaps have
added that it should dispose them to goodness. It is much more
likely, I suggest, that he would have given this answer to a question
he never put to himself than the answer that Meinecke attributes to
him.

It is also misleading to say, as Villari does, that Machiavelli 'like the
ancients ... sacrifices the individual to the state, but in his opinion the

23 As Professor Whitfield points out, Machiavelli seldom uses *virtù* in the plural;
when he does so, he has in mind, not the *virtù* discussed in this article, but
good or evil qualities more generally. See Whitfield, *Machiavelli*, 98.
24 Gilbert, *Chief Works*, I, 220
25 Ibid., 201

174 The Political Calculus

state is indifferent to every activity save the political and the military, and is solely engaged in guarding the security of its own existence and increasing its own strength.'[26] For this, too, is to assume that Machiavelli raised questions he did not raise, and gave or implied certain answers to them. No doubt, he admired the Romans for their willingness to make great sacrifices for the republic. But he never enquired what the citizens should be willing to do for the political community he belongs to. He made no attempt, as later writers were to do, to define the limits of the duty of the individual to the state, or to argue that there are no limits. If we take the political writers most concerned for the individual, his rights and aspirations – such liberals as Constant, Humboldt, and the younger Mill – we do not find them denying that the citizen ought to be called upon to risk his life for the state, or to make other great sacrifices for it. They do, of course, define the obligations of the state to its citizens, and they argue or imply that citizens have a moral right, under certain circumstances, to disobey or resist their rulers. That is why we call them liberals. They do what Machiavelli never attempted. But that does not give us the right to conclude that Machiavelli, who addressed his mind to quite other problems, took up a position opposed to theirs. If to sacrifice the individual to the state is to approve his risking his life in defence of it, then most liberals sacrifice him; and if it is to deny that he ever has the right to resist his rulers, then Machiavelli does not sacrifice him. To say that he does or does not is equally misleading; for it is to suggest that he answers a question that he never even puts to himself.

The writers who speak of him in this way are perhaps moved to do so by what he says about *virtù*. Since the questions of deepest concern to him in both *The Prince* and the *Discourses* relate to the state and its establishment and preservation, it is only to be expected that he should attend particularly to the qualities which he believes men must possess if the state is to be well-ordered and strong. These are the qualities that make up what he calls *virtù*. He admires them, or some of them, very much, even when they are manifest in what he thinks are necessary 'crimes.' He expresses much louder admiration for these qualities than he does for goodness as distinct from *virtù*. But then they are more directly relevant to the questions he puts and tries to answer. There is no warrant for saying that he looks upon

26 Villari, *Life and Times of Machiavelli*, bk.II, ch.2, 95

175 In Search of Machiavellian *Virtù*

virtù as higher than goodness, or thinks of it as the purpose of the
state, or that he sacrifices the individual to the state – whatever that
may mean.

Chabod says that Machiavelli's absorbing passion is for politics, and
that he takes little interest in anything else. This is substantially true;
for Machiavelli, though he speaks of other things, especially in his
plays and letters, speaks of them much as he does of politics. As, for
example, when he speaks of love – or, rather, of the pursuit of women.
Here too there is something definite to be attained, and the pursuer
must be resourceful, skilful, and bold if he is to attain it. Love, as
Machiavelli speaks of it, is an activity less absorbing, less admirable,
less fruitful of glory, than government and war, but in several respects
it is similar. It is a game, perhaps, a distraction, and yet is not unlike
the serious business from which it distracts. I speak, of course, not
of any theory about love to be found in Machiavelli's writings, nor of
his treatment of women, but only of an attitude to love revealed in
his two plays and some of his letters.
   'The truth,' says Chabod, 'is that Machiavelli leaves the moral ideal
intact and he does so because it does not concern him.'[27] Perhaps it
would be better to say that it does not concern him directly; for, as
we have seen, he holds that a community cannot be well ordered for
long, nor formidable to others, unless its members are honest and
good – unless, like the old Romans and the Germans of his day, they
have *bontà* and not merely *virtù*. And *bontà* has more of morality
about it than has *virtù*. But Machiavelli has little to say about it, and
has nowhere a word of sympathy for the troubled conscience. As
Chabod puts it, 'he is ignorant, not only of the eternal and the transcendent, but also of the moral doubt and the tormenting anxiety that
beset a conscience turned in upon itself.'[28]
   Ridolfi expresses a different opinion, and speaks of 'the intimate
religious foundation of his conscience which breathes from all his
works.'[29] It seems to have breathed for few besides Ridolfi. By all

27 Federico Chabod, *Machiavelli and the Renaissance*, tr. D. Moore (London
    1958), 142
28 Ibid., 93
29 Roberto Ridolfi, *The Life of Niccolò Machiavelli*, tr. Cecil Grayson (London
    1963), 253

176 The Political Calculus

means, let us take care how we speak of Machiavelli. Let us not say
that he was without religion or that he was untroubled by conscience, or – as some have said – that his *Exhortation to Penitence* was
not a moment of piety in his life but a 'frivolous joke.' Chabod, taken
literally may well be wrong; Machiavelli was perhaps not 'ignorant
of the eternal and transcendent' and was almost certainly (being intelligent, sensitive, and self-critical) often a prey to moral doubt and
anxiety. No man reveals all that is in him in the writings he leaves
behind him. But the fact remains that Machiavelli has much to say
about *virtù* and little about moral goodness, and that *virtù*, as he
speaks of it, has nothing to do with conscience. Machiavelli was not
entirely a political animal; no man ever is. Yet the spirit that 'breathes
from all his works' is political.

Not only because he writes mostly about politics and war but also –
and above all – because the image of man that his writings project is,
in a broad sense of the word, political. He seems to admire above all
the man who knows what he wants and who acts resolutely and intelligently to get it. Such a man need not be engaged in politics or
war; he need not be a ruler or a general, a citizen or a soldier. He can
be anything, if only he has definite aims making large demands on
him, and has strength of mind and ability enough to meet them. Machiavelli never said that the qualities he so much admired are displayed only in politics and war, and we are not to conclude that he
thought so. Yet they are displayed largely in these two spheres, and
they are the spheres in which he took the deepest interest. The man
who knows what he wants and acts resolutely to get it must often,
especially if he has some large and difficult aim, use others for his
purposes. He need not always do so (he may be an artist) but often
he must. He is a wielder of power and influence. So the sphere of
virtù, though it is wider than just politics and war, is nevertheless in
a broad sense political. It consists above all of activities in which men
work together, or against one another, or make use of each other, in
the pursuit of definite aims.

It consists of only a part of life. Now, in general, it is no criticism
of a man to say that he is concerned with only a part of life. If he
makes his theme clear to his readers and leaves nothing important
out of account, they have no cause of complaint. The economist
studies only a part of human behaviour, and when he makes assumptions about the motives, aims, and capacities of men, presumably

177 In Search of Machiavellian *Virtù*

makes only such as he thinks are relevant to his purpose. Nobody is moved to say of Ricardo that he is ignorant of the eternal and the transcendent, or of moral doubt and anxiety. And if anyone did say it, we should think it beside the point. But when Chabod says it of Machiavelli, we think it a point worth making, whether we agree with him or not. We think this, not because Machiavelli's subject is politics and not economics, but because of the way he writes about it, the quality of his interest in it. He does not go about his business as Ricardo does about his; he does not attempt a systematic explanation of just one sphere of human activity, making only such assumptions about men's aims and capacities as he thinks necessary to his limited purpose. Unsystematic though he is, limited though his interests are, he makes large and bold statements about man, so that his readers get the impression that he claims to be taking the measure of their species. And the impression is not mistaken.

Machiavelli is a great writer whose moods and feelings infect his readers. What he admires is indeed admirable, and also rare. Firmness of purpose, presence of mind, resourcefulness, the ability to see more clearly and further than others, fortitude in adversity: these qualities and the others that make up *virtù* are everywhere exalted. It is through them, above all, that man makes his presence felt in the world, and in them that he takes pride. *Virtù* is opposed to *fortuna*, to chance, to the unforeseen, to the external and the hostile. Machiavelli appeals to sentiments that are strong in most men – to men without religion as much as those with it. To display *virtù* is not to do God's will, nor is it to behave morally; it is to make your will and your person count for something in the eyes of other men and your own. Which is not to say that *virtù* cannot be displayed in the service of God or in acting morally. Machiavelli, who in some moods despised Savonarola, in others admired him; he admired him for what he had of *virtù* (courage, a strong will, and fortitude) and despised him for what he lacked (understanding and foresight).

There is a perverse streak in Machiavelli. He likes to make himself out worse than he is. He likes at times to shock his contemporaries, and he has shocked posterity to the threshold of our own 'unshockable' age. Yet his 'phiiosophy' is not so much immoral as it is defective. For, unlike the 'political scientist' of today, he does present us with something that deserves to be called a philosophy: with reflections upon what is essentially human about man. He has a philoso-

178 The Political Calculus

phy in the sense that Montaigne – who is even less systematic than
he is – has one.

If we conceive of man as Machiavelli describes him we miss a great
deal that is distinctively human about him. We forget that he is a contemplative being and a problem to himself, that he is as much frustrated as inspired by his imagination, that many of his purposes – no
matter how exalted and powerful he is – are half-formed and change
imperceptibly. Above all, we forget that much that makes life seem
valuable to him comes of his uncertainties and hesitations, his doubts
and anxieties, his sense that there is more to him than he is aware of,
his not quite knowing what he is moving towards even though he is
to some extent self-propelled. Those who do not know what they
want and are not resolute in trying to get it are not necessarily poor
in spirit. Men are not always allies or enemies, masters or servants, in
the pursuit of definite aims; they are also involved with one another,
and with the groups and communities they belong to, in ways that
are comforting or hurtful, exciting or depressing, and yet unrelated
to such aims. These sides of life are just as much specifically human,
setting man apart from the other animals, enriching his imagination,
sharpening his intelligence, deepening his emotions, as the formation
and pursuit of clear and realistic aims.

Machiavelli did not deny this; he merely took no account of it. If
he had neglected it because it was not relevant to his purpose, there
would be no objecting to him on that score. If he had been what we
today call a political scientist, it would be absurd to complain that
he had too political a conception of man. But he was not a political
scientist in that sense; he did not aim at explaining systematically a
limited but important sphere of human activity. True, he wrote very
largely (though unsystematically) about politics; but in the course of
doing so he indulged in reflections about man that suggest that man
is pre-eminently political in the sense that what he values most in his
own species are rare qualities finding their largest scope in politics
and war, or in activities similar to them. It may be true that man admires these qualities as much as any, but it is not true that they,
more than others, give savour to his life. Machiavelli did not say they
do but he wrote as if he thought they did. He made altogether too
much of *virtù*, especially the heroic kind.

[9]

The Theme of *Gloria* in Machiavelli*

IN chapter XXV of *Il Principe*, Machiavelli refers very briefly to men's goals, saying that 'in the things that lead to the end that everyone has in view, namely glory and riches (*cioè glorie*[1] *e ricchezze*), men proceed in different ways.'[2] L. Arthur Burd observes that 'Machiavelli dispatches in this one short sentence a question which was usually discussed at length in the earlier political manuals: what is it, namely, that furnishes the motives of action?'[3] Glory was one of the most important ideas in Renaissance thought,[4] and Machiavelli's thought can be understood only imperfectly if the part that *gloria* played in it is not grasped; yet inexplicably this theme has been almost entirely neglected.[5]

---

* I am indebted to Professor Michael Oakeshott, Dr. Cecil H. Clough, Mr. Paolo L. Rossi, and Dr. Francesco Badolato for comments on an earlier draft.

Page references are to the Feltrinelli [Milan] edition of Machiavelli's *Opere*, the following volumes of which are cited: I – *Il Principe e Discorsi sopra la prima deca di Tito Livio*, 1960; II – *Arte della guerra e scritti politici minori*, 1961; VI – *Lettere*, 1961; VII – *La vita di Castruccio Castracani da Lucca e Istorie fiorentine*, 1962. Vols. I and II are edited by Sergio Bertelli (whose notes are cited as *Bertelli*), vols. VI and VII by Franco Gaeta (cited as *Gaeta*).

Russo= *Il Principe e pagine dei 'Discorsi' e delle 'Istorie,'* ed. Luigi Russo (Florence, 1931); *Carli*=Niccolò Machiavelli, *Le opere maggiori* . . . , scelta e commento di Plinio Carli (Florence, 1923); *Burd*=*Il Principe*, ed. L. Arthur Burd (Oxford, 1891).

In my quotations, both in the text and also in the notes, I reproduce the accents as found in the editions and commentaries. In other cases, I use Italian accents in accord with contemporary usage.

[1] Some texts have the singular *gloria*.

[2] *Princ.* XXV (pp. 99–100): 'li uomini, nelle cose che li 'nducono al fine, quale ciascuno ha innanzi, cioè glorie e ricchezze, procedervi variamente.'

[3] *Burd*, p. 360.

[4] There is no survey of the idea in Italian thought; for France, see Françoise Joukovsky, *La Gloire dans la poésie française et néolatine du XVI* siècle (Geneva, 1969).

[5] Leo Strauss, in his *Thoughts on Machiavelli* (Glencoe, 1958), discusses *gloria* intermittently in ch. IV. Other writers have referred to *gloria* or discussed it briefly. E.g., Pasquale Villari, in *Niccolò Machiavelli e i suoi tempi*, has a few pages on the subject (see especially vol. II [Florence, 1881], chs. 2 and 3), but he attempts neither analysis nor synthesis. A recent short treatment of the topic is Victor A. Santi's 'Parole di Machiavelli: "Gloria," ' *Lingua nostra*, 34 (1973), 108–110.

Machiavelli was by no means a systematic writer and *gloria*, like many other important themes, is discussed in various passages in different works, though most of his reflections on it are to be found in the *Discorsi*. What I propose to do is to reconstruct what he said about it, giving a systematic account of what Machiavelli himself said only in an unsystematic way, with varying degrees of explicitness. Particular attention will be paid to his explicit statements but I shall also try to elicit, necessarily in a tentative way, what seems to be implied in the views that he expresses. I shall first examine what he understood by *gloria*, considering not only its synonyms but also its antonyms, since the terms with which it is contrasted shed some light on its meaning. I shall then examine the ways in which, according to Machiavelli, men could acquire *gloria*, inquiring further what kinds of men sought it, in his opinion, and bringing into consideration *ricchezze*, the term with which it is linked in the passage quoted from *Il Principe*.

SYNONYMS AND ANTONYMS OF 'GLORIA'

The synonyms of *gloria* are *fama* (fame), *onore* (honour), *laude* (praise), *stima* (esteem),[6] and *riputazione* (reputation). Machiavelli does not actually say that they are synonyms but it is obvious from the way that he uses these words that they are often indistinguishable.[7] A few examples will suffice to prove the point. In the *Discorsi* he speaks of 'worldly honour' (*l'onore del mondo*) and a little later in the same paragraph he speaks of 'worldly glory' (*mondana gloria*).[8] Again, in the *Istorie fiorentine*, he speaks of the 'glorious' character of the First Crusade, because of the large areas that fell under the Christian sway, and later in the same paragraph says that the *virtù* of Saladin and internal discords resulted in the Crusaders being driven out from the lands 'that with so much honour (*con tanto onore*) they had succeeded in conquering.'[9] Finally, he says in the *Discorsi* that Decius Mus acted in one way to achieve *gloria*, whereupon his fellow consul Fabius Maximus Rullianus acted in a different way to achieve 'no less honour' (*non . . . manco onore*).[10]

The other words mentioned are also clearly used as synonyms. Thus,

---

[6] *Stima* is used as a synonym of *gloria* in *Princ.* XXI.

[7] They are certainly not perfect or complete synonyms, and the problems that this raises will be considered later (see below, pp. 618–621). It is necessary to consider carefully the context before it can be said that these words are used as exact synonyms.

[8] *Disc.* II, 2 (p. 282).

[9] *Ist. fior.* I, 17 (p. 102).

[10] *Disc.* III, 45 (p. 501).

RENAISSANCE QUARTERLY

he concludes *Discorsi*, Book III, chapter 20, by saying that in the following chapter he will discuss the reasons for the 'great fame (*gran fama*) and victories' of Hannibal. In that chapter he says that *gloria* and *riputazione* can be achieved in completely different ways; he refers in one place to Hannibal's *riputazione* and a few lines later to his *gloria*. And in *Discorsi*, I, 10, *gloria*, *fama*, *onore*, and *laude* are used interchangeably.

The antonyms of gloria are *vergogna* (shame, disgrace),[11] *ignominia* (ignominy),[12] *disonore* (dishonour),[13] and *infamia* (infamy),[14] all of which men, and particularly rulers, seek to avoid, because they cause one to be held in contempt, lead to a deterioration in one's position, and can easily result in the loss of one's state or 'ruin' (*rovina*).[15]

WHAT IS GLORY?

In what, then, does glory consist? Machiavelli speaks in various places about different types and conceptions of glory: true glory (*vera gloria*),[16] false glory (*falsa gloria*),[17] common glory (*gloria comune*),[18] the glory of individuals,[19] glory in the arts,[20] religious glory,[21] and worldly glory (*mondana gloria*[22] or *la gloria del mondo*).[23] He never attempts a comprehensive analysis. Nevertheless, there is an illuminating discussion of glory in *Discorsi*, II, 2, where he considers why in ancient times men were greater lovers of liberty than in his own day. He attributes it to the differences between ancient and modern education (*educazione*),[24] which in turn is traced to the difference between ancient religion and 'our religion,' that is, Christianity. The former valued very highly worldly honour (*l'onore del mondo*), considering it the highest good (*il*

---

[11] *Princ.* XXIV (p. 97); *Disc.* II, 24 (p. 353); *Ist. fior.* II, 32 (p. 186), III, 17 (pp. 247–248); *Arte d. guerra*, VII (p. 520).

[12] *Disc.* III, 41 (p. 494; twice).

[13] *Ist. fior.* III, 17 (pp. 247–248).

[14] *Disc.* I, 10 (p. 159).

[15] *Ist. fior.* V, 11 (p. 345).

[16] *Ist. fior.* II, 1 (p. 138), III, 5 (p. 220).

[17] *Disc.* I, 10 (p. 156).

[18] *Ist. fior.* III, 5 (p. 220), and see below, p. 592.

[19] See below, pp. 591–592.

[20] *Disc.* II, Proemio (p. 272).

[21] *Disc.* II, 2 (p. 282).

[22] *Ibid.*

[23] *Disc.* I, 10 (p. 159).

[24] *Educazione* (like the French *éducation*) has always had a wider meaning than 'education' usually has; it refers to the whole process of forming both character and mind (though the latter is sometimes distinguished from it and called *istruzione*).

GLORIA IN MACHIAVELLI   591

sommo bene). Its ceremonies were both 'magnificent' and 'ferocious,' encouraging men to be strong and warlike.

Moreover, ancient religion beatified only men full of worldly glory (*mondana gloria*), such as leaders of armies and rulers of republics. Our religion has glorified (*glorificato*) humble and contemplative men more than men of action. It has, then, seen humility, abjection, and contempt of the world (*dispregio delle cose umane*)[25] as the supreme good, while the other saw it as greatness of spirit, bodily strength, and all the other things that make men strong.[26]

Judgments made about glory, then, will depend both on the values held by those who pass judgment and on their views about the character of particular actions. To achieve glory, to be (or be considered) glorious, is to be 'glorified,' 'beatified,' 'honoured,' accorded fame. For Machiavelli, glory seems to consist essentially in the external recognition of outstanding deeds or achievements. Actions may be 'glorious' (or deserving of the highest praise) without their meritorious character being recognised; Machiavelli does not consider this possibility, although he does discuss undeserved glory. The saints canonised by the Church are of course the supreme example in our civilisation of men and women who have achieved spiritual or religious glory.[27] But, as might be expected, this is not the kind of glory that interests Machiavelli. Nor is he concerned with the glory achieved by artists, although he attributes to it an intrinsic clarity that time does little to diminish or to augment.[28] He is concerned with 'worldly glory,' with 'that which

[25] Treatises *de contemptu mundi* were common in medieval times, one of the best known having been written by Innocent III. And at papal coronations it had long been customary to burn three reeds while a priest chanted three times, 'Pater sancte, sic transit gloria mundi.'

[26] *Disc.* II, 2 (p. 282): 'La religione antica, oltre a di questo, non beatificava se non uomini pieni di mondana gloria; come erano capitani di eserciti e principi di republiche. La nostra religione ha glorificato più gli uomini umili e contemplativi che gli attivi. Ha dipoi posto il sommo bene nella umiltà, abiezione, e nel dispregio delle cose umane: quell'altra lo poneva nella grandezza dello animo, nella fortezza del corpo ed in tutte le altre cose atte a fare gli uomini fortissimi.'

[27] The glory of God, the martyrs, and the other saints are important themes in the Bible, the writings of theologians, and also in the liturgy. (E.g., glory is the leading motif of the prayer *Gloria in excelsis Deo*, the salutation *Gloria tibi, Domine* precedes the reading of the Gospel, which is followed by the synonymous salutation *Laus tibi, Christe*.) See A. Michel, 'Gloire,' *Dictionnaire de théologie catholique*, VI (Paris, 1947), cols. 1386–1388 and 1393–1432; A. J. Vermeulen, *The Semantic Development of Gloria in Early-Christian Latin* (Nijmegen, 1956); Matthias Heghmans, *Gloria Dei: Ein biblisch-theologischer Begriff nach den Schriftkommentaren des hl. Thomas von Aquin* (Siegburg, 1968).

[28] *Disc.* II, Proemio (p. 272): '. . . le arti . . . hanno tanta chiarezza in sé che i tempi possono tòrre o dare loro poco più gloria che per loro medesime si meritino.'

pertains to human life and affairs.'[29] The question that needs to be asked, then, is not, What is glory? but, What is worldly glory? What is it that men do in this sphere that entitles them to the approbation or praise of other men to the extent of receiving the supreme accolade of 'glory,' 'fame,' or a great 'reputation'? An examination of Machiavelli's works shows that it is great deeds in politics, diplomacy, or war. Glory is gained by those whose deeds are memorable (*degna di memoria*),[30] by those who 'do great things' (*fare gran cose*)[31] or 'undertake great enterprises' (*fare le grande imprese*).[32] The individuals to whom Machiavelli ascribes glory are all mythical heroes, rulers, or generals.[33]

Glory is also attributed to certain peoples or groups: they shared a common glory. For four hundred years the Roman people were lovers of glory (*amatori della gloria*),[34] aiming at domination and glory;[35] the Etruscans achieved great political and military glory, and a very praiseworthy level of culture and religion;[36] the first Crusaders achieved much glory;[37] and the Venetians achieved both security and glory when

[29] *Ibid.*: 'quelle [cose] pertinenti alla vita e costumi degli uomini.'

[30] *Ist. fior.* VI, 29 (p. 433), VII, 32 (p. 501).

[31] *Princ.* XVI (p. 67), XVIII (p. 72); *Disc.* II, 13 (p. 312).

[32] *Princ.* XXI (p. 89).

[33] Achilles (*Princ.* XIV [p. 64]), Cyrus (*ibid.*), Alexander the Great (*Princ.* XIV [p. 64]; *Disc.* I, [p. 126], II, 27 [p. 361]), Romulus (*Disc.* I, 10 [p. 159]), Scipio Africanus (*Princ.* XIV [p. 64], XVII [p. 70]; *Disc.* III, 21 [p. 448], III, 34 [p. 479]), Furius Camillus (*Disc.* I, 8 [p. 150]), Marcus Fabius (*Disc.* I, 36 [p. 214]), Gnaeus Manlius (*ibid.*), Hannibal (*Disc.* II, 27 [p. 362], III, 21 [p. 348]), Fabius Maximus Cunctator (*Disc.* III, 9 [p. 417]), Claudius Nero (*Disc.* III, 17 [p. 439]), Manlius Torquatus (*Disc.* III, 22 [pp. 448–449]), Valerius Corvinus (*ibid.*), Posthumius (*Disc.* III, 42 [p. 495]), Pontius (*Disc.* III, 42 [pp. 495–496]), Decius Mus (*Disc.* III, 45 [p. 501]), Fabius Maximus Rullianus (*ibid.*), Octavian (*Disc.* I, 52 [p. 248]), Marcus Aurelius (*Princ.* XIX [p. 84]), Theodosius (*Ist. fior.* I, 1 [p. 73]), the Turkish sultans Mahomet II (*Disc.* I, 19 [p. 184]) and Selim I (*ibid.*), Castruccio Castracani (*Ist. fior.* II, 30 [p. 183]; *Castruccio Castracani e Ist. fior,* p. 32), Michele di Lando (*Ist. fior.* III, 17 [p. 247]), Francesco Sforza (*Ist. fior.* VI, 8 [p. 400]), Cosimo de' Medici (*Ist. fior.* VII, 5 [p. 460], VII, 6 [p. 463]), Lorenzo de' Medici (*Discursus florentinarum rerum post mortem iunioris Laurentii Medices* in *Arte della guerra e scritti politici minori,* p. 276), Roberto Malatesta (*Ist. fior.* VIII, 24 [p. 553]), Ottaviano Fregoso (*Disc.* II, 24 [p. 353]), Ferdinand the Catholic (*Princ.* XXI [p. 89]), Fabrizio Colonna (*Arte d. guerra,* I [p. 329]).

[34] *Disc.* I, 58 (p. 264); in *Disc.* I, 36 (p. 214), they are said to have been great lovers (*amatori grandi*) of glory.

[35] *Disc.* II, 9 (p. 301): 'avendo Roma per fine lo imperio e la gloria.'

[36] *Disc.* II, 4 (p. 291): 'somma gloria d'imperio e d'arme, e massime laude di costumi e di religione.' In view of what he says in *Disc.* II, Proemio (p. 272) [see above, n. 28], the use of *laude* is probably just a stylistic variation (as *massime* is doubtless used to avoid repeating *somma*), though he may have thought *laude* a more appropriate word to use about *costumi* and *religione*.

[37] *Ist. fior.* I, 17 (p. 102).

GLORIA IN MACHIAVELLI   593

they fought their own wars, before using mercenaries in the fifteenth century.[38]

It was a common view in the ancient world that no man should be called fortunate, happy, or successful until he was dead;[39] likewise, it has sometimes been thought that, for Machiavelli, a man cannot be said to be 'glorious' until his career or life is finished.[40] It seems to me, however, that a distinction should be made between 'temporary' and 'permanent' glory. Temporary glory is that achieved through particular actions, feats, campaigns, or victories, and it may be tarnished or forfeited by later misadventures, mistakes, misdeeds, or crimes. A second kind of temporary glory should perhaps be distinguished: 'temporary' not in the sense that it may be forfeited during a man's lifetime, but in that after his death it may fade, for with the passing of time deeds or achievements that once dazzled men may seem less than glorious, either because they no longer appear remarkable or because they are thought to merit criticism rather than praise. Permanent glory is the settled verdict of posterity or 'history' that a man's deeds or career are of such a character as to entitle him to be considered 'glorious,' to be 'glorified,' 'celebrated,' or 'honoured' as a great man. This is the sort of glory epitomised in such epithets as Alexander 'the Great' or Lorenzo 'the Magnificent.' There is doubtless a certain arbitrariness in the awarding of these titles, for while those to whom they are given are always great men, others perhaps equally distinguished are not so favoured.[41]

Machiavelli was well aware of the variability of human judgments, and contrasts the obvious glory of works of art and those who created them with the glory achieved in human affairs (*la vita e costumi degli uomini*), 'for which the evidence is not so obvious.'[42] Men are very much inclined to praise unduly the period of their youth and also ancient times, for the knowledge of which they depend on the accounts of historians.[43] And Machiavelli shows considerable scepticism about

---

[38] *Princ.* XII (p. 56); *Ist. fior.* I, 39 (p. 135); *Arte d. guerra*, I (p. 348).

[39] E.g., Ecclesiasticus XI.30; Aeschylus, *Agamemnon*, 928; Euripedes, *Daughters of Troy*, 510; *Andromache*, 100; Sophocles, *Oedipus Tyrannus*, 1529; *Trachiniae*, 1; Ovid, *Metamorphoses*, III, 136.

[40] Phrases like *dopo la morte li rende gloriosi* (*Disc.* I, 10 [p. 159]) have perhaps given rise to this idea. Bacon, in his essay *Of Death*, says: 'Death hath this also, that it openeth the gate to good fame,' which seems to imply that 'good fame' is not achieved in this life.

[41] Was Innocent III less 'great' than Gregory the Great or Leo the Great?

[42] *Disc.* II, Proemio (p. 272): 'delle quali non se ne veggono sí chiari testimoni.'

[43] *Disc.* II, Proemio (p. 271).

RENAISSANCE QUARTERLY

historical knowledge, emphasising that 'we do not know the whole truth about the past.'[44] One of the reasons is that historians

often conceal things that discredit those times, while other things that tend to glorify them are magnified or exaggerated. Most writers are so seduced by the success of conquerors that, in order to render their victories glorious, they exaggerate not only the valour of their deeds but also those of their enemies.[45]

The result is that later generations marvel at the greatness of those men and their times and are constrained to praise and admire them exceedingly.[46] Some great historical figures receive more glory than they merit while others receive glory that they do not deserve at all. An example of the latter is Julius Caesar. Machiavelli warns us not to be deceived by 'the glory of Caesar,' although he was greatly praised by historians, 'because those who praise him were corrupted by his success and intimidated by the long duration of the empire, since those rulers who took his name did not allow writers to speak freely about him.'[47] This, then, is false glory (*falsa gloria*), glory that is either exaggerated or altogether undeserved.

HOW POLITICAL GLORY IS ACQUIRED

What, then, are the various ways in which, according to Machiavelli, men can attain worldly glory? Let us consider first the political sphere. The way that wins the highest glory is to found or reform republics or kingdoms, for after those who found, reform, or lead religions these men receive the highest praise.[48] The fullest discussion of this matter is in *Discorsi*, I, 10, whose theme is that while founders of tyrannies deserve condemnation (*sono vituperabili*), founders of kingdoms or republics deserve praise (*sono laudabili*). Everlasting honour (*perpetuo . . . onore*) is their reward, much fame, glory, or honour (*quanta fama, quanta gloria, quanto onore*), as well as security, peace, and tranquillity of mind, whereas founding a tyranny brings one much infamy and condemnation (*quanta*

---

[44] *Ibid.*: 'delle cose antiche non s'intenda al tutto la verità.'

[45] *Ibid.*: 'di quelle il più delle volte si nasconda quelle cose che recherebbono a quelli tempi infamia, e quelle altre che possano partorire loro gloria si rendino magnifiche ed amplissime. Perché il più degli scrittori in modo alla fortuna de' vincitori ubbidiscano che, per fare le loro vittorie gloriose, non solamente accrescano quello che da loro è virtuosamente operato, ma ancora le azioni de' nimici.'

[46] *Ibid.*

[47] *Disc.* I, 10 (p. 157).

[48] *Disc.* I, 10 (p. 156).

infamia, vituperio, biasimo), as well as dangers and troubles.[49] In short, one path leads to glory and security, the other to condemnation and fear;[50] one path 'enables one to live securely, and dying leave a glorious name (*e dopo la morte li rende gloriosi*), the other makes one live in continual difficulties, and leave behind an everlasting infamy (*sempiterna infamia*).'[51] Machiavelli draws the conclusion that a ruler who seeks worldly glory (*la gloria del mondo*) 'should want to possess a corrupt state, not to ruin it completely like Caesar, but to reform it like Romulus,'[52] for 'heaven cannot give men greater opportunities of *gloria*.'[53]

Machiavelli also takes up this theme in a slightly later piece,[54] *Discursus florentinarum rerum post mortem iunioris Laurentii Medices*, which he addressed to the Medici pope, Leo X, urging that he should ensure that Florence have 'a stable form of government for your own *gloria* and for the well being of your friends.'[55] Toward the end, he speaks in general terms about *fama*, *onore*, and *gloria*. If Leo follows his advice, the resultant unity will bring 'peace to the city and everlasting fame (*fama perpetua*) to Your Holiness.'

I believe that the greatest honour (*onore*) that men can receive is that which is freely given to them by their country (*patria*), and the greatest good (*bene*) that one can achieve, and the most pleasing to God, is that done for one's country. Next to this, no man is so exalted (*esaltato*) as much for any action as those who have with laws and institutions reformed republics and kingdoms; after the gods, these are the most praised (*laudati*).[56]

The order of precedence differs from that in *Discorsi*, I, 10, though there is not necessarily a contradiction, because one way of serving one's country is to reform it. Nothing is said here about those who found or reform religions, since it is not relevant to his theme.

He adds that very few men have had the opportunity of doing this, and fewer still have succeeded.

And this *gloria* has been so much esteemed (*stimata*) by men seeking only *gloria*, that being unable actually to make a republic, they have constructed one in their writings,

---

[49] *Ibid.*
[50] *Disc.* I, 10 (p. 158).
[51] *Disc.* I, 10 (p. 159).
[52] This is the theme of *Disc.* I, 9.
[53] *Disc.* I, 10 (p. 159).
[54] It was probably written in 1519 or 1520; Lorenzo died in May 1519, Leo in December 1521.
[55] *Arte della guerra e scritti politici minori*, p. 267.
[56] *Ibid.*, p. 275.

as Aristotle, Plato, and many others have done. . . . Therefore, heaven can give no greater gift to a man, nor show him a more glorious path (*piú gloriosa via*) than this. And among so much good fortune that God has bestowed on your family and Your Holiness personally, this is the greatest, namely, the power and the material to make yourself immortal, and thus greatly surpass the *gloria* of your father and ancestors.[57]

This is an extremely frank exhortation to a pope to seek the glory of this world.

Machiavelli discusses in chapter XXIV of *Il Principe* why Italian rulers have lost their states. He observes that if the advice given in the preceding chapters is followed, a new ruler can establish himself in power even more securely than one who has the advantage of being a hereditary ruler.

And so he will have the double glory (*duplicata gloria*) of founding a new state and of strengthening and adorning it with good laws, good arms, good friends, and good examples. But a hereditary ruler who loses his state, through lack of prudence or skill (*prudenzia*), incurs a double disgrace (*duplicata vergogna*).[58]

Stefano Porcari was a learned and spirited Roman noble, who conspired against Pope Nicholas V in 1452.

As is the wont of men who thirst for glory (*appetiscono gloria*), he wanted to do or at least attempt something remarkable (*qualche cosa degna di memoria*); and he decided that he should try to take away his *patria* from the popes and restore its ancient ways (*antico vivere*), hoping that, if he succeeded, he would be called the new founder and second father of that city.[59]

But since Porcari's prudence and skill did not match the grandeur of his vision, his conspiracy failed and he was executed. Machiavelli observes that although

one could praise his purpose, his way of carrying it out (*il giudicio*)[60] will always be condemned, because such enterprises (*simili imprese*), although intrinsically and in theory not without *gloria*, in practice almost always bring certain ruin.[61]

It may be that Machiavelli's reserve is due partly to the fact that the *Istorie fiorentine* was commissioned by and dedicated to a pope, and he

---

[57] *Ibid.*, pp. 275–276.
[58] *Princ.* XXIV (p. 97).
[59] *Ist. fior.* VI, 29 (p. 433).
[60] *Gaeta* (*Ist. fior.*, p. 435) glosses *giudicio*: 'il piano per realizzarla.'
[61] *Ist. fior.* VI, 29 (p. 435): 'E veramente puote essere da qualcuno la costui intenzione lodata, ma da ciascuno sarà sempre il giudicio biasimato, perché simili imprese, se le hanno in sé nel pensarle alcuna ombra di gloria, hanno nello esequirle quasi sempre certissimo danno.'

would not have wanted to seem to be encouraging plots against the Papal State, but the words *simili imprese* may refer to conspiracies undertaken with an imprudence bordering on folly.

Founding or reforming republics or kingdoms, which brings so much glory, implies establishing laws and institutions that will have a long life, encouraging religion and good habits among the people: 'The well being of a republic or kingdom consists not in having a ruler who governs wisely while he lives, but in establishing order in such a way that it will endure after his death.'[62]

The ways in which a ruler can earn esteem is the theme of chapter XXI of *Il Principe*.[63] 'Nothing,' he says, 'makes a ruler esteemed so much as undertaking great enterprises (*grande imprese*) and extraordinary deeds.' He takes as his first example Ferdinand of Aragon who, 'from being a weak king, has become the most famous and glorious king of Christendom; and if his actions are considered, it will be found that all are great and some are extraordinary.'[64] In relations with other states, a ruler earns esteem by being 'a real friend or an outright enemy,' for those who try to avoid committing themselves and choose the middle way of neutrality usually come to grief.[65] But he must recognise that usually it is not possible to follow entirely safe policies, 'since it is in the nature of things that in trying to avoid one difficulty one runs into another.' Prudence, which is an indispensable quality of outstanding rulers, 'consists in being able to perceive the nature of these difficulties and in taking the least harmful course.'[66]

In the government of his state, a ruler should do remarkable things, 'and when someone . . . does something unusually good or bad, the ruler should contrive to reward or punish him in such a way that it causes comment,' as was the practice of Barnabò Visconti of Milan.[67]

---

[62] *Disc.* I, 11 (p. 162). Machiavelli believed that, if a republic or kingdom was to be properly established or reformed, it must be conceived and carried out by one man (*Disc.* I, 9 [p. 153]).

[63] 'Quod principem deceat ut egregius habeatur.'

[64] *Princ.* XXI (p. 89): 'd'uno re debole è diventato per fama e per gloria el primo re de' Cristiani; e, se considerrete le azioni sua, le troverrete tutte grandissime e qualcuna estraordinaria.'

[65] *Princ.* XXI (p. 91).

[66] *Princ.* XXI (p. 92).

[67] *Princ.* XXI (p. 90). And in *Disc.* III, 34 (p. 480), he says that remarkable actions 'are necessary not only for those citizens who want to acquire a reputation (*fama*) in order to obtain office (*gli onori*) in their republic, but also for rulers (*principi*) in order to maintain their reputation (*riputazione*) . . . because nothing makes the ruler (*il signore*) so much

He should encourage the arts and honour those who excel in them.[68] There are doubtless two reasons for this policy. Artistic and intellectual life will flourish, which is presumably both desirable in itself and will have beneficial effects on civic life. Moreover, it was a commonplace[69] that outstanding deeds or achievements are soon forgotten unless they are recorded in a memorable way;[70] and a ruler who is a patron of the arts can expect to be celebrated by the writers and artists whom he has favoured. His name will be perpetuated and, if his other deeds are outstanding, he will achieve glory in the eyes of posterity.[71] He should also encourage trade, agriculture, and the other worthwhile activities of men; at appropriate times, he should hold festivals and spectacles for the people. He should avoid aloofness, and show himself to be humane and munificent, 'always being careful, however, to maintain the dignity appropriate to his position.'[72] In short, when his city or state flourishes, the ruler's reputation will be enhanced.[73] The most important thing to

---

esteemed as unusual deeds or sayings in keeping with the common good that show him to be magnanimous, generous, or just, and which become proverbial among his subjects.'

[68] *Princ.* XXI (p. 92).

[69] Cicero, *Pro Archia poeta*, vi, ix–xii; Seneca, *Epist.* XXI; Boethius, *De consolatione philosophiae*, II, vii, 45; Petrarch, *Rime*, CLXXXVII.

[70] If this is true of the actions of rulers (even of founders or reformers of states), it is probably even more true of those of generals, whose deeds are of their nature more ephemeral. Feats of war may be compared to sporting deeds. The continuing fame of sportsmen owes much to those who have written about them. Those who saw their outstanding performances die, and their glory soon fades, if they are not lauded by fine writers, as Neville Cardus celebrated the genius of cricketers like Grace, Trumper, Fry, and Maclaren, who are still highly reputed by the *cognoscenti*, even if they are indeed no longer exactly household names. And because cricket has attracted the interest of literary men more than other games, the fame of great cricketers is more likely to endure in England than that of other great sportsmen.

Who now remembers Garrick or Kean? Because there is no lasting record of their achievements, the fame of stage actors tends to fade more rapidly than that of film actors of comparable skill. The work of the latter may be examined in the same way as that of painters or sculptors, whose finest achievements enabled them, Machiavelli thought, to attain permanent glory.

[71] A good example is Lorenzo de' Medici, known to posterity as 'the Magnificent.' His reputation derives partly from his political skill, which ensured peace in Florence from 1480 until his death in 1492, partly from his literary talents, but above all from the flourishing artistic and intellectual life of Florence, which owed much to his patronage. See *Ist. fior.* VIII, 36 (pp. 575–577).

[72] *Princ.* XXI (p. 93). Lorenzo de' Medici sometimes failed in this respect. See *Ist. fior.* VIII, 36 (p. 576).

[73] The building of cities can glorify a ruler. When Alexander the Great 'wanted to build a city to increase his *gloria*, the architect Deinocrates showed him how he could build it on Mount Athos which, apart from being impregnable, would enable a city to be

be remembered by a ruler who wishes to be esteemed or glorious is that he 'must contrive to achieve through all his actions the reputation of a great man of surpassing excellence.'[74]

Advisors of princes or republics can also achieve glory. Machiavelli says that when an advisor advocates a course of action that, although criticised by all other courtiers or leading men, is nevertheless followed and results in success, he will acquire glory.[75] Glory of this sort apparently consists in a reputation for political wisdom, in being considered a man of much discernment and foresight in political or military affairs. Machiavelli also says that even when failure or disaster (*qualche rovina*) results from disregarding the modestly offered[76] counsel of an advisor, he will acquire great glory, 'and although one cannot enjoy *gloria* acquired through the misfortunes or difficulties (*mali*) of one's ruler or state, nevertheless it is of some value' (*è da tenerne qualche conto*).[77]

Machiavelli's reasoning may seem somewhat curious, but it can perhaps be explained as follows. If the failure is not overwhelming, the glory acquired is the high regard in which the advisor is held by the ruler or the citizens; if the ruin of the state results, the advisor achieves the glory of being acknowledged by posterity as a man of singular sagacity. When Machiavelli says that one cannot enjoy (*godere*) glory of this kind, he apparently means that such a reputation can afford no pleasure or satisfaction to the advisor.

HOW MILITARY GLORY IS ACQUIRED

If politics is the sphere in which the highest glory can be achieved, war also offers many opportunities; indeed, there are many more references in Machiavelli's writings to military than to political glory. Military glory is most easily achieved by leaders or generals (*capitani*): because they bear most responsibility, when things turn out well most of the

---

built resembling the human form, something both unusual and striking, and worthy of his greatness' (*degna della sua grandezza*). But since Deinocrates had failed to consider how the inhabitants could live there, his plan was rejected (*Disc.* I, 1 [p. 128]), and Alexander built Alexandria, 'not to live there but to enhance his *gloria*' (*Disc.* I, 1 [p. 126]).

74 *Princ.* XXI (p. 90): 'E sopra tutto uno principe si debbe ingegnare dare di sé in ogni sua azione fama di uomo grande e di nome eccellente.'

75 *Disc.* III, 35 (pp. 482–483). Machiavelli says, however, that this has dangers when things do not go well. The advisor may be ruined, since men tend to judge advice by the results, and are always ready to seek scapegoats.

76 He suggests that advice be offered 'without passion and modestly,' in order to avoid the dangers that advisors run when things go badly.

77 *Disc.* III, 35 (p. 483).

credit naturally accrues to them, just as in defeat they will normally have to bear most of the blame or suffer the disgrace. Soldiers in subordinate positions may gain glory for acts of bravery and skill;[78] they cannot claim credit for victories, although they naturally share in the common or collective glory gained when an army is victorious.

Just as the greatest political glory is gained by those who found kingdoms or republics, and create durable institutions and laws, the greatest military glory is achieved by generals who both build fine armies and obtain victories.

Double *gloria* and praise (*laude*) is merited by those generals who have not only defeated their enemies but, before engaging them, have had to train the armies and make them good, because in so doing they display two sorts of skill (*doppia virtù*). And this is so rarely found that the reputation of many generals would be much less than it is, if both these tasks had been required of them.[79]

The normal way of acquiring military glory is to be victorious in battle,[80] or to perform valorous deeds.[81] Machiavelli often speaks of those who gained glory in these ways: Furius Camillus won great honour and glory when he liberated Rome from the Gauls;[82] the consuls Marcus Fabius and Gnaeus Manlius won a very glorious victory against the Veienti and the Etruscans;[83] Ottaviano Fregoso gloriously captured the fortress of Genoa from the French;[84] Castruccio Castracani acquired much glory when he defeated the Pistoians and made them accept him as their ruler;[85] Roberto Malatesta of Rimini gained glory when he won the bloody battle of Campomorto in 1482;[86] Florence fought many wars between 1381 and 1434, winning great glory.[87]

---

[78] As do those who receive such awards as the Victoria Cross.

[79] *Disc.* III, 13 (pp. 430–431). See also *Arte d. guerra*, VII (p. 515).

[80] *Disc.* III, 42 (p. 496).

[81] E.g., Scipio's deeds in his youth (see below, p. 603) and Decius Mus's sacrifice of his life in battle (*Disc.* III, 45 [p. 501]).

[82] *Disc.* I, 8 (pp. 149–150).

[83] *Disc.* I, 36 (p. 214).

[84] *Disc.* II, 24 (p. 353).

[85] *Ist. fior.* II, 30 (p. 183).

[86] *Ist. fior.* VIII, 24 (pp. 552–553).

[87] *Ist. fior.* III, 29 (p. 270). For other references to glory acquired through victory or military prowess, see: *Princ.* XII (p. 56); *Disc.* I, 29 (pp. 197–198), I, 30 (p. 201), I, 52 (p. 248), II, Proemio (pp. 271–272), II, 1 (p. 277), II, 4 (p. 291), II, 27 (p. 362), II, 33 (p. 377), III, 9 (p. 417), III, 13 (p. 430), III, 17 (p. 439), III, 21 (pp. 446–448), III, 22 (pp. 448–449), III, 34 (p. 479), III, 40 (p. 493), III, 42 (p. 496); *Ist. fior.* III, 17 (p. 247), III, 29 (p. 269); *La vita di Castruccio Castracani . . . e Istorie fiorentine*, p. 32; *Arte d. guerra*, I (p. 329).

GLORIA IN MACHIAVELLI

Being defeated, however, does not necessarily mean that glory is lost or cannot be won. Machiavelli says that in any military action[88]

glory can be gained; being victorious is the usual way, but in defeat it can also be acquired either by showing that the defeat was not one's own fault[89] or else by at once performing some valorous action (*qualche azione virtuosa*) that cancels it.[90]

This is what the consul Posthumius did after the defeat and disgrace at the Caudine Forks.[91] Machiavelli says elsewhere that 'even in defeat one should try to acquire *gloria*, and there is more *gloria* in being overcome by force' than in losing for other reasons.[92] It remains very obscure, however, why defeat because of the enemy's superior strength should bring *gloria*, although it clearly should not incur disgrace. If the Venetians had possessed real skill and valour (*virtú*), after the partial defeat at Agnadello in 1509 'they could easily have reformed their ranks and been able to have won or to have lost more gloriously (*piú gloriosamente*) or else to have made a more honourable peace (*accordo piú onorevole*).'[93] When Hannibal returned from Italy, he found the Carthaginians hard pressed by the Romans; he first sought peace, but when that was refused, he resolved to fight, 'judging that he might be able to win or, if he lost, to lose gloriously (*perdere gloriosamente*).'[94] The Roman legate Lucius Lentulus, after the defeat at the Caudine Forks, emphasised that Rome must be saved at all costs, 'either through shameful or glorious means (*o con ignominia o con gloria*),[95] for if the army were saved, Rome would

---

[88] He says 'in any action' (*in qualunque azione*) but it is evident from the context that he means 'in any military action.'

[89] It is not at all obvious why this should result in glory; one would expect him to have said that it does not bring disgrace.

[90] *Disc.* III, 42 (p. 496): 'in qualunque azione si può acquistare gloria: perché nella vittoria si acquista ordinariamente; nella perdita si acquista o col mostrare tale perdita non essere venuta per tua colpa, o per fare subito qualche azione virtuosa che la cancelli.'

[91] *Disc.* III, 42 (pp. 495–496). He urged the Senate not to accept the peace made at Caudium, 'saying that it did not bind the Roman people but only himself and the others who had made it, and that, if the people wanted to be free from all obligation,' to send him and the others to the Samnites as hostages. This plan was accepted, but Posthumius was fortunate, for the Samnites sent them back to Rome, with the result that in Rome 'Posthumius received more glory in defeat (*piú glorioso per avere perduto*) than Pontius received from the Samnites for having won.'

[92] *Disc.* III, 10 (p. 422): 'si debbe eziandio perdendo volere acquistare gloria; e piú gloria si ha ad essere vinto per forza che per altro inconveniente che ti abbi fatto perdere.'

[93] *Disc.* III, 31 (p. 472).

[94] *Disc.* II, 27 (p. 362).

[95] According to Livy (IX, 4), Lentulus' words were: 'ea caritas patriae est, ut tam ignominia eam quam morte nostra, si opus sit, servemus.' Mario Bonfantini (Niccolò

be able to wipe out the shame, but if it were destroyed, even if the soldiers were to die gloriously, Rome and its liberty would be lost.'[96]

MILITARY GLORY ATTAINABLE IN VERY DIFFERENT WAYS

Machiavelli says in chapter xxv of *Il Principe* that in pursuit of glory men act in different ways. He does not develop the point there;[97] the fullest discussion of the relation between character, ways of acting, the results obtained, and the reputation or glory that accrues, is in the *Discorsi*, although most attention is paid to military glory. There are in fact two separate problems: first, why different (indeed, contrary) ways of acting should both be successful (or unsuccessful); secondly, why different or contrary ways of acting should both result in glory or a great reputation.

Let us examine the cases that Machiavelli considers. Hannibal[98] achieved glorious results in Italy for sixteen years;[99] he enjoyed many victories and suffered but few reverses. Moreover, his victories were obtained in difficult circumstances, far from Carthage, which failed to give him adequate support. The reasons for his success were his consummate skill as a strategist and tactician, his bravery, audacity, ingenuity, and resourcefulness, his harshness (or cruelty), and his long run of successes (for continual success breeds further success). Machiavelli gives no examples of his harshness, but he emphasises that it was one of the main reasons for his success and glory, for 'although his army was composed of men from different nations, there were never any internal dissensions or plots against him.'[100] This fact has aroused the admiration of all historians; 'what kept his army united and quiet was the great fear (*terrore*) that he inspired personally, together with respect for the repu-

---

Machiavelli, *Opere* [Milan, 1954], p. 411) comments: 'Dove a "morte", del testo di Livio, M. sostituisce *gloria*, come se il sacrificio della fama che onora e innalza l'uomo, e lo fa quasi immortale, si debba considerare assai più grave che quello della vita. Criterio caratteristico del Rinascimento.' But *Carli* (p. 234) justifies Machiavelli's choice of words, pointing out that, according to Livy, Lentulus had said a little earlier: 'mortem pro patria praeclaram esse fateor.'

[96] *Disc.* III, 41 (pp. 494–495).

[97] He does not discuss the different ways in which men act, but in terms of success and failure, not of glory.

[98] Machiavelli's sources were entirely Roman, and hostile to Hannibal. We are concerned only with the judgments that Machiavelli makes about Hannibal, on the basis of the sources available, not with how far his account corresponds to the truth.

[99] *Disc.* II, 27 (p. 362): 'Annibale partito d'Italia, dove era stato sedici anni glorioso.'

[100] *Disc.* III, 21 (p. 448).

tation (*riputazione*) that his bravery and skill (*virtú*) brought him.'[101] As for the charge of treachery (*poca fede, infideltà*), Machiavelli again gives no examples, except of those stratagems that are properly employed in war (being an essential part of the armoury of a great general),[102] and which are praiseworthy or glorious (*laudabile e gloriosa*) when attended by success.[103]

Machiavelli also discusses Scipio Africanus, and what he says shows how glory may be lost. Scipio was a great general, achieving many glorious victories both in Spain and Africa. When he was still very young he defended his father on the Ticino, and greatly encouraged the demoralised young Romans after the disastrous defeat at Cannae. These two actions 'established his *riputazione*, paving the way to the triumphs of Spain and Africa,' and 'brought him even more *gloria*' than they did.[104] However, his humanity and benevolence (*umanità e piatà*),[105] which aroused such admiration in Spain, also caused him much difficulty, for 'his soldiers together with some of his friends rebelled against him in Spain' and 'to overcome them he was obliged to resort to those harsh measures (*crudeltà*) that he had avoided.'[106] And Machiavelli says that these troubles were 'caused only by his not being feared,' for men are so restless and ambitious that affection earned by humanity, as in the case of Scipio, is easily forgotten.[107]

The account of Scipio's actions given in *Il Principe* is slightly different,[108] and the conclusions drawn seem to be very much at variance. The rebellion of his soldiers was caused only by his too great benevolence (*pietà*), which allowed the soldiers more liberty than was compatible with military discipline. He was rebuked for this in the Senate by Fabius Maximus, who called him a corrupter of the Roman militia.[109]

---

101 *Ibid.* The same view of the matter is found in *Princ.* XVII (pp. 70–71).

102 Thus Hannibal feigned flight in order to trap the Roman army near Lake Trasimene, and attached blazing faggots to the horns of his cattle to evade Fabius Maximus Cunctator (*Disc.* III, 40 [p. 493]).

103 *Disc.* III, 40 (p. 493).

104 *Disc.* III, 34 (p. 479).

105 *Disc.* III, 21 (p. 446). Machiavelli refers three times to his fine 'act of chastity (*castità*) in restoring a beautiful young wife unharmed to her husband'; he says that 'the news (*fama*) of that action endeared him to all Spain' and 'gave him more *riputazione* than his besieging of New Carthage' (*Disc.* III, 20 [p. 445]). See also *Disc.* III, 34 (pp. 479–480), *Arte d. guerra*, VI (p. 490).

106 *Disc.* III, 21 (p. 447).

107 *Ibid.*

108 Nothing is said about his using harsh measures to suppress the rebellion.

109 *Princ.* XVII (p. 71).

RENAISSANCE QUARTERLY

Moreover, when Quintus Pleminius, one of his legates, ravaged Locri,

because Scipio was easygoing (*natura facile*) he neither avenged the inhabitants nor punished the legate for his insolence; and a Senator who wished to excuse Scipio said that there were many men who knew better how to avoid errors than to correct those of others.[110]

Machiavelli observes that

if Scipio had continued to command armies, his character would eventually have destroyed (*violato*)[111] his *fama* or *gloria*, but since his actions were controlled by the Senate this harmful (*dannosa*) quality was not only concealed (*si nascose*)[112] but contributed to his *gloria*.[113]

In the *Discorsi*, he says that Scipio was as successful and glorious as Hannibal; in *Il Principe*, he implies that humanity or an indulgent character is in fact inimical to military success and glory, unless a general with such a character is controlled by his civil superiors. Yet such control is not really compatible with effective military command, and with the freedom that the Romans were accustomed to allow their generals.[114]

In the next chapter, Machiavelli discusses why the harshness (*durezza*) of Manlius Torquatus and the humanity (*comità*) of Valerius Corvinus brought them the same degree of glory; 'they displayed equal bravery and skill (*virtú*), and were honoured to the same degree by the Romans, sharing the same *gloria*.'[115]

Another Roman general who achieved glory was Fabius Maximus Cunctator, partly because he won some victories, but mainly because he prevented Hannibal from conquering Rome after the Romans had suffered three successive defeats. Fabius 'proceeded with his army very cautiously, without . . . the usual Roman audacity.'[116] In these difficult circumstances, Rome was very fortunate to find 'a commander whose

---

[110] *Ibid.*

[111] Some commentators interpret *violato* as meaning *macchiato* (tarnished) but I think Carli (p. 85) is right to say that it is 'piú forte che *macchiato o oscurato*.'

[112] *Russo* (p. 144) glosses *non solum si nascose*: 'Non produsse, cioè, tristi conseguenze manifeste.' Machiavelli seems to be referring here to the events at Locri rather than to the rebellion.

[113] *Princ.* XVII (p. 71): 'La qual natura arebbe col tempo violato la fama e la gloria di Scipione, se elli avessi perseverato nello imperio [*Bertelli* (*Princ.*, p. 71): comando militare]; ma, vivendo sotto el governo del Senato, questa sua qualità dannosa non solum si nascose, ma li fu a gloria.'

[114] This is the theme of *Discorsi*, II, 33, and he praises the Romans for this practice.

[115] *Disc.* III, 22 (pp. 448–449): 'di pari virtú, di pari trionfi e gloria vissono in Roma.'

[116] *Disc.* III, 9 (p. 417).

slowness (*tardità*) and caution kept the enemy at bay.' Fabius, too, was fortunate, for he 'could not have found circumstances more suitable for his way of acting, and because of this he was *glorioso*.' Machiavelli claims that Fabius acted as he did

because it came naturally to him (*per natura*), not because he chose to (*non per elezione*), as is proved by the fact that when Scipio wanted to take the armies to Africa to finish the war, Fabius was very much opposed to it, as if he could not change his methods or habits; so that if it had been left to him, Hannibal would still be in Italy.[117]

It would be misleading to conclude that Machiavelli thought Fabius owed his success and glory to luck, for his good qualities undoubtedly contributed markedly to his success; rather he was fortunate to have that opportunity of displaying these qualities. *Le mérite des hommes a sa saison aussi bien que les fruits*;[118] in other times he would have been relatively unsuccessful, and would not have achieved glory.

Machiavelli ends his comparison of Hannibal and Scipio in the *Discorsi* by saying that

it matters little what method a general follows, provided that he is skilful (*virtuoso*) and that his ability (*virtù*) makes him highly regarded (*riputato*) by men. For when his skill is great, as was Hannibal's and Scipio's, it cancels all those errors that result from being too much loved or too much feared.[119]

He adds that Scipio and Hannibal achieved the same results, the former by praiseworthy (*laudabili*) methods, the latter by detestable (*detestabili*) ones.

Machiavelli may not have thought that all was fair in war, but there does not seem to be any sort of conduct that debars a man from military glory. And whereas to be 'glorious' in politics, it is not enough to be successful[120] (and what exactly constitutes success is less straightforward), success in battle or war ordinarily seems sufficient to render a general glorious.[121]

---

117 *Ibid.*

118 La Rochefoucauld, *Maximes* (1678 ed.), 291.

119 *Disc.* III, 21 (p. 447): 'Importa . . . poco ad uno capitano per qualunque di queste vie e' si cammini, pure che sia uomo virtuoso e che quella virtù lo faccia riputato intra gli uomini. Perché quando la è grande, come la fu in Annibale ed in Scipione, ella cancella tutti quegli errori che si fanno per farsi troppo amare o per farsi troppo temere.'

120 See below, pp. 610–618.

121 In *La vita di Castruccio Castracani . . . e Istorie fiorentine* (p. 36), Machiavelli has Castruccio say that it is victory, not the way in which it is achieved, that brings glory.

'VIRTÙ' AND MILITARY GLORY

Nevertheless, since military success is not always merited, the relation between ability or skill (*virtù*),[122] success, and glory needs to be considered. Machiavelli says in the *Istorie fiorentine* that 'order arises from disorder or ruin, *virtú* from order, and from *virtú* results *gloria* and success.'[123] The connection between *virtù* and glory is frequently emphasised: the old Venetians fought their own wars with great *virtù* and achieved glorious results,[124] whereas at Agnadello the Venetians did not win glory because they lacked *virtù*;[125] it was the *virtù* of Furius Camillus that drove the Gauls from Rome, bringing him so much glory;[126] Hannibal, Scipio, Manlius Torquatus, and Valerius Corvinus achieved glory through their *virtù*; generals who both form strong armies and win victories show two kinds of *virtù*, and merit double glory.[127]

There is an interesting discussion of the relation between *virtù* and glory in *Discorsi*, I, 29. Difficulties arise when a people or a ruler send a general on an important expedition: 'when that general gains much *gloria* by winning,' they are obliged to reward him. Nevertheless, ingratitude is exceedingly common, for the following reason.

> The general who through his *virtú* has acquired territory (*imperio*) for his master by overcoming the enemy, and covered himself with *gloria* and his soldiers with booty, necessarily acquires so much *riputazione* in the eyes of his soldiers, his enemies, and the ruler's subjects that his victory bodes ill for the ruler who sent him.[128]

Since great generals tend to be ambitious, rulers tend to be suspicious, and consider ways of avoiding the danger that they think threatens them, either by killing the general or by taking away his reputation, which they do,

> by cleverly putting it about that the victory was achieved not through his *virtú* but

---

[122] The most common meanings of *virtù* in Machiavelli's writings are ability, skill, energy, determination, or courage, in politics or war, although the word is sometimes used in other senses. See my 'The Senses of *Virtù* in Machiavelli,' *European Studies Review*, 3 (1973), 315–345.

[123] *Ist. fior.* v, 1 (p. 325): 'dalla rovina nasce l'ordine, dall'ordine virtú, da questa, gloria e buona fortuna.'

[124] *Princ.* XII (p. 56).

[125] *Disc.* III, 31 (p. 472).

[126] *Disc.* I, 8 (pp. 149–150).

[127] *Disc.* III, 13 (pp. 430–431). For other instances of the linking of *virtù* and military glory, see *Disc.* I, 30 (p. 201), I, 43 (p. 231), II, Proemio (p. 271), II, 24 (p. 353); *Ist. fior.* v, 1 (p. 326), VIII, 23 (pp. 552–553).

[128] *Disc.* I, 29 (p. 198).

through luck (*fortuna*), or the weakness or cowardice (*viltà*) of the enemy, or because of the skill (*prudenza*) of the other leaders who were with him.[129]

This surely implies that military success that is not attributable in considerable measure to the *virtù* of the victorious general should not advance his reputation or merit glory.

It may be concluded, I think, that Machiavelli sees victory in war as leading 'naturally' to glory for the victor; that is, in fact, victors will ordinarily be honoured or glorified. And if a general is habitually successful or victorious he will achieve a glorious reputation while he lives and it should be endorsed by posterity, for continual success would hardly be possible if he lacks *virtù*. But when a general's ability contributes little or nothing to the victory and he is nonetheless glorified undeservedly, his is a false glory, as discerning observers will doubtless perceive. Genuine military glory, then, is largely the result of skill and bravery, of military *virtù*.

'Fortune,' however, may play some part, without causing the general to forfeit the glory of victory, as the career of Fabius Maximus shows. It does not follow, therefore, that military *virtù* necessarily leads to success and glory.[130] Whether one is successful will depend on a variety of factors: the ability and courage of one's officers and soldiers; on the strength and morale of the opposing army and the resourcefulness of its general; on unforeseen (and sometimes unforeseeable) factors, such as the weather,[131] illness or disease;[132] and on whether one's talents (which are always limited, however great they are) are appropriate for the campaign undertaken; in short, on whether the circumstances or the times are congenial.

Those who do not achieve military glory are generals who do not conquer or who are frequently or easily defeated.[133] They acquire in-

---

[129] *Disc.* I, 29 (p. 197).

[130] Grattan Freyer, 'The Ideas of Machiavelli,' *Scrutiny*, 8 (1939–40), 20, says: 'If a man has both *virtù* and Fortune with him he will achieve *la gloria*. With Fortune but without *virtù* he may achieve success, but not *la gloria*.'

[131] E.g., heavy and unseasonal rain just before the crucial battle of Fornovo in 1495 caused the River Taro to swell and the ground to become slippery, giving rise to unexpected difficulties.

[132] E.g., Francesco Sforza, a general of great *virtù*, had to abandon a siege because many of his men fell ill (*Ist. fior.* v, 23 [p. 363]).

[133] Obviously, being defeated will not enhance a general's reputation, but a successful general may suffer some reverses without its being tarnished (as with Hannibal), especially if the defeated army has fought valorously against a much stronger enemy. Whether glory is lost, then, will depend on the circumstances.

stead a reputation for mediocrity, incapacity, indolence, or cowardice; and the same is true of armies. One may distinguish between generals who do not aim at success and glory, or who are satisfied by occasional victories (and Machiavelli thought that most mercenary leaders were of this type), and those who try but are simply incompetent.

'VIRTÙ' AND POLITICAL GLORY

Political glory, like military glory, is the natural fruit of *virtù*,[134] although here, too, being *virtuoso* does not necessarily lead to glory, because whether one is successful will depend partly on *fortuna*.[135] *Virtù*, political ability, ingenuity, resourcefulness, and foresight are almost indispensable qualities for rulers who would perform remarkable deeds and undertake great enterprises. Rulers who lack *virtù*, who are weak, inefficient, imprudent, cowardly, or lacking in spirit, achieve not glory, but a reputation for mediocrity or incompetence; they are held in little account or despised. As with military leaders, a distinction may be made between rulers whose attempts to seek glory are nullified by their lack of skill[136] and those who do not aim at glory. Machiavelli pays most attention to the latter.

The later Roman emperors 'liked the shade (*ombra*) more than the sun,'[137] a quiet life rather than one that was active and vigorous; they tried to buy off such neighbouring peoples as the Parthians and the Germans. This was a path that led to ruin;[138] previously 'the Romans had sought domination and *gloria*, and were not content with a quiet, peace-

---

[134] Cosimo and Lorenzo de' Medici are examples of men of *virtù* who achieved political glory. For the former, see *Ist. fior.* VII, 5–6 (pp. 458–463); for the latter, see *Ist. fior.* VIII, 36 (pp. 573–577), where *reputazione* and *fama* are attributed to him, and *Discursus florentinarum rerum post mortem iunioris Laurentii Medices* (*Arte della guerra e scritti politici minori*, p. 276), where there is a reference to his *gloria*.

[135] E.g., in *Discorsi*, III, 30 (p. 467), when discussing how envy should be dealt with, he observes that when *fortuna* is so favourable to an able man (*uomo virtuoso*) that his rivals die naturally, he can become *glorioso* without violence (*scandolo*), demonstrating his *virtù* without difficulty and without injuring anyone.

[136] Piero Soderini, *gonfaloniere* for life in Florence between 1502 and 1512, is perhaps an example. It is true that Machiavelli does not actually say that he sought glory, but he emphasises that Soderini did his best for the city. Nevertheless, because he was incapable of dealing effectively with his political enemies, they brought about his downfall and that of the regime. See *Disc.* I, 52 (pp. 247–248), III, 3 (pp. 386–387), III, 9 (p. 418), III, 30 (p. 468).

[137] *Disc.* II, 30 (p. 370). These words also occur in *Arte d. guerra*, I (p. 345), where they are used literally, not figuratively.

[138] *Disc.* II, 30 (p. 370).

ful existence.'[139] Italy in the fifteenth century also provided many examples of rulers who did not seek glory. The Italian states were mostly
governed by mediocre rulers (*minori principi*) who, being slothful (*oziosi*),[140] 'did not seek *gloria* at all but wanted to live in much comfort and
security or to increase their wealth.'[141] In *Dell'arte della guerra*, Machiavelli paints a very vivid picture of their attitudes and habits.[142] The
consequences quickly became apparent after 1494, when most of these
states were repeatedly ravaged and destroyed; their rulers 'lost their
states in a shameful way, without displaying any *virtù* at all.'[143] In chapter XXIV of *Il Principe*, he criticises these rulers severely, saying that they
all suffered the shame (*vergogna*) of losing their states, while those who
had had the advantage of being hereditary rulers incurred a double
shame. He analyses the reasons for their ruin, and finds that they were
ill-equipped militarily and had not succeeded in gaining the friendship
of the people or had not known how to deal with the nobles. They
lacked prudence and displayed instead indolence and lack of spirit (*ignavia*). Like *ozio*, *ignavia* is an antonym of *virtù*: A. R. Ferrarin charac-
terises it as 'fundamental lack of *virtù*,'[144] and Allan H. Gilbert aptly
says that 'under *ignavia* can be summed up most defects of the ruler who
loses his state.'[145] In quiet times they never thought that things might
change and made no provision for the future.[146] They failed to build
strong armies by training their subjects,[147] relying instead on merce-

---

139 *Disc.* II, 9 (p. 301): 'avendo Roma per fine lo imperio e la gloria e non la quiete.'

140 *Ist. fior.* I, 39 (pp. 135–136): 'Di questi adunque oziosi principi e di queste vilissime
armi sarà piena la mia istoria.' *Ozio* is a common antonym of *virtù* in Machiavelli's
writings.

141 *Ist. fior.* I, 39 (p. 135): 'non mossi da alcuna gloria ma per vivere o più ricchi o
più sicuri.'

142 *Arte d. guerra*, VII (p. 518): 'Before they felt the blows of the ultramontane wars, our
Italian rulers believed that it was enough for a prince to know how to deliver a sharp
retort in his court, write a fine letter, show himself to be quick and witty in speech, know
how to deceive, adorn himself with gems and gold, have a better table and finer apart-
ments than other men, live very lasciviously, be rapacious and haughty towards subjects,
live very indolently (*marcirsi nello ozio*), give military posts to favourites, scorn anyone
who tried to show them some praiseworthy path (*lodevole via*).'

143 *Arte d. guerra*, VII (p. 517): 'perdendo ignominiosamente lo stato, e sanza alcuno
esemplo virtuoso.'

144 Niccolò Machiavelli, *Scritti politici* (Milan, 1939), I, 117: 'radicale mancanza di
virtù.'

145 *Machiavelli's Prince and Its Forerunners* (Durham, N.C., 1938), p. 194.

146 *Princ.* XXIV (p. 98).

147 A ruler who 'has many men but lacks soldiers should blame his own laziness
(*pigrizia*) and lack of wisdom (*poca prudenza*), not the weakness or cowardice (*viltà*) of
his men' (*Disc.* III, 38 [p. 490]).

610   RENAISSANCE QUARTERLY

naries; and they certainly did not lead their armies into battle,[148] 'as
those who are *virtuosi* always do, thus ensuring that when they are victorious, the *gloria* and the territory conquered belong only to them.'[149]

CONDUCT INCOMPATIBLE WITH POLITICAL GLORY

Apart from ruling weakly, ineffectually, or unsuccessfully, there are
other modes of action that are incompatible with glory. In order to be
'glorious,' it is not enough for a ruler to be 'successful'; his methods
must not be dishonourable. Those who flourish through treachery or
breach of faith should not be considered glorious. In the *Discorsi*, Machiavelli contrasts the use of deception or stratagems (*fraude*) in war,
which bring glory when they succeed, with treachery (*fraude*) in politics
or diplomacy.

I do not mean that the *fraude* that consists in the breaking of pledged faith and treaties
is glorious, because even if it sometimes brings you power (*stato e regno*) . . . it will
never gain you *gloria*.[150]

Those who seize power by criminal means (*via scellerata e nefaria*),[151]
by treacherous violence, also forfeit any claim to glory. Agathocles and
Julius Caesar have the dubious distinction of being the only successful
or great men to whom glory is explicitly denied. Agathocles' character
and career are discussed in chapter VIII of *Il Principe*, which is concerned
with 'Those Who Have Attained Power by Villainy.'[152] Machiavelli
says that 'as he rose to power, he always led a wicked life.'[153] After be-

[148] Machiavelli remarks in *Discorsi*, III, 10 (p. 419), that they refrain from this to avoid
danger (*per fuggire i pericoli*), and that, on the rare occasions when modern rulers personally lead their armies, 'it is done for show (*a pompa*) and not for any praiseworthy
reason.'

[149] *Disc.* I, 30 (p. 201). Machiavelli recommends rulers to follow this practice 'to avoid
the necessity either of remaining suspicious or of being ungrateful' to their conquering
generals.

[150] *Disc.* III, 40 (p. 493): 'io non intendo quella fraude essere gloriosa che ti fa rompere
la fede data ed i patti fatti: perché questa, ancora che la ti acquisti qualche volta stato e
regno . . . la non ti acquisterà mai gloria.'

[151] *Princ.* VIII (p. 40). *Scellerata* means 'villainous' or 'wicked,' and *Russo* (p. 89), glossing *nefaria*, says that it '[a]ccentua il significato di scellerata: nefario è cio che è contrario
a ogni legge umana e divina.'

[152] 'De his qui per scelera ad principatum pervenere.'

[153] *Princ.* VIII (p. 41): 'tenne sempre, per li gradi della sua età, vita scellerata.' Most
commentators take *per li gradi della sua età* to mean 'throughout his life' but Giuseppe
Lisio (*Il Principe* [Florence, 1900], p. 57) glosses it 'gli anni della fanciullezza e della
gioventú, considerate come i gradi ascendenti della vita.' Machiavelli's source was Jus-
tinus, and Lisio points out that the phrase corresponds to that used in Book XXII of his

coming *praetor* of Syracuse, he decided to become ruler through violence (*con violenzia*); he tricked the most important citizens into attending a meeting, at which, with the help of Hamilcar, the Carthaginian
general, they were all massacred. Thereafter, he held his position without any civil strife, and successfully fought his enemies, both in Sicily
and abroad. Machiavelli, however, insists that he was not 'glorious':

> Yet it cannot be called *virtú* to kill one's fellow citizens or betray one's friends, be
> treacherous, merciless, and irreligious. One can attain power (*imperio*) by acting in
> these ways, but not *gloria*.[154]

Agathocles overcame difficulties and dangers with much courage and
ability (*virtú*), and displayed such greatness of spirit (*grandezza dello
animo*) that

> he cannot be judged inferior to any great leader (*eccellentissimo capitano*). Yet because
> of his terrible cruelty and inhumanity, and his countless atrocities (*scelleratezze*), he
> cannot be celebrated (*celebrato*) among the most excellent men (*eccellentissimi uomini*).[155]

It seems that he deserves credit for his martial spirit and deeds (that is,
as a *capitano*) after he became ruler; what blackens his reputation is how
he became ruler, because he treacherously slaughtered his friends and
fellow citizens. Trickery and violence are to be condemned in a ruler or
an aspiring ruler. And even his subsequent career cannot absolve him in
Machiavelli's eyes, although by benefitting his subjects he may in some
measure have redeemed himself with God and with men.[156] The stain
incurred by the way he seized power is indelible, like an original sin.

Machiavelli discusses in the *Discorsi* the character and deeds of Cyrus
the Great.[157] Although at first sight Cyrus resembles Agathocles, there
are significant differences. Machiavelli says that Xenophon shows 'how
many honours (*onori*) and victories and how much good reputation

---

history: 'non honestiorem pueritiam quam principia originis habuit.' Moreover, Machiavelli makes it clear that Agathocles later mended his ways (*Princ.* VIII [p. 44]).

[154] *Princ.* VIII (p. 42): 'Non si può ancora chiamare virtú ammazzare li sua cittadini,
tradire li amici, essere sanza fede, sanza pietà, sanza relligione; li quali modi possono fare
acquistare imperio, ma non gloria.'

[155] *Ibid. Carli* (p. 52) observes: 'Non per nulla dice qui *uomini*, e di sopra ha detto
capitano: gran capitano Agàtocle sí; *grande uomo* no, perché del grande uomo è propria
quella virtú machiavellica piena, da cui solo può venir "gloria." '

[156] *Princ.* VIII (p. 44).

[157] The details of Cyrus' career are very obscure, and Xenophon's *Cyropaedia* is largely
fictitious. He used Cyrus in order to illustrate his views on war and politics (as Machiavelli himself used Castruccio Castracani); the correctness of Machiavelli's account of
Cyrus does not concern us.

(*buona fama*) Cyrus acquired through being humane and affable, and not being haughty (*superbo*), cruel, lustful (*lussurioso*), or having any other vice that stains (*macchi*) the reputations of men.'[158] Yet in an earlier chapter he says that Xenophon shows how Cyrus could not have prospered without deceit, 'for Cyrus's first expedition against the king of Armenia was full of trickery (*fraude*), and it was through cunning (*inganno*) and not force (*forza*) that he succeeded in taking that kingdom.'[159] Moreover, Cyrus 'deceived his maternal uncle Cyaxares, king of the Medes, in various ways, and Xenophon shows that without that deceit (*fraude*) he could not have achieved the greatness (*grandezza*) that he did.'[160] The moral is clear: ' a ruler or general (*principe*)[161] who wants to do great things (*fare gran cose*) must learn how to deceive (*ingannare*).'[162] Machiavelli says that Cyrus achieved glory;[163] we should apparently conclude that, since in war no means are dishonourable, the use of deceit is no hindrance to achieving glory, even in wars designed to seize the states of other rulers. The case of Cyrus seems sufficiently different from that of Agathocles for there to be no reason for denying him glory.

Giovanpaolo Baglioni of Perugia was a ruler who did not achieve glory. He failed to act in the appropriate way when a great opportunity presented itself. Pope Julius II wanted to remove the rulers who were flourishing in the Papal States, and in September 1506 he arrived at Perugia. Acting with his customary impetuosity, he did not wait for his troops but entered the city accompanied only by the cardinals and a few soldiers. Julius succeeded in carrying off Baglioni and installing an obedient governor, despite the fact that Baglioni had many soldiers. Machiavelli says that Baglioni displayed much cowardice (*viltà*), and 'it was not understood why he had not earned undying fame (*perpetua fama*) by quickly ridding himself of (*oppresso ad un tratto*)[164] his enemy, and enriched himself with booty, for the cardinals . . . had many valu-

---

[158] *Disc.* III, 20 (p. 445).

[159] *Disc.* II, 13 (p. 311).

[160] *Disc.* II, 13 (p. 312).

[161] *Principe* usually means 'prince' or 'ruler' but sometimes it is used of generals (e.g., of Hannibal in *Princ.* XVII [p. 70]), and since in *Disc.* II, 13, Machiavelli is discussing both political and military success (although the former is certainly emphasised rather more), *principe* here probably means 'ruler' or 'general.'

[162] *Disc.* II, 13 (p. 312).

[163] *Princ.* XIV (p. 64).

[164] The word *oppresso* is ambiguous, but here it almost certainly means 'killed.' For discussion of this point, see below, n. 171.

ables with them.'[165] It could not have been through goodness (*per bontà*) or scruples of conscience (*per conscienza*), since he was an evil man.[166] The explanation of his conduct must be that

men do not know how to be 'honourably' bad (*onorevolmente cattivi*)[167] or completely good (*perfettamente buoni*), and that they do not know how to commit a crime (*una malizia*) that is great (*ha in sé grandezza*) or in some way magnanimous (*generosa*). Thus, although Giovanpaolo did not worry about a reputation for open incest and parricide, when he had a fine opportunity (*giusta occasione*) he did not know how, or rather did not dare, to do something for which everyone would have admired his spirit (*animo*). He would have had an everlasting reputation (*memoria eterna*), as having been the first to show these prelates that those who live and rule as they do merit little esteem; and the magnitude (*grandezza*) of his action would have overcome (*superato*)[168] all the notoriety (*infamia*) and all the dangers that might have resulted from it.[169]

This chapter presents some difficulties, mainly because of certain ambiguous words and phrases. While it is clear that Baglioni did not gain glory, it is not obvious whether Machiavelli would have considered him glorious if he had acted in the way suggested. Apart from other considerations, a glorious reputation seems precluded by the way that he came to power, for his murders differed only in scale from those of Agathocles.[170] It is made quite clear that Baglioni was a very wicked man. Would he have been even more wicked, in Machiavelli's opinion,

---

[165] *Disc.* I, 27 (p. 195).

[166] He lived incestuously with his sister, and had killed his cousins and nephews in order to rule.

[167] The theme of *Discorsi*, I, 27, is that 'Very Few Men Are Entirely (*al tutto*) Bad or Good,' and Baglioni is the sole example considered; it is not obvious why Machiavelli introduces the unexpected word *onorevolmente* to qualify *cattivi*. In *Dell'arte della guerra*, I (p. 336), he says that men who live only by fighting find much difficulty in peaceful times and that when 'they do not have enough ability (*virtú*) to join together to achieve a "worthwhile" villainy (*una cattività onorevole*), they are forced by necessity to become brigands, and the authorities are forced to suppress them.' *Bertelli* (*Arte d. guerra*, p. 336) glosses *una cattività onorevole* as 'una malvagità che abbia in sé della grandezza' and draws attention to the words *onorevolmente cattivi* in *Discorsi*, I, 27.

[168] It is not at all obvious how the *grandezza* of the action could have overcome the resultant perils.

[169] *Disc.* I, 27 (pp. 195–196): 'si conchiuse, nascesse che gli uomini non sanno essere onorevolmente cattivi o perfettamente buoni, e come una malizia ha in sé grandezza o è in alcuna parte generosa, e' non vi sanno entrare. Cosí Giovampagolo, il quale non stimava essere incesto e publico parricida, non seppe, o a dir meglio non ardí, avendone giusta occasione, fare una impresa dove ciascuno avesse ammirato l'animo suo, e avesse di sé lasciato memoria eterna sendo il primo che avesse dimostro a' prelati quanto sia da stimare poco chi vive e regna come loro, ed avessi fatto una cosa la cui grandezza avesse superato ogni infamia, ogni pericolo che da quella potesse dependere.'

[170] Indeed, in one respect they were worse, because he had killed his own relatives.

if he had killed[171] the pope and the cardinals? It seems likely that he would, but that he would have been magnificently bad, wicked in the grand manner.[172] When Machiavelli says that Baglioni could have achieved everlasting *fama*, he is presumably using the word either in the neutral sense that it sometimes had or else in the sense of 'bad fame,'[173] or fame achieved through actions remarkable for their badness and boldness.

It seems likely that Machiavelli simply means that if Baglioni had killed the pope, his would have become a household name, inspiring a certain admiration[174] for his audacity in committing the almost unheard of crime[175] of killing the spiritual leader of Christendom, as well as general condemnation of his wickedness. His would have been wickedness of a heroic sort, but his name would not have been 'glorious.'[176]

Machiavelli's attribution of 'glory' to Ferdinand of Aragon[177] pre-

[171] He could of course have held the pope and cardinals prisoners, but not indefinitely. Apart from the fact that public opinion would have been aroused, eventually he would have been obliged either to kill them or release them (and even if the release were conditional on a papal promise not to harm him, promises extracted under coercion would not have been considered binding [see *Disc.* III, 42]).

[172] J. H. Whitfield, *Machiavelli* (Oxford, 1947), pp. 100–101, aptly cites La Rochefoucauld's maxim (*Maximes*, 185): 'Il y a des héros en mal comme en bien.' It must be conceded, however, that it is possible to interpret the chapter differently. It might be thought that Machiavelli is insinuating that Baglioni would have performed a public service (and his 'crime' thus have been *generosa*) if he had dispatched the pope and cardinals, and that it is implied that his action (because of its *grandezza*?) would not really have been infamous. Yet when the self-seeking, ambitious character of Baglioni is considered, it is difficult to see how the action could have been *generosa*; he would have acted thus simply to save his own skin.

[173] Although perhaps not quite so common in the sixteenth century as the sense of 'good fame,' it was nevertheless a fairly frequent usage, reflecting the ambiguity of *fama* in classical Latin. Felice Alderisio, *Machiavelli* (Turin, 1930), p. 46, n. 2, observes: 'M. dice "fama" e non già "gloria," giacchè la memoria eterna che il Baglioni avrebbe potuto lasciare sarebbe dovuta sì ad una "tristizia grande e generosa," ma sempre ad una tristizia.'

[174] Doubtless it would have been a grudging admiration on the part of those who condemned his action.

[175] No pope had been killed for more than six centuries; in 1303 when Boniface VIII was manhandled by the emissaries of Philip the Fair at Anagni shortly before his death, there was widespread shock and condemnation of the French action.

[176] On this reading, then, Machiavelli's attitude to Baglioni is similar to that of Guicciardini, who said that he could have captured the pope and all his court 'if in so great a matter he had known how to make ring round the whole world the treachery (*perfidia*) that had already blackened (*infamato*) his name in matters so much less important' (*Storia d'Italia*, VII, 3).

[177] *Princ.* XXI. See above, p. 597.

GLORIA IN MACHIAVELLI　　　　615

sents great difficulties. It cannot be doubted that Ferdinand was a very successful ruler but, as we have seen, success alone does not bring glory. It is not enough to do 'great things'; they must not be done dishonourably. Machiavelli says explicitly in the *Discorsi* that breaking treaties and acting treacherously may bring success but never glory.[178] Yet in *Il Principe* he makes it abundantly clear that this was precisely the way that Ferdinand prospered, saying that he resorted to a 'pious cruelty' of almost unexampled wretchedness when he despoiled and expelled the Spanish Jews and Moslems, and used the same pretext (*mantello*) of religion in his invasion of North Africa.[179] And at the end of chapter XVIII of *Il Principe*, he had Ferdinand in mind when he says that

a certain ruler of the present day,[180] whom it is better not to name, has always preached peace and good faith, while being a great enemy of both; and if he had practised them, he would before this have certainly lost either his *reputazione* or his state.[181]

His 'reputation' means his 'fame' or 'glory'; losing it, he would have become a ruler of little account. One would have expected Machiavelli to have classified Ferdinand with Agathocles, as a ruler who was successful but not 'glorious.' This judgment about Ferdinand's fame or glory is perhaps primarily a statement about the esteem that Ferdinand actually enjoyed; nevertheless Machiavelli does not dissent from it, saying that it was undeserved, as he did of Caesar's glory.

Men who destroy things that are good or valuable are 'infamous,' not glorious. What is condemned is not the use of force but its use for destructive instead of for constructive purposes.[182] Romulus is praised because he used force in order to build a state;[183] Julius Caesar is condemned because he destroyed the Roman republic.[184]

---

[178] *Disc.* III, 40 (p. 493).

[179] *Princ.* XXI (p. 90): 'per possere intraprendere maggiore imprese, servendosi sempre della relligione, si volse a una pietosa crudeltà, cacciando e spogliando el suo regno, de' Marrani, né può esser questo esemplo piú miserabile né piú raro. Assaltò sotto questo medesimo mantello l'Affrica.'

[180] All the commentators who gloss this phrase interpret it as an allusion to Ferdinand.

[181] *Princ.* XVIII (p. 74): 'Alcuno principe de' presenti tempi, quale non è bene nominare, non predica mai altro che pace e fede, e dell'una e dell'altra è inimicissimo; e l'una e l'altra, quando e' l'avessi osservata, li arebbe piú volte tolto o la reputazione o lo stato.'

[182] *Disc.* I, 9 (p. 154): 'colui che è violento per guastare, non quello che è per racconciare, si debbe riprendere.'

[183] *Disc.* I, 9 (pp. 153–155).

[184] *Disc.* I, 10 (p. 157). Later in the same chapter (p. 159), Caesar is said to have ruined (*guastare*) Rome. Cf. *Disc.* I, 37 (p. 218): 'Cesare . . . fu primo tiranno in Roma, talché mai fu poi libera quella città.'

The most emphatic condemnation of the destroyers of good things and the founders or cultivators of bad is in *Discorsi*, I, 10, where he criticises those who found tyrannies.

Infamous and detestable . . . are those men who destroy religions, who undermine kingdoms and republics, who are enemies of the *virtú*,[185] of letters, and of every other art that is useful to men or increases human dignity; such as those who are impious, violent, ignorant, worthless, slothful, or base.[186]

Tyrants (*tiranni*)[187] merit condemnation because tyranny (*tirannide*) is antithetical to the rule of law and civic freedom. They govern in their own interests rather than in those of their subjects; they are 'ambitious,' considering their own good or that of their families or descendants, not the common good.[188] Although Machiavelli sometimes[189] distinguishes

---

[185] The word *virtù* probably does not mean 'virtues' or 'good qualities' but refers to the words that follow it.

[186] *Disc.* I, 10 (p. 156): 'Sono . . . infami e detestabili gli uomini distruttori delle religioni, dissipatori de' regni e delle republiche, inimici delle virtú, delle lettere e d'ogni altra arte che arrechi utilità e onore alla umana generazione, come sono gl'impii, i violenti, gl'ignoranti, i dappochi, gli oziosi, i vili.'

[187] A 'tyrant' is characterised as an 'absolute ruler' (*principe assoluto*) in *Disc.* III, 26 (p. 460), and here, as elsewhere (e.g., *Disc.* III, 6), the tendency of tyrants to harm their subjects is emphasised. In *Disc.* I, 25 (p. 193), 'uno vivere politico' (which may be either a *republica* or a *regno*) is contrasted with 'una potestà assoluta, la quale dagli autori è chiamata tirannide.' '[U]no vivere civile e libero' is contrasted with 'uno assoluto e tirannico' in *Disc.* I, 9 (p. 154), and a 'tyranny' with a 'free state' (*stato libero*) in *Disc.* III, 3 (p. 386), where he discusses how Piero Soderini might have acted, and implies that 'pigliare istraordinaria autorità e rompere con le leggi la civile equalità' would have been a tyrannical act (even if justified in the circumstances).

Sometimes, however, Machiavelli uses *tiranno* in the sense of 'usurper.' Thus in *Ist. fior.* I, 30 (p. 123), he says that Pope Benedict XII 'fece uno decreto che tutti i tiranni di Lombardia possedessino le terre, che si avevano usurpate, con giusto titulo.' But after Benedict's death, the Emperor Louis IV, 'per non essere ancora egli meno liberale delle cose d'altri che si fusse stato il papa, donò a tutti quegli che nelle terre della Chiesa erano tiranni le terre loro, acciò che con la autorità imperiale le possedessero.' Pope Julius II's policy of removing these *tiranni* is referred to in *Disc.* I, 27. *Russo* (p. 222), glossing *tiranno* at the beginning of this chapter, says: 'Qui, sinonimo di signore' (i.e., 'ruler'), but from the context (and in the light of the above passage in *Ist. fior.*) it seems to me to have the sense of 'usurper.'

[188] For Machiavelli, *ambizione* is essentially a derogatory term (e.g., *Disc.* I, 2 [p. 132], I, 9 [p. 154], I, 10 [p. 158]); a man who is *ambizioso* is self-seeking, and Machiavelli frequently contrasts actions motivated by ambition with those motivated by the public or common good (e.g., *Disc.* III, 3 [p. 387], III, 11 [p. 423], III, 12 [p. 427], III, 22 [p. 452]).

[189] Founders and reformers of kingdoms (*regni*), as well as of republics (*republiche*), are praised in *Discorsi*, I, 9, and in the following chapter founders of both republics and kingdoms are said to be worthy of praise, and founding a republic or a kingdom is explicitly contrasted with founding a tyranny.

between princes and tyrants, it must be admitted that the distinction is not always observed, because he also says that the common good is held in high regard only in republics,[190] and that 'usually what a prince (*principe*) does for himself harms his city and what is done for the city harms him.'[191] He then discusses what happens when a tyranny replaces a free community (*uno vivere libero*), saying that even when there arises an able tyrant (*tiranno virtuoso*)

who through his spiritedness and military skill (*virtú d'arme*) extends his state, no bene-fit accrues to that republic (*republica*)[192] but only to him; he cannot honor any of those good and able citizens over whom he rules, because he would then be suspicious of them.[193]

There are, however, exceptions to the generalisation that princes are not concerned with promoting the common good. King Agis tried un-successfully to restore the laws of Lycurgus in Sparta; his successor, Cle-omenes, also sought to achieve the same good for his country,[194] and thinking that the ambitious Ephors would prevent his achieving some-thing so useful for the people (*utile a molti*), he had them killed, and restored the ancient laws.[195] Timoleon of Corinth and Aratus of Sicyon, too, were good princes (*principi buoni*),[196] worthy of being imitated; their rule so satisfied their subjects that 'although they several times tried to retire, they were not permitted to.'[197] It should probably be con-

---

[190] *Disc.* II, 2 (p. 280): 'non il bene particulare ma il bene comune è quello che fa grandi le città. E sanza dubbio questo bene comune non è osservato se non nelle re-publiche.'

[191] *Ibid.*: 'quando vi è uno principe ... il piú delle volte quello che fa per lui offende la città, e quello che fa per la città offende lui.'

[192] The use of *republica* for a state ruled by a 'tyrant' is indicative of Machiavelli's loose use of terms.

[193] *Disc.* II, 2 (p. 280): 'E se la sorte facesse che vi surgesse uno tiranno virtuoso, il quale per animo e per virtú d'arme ampliasse il dominio suo, non ne risulterebbe alcuna utilità a quella republica, ma a lui proprio: perché e' non può onorare nessuno di quegli cittadini che siano valenti e buoni che egli tiranneggia, non volendo avere ad avere sospetto di loro.'

[194] *Disc.* I, 9 (p. 155): 'fare questo bene alla sua patria.'

[195] *Ibid.*

[196] *Principe* is also used loosely by Machiavelli. Sometimes it means 'hereditary ruler,' sometimes simply 'ruler' (as in *Disc.* I, 26, where he says that from being a petty king [*piccol re*], Philip of Macedon became *principe* of Greece); occasionally it means 'leader' or 'general' (see above, n. 161).

[197] *Disc.* III, 5 (p. 390).

cluded, then, that the distinction between 'prince' and 'tyrant' stands, and that whereas a prince may attain glory, a tyrant cannot.[198]

GLORY AS A GOAL OR MOTIVE

It remains to consider the extent to which Machiavelli thought that men were motivated by glory or conceived of it as a goal to be sought. He says in chapter xxv of *Il Principe* that men aim at glory and riches. Does he mean that all men seek both, that some men seek both, or that some seek glory while others seek riches? It hardly seems plausible to maintain that fame was the spur for a Florentine artisan, a Venetian merchant, or a Roman peasant. Most men do not leave any mark in history, nor do they try to. Their destiny is obscure, their annals are short and simple; they are 'to fame unknown.'[199]

Burd thought Machiavelli's remark worthy of note, but hardly any later commentators have followed him. Manfredo Vanni suggests that it is a 'comprehensive classification of human goods—moral and material.'[200] This seems a plausible interpretation but a major difficulty in accepting it is that 'moral goods' is a much broader concept than 'glory.' And although *onore, riputazione, fama*, and *laude* are synonyms of *gloria*, they are by no means exact synonyms.

Although *fama* is often equivalent to *gloria*, sometimes it means 'rumour'[201] or 'news.'[202] Occasionally it means a reputation that one acquires not for public but for private actions. Machiavelli says that a man who keeps respectable company acquires a good reputation (*buono nome*), because the company that one keeps is a most reliable indication of one's character;[203] and sometimes 'some noteworthy or remarkable action, even in private life, will bring a man to public notice' (*publica*

---

[198] Leo Strauss, however, in his *Thoughts on Machiavelli* (Glencoe, 1958), emphasises the blurring of the difference between republics and principalities in the *Discorsi* (pp. 265–266) and argues that there is 'no essential difference between the public-spirited founder of a republic and the selfish founder of a tyranny' (p. 273).

[199] Thomas Gray, *Elegy in a Country Churchyard*.

[200] Vanni's edition of *Il Principe* (Milan, 1966), p. 134: '*glorie e ricchezze. Distinzione comprensiva dei beni umani: beni morali e materiali.*'

[201] *Disc.* III, 34 (p. 478): 'Dico adunque come il popolo nel suo distribuire va dietro a quello che si dice d'uno per publica voce e fama quando per sue opere note non lo conosce altrimenti, o per presunzione o opinione che si ha di lui.'

[202] E.g., *Disc.* III, 20 (p. 445) [see above, n. 105]; *Ist. fior.* v, 27 (p. 370), VII, 27 (p. 493).

[203] *Disc.* III, 34 (p. 478).

fama).[204] Moreover, *fama* sometimes has a bad sense:[205] unlike *gloria*, it can be achieved through bad actions. Machiavelli observes that 'many men, not having had the opportunity to acquire *fama* by praiseworthy deeds, have contrived to acquire it by evil deeds.'[206]

And whereas *gloria* always implies fame that is good as well as great, a reputation (*riputazione*) may be either good or bad, restricted or local, as well as widespread or universal. Moreover, *riputazione* is a different sort of word from *gloria*: a reputation is always 'for something'—for great deeds sometimes but also for certain abilities or qualities, for piety, learning, etc. It was a reputation for honesty or impartiality that Savonarola lost,[207] and it was a reputation for being a lover of Florentine liberty that Piero Soderini enjoyed as he rose to power in that city.[208]

Laude, too, although it is sometimes linked as a synonym with *gloria*, often has a different meaning. Not only great achievements merit praise. Men may be lauded for their motives, as Machiavelli praises Julius II because he acted in order to aggrandise the Church and not for any private end.[209] Again, men who are in no way glorious may be praised for certain good qualities, as Alexander Severus was, because 'in the fourteen years that he was emperor, he killed no one without trial; nevertheless, being thought effeminate and too much under his mother's influence,

---

[204] *Ibid.*

[205] Although Machiavelli never speaks of 'bad fame' (preferring instead *infamia*), he sometimes speaks of 'good' fame (*buona fama*), e.g., *Disc.* I, 52 (p. 247), III, 20 (p. 445), which would be unnecessary if *fama* were always good.

[206] *Ist. fior.*, Proemio (p. 70): 'molti, non avendo avuta occasione di acquistarsi fama con qualche opera lodevole, con cose vituperose si sono ingegnati acquistarla.' And in *Arte d. guerra*, I (p. 337), a distinction is made between generals who 'acquistarono fama come valenti uomini, non come buoni' and those who 'acquistarono gloria come valenti e buoni.'

The fifteenth-century writer Cristoforo Landino in his *Comento* on Dante's *Divina Commedia* (Venice, 1520, p. 324) distinguishes between *fama* and *gloria*: 'Benché fama e gloria a molti paiano quasi quel medesimo, nientedimeno fama è notizia molto frequente d'alcuna cosa, gloria è notizia chiara d'alcuna cosa con lode. Adunque la fama può essere di cosa che né splendore né laude alcuna seco adduce, ma la gloria non può essere sanza quelle.' And the sixteenth-century writer Bernadino Daniello in his commentary on Dante (Venice, 1565, p. 483) makes a similar distinction: 'Non è la gloria e la fama una cosa medesima; ma sono l'una dall'altra differenti in questo, che la fama può esser delle opere così oscure come chiare, ma la gloria è solamente delli illustri.' For a discussion of the distinction the Romans made between *gloria* and *fama*, see Donald C. Earl, *The Moral and Political Tradition of Rome* (London, 1967), p. 30.

[207] *Disc.* I, 45 (p. 234).

[208] *Disc.* I, 52 (p. 247).

[209] *Princ.* XI (p. 52).

620   RENAISSANCE QUARTERLY

he became despised, his army plotted against him and killed him.'[210]

Onore, though sometimes having the same meaning as *gloria*, is, of all these synonyms, that with the widest range of meanings. Although Machiavelli does not make the distinction, 'social' honour should be distinguished from 'public' honour (which is acquired in politics or war). For Machiavelli, all men (except perhaps those in the very lowest condition of life)[211] can possess social honour; it may therefore be called a 'universal' value.[212] It consists in being respected by one's fellows, and seems to be conceived of by Machiavelli essentially as something to be preserved.[213] Men can lose it by their own misdeeds or those of their families or associates or by being subjected to insults or injuries.[214] Social honour is quite different from public honour, fame or glory; whereas the former is ordinary, the latter is extraordinary, and must be achieved or won. The antonym of social honour is always dishonour, but public honour or glory may be contrasted with obscurity as well as with dishonour.[215]

[210] *Princ.* xix (p. 80).

[211] Those whom he describes as being of *sangue vile* or *infima fortuna*.

[212] This all-pervading sense of honour has remained a characteristic not only of Italian society but of all Mediterranean societies. See Jean G. Péristiany, ed., *Honour and Shame: The Values of Mediterranean Society* (London, 1965); J. K. Campbell, *Honour, Family and Patronage: A Study of Institutions and Moral Values in a Greek Mountain Community* (Oxford, 1964), esp. ch. x; J. Davis, 'Honour and Politics in Pisticci,' *Proceedings of the Royal Anthropological Institute of Great Britain and Ireland* (1969), pp. 69–81.

Until 1969, adultery was a legal offence in Italy, and even if duels are no longer fought in defence of honour, the concept of *delitto d'onore* retains its force. According to article 587 of the Italian penal code, a person who kills in defence of honour incurs a sentence of between three and seven years instead of a much longer sentence.

Honour is seen also as an attribute of institutions. John C. Adams and Paolo Barile (*The Government of Republican Italy* [London, 1962], p. 215) discuss *vilipendio*, 'a crime that consists of a disrespectful statement or action towards certain public institutions and the persons who direct them.' They observe that it rests on the hypothesis that 'persons and institutions have a kind of honor that can be damaged by the public statement of uncomplimentary opinions or facts.'

[213] See below, pp. 622–625.

[214] And the dishonour is increased when insults or injuries are public or widely known (e.g., the case of Pausanias, discussed in *Disc.* ii, 28 [p. 364]), especially perhaps when it is publicised by the offender (e.g., *Ist. fior.* vii, 33 [p. 503]).

[215] Schopenhauer, in his perceptive discussion of these matters in *Aphorismen zur Lebensweisheit*, ch. iv, expresses a similar view: 'Ruhm muss daher erst erworben werden: die Ehre hingegen braucht bloss nicht verloren zu gehn. Dem entsprechend ist Ermangelung des Ruhmes Obskurität, ein Negatives; Ermangelung der Ehre ist Schande, ein Positives.' See Schopenhauer's *Sämmtliche Werke*, ed. J. Frauenstädt, 2nd ed., v (Leipzig, 1922), 385.

Even public honour is not always the same as glory. Whereas glory is always accorded for personal merits (real or perceived), some sorts of public honour may have nothing to do with merit. Guests of honour are not necessarily honourable or deserving of honour.[216] And some men are treated with honour because of the office they hold. Moreover, *onore* (like the Latin *honor*) sometimes means an office or post in a state. The honour accorded to victorious generals in the Roman 'triumphs' is an example of honour that is the same as glory; like victorious athletes who run laps of honour, they were thought to merit it.[217]

Gloria, then, has a narrower and a more exalted meaning than *onore* and the other synonyms, and may be aptly defined as 'very great fame or honour that is generally recognized, acquired through extraordinary merits or talents, through valorous deeds or great enterprises.'[218] Glory is a reputation for great deeds in the public sphere, and Machiavelli never attributes it except to those prominent in politics or war. It is impossible, therefore, to accept Vanni's view that *glorie e ricchezze* is a comprehensive classification of human goods.

Nevertheless, Machiavelli has much to say about men's desires both for glory, honour, or esteem, and for material possessions or riches, and it is necessary to consider this more fully. Sometimes he contrasts *gloria* with *ricchezze*[219] or acquisitions (*acquisto*),[220] but more often it is *onore* that he contrasts with *roba*,[221] *ricchezze*,[222] *sustanze*,[223] and *utile*.[224]

Men in general are attached both to possessions and to honour. In *Il Principe*, he says that 'the desire to acquire is really very natural and or-

---

[216] The rascally Oliverotto Euffreducci, planning to murder his uncle, Giovanni Fogliano, ruler of Fermo, wrote to him saying that he wished to come to Fermo in a way that did him honour (*voleva venire onorevole*), accompanied by a hundred of his friends and servants. He pointed out that his being received honourably would also honour Fogliano, who had raised him (*Princ.* VIII [pp. 42–43]).

[217] And when a defeated army is permitted to depart 'honourably' with their arms, glory is certainly not gained but dishonour is avoided. This is what was denied to the Romans after their defeat at the Caudine Forks.

[218] *Grande dizionario della lingua italiana* (Turin, 1970), VI, 930: *Gloria*: 'Fama e onore altissimi e universalmente riconosciuti che si acquistano per meriti e virtù straordinari, per imprese valorose, per opere grandi.'

[219] *Princ.* XXV (p. 100).

[220] *Disc.* I, 29 (p. 201).

[221] *Disc.* I, 37 (p. 218), III, 6 (pp. 391–392); *Princ.* XIX (p. 75).

[222] *Disc.* I, 40 (p. 228).

[223] *Disc.* I, 37 (p. 216).

[224] *Disc.* I, 50 (p. 244).

dinary,'[225] and although he has in mind particularly the acquisition of territory or states, it seems reasonable to interpret it as applying to possessions of all kinds. In the *Discorsi*, he says that nature has created men with unlimited desires but limited abilities.[226] Hostility and wars arise, partly because men desire to acquire more, partly because they fear to lose what they already possess. And he observes that honours and possessions (*gli onori e le sustanze*) are most esteemed by men.[227] His examination of the operation of the agrarian laws in ancient Rome, however, leads him to conclude that 'men esteem property (*roba*) even more than positions of honour (*onori*); for the Roman nobility always yielded to the people about such positions (*onori*), but when property was at stake' they defended it with great obstinacy.[228] Men are attached to their property almost as much as to their lives,[229] doubtless because property is a prerequisite for living or living well, and because possessions are dear to them (being seen as an extension or expression of their personalities).

In chapter XVII of *Il Principe*, Machiavelli emphasises that a ruler should avoid being hated by his subjects, and that he must 'refrain from taking the property (*roba*) of his citizens and subjects, and from interfering with their women.'[230] He may take life, if there is 'a proper and obvious reason,' but 'above all, one must not touch the property of others, for men forget more easily the death [i.e., the killing] of a father than the loss of their patrimony.'[231] This might be taken as implying that 'honour' is less important than property (for such a killing of one's father must involve dishonour), but in a piece written in 1512 Machiavelli observes that the reason is that a dead relative cannot be brought

---

[225] *Princ.* III (p. 23): 'È cosa veramente molto naturale et ordinaria desiderare di acquistare.'

[226] *Disc.* I, 37 (p. 215): 'la natura ha creato gli uomini in modo che possono desiderare ogni cosa e non possono conseguire ogni cosa.'

[227] *Disc.* I, 37 (p. 216).

[228] *Disc.* I, 37 (p. 218).

[229] In *Arte d. guerra*, IV (p. 440), generals who wish their soldiers to fight well are advised not to let them send their possessions home or to leave them in a safe place, 'so that they understand that, if they flee to save their lives, they will lose their goods (*roba*), the love of which is usually not less effective than the desire to live in making men fight strongly.'

[230] *Princ.* XVII (p. 70).

[231] *Ibid.*: 'sopra a tutto, astenersi dalla roba d'altri; perché li uomini sdimenticano piú presto la morte del padre che la perdita del patrimonio.' See also *Disc.* III, 23 (p. 455).

back to life, whereas men can always hope that a change of ruler or regime might lead to their property being restored.[232]

Machiavelli returns to this theme in chapter XIX, which is concerned with the avoidance of contempt and hatred, observing that a ruler incurs hatred

above all, for being rapacious and for taking the property and women of his subjects; one must refrain from doing this. Most men will be happy if they are not deprived of either property or honour, and one will then have to deal only with the ambition of the few.[233]

Machiavelli discusses the injuries committed by rulers in *Discorsi*, III, 6, which is concerned with conspiracies; he distinguishes between injuries relating to life (*sangue*), property (*roba*), and honour (*onore*). Apart from threats to their lives

offences against property and honour are what weigh most heavily with men. And a ruler should always be very careful about these matters, because even if one strips a man of all his property he may still revenge himself with his knife. And if a man is completely dishonoured, he will harbour a desire for revenge. And of offences against honour, those against women are the most important, and then offences against one's own person (*vilipendio della sua persona*).[234]

Although Machiavelli does not actually say so, possessions and honour should probably be regarded as closely linked; for the seizure of one's property results in dishonour as well as impoverishment. It is perhaps significant that Machiavelli usually speaks of possessions as *roba* (or *patrimonio*) rather than as 'riches' (*ricchezze*); despite what he says in *Discorsi*, I, 37, he probably thought that most men see them as things more to be preserved than increased.

All men, then, desire to preserve their possessions and guard their honour. And the vast majority wish, above all, not to be oppressed or interfered with. According to Machiavelli, this is the dominant charac-

232 Niccolò Machiavelli, *Opere complete* (Florence, 1857), p. 1146 (cited by *Burd*, p. 294): 'Gli uomini si dolgono più d'uno podere che sia loro tolto, che d'uno fratello o padre che fussi loro morto, perché la morte si dimentica qualche volta, la roba mai. La ragione è in pronta; perché ognun sa che per la mutazione d'uno stato, uno fratello non può risuscitare, ma e' può bene riavere el podere.'
233 *Princ.* XIX (p. 75): 'Odioso lo fa, sopr'a tutto . . . lo essere rapace et usurpatore della roba e delle donne de' sudditi: di che si debbe astenere; e qualunque volta alle universalità delli uomini non si toglie né roba né onore, vivono contenti, e solo si ha a combattere con la ambizione di pochi.'
234 *Disc.* III, 6 (pp. 391–392).

teristic of the masses.[235] They do not seek glory but they wish to preserve their good names.

What about other men, those who do not belong to 'the masses'? Machiavelli is most interested in those who are active in war, politics, and diplomacy. He says little about the typical character of soldiers but when discussing the Roman emperors he emphasises the 'cruelty and avarice of the soldiers,' remarking that

> it was difficult to satisfy both the soldiers and the people; for the people liked tranquillity and therefore preferred moderate rulers, while the soldiers liked rulers of military spirit, who were insolent, cruel, and rapacious. And they wanted these qualities to be exercised on the people, so that they could have double pay and satisfy their own avarice and cruelty.[236]

Whereas generals usually desire military success and glory, soldiers (especially mercenaries) tend to desire victory in order to secure the spoils of war.[237] *Discorsi*, I, 43, is concerned with the theme that 'Those Who Fight for Their Own *Gloria* Are Good and Faithful Soldiers,' and he stresses the difference between 'a contented army . . . that fights for its own *gloria*' and one 'that fights for the ambition of others,' as mercenary armies do. Although it may be concluded that soldiers fighting for their country are motivated by glory, it is probably not so strong as the desire for booty, partly because victory brings a soldier only a share of the collective glory, partly because no man lives by glory alone and the more concrete fruits of victory seem more attractive.

The qualities that Machiavelli attributes to those active in public life are ambition (a desire to advance oneself and one's own interests), arrogance, haughtiness, a disposition to command and oppress the masses.[238] These are the dominant traits of what may be called 'the ruling classes.' Members of great families usually play a part in public affairs[239] and expect to occupy important posts (*gradi* or *onori*); they are easily offended

---

[235] E.g., *Princ.* XVII (p. 70), XIX (p. 75); *Disc.* I, 16 (p. 176), II, 28 (pp. 363–365), III, 6 (pp. 391–392).

[236] *Princ.* XIX (pp. 78–79).

[237] E.g., in *Discorsi*, I, 29 (p. 198), he says that when a general conquers territory for a ruler, 'he covers himself with *gloria* and his soldiers with booty (*ricchezze*).' See also *Disc.* III, 23 (p. 454).

[238] E.g., *Princ.* IX (pp. 45–46), XIX (pp. 77–78); *Disc.* I, 2 (p. 134), I, 3 (p. 135), I, 5 (pp. 139, 141), I, 9 (p. 155), I, 16 (pp. 175–176), I, 37 (p. 218), I, 40 (pp. 227–228), I, 41 (p. 230); *Ist. fior.* III, 1 (p. 212).

[239] Machiavelli emphasises that important men cannot expect to retire from public life (*Disc.* III, 2 [p. 385]).

if their expectations are disappointed, or if their honour is slighted in other ways. If they already have important posts, they want to keep them. They naturally tend to seek political or military glory but, since they want to preserve their social position, they are also very attached to their property. Ministers or officials desire honours and riches, which wise rulers bestow plentifully in order to keep them contented and faithful.[240]

It is clear, however, that Machiavelli did not think that all men prominent in public life sought glory. Mediocre rulers or generals, easily satisfied by a quiet or comfortable life, do not seek it.[241] It might be assumed that important rulers aim at glory but this assumption may not be correct. Thus Machiavelli advises Raffaello Girolami, who was about to go to the Spanish Court as Florentine envoy, to observe carefully whether the Emperor Charles V 'is inclined to war or peace, whether he is moved by *gloria* or by some other passion.'[242]

Nevertheless, Machiavelli gives much weight to glory as a motive or goal. Although men sometimes perform great or glorious deeds because they are impelled by 'necessity,' by the exigencies of the situations in which they find themselves (and so glory is, as it were, thrust upon them),[243] the impulse is often as much internal as external; some men have a natural inclination to seek glory. The ancient Romans, who were great lovers of glory,[244] understood this very well. The theme of *Discorsi*, II, 33, is that their generals were given a free hand so that they could act more effectively,[245] and the case of the consul Fabius Maximus Rullianus is discussed at length. The senators thought that close supervision would diminish the glory that he would gain from victories. They wanted Fabius to act as seemed best to him 'and the glory to be all his, judging that the love of glory would be a sufficient constraint and inducement for him to operate well.'[246] It was the desire for glory that led to the ruin of Manlius Capitolinus. Being envious of the honours accorded to Furius Camillus, and thinking that his services to Rome

[240] *Princ.* XXII (p. 94).
[241] See above, pp. 607–610.
[242] *Memoriale a Raffaello Girolami* . . . (*Arte della guerra e scritti politici minori*, p. 286): 'se egli ama la guerra o la pace, se la gloria lo muove o altra sua passione.'
[243] *Disc.* III, 12 (p. 425).
[244] *Disc.* I, 36 (p. 214), II, 9 (p. 301).
[245] 'Come i Romani davano agli loro capitani degli eserciti le commissioni libere.'
[246] *Disc.* II, 33 (p. 378).

merited equal esteem, he stirred up sedition, and was executed.[247] His previous fine deeds were cancelled by his ambition, which blinded him to the appropriate way to act. And Machiavelli draws the conclusion that 'in corrupt states the means of attaining *gloria* are different from those appropriate in states that are still incorrupt.' In other words, 'men in their actions and especially in great matters should consider the times and circumstances and act accordingly.'[248] Claudius Nero, who had allowed himself to be tricked by Hasdrubal in Spain when he had the Carthaginian general at his mercy, and had in consequence suffered 'great dishonour and contempt,' later undertook a very risky manoeuvre against the Carthaginians, and being reproached, said, according to Machiavelli,[249] that 'he knew that if he succeeded he would regain the *gloria* that he had lost in Spain, but that if he failed . . . he would be revenged against the city and the citizens that had offended him so ungratefully and imprudently.'[250] Alexander the Great, besieging the republic of Tyre, perceived that its long and stout resistance threatened to tarnish his glory, and tried to reach an agreement with the city.[251] The Duke of Athens thought that it was 'the mark of a pusillanimous man not to undertake a glorious enterprise because its success could not be guaranteed.'[252] Michele di Lando sought glory by attacking his enemies rather than waiting for them to assault him.[253] And in the last chapter of *Il Principe*, Machiavelli urges the Medici to take the lead in the glorious enterprise of freeing Italy from foreign domination, reminding them that although God has provided a fine opportunity, 'the rest must be done by you; God does not want to do everything, in order not to deprive us of our freedom (*libero arbitrio*) and of the share of *gloria* that belongs to us.'[254]

[247] *Disc.* I, 8 (p. 150).
[248] *Disc.* III, 8 (p. 415).
[249] Several commentators point out that there are some confusions in Machiavelli's account; e.g., that, according to Livy, it was Livius Salinator who spoke the words quoted.
[250] *Disc.* III, 17 (p. 439).
[251] *Disc.* II, 27 (p. 361).
[252] *Ist. fior.* II, 35 (p. 194).
[253] *Ist. fior.* III, 17 (p. 247).
[254] *Princ.* XXVI (p. 103). For other references to glory as a motive or goal, see *Princ.* VII (p. 33), XIV (p. 64), XXIV (p. 97); *Disc.* I, 1 (pp. 126, 128), I, 10 (pp. 156–159), I, 30 (p. 201), I, 36 (p. 214), I, 43 (p. 231), I, 58 (p. 264), II, Proemio (p. 271), II, 9 (p. 301), II, 22 (p. 344), II, 27 (p. 362), III, 35 (p. 483), III, 45 (p. 501); *Ist. fior.* II, 32 (p. 186), III, 5 (pp. 219, 220), IV, 28 (p. 314), V, 8 (p. 339), V, 11 (pp. 344–345), VI, 4 (p. 393), VI, 29 (p. 433),

While it is evident that Machiavelli did not consider that tyrants and ambitious men (like Agathocles) achieved glory, it is not so clear whether he thought that they sought glory. It should probably be inferred from what he says in *Discorsi*, I, 10, that he believed that such men did seek glory, but of a false or perverted kind. He says that although men will praise what ought to be praised and condemn what ought to be condemned, in practice 'nearly all men, seduced by a false good and a false glory (*falsa gloria*), either consciously or unconsciously, allow themselves to follow paths that deserve more blame than praise.'[255]

*

The reconstruction of Machiavelli's thoughts about glory is now complete; I have put together what seems to go together. The account given has been constructive rather than critical, and it is to be hoped that it does no violence to his thought, in other words, that it is the sort of account he would have written if he had set down systematically his thoughts on the subject. It remains to comment briefly on the leading features of his thinking about glory, and to remark some of its limitations.

These limitations are the natural consequence of Machiavelli's cast of mind. He was predominantly concerned with what he saw as concrete realities, and his treatment of them is usually orderly and well presented. Thus when he discusses mercenary, auxiliary, and mixed troops,[256] he defines his terms (as far as is necessary) and treats systematically the advantages and disadvantages of these forms of militia. He was, of course, also concerned with the ideals that men pursue (and with those that they should pursue) but he was less interested in questions of this sort; and in treating ideas or concepts (e.g., *virtù, fortuna, necessità*) he usually[257] did not think it appropriate to define or elaborate them.

It is in no way surprising, therefore, that his thinking about glory is

---

VII, 26 (p. 492), VII, 32 (pp. 501–502); *Arte d. guerra*, I (p. 338); *Allocuzione fatta ad un magistrato (Arte della guerra e scritti politici minori*, p. 137), *Discursus florentinarum rerum post mortem iunioris Laurentii Medices (op. cit.*, pp. 275–276); *Lettere*, pp. 254, 260, 270, 277, 288, 352.

255 *Disc.* I, 10 (p. 156). Cf. the comments in *Ist. fior.* III, 5 (pp. 219–220), about 'quello appetito non di vera gloria, ma di vituperosi onori dal quale dependono gli odi, le nimicizie, i dispareri, le sètte.'

256 *Princ.* XII–XIII.

257 There are exceptions; e.g., *prudenzia* is defined in *Princ.* XXI (p. 92) [see above, p. 597], and there is a rather peculiar definition of *onore* in *Disc.* II, 23 (p. 347).

not notable for its conceptual grasp. He throws no light at all on the meaning of glory; indeed, what exactly he understands by it has to be inferred,[258] and no consideration is given to the relations between different kinds of glory. Thus the relation between political and military glory is not explored. And, consequently, some discrepancies are to be discerned. In view of what Machiavelli says about Julius Caesar's lack of genuine glory,[259] it may be wondered why he should ascribe glory to Octavian.[260] But it is clear that he is referring to the military glory that Octavian won, and is not concerned with his political role. In Machiavelli's discussion of Caesar, it is the part that he played in ruining the Roman republic that is considered, and whether Caesar's military exploits merited glory is irrelevant. Again, when Machiavelli denies glory to Agathocles,[261] because of the criminal way in which he seized power, it is evident that he has political glory in mind. Yet he emphasises how ably and successfully Agathocles conducted his military campaigns; may it not be said that Agathocles acquired (or merited) military glory? It might be inferred that, if Machiavelli had discussed the relationship between political and military glory, he would have said that acting in ways that are incompatible with political glory does not prevent a man from meriting or gaining military glory. The relationship between political and military glory, then, remains somewhat obscure. Nevertheless, what is clear is that there is a moral element in Machiavelli's notion of political glory, that he thought that there were modes of conduct incompatible with political glory, whereas this element is absent from his notion of military glory, for this sort of glory is achieved through deserved success in war, whatever the methods used. In short, Machiavelli says much about the actions or methods that gain glory, do not gain it, or cause it to be tarnished or lost, and, despite a few ambiguities, oddities, and obscurities, it may be said to compose a consistent doctrine.

Machiavelli's emphasis on worldly glory as a goal is very striking, and perhaps this aspect of his thought is of most importance. For him, the desire for worldly glory was far from being 'that last infirmity of noble mind.'[262] 'Scorning delights' (or the *ombre* of the palace or tent)

---

[258] See above, p. 589.
[259] See above, pp. 594 and 610.
[260] *Disc.* I, 52 (p. 248).
[261] See above, pp. 610–611.
[262] Milton, *Lycidas*, line 71.

and 'living laborious days' attending to affairs of state or engaged in military campaigns was highly praiseworthy. Machiavelli's ideal was not an easy, indolent life but one that was active and energetic, exploiting one's *virtù* to the full. The detailed attention that he pays to military glory is significant. Even if he believed political glory to be of higher value, he thought that rulers should also be skilled in military matters, and capable of achieving military glory.[263] This sort of glory, of course, is almost always gained through war; as Hobbes observes, 'there is no honour military but by war.'[264] Yet war exacts its toll; men will die or be wounded; it brings rapine, destruction, and ruin. The path that leads some men to glory will lead others to their graves; but Machiavelli shows little awareness of this darker side, and certainly did not see military glory (as Lincoln did) as an 'attractive rainbow that rises in showers of blood.'[265]

Machiavelli's emphasis on worldly glory as a goal runs counter to the dominant trend of Christian thought and reveals a way of thinking characteristic of the ancient world, of the Greeks and perhaps especially of the Romans. Glory or fame occupied an important place in Roman thought,[266] as is testified by the writings of historians like Sallust, Livy, and Tacitus, and poets like Virgil and Ovid. Yet emphasis on the ideal of glory often went together with an awareness of its insubstantiality. Even Cicero, who wrote much about glory (he composed a treatise *De gloria*—now lost), and stressed its value,[267] acknowledged that a man could not *enjoy* genuine or lasting glory.[268] Again, there is scarcely a hint of this in Machiavelli's writings; he neglects what might be called the psychology of the search for glory.

The ancient attitude to worldly glory was rejected by Christian

---

263 Freyer, 'The Ideas of Machiavelli,' p. 20, remarks that 'the idea [*gloria*] is only pragmatically moral' and says that coming 'neither from closet virtue nor from selfishly ambitious achievement, it must be civic renown, and in the constant flux of warring peoples, civic renown becomes inevitably military renown, almost inevitably military conquest.'

264 *Leviathan*, ch. 11.

265 Abraham Lincoln, *Complete Works*, ed. John G. Nicolay and John Hay (New York, 1894), I, 106.

266 Ulrich Knoche, 'Der römische Ruhmesgedanke,' *Philologus*, 89 (1934), 102–124; Donald C. Earl, *The Political Thought of Sallust* (Cambridge, 1961), esp. ch. I; *idem*, *The Moral and Political Tradition of Rome*, passim.

267 E.g., *Pro Archia poeta*, vi–xii; *Pro Milone*, xxxv; *Tusc. Disp.* III, ii; *De Officiis*, II, ix–xiv.

268 *Tusc. Disp.* I, xxxviii. Cf. *Pro Archia*, xii.

writers, not only by spiritual and unworldly men like Thomas a Kempis,[269] but also by such theologians and philosophers as St. Augustine and St. Thomas Aquinas. In *De Civitate Dei*, Augustine maintains that the desire for human honour should be avoided, 'the glory of the righteous being wholly in God.'[270] 'To the virtuous,' he says, 'contempt of glory is a great virtue.'[271] Aquinas, in *De Regimine Principum*, is less outspoken; but he claims both that 'human glory' is an insufficient reward for the kingly office,[272] and that it can lead to various evils, such as the attempt to gain military glory by making wars. The genuine reward for good kings, in his view, is the 'incorruptible crown of heavenly glory.'[273]

With the renewed interest in, and study of, the classical world, some of the ancient values became increasingly admired in Renaissance Italy; the emphasis on the individual and the place that he could mark out for himself in the world led naturally to a view of 'human glory' that owed more to classical (or pagan) ideas than to those of Christianity.[274] Burckhardt emphasised such phenomena as the cult of the famous men of antiquity, the cult of birthplaces and graves, the coronation of poets, and the interest in biographical studies and writings that preserved and enhanced the glory of great deeds.[275] In the fifteenth and sixteenth centuries, concern with worldly reputation, fame or glory, was very characteristic of enterprising and thoughtful Italians in many spheres, and this concern was reflected in the writings of those who observed and meditated on human nature and conduct: in, among others, Lorenzo de' Medici[276] and Baldesar Castiglione,[277] and in Machiavelli's younger

---

[269] *De Imitatione Christi*, I, 3; II, 6; III, 40, 41.

[270] *De Civitate Dei*, V, 14.

[271] *Ibid.*, V, 19. For a discussion of Augustine's views about *gloria*, see Earl, *The Moral and Political Tradition of Rome*, pp. 127–131.

[272] *De Regimine Principum*, VII.

[273] *Ibid.*, VIII and IX.

[274] Although Dante acknowledged the fragility of fame or worldly glory (*Purg.* XI, 79–117; *Par.* XVI, 79–87), he certainly desired it, and it is an important theme in his writings (see *Inf.* II, 58–60; XV, 106–107; XVI, 66–69; XXIV, 46–57; XXX, 91–93; XXXI, 116, 127; *Purg.* VII, 16–18; VIII, 124–126; X, 73–76; XVIII, 136–138; *Par.* II, 16–18; VI, 48, 112–117; IX, 37–42; XXV, 1–9; *De Monarchia*, I, 1). Petrarch's attitude to glory was very similar, and it is one of his constant themes (e.g., in the *Trionfi*, especially those of *Fama*, *Tempo* and *Eternità*; *Rime*, CLXXXVII, CCLXIV).

[275] Jacob Burckhardt, *The Civilisation of the Renaissance in Italy* (London, 1950), pp. 87–93.

[276] *Rappresentazione di S. Giovanni e Paolo*, 25–30, 133–139.

[277] *Il Libro del Cortegiano*, I, 43, 45, 46.

GLORIA IN MACHIAVELLI   631

contemporaries Francesco Guicciardini[278] and Donato Giannotti.[279] It was not Machiavelli's way to formulate ideas or ideals with any degree of system, but in no writer of his times is the theme of glory more prominent; he expressed common ideas about fame or glory explicitly and vividly.

University of Lancaster   RUSSELL PRICE

[278] *Ricordi*, ed. Raffaele Spongano (Florence, 1951). Sometimes he expressed his views in terms of *gloria* (e.g., C32, C72), sometimes in terms of *onore* (e.g., C15, C118).

[279] *Della republica fiorentina*, II, 20: 'è da notare, che quattro sono le cose dalle quali gli uomini sono mossi; cioè roba, onore, danno o ignominia: ma perché chi teme ignominia è cupido d'onore, e chi teme il danno è cupido della roba, vengono ad essere due le cose che muoveno gli uomini a pigliare qualche impresa; cioè roba e onore.'

[10]

Sixteenth Century Journal
IX,4 (1978)

Cicero's *De Officiis* and Machiavelli's *Prince*

Marcia L. Colish
Oberlin College

Machiavelli's classical sources are a subject which students of his political thought have scarcely neglected. The Roman historians, Polybius, Homer, Aristotle, and Seneca have all received their due.[1] The subject of *virtu*, or, more loosely, Machiavelli's ethical thought, has also stimulated extensive scholarly interest.[2] This being the case, it is surprising to note that no one has explored systematically the connections between Cicero's *De officiis* and Machiavelli's *Prince*. This oversight is indeed curious. The *De officiis* was read and copied more frequently than any other single work of classical Latin prose in the Middle Ages and Renaissance and it played an important formative role in the ethos of the Florentine civil humanists. Scholars have by no means ignored Cicero's place in the thought of trecento and quattrocento Florentines. Yet, the commentators who have compared Machiavelli with Cicero have confined themselves to isolating parallels

[1]On Machiavelli's education see Felix Gilbert, *Machiavelli and Guicciardini: Politics and History in Sixteenth-Century Florence* (Princeton, 1965), pp. 162 ff., 318-22; Roberto Ridolfi, *Life of Niccolo Machiavelli*, trans. Cecil Grayson (Chicago, 1963), ch. 1. On his classical sources see in general Georg Ellinger, *Die antiken Quellen der Staatslehre Machiavelli's*, Sonderabdruck aus der *Zeitschrift fur die gesamte Staatswissenschaft* (Tubingen, 1888) and Friedrich Mehmel, "Machiavelli und die Antike," *Antike und Abendland*, 3 (1948), 152-86. On Machiavelli and Tacitus see Kenneth Charles Schellhase, "Tacitus in the Political Thought of Machiavelli," *Il Pensiero Politico*, 4 (1971), 381-91 and his more recent *Tacitus in Renaissance Political Thought* (Chicago, 1976), ch. 1; on Machiavelli and Livy see J. H. Whitfield, "Machiavelli's Use of Livy," in *Livy*, ed. T. A. Dorey (London, 1971), pp. 73-96; on Machiavell and Frontinus see Neal Wood, "Frontinus as a Possible Source for Machiavelli's Method," *Journal of the History of Ideas*, 28 (1967), 243-48; on Machiavelli and Seneca see Niccolo Machiavelli, *Il principe*, ed. L. Arthur Burd (Oxford, 1891), p. 335 note 2; Allan H. Gilbert, *Machiavelli's Prince and Its Forerunners: The Prince as a Typical Book De Regimine Principum* (Durham, 1938), p. 150; Neal Wood, "Some Common Aspects of the Thought of Seneca and Machiavelli," *Renaissance Quarterly*, 21 (1968), 11-23; on Machiavelli and Homer see John H. Geerken, "Heroic Virtue: An Introduction to the Origins and Nature of a Renaissance Concept," Yale Ph.D. dissertation, 1967 (Ann Arbor: University Microfilms, 1968), esp. ch. 4-6; his conclusions are summarized in "Homer's Image of the Hero in Machiavelli: A Comparison of Arete and Virtu," *Italian Quarterly*, 14 (1970), 45-90; on Machiavelli and Polybius see Arnaldo Momigliano, "Polybius' Reappearance in Western Europe," in *Polybe*, Entretiens sur l'antiquite classique, 20 (Vandoeuvres-Geneve, 1974), 347-72, which supercedes the hypotheses of J. H. Hexter, "Seyssel, Machiavelli, and Polybius VI: The Mystery of the Missing Translation," *Studies in the Renaissance*, 3 (1956), 75-96 and Gennaro Sasso, *Studi su Machiavelli* (Napoli, 1967), pp. 161-280.

[2]See in particular J. H. Whitfield, "The Doctrine of Virtu," *Italian Studies*, 3 (1946-48), 28-33 and Neal Wood, "Machiavelli's Concept of *Virtu* Reconsidered," *Political Studies*, 15 (1967), 159-72. Excellent reviews of the most recent literature on this topic are provided by John H. Geerken, "Machiavelli Studies since 1969," *JHI*, 37 (1976), 360-63 and Russell Price, "The Senses of Virtu in Machiavelli," *European Studies Review*, 3 (1973), 315-45.

82   The Sixteenth Century Journal

between his writings and the *De officiis*. Their reading of the *De officiis* has been all too casual and they have generally stressed the idea that Machiavelli made a decisive departure both from the *De officiis* itself and from its use by his medieval and Renaissance predecessors.

However, a sustained analysis of the *De officiis* in comparison with the *Prince* will show that Cicero's work was capable of providing Machiavelli with much more than a few isolated *topoi* or with an ethical ideal against which he could formulate his own, more pragmatic position. The *De officiis* could supply Machiavelli with these things but it also could provide him with a way of defining his ethical terminology and a structural framework for the analysis of the ethics of public life. Machiavelli could, and, it is argued in this paper, did apply this Ciceronian bequest in a positive as well as in a negative way, conscious of how his simultaneously straightforward and ironic uses of Cicero would resonate in the ears of his contemporaries. This contention requires a close reading of the *De officiis*, since it is this side of the comparison that has received short shrift. We need to see what is actually going on in this treatise before we will be in any position to assess the extent to which Machiavelli may be standing Cicero on his head in the *Prince*.

The aspect of this thesis that is the easiest to demonstrate is the sheer accessibility of the *De officiis* in the Middle Ages and Renaissance and the intimate familiarity with it that characterized Florentine thought up through Machiavelli's day. The evidence to this effect, from the manuscript tradition, from the direct and indirect *testimonia*, and from the flood of both handwritten texts and printed editions in the fifteenth century is, in a word, overwhelming.[3] More than 600 manuscripts of the *De officiis* survive. It is one of a handful of classical Latin works whose textual tradition can be traced with confidence back to antiquity. The indirect tradition is so massive and complex that it is too intractable to be useful to modern editors in establishing the text. Vernacular translations, no less than Latin texts, abounded in the Middle Ages, including Italian, German, and Icelandic versions and thirty-eight in Old French alone. The multiplication of Latin manuscripts reached its high-water mark in the Renaissance and no less than thirty-four printed editions were published in the fifteenth century. Florentine readers in that period would have faced no difficulties in con-

[3]On what follows in the next two paragraphs see in particular Paolo Fedeli, "Il 'De officiis' di Cicerone: Problemi e atteggiamenti della critica moderna," *Aufstieg und Niedergang der romischen Welt: Geschichte und Kultur Roms im Spiegel der neueren Forschung*, ed. Hildegard Temporini (Berlin, 1973), IV, part 1, pp. 357-427; N. E. Nelson, "Cicero's *De officiis* in Christian Thought: 300-1300," *Essays and Studies in English and Comparative Literature*, University of Michigan Publications in Language and Literature, 10 (Ann Arbor, 1933), pp. 59-160; Marcus Tullius Cicero, *Les Devoirs*, ed. and trans. Maurice Testard (Paris, 1965), I, pp. 67-77, 86-92. Of more limited use are J. T. Muckle, "The Influence of Cicero in the Formation of Christian Culture," *Proceedings and Transactions of the Royal Society of Canada*, 3rd ser., 42 (1948), pp. 113-25 and Ettore Paratore, "Cicerone attraverso i secoli," *Marco Tullio Cicerone*, Scritti commemorativi pubblicati nel bimillenario della morte, Istituto di studi romani, Centro di studi ciceroniani (Firenze, 1961), pp. 243-46.

sulting the *De officiis*. The catalogue of the library of San Marco, compiled at the end of the fifteenth century, lists four quattrocento manuscript copies and one printed edition, published in Venice in 1482.[4]

Even more extensive are the uses to which the *De officiis* was put from the patristic age up through the quattrocento. During the Middle Ages, it was the most authoritative, most frequently cited, and most commonly imitated treatise on classical ethics, considered both in itself and in conjunction with Christian ethics. Cicero's influence outstripped that of all other classical authors on topics such as social utility, civic virtue, the application of moral rules to times, places, and circumstances, and the relations between virtue and expediency. From the days of St. Ambrose onward the *De officiis* was a popular model for treatises on the duties of churchmen. From the days of Lactantius onward it provided guidelines for the ethics of statesmanship and public service, a theme reformulated in the genre of the mirror of princes as early as the Carolingian period. By the thirteenth century the *De officiis* was being used with increasing frequency, along with Aristotle's *Politics* and the pseudo-Plutarchan *Institutio Traiani*, by Italian lay authors seeking models for governance in the city-state republics. Florentines, or men in the employ of Florence, led the field, from Giovanni Nanni to Albertano da Brescia to Brunetto Latini to Dante.

It was Petrarch who launched Cicero on the distinctive course he was to sail in the Florentine humanist tradition. Cicero was important to Petrarch for many reasons--as a stylistic and formal model, as an exponent of the union of wisdom, virtue, and eloquence, and as an existential analogue of his own tensions over the active versus the contemplative life, no less than as a defender of republican institutions and as an authority on the attributes of the virtuous and successful statesman.[5] As is well known, this constellation of ideas was assimilated by a series of Florentine civic thinkers in the fourteenth and fifteenth centuries, who combined Petrarch's Ciceronianism with a number of other complementary sources.[6] One of the

[4]Berthold L. Ullman and Philip A. Stadter, *The Public Library of Renaissance Florence: Niccolo Niccoli, Cosimo de' Medici and the Library of San Marco*, Medioevo e umanesimo, 10 (Padova, 1972), cat. numbers 864, 874, 876, 878, 883. The last noted is the printed edition.

[5]The best study of Petrarch's use of Cicero in this connection is Arpad Steiner, "Petrarch's *Optimus Princeps*," *Romanic Review*, 25 (1934), 99-111. (I am indebted to Benjamin G. Kohl for this reference.) In more general terms see also Aldo S. Bernardo, *Petrarch, Scipio and the "Africa": The Birth of Humanism's Dream* (Baltimore, 1962), pp. 5, 9-10, 98-102 and passim; and Walter Ruegg, *Cicero und der Humanismus: Formale Untersuchungen uber Petrarca und Erasmus* (Zurich, 1946), pp. 7-63.

[6]Hans Baron, "Cicero and the Roman Civic Spirit in the Middle Ages and Early Renaissance," *Journal of the John Rylands Library*, 22 (1938), 73-97; *The Crisis of the Early Italian Renaissance: Civic Humanism and Republican Liberty in an Age of Classicism and Tyranny*, rev. ed. (Princeton, 1966), pp. 121-34; "La rinascita dell'etica statale nell'umanesimo fiorentino del quattrocento," *Civilta moderna*, 7 (1935), pp. 3-31; "Franciscan Poverty and Civic Wealth as Factors in the Rise of Humanistic Thought," *Speculum*, 13 (1938), pp. 1-37.

84 The Sixteenth Century Journal

most impressive features of the use of the *De officiis* from the Middle Ages up through the quattrocento, a feature of this tradition that has sometimes been ignored, is its preservation of the values of political realism and expediency, its stress on the active life of public service, and its conception of virtue as decisive and energetic activity and not merely as an inner mental intentionality.[7] There was also a more idealistic use of Cicero, reinforced by the medieval theologians who had appropriated the *De officiis* for more strictly ecclesiastical purposes. This theological tradition elevated the *honestum* over the *utile* and placed the value of expediency under the rule of a higher law, whether natural or divine. Some scholars have tried to confine the medieval and Renaissance influence of the *De officiis* prior to Machiavelli to the theological strand in the tradition, underestimating its other aspect, an approach that has led them to see Machiavelli as effecting a sharp break with his classical, Christian, and humanistic forebears.[8] Correctives to this one-sided interpretation have been provided by a number of recent studies which have examined the medieval and Renaissance tradition of the *De officiis* in a more evenhanded manner. But, since Machiavelli was at the same time fully capable of using the *De officiis* directly, we must also go back to Cicero himself.

Several attempts to assemble parallels between the *De officiis* and the *Prince* have been made, although the scholars who have assembled them have been disinclined to do very much with them once having acknowledged their existence.[9] The one most frequently noted is Cicero's reference to the lion and the fox, under the rubric of the ruler's need to play

[7]These aspects have been noted by Isaiah Berlin, "The Originality of Machiavelli," *Studies in Machiavelli*, ed. Myron P. Gilmore (Firenze, 1972), pp. 163, 180, 200; Geerken, "Heroic Virtue," 58-73, 79, 304 n. 7, and appendix 4, although he attributes this position primarily to Homeric influence; Nelson, "Cicero's *De Officiis*," *loc. cit.*, 62 and passim; J. H. Whitfield, *Machiavelli* (Oxford, 1947), pp. 99-101, 103; "The Doctrine of Virtu," *loc. cit.*; Wood, "Machiavelli's Concept of *Virtu*," *loc. cit.*, p. 160.

[8]The most important statements of this view are Felix Gilbert, "The Humanist Concept of the Prince and *The Prince* of Machiavelli," *Journal of Modern History*, 11 (1939), pp. 449-83, esp. part II; "Machiavellism," in *History: Choice and Commitment* (Cambridge, Mass., 1977), pp. 155-56; Gioacchino Paparelli, "Virtu e fortuna nel medioevo, nel rinascimento e in Machiavelli," *Cultura e scuola*, 9 (1970), pp. 76-89; Niccolo Machiavelli, *The Discourses*, trans. Leslie J. Walker, with a new intro. and appendix by Cecil H. Clough (London, 1975), II, p. 288.

[9]The most exhaustive list is provided by Walker, *op. cit.*, II, table 13, pp. 277-79. Walker contradicts himself in a most peculiar manner, however. Despite the citations he lists, he asserts, on the one hand, "that in the *Prince* there is no reference to Cicero at all, . . .(suggesting) that with Cicero's works Machiavelli had no acquaintance," II, p. 277; while on the other hand, he says, "It would seem, then, to be almost certain that Machiavelli had read the *De Officiis* but the result was not that he found himself in agreement with Cicero's doctrine . . . but that he took up on the main issue a diametrically opposed position," II, p. 288.

the role of the beast on occasion.[10] Next is the parallel idea in Cicero and Machiavelli that circumstances alter cases, suspending at times the moral rules that would otherwise be binding.[11] Other parallels include the question of whether it is safer to rule through love or fear[12] and whether and how the ruler should exercise liberality,[13] along with the advice that he should refrain from seizing other people's property[14] and the ideas that people are generally selfish[15] and that prudence consists in choosing the lesser evil as good.[16] Like the maxim *"fortuna fortes adiuvat,"* which Cicero cites in his *Tusculan Disputations* and which most of the Roman historians repeat in one form or another and which Machiavelli recycles in the twenty-fifth chapter of the *Prince*, these notions are not what any reader conversant with the classics would regard as shattering new insights into politics or the human condition. They are essentially commonplaces, recognized and used as such by all concerned from Cicero's day to Machiavelli's.

Much more important is Cicero's overall argument in the *De officiis*, the way he defines his terms, and the resonances with Cicero's personal situation which Machiavelli may well have felt at the point in his own life when he was writing the *Prince*.[17] Cicero had attained the consulate, the

[10]Marcus Tullius Cicero, *De officiis* 1.11.34, 1.13.41., ed. Testard: Niccolo Machiavelli, *Il Principe* 18, in *Il principe e altri scritti*, ed. Gennaro Sasso (Firenze, 1963). Among scholars who have noted this parallel see Burd, *op. cit.*, 301 n. 1, 302 n. 2; Ellinger, *op. cit.*, 49-50; Mehmel, "Machiavelli und die Antike," *loc. cit.*, 159; Giuseppe Prezzolini, *Machiavelli*, trans. Gioconda Savini (New York, 1967), 98-99; Sasso, comm. on his ed. of *Il principe*, 151 notes 2, 7. Eric W. Cochrane, "Machiavelli: 1940-1960," *J. of Mod. Hist.*, 33 (1961), 129, describes this parallel as a generally recognized one, although his citation to the relevant passage of *De off.* is incorrect.

[11]*De off.* 1.10.31-32: *Il principe* 25. Noted by Berlin, "The Originality of Machiavelli," *loc. cit.*, p. 200; Whitfield, *Machiavelli*, pp. 68, 70-71, 74, although Whitfield attributes the citation to Book 4 of the *De off.*, which has only three books.

[12]*De off.* 2.7.23: *Il principe* 17, 19, 20. Noted by Burd, *op. cit.*, p. 355 n. 2; A. H. Gilbert, *op. cit.*, p. 150.

[13]*De off.*, 1.14.42-1.16.52, 2.15.52-2.18.64: *Il principe* 15-16. Noted by Burd, *op.cit.*, pp. 286-87 n. 15; A. H. Gilbert, *op. cit.*, 89; Whitfield, *Machiavelli*, 124.

[14]*De off.* 1.14.42: *Il principe* 16, 17, 19. Noted by Ellinger, *op. cit.*, pp. 50-51.

[15]*De off.* 1.25.46, 3.17.70: *Il principe* 18. Noted by Burd, *op. cit.*, p. 303 n. 9.

[16]*De off.* 3.13.53-3.15.61: *Il principe* 21. Noted by Burd, *op. cit.*, pp. 344-45 n. 8.

[17]An excellent analysis of the *De off.* with a guide to the literature on this work is supplied by Klaus Bringmann, *Untersuchungen zum spaten Cicero*, Hypomnemata, 29 (Gottingen, 1971), pp. 229-50. Other good recent assessments include Domenico Romano, "Motivi politici ed autobiografici nel 'De officiis' di Cicerone," *Annali del Liceo classico "G. Garibaldi" di Palermo*, n.s. 5-6 (1968-69), 21-31 and Testard, intro. to his ed. of *De off.*, I, pp. 52-66. The existential parallel with Machiavelli as the author of the *Prince* has been misunderstood by the Machiavelli scholar who noted it thus far, Martin Fleisher, "A Passion for Politics: The Vital Core of the World of Machiavelli," in *Machiavelli and the Nature of Political Thought*, ed. Martin Fleisher (New York, 1972), p. 118.

highest office in the Roman Republic. But Julius Caesar's rise to power had
relegated him to the status of a political outsider. It took Cicero several
years to internalize this state of affairs, although it may be doubted whether
his personal and partisan hopes were ever completely dimmed. He was
forced to spend his last years in retirement, writing a series of philosophical
works on political theory, law, theology, cosmology, and ethics. In these
works he sought simultaneously to console himself, to advertise his
qualifications for public office, to accuse his enemies, to advocate the
republican form of government, and to develop a rationale for *otium lit-
terarium* as the conduct of statecraft by other means. The *De officiis* was
Cicero's last work and it reflects all of these concerns. It is also the last in a
series of ethical writings in which he sought to formulate his own moral
philosophy. For this purpose he drew heavily on the ethics of Stoicism,
particularly on the middle Stoic Panaetius,[18] but he redefined Stoic terminology and criteria significantly in the light of other moral values which
he prized and as a function of his own personal vision of politics.[19]

The *De officiis* consists of three books, the first treating the *honestum*,
the second treating the *utile*, and the third seeking to reconcile them. At
least, that is Cicero's ostensible program. The initial problem and terminology are Stoic. Had he used his terms in a Stoic sense he would have
defined the *honestum* as the *summum et unicum bonum* and the *utile* as a
synonym of the Stoic preferables, or *adiaphora*, conducive to virtue under
certain circumstances but, taken by themselves, as morally neutral en bloc.
The reconciliation of the *honestum* and the *utile* would be achieved simply
by asserting that the *honestum*, being intrinsically good and an end in itself,
should be the changeless criterion by which the admissability of the *utile*
should be judged. However, this is not the argument which Cicero in fact
puts forth in the *De officiis*. Instead, he elevates the *utile* to the level of an
ethical criterion in its own right, making it the norm of the *honestum*. He

---

[18]*De off.* 1.1.2, 1.2.6; *Ad Atticum* 420.4, ed. and trans. D. R. Shackleton Bailey, 6 vols.
(Cambridge, 1965-68).

[19]On Cicero's sources for this work see the intro. to the literature provided by Testard,
intro. to his ed. of *De off.*, I, 25-49; also Fedeli, "Il 'De officiis' di Cicerone," *loc. cit.*, pp. 361-
75; Philipp Finger, "Das stoische und das akademische Fuhrerbild in Cicero's Schrift De officiis
(1. Buch)," *Neue Jarhbucher fur Antike und deutsche Bildung*, 5 (1942), 1-20; Hans Armin
Gartner, *Cicero und Panaitios: Beobachtungen zu Ciceros De officiis*, Berichte der
Heidelberger Akademie der Wissenschaften, philosophischhistorische Klasse, 5 (Heidelberg,
1974); Heinrich Jungblut, "Cicero und Panatius im zweiten Buch uber die Pflichten," *Beilage
zum Programm des Lessing-Gymnasiums zu Frankfurt a. M. Ostern 1910* (Frankfurt, 1910);
Georg Kilb, "Ethische Grundbegriffe der alten Stoa und ihre Ubertragung durch Cicero," in
Das neue Cicerobild, ed. Karl Buchner, Wege der Forschung, 27 (Darmstadt, 1971), pp. 38-64.
Quinto Cautadella, "Sulle fonti del 'De officiis' di Cicerone," *Atti del I congresso internazionale di studi ciceroniani, Roma, aprile 1959* (Roma, 1961), II, pp. 479-91 stresses
Platonic sources and Ettore Lepore, *Il princeps ciceroniano e gli ideali politici della tarda
repubblica* (Napoli, 1954), p. 387 stresses Aristotelianism.

also redefines the *honestum* itself, treating it not as Stoic virtue, which he sees as inhuman and unattainable in practice, but as the *medium officium*, the intermediate duty of the public man, which can be achieved in the real world and which pertains to the *usus vitae*, the needs of daily life.[20]

Cicero begins his scaling down and redefinition of the *honestum* in his discussion of the four cardinal virtues in Book One. Wisdom is not the leading virtue in the group, since the other virtues are more directly concerned with those things on which the practical business of life depends, *"quibus actio vitae continetur."*[21] Still, he says, wisdom, as the quest for truth, has its application in the avoidance of credulity and excessive concern for subjects that are obscure or useless.[22] Rather than judging what is useful, wisdom itself is thus subjected to the norm of utility. Justice, for Cicero, is the paramount virtue, for the duties flowing from it above all *"pertinent ad hominum utilitatem."*[23] Cicero combines the traditional Platonic and Aristotelian *suum cuique* formula with the defense of private rights drawn from Roman law. Justice prevents us from injuring others, except when we are punishing injuries, and it leads us to use common possessions for the common good and private property for private interests. In applying these principles Cicero stresses at some length that circumstances alter cases. There are some occasions when cruelty is in order and when we are excused from the normal obligations of trust, truthfulness, and good faith. One criterion which Cicero invokes in this connection is equity and common sense. But a second criterion which he invokes is prudence and necessity. In particular, political life frequently requires us to apply the latter rule. We should conduct war and peace without guile or violence, if possible. But, while such strategies are bestial rather than human, we may have to use them as a last resort. This is the context in which Cicero mentions the famous analogy of the lion and the fox.[24] Cicero also treats the topic of beneficence and liberality as a subspecies of justice, applying the same general norms.[25] We should be liberal, he says, so as to harm no one and so as to benefit ourselves and our friends, measuring our generosity according to the services that the recipient has rendered or is likely to render *"ad nostras utilitates."*[26] The needs of the recipient are the least important consideration. Thus Cicero adjusts his major virtue, justice, to expediency.

[20]*De off.* 1.3.7-10.

[21]*De off.* 1.5.17.

[22]*De off.*1.6.18-19.

[23]*De off.* 1.43.155.

[24]For this whole discussion of justice, *De off.* 1.7.20-1.13.41, with the lion and fox passage at 1.13.41.

[25]*De off.* 1.14.42-1.18.59.

Machiavelli II

The same kind of analysis holds true for courage and temperance. For Cicero courage is practical not only because it endows its possessor with equanimity but also because it enhances his wealth and family position, *"cum in augendis opibus utilitatibusque et sibi et suis comparandis."*[27] While, on the one hand, Cicero asserts that no one attains true glory who has achieved a reputation for courage by treachery,[28] he observes, on the other hand, that courage bespeaks the desire to perform deeds that are simultaneously great and useful in the highest degree, *"res geras magnas illas quidem et maxime utiles."*[29] Striking a note of personal propaganda, he adds that statesmanship and scholarship may be more courageous than military service, underlining the point by quoting a line from the poem he wrote on his own consulship, *"cedant arma togae, concedat laurea laudi."*[30] The final virtue, temperance or *decorum*, which governs the exercise of the other three, is oriented to physical exertion and not mere mental activity, *"actio quaedam, non solum mentis agitatio."*[31] Temperance is useful in that it enhances our reputation and wins public approbation.[32] In applying temperance to oneself, Cicero counsels, one should remember that the *"finis est usus"* and that one's vocation should be *"non mediocris utilitas."*[33] It is clear from Cicero's definitions and applications of these four cardinal virtues that he does not regard them as ends in themselves or as their own rewards. His first step toward reconciling the *honestum* and the *utile* therefore has been to reformulate the *honestum* itself as a mode of the *utile*.

Cicero proceeds to reshuffle his ethical terminology along the same lines in Books Two and Three. Each of these books is designed to show that the *honestum* and the *utile* are not in conflict. In Book Two Cicero seeks to prove this point by arguing that the *utile* is itself a worthy end and that the *honestum* is a practical means to that end. The *utilia*, he says, are valuable because they enable us to manipulate others in our own interest. All of the virtues, and most especially justice, inspire confidence and respect in our fellow men. Thus, if we possess these virtues, we will be able to bend others to our will most easily. It is in this context that Cicero raises the question of whether it is better to rule through love or fear. He assesses these alter-

[26]*De off.* 1.14.45.

[27]*De off.* 1.5.17.

[28]*De off.* 1.19.62.

[29]*De off.* 1.20.66.

[30]*De off.* 1.22.77.

[31]*De off.* 1.5.17.

[32]*De off.* 1.28.98.

[33]*De off.* 1.39.138, 1.42.151.

natives in terms of their impact on political stability and the power of the ruler. Fear, he notes, is a poor safeguard. Those who rule by fear, in a state hitherto free, will find themselves especially in danger insofar as freedom suppressed and then regained bites with sharper teeth than freedom never interrupted.[34] Since virtue is useful, he continues, it is important to make it visible to others. Cicero provides a long list of ways in which virtuous persons can effectively publicize their reputations, beginning this section of the book with the injunction that the virtues one seeks to advertise must be virtues that one actually possesses. The essence of the problem, he says, is to be what we wish to be thought to be. Hypocrisy wins no glory; but, equally important, it simply does not work.[35] Sooner or later the hypocrite will be found out. In the long run, it requires less effort to possess virtue than to try to fake it.

In Book Three Cicero continues his reconciliation of the *honestum* and the *utile*, this time from another direction. In the second book he had argued that virtue is expedient; here he argues that immorality is inexpedient. There are certain actions, such as tyrannicide and some forms of civil disobedience, which are good and expedient even though they violate the moral law.[36] But, in general, Cicero seeks to show that injuring others benefits neither the individual who commits the injury nor society at large. The advantage that seems to be served by wrongdoing will emerge as only apparent, not real, or as easily lost, or as prone to boomerang. Moral obloquy brings shame, not glory: "If office is sought for the sake of glory, crime should be avoided, for there can be no glory in crime; but if it is power for its own sake that is sought, by whatever means, it cannot be useful if it is associated with infamy."[37] Honesty is therefore the best policy, for it alone gets results.

In the *De officiis* Cicero is clearly taking a giant step away from the defense of the *honestum* as a higher law that gives whatever limited value it can to the *utile*. Instead, as we have seen, he has assimilated the *honestum* to the *utile* by recasting the traditional meaning of the terms. Yet, the *De officiis* cannot be seen as an exercise in unadulterated pragmatism. For Cicero the *honestum*, or the common good, and the *utile*, or individual interest, cannot conflict because man is part of a larger social and moral whole, which makes radical individualism unacceptable as a basis for ethical action. In cases where the two values appear to conflict, utility, to be

[34] *De off.* 2.7.23-24. For this whole topic, 2.3.9-2.12.43.

[35] *De off.* 2.12.43-2.13.44. For this whole topic, 2.9.31-34, 2.11.39, 2.12.43-2.25.89.

[36] *De off.* 3.4.19-20, 3.5.21-3.7.33.

[37] *De off.* 3.32.87: "*Si gloriae causa imperium expetendum est, scelus absit, in quo non potest esse gloria; sin opes expetuntur quoquo modo, non poterunt utiles esse cum infamia.*" For this whole topic, 3.4.19-3.22.87.

sure, is the norm invoked to resolve the conflict. But it is utility on a social level, *utilitas rei publicae*. Even in cases where exceptions can be made to this rule, the spirit of the rule, that is, social utility, provides the grounds for departing from it.[38] Cicero's stress on the norm of social utility is evident in his definitions of the cardinal virtues no less than in his analysis of individual advantage. In the case of the virtues, he recognizes private rights that do not have to be sacrificed so long as they do not interfere with the rights of others. In the case of personal interests, they cannot be promoted without virtue, which must really be possessed in order to be truly useful. Cicero believes that a sound public order will maintain and protect private rights while a sound moral order will eliminate conflict between the individual and the group. It is true that he removes the conflict between the *honestum* and the *utile* by treating them both as forms of the *utile*. In that sense he seeks to bring the Stoic ideal down to earth. But it is also true that the harmony between public and private goods which he envisions is predicated in turn on a political and ethical ideal of his own, a good society in which the individual and the public good would truly be reciprocal if not identical. This good society is bound indissolubly in Cicero's mind with the Roman Republic.

Both Cicero's defense of expediency and his association of civic virtue with an ideal republican constitution find their resonances in Machiavelli's *Prince*. Machiavelli's double use of Cicero's *De officiis* can be seen most clearly if we keep two well known features of the *Prince* in mind: first, Machiavelli's apparent contrast between the qualities that make for success and those that make for glory, and, second, the fact that he excerpted the *Prince* from his *Discourses*, positing one set of political and moral dynamics for principalities and another for republics.

In the first case, Machiavelli leans heavily on the structure used by Cicero in Books Two and Three of the *De officiis*, raising some of the same questions: Should the ruler be liberal or frugal, cruel or merciful? Should he rule through love or fear? Should he rule through good faith or trickery? Like Cicero, Machiavelli emphasizes the *utile* and treats the virtues as means to the ends of the ruler's power and security. Like Cicero, he thinks that times and circumstances alter our moral obligations. His advice is sometimes diametrically opposed to Cicero's. Thus, he argues that frugality is preferable to liberality.[39] A still more striking departure from Cicero is Machiavelli's advocacy of dissimulation. Where Cicero asserts that all efforts to fake the virtues are doomed to failure, Machiavelli insists that people judge by appearances and results, and that the prince should therefore not hesitate to imitate those virtues which are useful but which he

[38] *De off.* 3.3.12-3.4.17, 3.4.20, 3.5.21-3.6.32, 3.7.34-3.9.39.

[39] *Il principe* 16.

does not himself possess. It is not necessary to have all the virtues, he argues, but it is necessary to appear to have them.[40] On the other hand, Machiavelli's advice is often quite similar to Cicero's. Thus, he agrees that cruelty is sometimes desirable as the lesser of two evils,[41] that the ruler must know how to act as the lion and the fox, that breaches of faith may be reasonable in certain situations,[42] and that it is important for the ruler to avoid the people's hatred.[43]

In the latter connection, he also agrees with Cicero that the best way to avoid hatred and to gain popularity and reputation is to act in ways that promote the common weal. Machiavelli here advises the prince to respect private rights, to be firm and consistent, to perform great deeds, to be generous, to patronize the arts and sciences, to foster commerce, industry, and agriculture, and to underwrite public festivals.[44] In other words, he counsels the ruler to practice the virtues of justice, magnanimity, courage, beneficence, and concern for the cultural and economic well-being of the community. He also observes that the prince should choose confidential ministers who are wise men, adding that it is impossible for a ruler to obtain good advice unless he is wise himself. For if the prince lacked wisdom, he would be incapable of assessing the quality of the advice given and of the men who give it. Nor would he inspire wise men to serve him unless he showed himself worthy of their confidence and respect.[45]

It thus emerges that Machiavelli, like Cicero, thinks that, in the long run, the best way to achieve the appearance of virtue is actually to be what one appears to be. And, like Cicero, he argues that the virtues should be cultivated because they are useful and that they will prove most useful to the prince if he cultivates the ones that yield some benefit to society at large. At the beginning of the *Prince* Machiavelli raises the question of whether success and glory, and the strategies apposite to them, are in conflict. He seems to answer in the affirmative. Reviewing the policies of Agathocles of Syracuse and other new princes, ancient and modern, he says that it cannot be called virtue to kill one's fellow citizens, to betray one's friends, to lack fidelity, mercy, and religion. Such traits may enable a ruler to gain power, but not glory.[46] But at the end of the *Prince*, having given his own advice to the ruler, he observes that the reputation which the prince gains through

[40]*Il principe* 15, 18.

[41]*Il principe* 17.

[42]*Il principe* 18.

[43]*Il principe* 17, 19.

[44]*Il principe* 19, 21.

[45]*Il principe* 22-23.

policies conducive to the general good will bring glory to him and general happiness to his people.[47] Both Machiavelli's conception of the *honestum* and the *utile* in this context and the way in which he harmonizes the one with the other have a great deal in common with Cicero's position.

The principal dimension that is present in the *De officiis* and which Machiavelli deliberately omits from the *Prince* is the dimension of civic virtue. This topic fascinates Cicero to the point of obsession and it is, of course, a theme that Machiavelli analyzes and agonizes over again and again in the *Discourses* and the *History of Florence*, in his efforts to locate this virtue preeminently in republican constitutions and in his persistent inability to account for the fact that polities of this type have repeatedly failed to preserve their liberty.[48] On the one hand, a republican constitution is no guarantee of civic virtue, a conclusion which Machiavelli feels compelled to draw from the historical evidence before his eyes, thus parting company with Cicero and with his predecessors in the civic humanist tradition. On the other hand, he is deeply committed to republican institutions and sincerely wants to believe that they alone engender the kind of civic ethos which he values. As he puts it in the famous passage from the *Discourses*: "It is not private interest but the common good that makes cities great. And, without doubt the common good is observed only in republics, for they carry out everything that advances it."[49] Now a principality may have a ruler who possesses *virtu*, but it cannot have a population that functions as a moral community in a positive sense, possessing the corporate attribute of civic virtue. The leaders whom Cicero addresses in the *De officiis* are an aristocracy, but in his own mind they represent and inspire the virtues that the whole community can and should manifest. Machiavelli, by contrast, has difficulty envisioning such an organic moral relationship between the ruler and the ruled in a principality. Or, perhaps more precisely, he has difficulty envisioning it in the case of the Medici ruler for whom the *Prince* was intended. His omission of the *topos* of civic virtue from the *Prince* therefore can be seen as an ironic comment on princes, in general and in particular. It is certainly an omission which contemporary readers, steeped as they were in Cicero's *De officiis*, were bound to notice.

[46]*Il principe* 8.

[47]*Il principe* 26. The subject of glory has been given exhaustive study in the recent paper by Russell Price, "The Theme of *Gloria* in Machiavelli," *Renaissance Quarterly*, 30 (1977), esp. pp. 594-99, 606-31, although he does not see any connection between Machiavelli and the *De officiis* on this topic.

[48]On this question see most recently Marcia L. Colish, "The Idea of Liberty in Machiavelli," *JHI*, 32 (1971), 330-50 and the literature cited therein.

[49]*Discorsi* 2.2, ed. Sergio Bertelli, in Niccolo Machiavelli, *Opere*, 8 vols. (Milano, 1960-65), I, p. 280. My trans. is given.

    One would like to think that, as evening fell and Machiavelli shook the
dust and grime from his clothes after a day passed in the desultory activities
that occupied him at Sant' Andrea, when he put on his curial robes and
retired to commune with the ancients, one of those ancients was Cicero and
that Machiavelli had a copy of the *De officiis* at hand. It seems unlikely that
he would have failed to notice the analogies between Cicero and himself,
politicians ill-used and in exile, cut off from the life that was meat and drink
to them. The similarities in conceptualization and argument between the *De
officiis* and the *Prince* are too striking and too extended to be dismissed
under the heading of Machiavelli's use of the commonplace tradition. They
are certainly substantial enough to refute the view that he was referring to
Cicero merely in order to turn him inside out. Untested assumptions about
the ethical content and directionality of Cicero's argument in the *De officiis*
seem to have been responsible for this misapprehension. The remedy is for
Machiavelli scholars to read Cicero with as knowing, as sympathetic, and
as critical an eye as Machiavelli and his contemporaries directed at him.

[11]

Canadian Journal of Political and Social Theory/Revue canadienne de théorie politique et sociale, Vol. 2, No. 3 (Fall/Automne 1978).

MACHIAVELLI AND GUICCIARDINI: ANCIENTS AND MODERNS

J. G. A. Pocock

This essay's aim[1] is to examine the contention, put forward by such diverse scholars as Friedrich Meinecke, Leo Strauss and Felix Gilbert, that Machiavelli's thought and that of other Florentines such as Bernardo Rucellai, marked the start of thinking about "modern" politics and history. It also attempts to consider the paired terms "ancient" and "modern" — what they may mean and have meant, and how far it has been or may be useful to examine the two Florentines in the context of the relation between antiquity and modernity.

Leo Strauss held that we were living in times when modernity had itself become a problem. One might say that the word has always been used to denote a consciously problematical view of the human condition; but doubtless it was some highly self-confident brand of progressivist or dialectical modernism that Strauss had chiefly in mind. At a much simpler level, we can agree that the concept of modernity always presents a rather obvious problem, that of definition. Must we always mean the same thing? It would not be hard to show that the word *modern* is what we make of it; its meaning depends largely upon what we choose to place before it.

If we ask whether there is a sense in which Machiavelli and Guicciardini have been, or may be, said to mark the beginnings of *modern* political thinking, the elementary thought should soon occur to us that what preceded them ought to be termed not *ancient* but medieval. The discussion as to whether their thinking was in fact modern usually becomes a discussion of whether it can be effectively characterised as a breakaway from modes of thinking which can be characterised as *medieval*. This is a great deal more than a difference of terminology. Machiavelli and Guicciardini lived in a culture intellectually dominated by the ideas of the Renaissance humanists, and although these scholars did not use such words as *medieval*, they did have a vividly generalised notion of a period in time which separated them from

93

J.G.A. POCOCK

those whom they called *the ancients*. This period seemed to them one of barbarism and scholasticism, and they aimed to annul it and escape from it by returning to the ancients, reading their works and imitating their actions. The humanists were *ancients*, as this term was to be used later on, in the days of the "quarrel between the ancients and the moderns", when it denoted those who thought direct imitation of the Greeks and Romans possible and necessary. The point is that we have now a three-part instead of a two-part division of Western cultural history, and *ancient* is being used as the antithesis, not of *modern*, but of something which will soon be known as *medieval*. The Christian civilisation of post-Roman Latinity (or the Latin civilisation of post-Roman Christianity) is seen as occupying the interval between the ancients and the return to them, and the nearest thing to being modern that has so far appeared is being an ancient in the sense of one who would return to the ancients and imitate them. Machiavelli and Guicciardini differed as to how far this imitation was possible in politics, and we shall return to their debate; but they were discussing the governing assumption of their culture, namely that it was possible.

It is implicit in all this that the humanists understood the Christian Latinity which they called barbarous, the medieval, as a radical denial of ancient values, and so it had been. But equating the Christian with the barbarous was a dangerous game, not to be played to a finish until the time of the *philosophes*; and given that with some exceptions — of whom Machiavelli may have been one — the humanists did not wish to break with Christian values and beliefs, there was a formidable tension between retention of these beliefs and direct imitation of the pagan authors. All that the humanists were bringing about was a sharp increase in the risks of a game as old as the Fathers of the Church, and even the neo-pagans among them were ancients, not moderns.

Strauss was certainly not ignorant of the meaning of the word *medieval*, and he knew that among its many meanings it denoted a period during which the values of ancient political philosophy had in some ways been denied and set aside in favour of those of monotheist religion. He rightly held, however, that in so far as there had continued to be political philosophy, it had been the philosophy of Plato and Aristotle, and he held — with considerable justification — that the gulf between this and the revealed religions had in many ways been bridged, so that there continued to be a grand tradition of ancient philosophy throughout the medieval centuries. He pointed out that for Plato and Aristotle, political philosophy culminated in the knowledge of a God, and he believed (correctly) that there had always been minds at work in the monotheist systems labouring to reconcile the God of revelation with the God of philosophy. His insistence that this could only be done with the aid of esoteric teaching might have got him into trouble in the medieval University of

MACHIAVELLI AND GUICCIARDINI

Paris, where such problems were notoriously open to public disputation; but it was in Christian Paris, more than in Muslim Spain which perhaps Strauss better understood, that the justification of philosophy in a monotheist setting became the justification of Aristotelian political society in the setting of the monotheist universe, that the city was presented as leading to the knowledge of God. Here Strauss' highly individual interpretation joins hands with many far more simplistic accounts of Machiavelli as *modern* in the sense of *not medieval*.

It is with the Christianised Aristotelianism of the schoolmen that these accounts all begin, and from this Aristotelianism that they see Machiavelli as departing. The textbooks of historical political philosophy all do this, with or without an interlude on the subject of Marsilius of Padua; and Strauss's *Thoughts on Machiavelli* is essentially an immensely elaborate account of how Machiavelli *intended* to break with *ancient* political philosophy, and *intended* to say many things which Strauss considered the necessary consequences of this breach.

Now one may doubt that this is a correct interpretation of Machiavelli's intentions, or of the ideas which he communicated to other people. This does not mean that if you compare his doctrines with those of the Aristotelian tradition, important implications will not appear; but one may doubt whether it was his intention to express these implications, or whether he or his readers considered assent or dissent from the Aristotelian tradition the most important question before them. One might say merely that Strauss and others like him are historically wrong but may be philosophically right: that the contrast between Aquinas and Machiavelli is there even if the latter did not mean to express it; but in fact the problem does not stop there. Strauss's view of political philosophy does entail a view of its history — a movement from *ancient* (meaning Aristotelian) to *modern* (meaning the negation of *ancient*) — and if you reject this as the historical scheme in which Machiavelli is to be located, it does follow that you read him as expressing other political, if not philosophical, meanings than those read into him by Strauss.

If we locate Machiavelli and Guicciardini among the Florentine civic humanists, the case for characterising them as dissenters from the Aristotelian tradition is weakened. The humanist line of thought, prevalent for over a century, was the work of writers who had been trained in humanist studies and in the Florentine chancellery and other public offices, not in any school where philosophical disputation was a principal means of communication. As Hans Baron and his critics[2] point out, Florentine intellectual culture was more rhetorical than philosophical, and the problems debated in universities were not necessarily those which gave rise to its political ideas. A thinker in the tradition of Platonic philosophy may reply that it is a grave error to discuss politics rhetorically rather than philosophically, and may succeed in showing

J.G.A. POCOCK

that Florentine political thought has characteristics which are the result of this error. To do so, however, will be philosophical criticism rather than an historical account of what those thinkers meant to say or were understood to say by others. In fact, Machiavelli had nothing whatever to say about the Aristotelian political tradition, but it is not a necessary consequence — as Strauss and many after him have attempted to infer — that he meant by his silence to convey the message that it was not worth thinking about. He may simply not have been thinking about it.

This is not to say there are no traces in Florentine thought of the great syntheses of medieval Aristotelianism. In the sermons of Girolamo Savonarola, some of which Machiavelli may have heard, the teachings of St. Thomas Aquinas are unquestionably present, even though when Savonarola thinks he is quoting Aquinas he is sometimes quoting Tolomeo da Lucca's continuation of the *De Regimine Principum*[3]. Savonarola, however, was a Dominican friar, and Dominicans studied Aquinas for obvious reasons; we have to beware of constructing a succession of major philosophers and supposing that this necessarily supplies us with the historical context in which men did their thinking. The first critic so far known to have observed that Machiavelli's thought can be related to the Aristotelian tradition was Tommaso Campanella — another Dominican — about a hundred years later, and he wrote that the study of Aristotle could lead directly to the errors of Machiavelli[4]. This makes sense only by supposing that when Campanella said "Aristotle" he meant Aristotle as studied at Padua, or elsewhere in the late scholastic scene where syntheses such as St. Thomas's were generally accepted, and secular philosophy and politics were much more likely to exist in defiance of their conformity with the Christian faith. The late scholastic scene disintegrates as we look at it; the synthesis of religion and philosophy was not universal, and it was possible to construct schemes of political thought without reference to Aristotelian philosophy at all. The presumption that Machiavelli must be viewed as *modern* because he departs from a *medieval* or *ancient* mainstream or "great tradition" — the last phrase was a favourite with Strauss — is not historically self-evident.

Hans Baron demonstrates that the civic humanist mode of political thought had been autonomous for rather more than a century before Machiavelli's time; and the doctrines against which it contended were not those of Thomas Aquinas. It is not clear that Strauss maintained they were, but for this very reason it may be held that his account of pre-Machiavellian thought is less than satisfactory. When he approached the great question of the relation between political philosophy and revealed religion, his eye was very often upon medieval Jewish rather than Christian thought, and for this reason it was fixed more upon prophecy than upon grace. The Christian challenge to the primacy of political philosophy was expressed for all time by St.

MACHIAVELLI AND GUICCIARDINI

Augustine; and what Augustine desired to say was that souls were brought to salvation by the freely operating grace of God, and that this grace operated through the sacramental institutions of the Church and not through the political institutions of secular justice. The *civitas terrena* was very seldom just, and when it was, its justice did not lead to salvation. Secular time, in which the political city had its being, had very little to do with the processes of salvation and redemption, and the specifically political virtues — grouped by Augustine under the Sallustian title of *libido dominandi* — might not be virtues at all. Now it simply cannot be maintained that the vindication of politics as a thing natural to man — which scholastic theologians attempted during and after the thirteenth century — healed up the breach between *civitas terrena* and *civitas Dei* as if it had never been. The eve of that great Augustinian revolt which we call the Protestant Reformation, was the era of Machiavelli and Guicciardini. However superb we may find the great attempts to articulate it, the medieval synthesis was not even in ruins; it had never been achieved, and one of the consequences is that Florentine political thought is not an attempt at a new political philosophy, but an attempt to constitute political thought on a new basis which, since it did not address itself to the relations of philosophy and grace, had better not be called philosophy at all. It was rhetoric, the attempt to use language as a means of action; and the values to which it appealed were those of the *vita activa*.

The Florentine humanists saw themselves as rhetoricians, as thinkers in action aiming to speak and write so as to reconstitute a world of civic action, and in so speaking they reiterated one of the cardinal phrases of the Hellenic and European tradition: that man is by nature a political animal, incomplete unless enacting and declaring himself within a scheme of civic relationships. Now although this is one of the fundamental premises of political philosophy, it had been insisted on by Plato, and in his own way by Aristotle, that political existence is imperfect unless completed by philosophy. The humanist emphasis on the *vita activa* can be read as a return to the world of Pericles and Alcibiades, to action as it had been before it was questioned by Socrates. True, and very important; but (1) such a return was radically ancient and not modern; (2) we further misinterpret the whole problem of antiquity if we do not realise that the ancients sought after by the humanists were not pre-Socratic Greeks but middle-Stoic Romans; (3) the doctrine that citizenship must be completed by philosophy had been drastically altered by Augustine and other Fathers, who had created a universe in which philosophy was transformed into grace. Strauss saw in history the unremitting struggle of the philosophers to reconquer grace for themselves, but he seems to have thought that the philosophers had usually won. There would not have been a Protestant Reformation if they had won, and there might not have been a humanist revival in politics either.

J.G.A. POCOCK

Given a world in which grace — however much degraded and corrupted by the Church — held against the competition of philosophy the role of completing and perfecting political nature, there could be only two — but overlapping — outcomes for the humanist revival of the assertion that man was by nature political and that the city perfected his nature. Either citizenship must be seen as doing the work of grace — as is proclaimed in the sermons of Savonarola[5] — or it must do its own work in some indifference to the work of grace, as seems to be the message of Machiavelli. We do not understand the sixteenth century if we suppose that ancient philosophy held the field intact against the onslaughts of grace; and to treat the history of philosophy by itself, and organize it into *ancient* and *modern*, may well encourage us to do so.

If we look at the history of what some call civic humanism and others classical republicanism[6], we may see the following. Certain Florentine humanists revived the doctrine that the republic or polis contained all that was necessary to the completion of human life on earth; and they did so in a Christian context where the *civitas terrena* of politics was set over against the *civitas Dei* of grace. For reasons connected with the sharpness of this antithesis, they described the republic in terms of the *vita activa* instead of the *vita contemplativa*, and it is correct to point out that this was likely to entail some abandonment of the Athenian postulate that action must be completed by philosophy; but we mistake the historical context if we suppose that Augustinian grace had been re-absorbed by Thomist or Aristotelian philosophy. These Florentines depicted their own republic as an inheritor or revival of the ancient republic typified by Rome, and in so doing reiterated the humanist vision of an interval of barbarism — which was also an interval of Christianity — separating antiquity and themselves: an interval, in this case, of Christian empire and papacy. They had now raised for themselves a two-sided problem in historical understanding, such as neither ancient philosophers nor ancient historians had confronted. How had this interlude of empire, papacy and (if they thought about it) feudalism come to exist? If the republic was the norm of political life, what explained its decline and replacement by empire in the Roman case, its revival and all too evident instability in the Florentine case, its apparent serenity and unalterability in the case of Venice? These were historical problems, to which philosophy suggested some answers, but by no means all that might be put forward. The experiment in recovering antiquity produced a great gulf in the humanist understanding of time, which must be filled by adducing sacred or secular ideas about history; and there was the further difficulty that the republic had seldom been depicted as a sacred entity, linked with the fulfilment of the Christian redemption.

It may next be argued that history — the succession of events in secular time — could be depicted either as the work of grace, or with the aid of a sharply

98

MACHIAVELLI AND GUICCIARDINI

limited secular vocabulary. The republic could — although traditions to this effect were somewhat lacking — be said to do the work of grace, bringing human life nearer to salvation by perfecting its political form and earthly justice. This is going on in the sermons of Savonarola, who found means of expressing this doctrine in ways not incompatible with the language of orthodox Thomism: *gratia non tollit naturam, sed perficit.* The republic, however, because of its secular character and its historical instability, must be thought of as existing at specific and separated moments of secular time; and the only way to say that it perfected human life, or restored human life to its original nature — which must be the work of grace — was to say that these were the moments at which grace operated in secular time to do its work of redemption. This in turn could only be said by recourse to the prophetic and apocalyptic, eschatological and millenarian, terminologies of the Christian vocabulary, and Savonarola was neither the first nor the last to find that to be a republican was also to be a prophet. In pursuit of the logic of the prophetic vocabulary, he came to denounce the Pope as Antichrist, and found that this was too much even for the Florentines, who were accustomed to treating the Pope with disrespect, but never forgot to count the political costs of doing so.

Machiavelli and Guicciardini may be brought back into the story here. They both felt considerable respect for Savonarola, both for his role in restoring popular government and for the astonishing effect which his prophecies had upon the Florentine mind; but they did not believe that his prophecies were genuine, and they had noted his ultimate failure — connected like his rise with the French invasion of 1494, which had rendered republican survival more precarious than ever. They therefore concluded that the survival of republics was a secular problem, to be understood if not mastered by mobilising that sharply limited vocabularly for the understanding of secular events described a moment ago. This was organised around the key concepts of custom and fortune. If a secular political structure could be anchored deeply enough in remembered experience and custom, it might acquire a stability which fortune — the symbol of instability in secular and political affairs — would find hard to overthrow. If not, however, every political action was itself the product of this same fortune, its apparent success in achieving stability occurring as fortune's wheel swung upwards, its ultimate failure and downfall occurring as the wheel swung down. In so far as human actions were not rewarded by grace, they were all governed by the wheel of fortune. There were moral qualities and political skills which it was appropriate for men to display in the confrontation with fortune; there was civic and heroic virtue, there was prudence and caution, there was understanding of how a polity might be balanced and rendered just and stable. These were not non-moral qualities, but if one thought of them as existing apart from the operation of grace, they were unlikely to enjoy ultimate

J.G.A. POCOCK

political success — especially on the presumption that only grace could save a city — and they were unlikely to lead to the salvation of souls. Any Christian moralist must say that to save souls was more important than to save the city; but the reply had always been possible that if it was good to save the city, this end must be sought by means other than those which led to the salvation of souls. As early as 1420 — and in a time of conflict with the Papacy — Gino di Neri Capponi had written that Florence needed men who cared more for the good of the city than for the good of their own souls[7]; a phrase Machiavelli was to repeat. Savonarola had seemed to show that only if Florence were a holy city governed in the fulfilment of prophecy were these two ends the same, and he had not brought holiness and Florence together.

In the wake of his failure — and also because they saw that a republic must always be something more than a customary community — Machiavelli and Guicciardini, together with other Florentine writers, set out to see what might be done for a city by those virtues defined by the contention with fortune rather than by the expectation of grace. Since they did not expect to save souls by what they envisaged doing, they accepted that their means would be imperfectly moral; they aimed at achieving stability and success, but they did not expect final success in the contention with fortune either. They might therefore have been orthodox and pious Augustinians, who held that the first priority was to save the *civitas terrena* even though action in this field could never be action in the *civitas Dei*. They were not, however; expressions of Christian faith are lacking in their works, and Machiavelli is prepared to judge the faith severely by the standards of the *civitas terrena*. The paradox is that all this had come about because the civic humanists had repeated the Aristotelian doctrine that man is by nature a political animal in the Augustinian context of a sharp separation between the world of politics and the world of grace. Given the Christian conviction that the only intelligible history is the history of grace, but that grace does not need history in order to be effective — given also the brutal experience of instability that beset the Florentine republic in every generation — the effect had been to make the republic's chief problem that of existence in a history that neither grace nor philosophy could explain. There was a republican rhetoric that could do much towards explaining it; but since only grace (and perhaps philosophy) could furnish final explanations, the theory and practice of republican existence would never bring moral, or political, or historical completeness. To adhere to natural politics in an Augustinian universe must lead to ambivalence and ultimately to historicism. When Guicciardini asks himself why a republic is necessary for Florence, he does not answer in terms of the nature of politics nor the nature of man, but of the nature of the Florentines. They are that way, he says; their history has made them such that they will never be content without a republic, but they are most unlikely ever to achieve one[8]. The only nature here is second nature,

MACHIAVELLI AND GUICCIARDINI

that which is produced by history; but the point is less that Guicciardini has abandoned the philosophical principle that men are by nature political and need philosophy in order to perfect their politics, than that to assert human politicality in an Augustinian universe was to leave it ultimately intelligible only in a history which must be either sacred or secular. Augustine had told the Florentines this would happen; but political animals they were, and they went ahead, between 1494 and 1530, to face the choices expressed in the writings of Savonarola and Machiavelli.

Machiavelli's drastic innovation was to isolate and apply the Roman notion of *virtù*, that dominant and ruling quality by which men confronted fortune and overcame it insofar as it was ever possible to do so. In *Il Principe* he developed this notion in connection with the figure of the "new prince", who — unlike the "born prince", who was so far legitimised by custom that he had little to fear from fortune and little need of *virtù* — had made himself ruler by means that disturbed the customs of his subjects and left him exposed to fortune and needing all the *virtù* he could display. This kind of adventurer was no longer common even in Italy, and in later centuries only Napoleon Bonaparte exemplified the combination of *condottiere* and legislator which Machiavelli sketched in his portrait. We have to remember how carefully the new prince was defined by the abnormality of his situation before leaping to the conclusion that he is intended to be a type of political actor as such. It is true that *virtù* is defined as not only that which he needs as a consequence of his usurpation, but that which moved him to perform the usurpation in the first place. This is linked with a study of innovation as destroying the conditions which might have made it legitimate; but *Il Principe* may be intended as a study and typology of innovation rather than of political action. Once again, when Machiavelli explains how the "new prince" must and should behave immorally in order to maintain his position, we should not let our indignation at the suggestion that *any* political being should behave like this lead us into supposing that we are being told that *all* political beings should. The new prince is living in a world of disorder which is often of his own creating, and it does not seem that he is going to find a way out of it. He cannot change the nature of his subjects by teaching them new customs, and he cannot alter his own nature as fact as his circumstances will alter; this is why fortune will always have power over him[9]. He is not the author of a new political order, but a successful rider on the wheel of fortune in a politics permanently disordered by his own act. In consequence, though he is constantly adjured to study and imitate the lessons of anitiquity, this does not mean that there is any classical type — certainly not Cesare Borgia — on whom he can permanently model himself. The new princes of the past, like those of the present, lived in disordered, not in patterned circumstances; none of their actions could be proof against fortune, and every situation in which the

101

J.G.A. POCOCK

prince might find himself had the uniqueness of irrationality. We shall have to ask the question: is this or is this not modernity?

In his greater work the *Discorsi*, Machiavelli turned his attention from the prince to the citizen and considered the political structure of republics. For reasons which need not be considered in detail here, he resolved that the most interesting republic to study was the armed and expansive city, like republican Rome, which alone would give arms to its non-noble citizens and in consequence admit them to political rights. There was an intrinsic relationship between expansion of the city and the extension of citizenship, or between imperialism and democracy. The nobles gave the people arms because they were needed in the legions, and the people employed their arms in claiming their political rights. There would always be tension between the two but this would make the city more warlike and more free; a belief which Guicciardini found he could not accept, since there could be neither rule nor law without order, even if this must be imposed by authority. Leo Strauss' *Thoughts on Machiavelli* consists largely of a series of arguments to the effect that this creative tension between nobles and people is a deception, and that the *Discorsi* consists of a series of covert instructions to the rulers on how the ruled may be manipulated and deceived. The arguments are tortured and the conclusions exaggerated. The relation between nobles and people is ambiguous; it is assumed that the nobles will try to deceive, as the people will try not to be deceived, and that the victory of either may be occasionally desirable, just as the tension between the two will be permanently valuable. Every reader of Machiavelli's age and the next who considered the matter, seemed to see clearly that he was a *popolano* who advocated non-noble participation in government, and in grounding this in popular possession of arms, ensured in his theory that the people's role would be more than a merely deferential one. A central theme is that possession of arms and possession of political capacity are one and the same, and that *virtù* rests upon both. Unlike the *virtù* of the new prince, that of the citizen entails law and liberty, obedience and equality; it has a complex moral code. Because its end is the expansiveness of the city, without which it cannot exist, it is not identical with Christian morality, and the historical world which *virtù* creates is incompatible with that created by Christian redemption. A city's *virtù* grows by destroying the *virtù* of others; when one city rules the whole world, its *virtù* will corrode and degenerate; there will be a collapse, a cataclysm, and the process will begin again[10]. This vision of history is not modern; it is Roman and pre-Christian, though it flourished for a while in early modern history.

Guicciardini liked to consider himself a more cautious thinker than Machiavelli, and was more closely aligned with the Florentine political aristocracy, although these were not nobility. He held prudence rather than *virtù* to be the quality with which men sought to guide themselves through

MACHIAVELLI AND GUICCIARDINI

disordered political and moral situations, although this quality too was imperfectly moral. The difference is that through *virtù* one can hope to impose one's own pattern on these situations, whereas through prudence one aims only to diagnose situations which one cannot control and guide oneself accordingly. For this reason Guicciardini held that Machiavelli had overestimated the extent to which it was possible to imitate the actions of antiquity; not only did the situations which had existed in the past not recur in identical form in the present — Machiavelli knew this well enough — but one could not, so to speak, make them recur by the imposition of *virtù* on the present. If we look closely at Guicciardini's criticisms of Machiavelli one finds him repeatedly saying that we cannot imitate the actions of the early Romans unless we command legions of armed citizens[11]. It is a cardinal fact about his own times that Florence did not command a citizen militia — although he agrees that it would be a very good thing, morally as well as politically, if there were one. There is need of the sagacity of a wise and prudent few, who can guide the city's policy in situations which arms cannot command. So far there is little disagreement with Machiavelli in principle or theory, but Guiccciardini does go on to express doubt whether there ever existed the intimate relationship between arms and citizenship which Machiavelli had detected at Rome. The plebians were not good citizens because their arms made them so; military discipline was an independent variable, founded by the kings rather than the consuls, which held Rome together when the dissensions of nobles and people, inherent in the republic's political structure, would otherwise have torn the city apart[12].

What seems to be happening here is that Guicciardini's rejection of the *virtù* which can control the present is increasing his scepticism as to the extent to which we can guide ourselves by knowing the past, and consequently his awareness of the incoherence and elusiveness of all historical situations past and present. In addition to his *Considerations on Machiavelli's Discourses*, his *Ricordi* — a collection of political maxims — developed a series of warnings about the extreme difficulty of applying prudence itself to the understanding of history and politics, and how easy it is to let one's sensitivity to the complexity of things betray one into believing that one has comprehended them, whereas it is the contrary lesson that one ought to be learning[13]. In his last and greatest work, the *History of Italy*, we seem to see him in retirement from active politics, moving towards the belief that nothing is left but to write the history of events, seeking less to understand the forces which made them happen than the forces which made men — including the author himself — constantly mislead themselves as they tried to understand and control them[14]. This pessimism and historicism present the extreme outcome of the civic humanists' discovery that the life of political societies took place in secular time, and that secular time was controlled by neither

J.G.A. POCOCK

philosophy nor grace. The further discovery that secular action could be assured of neither morality nor success was common to both Machiavelli and Guicciardini, and had nothing whatever that was new about it. What was new — or at least un-medieval — about them was their belief that men were morally and politically obliged to undertake action whose morality could not be assured. The polis had its morality, which was not the morality of the *civitas Dei*, and consequently neither morality was complete. Machiavelli expressed this in the image of the centaur, half man and half beast; and the secular time in which the centaur had his being can be appropriately termed history.

There seems a sound case, then, for the view that the Florentines arrived at a position of historicism, of insisting that the crucial characteristic of moral and political life is that it is lived in history. Historicism sounds very modern, in the sense that it is neither ancient nor medieval, yet the variety of historicism we have been looking at was compounded wholly out of the tension between ancient and medieval materials. The civic humanists sought to imitate the actions of antiquity, and to assert the primacy of political values, which is an ancient ideal; they did so in the context of Augustine's radical separation between the values of citizenship and those of redemption, between the secular history which contained the former and the sacred history which led to the latter, and these are postulates of medieval thought. Out of this tension emerged the Florentine variety of historicism; but is this historicism to be termed modern? It depends what one means by the word, and one needs some canons for its use.

I have challenged the idea of a transition from ancient to modern, on the grounds that the medieval world was profoundly divided between Athenian, Roman and Christian values. Leo Strauss' vision of history, although he might not have owned to having one[15], was focussed on the history of political philosophy, and on the assumption that Aristotelians had bridged the gap between political philosophy and redemptive grace. There may be a case for continuing to organise the history of political philosophy into ancient and modern, but the Augustinian position involved a denial that there could be such a thing as political philosophy at all, and I have been advancing the paradox that the Florentine predicament had more in common with that. They were trying to act and to imitate in a world where secular and sacred were so sharply divided that imitation proved destructive of all except history. Negating philosophy was a philosophical act for Strauss, and had philosophical consequences; this is an intelligible position, but he tells us he first considered Hobbes the founder of modern political philosophy, and later came to think it was Machiavelli. There is an important crux here. We know that Hobbes aimed to set up a modern political philosophy because he tells us so himself; he says that for two thousand years Western thought has been dominated by

104

MACHIAVELLI AND GUICCIARDINI

Athenian philosophy; the political and philosophical consequences have been disastrous, and that there is need for something else[16]. He proceeds to set up what is certainly a philosophy and certainly political; this is certainly modern in the sense that it differs radically from the ancient and medieval. Now the trouble about Machiavelli, and Guicciardini too, is that they do not say anything about philosophy or philosophers at all; or if some limited transitory allusions consider political philosophy, they signal the author's intentions of doing something so different that it will not be a different kind of philosophy, but something else altogether. This is what they proceed to do; they explore the idea of imitation so radically that doing so becomes an exploration of the idea of history. This is open to philosophical criticism; it has consequences in the historical world with which the philosopher may have to reckon as he tries to express his philosophy as a denizen of that world, but it is not philosophy, but something else. Strauss' attempts to show that Machiavelli was trying to create a new philosophy in the same way that Thomas Hobbes was are unbelievably complicated and indirect, and they end with nothing more than the contention that he was covertly preaching a pseudo-normative doctrine of amoral individualism, which many have found in his writings and equated it with Hobbes, as did Strauss. Machiavelli's explorations of the problem of history, on which Guicciardini commented, are altogether subordinated. I suggest the attempt was misconceived, Machiavelli was not a political philosopher, and the historical context which makes him intelligible is not one in which political philosophy is the dominant presence.

The idea of basing action upon imitation is, in a sense, pre-philosophcal. Socrates and Plato set out to show that it was not enough, and the latter might well have said that the humanists of the Renaissance were making the same mistake as those Athenians who tried to base action upon imitation of the heroes of epic poetry. The Florentines developed an independent enquiry into the moral and political imperfection — which was at the same time a moral and political necessity — of imitating the actions of ancient history. The ancients did not conduct such an enquiry, but discovering how difficult it is to imitate the actions of antiquity is not enough to make you a modern if you go on trying to do it and do not discover any alternative principles on which action can be based. The discovery which Machiavelli and Guicciardini made of the enormous difficulty and imperfection of action in historic time is based on the discovery that secular time is not controlled by grace or rendered intelligible by philosophy; it is not based on the discovery that secular processes in history are perpetually producing objective conditions which have not existed before, and this is the essential condition of anything we can call a consciousness of modernity. Hobbes may have intended to produce a philosophy unlike any that had existed previously, but I doubt if this means he had any modern sense of historical process. His historical scheme remains

105

J.G.A. POCOCK

prophetic and eschatological[17]; but Machiavelli had no such intention. When he talks of the need for "new modes and orders", he means that such modes and orders must be securely founded on the practice of antiquity and will be new in the normal pre-modern sense that they will be renewed, "the world's great age begins anew, the golden years return." Since all such imitation is carried out in a world subject to fortune, there is a probability that such a *renovatio* will turn out to be an *innovatio*, that self-destructive mode of action which removes the conditions on which it was founded. The Machiavellian doctrine of action, then is neither ancient nor modern in any simple sense; but the paradigm remains that of imitating antiquity in the knowledge that this is not altogether possible. Guicciardini, who thinks that Machiavelli over-simplifies the case, does not differ from him as to the paradigm; while Hobbes is a modern who has not become a historicist.

Towards the end of Hobbes' lifetime — and more than a century after the end of Machiavelli's and Guicciardini's — there raged that "quarrel of the ancients and moderns" from which our usage of the last term is largely derived. An *ancient* was one who still thought it of paramount importance to imitate antiquity; a *modern* was one who did not; but there were two distinguishable if overlapping reasons for being a modern. One might believe that one had succeeded in something which the Greeks and Romans had attempted but failed to do; or one might believe that one had discovered how to do something which they had never attempted, and shown that they had been on the wrong track or that their enterprise was now unnecessary. The frame of mind which holds that imitation of antiquity is highly desirable but almost impossibly difficult will not supply modernity in the former sense, and will supply it in the latter only if, as the result of the tension between theory and practice, "modes and orders" which are in fact new have been discovered and exploited. Had anything of the kind occurred in the wake of Machiavelli and Guicciardini? It seems unlikely. There had been a widespread investigation of *raison d'état*, which owed a great deal to them both[18]; but for the most part this was a further development of the casuistical problems[19] which arose when it was admitted that the morality of state action differed from the morality of private action, and the consequent attempt to identify the "interest of states", and show how these determined action of the former kind, had not yet shown that the modern state differed in character or purpose from the ancient. Furthermore, when we encounter the "quarrel of ancients and moderns" in a strictly political form, and it is asked for the first time whether the modern political individual is a different sort of being from the ancient, we find, regularly employed to define the ancient and criticise the modern, Machiavelli's equation between arms-bearer and citizen. He insists that it is the possession of arms which endows the individual with political autonomy and the capacity for virtue in either a classical or a Machiavellian sense.

MACHIAVELLI AND GUICCIARDINI

Strauss contended that Machiavelli, like Hobbes, was the author of a radical individualism which depicted men as seeking private good first and public good second; but what we find, towards the year 1700, is a persistent contrast between the ancient or medieval warrior whose arms permitted him to engage in his own government, and the individual of commercial and cultivated society who preferred to purchase the goods which commerce made possible, while paying others to defend him, govern him and represent him[20]. The latter is the archetype of modernity and is only very indirectly the heir of Hobbes. If this is so, Machiavelli and even Guiciardini rank among the ancients in the great quarrel, both because they knew no positive alternative to imitation of the ancients and because they tended — Machiavelli less equivocally, on the whole, than his friend and critic — to depict the political individual in the shape of classical citizen.

In conclusion, the Florentines rank as ancients rather than moderns; and if it be objected that an *ancient* in this sense is still a modern phenomenon, both because to imitate antiquity is not to be an antique man and because the imitation of antiquity is a post-medieval ideal, I reply that modernity appears only when there are secular means of knowing oneself to be a different sort of secular being from an antique man. The struggle for imitation and revival produced an acute awareness of history and a pre-modern species of historicism; but there is a profound difference between an historicism which presents history as a secular flux ruled by fortune, and one which presents it as a secular process and transformation. It was the advent of commercial society which convinced theorists after 1700 that the world had changed and the classical ideal of citizenship ceased to be viable[21]. Their historicism consisted in visualising, with Rousseau, the historical process which had rendered man civilised as one and the same with that which had deprived him of his political virtue. From there the path lay towards Kant, Hegel and Marx, towards the attempt to identify consciousness of self with consciousness of the contradictions of the historical process. To all of this the Florentines' contribution seems to have consisted less in the architecture of modernity than in the neo-classical antithesis against which it was shaped. They were moderns only in the sense that they were ancients.

History
Johns Hopkins University

J.G.A. POCOCK

Notes

1. Based upon a lecture given under the auspices of the History and Political Science Departments of Simon Fraser University, July 17, 1978.

2. Baron, *The Crisis of the Early Italian Renaissance*, Princeton University Press, 1966. Jerrold E. Seigel, *Rhetoric and Philosophy in Renaissance Humanism*, Princeton University Press, 1968. George Holmes, *The Florentine Enlightenment, 1400-1450*, London: Weidenfeld and Nicolson, 1969.

3. See Charles T. Davis, "Roman Patriotism and Republican Propaganda: Ptolemy of Lucca and Pope Nicholas III", *Speculum*, L, 3, 1975, pp. 411-33.

4. Rodolfo De Mattei, *Dal Premachiavellismo all'Antimachiavellismo*, Florence: G. C. Sansoni, 1969, pp. 159-60.

5. Donald Weinstein, *Savonarola and Florence: Prophecy and Patriotism in the Renaissance*, Princeton University Press, 1970.

6. In the next few paragraphs I summarise arguments to be found in my *The Machiavellian Moment: Florentine Political Thought and the Atlantic Republican Tradition*, Princeton University Press, 1975.

7. L. Muratori, *Rerum Italicorum Scriptores*, Milan: 1723-51, vol. XVIII, col. 1149. Renzo Sereno, "The *Ricordi* of Gino di Neri Capponi", *American Political Science Review*, 52, 4, 1958, pp. 1118-22.

8. Roberto Palmarocchi, ed., *Francesco Guicciardini: Dialogo e Discorsi del Reggimento di Firenze*, Bari: Laterza, 1932, pp. 94-5, 223, 261-62. *Machiavellian Moment*, pp. 125-6, 142-3, 250-1.

9. *Il Principe*, ch. XXV. *Machiavellian Moment*, pp. 96-7, 179-80.

10. *Discorsi*, II, 5; *Machiavellian Moment*, pp. 216-8.

11. *Considerations on the Discourses of Machiavelli*, in *Selected Writings*, ed. and trans. Cecil and Margaret Grayson, London: Oxford University Press, 1965, pp. 69, 117; *Ricordi*, trans. Mario Domandi, *Maxims and Reflections of a Renaissance Statesman*, New York: Harper Torchbooks, 1965, p. 69; Palmarocchi, *Dialogo e Discorsi*, pp. 68, 90-93, 155. See Herbert Butterfield, *The Statecraft of Machiavelli*, London: G. Bell, 1955, *Machiavellian Moment*, pp. 239, 245-48, 268-70.

12. *Dialogo e Discorsi*, pp. 148-58.

13. *Machiavellian Moment*, pp. 267-8.

14. Mark Phillips, *Francesco Guicciardini: The Historian's Craft*, University of Toronto Press, 1977. Felix Gilbert, *Machiavelli and Guicciardini: Politics and History in Sixteenth-Century Florence*, Princeton University Press, 1965.

15. *Cf.* John Gunnell, "The Myth of the Tradition", *American Political Science Review*, 72, 1, 1978, pp. 122-34.

16. *Leviathan*, ch. 46.

MACHIAVELLI AND GUICCIARDINI

17. Pocock, "Time, History and Eschatology in the Thought of Thomas Hobbes", in *Politics, Language and Time*, New York: Atheneum, 1971.

18. Friedrich Meinecke, *Der Idee der Staatsräson*, English translation, *Machiavellism*, New Haven: Yale University Press, 1957. E. Thuau, *Raison d'état et pensée politique à l'epoque de Richelieu*, Paris: Colin, 1966. W. F. Church, *Richelieu and Reason of State*, Princeton University Press, 1972. Although Machiavellian elements are evident in these writers, the role of Guicciardini has been little studied; see forthcoming work by Lionel A. McKenzie, Johns Hopkins University.

19. See George L. Mosse, *The Holy Pretence: A Study in Christianity and Reason of State from William Perkins to John Winthrop*, Oxford: Basil Blackwell, 1957.

20. *Machiavellian Moment*, ch. 13.

21. Joseph E. Cropsey, *Polity and Economy: An Interpretation of the Principles of Adam Smith*, The Hague: Nijhoff, 1957. *More Straussiano*, he links the pursuit of wealth in Smith directly with the fear of violent death in Hobbes. For discussion, see Donald Winch, *Adam Smith's Politics: An Essay in Historiographic Revision*, Cambridge University Press, 1978.

[12]

The Originality of Machiavelli

I

THERE is something surprising about the sheer number of interpretations of Machiavelli's political opinions.[1] There exist, even now,
over a score of leading theories of how to interpret *The Prince* and *The
Discourses* – apart from a cloud of subsidiary views and glosses. The
bibliography of this is vast and growing faster than ever.[2] While there
may exist no more than the normal extent of disagreement about the
meaning of particular terms or theses contained in these works, there
is a startling degree of divergence about the central view, the basic
political attitude of Machiavelli.

This phenomenon is easier to understand in the case of other
thinkers whose opinions have continued to puzzle or agitate mankind
– Plato, for example, or Rousseau, or Hegel, or Marx. But then it
might be said that Plato wrote in a world and in a language that we
cannot be sure we understand; that Rousseau, Hegel, Marx were

---

[1] The first draft of this paper was read at a meeting of the British section
of the Political Studies Association in 1953. I should like to take this opportunity of offering my thanks to friends and colleagues to whom I sent it for
their comments. They include A. P. d'Entrèves, Carl J. Friedrich, Felix
Gilbert, Myron Gilmore, Louis Hartz, J. P. Plamenatz, Lawrence Stone and
Hugh Trevor-Roper. I have greatly profited from their criticisms, which
have saved me from many errors; for those that are left I am, of course, alone
responsible.

[2] The full list now contains more than three thousand items. The biblio-
graphical surveys that I have found most valuable are P. H. Harris, 'Progress
in Machiavelli Studies', *Italica* 18 (1941), 1–11; Eric W. Cochrane,
'Machiavelli: 1940–1960', *Journal of Modern History* 33 (1961), 113–36;
Felix Gilbert, *Machiavelli and Guicciardini* (Princeton, 1965); Giuseppe
Prezzolini, *Machiavelli anticristo* (Rome, 1954), trans. into English as
Machiavelli (New York, 1967; London, 1968); De Lamar Jensen (ed.),
Machiavelli: Cynic, Patriot, or Political Scientist? (Boston, 1960); and
Richard C. Clark, 'Machiavelli: Bibliographical Spectrum', *Review of
National Literatures* 1 (1970), 93–135.

AGAINST THE CURRENT

prolific theorists, whose works are scarcely models of clarity or consistency. But *The Prince* is a short book : its style is usually described
as being singularly lucid, succinct and pungent – a model of clear
Renaissance prose. *The Discourses* is not, as treatises on politics go, of
undue length, and it is equally clear and definite. Yet there is no consensus about the significance of either; they have not been absorbed
into the texture of traditional political theory ; they continue to arouse
passionate feelings ; *The Prince* has evidently excited the interest and
admiration of some of the most formidable men of action of the last
four centuries, especially of our own, men not normally addicted to
reading classical texts.

There is evidently something peculiarly disturbing about what
Machiavelli said or implied, something that has caused profound and
lasting uneasiness. Modern scholars have pointed out certain real or
apparent inconsistencies between the (for the most part) republican
sentiment of *The Discourses* (and *The Histories*) and the advice to
absolute rulers in *The Prince*; indeed there is a difference of tone
between the two treatises, as well as chronological puzzles : this raises
problems about Machiavelli's character, motives and convictions
which for three hundred years and more have formed a rich field of
investigation and speculation for literary and linguistic scholars,
psychologists and historians.

But it is not this that has shocked western feeling. Nor can it be
only Machiavelli's 'realism' or his advocacy of brutal or unscrupulous
or ruthless policies that has so deeply upset so many later thinkers, and
driven some of them to explain or explain away his advocacy of force
and fraud. The fact that the wicked are seen to flourish or that immoral
courses appear to pay has never been very remote from the consciousness of mankind. The Bible, Herodotus, Thucydides, Plato, Aristotle
– to take only some of the fundamental works of western culture –
the characters of Jacob or Joshua or David, Samuel's advice to Saul,
Thucydides' Melian dialogue or his account of at least one ferocious
but rescinded Athenian resolution, the philosophies of Thrasymachus
and Callicles, Aristotle's advice to tyrants in the *Politics*, Carneades'
speeches to the Roman Senate as described by Cicero, Augustine's
view of the secular state from one vantage point, and Marsilio's from
another – all these had cast enough light on political realities to shock
the credulous out of uncritical idealism.

The explanation can scarcely lie in Machiavelli's tough-mindedness
alone, even though he did perhaps dot the i's and cross the t's more

THE ORIGINALITY OF MACHIAVELLI

sharply than anyone before him.[1] Even if the initial outcry – the reactions of, say, Pole or Gentillet – is to be so explained, this does not account for the reactions of those acquainted with the views of Hobbes or Spinoza or Hegel or the Jacobins and their heirs. Something else is surely needed to account both for the continuing horror and for the differences among the commentators. The two phenomena may not be unconnected. To indicate the nature of the latter phenomenon let me cite only the best known rival interpretations of Machiavelli's political views produced since the sixteenth century.

According to Alberico Gentili[2] and Garrett Mattingly,[3] the author of *The Prince* wrote a satire, for he certainly cannot literally have meant what he said. For Spinoza,[4] Rousseau,[5] Ugo Foscolo,[6] Luigi Ricci (who introduces *The Prince* to the readers of The World's Classics)[7] it is a cautionary tale; for whatever else he was, Machiavelli was a passionate patriot, a democrat, a believer in liberty, and *The Prince* must have been intended (Spinoza is particularly clear on this) to warn men of what tyrants could be and do, the better to resist them. Perhaps the author could not write openly with two rival powers – those of the church and of the Medici – eyeing him with equal (and not unjustified) suspicion. *The Prince* is therefore a satire (though no work seems to me to read less like one).

For A. H. Gilbert[8] it is anything but this – it is a typical piece of its period, a mirror for princes, a genre exercise common enough in the Renaissance and before (and after) it, with very obvious borrowings and 'echoes'; more gifted than most of these, and certainly more

---

[1] His habit of putting things *troppo assolutamente* had already been noted by Guicciardini. See 'Considerazioni intorno ai *Discorsi* del Machiavelli', book 1, chapter 3, p. 8 in *Scritti politici e ricordi*, ed. Roberto Palmarocchi (Bari, 1933).

[2] Alberico Gentili, *De legationibus libri tres* (London, 1585), book 3, chapter 9, pp. 101–2.

[3] Garrett Mattingly, 'Machiavelli's *Prince*: Political Science or Political Satire?', *American Scholar* 27 (1958), 482–91.

[4] Benedictus de Spinoza, *Tractatus politicus*, chapter 5, section 7.

[5] *Du contrat social*, book 3, chapter 6, note.

[6] *I sepolchri*, 156–8: 'che, temprando lo scettro a' regnatori,/gli allòr ne sfronda, ed alle genti svela/di che lagrime grondi e di che sangue . . .'.

[7] Luigi Ricci, preface to Niccolò Machiavelli, *The Prince* (London, 1903).

[8] Allan H. Gilbert, *Machiavelli's* Prince *and its Forerunners* (Durham, North Carolina, 1938).

AGAINST THE CURRENT

hard-boiled (and influential); but not so very different in style, content, or intention.

Giuseppe Prezzolini[1] and Hiram Haydn,[2] more plausibly, regard it as an anti-Christian piece (in this following Fichte and others)[3] and see it as an attack on the church and all her principles, a defence of the pagan view of life. Giuseppe Toffanin,[4] however, thinks Machiavelli was a Christian, though a somewhat peculiar one, a view from which Roberto Ridolfi,[5] his most distinguished living biographer, and Leslie Walker (in his English edition of *The Discourses*)[6] do not wholly dissent. Alderisio,[7] indeed, regards him as a sincere Catholic, although he does not go quite so far as Richelieu's agent, Canon Louis Machon, in his *Apology for Machiavelli*,[8] or the anonymous nineteenth-century compiler of *Religious Maxims faithfully extracted from the works of Niccolò Machiavelli* (referred to by Ridolfi in the last chapter of his biography).[9]

For Benedetto Croce[10] and all the many scholars who have followed him, Machiavelli is an anguished humanist, and one who, so far from seeking to soften the impression made by the crimes that he describes, laments the vices of men which make such wicked courses politically

[1] op. cit. (p. 25, note 2 above).

[2] Hiram Haydn, *The Counter-Renaissance* (New York, 1950).

[3] e.g. the Spaniards Pedro de Ribadeneira, *Tratado de la Religión* (Madrid, 1595), and Claudio Clemente (pseudonym of Juan Eusebio Nieremberg), *El Machiavelismo degollado* (Alcalá, 1637).

[4] Giuseppe Toffanin, *La fine dell'umanesimo* (Turin, 1920).

[5] Roberto Ridolfi, *Vita di Niccolò Machiavelli* (Rome, 1954), trans. by Cecil Grayson as *The Life of Niccolò Machiavelli* (London and Chicago, 1963).

[6] *The Discourses of Niccolò Machiavelli*, trans. with introduction and notes in 2 vols by Leslie J. Walker (London, 1950).

[7] Felice Alderisio, *Machiavelli: l'Arte dello Stato nell'azione e negli scritti* (Turin, 1930).

[8] As quoted by Prezzolini, op. cit. (p. 25, note 2 above), English version, p. 231.

[9] op. cit. (note 5 above), Italian version, p. 382; English version, p. 235.

[10] Croce ascribes to Machiavelli 'un'austera e dolorosa coscienza morale', *Elementi di politica* (Bari, 1925), p. 62. The idea that Machiavelli actually wishes to denounce naked power politics—what Gerhard Ritter in a volume of that name has called *Die Dämonie der Macht* — goes back to the sixteenth century (see Burd's still unsuperseded edition of *The Prince* (Oxford, 1891), pp. 31 ff.).

THE ORIGINALITY OF MACHIAVELLI

unavoidable – a moralist who 'occasionally experiences moral nausea'[1] in contemplating a world in which political ends can be achieved only by means that are morally evil, and thereby the man who divorced the province of politics from that of ethics. But for the Swiss scholars Walder, Kaegi and von Muralt[2] he is a peace-loving humanist, who believed in order, stability, pleasure in life, in the disciplining of the aggressive elements of our nature into the kind of civilised harmony that he found in its finest form among the well-armed Swiss democracies of his own time.[3]

For the neo-stoic Justus Lipsius and a century later for Algarotti (in 1759) and Alfieri[4] (in 1786) he was a passionate patriot, who saw in Cesare Borgia the man who, if he had lived, might have liberated Italy from the barbarous French and Spaniards and Austrians who were trampling over her and had reduced her to misery and poverty, decadence and chaos. Garrett Mattingly[5] could not credit this because it was obvious to him, and he did not doubt that it must have been no less obvious to Machiavelli, that Cesare was incompetent, a mountebank, a squalid failure; while Eric Vögelin seems to suggest that it is not Cesare, but (of all men) Tamerlane who was hovering before Machiavelli's fancy-laden gaze.[6]

For Cassirer,[7] Renaudet,[8] Olschki[9] and Keith Hancock,[10] Machiavelli is a cold technician, ethically and politically uncommitted, an objective analyst of politics, a morally neutral scientist, who (Karl

[1] op. cit. (p. 28, note 10 above), p. 66; see Cochrane's comment, op. cit. (p. 25, note 2 above), p. 115, note 9.

[2] For references see Cochrane, ibid., p. 118, note 19.

[3] 'The Swiss are most free [*liberissimi*] because the best armed [*armatissimi*].' *The Prince*, chapter 12.

[4] Vittorio Alfieri, *Del principe e delle lettere*, book 2, chapter 9. *Opere*, vol. 4, ed. Alessandro Donati (Bari, 1927), pp. 172–3.

[5] op. cit. (p. 27, note 3 above).

[6] Eric Vögelin, 'Machiavelli's *Prince*: Background and Formation', *Review of Politics* 13 (1951), 142–68.

[7] Ernst Cassirer, *The Myth of the State* (London and New Haven, Connecticut, 1946), chapter 12.

[8] Augustin Renaudet, *Machiavel: étude d'histoire des doctrines politiques* (Paris, 1942).

[9] Leonardo Olschki, *Machiavelli the Scientist* (Berkeley, California, 1945).

[10] W. K. Hancock, 'Machiavelli in Modern Dress: an Enquiry into Historical Method', *History* 20 (1935–6), 97–115.

AGAINST THE CURRENT

Schmid[1] tells us) anticipated Galileo in applying inductive methods
to social and historical material, and had no moral interest in the use
made of his technical discoveries – equally ready to place them at the
disposal of liberators and despots, good men and scoundrels. Renaudet
describes his method as 'purely positivist', Cassirer, as concerned with
'political statics'. But for Federico Chabod he is not coldly calculating
at all, but passionate to the point of unrealism;[2] Ridolfi, too, speaks of *il
grande appassionato*,[3] and De Caprariis[4] thinks him positively visionary.

For Herder he is, above all, a marvellous mirror of his age, a man
sensitive to the contours of his time, who faithfully described what
others did not admit or recognise, an inexhaustible mine of acute contemporary observation; and this is accepted by Ranke and Macaulay,
Burd and, in our day, Gennaro Sasso.[5] For Fichte he is a man of deep
insight into the real historical (or super-historical) forces that mould
men and transform their morality – in particular, a man who rejected
Christian principles for those of reason, political unity and centralisa-
tion. For Hegel he is the man of genius who saw the need for uniting
a chaotic collection of small and feeble principalities into a coherent
whole; his specific nostrums may excite disgust, but they are accidents
due to the conditions of their own time, now long past; yet, however
obsolete his precepts, he understood something more important – the
demands of his own age – that the hour had struck for the birth of the
modern, centralised, political state, for the formation of which he
'established the truly necessary fundamental principles'.[6]

[1] Karl Schmid, 'Machiavelli', in Rudolf Stadelmann (ed.), *Grosse Geschichts-
denker* (Tübingen/Stuttgart, 1949); see the illuminating review of Leonard
von Muralt, *Machiavellis Staatsgedanke* (Basel, 1945) by A. P. d'Entrèves,
English Historical Review 62 (1947), 96–9.

[2] In his original article of 1925 ('Del "Principe" di Niccolò Machiavelli',
Nuova rivista storica 9 (1925), 35–71, 189–216, 437–73; repr. as a book
(Milan/Rome/Naples, 1926)) Chabod develops Croce's view in a direction
closer to the conclusions of this article. See the English collection of Chabod's
essays on Machiavelli, *Machiavelli and the Renaissance*, trans. David Moore,
introduction by A. P. d'Entrèves (London, 1958), pp. 30–125 ('*The Prince*:
Myth and Reality') and *Scritti su Machiavelli* (Turin, 1964), pp. 29–135.

[3] op. cit. (p. 28, note 5 above), Italian version, p. 364.

[4] For reference see Cochrane, op. cit. (p. 25, note 2 above), p. 120, note 28.

[5] Gennaro Sasso, *Niccolò Machiavelli* (Naples, 1958).

[6] If Machiavelli's *Prince* is viewed in its historical context – of a divided,
invaded, humiliated Italy – it emerges not as a disinterested 'summary of
moral and political principles, appropriate to all situations and therefore to

THE ORIGINALITY OF MACHIAVELLI

The thesis that Machiavelli was above all an Italian and a patriot, speaking above all to his own generation, and if not solely to Florentines, at any rate only to Italians, and must be judged solely, or at least mainly, in terms of his historical context, is a position common to Herder and Hegel, Macaulay and Burd, De Sanctis and Oreste Tommasini.[1] Yet for Herbert Butterfield[2] and Raffaello Ramat[3] he suffers

none', but 'as a most magnificent and true conception on the part of a man of genuine political genius, a man of the greatest and noblest mind' (*Die Verfassung Deutschlands*, in *Schriften zur Politik und Rechtsphilosophie* (*Sämtliche Werke*, ed. Georg Lasson, vol. 7), 2nd ed. (Leipzig, 1923), p. 113). See p. 135 of the same work for Hegel's defence of 'die Gewalt eines Eroberers' conceived as a unifier of German lands. He regarded Machiavelli as a forerunner in an analogous Italian situation.

[1] Especially Tommasini in his huge compendium, *La vita e gli scritti di Niccolò Machiavelli nella loro relazione col Machiavellismo* (vol. 1, Rome/ Turin/Florence, 1883; vol. 2, Rome, 1911). In this connection Ernst Cassirer makes the valid and relevant point that to value – or justify – Machiavelli's opinions solely as a mirror of their times is one thing; to maintain that he was himself consciously addressing only his own countrymen and, if Burd is to be believed, not even all of them, is a very different one, and entails a false view of him and the civilisation to which he belonged. The Renaissance did not view itself in historical perspective. Machiavelli was looking for – and thought that he had found – timeless, universal truths about social behaviour. It is no service either to him or to the truth to deny or ignore the unhistorical assumptions which he shared with all his contemporaries and predecessors. The praise lavished upon him by the German historical school from Herder onwards, including the Marxist Antonio Gramsci, for the gifts in which they saw his strength – his realistic sense of his own times, his insight into the rapidly changing social and political conditions of Italy and Europe in his time, the collapse of feudalism, the rise of the national state, the altering power relationships within the Italian principalities and the like – might have been galling to a man who believed he had discovered eternal verities. He may, like his countryman Columbus, have mistaken the nature of his own achievement. If the historical school (including the Marxists) is right, Machiavelli did not do, and could not have done, what he set out to do.

But nothing is gained by supposing he did not set out to do it; and plenty of witnesses from his day to ours would deny Herder's assertion, and maintain that Machiavelli's goal – the discovery of the permanent principles of a political science – was anything but Utopian; and that he came nearer than most to attaining them.

[2] Herbert Butterfield, *The Statecraft of Machiavelli* (London, 1955).

[3] Raffaello Ramat, '*Il Principe*', in *Per la storia dello stile rinascimentale* (Messina/Florence, 1953), pp. 75–118.

AGAINST THE CURRENT

from an equal lack of scientific and historical sense. Obsessed by classical authors, his gaze is on an imaginary past; he deduces his political maxims in an unhistorical and *a priori* manner from dogmatic axioms (according to Lauri Huovinen)[1] – a method that was already becoming obsolete at the time in which he was writing; in this respect his slavish imitation of antiquity is judged to be inferior to the historical sense and sagacious judgement of his friend Guicciardini (so much for the discovery in him of inklings of modern scientific method).

For Bacon[2] (as for Spinoza, and later for Lassalle) he is above all the supreme realist and avoider of Utopian fantasies. Boccalini[3] is shocked by him, but cannot deny the accuracy or importance of his observations; so is Meinecke[4] for whom he is the father of *Staatsräson*, with which he plunged a dagger into the body politic of the west, inflicting a wound which only Hegel would know how to heal (this is Meinecke's optimistic verdict half a century ago, apparently withdrawn after the Second World War).

[1] Lauri Huovinen, *Das Bild vom Menschen im politischen Denken Niccolò Machiavellis* (*Annales Academiae Scientiarum Fennicae*, series B, vol. 74 (Helsinki, 1951), No 2).

[2] 'We are much beholden to Machiavelli and other writers of that class, who openly and unfeignedly declare and describe what men do, and not what they ought to do.' Bacon goes on to qualify this by explaining that to know the good one must investigate the evil, and ends by calling such approaches 'corrupt wisdom' (*De augmentis*, book 7, chapter 2, and book 8, chapter 2: quoted from *The Works of Francis Bacon*, ed. Spedding, Ellis and Heath (London, 1857–74), vol. 5, pp. 17 and 76). Compare Machiavelli's aphorism in a letter to Guicciardini, No 179 in the Alvisi edition (Niccolò Machiavelli, *Lettere familiari*, ed. Edoardo Alvisi (Florence, 1883)): 'io credo che questo sarebbe il vero modo ad andare in Paradiso, imparare la via dell'Inferno per fuggirla.' A. P. d'Entrèves has kindly drawn my attention to this characteristic passage; so far as I know there is no reason for supposing that Bacon had any knowledge of it. Nor, it may be, had T. S. Eliot when he wrote 'Lord Morley . . . intimates that Machiavelli . . . saw only half of the truth about human nature. What Machiavelli did not see about human nature is the myth of human goodness which for liberal thought replaces the belief in Divine Grace' ('Niccolò Machiavelli', in *For Lancelot Andrewes* (London, 1970), p. 50).

[3] Traiano Boccalini, *Ragguagli di Parnaso*, centuria prima, No 89.

[4] Friedrich Meinecke, *Die Idee der Staatsräson in der neueren Geschichte*, 2nd ed. (Munich/Berlin, 1927), trans. by Douglas Scott as *Machiavellism* (London, 1957).

32

THE ORIGINALITY OF MACHIAVELLI

But for König[1] he is not a tough-minded realist or cynic at all, but an aesthete seeking to escape from the chaotic and squalid world of the decadent Italy of his time into a dream of pure art, a man not interested in practice who painted an ideal political landscape; much (if I understand this view correctly) as Piero della Francesca painted an ideal city; *The Prince* is to be read as an idyll in the best neoclassical, neopastoral, Renaissance style (yet De Sanctis in the second volume of his *History of Italian Literature* denies it a place in the humanist tradition on account of Machiavelli's hostility to imaginative visions).

For Renzo Sereno[2] it is a fantasy indeed but of a bitterly frustrated man, and its dedication is the 'desperate plea'[3] of a victim of 'Fortune's great and steady malice'.[4] A psychoanalytic interpretation of one queer episode in Machiavelli's life is offered in support of his thesis.

For Macaulay he is a political pragmatist and a patriot who cared most of all for the independence of Florence, and acclaimed any form of rule that would ensure it.[5] Marx calls the *History of Florence* a 'masterpiece', and Engels (in the *Dialectics of Nature*) speaks of Machiavelli as one of the 'giants' of the Enlightenment, a man free from *petit-bourgeois* outlook. Soviet criticism is more ambivalent.[6]

---

[1] René König, *Niccolo Machiavelli: Zur Krisenanalyse einer Zeitenwende* (Zurich, 1941).

[2] Renzo Sereno, 'A Falsification by Machiavelli', *Renaissance News* 12 (1959), 159–67.

[3] ibid., p. 166.

[4] *The Prince*, dedication (trans. by Allan Gilbert in Machiavelli, *The Chief Works and Others*, 3 vols (Durham, North Carolina, 1965), vol. 1, p. 11: all quotations in this essay from Machiavelli's writings are given in this version, unless otherwise stated).

[5] For an extended modern development of this, see Judith Janoska-Bendl, 'Niccolò Machiavelli: Politik ohne Ideologie', *Archiv für Kulturgeschichte* 40 (1958), 315–45.

[6] The only extended treatment of Machiavelli by a prominent Bolshevik intellectual known to me is in Kamenev's short-lived introduction to the Russian translation of *The Prince* (Moscow, 1934), reprinted in English as 'Preface to Machiavelli', *New Left Review* No 15 (May–June 1962), 39–42. This unswervingly follows the full historicist-sociological approach criticised by Cassirer. Machiavelli is described as an active publicist, preoccupied by the 'mechanism of the struggles for power' within and between the Italian principalities, a sociologist who gave a masterly analysis of the 'sociological' jungle that preceded the formation of a 'powerful, national, essentially bourgeois'

AGAINST THE CURRENT

For the restorers of the short-lived Florentine republic he was
evidently nothing but a venal and treacherous toady, anxious to serve
any master, who had unsuccessfully tried to flatter the Medici in
the hope of gaining their favour. George Sabine (in his well-known
textbook)[1] views him as an anti-metaphysical empiricist, Hume or
Popper before his time, free from obscurantist, theological and
metaphysical preconceptions. For Antonio Gramsci[2] he is above all a
revolutionary innovator who directs his shafts against the obsolescent
feudal aristocracy and papacy and their mercenaries: his *Prince* is a
myth which signifies the dictatorship of new, progressive forces:
ultimately the coming role of the masses and of the need for the
emergence of new politically realistic leaders – *The Prince* is 'an
anthropomorphic symbol' of the hegemony of the 'collective will'.

Like Jakob Burckhardt[3] and Friedrich Meinecke,[4] C. J. Friedrich[5] and Charles Singleton[6] maintain that he has a developed conception of the state as a work of art; the great men who have founded or
maintain human associations are conceived as analogous to artists
whose aim is beauty, and whose essential qualification is understanding
of their material – they are moulders of men, as sculptors are moulders
of marble or clay.[7] Politics, in this view, leaves the realm of ethics,

---

Italian state. His almost 'dialectical' grasp of the realities of power, and freedom from metaphysical and theological fantasies, establish him as a worthy
forerunner of Marx, Engels, Lenin and Stalin. These opinions were brought
up at Kamenev's trial and pilloried by Vyshinsky, the prosecutor. See on this
Chimen Abramsky, 'Kamenev's Last Essay', *New Left Review* No 15 (May–
June 1962), 34–38; and, on the peculiar fate of Machiavelli in Russia, Jan
Malarczyk, *Politicheskoe uchenia Makiavelli v Rossii, v russkoi dorevolyut-
sionnoi i sovetskoi istoriografii* (*Annales Universitatis Mariae Curie-Sklod-
kowska*, vol. 6, No 1, section G, 1959 (Lublin, 1960)).

[1] George H. Sabine, *A History of Political Theory* (London, 1951).

[2] Antonio Gramsci, *Note sul Machiavelli*, in *Opere*, vol. 5 (Turin, 1949).

[3] Jakob Burckhardt, *The Civilization of the Renaissance in Italy*, trans.
S. G. C. Middlemore (London, 1929), part 1, chapter 7, pp. 104 ff.

[4] op. cit. (p. 32, note 4 above).

[5] C. J. Friedrich, *Constitutional Reason of State* (Providence, Rhode Island,
1957).

[6] Charles S. Singleton, 'The Perspective of Art', *Kenyon Review* 15 (1953),
169–89.

[7] See Joseph Kraft, 'Truth and Poetry in Machiavelli', *Journal of Modern
History* 23 (1951), 109–21.

THE ORIGINALITY OF MACHIAVELLI

and approaches that of aesthetics. Singleton argues that Machiavelli's originality consists in his view of political action as a form of what Aristotle called 'making' – the goal of which is a non-moral artefact, an object of beauty or use external to man (in this case a particular arrangement of human affairs) – and not of 'doing' (where Aristotle and Aquinas had placed it), the goal of which is internal and moral – not the creation of an object, but a particular kind – the right way – of living or being.

This position is not distant from that of Villari, Croce and others, inasmuch as it ascribes to Machiavelli the divorce of politics from ethics. Singleton transfers Machiavelli's conception of politics to the region of art, which is conceived as being amoral. Croce gives it an independent status of its own : of politics for politics' sake.

But the commonest view of him, at least as a political thinker, is still that of most Elizabethans, dramatists and scholars alike, for whom he is a man inspired by the Devil to lead good men to their doom, the great subverter, the teacher of evil, *le docteur de la scélératesse*, the inspirer of St Bartholomew's Eve, the original of Iago. This is the 'murderous Machiavel' of the famous four-hundred-odd references in Elizabethan literature.[1] His name adds a new ingredient to the more ancient figure of Old Nick. For the Jesuits he is 'the devil's partner in crime', 'a dishonourable writer and an unbeliever', and *The Prince* is, in Bertrand Russell's words, 'a handbook for gangsters' (compare with this Mussolini's description of it as a *'vade mecum* for statesmen', a view tacitly shared, perhaps, by other heads of state). This is the view common to Protestants and Catholics, Gentillet and François Hotman, Cardinal Pole, Bodin and Frederick the Great, followed by the

[1] Edward Meyer, *Machiavelli and the Elizabethan Drama* (Litterarhistorische Forschungen I: Weimar, 1897). See on this Christopher Morris, 'Machiavelli's Reputation in Tudor England', *Il pensiero politico* 2 (1969), 416–33, especially p. 423. See also Mario Praz, 'Machiavelli and the Elizabethans', *Proceedings of the British Academy* 13 (1928), 49–97; Napoleone Orsini, 'Elizabethan Manuscript Translations of Machiavelli's *Prince*', *Journal of the Warburg Institute* 1 (1937–8), 166–9; Felix Raab, *The English Face of Machiavelli* (London, 1964; Toronto, 1965); J. G. A. Pocock, 'Machiavelli, Harrington and English Political Ideologies in the Eighteenth Century', in *Politics, Language and Time* (London, 1972), pp. 104–47; and, most famous of all, Wyndham Lewis, *The Lion and the Fox* (London, 1951). Zera S. Fink in *The Classical Republicans* (Evanston, 1945), J. G. A. Pocock and Felix Raab stress his positive influence in seventeenth-century England, with Bacon and Harrington at the head of his admirers.

AGAINST THE CURRENT

authors of all the many anti-Machiavels, among the latest of whom
are Jacques Maritain[1] and Leo Strauss.[2]

There is prima facie something strange about so violent a disparity
of judgements.[3] What other thinker has presented so many facets to
the students of his ideas? What other writer – and he not even a recognised philosopher – has caused his readers to disagree about his purposes so deeply and so widely? Yet, I must repeat, Machiavelli does
not write obscurely; nearly all his interpreters praise him for his terse,
dry, clear prose.

What is it that has proved so arresting to so many? Let me deal with
some obvious answers. It is no doubt astonishing to find a thinker so
free from what we have been taught to regard as being the normal
intellectual assumptions of his age. Machiavelli does not so much as
mention natural law, the basic category in terms of which (or rather
the many varieties of which) Christians and pagans, teleologists and
materialists, jurists, theologians and philosophers, before and indeed
for many decades after him, discussed the very topics to which he
applied his mind. He was of course not a philosopher or a jurist:
nevertheless, he was a political expert, a well-read man of letters. The
influence of the old Stoic-Christian doctrine was not, by his time,
what it had once been in Italy, especially among the early humanists.
Still, having set himself to generalise about the behaviour of men in
society in a novel fashion, Machiavelli might have been expected, if
not to refute or reject explicitly, at least to deliver a glancing blow at
some of the assumptions which, he clearly thinks, have led so many to
their doom. He does, after all, tell us that his path has never before
been trodden by any man, and this, in his case, is no mere cliché: there
is, therefore, something extraordinary in the fact that he completely

[1] Jacques Maritain, 'The End of Machiavellianism', *Review of Politics* 4
(1942), 1–33.
[2] Leo Strauss, *Thoughts on Machiavelli* (Glencoe, Illinois, 1958).
[3] One of the best and liveliest accounts of the mass of conflicting theories
about *The Prince* is provided by E. W. Cochrane in the article cited above
on p. 25, note 2, to which this catalogue owes a great deal. For earlier conflicts see Pasquale Villari's standard and in some ways still unsuperseded *The
Life and Times of Niccolò Machiavelli*, trans. Linda Villari (London, 1898),
and the earlier works cited by him, e.g. Robert von Mohl, 'Die Machiavelli-
Literatur', in *Die Geschichte und Literatur der Staatswissenschaften* (Erlangen,
1855–8), vol. 3, pp. 519–91, and J. F. Christius, *De Nicolao Machiavelli
libri tres* (Leipzig, 1731). For later works see above, p. 25, note 2.

THE ORIGINALITY OF MACHIAVELLI

ignores the concepts and categories – the routine paraphernalia – in terms of which the best-known thinkers and scholars of his day were accustomed to express themselves. And, indeed, Gentillet in his *Contre-Machiavel* denounces him precisely for this. Only Marsilio before him had dared do this: and Neville Figgis thinks it a dramatic break with the past.[1]

The absence of Christian psychology and theology – sin, grace, redemption, salvation – need cause less surprise: few contemporary humanists speak in such terms. The medieval heritage has grown very thin. But, and this is more noteworthy, there is no trace of Platonic or Aristotelian teleology, no reference to any ideal order, to any doctrine of man's place in nature in the great chain of being, with which the Renaissance thinkers are deeply concerned – which, say, Ficino or Pico or Poggio virtually take for granted. There is nothing here of what Popper has called 'essentialism', *a priori* certainty directly revealed to reason or intuition about the unalterable development of men or social groups in certain directions, in pursuit of goals implanted in them by God or by nature. The method and the tone are empirical. Even Machiavelli's theory of historical cycles is not metaphysically guaranteed.

As for religion, it is for him not much more than a socially indispensable instrument, so much utilitarian cement: the criterion of the worth of a religion is its role as a promoter of solidarity and cohesion – he anticipates Saint-Simon and Durkheim in stressing its crucial social importance. The great founders of religions are among the men he most greatly admires. Some varieties of religion (e.g. Roman paganism) are good for societies, since they make them strong or spirited; others on the contrary (e.g. Christian meekness and unworldliness) cause decay or disintegration. The weakening of religious ties is a part of general decadence and corruption: there is no need for a religion to rest on truth, provided that it is socially effective.[2] Hence his veneration of those who set their societies on sound spiritual foundations – Moses, Numa, Lycurgus.

There is no serious assumption of the existence of God and divine law; whatever our author's private convictions, an atheist can read Machiavelli with perfect intellectual comfort. Nor is there piety towards authority, or prescription – nor any interest in the role of the

[1] John Neville Figgis, *Studies of Political Thought from Gerson to Grotius*, 2nd ed. (Cambridge, 1916).

[2] *Discourses* I 12.

37

AGAINST THE CURRENT

individual conscience, or in any other metaphysical or theological issue. The only freedom he recognises is political freedom, freedom from arbitrary despotic rule, i.e. republicanism, and the freedom of one state from control by other states, or rather of the city or *patria*, for 'state' may be a premature term in this connection.[1]

There is no notion of the rights of, or obligation to, corporations or non-political establishments, sacred or secular – the need for absolute centralised power (if not for sovereignty) is taken for granted. There is scarcely any historical sense: men are much the same everywhere, and at all times, and what has served well for the ancients – their rules of medicine, or warfare, or statecraft – will surely also work for the moderns. Tradition is valued chiefly as a source of social stability. Since there is no far-off divine event to which creation moves and no Platonic ideal for societies or individuals, there is no notion of progress, either material or spiritual. The assumption is that the blessings of the classical age can be restored (if fortune is not too unpropitious) by enough knowledge and will, by *virtù* on the part of a leader, and by appropriately trained and bravely and skilfully led citizens. There are no intimations of an irrevocably determined flow of events; neither *fortuna* nor *necessità* dominates the whole of existence; there are no absolute values which men ignore or deny to their inevitable doom.

It is, no doubt, this freedom from even such relics of the traditional metaphysics of history as linger on in the works of even such perfectly secular humanists as Egidio and Pontano, not to mention earlier authors of 'mirrors for princes', as well as Machiavelli's constant concern with the concrete and practical issues of his day, and not any mysterious presentiment of the coming scientific revolution, that gives him so modern a flavour. Yet it is plainly not these characteristics that have proved so deeply fascinating and horrifying to his readers

---

[1] See on this much-discussed issue the relevant theses of J. H. Whitfield in *Machiavelli* (Oxford, 1947), especially pp. 93–5, and J. H. Hexter in '*Il principe* and *lo stato*', *Studies in the Renaissance* 4 (1957), 113–35, and the opposed views of Fredi Chiapelli in *Studi sul linguaggio del Machiavelli* (Florence, 1952), pp. 59–73, Francesco Ercole in *La politica di Machiavelli* (Rome, 1926) and Felix Gilbert, op. cit. (p. 25, note 2 above), pp. 328–30. For an earlier version of Gilbert's anti-Ercole thesis see his 'The Concept of Nationalism in Machiavelli's *Prince*', *Studies in the Renaissance* 1 (1954), 38–48. H. C. Dowdall goes further and seems to maintain that it is, in effect, by inventing the word 'state' that Machiavelli founded modern political science ('The Word "State"', *Law Quarterly Review* 39 (1923), 98–125).

THE ORIGINALITY OF MACHIAVELLI

from his day to our own. 'Machiavelli's doctrine', wrote Meinecke, 'was a sword thrust in the body politic of Western humanity, causing it to cry out and to struggle against itself.'[1]

What was it that was so upsetting in the views of Machiavelli? What was the 'dagger' and the 'unhealed wound' of which Meinecke speaks, 'the most violent mutilation suffered by the human practical intellect'[2] which Maritain so eloquently denounced? If it is not Machiavelli's (ruthless, but scarcely original) realism, nor his (relatively original, but by the eighteenth century pretty widespread) empiricism that proves so shocking during all these centuries, what was it?

'*Nothing*,' says one of his commentators:[3] *The Prince* is a mere tabulation of types of government and rulers, and of methods of maintaining them. It is this and no more. All the 'feeling and controversy' occasioned by it evidently rest on an almost universal misreading of an exceptionally clear, morally neutral text.

I cite this not uncommon view for fairness's sake. My own answer to the question will be clearer if before offering it I state (in however brief and over-simplified a form) what I believe Machiavelli's positive beliefs to have been.

II

Like the Roman writers whose ideals were constantly before his mind, like Cicero and Livy, Machiavelli believed that what men – at any rate superior men – sought was the fulfilment and the glory that come from the creation and maintenance by common endeavour of a strong and well-governed social whole. Only those will accomplish this who know the relevant facts. If you make mistakes and live in a state of delusion, you will fail in whatever you undertake, for reality misunderstood – or worse still, ignored or scorned – will always defeat you in the end. We can achieve what we want only if we understand firstly ourselves, and then the nature of the material with which we work.

Our first task, therefore, is the acquisition of such knowledge. This, for Machiavelli, was mainly psychological and sociological: the best

[1] op. cit. (p. 32, note 4 above), p. 61 (English version, p. 49).

[2] op. cit. (p. 36, note 1 above), p. 3.

[3] Jeffrey Pulver, *Machiavelli: The Man, His Work, and His Times* (London, 1937), p. 227.

AGAINST THE CURRENT

source of information is a mixture of shrewd observation of contemporary reality together with whatever wisdom may be gleaned from
the best observers of the past, in particular the great minds of antiquity,
the sages whose company (as he says in his celebrated letter to Vettori)
he seeks when he gets away from the trivial occupations of his daily
life; these noble spirits, in their humanity, treat him kindly and yield
answers to his questions; it is they who have taught him that men are
in need of firm and energetic civil government. Different men pursue
different ends, and for each pursuit need an appropriate skill. Sculptors,
doctors, soldiers, architects, statesmen, lovers, adventurers each pursue
their own particular goals. To make it possible for them to do so,
governments are needed, for there is no hidden hand which brings all
these human activities into natural harmony. (This kind of approach
is wholly typical of the humanism of Machiavelli's country and his
time.) Men need rulers because they require someone to order human
groups governed by diverse interests and bring them security, stability,
above all protection against enemies, to establish social institutions
which alone enable men to satisfy their needs and aspirations. They
will never attain to this unless they are individually and socially
healthy; only an adequate education can make them physically and
mentally sturdy, vigorous, ambitious and energetic enough for effective
cooperation in the pursuit of order, power, glory, success.

Techniques of government exist – of that he has no doubt – although
the facts, and therefore the methods of dealing with them, may look
different to a ruler and to his subjects: this is a matter of perspective:
'those who draw maps of countries put themselves low down on the
plains to observe the nature of mountains . . . and to observe that of
low places put themselves high up on mountain tops'.[1] What is certain
is that unless there is a firm hand at the helm, the ship of state will
founder. Human society will collapse into chaos and squalor unless a
competent specialist directs it; and although Machiavelli himself gives
reasons for preferring freedom and republican rule, there are situations
in which a strong prince (the Duke of Valentino, even a Medici, if his
plea had any sincerity to it) is preferable to a weak republic.

All this Aristotle and the later Stoics would have endorsed. But
from the fact that there is such a thing as an art of government, indispensable to the attainment of goals that men in fact seek, it does not
follow that Machiavelli did not care to what uses it was applied, and
merely produced a handbook of scientific political 'directives' that was

[1] *The Prince*, dedication.

40

THE ORIGINALITY OF MACHIAVELLI

morally neutral, *wertfrei*. For he makes it all too plain what it is that he himself desires.

Men must be studied in their behaviour as well as in their professions. There is no *a priori* route to the knowledge of the human material with which a ruler must deal. There is, no doubt, an unchanging human nature the range of whose response to changing situations can be determined (there is no trace in Machiavelli's thought of any notion of systematic evolution or of the individual or society as a self-transforming entity); one can obtain this knowledge only by empirical observation. Men are not as they are described by those who idealise them – Christians or other Utopians – nor by those who want them to be widely different from what in fact they are and always have been and cannot help being. Men (at least his own countrymen for and about whom he was writing) seem to him for the most part to be 'ungrateful, wanton, false and dissimulating, cowardly and greedy . . . arrogant and mean, their natural impulse is to be insolent when their affairs are prospering and abjectly servile when adversity hits them.'[1] They care little for liberty – the name means more to them than the reality – and they place it well below security, property or desire for revenge. These last the ruler can provide to a reasonable degree. Men are easily corrupted, and difficult to cure. They respond both to fear and to love, to the cruel Hannibal and to the just and humane Scipio. If these emotions cannot be combined, fear is the more reliable : provided always that it does not turn to hate, which destroys the minimum of respect that subjects must retain for those who govern them.

Society is, normally, a battlefield in which there are conflicts between and within groups. These conflicts can be controlled only by the judicious use of both persuasion and force. How is this done? As in medicine, architecture or the art of war, we can obtain systematic knowledge of the required technique if only we will look at the practice (and the theory) of the most successful societies we know, namely those of classical times.

Machiavelli's theories are certainly not based on the scientific principles of the seventeenth century. He lived a hundred years before Galileo and Bacon, and his method is a mixture of rules of thumb, observation, historical knowledge and general sagacity, somewhat like

[1] This celebrated passage from the seventeenth chapter of *The Prince* is here given in Prezzolini's vivid rendering: see his 'The Christian Roots of Machiavelli's Moral Pessimism', *Review of National Literatures* 1 (1970), 26–37: 27.

AGAINST THE CURRENT

the empirical medicine of the pre-scientific world. He abounds in precepts, in useful maxims, practical hints, scattered reflections, especially historical parallels, even though he claims to have discovered general laws, eternally valid *regole generali*. An example of a triumph or a failure in the ancient world, a striking saying by an ancient author, carries more weight with him (as Butterfield and Ramat correctly note) than historical analysis of the type that was becoming common even in his own day, and of which Guicciardini was a master.

Above all he warns one to be on one's guard against those who do not look at men as they are, and see them through spectacles coloured by their hopes and wishes, their loves and hatreds, in terms of an idealised model of man as they want him to be, and not as he is and was and will be. Honest reformers, however worthy their ideals, like the worthy leader of the Florentine republic, Piero Soderini, whom Machiavelli served, or the far more gifted Savonarola (towards whom his attitude oscillates sharply), foundered and caused the ruin of others, largely because they substituted what should be for what is; because at some point they fell into unrealism.

They were men of very different quality. Savonarola had a strong will, whereas Soderini was, in Machiavelli's view, small-minded and indecisive. But what they had in common was an inadequate grasp of how to use power. At the crucial moment they both showed their lack of a sense of *verità effettuale* in politics, of what works in practice, of real power, of the big battalions. Machiavelli's texts contain frequent warnings against unreliable sources of information, émigrés for example, whose minds are distorted by their wishes and cannot attain to an objective view of the facts, and others whose reason (this is a humanist commonplace) is darkened by the passions that distort their vision.

What has led and will lead such statesmen to their doom? Often enough only their ideals. What is wrong with ideals? That they cannot be attained. How does one know this? This is one of the foundations upon which Machiavelli's claim to be a thinker of the first order ultimately rests. Machiavelli has a clear vision of the society which he wishes to see realised on earth, or if this sounds too grandiose for so concrete and applied a thinker, the society which he wishes to see attained in his own country, perhaps even in his own lifetime; at any rate within the predictable future. He knows that such an order can be created, because it, or something sufficiently close to it, has been

42

THE ORIGINALITY OF MACHIAVELLI

realised in Italy in the past, or in other countries – the Swiss or German cities for example, or the great centralised states in his own time. It is not merely that he wishes to create or restore such an order in Italy, but that he sees in it the most desirable condition that can, as both history and observation teach, be attained by men.

The data of observation are drawn mainly from contemporary Italy; as for history, it is for him what had been recorded by the great historians, the writers whom he most admires, Romans, Greeks, the authors of the Old Testament. Where have men risen to their full height? In Periclean Athens, and in the greatest period of human history – the Roman Republic before its decline, when Rome ruled the world. But he thinks well, too, of the reigns of the 'good' emperors, from Nerva to Marcus Aurelius. He does not feel that he needs to demonstrate that these were golden hours in the life of humanity; this, he believes, must be self-evident to anyone who contemplates these epochs and compares them with the bad periods – the last years of the Roman Republic, the collapse that followed, the barbarian invasion, the medieval darkness (although he may not have thought of it in these terms), the divisions of Italy, the weakness, the poverty, the misery, the defencelessness of the faction-ridden Italian principalities of his own day before the trampling armies of the great, well organised national states of the north and the west.

He does not trouble to argue this at length: it seems to him perfectly obvious (as it must have done to most men of his age) that Italy was both materially and morally in a bad way. He did not need to explain what he meant by vice, corruption, weakness, lives unworthy of human beings. A good society is a society that enjoys stability, internal harmony, security, justice, a sense of power and of splendour, like Athens in its best days, like Sparta, like the kingdoms of David and Solomon, like Venice as it used to be, but, above all, like the Roman Republic. 'Truly it is a marvellous thing to consider to what greatness Athens came in the space of a hundred years after she freed herself from the tyranny of Pisistratus. But above all, it is very marvellous to observe what greatness Rome came to after she freed herself from her kings.'[1]

The reason for this is that there were men in these societies who knew how to make cities great. How did they do it? By developing certain faculties in men, of inner moral strength, magnanimity, vigour, vitality, generosity, loyalty, above all public spirit, civic sense,

[1] *Discourses* II 2.

AGAINST THE CURRENT

dedication to the security, power, glory, expansion of the *patria*. The ancients developed these qualities by all kinds of means, among which were dazzling shows and bloodstained sacrifices that excited men's senses and aroused their martial prowess, and especially by the kind of legislation and education that promoted the pagan virtues. Power, magnificence, pride, austerity, pursuit of glory, vigour, discipline, *antiqua virtus* – this is what makes states great. Agesilaus and Timoleon, Brutus and Scipio, are his heroes; not Pisistratus or Julius Caesar who extinguished republican regimes and destroyed their spirit by exploiting human weaknesses. But there is no need to stay within Graeco-Roman confines; Moses and Cyrus are as deserving of respect as Theseus and Romulus – stern, sagacious and incorruptible men who founded nations and were rightly honoured by them.

What was done once can be done again. Machiavelli does not believe in the irreversibility of the historical process or the uniqueness of each of its phases. The glories of antiquity can be revived if only men vigorous and gifted and realistic enough can be mobilised for the purpose. In order to cure degenerate populations of their diseases, these founders of new states or churches may be compelled to have recourse to ruthless measures, force and fraud, guile, cruelty, treachery, the slaughter of the innocent, surgical measures that are needed to restore a decayed body to a condition of health. And, indeed, these qualities may be needed even after a society has been restored to health; for men are weak and foolish and perpetually liable to lapse from the standards that alone can preserve them on the required height. Hence they must be kept in proper condition by measures that will certainly offend against current morality. But if they offend against this morality, in what sense can they be said to be justified? This seems to me to be the nodal point of Machiavelli's entire conception. In one sense they can be justified, and in another not; these senses must be distinguished more clearly than he found it necessary to do, for he was not a philosopher, and did not set himself to the task of examining, or even spelling out, the implications of his own ideas.

Let me try to make this clearer. It is commonly said, especially by those who follow Croce, that Machiavelli divided politics from morals – that he recommended as politically necessary courses which common opinion morally condemns: e.g. treading over corpses for the benefit of the state. Leaving aside the question of what was his conception of the state, and whether[1] he in fact possessed one, it seems to

[1] See p. 38, note 1 above.

THE ORIGINALITY OF MACHIAVELLI

me that this is a false antithesis. For Machiavelli the ends which he advocates are those to which he thinks wise human beings, who understand reality, will dedicate their lives. Ultimate ends in this sense, whether or not they are those of the Judaeo-Christian tradition, are what is usually meant by moral values.

What Machiavelli distinguishes is not specifically moral from specifically political values;[1] what he achieves is not the emancipation of politics from ethics or religion, which Croce and many other commentators regard as his crowning achievement; what he institutes is something that cuts deeper still – a differentiation between two incompatible ideals of life, and therefore two moralities. One is the morality of the pagan world: its values are courage, vigour, fortitude in adversity, public achievement, order, discipline, happiness, strength, justice, above all assertion of one's proper claims and the knowledge and power needed to secure their satisfaction; that which for a Renaissance reader Pericles had seen embodied in his ideal Athens, Livy had found in the old Roman Republic, that of which Tacitus and Juvenal lamented the decay and death in their own time. These seem to Machiavelli the best hours of mankind and, Renaissance humanist that he is, he wishes to restore them.

Against this moral universe (moral or ethical no less in Croce's than in the traditional sense, that is, embodying ultimate human ends however these are conceived) stands in the first and foremost place, Christian morality. The ideals of Christianity are charity, mercy, sacrifice, love of God, forgiveness of enemies, contempt for the goods of this world, faith in the life hereafter, belief in the salvation of the individual soul as being of incomparable value – higher than, indeed wholly incommensurable with, any social or political or other terrestrial goal, any economic or military or aesthetic consideration. Machiavelli lays it down that out of men who believe in such ideals, and practise them, no satisfactory human community, in his Roman sense, can in principle be constructed. It is not simply a question of the unattainability of an ideal because of human imperfection, original sin, or bad luck, or ignorance, or insufficiency of material means. It is not, in other words, the inability in practice on the part of ordinary human

---

[1] For which he is commended by De Sanctis, and (as Prezzolini points out, op. cit., p. 25, note 2 above) condemned by Maurice Joly in the famous *Dialogue aux enfers entre Machiavel et Montesquieu* (Brussells, 1864), which served as the original of the forged *Protocols of the Learned Elders of Zion* (London, 1920).

45

AGAINST THE CURRENT

beings to rise to a sufficiently high level of Christian virtue (which may, indeed, be the inescapable lot of sinful men on earth) that makes it, for him, impracticable to establish, even to seek after, the good Christian state. It is the very opposite: Machiavelli is convinced that what are commonly thought of as the central Christian virtues, whatever their intrinsic value, are insuperable obstacles to the building of the kind of society that he wishes to see; a society which, moreover, he assumes that it is natural for all normal men to want — the kind of community that, in his view, satisfies men's permanent desires and interests.

If human beings were different from what they are, perhaps they could create an ideal Christian society. But he is clear that human beings would in that event have to differ too greatly from men as they have always been; and it is surely idle to build for, or discuss the prospects of, beings who can never be on earth; such talk is beside the point, and only breeds dreams and fatal delusions. What ought to be done must be defined in terms of what is practicable, not imaginary; statecraft is concerned with action within the limits of human possibility, however wide; men can be changed, but not to a fantastic degree. To advocate ideal measures, suitable only for angels, as previous political writers seem to him too often to have done, is visionary and irresponsible and leads to ruin.

It is important to realise that Machiavelli does not wish to deny that what Christians call good is, in fact, good, that what they call virtue and vice are in fact virtue and vice. Unlike Hobbes or Spinoza (or eighteenth-century *philosophes* or, for that matter, the first Stoics), who try to define (or redefine) moral notions in such a way as to fit in with the kind of community that, in their view, rational men must, if they are consistent, wish to build, Machiavelli does not fly in the face of common notions — the traditional, accepted moral vocabulary of mankind. He does not say or imply (as various radical philosophical reformers have done) that humility, kindness, unworldliness, faith in God, sanctity, Christian love, unwavering truthfulness, compassion, are bad or unimportant attributes; or that cruelty, bad faith, power politics, sacrifice of innocent men to social needs, and so on, are good ones.

But if history, and the insights of wise statesmen, especially in the ancient world, verified as they have been in practice (*verità effettuale*), are to guide us, it will be seen that it is in fact impossible to combine Christian virtues, for example meekness or the search for spiritual

46

THE ORIGINALITY OF MACHIAVELLI

salvation, with a satisfactory, stable, vigorous, strong society on earth. Consequently a man must choose. To choose to lead a Christian life is to condemn oneself to political impotence: to being used and crushed by powerful, ambitious, clever, unscrupulous men; if one wishes to build a glorious community like those of Athens or Rome at their best, then one must abandon Christian education and substitute one better suited to the purpose.

Machiavelli is not a philosopher and does not deal in abstractions, but what his thesis comes to is of central concern to political theory: that a fact which men will not face is that these two goals, both, evidently, capable of being believed in by human beings (and, we may add, of raising them to sublime heights), are not compatible with one another. What usually happens, in his view, is that since men cannot bring themselves resolutely to follow either of these paths wherever they may lead ('men take certain middle ways that are very injurious; indeed, they are unable to be altogether good or altogether bad'),[1] they try to effect compromises, vacillate, fall between two stools, and end in weakness and failure.

Anything that leads to political ineffectiveness is condemned by him. In a famous passage in the *Discourses* he says that Christian faith has made men 'weak', easy prey to 'wicked men', since they 'think more about enduring their injuries than about avenging them'.[2] The general effect of Christian teaching has been to crush men's civic spirit, and make them endure humiliations uncomplainingly, so that destroyers and despots encounter too little resistance. Hence Christianity is in this respect compared unfavourably with Roman religion, which made men stronger and more 'ferocious'.

Machiavelli modifies this judgement on Christianity in at least two passages in the *Discourses*. In the first he observes that Christianity has had this unfortunate effect only because it was misinterpreted in a spirit of *ozio* – quietism or indolence – for there is surely nothing in Christianity which forbids 'the betterment and the defence of our country'.[3] In the second passage he declares that 'If religion of this sort had been kept up among the princes of Christendom, in the form in which its giver founded it, Christian states and republics would be more united, much more happy than they are',[4] but the decadent Christianity of the church of Rome has had the opposite effect – the

---

[1] *Discourses* I 26.
[3] ibid.
[2] ibid. II 2.
[4] ibid. I 12.

AGAINST THE CURRENT

papacy has destroyed 'all piety and all religion' in Italy, and her unity too.

Even if these passages are taken literally, and are not viewed as pieces of minimum lip-service to avert clerical censorship or persecution, what they assert is that if the church had developed a patriotic and thoroughly militant outlook, on the lines of Roman *antiqua virtus*, and had made men virile, stern, devout and public-spirited, it would have produced more satisfactory social consequences. What it has done is to lead, on the one hand, to corruption and political division – the fault of the papacy – and on the other, to other-worldliness and meek endurance of suffering on earth for the sake of the eternal life beyond the grave. It is this last strain that dissolves the social fabric and helps bullies and oppressors.

In his political attack on the church of Rome, shared by Guicciardini and others in his time, Machiavelli might have found enthusiastic allies in the Reformation (there is no evidence, so far as I know, that news of the 'monks' quarrel' had ever reached his ears). His demand for a Christianity which did not put the blessings of a pure conscience and faith in heaven above earthly success, and exalted love of glory and self-assertion above meekness and resignation, might have been more difficult to meet. Machiavelli finds nothing to criticise in pagan Roman religion at its most vigorous; he demands a similar religion – not necessarily wholly unchristian, but muscular enough to be, for practical purposes, not less effective. It does not seem unreasonable to conclude from this (as Fichte[1] and Prezzolini[2] tell us) that he is an implacable critic of truly Christian institutions, rather than their champion. In this he is followed by all those later thinkers who share with him either his conception of man and his natural needs (eighteenth-century materialists, Nietzsche, social Darwinists) or (like Rousseau and some nineteenth-century positivists) his civic ideals.

It is important to note that Machiavelli does not formally condemn Christian morality, or the approved values of his own society. Unlike systematic moralists like Hobbes or Spinoza he does not attempt to redefine terms to conform with an egoistic rationalism, so that such Christian virtues as, say, pity, humility, self-sacrifice, obedience are shown to be weaknesses or vices. He transposes nothing: the things men call good are indeed good. Words like *buono, cattivo, onesto, inu-*

[1] *Fichte's Werke*, ed. Immanuel Hermann Fichte (Berlin, 1971), vol. 11, pp. 411–13.

[2] op. cit. (p. 25, note 2 above), English version, p. 43.

THE ORIGINALITY OF MACHIAVELLI

mano etc. are used by him as they were in the common speech of his time, and indeed of our own. He merely says that the practice of these virtues makes it impossible to build a society which, once it is contemplated, in the pages of history or by the political imagination, will surely awaken in us – in any man – a great longing.

One of the crucial passages is to be found in the tenth chapter of the first book of the *Discourses* : he is distinguishing between the good and the bad Roman emperors on the lines of Tacitus or Dio, and adds 'if a prince is of human birth, he will be frightened away from any imitation of wicked times and will be fired with an immense eagerness [*immenso desiderio*] to follow the ways of good ones' – 'good' in some non-Christian sense, evidently. Whitfield thinks that he is not pessimistic or cynical. Perhaps not cynical – that is a fine point : the line between cynicism (and indeed pessimism too) and an unflinching realism is at times not easy to draw. But Machiavelli is not, in the usual sense of the word, hopeful. Yet like every humanist thinker from his own day to ours, he believes that if only the truth were known – the real truth, not the fairy tales of shallow moralists – it would help to make men understand themselves and make them go farther.

He believes also that the qualities that men need in order to revive these *buoni tempi* are not compatible with those that are urged upon them by Christian education. He does not seek to correct the Christian conception of a good man. He does not say that saints are not saints, or that honourable behaviour is not honourable or to be admired ; only that this type of goodness cannot, at least in its traditionally accepted forms, create or maintain a strong, secure and vigorous society, that it is in fact fatal to it. He points out that in our world men who pursue such ideals are bound to be defeated and to lead other people to ruin, since their view of the world is not founded upon the truth, at least not upon *verità effettuale* – the truth that is tested by success and experience – which (however cruel) is always, in the end, less destructive than the other (however noble).

If the two passages mentioned above[1] are to be taken literally, Christianity, at least in theory, could have taken a form not incompatible with the qualities that he celebrates ; but, not surprisingly, he does not pursue this line of thought. History took another turn. The idea of such a Christian commonwealth – if he gave it a serious thought – must have seemed to him as Utopian as a world in which all

[1] See p. 47, notes 3 and 4 above.

49

AGAINST THE CURRENT

or even most men are good. Christian principles have weakened men's civic virtues. Speculation on the form that Christianity might have taken, or could, in unlikely circumstances, still take, can for him only be an idle (and dangerous) pastime.

Christians as he knew them in history and his own experience, that is, men who in their practice actually follow Christian precepts, are good men, but if they govern states in the light of such principles, they lead them to destruction. Like Prince Myshkin in Dostoevsky's *The Idiot*, like the well-meaning *Gonfalonieri* of the Florentine Republic, like Savonarola, they are bound to be defeated by the realists (the Medici or the Pope or King Ferdinand of Spain) who understand how to create lasting institutions; build them, if need be, on the bones of innocent victims. I should like to emphasise again that he does not explicitly condemn Christian morality: he merely points out that it is, at least in rulers (but to some degree in subjects too), incompatible with those social ends which he thinks it natural and wise for men to seek. One can save one's soul, or one can found or maintain or serve a great and glorious state; but not always both at once.

This is a vast and eloquent development of Aristotle's *obiter dictum* in the *Politics* that a good man may not be identical with a good citizen (even though Aristotle was not thinking in terms of spiritual salvation). Machiavelli does not explicitly rate either way of life above the other. When he says 'hate is incurred as much by means of good deeds as of bad',[1] he means by 'good deeds' what any man brought up to live by Christian values means. Again, when he says that good faith, integrity are 'praiseworthy'[2] even if they end in failure, he means by 'praiseworthy' that it is right to praise them, for of course what is good (in the ordinary sense) *is* good. When he praises the 'chastity, affability, courtesy, and liberality'[3] of Scipio or Cyrus or Timoleon, or even the 'goodness' of the Medici Pope Leo X, he speaks (whether he is sincere or not) in terms of values that are common to Cicero and Dante, to Erasmus and to us. In the famous fifteenth chapter of *The Prince* he says that liberality, mercy, honour, humanity, frankness, chastity, religion, and so forth, are indeed virtues, and a life lived in the exercise of these virtues would be successful if men were all good. But they are not; and it is idle to hope that they will become so. We must take men as we find them, and seek to improve them along possible, not impossible, lines.

[1] *The Prince*, chapter 19.   [2] ibid., chapter 18.
[3] ibid., chapter 14.

THE ORIGINALITY OF MACHIAVELLI

This may involve the benefactors of men – the founders, educators, legislators, rulers – in terrible cruelties. 'I am aware that everyone will admit that it would be most praiseworthy for a prince to exhibit such of the above-mentioned qualities as are considered good. But because no ruler can possess or fully practise them, on account of human conditions that do not permit it',[1] he must at times behave very differently in order to compass his ends. Moses and Theseus, Romulus and Cyrus all killed; what they created lasted, and was glorious; '. . . any man who under all conditions insists on making it his business to be good will surely be destroyed among so many who are not good. Hence a prince . . . must acquire the power to be not good, and understand when to use it and when not to use it, in accord with necessity.'[2] 'If all men were good, this maxim [to break faith if interest dictates] would not be good, but . . . they are bad.'[3] Force and guile must be met with force and guile.

The qualities of the lion and the fox are not in themselves morally admirable, but if a combination of these qualities will alone preserve the city from destruction, then these are the qualities that leaders must cultivate. They must do this not simply to serve their own interest, that is, because this is how one can become a leader, although whether men become leaders or not is a matter of indifference to the author – but because human societies in fact stand in need of leadership, and cannot become what they should be, save by the effective pursuit of power, of stability, *virtù*, greatness. These can be attained when men are led by Scipios and Timoleons or, if times are bad, men of more ruthless character. Hannibal was cruel, and cruelty is not a laudable quality, but if a sound society can be built only by conquest, and if cruelty is necessary to it, then it must not be evaded.

Machiavelli is not sadistic; he does not gloat on the need to employ ruthlessness or fraud for creating or maintaining the kind of society that he admires and recommends. His most savage examples and precepts apply only to situations in which the population is thoroughly corrupt, and needs violent measures to restore it to health, e.g. where a new prince takes over, or a revolution against a bad prince must be made effective. Where a society is relatively sound, or the rule is traditional and hereditary and supported by public sentiment, it would be quite wrong to practise violence for violence's sake, since its results would be destructive of social order, when the purpose of government is to create order, harmony, strength. If you are a lion and a fox you

[1] ibid., chapter 15.   [2] ibid.   [3] ibid., chapter 18.

51

AGAINST THE CURRENT

can afford virtue – chastity, affability, mercy, humanity, liberality, honour – as Agesilaus and Timoleon, Camillus, Scipio and Marcus did. But if circumstances are adverse, if you find yourself surrounded by treason, what can you do but emulate Philip and Hannibal and Severus?

Mere lust for power is destructive: Pisistratus, Dionysius, Caesar were tyrants and did harm. Agathocles, the tyrant of Syracuse, who gained power by killing his fellow citizens, betraying his friends, being 'without fidelity, without mercy, without religion',[1] went too far, and so did not gain glory; 'his outrageous cruelty and inhumanity together with his countless wicked acts'[2] led to success, but since so much vice was not needed for it, he is excluded from the pantheon; so is the savage Oliverotto da Fermo, his modern counterpart, killed by Cesare Borgia. Still, to be altogether without these qualities guarantees failure; and that makes impossible the only conditions in which Machiavelli believed that normal men could successfully develop. Saints might not need them; anchorites could perhaps practise their virtues in the desert; martyrs will obtain their reward hereafter; but Machiavelli is plainly not interested in these ways of life and does not discuss them. He is a writer about government; he is interested in public affairs; in security, independence, success, glory, strength, vigour, felicity on earth, not in heaven; in the present and future as well as the past; in the real world, not an imaginary one. And for this, given unalterable human limitations, the code preached by the Christian church, if it is taken seriously, will not do.

Machiavelli, we are often told, was not concerned with morals. The most influential of all modern interpretations – that of Benedetto Croce, followed to some extent by Chabod, Russo and others – is that Machiavelli, in Cochrane's words,[3] 'did not deny the validity of Christian morality, and he did not pretend that a crime required by political necessity was any less a crime. Rather he discovered . . . that this morality simply did not hold in political affairs and that any policy based on the assumption that it did would end in disaster. His factual, objective description of contemporary political practices, then, is a sign not of cynicism or of detachment, but of anguish.'

This account, it seems to me, contains two basic misinterpretations. The first is that the clash is one between 'this [i.e. Christian] morality' and 'political necessity'. The implication is that there is an incompatibility between, on the one hand, morality – the region of ultimate

[1] *The Prince*, chapter 8.   [2] ibid.   [3] op. cit. (p. 25, note 2 above), p. 115.

THE ORIGINALITY OF MACHIAVELLI

values sought after for their own sakes – values recognition of which alone enables us to speak of 'crimes' or morally to justify and condemn anything; and on the other, politics – the art of adapting means to ends – the region of technical skills, of what Kant was to call 'hypothetical imperatives', which take the form 'If you want to achieve *x* do *y* (e.g. betray a friend, kill an innocent man)', without necessarily asking whether *x* is itself intrinsically desirable or not. This is the heart of the divorce of politics from ethics which Croce and many others attribute to Machiavelli. But this seems to me to rest on a mistake.

If ethics is confined to, let us say, Stoic, or Christian or Kantian or even some types of utilitarian ethics, where the source and criterion of value are the word of God, or eternal reason, or some inner sense or knowledge of good and evil, of right and wrong, voices which speak directly to individual consciousness with absolute authority, this might have been tenable. But there exists an equally time-honoured ethics, that of the Greek *polis*, of which Aristotle provided the clearest exposition. Since men are beings made by nature to live in communities, their communal purposes are the ultimate values from which the rest are derived, or with which their ends as individuals are identified. Politics – the art of living in a *polis* – is not an activity which can be dispensed with by those who prefer private life: it is not like seafaring or sculpture which those who do not wish to do so need not undertake. Political conduct is intrinsic to being a human being at a certain stage of civilisation, and what it demands is intrinsic to living a successful human life.

Ethics so conceived – the code of conduct, or the ideal to be pursued by the individual – cannot be known save by understanding the purpose and character of his *polis*: still less be capable of being divorced from it, even in thought. This is the kind of pre-Christian morality which Machiavelli takes for granted. 'It is well known', says Benedetto Croce,[1] 'that Machiavelli discovered the necessity and the autonomy of politics, politics which is beyond moral good and evil, which has its own laws against which it is futile to rebel, which cannot be exorcised and banished from the world with holy water.' Beyond good and evil in some non-Aristotelian, religious or liberal-Kantian sense; but not beyond the good and evil of those communities, ancient or modern, whose sacred values are social through and through. The art of colonisation or of mass murder (let us say) may also have their 'own laws against which it is futile to rebel' for those who wish to practise them

[1] op. cit. (p. 28, note 10 above), p. 60.

AGAINST THE CURRENT

successfully. But if or when these laws collide with those of morality, it is possible and indeed morally imperative to abandon such activities.

But if Aristotle and Machiavelli are right about what men are (and should be – and Machiavelli's ideal is, particularly in the *Discourses*, drawn in vivid colours), political activity is intrinsic to human nature, and while individuals here and there may opt out, the mass of mankind cannot do so; and its communal life determines the moral duties of its members. Hence in opposing the 'laws of politics' to 'good and evil' Machiavelli is not contrasting two 'autonomous' spheres of acting – the 'political' and the 'moral': he is contrasting his own 'political' ethics to another conception of it which governs the lives of persons who are of no interest to him. He is indeed rejecting one morality – the Christian – but not in favour of something that cannot be described as a morality at all, but only as a game of skill, an activity called political, which is not concerned with ultimate human ends, and is therefore not ethical at all.

He is indeed rejecting Christian ethics, but in favour of another system, another moral universe – the world of Pericles or of Scipio, or even of the Duke Valentino, a society geared to ends just as ultimate as the Christian faith, a society in which men fight and are ready to die for (public) ends which they pursue for their own sakes. They are choosing not a realm of means (called politics) as opposed to a realm of ends (called morals), but opt for a rival (Roman or classical) morality, an alternative realm of ends. In other words the conflict is between two moralities, Christian and pagan (or as some wish to call it, aesthetic), not between autonomous realms of morals and politics.

Nor is this a mere question of nomenclature, unless politics is conceived as being concerned not (as it usually is) with means, skills, methods, technique, 'know how', Croce's *pratica* (whether or not governed by unbreakable rules of its own), but with an independent kingdom of ends of its own, sought for their own sake, a substitute for ethics.[1] When Machiavelli said (in a letter to Francesco Vettori) that he loved his native city more than his own soul, he revealed his basic moral beliefs, a position with which Croce does not credit him.[2]

[1] Meinecke, Prezzolini (op. cit. (p. 25, note 2 above), English version, p. 43) and Ernesto Landi, 'The Political Philosophy of Machiavelli', trans. Maurice Cranston, *History Today* 14 (1964), 550–5, seem to me to approach this position most closely.

[2] Benedetto Croce, 'Per un detto del Machiavelli', *La critica* 28 (1930), 310–12.

THE ORIGINALITY OF MACHIAVELLI

The second thesis in this connection which seems to me mistaken is the idea that Machiavelli viewed the crimes of his society with anguish. (Chabod in his excellent study, unlike Croce and some Croceans, does not insist on this.) This entails that he accepts the dire necessities of the *raison d'état* with reluctance, because he sees no alternative. But there is no evidence for this: there is no trace of agony in his political works, any more than in his plays or letters.

The pagan world that Machiavelli prefers is built on recognition of the need for systematic guile and force by rulers, and he seems to think it natural and not at all exceptional or morally agonising that they should employ these weapons wherever they are needed. Nor is the distinction he draws that between the rulers and the ruled. The subjects or citizens must be Romans too: they do not need the *virtù* of the rulers, but if they also cheat, Machiavelli's maxims will not work; they must be poor, militarised, honest and obedient; if they lead Christian lives, they will accept too uncomplainingly the rule of mere bullies and scoundrels. No sound republic can be built of such materials as these. Theseus and Romulus, Moses and Cyrus, did not preach humility or a view of this world as but a temporary resting place to their subjects.

But it is the first misinterpretation that goes deepest, that which represents Machiavelli as caring little or nothing for moral issues. This is surely not borne out by his own language. Anyone whose thought revolves round central concepts such as the good and the bad, the corrupt and the pure, has an ethical scale in mind in terms of which he gives moral praise and blame. Machiavelli's values are not Christian, but they are moral values.

On this crucial point Hans Baron's criticism of the Croce-Russo thesis[1] seems to me correct. Against the view that for Machiavelli politics were beyond moral criticism Baron cites some of the passionately patriotic, republican and libertarian passages in the *Discourses* in which the (moral) qualities of the citizens of a republic are favourably compared with those of the subjects of a despotic prince. The last chapter of *The Prince* is scarcely the work of a detached, morally neutral observer, or of a self-absorbed man, preoccupied with his own inner personal problems, who looks on public life 'with anguish' as the graveyard of moral principles. Like Aristotle's or Cicero's, Machiavelli's

---

[1] Hans Baron, 'Machiavelli: the Republican Citizen and the Author of "The Prince"', *English Historical Review* 76 (1961), 217–53, *passim*.

55

AGAINST THE CURRENT

morality was social and not individual : but it is a morality no less than theirs, not an amoral region, beyond good or evil.

It does not, of course, follow that he was not often fascinated by the techniques of political life as such. The advice given equally to conspirators and their enemies, the professional appraisal of the methods of Oliverotto or Sforza or Baglioni, spring from typical humanist curiosity, the search for an applied science of politics, fascination by knowledge for its own sake, whatever the implications. But the moral ideal, that of the citizen of the Roman Republic, is never far away. Political skills are valued solely as means – for their effectiveness in recreating conditions in which sick men recover their health and can flourish. And this is precisely what Aristotle would have called the moral end proper to man.

This leaves still with us the thorny problem of the relation of *The Prince* to the *Discourses*. But whatever the disparities, the central strain which runs through both is one and the same. The vision – the dream – typical of many writers who see themselves as tough-minded realists – of the strong, united, effective, morally regenerated, splendid and victorious *patria*, whether it is saved by the *virtù* of one man or many – remains central and constant. Political judgements, attitudes to individuals or states, to *fortuna*, and *necessità*, evaluation of methods, degree of optimism, the fundamental mood – these vary between one work and another, perhaps within the same exposition. But the basic values, the ultimate end – Machiavelli's beatific vision – does not vary.

His vision is social and political. Hence the traditional view of him as simply a specialist on how to get the better of others, a vulgar cynic who says that Sunday school precepts are all very well, but in a world full of evil men you too must lie, kill and so on, if you are to get somewhere, is incorrect. The philosophy summarised by 'eat or be eaten, beat or be beaten' – the kind of wordly wisdom to be found in, say, Mazzei[1] or Giovanni Morelli,[2] with whom he has been compared – is not what is central in him. Machiavelli is not specially concerned with the opportunism of ambitious individuals ; the ideal before his eyes is a shining vision of Florence or of Italy ; in this respect he is a typically impassioned humanist of the Renaissance, save that his ideal is not artistic or cultural but political, unless the state – or regenerated Italy– is considered, in Burckhardt's sense, as an artistic goal. This is very

[1] Ser Lapo Mazzei, *Lettere di un notaro a un mercante del secolo XIV*, ed. Cesare Guasti, 2 vols (Florence, 1880).

[2] Giovanni di Pagolo Morelli, *Ricordi*, ed. Vittore Branca (Florence, 1956).

THE ORIGINALITY OF MACHIAVELLI

different from mere advocacy of toughmindedness as such, or of a realism irrespective of its goal.

Machiavelli's values, I should like to repeat, are not instrumental but moral and ultimate, and he calls for great sacrifices in their name. For them he rejects the rival scale – the Christian principles of *ozio* and meekness – not, indeed, as being defective in itself, but as inapplicable to the conditions of real life; and real life for him means not merely (as is sometimes alleged) life as it was lived around him in Italy – the crimes, hypocrisies, brutalities, follies of Florence, Rome, Venice, Milan. This is not the touchstone of reality. His purpose is not to leave unchanged or to reproduce this kind of life, but to lift it to a new plane, to rescue Italy from squalor and slavery, to restore her to health and sanity.

The moral ideal for which he thinks no sacrifice too great – the welfare of the *patria* – is for him the highest form of social existence attainable by man; but attainable, not unattainable; not a world outside the limits of human capacity, given human beings as we know them, that is, creatures compounded out of those emotional, intellectual and physical properties of which history and observation provide examples. He asks for men improved but not transfigured, not superhuman; not for a world of ideal beings unknown on this earth, who, even if they could be created, could not be called human.

If you object to the political methods recommended because they seem to you morally detestable, if you refuse to embark upon them because they are, to use Ritter's word, 'erschreckend', too frightening, Machiavelli has no answer, no argument. In that case you are perfectly entitled to lead a morally good life, be a private citizen (or a monk), seek some corner of your own. But, in that event, you must not make yourself responsible for the lives of others or expect good fortune; in a material sense you must expect to be ignored or destroyed.

In other words you can opt out of the public world, but in that case he has nothing to say to you, for it is to the public world and to the men in it that he addresses himself. This is expressed most clearly in his notorious advice to the victor who has to hold down a conquered province. He advises a clean sweep: new governors, new titles, new powers and new men; he should 'make the rich poor, the poor rich, as David did when he became king: "the poor he filled with good things and the rich he sent away empty". Besides this, he should build new cities, overthrow those already built, change the inhabitants from one place to another; and in short he should leave nothing in that province

AGAINST THE CURRENT

untouched, and make sure that no rank or position or office or wealth is held by anyone who does not acknowledge it as from you.'[1] He should take Philip of Macedon as his model, who 'grew in these ways until he became lord of Greece'.

Now Philip's historian informs us – Machiavelli goes on to say – that he transferred the inhabitants from one province to another 'as herdsmen transfer their herds' from one place to another. Doubtless, Machiavelli continues,

> These methods are very cruel, and enemies to all government not merely Christian but human, and any man ought to avoid them and prefer to live a private life rather than to be a king who brings such ruin on men. Notwithstanding, a ruler who does not wish to take that first good way of lawful government, if he wishes to maintain himself, must enter upon this evil one. But men take certain middle ways that are very injurious; indeed, they are unable to be altogether good or altogether bad.[2]

This is plain enough. There are two worlds, that of personal morality and that of public organisation. There are two ethical codes, both ultimate; not two 'autonomous' regions, one of 'ethics', another of 'politics', but two (for him) exhaustive alternatives between two conflicting systems of value. If a man chooses the 'first good way', he must, presumably, give up all hope of Athens and Rome, of a noble and glorious society in which human beings can thrive and grow strong, proud, wise and productive; indeed, they must abandon all hope of a tolerable life on earth: for men cannot live outside society; they will not survive collectively if they are led by men who (like Soderini) are influenced by the first, 'private' morality; they will not be able to realise their minimal goals as men; they will end in a state of moral, not merely political, degradation. But if a man chooses, as Machiavelli himself has done, the second course, then he must suppress his private qualms, if he has any, for it is certain that those who are too squeamish during the remaking of a society, or even during its pursuit and maintenance of its power and glory, will go to the wall. Whoever has chosen to make an omelette cannot do so without breaking eggs.

Machiavelli is sometimes accused of too much relish at the prospect of breaking eggs – almost for its own sake. This is unjust. He thinks these ruthless methods are necessary – necessary as means to provide

[1] *Discourses* I 26.   [2] ibid.

THE ORIGINALITY OF MACHIAVELLI

good results, good in terms not of a Christian, but of a secular, humanistic, naturalistic morality. His most shocking examples show this. The most famous, perhaps, is that of Giovanpaolo Baglioni, who caught Julius II during one of his campaigns, and let him escape, when in Machiavelli's view he might have destroyed him and his cardinals and thereby committed a crime 'the greatness of which would have transcended every infamy, every peril that could have resulted from it'.[1]

Like Frederick the Great (who called Machiavelli 'the enemy of mankind' and followed his advice),[2] Machiavelli is, in effect, saying 'Le vin est tiré: il faut le boire.' Once you embark on a plan for the transformation of a society you must carry it through no matter at what cost: to fumble, to retreat, to be overcome by scruples, is to betray your chosen cause. To be a physician is to be a professional, ready to burn, to cauterise, to amputate; if that is what the disease requires, then to stop half-way because of personal qualms, or some rule unrelated to your art and its technique, is a sign of muddle and weakness, and will always give you the worst of both worlds. And there are at least two worlds: each of them has much, indeed everything, to be said for it; but they are two and not one. One must learn to choose between them, and having chosen, not look back.

There is more than one world, and more than one set of virtues: confusion between them is disastrous. One of the chief illusions caused by ignoring this is the Platonic-Hebraic-Christian view that virtuous rulers create virtuous men. This according to Machiavelli is not true. Generosity is a virtue, but not in princes. A generous prince will ruin the citizens by taxing them too heavily, a mean prince (and Machiavelli does not say that meanness is a good quality in private men) will save the purses of the citizens and so add to public welfare. A kind ruler – and kindness is a virtue – may let intriguers and stronger characters dominate him, and so cause chaos and corruption.

Other writers of 'mirrors for princes' are also rich in such maxims, but they do not draw the implications; Machiavelli's use of such generalisations is not theirs; he is not moralising at large, but illustrating a specific thesis: that the nature of men dictates a public morality which is different from, and may come into collision with, the virtues of men who profess to believe in, and try to act by, Christian precepts. These may not be wholly unrealisable in quiet times, in private life.

[1] ibid. I 27.

[2] It is still not clear how much of this Frederick owed to his mentor Voltaire.

AGAINST THE CURRENT

But they lead to ruin outside this. The analogy between a state and people and an individual is a fallacy : 'a state and a people are governed in a different way from an individual' ;[1] 'not individual good but common good is what makes cities great'.[2]

One may disagree with this. One may argue that the greatness, glory and wealth of a state are hollow ideals, or detestable, if the citizens are oppressed and treated as mere means to the grandeur of the whole. Like Christian thinkers, or like Constant and the liberals, or like Sismondi and the theorists of the welfare state, one may prefer a state in which citizens are prosperous even though the public treasury is poor, in which government is neither centralised nor omnipotent, nor, perhaps, sovereign at all, but the citizens enjoy a wide degree of individual freedom; one may contrast this favourably with the great authoritarian concentrations of power built by Alexander or Frederick the Great or Napoleon, or the great autocrats of the twentieth century.

If so, one is simply contradicting Machiavelli's thesis: he sees no merit in such loose political textures. They cannot last. Men cannot long survive in such conditions. He is convinced that states which have lost the appetite for power are doomed to decadence and are likely to be destroyed by their more vigorous and better armed neighbours; and Vico and modern 'realistic' thinkers have echoed this.

Machiavelli is possessed by a clear, intense, narrow vision of a society in which human talents can be made to contribute to a powerful and splendid whole. He prefers republican rule in which the interests of the rulers do not conflict with those of the ruled. But (as Macaulay perceived) he prefers a well-governed principate to a decadent republic: and the qualities he admires and thinks capable of being welded into – indeed, indispensable to – a durable society, are not different in *The Prince* and the *Discourses* : energy, boldness, practical skill, imagination, vitality, self-discipline, shrewdness, public spirit, good fortune, *antiqua virtus*, *virtù* – firmness in adversity, strength of character, as celebrated by Xenophon or Livy. All his more shocking maxims – those responsible for the 'murd'rous Machiavel' of the

[1] '. . . una repubblica e un popolo si governa altrimenti che un privato', *Legazioni all'Imperatore*, quoted by L. Burd, op. cit. (p. 28, note 10 above), p. 298, note 17.

[2] *Discourses* II 2. This echoes Francesco Patrizzi's 'aliae sunt regis virtutes, aliae privatorum', in *De regno et regis institutione*, quoted by Felix Gilbert in 'The Humanist Concept of the Prince and *The Prince* of Machiavelli', *Journal of Modern History* 11 (1939), 449–83: 464, note 34.

THE ORIGINALITY OF MACHIAVELLI

Elizabethan stage – are descriptions of methods of realising this single end: the classical, humanistic and patriotic vision that dominates him.

Let me cite a round dozen of his most notoriously wicked pieces of advice to princes. You must employ terrorism or kindness, as the case dictates. Severity is usually more effective, but humanity, in some situations, brings better fruit. You may excite fear but not hatred, for hatred will destroy you in the end. It is best to keep men poor and on a permanent war footing, for this will be an antidote to the two great enemies of active obedience – ambition and boredom – and the ruled will then feel in constant need of great men to lead them (the twentieth century offers us only too much evidence for this sharp insight). Competition – divisions between classes – in a society is desirable, for it generates energy and ambition in the right degree.

Religion must be promoted even though it may be false, provided it is of a kind which preserves social solidarity and promotes manly virtues, as Christianity has historically failed to do. When you confer benefits (he says, following Aristotle), do so yourself; but if dirty work is to be done, let others do it, for then they, not the prince, will be blamed, and the prince can gain favour by duly cutting off their heads; for men prefer vengeance and security to liberty. Do what you must do in any case, but try to represent it as a special favour to the people. If you must commit a crime do not advertise it beforehand, since otherwise your enemies may destroy you before you destroy them. If your action must be drastic, do it in one fell swoop, not in agonising stages. Do not be surrounded by over-powerful servants – victorious generals are best got rid of, otherwise they may get rid of you.

You may be violent and use your power to overawe, but you must not break your own laws, for that destroys confidence and disintegrates the social texture. Men should either be caressed or annihilated; appeasement and neutralism are always fatal. Excellent plans without arms are not enough or else Florence would still be a republic. Rulers must live in the constant expectation of war. Success creates more devotion than an amiable character; remember the fate of Pertinax, Savonarola, Soderini. Severus was unscrupulous and cruel, Ferdinand of Spain is treacherous and crafty: but by practising the arts of both the lion and the fox they escaped both snares and wolves. Men will be false to you unless you compel them to be true by creating circumstances in which falsehood will not pay. And so on.

These examples are typical of 'the devil's partner'. Now and then doubts assail our author: he wonders whether a man high-minded

61

AGAINST THE CURRENT

enough to labour to create a state admirable by Roman standards will be tough enough to use the violent and wicked means prescribed; and conversely, whether a sufficiently ruthless and brutal man will be disinterested enough to compass the public good which alone justifies the evil means. Yet Moses and Theseus, Romulus and Cyrus, combined these properties.[1] What has been once, can be again: the implication is optimistic.

All these maxims have one property in common: they are designed to create or resurrect or maintain an order which will satisfy what the author conceives as men's most permanent interests. Machiavelli's values may be erroneous, dangerous, odious; but he is in earnest. He is not cynical. The end is always the same: a state conceived after the analogy of Periclean Athens, or Sparta, but above all the Roman Republic. Such an end, for which men naturally crave (of this he thinks that history and observation provide conclusive evidence), 'excuses' any means; in judging means, look only to the end: if the state goes under, all is lost. Hence the famous paragraph in the forty-first chapter of the third book of *The Discourses* where he says, 'when it is absolutely a question of the safety of one's country, there must be no consideration of just or unjust, of merciful or cruel, of praiseworthy or disgraceful; instead, setting aside every scruple, one must follow to the utmost any plan that will save her life and keep her liberty.' The French have reasoned thus: and the 'majesty of their king and the power of their kingdom' have come from it. Romulus could not have founded Rome without killing Remus. Brutus would not have preserved the Republic if he had not killed his sons. Moses and Theseus, Romulus, Cyrus and the liberators of Athens had to destroy in order to build. Such conduct, so far from being condemned, is held up to admiration by the classical historians and the Bible. Machiavelli is their admirer and faithful spokesman.

What is there, then, about his words, about his tone, which has caused such tremors among his readers? Not, indeed, in his own lifetime – there was a delayed reaction of some quarter of a century, but after that it becomes one of continuous and mounting horror. Fichte, Hegel, Treitschke 'reinterpreted' his doctrines and assimilated them to their own views. But the sense of horror was not thereby greatly mitigated. It is evident that the effect of the shock which he administered was not a temporary one: it has lasted almost to our own day.

[1] Hugh Trevor-Roper has drawn my attention to the irony of the fact that the heroes of this supreme realist are all, wholly or in part, mythical.

THE ORIGINALITY OF MACHIAVELLI

Leaving aside the historical problem of why there was no immediate contemporary criticism, let us consider the continuous discomfort caused to its readers during the four centuries that have passed since *The Prince* was placed upon the Index. The great originality and the tragic implications of Machiavelli's theses seem to me to reside in their relation to a Christian civilisation. It was all very well to live by the light of pagan ideals in pagan times; but to preach paganism more than a thousand years after the triumph of Christianity was to do so after the loss of innocence – and to be forcing men to make a conscious choice. The choice is painful because it is a choice between two entire worlds. Men have lived in both, and fought and died to preserve them against each other. Machiavelli has opted for one of them, and he is prepared to commit crimes for its sake.

In killing, deceiving, betraying, Machiavelli's princes and republicans are doing evil things, not condonable in terms of common morality. It is Machiavelli's great merit that he does not deny this.[1] Marsilio, Hobbes, Spinoza, and, in their own fashion, Hegel and Marx, did try to deny it. So did many a defender of the *raison d'état*, imperialist and populist, Catholic and Protestant. These thinkers argue for a single moral system: and seek to show that the morality which justifies, and indeed demands, such deeds, is continuous with, and a more rational form of, the confused ethical beliefs of the uninstructed morality which forbids them absolutely.

From the vantage point of the great social objectives in the name of which these (prima facie wicked) acts are to be performed, they will be seen (so the argument goes) as no longer wicked, but as rational – demanded by the very nature of things – by the common good, or man's true ends, or the dialectic of history – condemned only by those who cannot or will not see a large enough segment of the logical, or theological, or metaphysical, or historical pattern; misjudged, denounced only by the spiritually blind or short-sighted. At worst, these 'crimes' are discords demanded by the larger harmony, and therefore, to those who hear this harmony, no longer discordant.

Machiavelli is not a defender of any such abstract theory. It does not occur to him to employ such casuistry. He is transparently honest

[1] This is recognised by Jacques Maritain (see his *Moral Philosophy* (London, 1964), p. 199) who conceded that Machiavelli 'never called evil good or good evil'. *Machtpolitik* is shown to be what it is: the party with the big battalions; it does not claim that the Lord is on its side: no *Dei gesta per Francos*.

AGAINST THE CURRENT

and clear. In choosing the life of a statesman, or even the life of a citizen with enough civic sense to want your state to be as successful and as splendid as possible, you commit yourself to rejection of Christian behaviour.[1] It may be that Christians are right about the well-being of the individual soul, taken outside the social or political context. But the well-being of the state is not the same as the well-being of the individual – they 'are governed in a different way'. You will have made your choice: the only crimes are weakness, cowardice, stupidity, which may cause you to draw back in midstream and fail.

Compromise with current morality leads to bungling, which is always despicable, and when practised by statesmen involves men in ruin. The end 'excuses' the means, however horrible these may be in terms of even pagan ethics, if it is (in terms of the ideals of Thucydides or Polybius, Cicero or Livy) lofty enough. Brutus was right to kill his children: he saved Rome. Soderini did not have the stomach to perpetrate such deeds and ruined Florence. Savonarola, who had sound ideas about austerity and moral strength and corruption, perished because he did not realise that an unarmed prophet will always go to the gallows.

If one can produce the right result by using the devotion and affection of men, let this be done by all means. There is no value in causing suffering as such. But if one cannot, then Moses, Romulus, Theseus, Cyrus are the exemplars, and fear must be employed. There is no sinister Satanism in Machiavelli, nothing of Dostoevsky's great sinner, pursuing evil for evil's sake. To Dostoevsky's famous question 'Is everything permitted?', Machiavelli (who for Dostoevsky would surely have been an atheist) answers 'Yes, if the end – that is, the pursuit of a society's basic interests in a specific situation – cannot be realised in any other way.'

This position has not been properly understood by some of those who claim to be not unsympathetic to Machiavelli. Figgis, for example,[2] thinks that he permanently suspended 'the *habeas corpus* acts of the whole human race', that is to say, that he advocated methods of terrorism because for him the situation was always critical, always

---

[1] At the risk of exhausting the patience of the reader, I must repeat that this is a conflict not of pagan statecraft with Christian morals, but of pagan morals (indissolubly connected with social life and inconceivable without it) with Christian ethics, which, whatever its implication for politics, can be stated independently of it, as, e.g., Aristotle's or Hegel's ethics cannot.

[2] op. cit. (p. 37, note 1 above), p. 76.

THE ORIGINALITY OF MACHIAVELLI

desperate, so that he confused ordinary political principles with rules needed, if at all, only in extreme cases.

Others – perhaps the majority of his interpreters – look on him as the originator or at least a defender of what later came to be called 'raison d'état', 'Staatsräson', 'ragion di stato' – the justification of immoral acts when undertaken on behalf of the state in exceptional circumstances. More than one scholar has pointed out, reasonably enough, that the notion that desperate cases require desperate remedies – that 'necessity knows no law' – is to be found not only in antiquity but equally in Aquinas and Dante and other medieval writers long before Bellarmino or Machiavelli.

These parallels seem to me to rest on a deep but characteristic mis-understanding of Machiavelli's thesis. He is not saying that while in normal situations current morality – that is, the Christian or semi-Christian code of ethics – should prevail, yet abnormal conditions can occur, in which the entire social structure in which alone this code can function becomes jeopardised, and that in emergencies of this kind acts which are usually regarded as wicked and rightly forbidden, are justified.

This is the position of, among others, those who think that all morality ultimately rests on the existence of certain institutions – say Roman Catholics who regard the existence of the church and the papacy as indispensable to Christianity – or nationalists who see in the political power of a nation the sole source of spiritual life. Such persons maintain that extreme and 'frightful' measures needed for protecting the state or the church or the national culture in moments of acute crisis may be justified, since the ruin of these institutions may fatally damage the indispensable framework of all other values. This is a doctrine in terms of which both Catholics and Protestants, both con-servatives and communists, have defended enormities which freeze the blood of ordinary men.

But this is not Machiavelli's position. For the defenders of the *raison d'état*, the sole justification of these measures is that they are exceptional – that they are needed to preserve a system the purpose of which is precisely to preclude the need for such odious measures, so that the sole justification of such steps is that they will end the situa-tions that render them necessary. But for Machiavelli these measures are, in a sense, themselves quite normal. No doubt they are called for only by extreme need; yet political life tends to generate a good many such needs, of varying degrees of 'extremity'; hence Baglioni, who

65

AGAINST THE CURRENT

shied away from the logical consequences of his own policies, was clearly unfit to rule.

The notion of *raison d'état* entails a conflict of values which may be agonising to morally good and sensitive men. For Machiavelli there is no conflict. Public life has its own morality, to which Christian principles (or any absolute personal values) tend to be a gratuitous obstacle. This life has its own standards: it does not require perpetual terror: but it approves, or at least permits, the use of force where it is needed to promote the ends of political society.

Sheldon Wolin[1] seems to me right in insisting that Machiavelli believes in a permanent 'economy of violence' – the need for a consistent reserve of force always in the background to keep things going in such a way that the virtues admired by him and by the classical thinkers to whom he appeals can be protected and allowed to flower. Men brought up within a community in which such force, or its possibility, is used rightly, will live the happy lives of Greeks or Romans during their finest hours. They will be characterised by vitality, genius, variety, pride, power, success (Machiavelli scarcely ever speaks of arts or sciences); but it will not, in any clear sense, be a Christian commonwealth. The moral conflict which this situation raises will trouble only those who are not prepared to abandon either course: those who assume that the two incompatible lives are in fact reconcilable.

But to Machiavelli the claims of the official morality are scarcely worth discussing: they are not translatable into social practice: 'If all men were good . . .', but he feels sure that men can never be improved beyond the point at which considerations of power are relevant. If morals relate to human conduct, and men are by nature social, Christian morality cannot be a guide for normal social existence. It remained for someone to state this. Machiavelli did so.

One is obliged to choose: and in choosing one form of life, give up the other. That is the central point. If Machiavelli is right, if it is in principle (or in fact: the frontier seems dim) impossible to be morally good and do one's duty as this was conceived by common European, and especially Christian ethics, and at the same time build Sparta or Periclean Athens or the Rome of the Republic or even of the Antonines, then a conclusion of the first importance follows: that the belief that the correct, objectively valid solution to the question of how men should live can in principle be discovered, is itself in principle not

[1] Sheldon S. Wolin, *Politics and Vision* (London, 1960), pp. 220–24.

THE ORIGINALITY OF MACHIAVELLI

true. This was a truly *erschreckend* proposition. Let me try to put it in its proper context.

One of the deepest assumptions of western political thought is the doctrine, scarcely questioned during its long ascendancy, that there exists some single principle which not only regulates the course of the sun and the stars, but prescribes their proper behaviour to all animate creatures. Animals and sub-rational beings of all kinds follow it by instinct; higher beings attain to consciousness of it, and are free to abandon it, but only to their doom. This doctrine, in one version or another, has dominated European thought since Plato; it has appeared in many forms, and has generated many similes and allegories; at its centre is the vision of an impersonal Nature or Reason or cosmic purpose, or of a divine Creator whose power has endowed all things and creatures each with a specific function; these functions are elements in a single harmonious whole, and are intelligible in terms of it alone.

This was often expressed by images taken from architecture: of a great edifice of which each part fits uniquely in the total structure; or from the human body as an all-embracing organic whole; or from the life of society as a great hierarchy, with God as the *ens realissimum* at the summit of two parallel systems – the feudal order and the natural order – stretching downwards from Him, and reaching upwards to Him, obedient to His will. Or it is seen as the Great Chain of Being, the Platonic-Christian analogue of the world-tree Ygdrasil, which links time and space and all that they contain. Or it has been represented by an analogy drawn from music, as an orchestra in which each instrument or group of instruments has its own tune to play in the infinitely rich polyphonic score. When, after the seventeenth century, harmonic metaphors replaced polyphonic images, the instruments were no longer conceived as playing specific melodies, but as producing sounds which, although they might not be wholly intelligible to any given group of players (and might even sound discordant or superfluous if taken in isolation), yet contributed to the total pattern perceptible only from a loftier standpoint.

The idea of the world and of human society as a single intelligible structure is at the root of all the many various versions of natural law – the mathematical harmonies of the Pythagoreans, the logical ladder of Platonic Forms, the genetic-logical pattern of Aristotle, the divine *Logos* of the Stoics and the Christian churches and of their secularised offshoots. The advance of the natural sciences generated more

67

AGAINST THE CURRENT

empirically conceived versions of this image as well as anthropomorphic similes: of Dame Nature as an adjuster of conflicting tendencies (as in Hume or Adam Smith), of Mistress Nature as the teacher of the best way to happiness (as in the works of some French Encyclopedists), of Nature as embodied in the actual customs or habits of organised social wholes; biological, aesthetic, psychological similes have reflected the dominant ideas of an age.

This unifying monistic pattern is at the very heart of traditional rationalism, religious and atheistic, metaphysical and scientific, transcendental and naturalistic, that has been characteristic of western civilisation. It is this rock, upon which western beliefs and lives had been founded, that Machiavelli seems, in effect, to have split open. So great a reversal cannot, of course, be due to the acts of a single individual. It could scarcely have taken place in a stable social and moral order; many beside him, ancient sceptics, medieval nominalists and secularists, Renaissance humanists, doubtless supplied their share of the dynamite. The purpose of this essay is to suggest that it was Machiavelli who lit the fatal fuse.

If to ask what are the ends of life is to ask a real question, it must be capable of being correctly answered. To claim rationality in matters of conduct was to claim that correct and final solutions to such questions can in principle be found.

When such solutions were discussed in earlier periods, it was normally assumed that the perfect society could be conceived, at least in outline; for otherwise what standard could one use to condemn existing arrangements as imperfect? It might not be realisable here, below. Men were too ignorant or too weak or too vicious to create it. Or it was said (by some materialistic thinkers in the centuries following *The Prince*) that it was technical means that were lacking, that no one had yet discovered methods of overcoming the material obstacles to the golden age; that we were not technologically or educationally or morally sufficiently advanced. But it was never said that there was something incoherent in the very notion itself.

Plato and the Stoics, the Hebrew prophets and Christian medieval thinkers and the writers of Utopias from More onward had a vision of what it was that men fell short of; they claimed, as it were, to be able to measure the gap between the reality and the ideal. But if Machiavelli is right, this tradition – the central current of western thought – is fallacious. For if his position is valid then it is impossible to construct even the notion of such a perfect society, for there exist at least two

THE ORIGINALITY OF MACHIAVELLI

sets of virtues – let us call them the Christian and the pagan – which are not merely in practice, but in principle incompatible.

If men practise Christian humility, they cannot also be inspired by the burning ambitions of the great classical founders of cultures and religions; if their gaze is centred upon the world beyond – if their ideas are infected by even lip-service to such an outlook – they will not be likely to give all that they have to an attempt to build a perfect city. If suffering and sacrifice and martyrdom are not always evil and ines-capable necessities, but may be of supreme value in themselves, then the glorious victories over fortune which go to the bold, the impetuous and the young might neither be won nor thought worth winning. If spiritual goods alone are worth striving for, then of how much value is the study of *necessità* – of the laws that govern nature and human lives – by the manipulation of which men might accomplish unheard-of things in the arts and the sciences and the organisation of social lives?

To abandon the pursuit of secular goals may lead to disintegration and a new barbarism; but even if this is so, is it the worst that could happen? Whatever the differences between Plato and Aristotle, or of either of these thinkers from the Sophists or Epicureans or the other Greek schools of the fourth and later centuries, they and their disciples, the European rationalists and empiricists of the modern age, were agreed that the study of reality by minds undeluded by appearances could reveal the correct ends to be pursued by men – that which would make men free and happy, strong and rational.

Some thought that there was a single end for all men in all circum-stances, or different ends for men of different kinds or in dissimilar historical environments. Objectivists and universalists were opposed by relativists and subjectivists, metaphysicians by empiricists, theists by atheists. There was profound disagreement about moral issues; but what none of these thinkers, not even the sceptics, had suggested was that there might exist ends – ends in themselves in terms of which alone everything else was justified – which were equally ultimate, but incom-patible with one another, that there might exist no single universal overarching standard that would enable a man to choose rationally between them.

This was indeed a profoundly upsetting conclusion. It entailed that if men wished to live and act consistently, and understand what goals they were pursuing, they were obliged to examine their moral values. What if they found that they were compelled to make a choice

AGAINST THE CURRENT

between two incommensurable systems, to choose as they did without
the aid of an infallible measuring rod which certified one form of life
as being superior to all others and could be used to demonstrate this
to the satisfaction of all rational men? Was it, perhaps, this awful
truth, implicit in Machiavelli's exposition, that has upset the moral
consciousness of men, and has haunted their minds so permanently
and obsessively ever since?

Machiavelli did not himself propound it. There was no problem
and no agony for him; he shows no trace of scepticism or relativism;
he chose his side, and took little interest in the values that this choice
ignored or flouted. The conflict between his scale of values and that of
conventional morality clearly did not (*pace* Croce and the other defenders of the 'anguished humanist' interpretation) seem to worry Machiavelli himself. It upset only those who came after him, and were not
prepared, on the one hand, to abandon their own moral values (Christian or humanist) together with the entire way of thought and action
of which these were a part; nor, on the other hand, to deny the validity
of, at any rate, much of Machiavelli's analysis of the political facts, and
the (largely pagan) values and outlook that went with it, embodied in
the social structure which he painted so brilliantly and convincingly.

Whenever a thinker, however distant from us in time or culture,
still stirs passion, enthusiasm or indignation, or any kind of intense
debate, it is generally the case that he has propounded a thesis which
upsets some deeply established *idée reçue*, a thesis which those who wish
to cling to the old conviction nevertheless find it hard or impossible to
dismiss or refute. This is the case with Plato, Hobbes, Rousseau,
Marx.

I should like to suggest that it is Machiavelli's juxtaposition of the
two outlooks – the two incompatible moral worlds, as it were – in the
minds of his readers, and the collision and acute moral discomfort
which follow, that, over the years, has been responsible for the desperate efforts to interpret his doctrines away, to represent him as a
cynical and therefore ultimately shallow defender of power politics,
or as a diabolist, or as a patriot prescribing for particularly desperate
situations which seldom arise, or as a mere time-server, or as an em-
bittered political failure, or as a mere mouthpiece of truths we have
always known but did not like to utter, or again as the enlightened
translator of universally accepted ancient social principles into empirical terms, or as a crypto-republican satirist (a descendant of Juvenal,
a forerunner of Orwell); or as a cold scientist, a mere political techno-

THE ORIGINALITY OF MACHIAVELLI

logist free from moral implications; or as a typical Renaissance publicist practising a now obsolete genre; or in any of the numerous other roles that have been and are still being cast for him.

Machiavelli may have possessed some, at any rate, of these attributes, but concentration on one or other of them as constituting his essential, 'true' character, seems to me to stem from reluctance to face, still more discuss, the uncomfortable truth which Machiavelli had, unintentionally, almost casually, uncovered; namely, that not all ultimate values are necessarily compatible with one another – that there might be a conceptual (what used to be called 'philosophical') and not merely a material obstacle to the notion of the single ultimate solution which, if it were only realised, would establish the perfect society.

III

Yet if no such solution can, even in principle, be formulated, then all political and, indeed, moral problems are thereby transformed. This is not a division of politics from ethics. It is the uncovering of the possibility of more than one system of values, with no criterion common to the systems whereby a rational choice can be made between them. This is not the rejection of Christianity for paganism (although Machiavelli clearly preferred the latter), nor of paganism for Christianity (which, at least in its historical form, he thought incompatible with the basic needs of normal men), but the setting of them side by side, with the implicit invitation to men to choose either a good, virtuous, private life, or a good, successful, social existence, but not both.

What has been shown by Machiavelli, who is often (like Nietzsche) congratulated for tearing off hypocritical masks, brutally revealing the truth, and so on, is not that men profess one thing and do another (although no doubt he shows this too), but that when they assume that the two ideals are compatible, or perhaps are even one and the same ideal, and do not allow this assumption to be questioned, they are guilty of bad faith (as the existentialists call it, or of 'false consciousness', to use a Marxist formula), which their actual behaviour exhibits. Machiavelli calls the bluff not just of official morality – the hypocrisies of ordinary life – but of one of the foundations of the central western philosophical tradition, the belief in the ultimate compatibility of all genuine values. His own withers are unwrung. He has made his choice. He seems wholly unworried by, indeed scarcely aware of, parting company with traditional western morality.

AGAINST THE CURRENT

But the question that his writings have dramatised, if not for himself, then for others in the centuries that followed, is this: what reason have we for supposing that justice and mercy, humility and *virtù*, happiness and knowledge, glory and liberty, magnificence and sanctity, will always coincide, or indeed be compatible at all? Poetic justice is, after all, so called not because it does, but because it does not, as a rule, occur in the prose of ordinary life, where, *ex hypothesi*, a very different kind of justice operates: 'a state and a people are governed in a different way from an individual'. Hence what talk can there be of indestructible rights, either in the medieval or the liberal sense? The wise man must eliminate fantasies from his own head, and should seek to dispel them from the heads of others; or, if they are too resistant, he should at least, as Pareto or Dostoevsky's Grand Inquisitor recommended, exploit them as a means to a viable society.

'The march of world history stands outside virtue, vice and justice,' said Hegel. If for 'the march of history' you substitute 'a well governed *patria*', and interpret Hegel's notion of virtue as it is understood by Christians or ordinary men, then Machiavelli is one of the earliest proponents of this doctrine. Like all great innovators, he is not without ancestry. But the names of Palmieri and Pontano, and even of Carneades and Sextus Empiricus, have left little mark on European thought.

Croce has rightly insisted that Machiavelli is not detached or cynical or irresponsible. His patriotism, his republicanism, his commitment, are not in doubt. He suffered for his convictions. He thought continually about Florence and Italy, and of how to save them. Yet it is not his character, nor his plays, his poetry, his histories, his diplomatic or political activities, that have gained him his unique fame.[1] Nor can

[1] The moral of his best comedy, *Mandragola*, seems to me close to that of the political tracts: that the ethical doctrines professed by the characters are wholly at variance with what they do to attain their various ends: virtually every one of them in the end obtains what he wants; if Callimaco had resisted temptation, or the lady he seduces had been smitten with remorse, or Fra Timoteo attempted to practise the maxims of the Fathers and the Schoolmen with which he liberally seasons his speeches, this could not have occurred. But all turns out for the best, though not from the point of view of accepted morality. If the play castigates hypocrisy and stupidity, the standpoint is not that of virtue but of candid hedonism. The notion that Callimaco is a kind of prince in private life, successful in creating and maintaining his own world by the correct use of guile and fraud, the exercise of *virtù*, a bold challenge to *fortuna*, and so on, seems plausible. For this see Henry Paolucci, Introduction to *Mandragola* (New York, 1957).

THE ORIGINALITY OF MACHIAVELLI

this be due only to his psychological or sociological imagination. His psychology is often excessively primitive. He scarcely seems to allow for the bare possibility of sustained and genuine altruism; he refuses to consider the motives of men who are prepared to fight against enormous odds, who ignore *necessità* and are prepared to lose their lives in a hopeless cause.

His distrust of unworldly attitudes, absolute principles divorced from empirical observation, is fanatically strong – almost romantic in its violence; the vision of the great prince playing upon human beings like an instrument intoxicates him. He assumes that different societies must always be at war with each other, since they have differing purposes. He sees history as an endless process of cut-throat competition, in which the only goal that rational men can have is to succeed in the eyes of their contemporaries and of posterity. He is good at bringing fantasies down to earth, but he assumes, as Mill was to complain about Bentham, that this is enough. He allows too little to the ideal impulses of men. He has no historical sense and little sense of economics. He has no inkling of the technological progress which is about to transform political and social life, and in particular the art of war. He does not understand how either individuals, communities or cultures develop and transform themselves. Like Hobbes, he assumes that the argument or motive for self-preservation automatically outweighs all others.

He tells men above all not to be fools: to follow a principle when this may involve you in ruin is absurd, at least if judged by worldly standards; other standards he mentions respectfully, but takes no interest in them: those who adopt them are not likely to create anything that will perpetuate their name. His Romans are no more real than the stylised figures in his brilliant comedies. His human beings have so little inner life or capacity for cooperation or social solidarity that, as in the case of Hobbes's not dissimilar creatures, it is difficult to see how they could develop enough reciprocal confidence to create a lasting social whole, even under the perpetual shadow of carefully regulated violence.

Few would deny that Machiavelli's writings, more particularly *The Prince*, have scandalised mankind more deeply and continuously than any other political treatise. The reason for this, let me say again, is not the discovery that politics is the play of power – that political relationships between and within independent communities involve the use of force and fraud, and are unrelated to the principles

73

AGAINST THE CURRENT

professed by the players. That knowledge is as old as conscious thought
about politics – certainly as old as Thucydides and Plato. Nor is it
merely caused by the examples that he offers of success in acquiring or
holding power – the descriptions of the massacre at Sinigaglia or the
behaviour of Agathocles or Oliverotto da Fermo are no more or less
horrifying than similar stories in Tacitus or Guicciardini. The proposition that crime can pay is nothing new in western historiography.

Nor is it merely his recommendation of ruthless measures that so
upsets his readers: Aristotle had long ago allowed that exceptional
situations might arise, that principles and rules could not be rigidly
applied to all situations; the advice to rulers in the *Politics* is tough-
minded enough; Cicero is aware that critical situations demand exceptional measures – *ratio publicae utilitatis, ratio status*, were familiar in
the thought of the Middle Ages. 'Necessity knows no law' is a Thomist sentiment: Pierre d'Auvergne says much the same. Harrington
said this in the following century, and Hume applauded him.

These opinions were not thought original by these, or perhaps any,
thinkers. Machiavelli did not originate, nor did he make much use of,
the notion of *raison d'état*. He stressed will, boldness, address, at the
expense of the rules laid down by calm *ragione*, to which his colleagues
in the *Pratiche Fiorentine*, and perhaps the Oricellari Gardens, may
have appealed. So did Leon Battista Alberti when he declared that
fortuna crushes only the weak and propertyless; so did contemporary
poets; so, too, in his own fashion, did Pico della Mirandola in his great
apostrophe to the powers of man, who, unlike the angels, can transform
himself into any shape – the ardent image which lies at the heart of
European humanism in the north as well as the Mediterranean.

Far more original, as has often been noted, is Machiavelli's divorce
of political behaviour as a field of study from the theological world-
picture in terms of which this topic is discussed before him (even by
Marsilio) and after him. Yet it is not his secularism, however audacious
in his own day, that could have disturbed the contemporaries of Voltaire or Bentham or their successors. What shocked them is something
different.

Machiavelli's cardinal achievement is, let me repeat, his uncovering
of an insoluble dilemma, the planting of a permanent question mark
in the path of posterity. It stems from his *de facto* recognition that ends
equally ultimate, equally sacred, may contradict each other, that entire
systems of value may come into collision without possibility of rational
arbitration, and that not merely in exceptional circumstances, as a

THE ORIGINALITY OF MACHIAVELLI

result of abnormality or accident or error – the clash of Antigone and Creon or in the story of Tristan – but (this was surely new) as part of the normal human situation.

For those who look on such collisions as rare, exceptional and disastrous, the choice to be made is necessarily an agonising experience for which, as a rational being, one cannot prepare (since no rules apply). But for Machiavelli, at least of *The Prince*, the *Discourses*, *Mandragola*, there is no agony. One chooses as one chooses because one knows what one wants, and is ready to pay the price. One chooses classical civilisation rather than the Theban desert, Rome and not Jerusalem, whatever the priests may say, because such is one's nature, and – he is no existentialist or romantic individualist *avant la parole* – because it is that of men in general, at all times, everywhere. If others prefer solitude or martyrdom, he shrugs his shoulders. Such men are not for him. He has nothing to say to them, nothing to argue with them about. All that matters to him and those who agree with him is that such men be not allowed to meddle with politics or education or any of the cardinal factors in human life; their outlook unfits them for such tasks.

I do not mean that Machiavelli explicitly asserts that there is a pluralism or even a dualism of values between which conscious choices must be made. But this follows from the contrasts he draws between the conduct he admires and that which he condemns. He seems to take for granted the obvious superiority of classical civic virtue and brushes aside Christian values, as well as conventional morality, with a disparaging or patronising sentence or two, or smooth words about the misinterpretation of Christianity.[1] This worries or infuriates those who

[1] e.g. in the passages from the *Discourses* cited above, or when he says, 'I believe the greatest good to be done and the most pleasing to God is that which one does to one's native city.' I must thank Myron Gilmore for this reference to *A Discourse on Remodelling the Government of Florence* (Gilbert, op. cit. (p. 33, note 4 above), vol. I, pp. 113–14). This sentiment is by no means unique in Machiavelli's works: but, leaving aside his wish to flatter Leo X, or the liability of all authors to fall into the clichés of their own time, are we to suppose that Machiavelli means us to think that when Philip of Macedon transplanted populations in a manner that (unavoidable as it is said to have been) caused even Machiavelli a qualm, what Philip did, provided it was good for Macedon, was pleasing to God and, *per contra*, that Giovanpaolo Baglioni's failure to kill the Pope and the Curia was displeasing to Him? Such a notion of the Deity is, to say the least, remote from that of the New Testament. Are the needs of the *patria* automatically identical with the will of the Almighty? Are those who permit themselves to doubt this in danger of

AGAINST THE CURRENT

disagree with him the more because it goes against their convictions without seeming to be aware of doing so — and recommends wicked courses as obviously the most sensible, something that only fools or visionaries will reject.

If what Machiavelli believed is true, this undermines one major assumption of western thought: namely that somewhere in the past or the future, in this world or the next, in the church or the laboratory, in the speculations of the metaphysician or the findings of the social scientist, or in the uncorrupted heart of the simple good man, there is to be found the final solution of the question of how men should live. If this is false (and if more than one equally valid answer to the question can be returned, then it is false) the idea of the sole true, objective, universal human ideal crumbles. The very search for it becomes not merely Utopian in practice, but conceptually incoherent.

One can surely see how this might seem unfaceable to men — believers or atheists, empiricists or apriorists — brought up on the opposite assumption. Nothing could well be more upsetting to those brought up in a monistic religious or, at any rate, moral, social or political system, than a breach in it. This is the dagger of which Meinecke speaks, with which Machiavelli inflicted the wound that has never healed; even though Felix Gilbert is right in thinking that he did not bear the scars of it himself. For he remained a monist, albeit a pagan one.

Machiavelli was doubtless guilty of much confusion and exaggeration. He confused the proposition that ultimate ideals may be incompatible with the very different proposition that the more conventional human ideals — founded on ideas of natural law, brotherly love, and

---

heresy? Machiavelli may at times have been represented as too Machiavellian; but to suppose that he believed that the claims of God and of Caesar were perfectly reconcilable reduces his central thesis to absurdity. Yet of course this does not prove that he lacked all Christian sentiment: the *Esortazione alla penitenza* composed in the last year of his life (if it is genuine and not a later forgery) may well be wholly sincere, as Ridolfi and Alderisio believe; Capponi may have exaggerated the extent to which he 'drove religion from his heart', even though 'it was not wholly extinct in his thought'. The point is that there is scarcely any trace of such *états d'âme* in his political writings, with which alone we are concerned. There is an interesting discussion of this by Giuseppe Prezzolini in his already cited article (p. 41, note 1 above), in which this attitude is traced to Augustine, and Croce's thesis is, by implication, controverted.

THE ORIGINALITY OF MACHIAVELLI

human goodness – were unrealisable and that those who acted on the opposite assumption were fools, and at times dangerous ones; and he attributed this dubious proposition to antiquity, and believed that it was verified by history. The first of these assertions strikes at the root of all doctrines which believe in the possibility of attaining, or at least formulating, final solutions; the second is empirical, commonplace, and not self-evident. The two propositions are not, in any case, identical or logically connected.

Moreover he exaggerated wildly: the idealised types of the Perilean Greek or the Roman of the old Republic may be irreconcilable with the ideal citizen of a Christian commonwealth (supposing such were conceivable), but in practice – above all in history, to which our author went for illustrations if not for evidence – pure types seldom obtain: mixtures and compounds and compromises and forms of communal life that do not fit into easy classifications, but which neither Christians, nor liberal humanists, nor Machiavelli would be compelled by their beliefs to reject, can be conceived without too much intellectual difficulty. Still, to attack and inflict lasting damage on a central assumption of an entire civilisation is an achievement of the first order.

Machiavelli does not affirm this dualism. He merely takes for granted the superiority of Roman *antiqua virtus* (which may be maddening to those who do not) over the Christian life as taught by the church. He utters a few casual words about what Christianity might have become, but does not expect it to change its actual character. There he leaves the matter. Anyone who believes in Christian morality, and regards the Christian commonwealth as its embodiment, but at the same time largely accepts the validity of Machiavelli's political and psychological analysis and does not reject the secular heritage of Rome – a man in this predicament is faced with a dilemma which, if Machiavelli is right, is not merely unsolved but insoluble. This is the Gordian knot which, according to Vanini and Leibniz, the author of *The Prince* had tied – a knot which can be cut but not undone.[1] Hence the efforts to dilute his doctrines, or interpret them in such a way as to remove their sting.

After Machiavelli, doubt is liable to infect all monistic constructions. The sense of certainty that there is somewhere a hidden treasure – the final solution to our ills – and that some path must lead to it (for,

[1] Quoted by Prezzolini, op. cit. (p. 25, note 2 above), English version, pp. 222–3.

AGAINST THE CURRENT

in principle, it must be discoverable); or else, to alter the image, the conviction that the fragments constituted by our beliefs and habits are all pieces of a jigsaw puzzle, which (since there is an *a priori* guarantee for this) can, in principle, be solved, so that it is only because of lack of skill or stupidity or bad fortune that we have not so far succeeded in discovering the solution, whereby all interests will be brought into harmony – this fundamental belief of western political thought has been severely shaken. Surely in an age that looks for certainties, this is sufficient to account for the unending efforts, more numerous today than ever, to explain *The Prince* and the *Discourses*, or to explain them away?

This is the negative implication. There is also one that is positive, and might have surprised and perhaps displeased Machiavelli. So long as only one ideal is the true goal, it will always seem to men that no means can be too difficult, no price too high, to do whatever is required to realise the ultimate goal. Such certainty is one of the great justifications of fanaticism, compulsion, persecution. But if not all values are compatible with one another, and choices must be made for no better reason than that each value is what it is, and we choose it for what it is, and not because it can be shown on some single scale to be higher than another; if we choose forms of life because we believe in them, because we take them for granted, or, upon examination, find that we are morally unprepared to live in any other way (although others choose differently); if rationality and calculation can be applied only to means or subordinate ends, but never to ultimate ends; then a picture emerges different from that constructed round the ancient principle that there is only one good for men.

If there is only one solution to the puzzle, then the only problems are firstly how to find it, then how to realise it, and finally how to convert others to the solution by persuasion or by force. But if this is not so (Machiavelli contrasts two ways of life, but there could be, and, save for fanatical monists, there obviously are, more than two), then the path is open to empiricism, pluralism, toleration, compromise. Toleration is historically the product of the realisation of the irreconcilability of equally dogmatic faiths, and the practical improbability of complete victory of one over the other. Those who wished to survive realised that they had to tolerate error. They gradually came to see merits in diversity, and so became sceptical about definitive solutions in human affairs.

But it is one thing to accept something in practice, another to

THE ORIGINALITY OF MACHIAVELLI

justify it rationally. Machiavelli's 'scandalous' writings begin the latter process. This was a major turning point, and its intellectual consequences, wholly unintended by its originator, were, by a fortunate irony of history (which some call its dialectic), the bases of the very liberalism that Machiavelli would surely have condemned as feeble and characterless, lacking in single-minded pursuit of power, in splendour, in organisation, in *virtù*, in power to discipline unruly men against huge odds into one energetic whole. Yet he is, in spite of himself, one of the makers of pluralism, and of its – to him – perilous acceptance of toleration.

By breaking the original unity he helped to cause men to become aware of the necessity of having to make agonising choices between incompatible alternatives in public and in private life (for the two could not, it became obvious, be genuinely kept distinct). His achievement is of the first order, if only because the dilemma has never given men peace since it came to light (it remains unsolved, but we have learnt to live with it). Men had, no doubt, in practice, often enough experienced the conflict which Machiavelli made explicit. He converted its expression from a paradox into something approaching a commonplace.

The sword of which Meinecke spoke has not lost its edge: the wound has not healed. To know the worst is not always to be liberated from its consequences; nevertheless it is preferable to ignorance. It is this painful truth that Machiavelli forced on our attention, not by formulating it explicitly, but perhaps the more effectively by relegating much uncriticised traditional morality to the realm of Utopia. This is what, at any rate, I should like to suggest. Where more than twenty interpretations hold the field, the addition of one more cannot be deemed an impertinence. At worst it will be no more than yet another attempt to solve the problem, now more than four centuries old, of which Croce at the end of his long life spoke as 'Una questione che forse non si chiuderà mai: la questione del Machiavelli'.[1]

---

[1] *Quaderni della 'Critica'* 5 No 14 (July 1949), 1–9.

[13]

II

The Moral Thought of
Renaissance Humanism *

IN THE WESTERN tradition that began with classical antiquity and continued through the Middle Ages down to modern times, the period commonly called the Renaissance occupies a place of its own and has its own peculiar characteristics. Historians have tried for a long time, and in various ways, to describe the civilization of the Renaissance. As a result, there has been so much controversy and difference of views that the so-called problem of the Renaissance has become the subject of an entire literature.

The traditional view of the Renaissance was formulated exactly 100 years ago by Jacob Burckhardt. In a most perceptive synthesis which focused on Italy in the fifteenth and early sixteenth century, he described the achievement of the period in the arts, literature, and scholarship, and stressed such general characteristics as individualism, the revival of antiquity, and the discovery of the world and of man. This picture was expanded and popularized by J. A. Symonds and others, among them those who stressed the pagan tendencies of the period more than Burckhardt had ever done. Other historians engaged in the task of analyzing the Renaissance as a broader European phenomenon, especially during the sixteenth century, and of exploring both the Italian influences and the national characteristics which the period assumed in each of the major European countries.

Burckhardt's views were challenged and criticized in a number of ways. Historians of the Middle Ages discovered that this

* Reprinted by permission from *Chapters in Western Civilization*, ed. by the Contemporary Civilization Staff of Columbia College, Vol. I, 3rd ed. (New York, Columbia University Press, 1961). 289–335.

period, especially in its later phases, had its own impressive achievements as a civilization, and was very far from a "dark age" that needed to make room for a period of "rebirth." In many instances, phenomena considered peculiar to the Renaissance were found to have had their counterparts or precedents in the Middle Ages. Historians of French literature, followed by those of other literatures, tended to minimize the Italian influences and to stress the independent contributions, during and before the Renaissance, of the other countries. Johan Huizinga, in his *Waning of the Middle Ages,* emphasized the thoroughly medieval features of so late a time as the fifteenth century, and his contribution is especially impressive since he focused on the Low Countries, an area that was at that time the chief artistic and economic center of Europe outside of Italy. While many historians, albeit with different evaluations, agreed that the Protestant and Catholic reformations of the sixteenth century put a sudden end to the secular and pagan culture radiating from Italy during the fifteenth century, others stressed the thoroughly religious character of the Renaissance in the northern countries, or even in Italy. One scholar, Giuseppe Toffanin, went so far as to suggest that Renaissance humanism was basically a Catholic reaction against the heretical tendencies inherent in the thought of the later Middle Ages. Continuity with the Middle Ages was the watchword of many historians who studied the economic and scientific development of the period—aspects that had been neglected by Burckhardt but have been particularly important in recent historical scholarship. Other historians speak of an actual economic and scientific decline during the fifteenth century, but this view is by no means shared by all specialists on the subject. These controversies are the more confusing since they affect even the chronological limits of the Renaissance period, whose beginning and end are subject to considerable fluctuation, depending on the persons or regions, developments or cultural aspects, on which the historian focuses his attention.

In the face of so much disagreement, one may only suggest that we apply the term Renaissance, which has by now become conventional, to the period in European history that goes at least from the middle of the fourteenth century to the beginning of the seventeenth. If we attach no value judgment to the term Renaissance, we shall not be surprised if we discover in the period many shortcomings as well as many achievements. If we grant that the Renaissance was a period of transition, we shall not be surprised to find in it many medieval as well as modern traits, and also some that are peculiar only to the Renaissance. There is no need to emphasize one of these aspects over the others for we can accept continuity as basic to history, while also realizing that historical continuity involves change as well as stability, and that a gradual change taking place over a period of several centuries is bound to be not only cumulative, but also to become considerable in the end. Each European country, we can also agree, made its own contribution to the civilization of the Renaissance, and did so in part by drawing upon its native medieval traditions, but Italy, both by the excellence of her own contributions and by the influence she exercised upon all other countries, occupied a position of cultural predominance that she never possessed before or after.

If the claim made by some older historians that the Renaissance was a period of revival after many dark centuries must now be subjected to severe qualification, the fact remains that writers of the period thought of their age as one that witnessed the rebirth of arts, letters, and learning after a long decay. Finally, in a complex, but articulated, civilization each area of culture may have its own distinct line of development. We have no reason to assume that the Renaissance, or any other period, must show the same characteristics, the same "style," the same rate of development or regional diffusion in art and literature, in politics, economy, or religion, in philosophy, or in the sciences. The perception of such a common style may be the ultimate aim of the historian of a period, but he cannot take it for granted at the start. Many of the controversies about the Renaissance are due to the tendency of historians to focus exclusively on one aspect of the culture of the period, to make one-sided generalizations on the basis of their favorite subject matter, and to ignore the other relevant aspects of the era. To approach a more objective view of the Renaissance, it seems preferable to respect the independence of the various fields of human endeavor, without denying or neglecting their mutual relations.

I

Within the broader outlines of Renaissance civilization, humanism may be considered as one of the more important, but limited, aspects or movements. The interpretation of Renaissance humanism, like that of the Renaissance itself, has been subject to a great deal of controversy and disagreement among recent historians. Moreover, humanism is even more difficult to define than is the Renaissance, since it is not enough to indicate its chronological limits. We must also try to describe its intellectual content and the range of its activities. This task is further complicated since the word *humanism* has come to stand for any kind of emphasis on human values. Quite naturally, when we hear Renaissance humanism mentioned, we think of an emphasis on human values that was supposedly current in the Renaissance period, or even was characteristic of that period. Humanism in this sense may certainly be found in the Renaissance, yet it was not as widespread as is often assumed. When historians speak of Renaissance humanism, they use the word in a sense that is different from our contemporary meaning. They are referring to a broad class of Renaissance intellectuals who are traditionally called humanists and who were active as teachers and secretaries, writers, scholars and thinkers; who exercised a wide and deep influence on all aspects of Renaissance civilization; and who left to posterity, along with the record of their lives and activities, vast writings that may be roughly classified as literature, historical and philological scholarship, and moral thought, but which often deal with such diverse subjects as philosophy and the sciences, literary and art criticism, education, government, and religion. The revival of antiquity generally associated with the Renaissance period, the thoroughgoing classicism that we notice in all its literary and artistic manifestations, is surely the direct or indirect effect of Renaissance humanism. When Georg Voigt, in 1859, described the earlier phases of Italian humanism, he emphasized its contributions to classical scholarship. Burckhardt and Symonds, without neglecting the impact of the humanists on Renaissance thought and literature, gave due importance to their work as historians and classical scholars. In later German scholarship this emphasis continued and was facilitated by the nineteenth-century use of the word *humanism,* then almost exclusively associated with the humanistic disciplines, that is, history and philology, and with the humanistic schools in which these disciplines were cultivated. On the other hand, because humanism seemed to predominate in Italian literature and civilization during the fifteenth century but to lose some of its importance during the sixteenth, Italian scholars tended to use "humanism" as a name for a period—mainly the fifteenth century —a period which scholars in other countries have called the early

Renaissance. Recently, the tendency has been to shift emphasis
from the scholarly and literary achievements of the humanists
and to define the movement in terms of certain ideas or ideals.
This tendency may be due to a declining respect for scholarship
as such, and to the feeling that Renaissance humanism must be
identified with a set of well-defined ideas if it is to be acceptable
to contemporary opinion. The modern undertones of the word
may also have played their part in the process. Konrad Burdach
assigned to humanism a religious origin and considered its secular orientation a later development. Giuseppe Toffanin believed
that Renaissance humanism was a Catholic reaction against certain heretical tendencies inherent in medieval thought. Douglas
Bush, thinking of northern rather than Italian humanists, identifies the core of Renaissance humanism as Christian humanism,
which shares with Thomas Aquinas the concern for harmony
between ancient reason and Christian faith. On the other hand,
Hans Baron placed in the center of his interpretation the civic
humanism of fifteenth-century Florence, which was primarily
concerned with the training of responsible citizens leading active
lives in a republican community. Finally, Eugenio Garin, in a
number of well-informed and influential studies, used the term
humanism as a common denominator for what was best in the
philosophical thought of the Renaissance, stressing its preoccupation with the human and moral problems of the layman and
its contrast with the theological orientation of medieval scholasticism.

II

There is some truth in most of these views, but it is difficult to
derive from them a clear and coherent picture of Renaissance
humanism that would do justice to the movement as a whole.
It is thus more useful perhaps to go back to the Renaissance
meanings of the terms *humanist* and *humanities,* from which the
modern term *humanism* is clearly derived. It seems that
"humanist," probably coined in the slang of university students,
designated a professional teacher of the humanities, and that
"humanities," or *Studia humanitatis,* was understood to include
such subjects as grammar, rhetoric, poetry, history, and moral
philosophy. This well-defined cycle of studies consisted, in other
words, of the subjects that would train a student to speak and
write well, both in prose and in verse and primarily in Latin

(which was still the accepted language of the schools and of the Church, of law, and of international diplomacy); it included the study and writing of history, and finally one of the philosophical disciplines—moral philosophy. Since the humanists were firmly convinced that it was necessary for each genre of writing to follow the models of ancient literature, the study of the Greek and Latin classics became a central and inseparable part of humanistic education: to study poetry meant to study the ancient poets as well as to learn how to write verse. In this way we can understand why Renaissance humanism was both literary and scholarly in its central concern, that classicism was at its heart, and why it spread through the influence of the humanists into all of Renaissance civilization. When the Renaissance scholars took over the classical term "humanities" for the studies in which they were interested, they meant to emphasize the human values inherent in these subjects, and the teaching of moral philosophy was an essential part of their program. In this way they were humanists also in the twentieth-century sense of the word. Yet Renaissance humanism, unlike its twentieth-century namesake, was strongly committed to a cultural program and ideal, and it is this ideal that all Renaissance humanists have in common. The particular philosophical, religious, or political ideas by which modern historians have tried to define Renaissance humanism are actually found in the writings of some humanists, and many of them are intrinsically quite significant. Yet since these ideas were not shared by all humanists, and since such a large part of the work of the humanists was not concerned with ideas at all, but was literary or scholarly in character, a proper definition or understanding of the movement as a whole cannot be based on them. On the other hand, since the main, and, as it were, professional concern of the humanists was limited to the humanities, we should not assume, as many scholars do, that humanism was identical with Renaissance civilization or Renaissance learning as a whole. Theology and law, medicine and mathematics, astronomy, astrology and alchemy, logic, natural philosophy and metaphysics, the vernacular literatures, the visual arts and music were all vigorously cultivated during the Renaissance but not primarily by the humanists. Each discipline had its own traditions and development, and was pursued by its own specialists. If all were strongly influenced by Renaissance humanism, this influence was largely external to the discipline itself and limited in its nature. It was owing to those humanists who had a personal interest or competence in one or more of these other disciplines, or to those specialists in the other disciplines who had enjoyed a humanist education in their youth, as became more and more the rule after the middle of the fifteenth century. The nature of this humanist influence is also characteristic: it consists primarily in the introduction of fresh classical sources and in the restatement of their ideas, in the vogue of classical quotations and allusions, in the use of the newly refined methods of historical and philological scholarship, and in an attempt to replace the specialized terminology of the medieval schools, their tight methods of arguing, their elaborate commentaries and disputed questions, by treatises, dialogues, and essays written in a smooth and elegant style.

Since moral philosophy, unlike the other philosophical disciplines, was considered a part of the humanities, we can easily understand that the moral thought of the Renaissance was closely associated with the humanist movement. A considerable part of the moral literature of the Renaissance was written by humanists, or by laymen with a humanist training, and practically all writers on moral subjects were influenced by humanism. The connection of this literature with humanism accounts for several of its peculiar features. Many, if not all, of the humanists were teachers, so that their moral thought was strongly centered on the education of the young. The humanists considered classical antiquity their major guide and model in thought and literature and their moral writings are accordingly studded with quotations from Greek and Roman authors, with episodes from classical history and mythology, with ideas and theories derived from ancient philosophers and writers. Finally, the humanists were professional rhetoricians, that is, writers and critics, who wished not only to say the truth, but to say it well, according to their literary taste and standards. They believed in the ancient rhetorical doctrine that a professional speaker and writer must acquire and show skill in making any idea that is related to his chosen topic plausible to his public. Consequently, a given idea is often expressed in phrases that aim at elegance rather than at precision, and many times, especially in a dialogue or in a speech, opinions may be defended with vigor and eloquence that are appropriate for the occasion, but do not express the author's final or considered view.

III

Moral teaching is often contained in literary genres cultivated by the humanists where a modern reader might not expect to find it. The humanists inherited from the ancient and medieval grammarians and literary critics the view that moral instruction is one of the main tasks of the poet. Hence there is a moral or even moralistic note in some of the poetry they wrote, and in the interpretation they gave of the ancient poets in the classroom and in their published commentaries. The humanists also followed ancient and medieval theory and practice in their belief that the orator and prose writer is a moral teacher and ought to adorn his compositions with pithy sentences quoted from the poets or coined by himself. To facilitate his task, a humanist would gather quotations and sentences in a commonplace book, and some writers would publish collections of sentences, proverbs, or historical anecdotes from which an author could freely quote on the appropriate occasion. Plutarch's *Apophthegmata*, in humanist translations, enjoyed great popularity for this reason, and Erasmus's *Adagia*, collected from many ancient sources and revised and enlarged several times by the author, was printed and used, though not always quoted, for several centuries.

Finally, another branch of study cultivated by the humanists, history, had moral significance for them. The humanists shared the view of many ancient and medieval authors that one of the tasks of historiography is to teach a moral lesson. Much Renaissance historiography is sustained by this belief. In the same way, the extensive biographical literature produced during the period is often animated by the desire to supply the reader with models worthy of imitation. The medieval lives of saints provided a precedent, since they too were written to provide the reader with models of pious conduct. But it makes a difference whether the persons whose lives are described as models of human conduct are Christian saints or ancient statesmen and generals, philosophers and poets, contemporary princes, citizens, or artists. The Renaissance continued to produce biographies of the saints, but it left a much larger number of secular biographies. The lives of famous ancients as written by Petrarch and other humanists were clearly intended to provide models for imitation, since classical antiquity was for the humanists the admired model in all fields of human endeavor. No wonder that in a famous hu-

manist controversy the relative superiority of the Romans Scipio
and Caesar served as a basis for discussing the merits of republican and monarchical government. When Machiavelli in his
Discourses on Livy holds out the institutions and actions of the
Roman republic as a model to his contemporaries, he follows
the practice of his humanist predecessors, and he states his underlying assumption more clearly than any of them had done:
human beings are fundamentally the same at all times, and
therefore it is possible to study the conduct of the ancients, to
learn from their mistakes and from their achievements, and to
follow their example where they were successful.

If we turn from these writings of the humanists in which a
moral or moralistic interest appeared to those works which deal
explicitly with moral philosophy, we may notice the favorite
genres used for this kind of literature. Most important are the
treatise and the dialogue, and later on, the essay. More marginal
forms are the oration and the letter, the most widespread forms
of humanist literature, which at times, serve to express moral
ideas. The letter was especially popular with the humanists, as
it allowed them to express their views in a personal and subjective fashion, although they considered letter-writing a branch
of literature, and gave the same polished elegance to their letters
as to their other literary compositions. To these we might add
the collections of sentences, proverbs, and commonplaces.

The language of these writings was usually Latin, but the use
of the vernacular appears especially in Tuscany, during the
fifteenth century, and becomes more widespread in the rest of
Italy and of Europe during the sixteenth. The choice of language
indicated the reading public to which an author wished to
address a given work. Latin writings were intended for an international audience of scholars and of educated alumni of humanist schools, while within a particular country or region works in
the vernacular were read chiefly by a middle class of ladies, businessmen, and artisans who were able to read and eager to be
entertained and instructed, but who usually knew no Latin and
lacked a humanist school education or a university training.

IV

The existence of this large body of moral literature written by
humanists and popularizers, and of the still larger body of humanist learning and literature, is in itself a significant historical

phenomenon. We are confronted with a vast body of secular learning, nourished from ancient sources and contemporary experience, and basically independent of, though not entirely unrelated to, the medieval traditions of scholastic philosophy and science, theology and law. As a part of this learning, or derived from it, we find a body of moral thought that is never opposed to religious doctrine—often explicitly harmonized with it—existing side by side with religious doctrine and claiming for its domain wider and wider areas of human life and experience. There are several medieval precedents for such secular moral thought, but these were different and more limited in scope. Certain moralists like Cicero, Seneca, and Boethius had enjoyed a continuous popularity throughout the Middle Ages, and medieval grammarians had tried to provide moral interpretations of ancient poets such as Ovid and Vergil. This tradition was apparently absorbed by Renaissance humanism in its beginnings in the fourteenth century. When Aristotle's writings were all translated into Latin and adopted as textbooks of philosophy at Paris and other universities during the thirteenth century, his *Ethics*, along with his *Politics*, his *Rhetoric*, and the *Economics* attributed to him, was expounded in the classroom, and a number of commentaries on these works owe their origin to this teaching tradition, although the course on ethics was an elective rather than a required course, and considered less important than logic or natural philosophy. Thus Aristotle's doctrines of the virtues and of the supreme good, and also his theory of the passions as presented in the *Rhetoric,* were well known to students of philosophy and to many others. When the humanists took over much of the teaching of ethics in the fifteenth century and wrote general treatises on moral subjects, they continued to use the Aristotelian writings, which recommended themselves by their topical completeness and the wealth of their detail, and the humanists often tended to follow his views though they might interpret them in a different way or combine them with theories derived from other sources. Finally, in the later Middle Ages there had developed a code of moral conduct for knights, that is, for a privileged class of laymen, and this code found its literary expression in lyrical poetry, in romances in verse and prose, and in a few theoretical treatises. The moral literature of the Renaissance was similarly intended for laymen rather than for clerics. Yet aside from its heavy classical equipment which had been lacking in the medieval literature of the knights, it was written by and for a different class of people: it had a different political, economic, and social foundation.

Renaissance humanism, which began in Italy toward the very end of the thirteenth century, at the earliest, cannot be explained as a delayed but direct result of the economic and political development of the city communities that began in the eleventh century. For even a theory of a "cultural lag," whatever that may mean, does not seem to supply the missing link, as there was, after all, a distinctive tradition of learning and literature in twelfth- and early thirteenth-century Italy that was not humanistic. On the other hand, an urban, not a feudal society provided at least the background of Renaissance civilization. The Renaissance humanists wrote their moral works for their fellow scholars, for their students, and for an elite of businessmen and of urbanized noblemen who were willing to adopt their cultural and moral ideas. During the sixteenth century, ever wider circles of the middle class seem to have taken interest in this literature.

Political theory was traditionally a part of ethics or a supplement to it, and the Renaissance moralists took a strong and sometimes primary interest in political theory. The nature of their political ideas varied a good deal according to circumstances. There was a tradition of civic and republican humanism, especially in Florence, and to a lesser degree in Venice, whose historical significance has been recently emphasized by Hans Baron and other scholars. Yet much Renaissance political thinking developed also along monarchical lines, especially during the sixteenth century. Both Machiavelli and Thomas More were also linked to the humanist movement.

Aside from the political treatises, the moral literature of the Renaissance addressed itself mainly to the private individual. The political and economic realities of the day are taken more or less for granted, and the purpose of the moral treatise is to give theoretical or practical instruction to the individual, especially to the young. The lines between decency and success are not always as clearly drawn as we might wish, and as a result, the word virtue came to have a curious ambiguity. It meant moral virtue, to be sure, but Machiavelli's *virtù* stood more for the strong character that assured political success, and the "virtuoso" was distinguished by intellectual and social skill rather than by moral excellence.

At this point, we might very well stop to consider the variety

MORAL THOUGHT OF HUMANISM   31

of meanings of the term "moral thought," both for the Renaissance and in its wider applications. When we speak of the morals of a person or a period, we think primarily of actual behavior, and assume that this behavior expresses some conscious or unconscious convictions, although it may be quite contrary to the professed ideals of the person and of the time. In this respect, the Renaissance, and especially the Italian Renaissance, enjoys a dubious reputation. In the popular view, which seems to find support in Symonds and other historians, the Italian Renaissance was a period of political ruthlessness, of crimes of violence and of passion; and the glittering melodrama of dagger and poison seems to provide an appropriate foil for the admired beauty of Renaissance poetry and painting. Examples of crime and cruelty were numerous in the Renaissance, in Italy and elsewhere, as they are in other periods of history, including the Middle Ages and our century. However, not all the stories and anecdotes that found their way from the Renaissance chroniclers and gossipwriters into modern textbooks of history are well documented, and those that we can accept were probably disapproved of in their own time as much as in ours. Moreover, it would be quite wrong to assume that such misdeeds dominated the picture of public or private life during the Renaissance. There were a great many decent people whose conduct agreed with the highest moral standards.

Yet, ignoring the actual conduct of people during the Renaissance or whatever secret or unexpressed thought may have guided them, and examining those moral ideas that we find more or less explicitly stated in the literature of the period, we find that moral subjects were discussed in a variety of ways. An author may describe the actual moral customs and manners of his time, either through examples, as is often done in narrative literature, or through a discussion of their general traits, without explicitly setting forth any standards of how people should behave. He may also, however, try to guide the conduct of people, especially of his younger readers, by prescribing how they should behave. Description and prescription are often confused in our contemporary discussions of moral and social problems, and they cannot always be kept apart in Renaissance literature, but it would help proper understanding of such discussions if the distinction is clearly kept in mind. In the literature which emphasizes the prescriptive aspect and tends to set standards for the young, we must distinguish between those authors who are mainly concerned with rules of prudence and expediency, and teach their readers how to behave in order to get along with other people and to have a successful career, and those who emphasize honesty and moral decency regardless of their practical consequences. In works of the latter kind there is often a mixture of ethical theory, which properly belongs to philosophy, and of moral exhortation and persuasion, which belongs to oratory and tends toward edification. Finally, there is the literature of strictly philosophical ethics, which intends to set forth general principles of moral thought and which is prescriptive only in an implicit way or by deducing rules of conduct from those general principles. This literature may take the form of systematic handbooks of ethics or of monographic treatises dealing with specific topics in ethics.

All these types are present in the moral literature of the Renaissance, and it would be wrong to say that any of them is limited to a particular phase of the period. However, the literature of the fifteenth and early sixteenth century is more frequently concerned with moralistic prescription and edification. As the sixteenth century progresses, rules of expediency and descriptions of manners and customs tend to prevail. One gets the impression of a more settled society in which standards of conduct and manners are well established and the main task of the young man is not to acquire valid ethical principles through independent critical thinking but rather to assure his success by learning how to adjust to life—that is, to the accepted modes of moral thought and conduct. This literature gains in historical and psychological interest what it loses in ethical solidity, and it leads the way towards such famous examples of seventeenth-century literature as Gracian, La Bruyère, or La Rochefoucauld.

V

In contrast to the books of manners stand the philosophical treatises on ethics that supply whatever theoretical structure and systematic thinking on moral problems there was during the Renaissance. Because of the general direction of Renaissance humanism, most, though not all, of their subject matter is derived from classical sources. The authors known during the Middle Ages, especially Aristotle, Cicero, and Seneca, continue to be important and in some ways become even more important, as there is a greater effort to interpret and to utilize them in great detail. Equally important are some other sources of ancient moral philosophy made available for the first time by humanist scholarship. These new sources include most of the writings of Plato and of the Neoplatonists, Stoic authors such as Epictetus and Marcus Aurelius, Sceptics like Sextus Empiricus, and Epicureans like Lucretius. Diogenes Laertius supplied new information on several schools of ancient thought, especially on Epicurus. Of equal, if not even greater, importance were a number of popular ancient moralists not identified with any particular school of philosophy, such as Xenophon and Isocrates, Plutarch and Lucian. The number both of their translations and of the quotations taken from them shows that they were among the favorite sources of Renaissance humanists.

The impact of these various sources and schools on the moral thought of the Renaissance was varied and complex. Moreover, the history of moral thought during the Renaissance is related to, but not identical with, the history of philosophy. Only a part of the moral literature of the period came from philosophers in the technical sense of the word, or was systematic in content. On the other hand, some of the most important philosophers of the Renaissance, and even entire groups and schools of Renaissance philosophy, such as the Aristotelians, the Platonists, and the philosophers of nature, were not interested primarily in ethics but made their major contributions to other parts of philosophy, especially logic, metaphysics, and natural philosophy. With these qualifications, we may say that there was a solid body of Aristotelian ethics throughout the Renaissance period. Its most obvious expressions are the numerous editions, translations, commentaries, and summaries of the ethical writings of Aristotle, among which the *Eudemian Ethics* now takes its proper place for the first time, and of their ancient and medieval interpreters. This literature has not been sufficiently explored until recent times, and we are just beginning to learn more about it. However, we may safely say of the Aristotelian ethics what has become apparent about Renaissance Aristotelianism in general. It continues in many ways the traditions of medieval Aristotelianism, which were very much alive at the universities, in Italy as elsewhere. On the other hand, there was among the humanists a strong tendency to recapture the genuine thought of Aristotle apart from its supposed distortions by medieval translators and commentators. Finally, there were all kinds of combinations on the part of Aristotelian philosophers, who tried to reconcile and

34   RENAISSANCE THOUGHT II

to synthesize what seemed to be valuable in the scholastic and
humanistic interpretations of Aristotle. In the study of ethics,
as in other disciplines, the main contribution of the humanists
to Aristotelian studies was to supply new translations based on
a better philological understanding of the Greek text. This is
more important than one might suspect. For in an author as
difficult and elusive as Aristotle, whose every word was (and still
is) considered by many thinkers as the ultimate source and
authority of philosophical truth, a different translation may be
equivalent to a different philosophy. Moreover, whereas the
medieval scholastics treated Aristotle pretty much in isolation,
the humanist Aristotelians read and interpreted Aristotle in close
conjunction with the other Greek philosophers and writers. On
the whole, the humanist Aristotelians were primarily interested
in Aristotle's ethical writings. Leonardo Bruni translated and
summarized only Aristotle's *Ethics, Politics* and *Economics,* while
Francesco Filelfo wrote a summary of ethics based on Aristotle.
Ermolao Barbaro, though not limited to Aristotle's ethical
writings, favored them in his lectures and in a summary of ethics.
Philip Melanchthon, Luther's colleague, wrote several treatises
on ethics, in which Aristotle's doctrine is preferred to that of
other ancient philosophers, and it was due to Melanchthon's
influence that the Reformed universities of Protestant Germany
continued to base their teaching of philosophy on the works of
Aristotle.

   As a result of this widespread study of Aristotle, practically
every writer of the period was acquainted with the main doctrines of Aristotelian ethics and was inclined to adopt them or
to discuss them. Aristotle's views that the supreme good of man
must include a minimum of external advantages and that the
contemplative life is the highest goal of human existence are as
familiar in the moral literature of the Renaissance as are his
distinction between moral and intellectual virtues, his definition
of the moral virtues as habits and as means between two opposite vices, and his detailed descriptions of individual virtues and
vices.

   Plato's influence on the moral thought of the Renaissance is
much more limited than Aristotle's, in spite of the well-known
role played generally by Platonism in Renaissance philosophy.
Plato's early dialogues, to be sure, deal with moral topics, and
were widely read in school, mainly in courses of Greek. Yet we
do not find any system of ethics based primarily on Plato, as so

many were on Aristotle. This is due partly to the unsystematic character of Plato's writings. More important, the leading Platonists of the Renaissance, like their late ancient and medieval predecessors, were interested in questions of metaphysics and cosmology rather than of ethics. They were not so much concerned with specific moral problems or theories but tended to reduce all ethical questions to the single task of attaining the contemplative life. Some of their specific theories that are relevant to moral thought we shall encounter later. The most important and widespread contribution of Platonism to the subject is the theory of love, based on the *Symposium* and *Phaedrus,* which was to constitute the subject matter of poems and lectures and of a special branch of prose literature. Among the moralists not committed to any special school of philosophy, quotations and borrowings from Plato were frequent, and became increasingly so after the rise of Florentine Platonism during the second half of the fifteenth century.

Stoic ethics as expressed in the writings of Seneca, and discussed in Cicero's philosophical works, had been a familiar ingredient of medieval moral thought, and continued to exercise a widespread influence during the Renaissance, when the writings of these Roman authors became even more popular than they had been before. The Stoic view that the supreme good of man consisted of virtue alone and that to secure virtue all passions must be thoroughly eradicated was generally known and often approved. Some Stoic theories appealed even to thinkers, such as Pomponazzi, who cannot be labeled as Stoic philosophers in their general orientation. Yet in contrast with this popular and eclectic Stoicism based on Cicero and Seneca, which permeated the moral thought of the fifteenth and early sixteenth century, it was only during the latter part of the sixteenth century that the Greek sources of ancient Stoicism became better known and that systematic attempts were made to restate Stoic philosophy (and especially Stoic ethics) in its original purity. The distinguished humanist, Justus Lipsius, compiled from the ancient sources a valuable handbook of Stoic ethics that was to enjoy great popularity during the seventeenth century, and the French writer, Guillaume Du Vair, gave a more literary expression to the same doctrine. Most Renaissance humanists found Stoic ethics uncongenial on account of its rigidity. The great vogue of pure Stoicism came only in the seventeenth century. In order to understand this later appeal, we must remember that the Stoics are rigorous only in their emphasis on the difference between virtue and vice, but reserve a very large area of human life to the things they call morally indifferent. Where questions of virtue and vice are not involved the Stoic sage is allowed and even encouraged to follow expediency. With virtue and vice often limited to a few ultimate decisions, the sway of expediency becomes very large indeed, and the Stoic moralist, while continuing to be rigorous in theory, may turn out to be lax, if not selfish, on most practical questions. The same may happen to the Platonist (and to the mystic), as soon as he has to act on matters unrelated to the life of contemplation.

The ethics of Epicurus, which proposed intellectual pleasure as the chief end of human life, was widely known in the Renaissance, and frequently discussed. Most humanists rejected Epicurean ethics and were more or less influenced by Cicero's unsympathetic account of that doctrine. Yet gradually the more favorable presentation of Epicurus in the works of Lucretius and Diogenes Laertius became better known, and Epicurus's emphasis on intellectual pleasure was more fully appreciated. Thus Epicurean ethics was endorsed by a few humanists, such as Lorenzo Valla and Cosimo Raimondi, and some of its tenets made an impression on thinkers whose general outlook was very different—for example, Marsilio Ficino.

Finally, ancient Scepticism had a number of followers in the Renaissance, especially in the sixteenth century, when the writings of Sextus became more widely known. The main appeal of Scepticism was in its claim that by abandoning all rigid doctrines and opinions we free ourselves from unnecessary worries and are left to face only the unavoidable necessities of life. If we wish to have a standard for our conduct, we should follow the customs of our country, at least in all matters that concern other people. In this way the boundaries between moral standards and established manners tend to be blurred, although there may remain a realm of personal and individual life in which we may think and do as we please. Scepticism in matters of reason is by no means incompatible with religious faith, as the example of Augustine may show; consequently this position had many more followers during the sixteenth century than is usually realized. The chief expression of this sceptical ethics is found in some of the essays of Montaigne, and in the writings of his pupil, Pierre Charron.

VI

The influence of ancient ethics on the Renaissance is not limited to an acceptance of the main systematic theories of antiquity by some Renaissance thinkers. The constant use of specific ancient ideas or sentences or examples in the discussion of moral topics is more widespread. This eclectic use of ancient material, for which some favorite author such as Cicero could serve as a classical model, is especially characteristic of the humanists and their popular followers. In this way, particular ideas or sentences taken from a given philosopher, such as Plato or Aristotle, were indiscriminately combined with those of other philosophers who held a very different position on major questions or with those of ancient moralists like Isocrates, Lucian, or Plutarch, who cannot even be credited with a coherent systematic position in philosophy. Thus the sharp boundaries between philosophical concepts or theories derived from different sources tend to vanish. Furthermore, Renaissance humanists were not so much interested as modern scholars are in emphasizing the distinctive traits of various periods, schools, and writers of antiquity or in playing up one against the other. They tended to admire ancient literature in all its periods and representatives (although some authors were more admired than others), and to be syncretistic as well as eclectic; that is, they liked to harmonize the views of various classical authors, and to extract from their writings a kind of common wisdom that could be learned, imitated, and utilized.

The numerous classical quotations that characterize most humanist treatises and even the essays of Montaigne, and which are apt to bore and annoy the modern reader, were not vain displays of empty erudition, although they might often serve this purpose. The quotations served as authorities—as confirmations of the validity of what the author was trying to say. Quotations from recognized authors were counted by ancient theorists of rhetoric among the forms of proof that an orator was supposed to produce. Augustine had emphasized the authority of Scripture as a chief source of theological discourse, and during the Middle Ages not only theology but each discipline of knowledge employed its standard authorities, along with rational arguments, in support of its theories. For a Renaissance humanist, a sentence from a classical writer served as such an authority, and if he added to his quotation what seems to us an arbitrary interpretation, he merely did what his predecessors and contemporaries also had done. In a period in which the emphasis is on authority and tradition, originality will assert itself in the adaptation and interpretation of the tradition. Moreover, there may be some originality even in the choice of one's quotations. It makes a difference whether an author keeps quoting the same passages that had been quoted by his predecessors or for the first time introduces new quotations, singling them out from their context and, as it were, discovering their significance.

The frequency of quotations and of commonplaces repeated in the moral literature of the Renaissance gives to all but its very best products an air of triviality that is often very boring to the modern critical reader, especially when he is acquainted with the ancient sources from which the quotations are drawn and in which they seem to have a much more subtle and precise meaning. If we want to do justice to these Renaissance writers we must try to understand the circumstances under which they wrote, and the purposes which they had in mind. Whenever many books of the same type are written, most of them are bound to be dull and mediocre, and only a few will stand out by reason of their authors' intellectual or literary merits. Human inventiveness seems limited, and repetition is the rule rather than the exception, even where no direct copying or plagiarism is involved. After all, no single reader was expected to read all the treatises on the same topic, just as a modern student will not read more than one or two textbooks on the same subject. Each treatise is addressed to its own readers, and must supply to them the same amount of general information that other readers may derive from other works on the same topic. This is even more the case with orations, which were delivered on only a single occasion and were published only incidentally when they happened to be very successful. An oration is composed to entertain and edify its audience by adapting general ideas to the occasion. While it was the custom in Florence to have each incoming group of magistrates treated to a speech in praise of justice, it was not so important that the orator should produce new or profound ideas about the meaning of justice—it was his job to impress his listeners with their duty to follow justice in the administration of their office. This was surely of great practical importance for the city as a whole. Since the oration was a principal form of humanist literature, the example might be

applied to its other branches. Each moral treatise had to exhort
and edify its readers by instructing them in matters of great
practical and human importance, and this was in most instances
more valuable than the presentation of novel or original
thoughts. In other words, we should not approach the average
moral literature of the Renaissance with excessive expectations
as to its depth or originality, but with an awareness of its limited
purposes, and a recognition that it was well suited to these
objectives.

VII

The frequency of ancient ideas and quotations in the moral
writings of the Renaissance humanists, and of humanist literature in general, raises another question that has been the subject
of much debate: what was the attitude of the Renaissance humanists toward Christianity, and in what sense and to what
extent were they inclined toward paganism? The charge of
paganism was made against the humanists by some theologians
of their own time, and it has been repeated by a number of
modern historians, some of whom have turned the charge into
praise. There were, however, very few attempts to revive the
pagan religions of classical antiquity, although this has been
charged by contemporaries and by modern scholars in a few
instances. Although much was made of pagan mythology in the
poetry and also in the prose treatises of the period, it was not
intended to replace the use of Christian religious thought and
imagery but to supplement it. In most instances it was no more
than a literary ornament sanctioned by ancient precedent. Where
it served a more serious intention, its use was justified by allegory
—by attributing to the pagan stories a hidden meaning that was
in accordance with Christian truth. This attitude culminates in
Pico della Mirandola's notion of a poetic theology, that is, of a
philosophical and theological truth that could be discovered
through the allegorical interpretation of pagan poetry and mythology. Yet the main impact of "paganism" on the moral
thought of the Renaissance consists in its heavy indebtedness to
ancient philosophical ideas, which we have already noted. The
task of assimilating the moral and philosophical thought of the
ancients to Christianity presented itself to the Church Fathers
and again to many medieval thinkers. From these earlier attempts, the Renaissance differed at least in degree, if not in

kind. The Church Fathers tended to fit Christianity into the
ancient modes of thought that had been previously familiar to
them and to their contemporaries. The humanists wanted to
adapt classical ideas to a previously accepted Christian view of
the world. Nevertheless, the affinity between the humanists and
the Church Fathers has been stressed with some justification by
modern historians like Toffanin, and the humanists themselves
were to some extent aware of this affinity. For when they defended "poetry," that is, humanist learning and the reading of
the pagan authors, against the theological critics of their own
time, they cited the precedent of the Church Fathers. No doubt
Bruni's translation of the letter in which Basil, one of the
Fathers, defended the reading of pagan poets by a Christian
youth owed its tremendous popularity to this issue. There were
many humanists who were not concerned with religious or theological problems, and did not touch on them in their writings.
Those who did, and they were important, never undertook a
general critique of the religious tradition such as appeared in
the eighteenth century. They usually praised the Bible and the
Church Fathers as the Christian classics, and attacked scholastic
theology as a barren distortion of original Christian doctrine
and piety. A few of them attacked the weaknesses they observed
in the Church of their time, and especially in monasticism. When
the humanists wrote about moral subjects, either they tried to
combine and to harmonize ancient and Christian ideas in the
manner of Erasmus, or they discussed moral topics on a purely
classical and secular basis—without however indicating any hostility toward Christianity, but rather taking for granted the
compatibility between the two, as was done by Alberti and many
other Italian humanists. In the sixteenth century, after the Protestant and Catholic reformations, we find humanist scholars and
moralists among the followers of both major camps, as well as
among those who favored some of the smaller heretical movements, or who tried hard to keep aloof from the religious struggle.
This shows once more, that Renaissance humanism as a whole
cannot be identified with a particular set of opinions or convictions, but is rather characterized by a cultural ideal and a range
of scholarly, literary, and intellectual interests that the individual
humanist was able to combine with a variety of professional,
philosophical, or theological convictions.

VIII

If we try to survey in more concrete detail the moral thought of the Renaissance period, it seems best to focus on the chief genres and themes of this literature, rather than on the ideas of individual writers and thinkers. The character of this literature, with its uncertain position between philosophical and popular thought, its dependence on classical sources, and its widespread eclecticism and triviality, seems to call for such an approach.

The most technical type of Renaissance literature on moral topics is the general treatise on ethics that was usually written for the use of students. Since Aristotle was and remained the chief basis of university instruction in the philosophical disciplines, many general treatises on ethics take the form of commentaries on Aristotle's *Nicomachean Ethics* and *Politics,* or of introductions, paraphrases, and summaries of those works. In the fifteenth century, the commentary of Donato Acciaiuoli and the *Compendium* of Ermolao Barbaro deserve mention; and in the sixteenth century there was Francesco Piccolomini, a Paduan, and a few other scholars such as Alessandro Piccolomini, who composed a handbook of Aristotelian ethics in Italian, indicating by this very fact that he was addressing himself to a broader educated public. Outside of Italy, the introductions of Jacques Lefèvre d'Etaples to Aristotle's writings on moral philosophy and Melanchthon's ethical writings represent the most influential attempts to restate Aristotle's ethics—especially his belief that the natural goods contribute to the supreme good of happiness and that the moral virtues are means between two opposite extremes —and to harmonize this natural ethics with the teachings of Scripture. John Case's moral questions on Aristotle, which originated in Oxford, are important as a rare example of a type of literature that must have flourished also at the English universities to a greater degree than is usually realized. More eclectic but still largely Aristotelian are the handbooks of Francesco Filelfo and of Sebastian Fox Morcillo. An early and very popular introduction to ethics, Leonardo Bruni's *Isagogicon Moralis Disciplinae,* follows Aristotle in the discussion of the moral and intellectual virtues, but advances a somewhat eclectic view on the supreme good. He bases the ultimate end of human life mainly on virtue but also grants some importance to external advantages and thus stays close enough to Aristotle's position, but at the same time he claims that this view is essentially identical with those of the Stoics and Epicureans. The most consistent attempt to present Stoic ethics in a systematic handbook was made by Justus Lipsius toward the end of the sixteenth century. Its major effects were to be felt only during the following century.

Aside from such handbooks of ethics, there are a number of more informal humanist treatises and dialogues in which the central topic of ancient ethics, that is, happiness or the supreme good, is discussed. Whereas Petrarch had blamed Aristotle for his belief that man may attain his ultimate end during the present life, an attitude echoed by Bartolommeo Fazio and others, many writers identified the goal of life with the knowledge and enjoyment of God but thought that this goal could be attained during the present life, at least by some people and for some time. This view was held especially by the leading Platonist, Marsilio Ficino, who wrote several short treatises on it. Bartolomeo Platina stresses endurance and wisdom in a Stoic sense, and Pietro Pomponazzi approaches Stoicism rather than the view of Aristotle when in his treatise on immortality he defines moral virtue as the task peculiar to human beings, and emphasizes that this virtue is its own reward, just as wickedness is its own punishment. Also the Epicurean view that pleasure is the supreme good found its defenders. The most famous of them, Lorenzo Valla, considers Epicureanism as the best among the pagan philosophies but endorses as his own view a kind of Christian Epicureanism in which the pleasures of the present life are abandoned for the sake of the pleasures, both physical and spiritual, which are promised in a future life to the faithful Christian.

A number of humanistic treatises deal with individual virtues, a subject that occupies a large part of Aristotle's *Ethics* and now is singled out for monographic treatment. Several of the virtues are discussed in the moral treatises of the Neapolitan humanist, Giovanni Pontano, such as courage, magnanimity, or prudence. Attempts to define the respective virtues are accompanied by a variety of moral rules and examples, and the concern is as much with stylistic elegance and moral edification, as with precise philosophical definitions or distinctions. Similar treatises were written by several Italian and other humanist writers.

A whole literature was dedicated to the highest virtue, wisdom, which was identified either with the attainment of pure knowledge, or with moral and practical ability in the affairs of life.

The latter tendency culminated in Pierre Charron, theologian and sceptical philosopher of the early seventeenth century. Analogous treatises were written on some specific vices such as ingratitude or avarice. There is a famous treatise on avarice by Poggio Bracciolini, in which some of the beneficial effects of this vice also are mentioned, in a way which some historians have tended to link with the spirit of modern capitalism.

IX

The humanist movement was closely identified with a reform of the program and curriculum of the secondary schools. Many of the humanists were professional tutors or school teachers, and it was through the training offered in the schools that most of the educated persons of the Renaissance period were influenced by humanist ideas, which they then carried into the larger spheres of public and professional life. Hence it was natural that the humanists would be very much concerned with the tasks and problems of education. The treatises on the education of the young form a large and important genre of humanist prose, and thanks to these treatises Renaissance humanism occupies as prominent a place in the history of educational theory as in that of educational practice.

The most influential early treatises were by Pier Paolo Vergerio the Elder and by Leonardo Bruni, to which we may add the treatise on education attributed to Plutarch that was translated by Guarino of Verona, who along with Vittorino da Feltre was the most famous and successful humanist teacher in fifteenth-century Italy. Other influential educational treatises were written by Maffeo Vegio and by Enea Silvio Piccolomini, a prominent humanist who entered the ecclesiastic career and finally became pope under the name of Pius II. Outside of Italy, educational treatises were written by many humanists such as Erasmus and Vives, by Wimpfeling and Camerarius in Germany, and by Ascham in England. These treatises were written either for the young students themselves or for the parents of prospective students to convince them of the value of a humanist education. A good deal of attention is paid to the praise of Greek and Latin literature, whose study formed the core of humanist instruction, and to the value of such an education for the future citizen or statesman. Often the author would offer actual reading lists, discussing the merits and educational value of specific classical authors and their different works. Aside from the genuine concern for a ruling class thoroughly imbued with a cultural heritage of unquestioned intellectual importance, the humanist educators laid much stress on the moral value inherent in the study of ancient literature, history, and philosophy. Through the reading of the classical authors, the student was to acquire a fund of moral ideas, sentences, and examples that would give him the necessary preparation to face the tasks of his own life. In stressing the moral value of a classical education, the humanists effectively countered the charge made by some theologians that the reading of the pagan poets and writers would corrupt the morals of the young. The humanists knew, of course, that there was much in ancient literature that could not stand muster before a strict Christian censor, and many of them did not hesitate to emulate it in prose and verse, pleading with Martial that their life was pure though their verse might be licentious. Yet they knew how to distinguish between a literature written by and for adults and the requirements of the education of the young. In their treatises on education they would usually omit from their reading list those ancient writings that gave rise to moral criticism, and Erasmus added the pointed remark that we should be careful not to imbibe the manners of the ancients along with their literature. In this way, the humanists managed to link their cultural ideals very closely with the moral aspirations of their time, and to make their educational program acceptable to all but the most narrow-minded theologians.

The actual human ideal of the Renaissance has often been characterized as that of the *uomo universale,* the universal man, or to use a modern phrase, the well-rounded personality. We rarely encounter this slogan in the literature of the period, but the actual life of persons like Leon Battista Alberti or Leonardo da Vinci seems to illustrate a quest for excellence in a great variety of pursuits, and the educational treatises of the time envisage a person who would achieve reasonable distinction in physical and artistic, intellectual and practical activities. This is also apparent in another large branch of literature that is concerned, not with education in general, but with the training of particular groups or classes of society.

A large number of treatises is dedicated to the education or the description of the good prince, and this literature has attracted a great deal of attention among historians of literature and of political thought. The "mirror of princes" was an important branch of literature during the later medieval centuries, and it has been shown that the ideal of the Christian king, based on Germanic customs and theological theories, was gradually transformed under the impact of the study of Roman law and of Aristotle's *Politics*. In fifteenth-century Italy, monarchical states were firmly established in Naples and Milan, and on a smaller scale, in Piedmont, Ferrara, and Mantua, not to speak of the numerous tiny and ephemeral principalities. It is against this background that the treatises on the best prince by humanists like Platina or Pontano and others must be understood. Important new sources for these treatises were several works of Isocrates and Plutarch that were widely diffused in a number of different translations. These humanist treatises were largely theoretical and gave much space to a list of the virtues that the prince should possess and to ancient examples of good conduct. It is characteristic that the tone of these treatises is secular rather than religious and that the reward promised to the good prince is everlasting fame rather than blessedness in a future life. The quest for fame was a central concern of the humanists and of their contemporaries, and the power of its appeal may be discovered in many episodes and writings of the period.

Another topic discussed in these treatises was the relation between virtue and expediency, and the authors of these usually concluded with Cicero that the most virtuous course of action is also in the long run the most advantageous. It has been pointed out by Allan Gilbert, Felix Gilbert, and other scholars that Machiavelli's *Prince*, though original in its extreme realism and its exclusive stress on expediency, is linked in its themes and problems with the late medieval and early humanist literature on the best prince. In the sixteenth century, the establishment of strong national monarchies outside of Italy forms the background for an important series of humanist treatises by Budé, Sepulveda, and others. The most famous is Erasmus's *Education of a Christian Prince*, which is explicitly introduced as a counterpart of Isocrates' treatise *Ad Nicoclem*, which Erasmus had translated. The prince is expected to read a number of ancient writers, in addition to the Bible. Among his suggestions for the administration of the state, Erasmus reminds the ruler that he is merely a member of the state, that his rule rests basically on the consent of the people, and that the public welfare is the only standard of the laws. Erasmus wants to limit the death penalty to extreme cases and urges the rulers to submit

46 RENAISSANCE THOUGHT II

their quarrels to arbitration, advocating on religious grounds the ideal of universal peace, a subject which he also treated elsewhere.

X

In fifteenth-century Italy, the ideal of republican liberty was as much alive as that of the monarchical state, as many humanist writings show. The Roman republic was as much a model for imitation as the Roman Empire, and it was no coincidence that the superiority of Scipio interpreted as a symbol of republican virtue was defended by Poggio, a Florentine citizen, against the claims of Caesar that were supported by Guarino, a subject of the Marquess of Ferrara. The comparison between different constitutions in the works of Plato, Aristotle, and Polybius found parallels in the writings of Francesco Patrizi, Aurelio Brandolini, and Machiavelli—who in his actual political career and in his *Discourses on Livy* attested his preference for the republican form of government. When Florentine political liberty was being undermined by the Medici regime, Alamanno Rinuccini wrote, but probably did not publish, his *De libertate*. Historians often exaggerate the significance of the fact that many of the city republics of the twelfth and thirteenth century succumbed to various forms of despotism during the fourteenth and fifteenth. The Venetian republic, ruled by its tightly restricted but responsible and educated nobility, became more powerful than ever, and was considered, on account of its wealth and stability, as a model by many political writers. The Florentine republic, which showed much less stability and underwent a variety of changes and revolutions, maintained its power and independence against several attacks from the outside and acquired, especially in the fifteenth century, a cultural and artistic predominance that was recognized throughout Italy and Europe. When Florence was threatened during the late fourteenth and early fifteenth century by the repeated attacks of the Visconti princes of Milan, who were expanding their rule over large areas of northern and central Italy, Florence mobilized against them her intellectual as well as her material resources. In this political crisis, many Florentine humanists emphasized the ideals of the republican state and of the responsible citizen called to govern that state. Hans Baron in a series of studies has forcefully described this civic humanism which flourished in Florence during the first half of the fifteenth century, and it certainly deserves attention as one of the most impressive phases of Renaissance humanism, even though it would be quite mistaken to identify Renaissance humanism as a whole with this Florentine civic humanism. There was a good deal of "despotic humanism" even in fifteenth-century Italy, and it would be quite impossible to comprise under the heading of "civic humanism" the entire political literature of the Renaissance period, let alone the large body of humanist literature that was not concerned with political problems at all. Florentine civic humanism found its best expression in the writings of Leonardo Bruni, Leon Battista Alberti, and Matteo Palmieri. Humanist learning is presented by them as serving the active life of the citizen involved in the affairs of his business and of his republic. He will not only occupy his leisure with the reading of the best authors, but will follow in his own life and activities the examples and precepts offered in their writings. It was not always mentioned but evidently understood that the prominent citizen was often called upon to deliver speeches, or to compose letters, of public importance, and that his humanist training would give him the necessary literary ability to accomplish these tasks with sufficient distinction to earn a good reputation for himself and for his city. Florentine history between 1434 and 1537 was characterized by a gradual transition from a republican form of government to the monarchy of the Medici—a development which was slowed and sometimes interrupted by a strong resistance on the part of the followers of the republican tradition. The political strife between the various parties was accompanied by literary controversy, as often happens, and the decline and fall of the Florentine republic thus produced a long series of political treatises defending the republican form of government and expounding the best ways to give it stability and perfection.

All Italian cities, whether their government was republican or monarchical, had a class of noble families of feudal or commercial antecedents. Its political influence varies greatly from place to place. In Venice, the nobles were the ruling class which monopolized all public office. In Naples, the feudal nobility possessed large landed property and traditional privileges, but the kings tended to reduce these privileges and to build a modern monarchy and a bureaucracy of trained persons directly responsible to them, just as the kings of England, France, and Spain were to do in the sixteenth century. In Florence, the older families were divided into bitterly opposed factions, and depending

48   RENAISSANCE THOUGHT II

upon the regime prevailing at a given time, some of them were
excluded from office or even exiled, while others shared the administration of the republic with able persons of more modest
origins. Everywhere, regardless of their political position, the
families of the nobility managed to maintain a good deal of
wealth and social prestige, and their style of life served as model
for the newcomers who established themselves through business
enterprises or political careers or even through professional success. However, with the exception of Naples and possibly Rome,
this nobility was no longer feudal in character but thoroughly
urbanized and hence may be called more appropriately a patri-
ciate. The humanists succeeded in gaining this important class
for their cause, educated their children, and impressed upon
them the conviction that they needed a good education by
humanist standards to be worthy of their social status. On the
other hand, the humanists cherished the ambition of attaining
for themselves a comparable social position, and at least some of
them succeeded. For the trained humanist could have a career
as chancellor or secretary of princes and republics, and thus was
able to contribute his share, along with the much larger body of
lawyers, to what was to be called in later centuries the *noblesse
de robe*. Against this background, it is quite understandable why
the humanists of the fifteenth century were interested in the
problem of nobility and why they should focus on the question
whether nobility is or should be based on birth or on personal
merit. The question had been discussed by a few late medieval
authors, and some of them had already emphasized the role of
personal merit as a basis of nobility. In the fifteenth century,
there was a whole series of treatises, *De Nobilitate,* in which this
problem is investigated further. In the treatises by Poggio Bracciolini, Buonaccorso da Montemagno, Bartolomeo Platina, and
the still unpublished but interesting dialogue of Cristoforo
Landino, the thesis that nobility rests on virtue is strongly defended. The problem is treated in typically humanist fashion
in the work of Buonaccorso da Montemagno, which enjoyed
tremendous popularity. Two Romans compete for the hand of a
noble woman, and support their claims in elaborate speeches,
one of them praising his illustrious ancestry, the other his personal achievements. The author does not tell us which of the
two married the girl, but the greater force seems to be in the
second speech which defends the claims of merit. The tendency
apparent in these treatises has led many scholars to consider the

preference for personal merit as against inherited nobility as typical of Renaissance humanism. This is to some extent justified, but not entirely so. The authors of the treatises we have mentioned were for the most part Tuscans. We should not overlook the fact that the claims of the Neapolitan nobility were defended by one of its members who was himself a humanist, Tristano Caracciolo, and those of the Venetian nobility by Lauro Querini, another well-known humanist who happened to be a Venetian nobleman himself. It is apparent once more how difficult it is to identify humanism as a whole with any given set of opinions, although these opinions may be held by some of its representatives. The common denominator is always, not a set of opinions, but a cultural and educational ideal.

XI

Another group of significant Renaissance moral treatises tries to describe, and to propose for imitation, the human ideal of the perfect citizen, magistrate, courtier, or gentleman. It is the ideal of a member of the ruling class, apart from its political connotations, held out as a model for young and old people alike. This genre, represented in the fifteenth century by some treatises of Alberti, Platina, and others, became especially important in the sixteenth. The most famous work of the group, Baldassarre Castiglione's *Book of the Courtier,* was translated into several languages and found imitators all over Europe. This work, which has great stylistic merit and occupies an important place in the history of Italian prose literature, clearly envisages a member of the aristocracy, and reflects many personal traits of its author who was active as a diplomat for many years in the service of the princes of Mantua and of the papal Curia. Castiglione's *Courtier* represents a human ideal of great breadth; it might be said to reflect the concept of the *uomo universale,* and it clearly exercised a civilizing influence upon the ruling classes of Renaissance Europe. Aside from the traditional knightly virtues of courage and physical prowess, the courtier is expected to have polished manners, to be an able participant in elegant conversation, to have a good literary education, and to be moderately accomplished in the arts of painting, music, and dance. An English counterpart is Sir Thomas Elyot's *Boke of the Governour,* in which moral and religious considerations play a some-

what larger role. Later in the century, the emphasis shifts more
and more to a description of manners practiced in good society
and to the requirements of polite conversation. Giovanni della
Casa's *Galateo*, and Stefano Guazzo's book *On Civil Conversation* were widely read, translated, and imitated, and form
the core of a large literature in all languages, usually described
as books of courtesy, of conduct, or of manners. Louis Wright
has shown that for England this literature more and more addressed itself not only to the members of the aristocracy, but also
to the middle class of merchants and professionals who were
eager to strengthen their social position by imitating the manners
of the older ruling class. This literature prepares the way for the
treatises on the perfect gentleman that were to be composed in
the seventeenth century. Yet it also contains a good many prudential rules and seems to be intended partly for the young man
of talent and modest means who is trying to get ahead in life
and make a career. The straight preaching of moral virtues, so
prominent in the early humanist treatises, now occupies less and
less space, although the possession of these virtues is taken more
or less for granted.

XII

Aside from the generalized ideal of the courtier or gentleman,
many treatises were written on the duties of persons who occupied a particular status, or practiced a particular profession.
There were books on the duties of a magistrate or ambassador,
or even on the duties of a bishop, in which moral prescriptions
were combined with advice concerning the practical conduct of
affairs. In the extensive literature of treatises on art that was
written during the Renaissance period, the technical rules of
the craft were embellished with moral advice for the artist. What
Cicero and Quintilian had required of the orator, namely that
he should combine moral stature and a general education with
the technical competence appropriate for his profession, was
now applied to all other professions, and especially to that of
the artist. The painter, the sculptor, and the architect not only
acquired a higher social status and prestige than they ever possessed before or afterwards, they also tended to combine artistic
skill with literary, scholarly, and scientific interests and competence—as we may see in the writings of Alberti, Piero della
Francesca, Leonardo, Dürer, Michelangelo, and Rubens—and

hence to appropriate for their profession the moral claims advanced originally by the humanist scholars.

One of the chief innovations brought about by the Protestant Reformation was the abolition of the monastic orders, which had played such an important role during the Middle Ages and which retained and even increased their importance in the modern Catholic world. The radical move of the Reformers was preceded, as is well known, by centuries of medieval attacks on the vices and shortcomings of the monks and friars, charges that were at least in part justified and that the Catholic Reformation of the sixteenth century tended to obviate. The humanists contributed their share to the critique of monasticism. Valla and others wrote against the monks, and Erasmus in his *Praise of Folly* poured a good deal of ridicule upon them. Yet it should be noted that Erasmus in this work did not spare any class of contemporary society, not even his own, the grammarians and rhetoricians; elsewhere he insists that the pious life was not a monopoly of the monastic orders, asserting an ideal of lay piety which he inherited from the "Modern Devotion," the Dutch mystic movement in whose schools he had received his first education. Yet he nowhere advocates the abolition of the orders. Among the earlier Italian humanists, we find several writers and scholars of distinction, such as Petrarch, Salutati, and Ermolao Barbaro, who actually came out in praise of the monastic life, and there were many learned monks, such as Ambrogio Traversari, who took a significant part in the humanist movement. Again it would be wrong to identify humanism as a whole with one or the other opinion on this important question.

A good deal has been written by Burckhardt and others about the place of women in Renaissance society. Women had not yet acquired an important place in professional life, and their activities were still largely confined to the house and the family. Yet within this limited range they were respected, and at least a few of them, especially the daughters of princes, noblemen, and scholars, received a literary and scholarly education and distinguished themselves as patrons of learning, or even as scholars and writers in their own right. Thus it is significant that one of the most important humanist treatises on education, Leonardo Bruni's *De studiis et litteris*, was dedicated to a woman. A series of treatises by fifteenth-century humanists deal with the family and with marriage, and hence have a good deal to say about the moral and practical duties of the housewife and mother. Famous and influential specimens of this literature are Francesco Barbaro's *De re uxoria,* and Alberti's treatise *Della famiglia.* The former emphasizes moral advice, and the latter contains charming pages on the way the wife of a wealthy citizen is supposed to assist her husband and to govern the household, servants, and children. In the sixteenth century, Castiglione in his *Courtier* devotes a special section of his work to the court lady, the female counterpart of his male subject, and Vives composed a significant treatise *On the Education of a Christian Woman.* Later in the century, in Italy as elsewhere, a whole series of treatises was written on the conduct of women, in which prudential rules played a large part and some advice was even offered on how to dress and how to use cosmetics.

XIII

A large segment of literature extending from the end of the fifteenth to the end of the sixteenth century deals with the subject of love. A famous medieval example had been Andreas Capellanus's book on courtly love, in which the customs of French chivalry received a more theoretical, though not a more philosophical, expression than in the lyric and epic poetry of the period. More philosophical was the lyric poetry of Cavalcanti, Dante, and their contemporaries in Italy, and the prose speculation on love began with Dante's *Vita Nuova* and *Convivio* as well as with the commentaries on Cavalcanti's obscure poem. This whole literature was given a new impulse and direction by Marsilio Ficino, the head of the Platonic Academy of Florence, and one of the leading Platonists of the Renaissance. He supplied to Western readers the first complete translations of Plato's *Symposium* and *Phaedrus* (parts of which had already been translated by Leonardo Bruni), and also published important commentaries on these two dialogues. In particular, the commentary on the *Symposium* became very famous. Basing himself primarily on Plato but transforming his doctrine under the influence of other philosophical, theological, and literary traditions, Ficino understood the love for another human being as a preliminary form and disguise of the basic love that each human being has for God and that finds its fulfillment only in the direct enjoyment and knowledge of God—a goal that is reached during the present life by only a few persons and for a short time, but will be attained forever in the future life by those who have aspired to it while on earth. Without rejecting sexual and earthly love, Ficino praises above all the pure and celestial love, that is, the mutual affection and friendship between two persons who are dedicated to the contemplative life and hence recognize that their mutual relationship is founded upon the love each of them has for God. This divine love Ficino claimed to define according to the teachings of Plato, and hence coining a term that was to become famous as well as ridiculous, he called it "Platonic" or "Socratic love." The doctrine of Platonic love constitutes only a small, though important, part of Ficino's philosophical system, but it enjoyed a wide popularity apart from the rest of his work, especially among poets and moralists. The notion of Platonic love was taken over and adapted by many poets, including Lorenzo de' Medici and Michelangelo. Moreover, Ficino's commentary on Plato's *Symposium* became the fountainhead of a whole literature of love treatises, in Italy and elsewhere, in which the philosophical notion of Platonic love was repeated, developed, and sometimes distorted. The authors of these treatises include distinguished philosophers, such as Pico della Mirandola, Leone Ebreo (from whom Spinoza seems to have borrowed his notion of the intellectual love of God), Francesco Patrizi, and Giordano Bruno, as well as famous writers like Bembo and Castiglione. For the last book of Castiglione's *Courtier* deals precisely with Platonic love along the lines defined by Ficino, and through this work the theory attained a very wide diffusion indeed. In the later treatises, the original link between Platonic love and the contemplative life was gradually lost, and the cult of Platonic love came to be a hypocritical disguise for refined sexual passion, or an empty game fashionable in good society. However, we should try to understand that originally it had a serious philosophical meaning, and that a good deal of serious talk and writing on love in the sixteenth century was shaped by the Platonist "philosophy of love."

XIV

Another typically humanist fashion in which the various forms of human life were discussed during the fifteenth and sixteenth century was the so-called comparison (*paragone*). Ancient rhetoric had insisted that it was the task of the orator to praise and to blame, and the praise of some virtue or quality was often combined with the blame of its contrary. To show their skill, orators even composed mock praises of bad or ridiculous things such as tyranny or baldness, and it was against this literary background and upon such models that Erasmus wrote his admirable *Praise of Folly*. Rhetorical contests left their traces in medieval Latin and vernacular poetry where the contrast between winter and spring, youth and old age are common themes. In humanistic literature, the rhetorical contest between two contrasts or rivals was a favorite sport, and we have encountered several examples already: the comparison between Scipio and Caesar, between republic and monarchy, and Buonaccorso's comparison between nobility by birth and by merit. In the same way, the merits and relative superiority of various arts, professions, or ways of life were frequently discussed. There are treatises on "arms and letters," debating the advantages of the military and the literary life. Leonardo da Vinci seriously argued that painting was superior to the other arts and sciences, and Michelangelo was consulted on the question of whether painting or sculpture was superior. The humanist defense of poetry, of which we have spoken before, took the form of attacking other learned disciplines, as in Petrarch's invectives against a physician. There was a whole literature on the relative merits of medicine and of law that had its roots in the rivalry of the university faculties and in which distinguished humanists such as Salutati and Poggio took an active part. Salutati sided with the jurists because the law had a greater significance for the life of the citizen and of the state. Several historians would like to consider this as the typically humanist position, but it happens that Poggio, no less a humanist than Salutati, voted in this contest in favor of medicine.

The argument used by Salutati in this discussion and on other occasions touches upon another more serious issue, the relative merits of the contemplative and of the active life. The distinction occurs already in Aristotle, who tends, along with most ancient philosophers, to consider the life of contemplation, rather than that of action, to be most perfect and desirable. A notable exception was Cicero, the Roman statesman, who insisted upon the political duties of the responsible citizen. During the Middle Ages, the life of contemplation was usually associated with the monastic ideal and was more or less persistently praised. In the Renaissance, we hear again several voices in praise of the active life, such as those of Salutati, Bruni, Alberti, and Palmieri, and these views have been emphasized by Hans Baron and other scholars as an important aspect of their civic humanism. Eugene Rice goes even further and treats the emphasis on the active life in these humanists, in some sixteenth-century writers and in Pierre Charron, as an important development leading away from the monastic ideal of the Middle Ages to the this-worldly and practical orientation of the modern age. Although it is significant that, from the fifteenth century on, the active life was finding more partisans among the writers of the age, the monastic life also had its defenders among the humanists, as we have seen, and even Salutati, one of the chief protagonists of the active life, wrote a whole treatise in praise of the monastic life, a fact that has puzzled several of his interpreters. Moreover, the ideal of the theoretical or contemplative life became dissociated during the Renaissance from the specific ideal of monasticism, and rather identified with the private existence of the scholar, writer, and scientist, no doubt under the influence of ancient philosophy, and this secularization of the contemplative life seems to me no less characteristic of the Renaissance (and of modern times) than the simultaneous emphasis on the claims of the active life. This tendency appears already in Petrarch's praise of solitude, and it is in this sense that the Platonists of the Florentine Academy praised the life of contemplation which occupied a central place in their philosophy. The most famous document in which the question is debated is Cristoforo Landino's *Camaldulensian Disputations*, a dialogue in which the active life is defended by Lorenzo de' Medici and the contemplative life by Leon Battista Alberti—and the victory seems to go to the latter. In the sixteenth century, Pomponazzi considers the theoretical life as superior but uses the practical life to define the end of man, as this life is peculiar to man and all human beings are able to have a part in it. In Montaigne there is a strong, though by no means exclusive, emphasis on the solitary life of contemplation, and most other philosophers take its superiority for granted, whereas the popular moralists insist on the needs and claims of the active life. Far from being resolved in the sixteenth century, the question is still with us. Whereas many writers decry the "ivory tower" of the intellectual, others would still insist on the right of the scholar, artist, or scientist to concentrate on his peculiar task. The rival claims of the active and contemplative life seem to illustrate a perennial human problem, and there seems to be no permanent answer to it, but each time, each profession, and each person will have to find a viable compromise.

Another similar question that was widely debated in Renaissance thought was the relation between the intellect and the
will, or between knowledge and love. This question overlaps that
of the contemplative and active life, but is not entirely identical
with it. For some partisans of the contemplative life, for example,
Petrarch, would still place will and love above intellect and
knowledge, since they consider the willing of the good and the
love of God as a part, and even as the most important part, of
the contemplative life. The problem occupies a very important
place in the history of Western thought. It has been rightly
asserted that the concept of will is absent from ancient Greek
philosophy. Plato, Aristotle, and other Greek thinkers know a
conflict between reason and desire, but they inherited from
Socrates the conviction that reason is capable by its own power
to know the good, to put it into practice, and to overcome the
resistance of any contrary desire. In the Christian view, this
Greek belief in the independent power of reason was far too
optimistic. In order to overcome his native propensity to evil
brought about by Adam's fall, man needed the grace of God.
On the basis of this Christian conception, Augustine formulated
his notion of the will. Aside from his faculty of knowing, man
has an independent faculty of willing. It is the will that was
corrupted by Adam's fall, and that must be purified by divine
grace if we are to attain the good. Medieval thought inherited
from Augustine this distinction between will and intellect, and
the relative merits of these two faculties became the subject of
important discussions, with Thomas Aquinas, among others,
emphasizing the superiority of the intellect, whereas Duns Scotus
and other "voluntarists" insisted, in accordance with Augustine,
on the superiority of the will. This question, in spite of its
scholastic origin, continued to occupy the humanists. Both
Petrarch and Salutati favored the superiority of the will. In the
Platonic Academy of Florence, the problem was evidently a
favorite topic of debate, as we may learn from Ficino's correspondence, and from the treatise of one of his pupils, Alamanno
Donati. Ficino himself apparently changed his view on the
matter in the course of his life, favoring at first the superiority
of the intellect but insisting in his later writings on the importance of the will and of love for the ascent of the soul to God.
His arguments show that the concept of will could be associated
with the life of contemplation no less than with that of action.

XV

Renaissance thought was interested not merely in moral rules of conduct or in the specific ways of life that an individual might choose according to his status or profession, but also in the general situation in which human beings find themselves on earth, in the chief forces determining this situation, and in the place man and his world occupy within the larger universe. There has been a widespread belief that Renaissance humanists held an optimistic view of life and were prone to enjoy this earth without caring as much for the future life after death as their medieval predecessors had. It is true that the concern with earthly life and its problems tended to increase from medieval to modern times. Nevertheless we must try to avoid exaggerated opinions. Even in Lorenzo de' Medici's famous lines, "Let him be happy who so desires, for we are not sure of the next day," which used to be quoted as the quintessence of the Renaissance view of life as frivolous and superficial, we have learned to hear melancholy undertones. Historians like Walser and Trinkaus have shown that the writers of the period were keenly aware of the miseries and ills of our earthly existence. Sickness and poverty, exile and imprisonment, the loss of friends and relatives were a common experience, and when Poggio and other humanists wrote about the misery of the human condition, they had no difficulty collecting ancient and modern examples to illustrate the frail and transitory state of earthly happiness. Lest we think that some classes of men are untouched by the miseries that befall the common lot, the humanists wrote special treatises about the unhappiness of scholars and of courtiers, and especially of princes. These treatises were full of examples from history, and they were intended to warn their readers not to trust their happiness, and to comfort the unhappy with the record of the ills suffered by others that were worse than their own. This chorus of lament may seem to be out of tune with many real and imagined traits of the period, but it is nearly universal. The Platonic philosopher Ficino invokes the shade of Heraclitus to weep at the misery of men, as he would laugh with Democritus at their folly.

This feeling that man has to suffer many vicissitudes and that the events of his life, whether good or bad, are largely beyond his control was interpreted by the writers and thinkers of the period in a variety of ways that were not always consistent with each other, but that lend a common note to the literature of the Renaissance. Divine providence was stressed by the theologians and never denied by any other thinkers, but popular and philosophical writers frequently played with the notions of fortune and fate.

The concept of chance was repeatedly discussed by ancient philosophers and played a role in the thought of Aristotle, and especially in that of Epicurus. In the moral thought of late antiquity, chance was given an important part in human affairs. and its power was even personified and worshiped as the goddess Tyche or Fortuna. During the Christian Middle Ages, Fortuna remained pretty much alive, not as a goddess, to be sure, but as an allegory and as an instrument of God. In the Renaissance the power of Fortuna is again very often mentioned. She appears in emblems and allegorical pictures as well as in the writings of the period. Statesmen and businessmen hoped that this blind and arbitrary power would bring them success, and Machiavelli devoted some striking pages to the description of its role in history and politics.

Many thoughtful persons were not satisfied with this whimsical rule of Fortuna over human affairs, but believed instead, or additionally, in the power of an inexorable fate. The view that all earthly events were rigidly determined by an unbroken chain of antecedent causes had been held by the ancient Stoics, and it was revived in a more or less modified form by Pomponazzi and other thinkers. Still more widespread was the belief in astrology, an elaborate system that presented itself as a science and tried to tie all earthly events, with the help of detailed but flexible rules, to the influence of the stars. This system, which had passed from the Babylonians into late antiquity and was transmitted through the Arabs to medieval Europe, was usually opposed by the theologians but was supported by the philosophers and scientists. During the Renaissance, astrology had a few opponents, such as Petrarch and Pico, but on the whole its prestige rose higher than ever before, both among scholars and laymen. The belief that all human affairs were governed by the motions of the stars was satisfactory to many people because it seemed to give some significance and regularity to the vicissitudes of life. The astrologers claimed to be able to predict the future of persons and countries, and in their passionate desire to know and to control their future, people were as little disturbed as in other times by the inherent contradiction in prophecy (for how can I change the future to my advantage if it is dependent on unchangeable laws, and how can I predict the future if I or others can do anything about it?) and as willing to forget the numerous predictions that were not confirmed by the outcome.

Different from the belief in fate is the theological doctrine of predestination, which also played an important part in the discussions of the period. Augustine had emphasized against the Pelagians that not only all earthly events but even our own moral choices and actions were foreordained by divine forethought and will, and the problem of how predestination can be reconciled with human free will gave rise to many difficulties in medieval theology and philosophy. The problem came to the fore with the Protestant Reformers, Luther and Calvin, who completely denied free will, something neither Augustine nor his medieval successors had clearly done. The question was of importance also to secular thinkers before the Reformation, as the example of Valla and Pomponazzi shows. Valla argued that it was easy to reconcile divine foreknowledge with human free will but considered the relationship between God's will and human freedom as a mystery of faith. Pomponazzi gave an intricate defense of predestination as well as of fate, but his attempt to make free will appear compatible with both of them seems neither clear nor convincing.

The concepts of fortune, of fate, and of predestination express in different ways and on different levels the feeling that human life is governed by divine and natural powers over which we have no control and to which we must submit more or less helplessly. Yet most Renaissance thinkers did not stop with the assertion of these superhuman powers, but tried in some way to uphold and defend the power of man over his own destiny, in the face of fortune and fate. The attempt is in itself significant even where it seems to be inconsistent or unsuccessful. Already the ancient Stoics, the most outspoken proponents of rigid fate, had struggled to assert the role of human freedom within a system of complete determinism. The later Stoics found their solution in the view that the wise man, while enduring patiently the external circumstances of his life which he is unable to change, is entirely free in his thought and in his moral attitude. In a more popular fashion, they opposed the power of reason and virtue to that of fortune and claimed for the wise man an inner victory even when he may seem to be outwardly defeated.

This is the keynote also of much humanist thinking and writing on the subject. In his extremely influential treatise on the remedies of good and bad fortune Petrarch opposes reason to the passions in good Stoic manner and exhorts his readers to overcome through virtue the hold that good and bad fortune alike have on our minds. Salutati also opposes virtue and wisdom to fate and fortune. The recurrent theme in Alberti's moral writings is the victory of virtue over fortune, and Ficino restates the same view, adding a Neoplatonic note by basing moral virtue on the life of contemplation. After having described the power of fortune, Machiavelli also insists that the prudent statesman is able to overcome, or at least to modify, the power of fortune. Guillaume Budé teaches his readers to despise the external circumstances of life, which fortune may give or take away. Just as these thinkers wish to oppose the power of fortune, Pico della Mirandola made a strenuous effort to oppose the power of fate. His elaborate attack against astrology was actually a defense of human freedom, and the arguments that he uses show very clearly that his attitude was prompted by moral and religious as well as by scientific considerations. This same concern for man's moral autonomy was to prompt such humanist thinkers as Erasmus and Sepulveda to defend free will against Luther's exclusive doctrine of predestination.

XVI

The themes and ideas that we have briefly discussed may illustrate the way in which Renaissance thinkers were preoccupied with moral and human problems. It has often been asserted that Renaissance thought, in contrast with medieval thought, was man-centered, not God-centered, or—to quote a rather unfriendly remark of Gilson—that the Renaissance was the Middle Ages minus God. Such statements are obviously exaggerated, since Renaissance thought as a whole was anything but indifferent to God, and since hardly any thinker of the period denied the existence of God, however his conception of God may have differed from various forms of religious orthodoxy. Yet the humanists who have attracted most of the attention of Renaissance historians were interested primarily in moral problems, frequently to the exclusion of theology and metaphysics, of natural philosophy and other learned disciplines. The very name "humanities," which they adopted for their studies, emphasized their concern with man in a programmatic fashion. No wonder that they were inclined to stress the importance of human problems and to extol the place of man in the universe. Already Petrarch argues in his treatise *On His Own and Other People's Ignorance* that it does not help us to know the nature of animals unless we also know the nature of man, and in his famous letter describing his ascent of Mont Ventoux he opposes his admiration for the human soul to the impression made upon him by mountains and the sea. It is significant that the latter passage is woven out of quotations from Seneca and Augustine, for the Renaissance doctrine of the dignity of man was nourished in many ways by classical and Christian sources. In the fifteenth century, the excellence of man was the theme of special treatises by Giannozzo Manetti and others. Especially in Manetti's treatise, the dignity of man is based not only on his biblical similarity to God, but above all on his varied achievements in the arts and sciences, which are described at great length. This favorite humanist theme then received a more metaphysical treatment at the hands of the Platonic philosophers. Marsilio Ficino dedicated several books of his chief work, the *Platonic Theology*, to man's achievements in the sciences and in government, emphasizing the universality of his knowledge and of his aspirations. When he restates the Neoplatonic conception that the universe is made of several degrees of being that extend from God at the summit to the corporeal world at the bottom, he intentionally revises the scheme in order to assign a privileged place in its center to the rational soul of man, thus making it the bond and knot of the universe, second in dignity only to God Himself. Pico della Mirandola went even further. In the famous *Oration,* which deals only in its first half with the dignity of man, and in other writings, he states that man does not occupy any fixed place in the universal hierarchy, but can freely choose his place in it. For he has no fixed nature but possesses all the gifts that had been distributed singly among the other creatures. Thus man is capable of leading many forms of life from the lowest to the highest. Pico's view is echoed in Vives's *Fable on Man;* man is introduced here as an actor capable of playing the roles of all other creatures. The central position of man in the universe, half way between animals and angels, is accepted also by Pomponazzi as a sign of man's excellence. Thus we may say that under the impact of a humanist tradition, systematic philosophers as different from each other as the Florentine Platonists and Pomponazzi assigned to man a privileged position in their conception of the universe. The emphasis on man's universal skill in the arts and sciences will recur in Francis Bacon's notion of the reign of man over nature, and thus there is an echo of the Renaissance glorification of man in the ideology that still underlies the technological aspect of modern natural science.

However, even on this issue that seems to be so close to the heart of Renaissance humanism, the period does not speak to us with a single voice. Even in the fifteenth century, Pope Innocent III's treatise *On Contempt for the World,* which constituted the foil and starting point of Manetti's work, was widely read and had its imitators. In the sixteenth century, a strong reaction against the excessive glorification of man may be noted. In the Protestant Reformers there was a tremendous emphasis on the depraved nature of man, and this view was probably expressed in conscious protest against the current stress on his dignity. Also Montaigne, otherwise so far removed from the theology of the Reformers and so close to humanist thought, goes a long way in his *Apology of Raymond de Sebond* to criticize the unfounded opinions on man's privileged place in the universe, and to insist on his humble position and on the vanity of his aspirations.

This Renaissance concern for man and his place in the universe may also account for the great prominence given during that period to the question of the immortality of the soul. The notion that the individual human soul is immortal had been strongly defended by Plato and the Neoplatonists, whereas Aristotle and other ancient philosophers held ambiguous or contrary opinions. Augustine had adopted the Neoplatonic view, and he was followed by all medieval Christian thinkers. With Renaissance Platonism, the question assumed a central importance that it had never before. Ficino actually designed his *Platonic Theology* around this problem and tried to demonstrate the immortality of the soul against the Aristotelians by a variety of arguments. This emphasis on immortality appealed to a large number of poets, philosophers, and theologians, and it is tempting to assume that it was under Platonist influence that the immortality of the soul was adopted at the Lateran Council of 1513 as an official dogma of the Catholic Church. When the leading Aristotelian philosopher, Pietro Pomponazzi, set out to show that personal immortality cannot be demonstrated by reason, he not only accepted it as an article of faith, but also stressed that the human soul, even according to reason, is immortal at least in some respect (*secundum quid*), on account of its high place among the material forms. Moreover, by returning to the problem many times in published treatises and unpublished questions and lectures, Pomponazzi showed how much he was puzzled by the question and how great an importance he attributed to it. On the other hand, his treatise of 1516 gave rise to a large number of written attacks upon his position by philosophers and theologians, and the question continued to be debated beyond the end of the sixteenth century. The statement that Renaissance students were interested in problems of the soul rather than of nature, often repeated after the nineteenth century French scholar Renan, is based upon the misinterpretation of an episode in which a group of students wanted to hear a course on Aristotle's *On the Soul* rather than on his *Meteorology*, but it contains a grain of truth that may well be based on better evidence.

It might be in order to indicate very briefly at this point in what ways the moral thought of the humanists, even though it was primarily concerned with individual conduct, also led to broader social, political, and humanitarian ideals. The theory of friendship occupied an important place in the ethics of Aristotle, Epicurus and Cicero, and its value is very often stressed in the letters and other writings of the humanists. In the Florentine Academy, the concept of friendship is closely associated with those of Christian and Platonic love, and Ficino liked to think that the members of his Academy were bound to one another and to himself, their common master, by a tie of Platonic friendship, thus forming a close community after the model of the ancient schools of philosophy.

In political thought, not only were the humanists concerned with the education of princes and magistrates, or with the relative merits of republican and monarchical government, but some of the Renaissance thinkers began to reflect on ideal commonwealths more perfect than the ones in existence. Thomas More's *Utopia*, a highly original work in spite of its obvious indebtedness to Plato's *Republic*, was the first of an important genre that was to flourish down to the eighteenth century. Its example was followed by Campanella, Bacon, and many lesser writers. The influence of this utopian literature on social and political reforms in modern times has been generally recognized. Another

contribution to social reform was Vive's treatise on assistance to
the poor, written at a time when the responsibility for public
relief was taken over by the cities in the Low Countries.

No less important was the contribution of Renaissance thought
to the development of the ideal of religious toleration. This ideal
arose first in the fifteenth century against the background of
medieval controversy with Judaism and Islam and of the echoes
of the polemics of the Church Fathers against ancient paganism.
In the sixteenth century, the problem acquired a new poignancy
in the face of religious dissent, persecution, and war within
Western Christendom. Without abandoning a belief in the superiority of his own religion, Nicolaus Cusanus advocated perpetual peace and toleration between the different creeds dividing
mankind. Ficino praised the solidarity and fellowship of all
human beings, and insisted that religion was natural to man,
and that all religions, though different in their practices and in
the degree of their perfection, contained a common core of truth
and expressed in some way the worship of the one true God.
Moreover, Ficino maintained that there was a basic harmony
between the true, Christian religion and the true, Platonic philosophy; and he accepted the apocryphal writings attributed to
Zoroaster, Hermes Trismegistus, Orpheus, and Pythagoras as
witnesses of an early pagan theology and philosophy that prepared the way for Plato and his followers, similarly as the Old
Testament foreshadowed the New. These notions added a new
and explicit force to the general humanist belief in the wisdom
of the ancients and its compatibility with Christian religious
teaching, and they exercised an enormous influence during the
sixteenth century. Equally important were the ideas of Pico della
Mirandola, who went even further. According to him, all known
philosophies and religions contained some elements of truth, and
he proposed to defend in a public disputation nine hundred
theses taken principally from ancient and medieval, Arabic and
Jewish, philosophers and theologians. In particular, he maintained that the writings of the Jewish Cabalists represented an
ancient oral tradition, and were in agreement with the teachings
of Christianity. In the second part of his famous oration, which
was actually composed as an introductory speech for his pro-
jected disputation, Pico eloquently expresses his belief in the
universality of truth in which every philosopher and theologian
participates to a greater or lesser degree. A hundred years later,
in his famous *Sevenfold Conversation*, which was widely circu-

lated in manuscript but not printed until recent times, Jean Bodin defends the claims of all the different religions. In the seventeenth century, Herbert of Cherbury laid the ground for deism by describing a natural religion consisting of the common core of all the various human creeds.

XVII

In spite of these broad and interesting ramifications, the moral thought of the Renaissance was fundamentally individualistic in its outlook. Of course, the term individualism has several meanings, and its applications to the Renaissance have aroused a good deal of controversy among historians. It cannot be denied that outstanding human individuals are found in other periods of history, including the Middle Ages, or that medieval nominalism emphasized the reality of the individual physical thing. When we speak of Renaissance individualism, the term should be understood in a different way. Above all, Renaissance thought and literature are extremely individualistic in that they aim, to a degree unknown to the Middle Ages and to most of ancient and modern times, at the expression of individual, subjective opinions, feelings, and experiences. Every humanist takes himself very seriously and thinks that everything he has heard and seen is eminently worth recording. Treatises on highly abstract subjects are intermixed with personal stories, gossip, flattery, and invective to a degree and in a manner of which a modern scholar, like his ancient or medieval predecessors, would be thoroughly ashamed. Hence the widespread Renaissance preference for the letter as a form of literary expression in which the author may speak in the first person, for the biography in which another person is vividly delineated in all his concrete qualities, and for the diary and autobiography in which both these traits are in a way combined. The rise of portrait painting in the visual arts seems to indicate the same general tendency. In a curious way, this individualism is blended in both art and literature with a strong classicism and formalism that might seem to be incompatible with it, but actually contributes to it a special color and physiognomy. Where moral precepts are involved, the literature is of course full of the most general rules, but these rules are addressed to the effort of the individual person, just as they are based on individual historical examples. This subjective and personal trait pervades most humanist literature, and it is apparent already in its first great representative, Petrarch. He vents his opinions, his likes and dislikes, his scruples and preoccupations, whereas objective statements on general problems are rather rare and incidental even in his philosophical writings. When we come to the end of the Renaissance, this subjective and personal character of humanist thought finds its most conscious and consummate philosophical expression in the *Essais* of Michel de Montaigne. Montaigne had received a humanist education, he knew Latin before he knew French, and his quotations from ancient authors, especially Plutarch and Seneca, fill many pages of his writings. The essay, in the form which he created and bequeathed to later centuries, is written in the first person, like the humanist letter, and is equally free in its style and structure: we might call the essay a letter written by the author to himself. Montaigne shares with the humanist his exclusive preoccupation with moral questions, his lack of interest in logic and metaphysics and the other learned disciplines, as well as his dislike for the scholastic type of learning. His philosophical position, though flexible, shows the impact of ancient skepticism, and to a lesser extent, of Stoicism. He writes on a variety of moral topics, often starting from classical examples or sentences. He would always refer to his personal experience, and draw the lesson for himself. His skepticism, from which he excepts only his religious faith, is prompted by observation and experience. He knows how complex and changeable all human affairs are. Circumstances alter all the time, and so do our moods. Most of his thoughts are prompted by introspection. What all humanists actually felt but did not express in so many words, he states most bluntly and clearly, namely, that he intends to talk primarily about himself and that his own individual self is the chief subject matter of his philosophizing. "Authors communicate themselves to the public by some peculiar and strange quality; I, for the first time, through my entire self, as Michel de Montaigne, not as grammarian or poet or lawyer. If the world complains that I speak too much of myself, I complain that the world does not think only of itself." (*Essais,* III, 2) Yet by making of his personal way of talking a philosophical program, by elevating introspection and the observation of actual human conduct to the rank of a conscious method, Montaigne already passes beyond the boundaries of humanist thought and literature, and leads the way toward the psychological study of moods and manners that was to characterize the moral literature of the seventeenth century.

XVIII

While a scholar may be concerned with the complexities of a historical period which he is trying to understand, the layman and the student look for a broad synthesis that selects and emphasizes those aspects of the past that are significant for them and for their time, and constitute, as it were, a contribution to contemporary civilization. Such a view seemed easy when there was an unquestioned faith in the present and future status of our civilization, and in its steady and almost inevitable progress. In our own time, this faith has been shattered in many ways. There is no doubt notable progress in technology and in the natural sciences, and there is a good deal of hope for social and political progress, as there should be, since such progress depends at least in part on our efforts, and hence is our own responsibility. Yet the future is not completely under our control and is, at least to that extent, uncertain. There is constant change but no steady progress in a variety of fields, and a growing awareness that every gain, though necessary and desirable, may have to be paid for by some loss. The present—shifting, complex, and inconsistent—ceases to be a firm measure for selecting what is significant in the past. Concentration on the present and rejection of the past are actually widespread at this moment, but such attitudes are lacking in wisdom and are not likely to last very long. Philosophers, linguists, critics of the arts and of literature, and practitioners of the social sciences often treat present realities as if they were absolutes, valid for all times and places, and as if there were no alternatives. This outlook is narrow and provincial, and one of the tasks of historical scholarship, so widely ignored, is to broaden our outlook, to open our eyes to the achievements of the past, even where they differ from our own. In historical recollection, we may vicariously relive what is gone because it is intrinsically significant, and hence we can understand it. And by thus preserving it, we keep it available for the future that may still make a use of it which we cannot now foresee. The study of history is highly important in any living tradition, and we like to think of ourselves as heirs of such a tradition, which we call Western civilization. If the future belongs to a broader world culture, which will contain many

68   RENAISSANCE THOUGHT II

strands other than those of the Western tradition, we still think
and hope that it will include what we consider to be the best
in the heritage of Western civilization.

If we look back upon the moral thought of Renaissance humanism for part of this heritage some of its most general traits
will become apparent. Many of them are related to the social
and professional situation in which most of the humanist writers
found themselves. As scholars and writers professionally concerned with the study of history and of the classics, as well as
with moral problems, they were thoroughly influenced by the
form and ideas of ancient literature and philosophy, but at the
same time eager to give expression to their personal feelings
and experiences. As a result of their work and efforts through
several centuries, the subject matter of the humanities was
established as a branch of secular learning that included moral
philosophy as distinct from, but not necessarily opposed to, theology and the natural sciences. It represented a peculiar combination of literature and scholarship that tended to disintegrate
in the following centuries, but it left a double heritage that has
more or less survived to the present day and that seems very
much worth preserving. On the one hand, there are the historical
and philological branches of knowledge that have greatly extended the range of their subject matter and refined the instruments of their research (as an echo of their origin in Renaissance
humanism they are still called, in old-fashioned French and
Italian, the moral sciences). On the other hand, there is a Renaissance tradition of literary culture that is not limited to formal
techniques but is concerned with broad human and philosophical problems, without accepting the limitations (and responsibilities) of professional philosophy. This latter tradition was
revived by nineteenth-century Romanticism and has recently
found an influential representative in George Santayana, the
American philosopher. After having surveyed the contributions
made by Renaissance humanism to moral thought, some of them
modest and trivial, we cannot help concluding with the hope
that its double heritage, scholarly and literary, though now
threatened by the onslaught of several competing forces may
survive in the future.

[14]

English Historical Review
© 1982 Longman Group Limited London

0013-8266/82/15020054/$02.00

Notes and Documents

New light on Machiavelli

THERE are three aspects of Machiavelli's ideas which raise particularly large issues for his biographers: their origins, the sort of world from which they came, and their relationship to his public life. It is unlikely that we will ever have a complete account of these things, because we have too few materials about certain corners of his life, and we know too little of the stages by which his thought evolved. These are the problems of all thinkers, but they are to be found in Machiavelli in a special form. We are utterly ignorant of his early life, his thought does not fit into a traditional category, and the 'active' and the 'contemplative' parts of his life were unusually close.

We know, for certain fact, hardly a thing about the first twenty-eight years of his life till he appears suddenly as an official in the Florentine chancery in 1498. We are puzzled by the violence of his political solutions and his unusual acceptance that the world is governed by two moralities. There, he still seems odd, even when he has been found a context amongst other Florentine writers of his age,[1] or when we realize that he was not proposing an immorality of public life, but rather the morality of the ancient city-state, which (so unlike the Christian) preferred public to private values as the basis of political life.[2] Is his thought odd or does it merely seem so? We would understand him better if we knew something of his formative years and if we could set beside the writings of his contemporary Florentines, some of their reactions to him and his ideas. Did they find them striking also, or is it us alone?

There is so much more too that we would like to know of his public life: whether his career was at all peculiar, whether he exercised mutely a minor role and what his contemporaries thought of it. Still more, it would be revealing to know more of his transitions from public to private life, because we can see that there lay the springs of his writings. His public life in the Florentine chancery from 1498 to 1512 gave him the experience; an enforced return to private life in 1512 gave him the opportunity and the reasons to write. Having written the *Prince* in 1513 he was yearning still more for public life, but the wish went unfulfilled. In the 1520s the cycle was again turned

---

1. R. von Albertini, *Das Florentinische Staatsbewusstsein im Übergang von der Republik zum Prinzipat* (Berne, 1955).
2. I. Berlin, 'The Originality of Machiavelli', in *Studies on Machiavelli* ed. M. P. Gilmore (Florence, 1972) pp. 147–206.

when a still more intimate relation emerged between his writing of the Florentine History and a last involvement in public life.

We will never know as much of all this as we might wish, but there are documents in the Florentine State Archives which can lighten our darkness. They tell us a crucial fact about Machiavelli's 'lost' years; they give us an insight into his unpopularity before 1512; they record one of the first reactions of a contemporary (arguably the first) to the ideas embodied in the *Prince*, and they inform us of two of the chief transitions of his life: from public to private life in 1513, and back again in 1526. In the one case they establish what it was that had implicated Machiavelli in the plot against the Medici in 1513 (and as such give us a clue to the origins of the *Prince*) and, in the other, provide some details of his last involvement in public life in the 1520s.

We have been in nearly total darkness about Machiavelli's youth. A tax record of his father, Messer Bernardo Machiavelli, lists Niccolò amongst his children in 1470.[1] The survival of his father's diary gives us some details of Niccolò's early education.[2] There is an allegedly late fifteenth-century manuscript of the *De Rerum Natura* of Lucretius, which may be in Machiavelli's hand[3] and two of his poems arguably belong to the years between 1492 and 1494.[4] On the basis of this literary evidence, Machiavelli has been made to fit into the 'humanist' circles of Lorenzo de' Medici. But Machiavelli's ideas (as we perceive them later) fit uncomfortably with the philosophy and the philology of late fifteenth-century Florence,[5] and if he had been 'contaminated' by close contact with the Medici, it would seem surprising that, in 1498, he should have leapt so high into the service of the popular government, only four years after its foundation.[6]

Otherwise nothing is known of his life until he appears suddenly in 1498, having been elected to head the Second Chancery in Florence. These 'lost years' have been the object of an intense speculation, and rightly so, because some knowledge of them might shed light on the genesis of his ideas. Recently it was announced that the knowledge had been gained: Machiavelli, in the years after 1489, had been living and working in Rome as the apprentice and cashier of a bank.[7] This dramatic claim was followed swiftly by a dramatic rebuttal: the Niccolò Machiavelli of the Roman bank was not the Niccolò Machiavelli of the *Prince*, but (as several proofs revealed) another of

1. R. Ridolfi, *The Life of Niccolò Machiavelli*, tr. C. Grayson (London, 1963) p. 258.
2. B. Machiavelli, *Libro di Ricordi* ed. C. Olschki (Florence, 1954).
3. S. Bertelli, 'Noterelle Machiavelliane. Un Codice di Lucrezio e Terenzio', *Rivista Storica Italiana*, lxxiii (1961) pp. 544–53; *cf. ibid.*, lxxvi (1964), pp. 774–92.
4. M. Martelli, 'Preistoria (Medicea) di Machiavelli', *Studi di Filologia Italiana*, xxix (1971), pp. 387 ff.
5. *Cf.* J. Najemy in *Speculum*, lii (1977), pp. 159–60.
6. A point also made by N. Rubinstein, 'Machiavelli and the world of Florentine politics', in *Studies on Machiavelli*, ed. M. P. Gilmore, pp. 5–6.
7. D. Maffei, *Il Giovane Machiavelli banchiere con Berto Berti a Roma* (Florence, 1973).

the same name.[1] Still we do not know where Machiavelli was living before 1498, whether in Florence or abroad, or what he was doing. Two documents, however, do survive in the Florentine archives, which shed light on one of these questions. Apart from the records of his father, these are the only documents so far discovered which reveal Machiavelli's existence before 1498.

They are documents preserved in the cartularies of Ser Bonaventura di Leonardo di Bonaventura, the notary who drew up Machiavelli's will in 1522.[2] The first is an act of proxy, a *procura* in Italian legal terminology, by Machiavelli's father; Messer Bernardo made Niccolò his proctor 'ad consentiendum et licentiam dandum domine Primavere eius filie'. This giving of consent by Machiavelli to his sister in their father's name probably refers to the handling of her dowry. It was drawn up in Florence on 28 April 1494.[3] The second document was drawn up by the same notary, also in Florence, in May 1497. In this, Primavera, now widowed, appointed her father as her proctor 'to exact all payments of the Monte' – presumably, the *Monte delle Doti*, or state dowry fund. In the same document she also appointed as her proctors, presumably for a like purpose (since the appointments are so closely conjoined) Ser Antonio di Parente d'Antonio, all notaries at the premises (*apoteca*) of a second notary, and her two brothers, Totto and Niccolò.[4] Neither document records the presence of Niccolò at the drawing up of the act, but, unless he was resident in Florence, his appointment in either case would seem to have had no point.

In 1498 Machiavelli entered upon his career in the Florentine chancery.[5] This lasted until 1512, and, suitably fermented, it provided the experience upon which his political thinking was later based. One peculiarity of this experience is that, seemingly, it was so 'secretarial' in character: how could such independent thinking (and such an independent character) have emerged from so dependent a role? One answer is that Machiavelli did find it easy to adapt himself to the demands of service. He accepted (and served) the needs of a master, and, in return, enjoyed much freedom. It may be that Machiavelli, as secretary, enjoyed more power and excited more hatred than is usually supposed. His part in the establishment of the Florentine militia is well known but his diplomatic role has sometimes been underestimated. Although some writers have considered that his diplomatic role was always too subservient to have justified much

1. M. Martelli, *L'Altro Niccolò di Bernardo Machiavelli* (Quaderni di Rinascimento, 1975).
2. A[rchivio di] S[tato] F[lorence], Not[arile] Antecos[imiano], B. 2684 fos. 102ʳ-5ʳ; ed. *Opere di Niccolò Machiavelli* ('Italia', 1813), i. cxxxix–cxliv.
3. A.S.F., Not. Antecos., B. 2674 fo. 29ᵛ; ed. in appendix, below, Doc. no. 1.
4. *Ibid.* fos. 124ʳ⁻ᵛ; ed. below, Doc. no. 2.
5. N. Rubinstein, 'The Beginnings of Niccolò Machiavelli's career in the Florentine Chancery', *Italian Studies*, xi (1956), pp. 72–91.

independence, in 1505, when he was sent on a legation to Mantua, he was given full diplomatic powers.[1] The freedom which Machiavelli came to enjoy around that time was due to the confidence of Piero Soderini, the Gonfalonier of Justice for Life, and the chief magistrate of the city.

There are two documents in Florence which give us a glimpse of Machiavelli's unpopularity in 1510 and 1511. They are both anonymous denunciations of Machiavelli, sent to the Eight of Ward, the chief criminal magistracy. In the first, which is dated 27 May 1510,[2] Machiavelli is accused of having committed an unnatural sexual act with a certain Lucretia, known as *La Riccia*, a courtesan with whom we know, from other sources, that Machiavelli was acquainted in 1514.[3] The second denunciation (dated 25 March 1511) accuses Machiavelli, in his capacity as chancellor of the Militia Officials (*Nove di Milizia*) of having appropriated a letter sent by a Florentine magistrate in the dominions to the Eight of Ward and germane to a judicial investigation.[4] This denunciation, like the first, was dismissed as unproven. It is not possible to know whether there was any truth in either of these charges, but it is fair to assume that the presenting of them is proof of Machiavelli's unpopularity.

His rise to a position of some influence, and his closeness to Soderini, had brought Machiavelli a certain notoriety; and some of his contemporaries considered him to be the sedulous instrument of Soderini's policies. Guicciardini and Cerretani, for example, both saw Machiavelli's mission to Germany in January 1508 as the product of Soderini's desire to have a loyal underling on the spot; they were wrong, but their error is instructive.[5] And when Filippo Strozzi agreed to marry Clarice de' Medici, Piero de' Medici's daughter, it was said that Soderini induced Machiavelli to write a denunciation of the marriage.[6]

It is not surprising that during such a career Machiavelli made enemies; the very fact of his closeness to the *Gonfaloniere a Vita* damned him in the eyes of many. In 1506 Alamanno Salviati, a leading opponent of Soderini's, described Machiavelli as a *ribaldo*,[7] and when an attempt was made, in December 1509, to have him sacked, possibly

1. J. N. Stephens, 'Machiavelli's *mandate* for his legation to Mantua (1505)', *Italian Studies*, xxxi (1976), pp. 17–21.
2. A.S.F., Otto di Guardia, epoca repubblicana, 147 fo. 17ᵛ; ed. below, Doc. no. 3.
3. R. Ridolfi, *op. cit.* p. 155.
4. A.S.F., Otto di Guardia, epoca repubblicana, 149 bis, fos. 93ʳ⁻ᵛ.
5. B. Cerretani, 'Storia Fiorentina', Biblioteca Nazionale Centrale, Florence, Fondo Principale, II, III, 74, fo. 344ʳ; F. Guicciardini, *Storie Fiorentine dal 1378 al 1509*, ed. R. Palmarocchi (Bari, 1931), p. 302; R. Devonshire Jones, 'Some observations on the relations between Francesco Vettori and Niccolò Machiavelli during the embassy to Maximilian I', *Italian Studies*, xxiii (1968), p. 94.
6. R. Ridolfi, *op. cit.* p. 121.
7. N. Machiavelli, *Lettere Familiari*, ed. E. Alvisi (Florence, 1883), p. 154: Biagio Buonaccorsi to Niccolò Machiavelli, 6 Oct. 1506.

on the grounds that his father was a tax debtor, there were many voices raised in its favour.[1] It is likely, therefore, that these denunciations are further evidence of this sort of rancour.

In November 1512 Machiavelli's fourteen years in Florentine public service came to an end, when he was sacked on the Medici's return to Florence. This sacking ushered in the second transition of Machiavelli's public and private life, and it was the greatest of them. The following fifteen months was a crucial period in Machiavelli's life. He was released from active occupation as a state servant and was desperately eager to regain it.[2] For both reasons he began to write the *Prince* and to think (as we know from a famous letter of 10 December 1513) of dedicating it to Giuliano de' Medici.[3]

What proved fatal for this ambition – what, perhaps, had already proved fatal – was Machiavelli's alleged involvement in the plot against the Medici in February 1513. The chief figures implicated in it were Pietro Paolo Boscoli, Agostino Capponi, Niccolò Valori and Giovanni Folchi. The former two were executed, the latter two were imprisoned. The conspiracy had come to light when Boscoli let slip a piece of paper which contained the names of a number of persons – apparently of persons sympathetic to their cause. One of these was Machiavelli.

He was arrested, tortured and later released. His biographers, although they have possessed no direct evidence of Machiavelli's role, have concluded that Machiavelli was not actively involved, and had uttered no more than some ill-considered words.[4] However the confession of one of the conspirators, Giovanni Folchi, is preserved amongst the Medici Papers in the Florentine State Archives and this throws light on what Machiavelli's jibes had been, on his attitude to the new government and it suggests a reason why he may have thought of dedicating the *Prince* to Giuliano de' Medici.

The Confession confirms the accepted view that Machiavelli had been no more than incautious in talking of the regime. It reveals, however, that, according to Alessandro Bonciani (quoted in the Confession) Machiavelli was intimate with Folchi. It reveals that he had discussed with him the deeds of Piero Soderini (*de' fatti del Ghonfaloniere*) and talked 'more of the wars than of the city'. What is still more interesting in the Confession is Machiavelli's judgment on the new Medici regime in Florence: '. . . he said that it appeared to him that this regime (*stato*) would not be governed without difficulty,

---

1. R. Ridolfi, *op. cit.* pp. 112–13.
2. For a different view: F. Gilbert, *Machiavelli and Guicciardini* (Princeton, 1965), pp. 160-1.
3. N. Machiavelli, *Lettere Familiari*, ed. E. Alvisi, pp. 305–10.
4. P. Villari, *Niccolò Machiavelli e i suoi Tempi* (Milan, 1895–7), ii. 198–204; R. Ridolfi, *op. cit.* pp. 135–6.

because it lacked someone to stand at the tiller, as Lorenzo de' Medici had properly done so'.[1]

This document is sufficiently interesting for what it reveals of Machiavelli's involvement in the plot, and his attitudes of the time. It has, however, a greater value. If we bring it into focus with two little-known papers written by Machiavelli some time after the Medici's return in 1512, and with the first dedication of the *Prince*, we may find a clue to the origin of that, his greatest work.

Both these two papers seem to have been drawn up in the first days of November 1512. The first is a memorial (sometimes described as a letter) which Machiavelli addressed to Cardinal de' Medici, that is, to Giovanni de' Medici, who was elected Pope Leo X in March 1513.[2] It was written some time after 29 September 1512 when five officials were appointed to recover Medici property which had been confiscated in 1494. It is an essay on the political unwisdom of the Medici recovering such lands, because of the disaffection that this would arouse in citizens, who, themselves, would be expropriated thereby of their lands.

The other piece is Machiavelli's *Ricordo ai Palleschi*,[3] as it has been entitled by its modern editors. This was probably written in early November 1512,[4] and, once again (despite the modern title), it was addressed to the Medici rather than to their supporters. It sought to persuade the Medici that their self-interest lay in dividing the leading citizens (the *grandi*) from the people and the way to do so was to avoid an attack upon Piero Soderini, the leader of the old regime. It was the *grandi*, according to Machiavelli, who were exciting hostility to Soderini in order to make themselves indispensable alike to the Medici and to the people. The Medici's true interest (he said) lay in discouraging this stratagem, dividing the *grandi* from the people and, thereby, forcing the former to side with them.

In the Folchi Confession Machiavelli is critical of the helmless state. In these memorials, he is telling the Medici how to rule. In the *Prince* (which Machiavelli at first intended to dedicate to Giuliano) he writes of how princes should rule. In both the former cases he is

---

1. A.S.F., Archivio Mediceo avanti il Principato, lxxxix, no. 38; ed. below, Doc. no. 5.

2. A.S.F., Le Carte Strozziane, 2nd ser., 86 fos. 34ʳ-5ᵛ new foliation (autograph); ed. in N.M., *Opere Complete* (Florence, 1857), p. 1146; *idem, Opere*, ed. A. Panella (Milan–Rome, 1938–9), ii. 778–9.

3. A.S.F., Carte Torrigiani, Busta V, ins. xxv (autograph); ed. *Ricordo di Niccolò Machiavelli ai Palleschi del 1512*, ed. C. Guasti (per le Nozze Bongi-Ranalli) (Prato, 1868); N.M., *Tutte le Opere Storiche e Letterarie*, ed. G. Mazzoni, M. Casella (Florence, 1929) pp. 791–2; *idem, Opere*, ed. A. Panella (Milan–Rome, 1938–9), ii. 717–20; *idem, Arte della Guerra e Scritti Politici Minori*, ed. S. Bertelli (Milan, 1961), pp. 225–7; J. J. Marchand, *Niccolò Machiavelli, i Primi Scritti Politici (1499–1512)* (Medioevo e Umanesimo, 23, 1975), pp. 533–5.

4. G. Sasso, *Niccolò Machiavelli, Storia del suo Pensiero Politico* (Naples, 1958), p. 179; J. J. Marchand, *op. cit.* p. 300. But *cf.* N. Rubinstein, 'Machiavelli and the world of Florentine politics', p. 20.

conscious of how the Medici must act if they are to survive. In the *Prince* he is conscious of the same general problem.

This may suggest a new way to look at the origins of the *Prince*. It may have begun not simply in Machiavelli recollecting in un-employed tranquillity his experience of government before 1512, or haphazardly dedicating it to Giuliano in the hope of recovering office. Nor did it have its origins in a desire (as Varchi claimed later) to tell Lorenzo de' Medici, its final dedicatee, how to make himself the 'absolute lord of Florence',[1] nor to tell Giuliano how to create a new state for himself in central Italy,[2] nor was it just the outcome of Machiavelli's interest in foreign affairs and of his correspondence with Francesco Vettori on that subject.[3] Nor yet did it originate in a desire to understand the career of the popular government which had just fallen,[4] nor simply (as the Folchi Confession might now suggest) in a desire to make good his incautious remarks in the spring of 1513, nor in any combination of these reasons.[5]

Rather, it can be suggested, the *Prince* may have arisen from an itch, which Machiavelli had been feeling since November 1512, to tell the Medici how to rule in order to survive: the failing helmsman must be taught to steer. It is no disproof of this to say that since Machiavelli intended to dedicate the *Prince* to Giuliano the work can have had no message for Florence, because Giuliano had already gone to live in Rome.[6] What is true of the final work may not have been true of its beginnings, and Machiavelli may have been itching to tell the Medici how to rule not just in Florence, but generally. The *Prince*, when it came to be written, was not just about Florence – it was a general work. It may, nevertheless, have taken root in Machiavelli's itch to tell the Medici how to rule (and not just in order to win their favour) and this may have continued to direct his thought when he wrote the *Prince*, although, by then, he was writing on the general plane.

In the end, the *Prince* was dedicated to Lorenzo de' Medici, duke of Urbino. And from 1513 to 1525 (with the exception of a brief employment by the *Otto di Pratica* in 1521) he continued to write: first (of his chief works) the *Discourses*, then the *Florentine History*. None of these books was printed before 1530 and we know all too little of their early history, and especially of their reception. There is, however, a

1. B. Varchi, *Storia Fiorentina*, ed. G. Milanesi (Florence, 1857–8), i. 200.
2. P. Villari, *op. cit.* iii. 378–82; *cf.* J. H. Whitfield, *Discourses on Machiavelli* (Cambridge, 1969), pp. 24–25, 67 ff.; C. H. Clough, *Machiavelli Researches* (Naples, 1967), pp. 31 ff.
3. R. von Albertini, *op. cit.* p. 55; G. Sasso, *op. cit.* pp. 206–7; J. R. Hale, *Machiavelli and Renaissance Italy* (London, 1961), p. 146.
4. *Cf.* N. Rubinstein, 'Machiavelli and the world of Florentine politics', p. 23.
5. F. Chabod, *Scritti su Machiavelli* (Turin, 1964), p. 211; *idem, Machiavelli and the Renaissance* (London, 1958), p. 39; C. Lefort, *Le Travail de l'oeuvre Machiavel* (Paris, 1972), p. 325.
6. C. H. Clough, *op. cit.* pp. 42–43. Incidentally, Giuliano did not leave for Rome in September 1513 (Clough, pp. 42, 48) but April.

letter in the diplomatic archives in Florence from Niccolò
Guicciardini to his father Luigi, dated 1517, which can take us a
certain way. It gives us the first sure reference to a reading of the
Prince that we possess. Previously we have had only the presentation
letter of Biagio Buonaccorsi, which was joined to his transcription of
the *Prince*.[1]

Our letter was written by Niccolò from Florence to Luigi in
Arezzo, where his father was Florentine Commissioner. The letter is
only dated 29 July, but it was evidently written in 1517, because it is
preserved in a volume of original letters, maintained in strict
chronological order, sandwiched between two letters which are dated
20 July and 31 July 1517.[2] It is partly given over to family affairs –
reports of his uncles, of Lodovico Alamanni, of his own studies, but
what interests us is his reply to an account by his father of the
movements of Spanish troops in the direction of Arezzo. What he
says is this:

> to me it appears, however, that if the enemy turned towards you, which you
> seem rather to suspect, it would not be easy to defend yourselves,
> considering the little constancy and faith of these Aretines towards the city;
> i.e. Florence, and it would be necessary (wishing to make sure of them) to do
> what Machiavelli, in his work *De Principatibus*, says that Iuriotto da Fermo
> did when he wished to become their lord, and even then one should not trust
> wholly in others.[3]

What Machiavelli had written of Oliverotto da Fermo (as Niccolò's
Iuriotto is more commonly called) in the *Prince*, was his method of
seizing the lordship of the city of Fermo by inviting its leading
citizens to a banquet where they were unceremoniously and un-
suspectingly murdered.[4]

This early reading of the *Prince*, the nature of the reaction to it, and
the men involved, are equally interesting. We notice the early title *De
Principatibus*, the one used by Machiavelli in his letter of 10 December
1513 and in most of the early manuscripts.[5] We notice this reading of
Machiavelli in the Guicciardini family: Luigi was the brother, and
Niccolò the nephew of Francesco Guicciardini, and both were
contributors to the intellectual life of Florence in the early sixteenth

1. *e.g.* A. M. Bandini, *Catalogus codicum italicorum Bibliothecae Mediceae Laurentianae
. . .* (Florence, 1778), cols. 230–1; F.-L. Polidori, 'Avvertimento', *Archivio Storico
Italiano*, Ser. I, vol. iv, pt. 2 (1853), pp. 394–5; A. Gerber, *Niccolò Machiavelli, Die
Handscriften, Ausgaben und Übersetzungen seiner Werke im 16. und 17. Jahrhunderts* (Gotha,
1912), p. 84n. (incomplete); N.M., *Il Principe*, ed. L. A. Burd (Oxford, 1891), p. 34;
idem, Opere ('Italia', 1813), i. xli–xliin.; C. H. Clough, *op. cit.* p. 29.
2. A.S.F., Signori, Dieci di Balia, Otto di Pratica, Missive Originali, 9.
3. A.S.F., Signori, Dieci di Balia, Otto di Pratica, Missive Originali, 9 fos. 95[r-v];
ed. below, Doc. no. 6.
4. *Il Principe*, cap. 8.
5. N. Machiavelli, *Lettere Familiari*, ed. Alvisi, pp. 305–10; A. Gerber, *op. cit.* pp.
82 ff.

century.[1] Luigi was known to Machiavelli, for before 1512 the latter had dedicated to him a poem on ambition.[2] Most of all we notice that this reference gives no support to the contention that what would have struck the first readers of the *Prince* was that it was another contribution to the traditional genre of 'Mirrors of Princes',[3] or at least that it caused them little scandal.[4] On the contrary, Niccolò Guicciardini seems to have been impressed by the 'immoral' Machiavelli. He quotes one of the chapters of the *Prince* where Machiavelli departs furthest from his forerunners,[5] and within it, moreover, he quotes one of the most notorious acts of *realpolitik* reported by Machiavelli. Indeed, this conclusion is reinforced by the fact that Niccolò Guicciardini wrenches Machiavelli's account of Oliverotto da Fermo from its context. In the *Prince* Machiavelli had referred to it as an example of the behaviour of princes who come to power by crime, and who are not to be praised because such actions win them not virtue or glory, but only power. Yet here, impliedly, Guicciardini has quoted the action as something to be praised and uses it as guidance on how to maintain power, when Machiavelli had emphasized that such acts of violence should only be perpetrated on the seizure of power. The legend of Machiavelli's immorality was already in the making.

This letter of Niccolò Guicciardini contains the first sure reference to a reading of the *Prince*, for besides it, there is only the prefatory letter of Biagio Buonaccorsi, which has been variously dated between 1514 and 1523. In several ways Buonaccorsi's is a less interesting testimony to the first reception of the *Prince* than is the Guicciardini letter. Its dating is insecure. Its literary purpose (it was composed as a formal dedication letter to his transcription of the *Prince*) meant that Buonaccorsi had set out to give a calculated description of the work's overall scope and interest, instead of revealing, in a spontaneous and *ex parte* fashion, what had struck him about it. Moreover Buonaccorsi stood in a peculiar relation to the work: he was acting as its professional copyist.[6]

For Machiavelli, working had led to writing and, finally, in 1525-6, his writing led him back to work. Till then the only time since 1512 when he had been able – briefly – to take up his old sort of career was a very minor mission on which he was sent to the Franciscan friars at Carpi in 1521. But in 1525 his writing of the *Florentine History* had led

1. R. von Albertini, *op. cit.* pp. 116 ff., 260 ff.
2. N. Machiavelli, *Tutte le Opere Storiche e Letterarie*, ed. Mazzoni, pp. 849-53, (casella).
3. L. A. Burd, introduction to N.M., *Il Principe*, ed. L. A. Burd (Oxford, 1891), p. 35; C. H. Clough, *op. cit.* pp. 52-53.
4. P. Villari, *op. cit.* ii. 423-4. But, *per contra*, N.M., *Opere*, ed. S. Bertelli (Milan, 1968) x. pp. xxxi–xxxii.
5. A. H. Gilbert, *Machiavelli's Prince and its Forerunners* (Durham N.C., 1938), p. 51.
6. M. Martelli, 'Preistoria (Medicea) di Machiavelli', pp. 382 ff.

him to think about the diplomatic and military plight of Italy, so close
to all his contemporaries since the French defeat at Pavia on 24
February 1525. He was brimfull of ideas for reform (no less
enthusiastic phrase would seem to do) and this led him to a last
involvement in public affairs. Once again there are documents which
can illumine some details of this last episode of his public life.

It began in May 1525 and it may have been precipitated (or
hastened) by domestic troubles at home. On 11 May 1525 he
'emancipated' his son Lodovico, that is, he set him legally free of
dependence upon him.[1] Lodovico was Machiavelli's second child and
in frequent trouble with the law. It seems unlikely that it was a
coincidence that on this very date, Lodovico had been sentenced by
the Eight of Ward for having assaulted a notary.[2] Whether or not
Machiavelli hastened to leave Florence to escape such troubles,
within a few weeks he was in Rome in order to present his Florentine
History to Pope Clement VII, to whom he had dedicated it. The book
and – more likely – Machiavelli's eager ideas enthused the Pope and
he sent him off to Francesco Guicciardini to pass on a plan for arming
the people of the Romagna. Back in Florence he was sent on a mission
to Venice to reclaim some debts which were owed to Florentine
merchants. His main chance, however, did not come until the
following year.

In the spring of 1526 the imperial threat to Italy led Pope Clement
VII to think of strengthening the Florentine defences and when he
did so he thought of Machiavelli. On 4 April Francesco Guicciardini
wrote to Machiavelli by order of the Pope, to seek his assistance.
Machiavelli replied the same day that he had met with the cardinal of
Cortona and he passed on some preliminary observations. He
reported that the following day he was to climb the walls, and to
discuss a new design for them with Count Pietro Navarra, the Spanish
military engineer.[3]

It has been said that this design 'was sent to Rome with a report
written by Machiavelli, which has been praised in recent times by
historians of military art. First it must have been praised by Clement
VII and his counsellors, as its author was at once called to Rome
where he succeeded in firing the Pope's enthusiasm and even that of
Guicciardini. He left again on 26 or 27 April'.[4]

A document from the Florentine archives reveals that the design
was made by Navarra and 'Signore Vitello' – presumably the
condottiere Vitello Vitelli and that it did not precede Machiavelli to

1. A.S.F., Not. Antecos. B. 2685 fo. 204ʳ: 'Nicolaus domini Bernardi de
Machiavellis, civis Florentinus etc., servatis etc., emancipavit etc. Lodovicum, eius
filium presentem et petentem etc., cui emancipationi decretum interposui etc.
rogantes etc.' The act is reported in A.S.F., Notificazioni di Atti di Emancipazione,
17 fo. 94ᵛ (where it is mis-dated 11.vi.1525).

2. G. Amico, *La Vita di Niccolò Machiavelli* (Florence, 1875), p. 614.

3. *Lettere Familiari*, ed. Alvisi, pp. 485-7.   4. R. Ridolfi, *op. cit.* p. 227.

Rome; but that rather he was deputed by the *Otto di Pratica* to bear it there himself. On 10 April it is recorded that that magistracy

deputed Niccolò Machiavelli to go to Rome to Our Lordship [the Pope] to bear the design made for the walls of the city by Pietro Navarra and by Signor Vitello, that is for 15 days and no more, beginning the day he leaves Florence.[1]

In fact he was away twenty days as a second document reveals. This records that he was paid 180 lire for his expenses at the rate of 9 lire a day.[2]

The former document gives Machiavelli no credit for this design, but this may reveal that the *Otto di Pratica* was doing less than justice to him. Certainly, on 27 April, Francesco Guicciardini wrote to his brother Luigi, who was a leading member of the regime in Florence that 'Machiavelli was the one who proposed this business, so you must treat him well during this visit and help him in any way necessary, for he has well earned his reward'.[3] In any case he had written an accompanying report,[4] and the enthusiasm for the whole affair seems certainly to have been his.

Machiavelli returned from Rome to be appointed Chancellor of the newly appointed Proctors of the Walls, but within a few weeks he departed for Lombardy. Ridolfi has commented that 'as we possess no instructions or letters patent issued to him by the Eight . . . it is not known whether he was sent out by the cardinal of Cortona or whether his friend the Lieutenant [i.e. Francesco Guicciardini] had him under his orders'.[5] There is, however, another document amongst the papers of the *Otto di Pratica*, which records payment to him for some 29 florins for this trip. This declares that he was sent to Lombardy 'with a commission from the magistracy'[6] (*i.e.* the *Otto di Pratica*), although in those years the cardinal of Cortona certainly exercised great influence upon the decisions of that magistracy.

Writing the *Florentine History* down to the death of Lorenzo the Magnificent had led Machiavelli to think closely about the plight of Italy in the 1520s, and thence he was drawn, briefly, into public life.

1. A.S.F., VIII di Pratica, Minutari e Ricordi, 2 fo. 133ᵛ: 'Deputato Niccolò Machiavelli a andare ad Roma a N.S. per portare el disegnio facto per le mura della ciptà da Pietro Navarra et dal Signor Vitello, cioè per 15 giorni et non più, cominciando el di partita di Firenze.'
2. A.S.F., VIII di Pratica, Ricordanze, 3 fo. 50ᶜ: 'Stantiato a Niccolò Machiavelli per vinti giorni che è stato absente a Roma mandato per il magistrato loro lire 180, ad ragione di lire 9 el giorno' (4 May 1526).
3. O. Tommasini, *La Vita e gli Scritti di Niccolò Machiavelli* (Rome, 1883–1911), ii. 1157.
4. ed. N.M., *Opere* ('Italia', 1813), iv. 459–68.
5. R. Ridolfi, *op. cit.* p. 229.
6. A.S.F., VIII di Pratica, Deliberazioni, Partiti, Condotte e Stanziamenti, 13 fo. 167ᵛ ink (157ᵛ pencil): 'Niccolò Machiavelli per andare a Messer Francesco Guicciardini in Lombardia con commissione del magistrato et per renderne conto fiorini ventinove d'oro, lire una piccoli.' (*Ibid.* vol. 14, fos. 11ʳ, 11ᵛ, 19ʳ contains payment for his later trip to Modena.)

Had he ever written the last chapters of the *Florentine History* (other than fragmentary notes) almost certainly they would have been moulded by this last 'experience of modern things'. That further transition from public to private life he never made. A year later, on 21 June 1527, he was dead.

University of Edinburgh   J. N. STEPHENS
University of Warwick   H. C. BUTTERS

Document no. 1
(A.S.F., Not. Antecos., B. 2674, fo. 29ᵛ)

Eadem die [28 Aprilis 1494] in populo Sancte Felicite, testibus Miniato Angeli Leonardi Grifi dicti populi et Dominico Gerardi Pieri Giani, populi Sancti Iacobi supra Arnura.

Procura — Dominus Bernardus Niholai[1] de Machiavellis fecit etc. suum procuratorem Nicolaum eius filium, ad consentiendum et licentiam dandum domine Primavere eius filie; volentem[1] procuratorem constituere et se obligare etc.

Document no. 2
(A.S.F., Not. Antecos., B. 2674, fos. 124ᶠ⁻ᵛ)[2]

1497 8 Maii, indictione 15, testibus Juliano Petri Guidi, *linaiolo*, Benedicto Tomei Christofani, populi Sancte Felicitatis in dicto Populo Sancte Felicitatis.

Domine Primavere domini Bernardi Niholai de Machiavellis et uxori olim Johannis Angeli de Vernaccis in mundualdum dedi Christofanum[3] Mactie de Careglis, presentem, etc.

Item incontinenti dicta domina Primavera cum licentia Domini Bernardi eius patris presentis etc. et cum licentia mundualdi etc. omni meliori modo etc. fecit etc. procuratorem etc. Dominum Bernardum, eius patrem, etc., presentem, etc. specialiter et nominatim ad exigendum omnes pagus Montis cuiusqunque generis cantantis, sub nomine dicte domine Primavere et exactionem finiendum etc. et ad faciendum im predictis que ipsa constituens facere posset etc. dans etc. promictens etc. obligans etc. rogans etc. per guarantigiam[4] etc.

Item incontinenti dicta domina dicto consensu patris et mundualdi etc. fecit etc. procuratores etc. Ser Antonium Parentis Antonii et Nicholaum et Tottum, eius fratres, filios dicti Domini Bernardi et quoslibet notarios apotece Ser Andree et quemlibet eorum in solidum etc. ad agendum etc. intrandum in tenutam etc. adcipiendum in solutum etc. adcusandum etc. et generaliter etc. dans etc. promictens etc. rogans etc. per guarantigiam[5] etc.

1. *sic.*
2. For two later documents relating to this case, see A.S.F., Not. Antecos., N. 4 (1499–1504) fos. 1ᶠ, 19ᵛ.
3. *sic.*   4. *obligans* (?) [cancelled] *etc.* MS.
5. quarantigiam MS.

Document no. 3
(A.S.F., Otto di Guardia, epoca repubblicana, 147, fo. 17ᵛ)

Tanburi addì 27 di maggio 1510.

Notifichasi a Voi, Signori Otto, chome Nicholò[1] di Messer   Nicholò
Bernardo Machiavelli fotte la Lucretia[1] vochata la Riccia nel culo.   La Lucre
Mandate per lei et troverete la verità. El notifichatore vule el quarto
vadia alle Murate.

30 Maii commissa citatio brigha falsa de dicta Riccia infra quintam
diem.[2]

Document no. 4
(A.S.F., Otto di Guardia, epoca repubblicana, 149 bis, fos. 93ʳ⁻ᵛ)

Addì xxv di marzo 1511.

Notifichasi a voi, Signori Otto, et querelandosi dice chome essendo
stata fatta una vituperosa chosa, et mai più udita in questa terra, che
dispiace a tutti e cittadini che l'anno udita, et dispiace per essere stata
fatta contro[3] al onore del vostro magistrato, et voi non avete stimato
quello, facendo vista di non vedere, ché se questo popolo avessi
pensato che avessi tenuto sì pocho conto del onore di cotesto luogho,
mai v'arebbe eletti a tale ofitio, perché chi non stima l'onore dell'
ufitio, non merita quello. Et molto più s'à a essere severo contro a
delitti commessi contro[4] al publicho che contro al privato, et più
s'ànno a punire; il contrario di che avete fatto. Et perché non abbiate
schusa con questo popolo, si notificha et querelando si dice chome.

Nicholò Machiavelli, cancelliere de' Nove, di questo mese essendoli
data una lettera da Giubileo d'Anghiari mandata da Lattantio Tedaldi,
vicario della Pieve, al vostro ufitio, detto Nicholò dolosamente, et per
fare verghogna al vostro ufitio, et per potere più arapinare che non fa,
si tenne decta lettera, nè mai l'à data, cosa molto di male exemplo. Nè è
huomo sì barbuto in questa terra che tale chosa avessi avuto animo di
fare. E sassi che avete l'esamine scripta di detto Giubileo et di Antonio
Peruzzi, et, però, non si allegha testimoni. Domandasi che faciate
iustitia. Et perché la chosa importa assai e più, non pensate che pare
bene non siate avezzi a ghovernare chose di stato. Però, si domanda
che se non sapete, o non volete, punire questo sì grande delitto, che lo
mandiate alla Quarantia, ché ne sarete commendati,[5] et ricomperete
l'onore vostro, e farete quanto siate oblighati alla patriale del vostro
ufitio.[6]

1. underlined MS.
2. *absoluta x lunii quia non constitit* margin with cancellation – stroke through body
of text MS.
3. *absolutus die xi Aprilis 1511 quia* [*propterea inter* (?) cancelled] *non constitit* margin
MS.
4. *allo* cancelled MS.
5. *commendati* changed from *commendate* MS.
6. stroke through body of text.

Document no. 5
(A.S.F., Archivio Mediceo avanti il Principato, lxxxix, no. 38)[1]

A dì primo di marzo 1512.[2]

Giovanni Folchi, examinato intr'al[3] palazo del Capitano in presentia di Pagolo di Piero de' Medici et Ghuglielmo Angiolini, due del numero delli Otto, et me, notaio infrascripto,[4] dixe:

Al proposito della ghuardia della città che credeva che fussi al proposito che e Medici havessino a passo alla chasa loro più parenti et amici si potessi, come hanno e chapi di parte delle terre della Chiesa (et questo ne' ragionamenti suoi chon Pietropagolo), in modo che Pietropagolo dixe, 'O, e bisognerebbe che cotesti parenti et amici appigionassino le chase loro et pigliassino di quelle d'altri vicine a detti Medici.'

Con Nicholò Machiavelli dixe havere parlato de' fatti del Ghonfaloniere, chome altra volta ha detto, et alsì di Giovambaptista Soderini, et più delle ghuerre che della città.

Et replichò il sonare di furto la champana, di che Pietropagolo lo interroghò, chome altra volta ha detto.

Et di Giuliano che Pietropagolo una volta lo domandò se Giuliano de' Medici[5] li pareva che andassi sicuro, et disse che li rispose che lui andassi sicurissimo; prima per la loro binignità, perché i Medici non feciono mai male a persona; l'altra perché in questa città non erano cittadini soldati chome sono a Bologna et Perugia.

Et che[6] Nicholò Machiavelli diceva che lo[7] pareva che questo stato non si potessi reggere senza difficultà, perché manchava di chi stesse a timone, chome stava sufficientemente Lorenzo de' Medici. Delle chose di fuora diceva che la legha non poteva stare sempre ad questo modo, et che facilmente[8] un dì si dissolverebbe.

Et che sfuggiva i ragionamenti di detto Nicholò, domandato perché, dixe perché Pagholo Vectori lo advertì che lui non usassi con Duccio, et lui dixe 'et io non userò anchora col Machiavello'. Et Pagolo li dixe 'Nè cotesto non dà noia'.

Et che[9] Alexandro Bonciani haveva detto a Simone Tornabuoni che erano[10] parechi che darebbono un dì delle schiene in terra, et che Giovanni Folchi tutto dì era col Machiavello.

Et che qualche volta Pietropagolo et lui leggevano la Politicha d'Aristotzile che parla del ghoverno delle città.

1. stamped numeration. The single sheet is also numbered, in pencil, 'F 89' (*i.e.* the fascile number) and, again, in pencil, '39'.
2. Florentine style, *i.e.* 1513.
3. changed from '*nel palazo*' MS.
4. *i.e.* Ser Zanobi Pace, chancellor of the *Otto di Guardia*, in whose hand this MS is written
5. *andava* cancelled MS.
6. three letters cancelled MS.
7. *lo* apparently changed from *li* MS.
8. falcilmente (*sic*) MS.
9. *Simone Tornabuoni* cancelled MS.
10. one word cancelled MS.

Document no. 6

(A.S.F., Signori, Dieci di Balia, Otto di Pratica, Missive Originali, 9, fos. 95ʳ·ᵛ)[1]

Honorande Pater etc. Intendo per una vostra ultima el iudicio fate di queste cose degli spagniuoli, che vi pare che, se non nasce qualche caso extraordinario, le cose habbino alla venuta di questi svizeri a posarsi in buono stato; et parmi che al modo le discorrete, le giudichiate benissimo. Ma poi, dall' altra parte, mi dà noia le cose che io intendo qua et da Jacopo, che è tornato di villa, et da Batista, et dagli altri, ché è secondo me, comunemente pocha speranza di bene, et non mi risolvo chi[2] sene inganni; perché mi presummo che voi che siate costì alla presentia, si può dire, intendiate queste per cose apunto,[3] et ancora credo che Jacopo, se non ci dà noia el desiderio cattivo, giudichi secondo quello intende, et pare ragionevole che non gli sieno detto le cose a rovescio d'elle. Sono mezo confuso, pure mi attengho al iuditio vostro per credere ne siate meglio ragguagliato di questi altri, benché continuamente Jacopo et Francesco mi dicono che voi ci pigliate su errore, et non siate advisato[4] bene delle cose ochorrente. Et[5] credo[5] che se voi fussi qua, et potessi udire a quello si risolvono, benché vi paia ragionevole debba succedere el contrario, per empiegli afatto, et mantenegli ne' loro errori, faresti vista di acchordarvi a loro pareri,[6] et anche forse per quello uscirebbono più larghi poi allo scrivere non fanno, vedendo voi essere di animo diverso et contrario dal loro. Ma a me, *tamen*, pare che se e nimici si voltassino verso voi, come mostrate havere qualche sospecto, dureresti non pichola faticha a difendervi, considerato la pocha fermezza et fede di cotesti aretini verso la città; et bisognerebbe, a volere assicurarsene, fare come dice el Machiavello in quella sua opera *De Principatibus* che fece Iuriotto da Fermo, quando sene volle insignorire, et anche poi non sarebbe da fidarsi al tutto degli altri; siché Iddio vene guardi et mandi piutosto cotesta peste adosso ad altri. Hammi male che costì sia, come scrivete, tanti grandissimi caldi, et conforterevi al riguardare, se non credessi che voi sanza altri richordi lo farete. La lettera vostra si dette a Jacopo, et del tutto[7] desiderate credo per lo apportatore vi rispondere. Francesco ha un pocho dello inpingue sconciamente et, però, se hoggi non vi rispondessi, non è da maravigliarsene.

Dello studiare mio non achade dire altro, se non come ogni giorno odo da Messer Lorenzo Petrucc(i)[8] una letione nella materia delle substitutione, et non credo perdere el tempo. Delle[9] cose di humanità vegho qualche volta,[10] cioè qualche storia, per piaciere et haverne

1. autograph. The numeration is stamped. The MS is also numbered, in ink, *71*.
2. *c* (of *chi*) written over *d* MS.
3. *apunto* changed from apunte MS.
4. *ragua* cancelled MS.
5. *se* cancelled MS.
6. *et* cancelled MS.
7. *credo* cancelled MS.
8. word run off the side of the page. MS.
9. *delle* changed from *della* MS.
10. *co* cancelled MS.

notitia. E mia libri che vennono da Bologna mi costeranno legati 8 duchati, che sciolti qua mi sono costi 6; vedretene poi alla tornata el conto. Lodovicho Alamanni[1] sene andò hiermattina in villa sua con la Gostanza per 4 mesi o circha, ché la camera della Gostanza la ha hauta la nuora per questo tempo.[2] Et parmi che *praeter eloquentiam et*[3] *vel loquentiam et ingenium acre* non vi sia molte altre cose, et alla tornata lo vedrete, che vi ho da dire mille belle cose. Delle ricolte et *similibus* non vene scrivo, perché so che apunto ne siate raguagliato da Mona Lisabella, che ci usa grandissima diligentia, alla quale porto quello honore et reverentia si conviene sanza voi melo richordassi, ché così è mio debito. Mona Simona si rachomanda a voi, et vorrebbe havessi questa licentia, et se voi non la havete hauta, per contentarla scrivetegli haverla, che queste donne fanno conto di certe frasche che è una morte. Hovvi ancora a scrivere come ho inteso dire che 6 mila fanti franzesi sono arrivati a Gienova, et non si sa perché, et harei da dire delle altre cose che le scriverrei, se non credessi che Jacopo, dal quale le intendo, vene advisassi. Non altro, se non che vi pregho[4] mi scriviate come havete fatto. Hora a voi mi rachomando. Adì 29 *Julii.*

Vostro Niccolò Guicciardini
in Firenze.

Magnifico viro Aloisio Guicciardino, generali commissario Florentino[5] *clarissimo patri honorando.*

In Arezo.

1. *se a n* cancelled MS.
2. *o circha . . . tempo* interlined MS.
3. *in* cancelled MS.
4. *vi pregho* interlined MS.
5. *florentino* partly lost MS.

[15]

On the Impersonality of the Modern State:
A Comment on Machiavelli's Use of *Stato*

HARVEY C. MANSFIELD, JR.
Harvard University

The modern state, by contrast to the Aristotelian regime, is essentially impersonal. For Machiavelli, stato is extremely personal; yet, it is argued, Machiavelli laid the foundation for the modern state in his general and impartial advice to acquire stato. *The argument proceeds by an analysis of Machiavelli's use of* stato, *after a brief consideration of its medieval counterparts.*

Nowadays when a person or party comes to power, it is said to take over *the* state or *the* government. It does not claim to advance *its* rule except through *the* state, as if to make it plain that the state does not belong, but is only delivered temporarily, in trust, to the winner of a struggle for power. The terms used may vary: in America, one speaks of the Reagan administration, consisting of Reagan, his lieutenants, and an assortment of Republicans, as having taken over the (federal) government; in France, *le gouvernement* or *le régime Mitterand* has acceded to *l'état*. But the impersonality of the modern state continues despite the variability of the terms used to express it. Even the Communists maintain the distinction, in theory, between their party and the state that the party has established and yet exists to serve.

The state or *the* government is not constituted by the current holders of power; rather, it is there before they arrive, waiting to be claimed, and it will continue after they have departed, waiting with equanimity and impartial regard for the next claimant. The state may be thought to have no interest, like a neutral, or to have its own interest, in order to serve as an arbiter, but in either case the essential point is that it does not belong to any of the contending parties or groups. The state has an existence independent of such parties or groups. Indeed, its independence seems to be constituted not so much by self-subsistence, which would make it resemble those parties or groups, as by abstraction from them. Whenever the state gets "a life of its own," we may fear tyranny, or hope for peace and reason, but we do not understand that life to be the same as the lives of parties or groups from which the state is abstracted. If this discussion sounds abstract, it is partly because the modern state is an abstraction. We moderns find abstractions easier to denounce than to do

without, and if we denounce the state as abstract, we mean, as Marx meant in denouncing Hegel, that it does not succeed in being abstract but remains a tool of the ruling party, group, or class. The ideal or standard of abstraction from personality is retained, or even heightened, in such denunciation.

Thus, when some modern person said *l'etat, c'est moi,* this was already a paradox, stating a conjunction of the impersonal with his person (Hartung, 1949; Rosen, 1961). He could not have said *c'est mon etat,* implying that this state rather than some other or none was his. Our modern notions of legitimate power seem bound up with the impersonality of the modern state. Even the vaunted rationality of the modern state seems designed to ensure its impersonality. Hegel's rational state was to be ruled by a universal class of bureaucrats educated to remove the partialities of ordinary persons, and Weber's bureaucratic office is an ideal-type of the modern attempt to deny that an office belongs to the officeholder.

Against this conception, one may set "the traditional idea of the prince maintaining his existing position and range of powers" (Skinner, 1978, vol. 2, p. 354). Such is Skinner's description of Machiavelli's usual or typical understanding of the relationship between prince and state. Skinner's impressive work, *The Foundations of Modern Political Thought,* aims to show how the modern state (or its foundations) evolved from this traditional idea of Machiavelli's to "the distinctively modern idea of the State as a form of public power separate from both the ruler and the ruled, and constituting the supreme political authority within a certain defined territory," which is to be found in Bodin's thought at the end of the sixteenth century.[1] I shall question Skin-

Received: January 3, 1983
Accepted for publication: March 14, 1983

[1]Skinner, 1978, vol. 2, p. 353; the definition of state is taken from Max Weber, vol. 1, p. x. See Tarcov (1982, pp. 63-64).

ner's description of Machiavelli's use of *stato* as traditional, but first I must endorse and elaborate his understanding of the traditional idea.

The traditional idea of the state comes from the notion of regime (*politeia*) in Plato and Aristotle, who do not make use of the term "state."[1] The regime, for them, means constitution in a fuller sense than the constitution of a modern state; it refers to the form or structure of the whole society and to its way of life as embodied in that structure. The offices or rules (*archai*) of the regime rule the society by giving that society its character; they are not separable from the society in such manner as to await impartially the winner of the power struggle within society. Only a democratic society, for example, consists with a democratic regime. A democratic regime, newly installed, proceeds as soon as it can to the democratizing of society and applies its principle of rule with partisan disregard for the neutrality of the "state" and the autonomy of "society."

Thus, says Aristotle, the city *is* chiefly the regime (*Politics* 1276b10-12). The city has territory and inhabitants, but these do not define it; one cannot make a city by constructing a wall around the Peloponnesus. Although a city must, of course, have a territory and a people, these are material for its *form*, which is its regime, and the city is defined chiefly by its form. It is not defined solely by its regime, because the regime is limited in what it can do by nature (for example, climate) and by human nature (the necessity to satisfy or to suppress human needs). It is also limited by custom, although custom, which consists anyway of practices established by the preceding regime or regimes, can sometimes change rapidly and utterly to the amazement of all who rely on it. The regime of a city is not, moreover, some hidden essence lying behind its territory and people; it is publicly visible in its offices and in the characteristic behavior of its rulers as its ordering (*taxis*). A democratic regime, for example, *looks* democratic, for what is most visible is that which is public, and the public is what the rulers do not need or desire to conceal, their rule.

Far from being impersonal and impartial, like the modern state, the Aristotelian regime reflects —and advances—the characteristic claim of the persons who rule. Such persons do not merely claim to promote their own self-interest in a greater whole that is common to society, but they promote themselves in a partisan view of the whole that is typically theirs, and they advance that view against the opposing view of their typical opponents, democrats versus oligarchs, for example. As men cannot help preferring themselves, so regimes are necessarily partisan. In this view, *l'état, c'est moi* would apply to every regime, including a democratic one; in Aristotle's terms, the *politeia* is the *politeuma*, the body of rulers. They are the regime, and the regime is theirs.

If a mixed regime could be made, which is doubtful, it would advance the claim to rule of all parties or the whole. It would be impartial by combining all parties rather than by not promoting any party or by remaining indifferent to which party wins the struggle for power. This regime would be partisan to the common interest of all in virtue rather than impartial in the maintenance of liberty to facilitate the self-promotion of each person and all parties. By means of this mixed regime, one could judge the partisan claims of the lesser regimes and sort those regimes into good and bad. Such judgment is asked for, one could say, by the claims of the regimes. It requires an elevation above ordinary partisanship that begins from ordinary partisanship and that does not issue in neutrality.

We may suppose that the impersonality of the modern state, such as we find it in the full clarity of Hobbes's political science, may have been intended to correct the partisanship of the Aristotelian regime. For in the Aristotelian understanding as Hobbes saw it, the regime was left exposed to the capture of religious parties, who used it with tyrannical zeal. We may suppose, then, that the impersonality of the modern state was the chosen instrument of secularization. That hypothesis cannot be elaborated or tested here.[3] But it does seem necessary to have before us a more complete picture of the alternative to the modern state than is usually supplied in discussions of the usage of "state," so that we do not leave the impression that such usage evolved in mere response to changing circumstances or by naive, groping discovery of the only truly conceivable political unit, the modern state. Whatever may have been the causes that established the modern state, it had to be conceived against the authority of classical political science; and if it is to be argued that political necessities alone brought about the modern state, then it must be shown why those very necessities were newly conceived to require a new ordering and a new politics. In writing the history of the modern state, historians, it may be gently suggested, need

---

[1] Plato *Republic* 473e, 501a, 544b-545d; *Statesman* 302b-303d; *Laws* 632c, 681d, 686c, 707d, 710d-e, 712e, 714b, 715b, 734e, 739e, 751a-c, 770e, 817b, 832c, 856b. Aristotle *Politics* 1247b32-9, 1275a38-b4, 1276b1-12, 1279a26-b10, 1280a8-25, 1281a12, 1289a8-20, 1297a6.

[3] See my attempts in Mansfield (1968, 1971).

clarification from political science.[4]

As far as I can see in the research of others, the classical understanding of the regime prevailed in medieval usage before Machiavelli. It is often not easy to see whether partisan regime or impersonal state is in question, because of the unhistorical habit, almost universal in medieval historians, of using the term "state" before it occurs or as it was not used in history (Chabod, 1964, p. 27). This habit is a form of superiority which implies that the observer knows what is going on better than the participant, as, for example, when the observer knows that the participant lives in a "medieval" period whereas the participant knew or conceived no such thing. Many medieval historians are in truth scholars of the unnoticed beginnings of modernity. Sometimes they speak of "the state" as taking shape, implying that the state is essentially modern; sometimes they contrast the "medieval state" with the "modern state," implying that the state is essentially universal. Although Aristotle founded his political science on the distinction between *polis* and *politeia,* one can find both terms (in their Latin equivalents, *civitas* and *respublica* or *politia*) translated as "state" (Kantorowicz, 1957, pp. 214-216; Post, 1964, pp. viii, 39; Tierney, 1982, pp. 23, 39). This is not to say that "state" was from the first used impersonally (I shall argue that Machiavelli's use of *stato* was not impersonal, much less that words are always used with full awareness of their meaning, or that meanings of words never change. But caution compels us to question whether the "state" is progressive or universal, as it may appear to us.

The word "state" does indeed occur in political contexts in the Middle Ages, but to name the regime, not a neutral, impersonal state. In this usage the Latin *status* does not stand alone, but requires some accompanying word or phrase to specify whose *status*.[5] The "State of the Church" (*status ecclesiae*) or "state of the realm" (*status regni*) has the general meaning of "state" as condition, still in use today, in which one must specify the condition of what. The condition implied is a condition of stability or a good condition, so that *status* could mean the welfare (of the realm) or the well-being (of the Church) which sets limits on the actions of the pope.[6] *Status* did

not mean the extent of effective power, when power is abstracted from its particular ends and is generalized as the power to do anything. When *status* comes to mean abstract, general power, effective for any end, we see the connection between state as a general or universal condition and state as sovereign, and we recognize the modern state.

To illustrate the meaning of *status,* we may consider Thomas Aquinas' commentary on Aristotle's *Politics* (c. 1260), an authoritative source because of its influence and because its object is political science, not legal argument. Neither Thomas in his commentary nor William of Moerbeke in his translation makes use of *status* for the discussion of the regime in the third book of the *Politics.* But *status* does enter the revision of Aquinas' commentary made by Ludovicus de Valentia in 1492 using Leonardo Bruni's translation of Aristotle from the early fifteenth century.[7] As instances of a general rejection of Moerbeke's Grecisms, *oligarchia* becomes *status paucorum,* and *democratia, status populuris.* This is done in a context where the *politia* (regime) is said to be nothing other than the *ordo dominantum* in the city (Aquinas, 1951, III.6, 385, 392-395). The "state of the few," then, is their domination; but it is also their condition, order, or way of life, which is the condition of the city where they dominate. This thoroughly unmodern identification of the *power* in a society with the *condition* of that society, which makes its politics responsible for its way of life, seems characteristic of medieval usage, and of Florentine usage as well, before Machiavelli.[8]

It is generally agreed that the modern state was constituted by an abstraction from personal to impersonal rule, but it is not generally appreciated how radical that abstraction was. To move from *status* with its concrete specification to *status* or state without such specification was not enough, if the state thus abstracted still refers to someone's or some group's personal rule, although it does not matter which. That state is no more abstract than Aristotle's regime, the term for which can stand alone but always signifies one or another form of personal rule. Skinner (1978, vol. 2, p. 356) finds the earliest impersonal use of "state"

---

[4]One should immediately add that clarification is needed from political science that is aware of the classical regime; see Post (1964, pp. 7, 247).

[5]See Condorelli (1923, 90:80); Dowdall (1923, p. 101); Post (1964, pp. 270, 371n); see the exceptions in Tierney (1963, p. 386) and Meyer (1950, p. 230).

[6]See Post (1964, pp. 298-306); Kantorowicz (1957, p. 271n); Tierney (1982, pp. 17, 64, 70); Powicke (1936, pp. 8-11).

[7]On this humanist outrage upon Aquinas, see Cranz (1978, pp. 171-173); Dondaine (1964, pp. 590-592); Grabmann (1941, p. 77); Martin (1952, pp. 41-47); Aquinas (1971, pp. 15-21).

[8]See Rubinstein (1971, pp. 313-326). But I cannot follow Rubinstein when he says that Leonardo Bruni, clarifying Aquinas, "distinguishes clearly between government and the groups of individuals controlling it" (p. 316). He seems to me clearly to equate the two, in accord with Aquinas and Aristotle.

852   The American Political Science Review   Vol. 77

to be, perhaps in Thomas Starkey's *A Dialogue between Reginald Pole and Thomas Lupset* (Starkey, 1948), completed in 1535. There one finds "the whole state" (p. 57), "the perfect state" (pp. 69, 111), and "a mixed state" (p. 165). But in these instances and in all others I could find (see esp. pp. 57, 64, 89, 99, 155, 164, 165, 167), "state" is used in the traditional Aristotelian sense of regime. For Starkey, the state was both the condition of being ruled and the rulers, with no hint of a distinction between state and society. Starkey used the term "state" impersonally, but he had by no means achieved the radical abstraction of an impersonal state.

Thus, to look for the rise of the modern state in the fashioning of sovereignty may be misleading, if it is done without attention to the peculiar character of sovereignty in the modern state. Modern sovereignty is impersonal, and the modern sovereign prescribes what he must (which may be much) only or mainly to keep the peace and his own power intact (see Calasso, 1957, p. 164). But if one is content to seek sovereignty in uncontested power, one will mistake the rediscovery of the regime in Aristotle's *Ethics* and *Politics,* which occurred in the thirteenth century, for the modern state.[9] The Aristotelian regime was not a way-station toward the modern state, however, but rather the greatest obstacle to its conception.

The rediscovery of the Aristotelian regime did undermine the legal character of medieval political thought. For according to Aristotle, the regime, or the human legislator, is the source of law, rather than law the source of the regime (*Politics* 1282b8-14, 1289a13-15). The reassertion of this truth could not fail to subvert the fundamental premises both of Roman law, the pretense by which an empire is presented as the choice of a republic, and of canon law, the claim that law has a divine source. Those who find the origin of the impersonal, modern state in the legal conceptions of medieval corporatism also underestimate the radical nature of the modern state. To realize the impersonality of the modern state, it is not enough merely to distinguish between person and office, since that separation is already accomplished in the offices of the Aristotelian regime. The modern state requires much more: that offices not be used for personal rule according to the opinions of the rulers. If this is to happen, the state as a corporation must be radically abstracted from the actual persons who govern through it. The medieval corporation, often called *universitas,* was the legal person of a preexisting group,

for example the monks of a monastery. It conferred a legal immortality on their group, thus a certain impersonality, but it did not require the monks to abstract from their character as monks when constituting the *universitas.*

A greater abstraction occurred when *universitas* was used to describe the community that was the source of law beyond communities existing under the law.[10] But again, although a legal person, the *universitas* was a particular community, a particular people having an existence before its legal existence; the legality conferred by incorporation was a baptism, not a creation (Michaud-Quantin, 1970, p. 55). Hence, as Brian Tierney explains the principle of medieval corporatism, the people command as *universitas* but obey as individuals (Tierney, 1982, pp. 57-58, 80). This is the precise opposite of the principle by which the modern state is incorporated; according to Hobbes and our present understanding, we are free as individuals and obey as citizens. The modern state is created by incorporation from the "state of nature" or something like it. The modern state is not merely a legalized, incorporated regime; it is artificial in order to abstract from any regime that might be lurking behind the medieval corporation.

With Machiavelli, however, we encounter a fundamental challenge to the classical regime which is expressed in his use of *stato.* At first sight Machiavelli's use of *stato* appears quite traditional (as Skinner says[11]) or Aristotelian, that is, quite foreign to us, for we are struck by the phrases *suo stato* and *loro stato,* which frequently inform us that the impersonal modern state is not in question.[12] At the same time we frequently encounter *lo stato* standing by itself, which might make us think that the impersonality of the modern state is under way. But such an impression would be misleading. With us *the* state sig-

---

[9]See Morrall (1971, p. 80), Ullmann (1961, p. 293; 1975, p. 272).

[10]See Tierney (1982, pp. 22-26, 36, 42, 73); Mochi Onory (1951, p. 259); Kantorowicz (1957, p. 272); Michaud-Quantin (1970, pp. 7, 40-41, 55, 57); Canning (1980, pp. 12-13, 31); Keen (1965, p. 110). See also John of Salisbury (*Policratus* IV 2) for the expression *universitas rei politicae;* this is a *universitas* of the regime which as such precedes the law but ought to live by the law. Understanding of the classical regime did not have to await the rediscovery of Aristotle's *Politics* a century later.

[11]Skinner (1978, vol. 2, p. 354); Post (1964, pp. 365-366); Ercole (1926, p. 66); DeVries (1957, pp. 70, 80-81); D'Entrèves (1967, p. 30); Hexter (1973, pp. 173-175).

[12]DeVries (1957, pp. 58-59); Chiappelli (1969, p. 36n; cf. 1952, pp. 59-73). See also *stato loro proprio,* "their own state," in *Florentine Histories* VI 8, and "those to whom the state belonged," *Florentine Histories* VII 2.

nifies something impersonal, and we do not use a possessive pronoun. When Machiavelli uses *lo stato* without a possessive pronoun, however, he seems always to imply one. Merely because the word *stato* in the Italian of Machiavelli and of his contemporaries had acquired the ability to stand alone by contrast to the Latin *status,* it does not follow that *stato* meant "impersonal state" any more than did *politia* in Moerbeke's translation of Aristotle's *politeia,* which also stood by itself. The phrases Skinner cites (1978, vol. 2, p. 354) as possible counter-examples suggesting a tincture of impersonality in Machiavelli's *stato*—*la maestrà dello stato, l'autorità dello stato, la mutazione dello stato*—prove on examination to refer to the majesty, authority, and change of *someone's* state. The someone may be collective, as in *stato di Firenze,* but that does not make Florence's state any less personal than Aristotle's *status popularis* (in Bruni's translation in Aquinas' commentary), which is a regime belonging to the people. If the *stato di Firenze* includes Pisa, that is because Pisa belongs to the Florentines.

When Machiavelli says at the end of the ninth chapter of *The Prince* that the wise prince should think of a way by which his citizens always have need *dello stato e di lui,* he distinguishes that prince from the state but hardly denies that the state is the prince's (cf. DeVries, 1957, p. 61; *Florentine Histories* VI 35). When he says in the same place that *lo stato* has need of the citizens, he obviously refers to that same prince's state. And in the eighteenth chapter of the *Discourses on Livy,* when he speaks of the difficulty of maintaining *lo stato libero* in a corrupt city, the difficulty is that of keeping free the state belonging to a corrupt people, not that of keeping an impersonal state free. For, as we learn in the sixteenth chapter, even the *libero stato* has partisan friends and enemies.

Stato can also appear in an objective genitive, as in *stato di Lombardia* and *stato di Asia* (*Florentine Histories* I 37; *The Prince,* chap. 4). These "states" did not belong to Lombardy and Asia, but they did belong to Filippo Visconti and Alexander, respectively. Machiavelli refers to *quello stato* "which had ruled from 1381 to 1434" in Florence (*Florentine Histories,* III 29), meaning "that state" that was held by and passed through many hands in those years. But neither many hands at one time nor different hands over time make Machiavelli's *stato* any more impersonal than Aristotle's regime.[13] Nor does a personifica-

tion of *stato,* which occurs rarely in Machiavelli, signify the presence of the modern impersonal state, because the state that is personified is still someone's, like the Aristotelian regime. *Né creda mai alcuno stato* ("nor should any state ever believe," *The Prince,* chap. 21) states clearly in the context what "the prince" should never believe, although "prince" here refers to the Venetians and the Florentines. And *il sospetto che lo stato aveva* ("the suspicion that the state had," *Florentine Histories* III 23) refers to the "princes of the state" soon after. *Questi stati tengono il cuore disarmato e le mani e li piedi armati* ("these states keep their hearts unarmed and their hands and feet armed," *Discourses on Livy,* II 30) refers to a mistake of both princes and republics in regard to their states. *Stato* is not made impersonal with its own verb any more than with the impersonal article so long as someone's or some party's personal state is meant (cf. DeVries, 1957, p. 79; Ercole, 1926, p. 77). One person's *stato* can be exchanged for another's (*Florentine Histories* VI 30); so *stato* is not as personal as an old shoe. As we shall see, *stato* is personal not because it suits you but because you have acquired it. The *arte dello stato* that Machiavelli said he had been studying for 15 years (in the letter of December 10, 1513 in which he casually announces he has completed *The Prince;* cf. letter of April 9, 1513) is the universal or impersonal art of maintaining personal domination (cf. Chiappelli, 1969, p. 36n). Without prolonging this discussion, I cannot say that I have found in any of Machiavelli's writings an instance of the impersonal modern state among his uses of *stato.*

This does not mean, however, that Machiavelli's *stato* is a regime in the traditional or classical sense. As J. H. Hexter has shown in his well-known study, *stato* in *The Prince* is used almost invariably in an exploitative sense: someone is almost always exploiting someone else by means of *lo stato.*[14] It might be better to say that *stato is* such exploitation,[15] and one might wish to avoid the anachronism "exploitation" and speak of

[14]Hexter (1973); Ercole (1926, p. 107); Sternberger (1974, pp. 42-43). Consider Machiavelli's famous joke: "For when the Cardinal of Rouen said to me that the Italians do not understand war, I replied to him that the French do not understand about the state" (*non si intendovano dello stato; The Prince,* chap. 3). Note the rare instances of *reggimento* in *Florentine Histories* II, 11, 32.

[15]Hexter (1973, p. 171) speaks almost in successive sentences of Machiavelli's *stato* as an instrument and as the object of exploitation. As instrument of exploitation *stato* implies the existence of something like "the state" with which to exploit others. Hexter seems here to slip into the error of presupposing the modern state, for

[13]Cf. DeVries (1957, p. 65) and Rubinstein (1971, p. 319). For Strayer (1970, p. 10), permanent, impersonal institutions, together with authority and loyalty, suffice to make a state; so he asserts, "certainly the Greek polis was a state." See Aristotle *Politics* 1301b6-13.

domination (*dominio*) or mastery (*signoria*) or empire (*imperio*) as Machiavelli does. Machiavelli comes as close as he ever does to a definition of *stato* in the first sentence of *The Prince:* "All states, all dominions [*dominii*] that have had and have empire [*imperio*] over men have been and are either republics or principalities."[16] Here "states," either republics or principalities, are in apposition to "dominions" that have "empire" over men. A quick survey of some features of Machiavelli's political thought will show how far this empire over men is from the Aristotelian regime (cf. Sternberger, 1974, pp. 38-39, 56-66).

Machiavelli's *stato* is someone's to acquire or to maintain. The state itself never acquires or maintains on its own account separate from the advantage of some person or group: this is the critical test that tells us Machiavelli's state is not impersonal (Ercole, 1926, pp. 150-151). But if *stato* is always the advantage of someone over someone else, acquiring and maintaining the state cannot be equally important. In the second chapter of *The Prince,* Machiavelli lets us think that the hereditary prince, who has not acquired his principality, is "the natural prince" because he maintains it more easily. But in the third chapter we are rudely informed of "the natural and ordinary desire to acquire," and in the sixth chapter we learn that those princes who acquire their states with difficulty and by virtue, in total contrast to hereditary princes, keep them with ease. Meanwhile, in the fifth chapter of the *Discourses,* Machiavelli says that those who want to maintain their possessions have the same wish as those who want to acquire, namely, the wish to acquire, since men do not think they possess anything securely unless they are acquiring something new. One cannot sit still to maintain what one has, we learn in the next chapter, because "all human things are in motion." Thus in both *The Prince* and the *Discourses,* for both princes and republics, acquisition comes first.

This conclusion, so contrary to Aristotle's politics as well as his ethics, cannot but affect Machiavelli's notion of *stato.*[17] I shall mention three changes it produces by comparison to Aristotle's

regime, in the ordering of the state, the claims it advances, and the neutrality it recommends.

First, whereas for Aristotle the regime is "some ordering of the inhabitants of the city" that remains visible in its form as long as the regime lasts, for Machiavelli the "order" or "orders" of the state must be subject to change.[18] Given the necessity to acquire and the consequent loosening of moral restraint, neither princes nor republics can afford to retain subordinates or maintain institutions that become inconvenient. Princes must be capable of using others as Cesare Borgia, himself the instrument of his father Alexander VI, used Remirro de Orco (*The Prince,* chap. 7); and in republics, "orders" must be manipulated with new "modes" and then changed into new orders when the "matter" of a city is becoming corrupted or when an emergency arises, for example the challenge to the Senate posed by ambitious leaders of the plebeians. In both cases the true ordering of the state is not what appears to the public, but what goes on behind the scenes; and this contrast is confirmed and expanded by the obvious importance of conspiracy in Machiavelli's political thought in comparison to Aristotle's (Mansfield, 1979, on *Discourses* III 6). What is visible in Machiavelli's state is not the character of power, but rather its effectual extent. With this difference we are on the way toward defining the state by its territory and people (cf. Shennan, 1974, p. 25).

Second, the necessity to acquire determines the characteristic claims of states. Since states must acquire, they must yield to, nay incite, the desire for glory in those men of a princely nature who most evince that desire. At the same time, the people must be conciliated and their desire for security satisfied when possible, if only to maintain the glory of princes and princely leaders in republics. If a common good is sought between princes and peoples, it must accommodate their diverse but complementary desires for glory and security, whatever the claims of regimes may be. Although Machiavelli keeps the traditional Roman distinction between principalities and republics, he does not stress the characteristically opposing claims of those regimes; he throws cold water both on the typical republican hatred for "the name of prince" and on princely disdain for the fickleness of popular government (*Discourses on Livy,* I 58, II 2). He erodes the traditional distinction with such phrases as "princes in the republic" and "civil principality" and with similar advice to both on how to misbehave. Despite their contrasting claims to virtue, states are to be judged by their "effectual truth" in acquiring glory and maintaining security. One hardly need add that,

---

which he indicated Chiappelli (pp. 173-175). For more on Machiavelli's *stato,* see Chabod (1967, pp. 631-637); Gilbert (1965, pp. 326-330); and Whitfield (1947, pp. 93-95).

[16]See Dowdall (1923, p. 110); Condorelli (1923, p. 87). Note that nothing is said in Machiavelli's sentence about the future.

[17]Aristotle *Politics* 1267a30-32 and Machiavelli *Discourses on Livy* I 6 (end); see also *Politics* 1257b38-1258a1, 1323a34-1323b21, 1365a6-8; *Nicomachean Ethics* 1129b1-3.

[18]*Politics* 1247b38; *Discourses on Livy* I 18.

for Machiavelli, glory and security are in this world. It was to prevent the appropriation of the classical regime and its claims of justice by the city of God and the "Christian republic" that he directed the attention of both republics and principalities toward worldly gain.

Thus, on returning to the first sentence of *The Prince*, we can see that Machiavelli's use of *stato* enables him to be neutral between republics and principalities. Whereas for Aristotle the better regimes are regimes in a truer sense than the worse ones,[17] for Machiavelli principalities are as much states as are republics. His well-known but not always well-examined preference for republics is carefully qualified: the common good "is not observed if not in republics," but it consists in the oppression of the few by the many, and to be conquered by a republic is the hardest slavery.[18] Nothing prevents a prince in a "civil principality" (*The Prince*, chap. 9) from benefiting the people as much as they may be in a free republic, and in any case Machiavelli sees quite clearly that *stato* won by collective selfishness has no moral superiority over that acquired by individual selfishness. The reason is that they hardly differ. Just as every prince needs a people, so every people needs a head—an ambitious tribune, consul, dictator, or senate—to direct it as a people in its acquisitions.

Machiavelli's neutrality is evident in his use of the medieval term for corporation, *università*, in chapter 19 of *The Prince*. Although in earlier chapters he had stressed the need for the prince to have the favor, or at least to avoid the hatred, of the people in order to maintain his state, he now suddenly changes his tune. Since the prince cannot help being hated by someone, Machiavelli discloses for the first time, he is at first compelled not to be hated by the *università* (that is, the people or everyone); but when he cannot do this, he must contrive to avoid the hatred of the most powerful *università* (in the plural), that is, the soldiers. Thus Machiavelli's preference for a democratic over an undemocratic policy is not absolute and is determined by necessity, not choice. In this statement of it he uses the medieval term *università* in both senses of corporation within the law and community that is the source of law, but with brusque disregard for law and legality.

I conclude that the path to the modern state was not by way of Machiavelli's republicanism, as Pocock (1975, pp. vii-viii) has argued. His repub-

licanism shows no more of the impersonality of the modern state than does his advice to princes. A republic is the *stato* of a certain group as a principality is the *stato* of the prince, in both cases an effectual acquisition. An effectual acquisition is one properly maintained, that is, continually refreshed with new acquisitions. Rather than in his republicanism, such as it was, Machiavelli's step toward the impersonality of the modern state can be seen in his impartial advice to all parties and persons to acquire when they can. The very universality of his advice to be partial to oneself requires that he be neutral between the parties he advises, for example between princes and republics (see Mansfield, 1981, pp. 293-305). Republicanism, therefore, is not a continuous tradition from ancient to modern times, for somewhere between ancient and modern republicanism the concept of the impersonal modern state was introduced. Aristotle lacks it, and Rousseau (*Social Contract* I 6) has it. This concept came not from within republicanism, but from an attitude of neutrality toward republics in the old sense of partisan regimes, which required a transformation of the republican spirit. To this consideration, one should add the impressive and obvious fact that everywhere in the West the modern state was, or was the work of, a monarchy.

Nonetheless, to say that the change from the personal state to the impersonal state was "the decisive shift," as Skinner does (1978, vol. 1, p. ix), is somewhat misleading. Rather, the decisive shift was from the personal state in the Aristotelian sense to the *acquisitive* personal state of Machiavelli. For this change provided the impartiality that is fundamental to the modern state. Implicit in Machiavelli's general advice to acquire was an impartial regard for all who might be capable of applying it. After this it was but a step (although a step Machiavelli did not take) to a state that might acquire for all and facilitate the acquisitions of all impartially (Orwin, 1978, *72*, 1226-1227). Thus the impersonal modern state was conceived, not in, but out of, the thought of the most personal political philosopher that we know, in the sense of recommending self-aggrandizement. That is why finding medieval anticipations of impersonality does not suffice to explain the modern state, for the modern state expresses Machiavelli's impartial acquisitiveness in its formulations of impersonal legality.

The state of *ragione di stato* appeared in 1589, soon after Machiavelli, in a book of that name by Giovanni Botero, a follower of Machiavelli. That state, as opposed to Machiavelli's, was said to be impartially acquisitive because the reasoning of its *ragione* was not the ruler's but the state's. Hence the state, unlike Machiavelli's, was not oppressive

---

[17]*Politics* 1275b1-3; see Plato, *Laws* 712e; *Statesman* 303c.

[18]*Discourses on Livy* II 2; cf. *Discourses* III 9, and see Mansfield (1979) on *Discourses* 1, 55, 58-59; II 2, 19.

Machiavelli II

to the ruled.²¹ But the full conception of the modern state had to await the political science of Hobbes.

What Skinner calls the "main elements" of the modern state gradually acquired between Machiavelli and Hobbes were mere materials assembled for Hobbes's construction on a foundation prepared by Machiavelli. It was Hobbes who distinguished state from society, thus allowing the state to represent society impartially; he who, to make this distinction, invented the concept of the state of nature yielding natural rights before natural duties and the right of self-preservation generalizing and legalizing Machiavelli's advice to acquire; and he it was who conceived the impersonal state as an artificial person whose words and deeds were "owned" by his subjects, not by himself. Only with a view to Hobbes could we know what the various anticipations of the modern state were anticipating, but the decision in the "decisive shift" to modernity was taken by Machiavelli.

References

Botero, G. *Della Ragion di Stato.* Bologna: Cappelli, 1930.

Calasso, F. *I Glossatori e la teoria della sovranità.* Milan: Guiffrè, 1957.

Canning, J. P. The corporation in the political thought of the Italian jurists of the thirteenth and fourteenth centuries. *History of Political Theory,* 1980, *1,* 9-32.

Chabod, F. Alcuni questioni di terminologia: stato, nazione, patria nel linguaggio del Cinquecento. In F. Chabod (Ed.). *Scritti sul Rinascimento.* Turin: Einaudi, 1967.

Chabod, F. Was there a Renaissance state? In H. Lubasz (Ed.). *The development of the modern state.* New York: Macmillan, pp. 27-36, 1964.

Chiappelli, F. *Nuovi studi sul linguaggio del Machiavelli.* Florence: Le Monnier, 1969.

Chiappelli, F. *Studi sul linguaggio del Machiavelli.* Florence: Le Monnier, 1952.

Condorelli, O. Per la storia del nome "stato." *Archivio Giuridico,* 1923, *89,* 223-235; *90,* 70-112.

Cranz, F. The publishing history of the Aristotle commentaries of Thomas Aquinas. *Traditio,* 1978, *34,* 157-192.

D'Entrèves, A. P. *The notion of the state.* Oxford: Clarendon Press, 1967.

DeVries, H. *Essai sur la terminologie constitutionelle chez Machiavel.* Amsterdam: University of Amsterdam doctoral thesis, 1957.

Dondaine, H. F. Le *Super Politicam* de Saint Thomas. *Revue des Sciences Philosophiques et Théologiques.* 1964, *48,* 585-602.

Dowdall, H. C. The word "state." *Law Quarterly Review.* 1923, *39,* 98-127.

Ercole, F. *La politica di Machiavelli.* Rome: Anonima Romana, 1926.

Friedrich, C. J. *Constitutional reason of state.* Providence, R.I.: Brown University Press, 1957.

Gilbert, F. *Machiavelli and Guicciardini.* Princeton, N.J.: Princeton University Press, 1965.

Grabmann, M. *Die mittelalterlichen Kommentare zur Politik des Aristoteles.* Munich: Sitzungsberichte der Bayerishen Akademie der Wissenschaften, 1941.

Hartung, F. L'état c'est moi. *Historische Zeitschrift,* 1949, *169,* 1-30.

Hexler, J. H. Il principe and lo stato. In J. H. Hexter (Ed.). *The vision of politics on the eve of the Reformation.* New York: Basic Books, 1973.

John of Salisbury. *Policraticus.* (2 vols.). (C. C. J. Webb, Ed.). Oxford: Clarendon Press, 1909. (Completed in 1159.)

Kantorowicz, E. H. *The king's two bodies' a study in medieval political theology.* Princeton, N.J.: Princeton University Press, 1957.

Keen, M. H. The political thought of the fourteenth-century civilians. In B. Smalley (Ed.). *Trends in medieval political thought.* New York: Barnes and Noble, 1965.

Machiavelli, N. *Lettere.* (F. Gaeta, Ed.). Milan: Feltrinelli Editore, 1961.

Machiavelli, N. *Opere politiche.* (M. Puppo, Ed.). Florence: Le Monnier, 1969.

Mansfield, H. C. Jr. Hobbes and the science of indirect government. *American Political Science Review,* 1971, *65,* 97-110.

Mansfield, H. C. Jr. *Machiavelli's new modes and orders: a study of the Discourses on Livy.* Ithaca, N.J.: Cornell University Press, 1979.

Mansfield, H. C. Jr. Machiavelli's political science. *American Political Science Review,* 1981, *75,* 293-305.

Mansfield, H. C. Jr. Modern and medieval representation. *Nomos,* 1968, *11,* 55-82.

Martin, C. The Vulgate text of Aquinas's commentary on Aristotle's *Politics. Dominican Studies,* 1952, *5,* 35-64.

Meyer, A. O. Zur Geschichte des Wortes Staat. *Die Welt als Geschichte,* 1950, *10,* 229-239.

Michaud-Quantin, P. *Universitas: Expressions du Mouvement Communautaire dans le Moyen-Age Latin.* Paris: Vrin, 1970.

Mochi Onory, S. *Fonti canonistiche dell' idea moderna dello stato.* Milan: Vita e Pensiero, 1951.

Morrall, J. B. *Political thought in medieval times.* 3rd ed. London: Hutchinson University Library, 1971.

Orwin, C. Machiavelli's unchristian charity. *American Political Science Review,* 1978, *72,* 1217-1228.

Pocock, J. G. A. *The Machiavellian moment.* Princeton, N.J.: Princeton University Press, 1975.

Post, G. *Studies in medieval legal thought.* Princeton, N.J.: Princeton University Press, 1964.

Powicke, F. M. Reflections on the medieval state. *Transactions of the Royal Historical Society.* 1936, *19,* 1-18.

²¹Botero (1930, pp. 9, 26-33); see Friedrich (1957, p. 4). *Ragione di stato* in Botero substitutes for fraud in Machiavelli, for when the *stato* becomes entitled to its own special reason, it no longer needs fraud. Cf. *per cagione dèllo stato* in Machiavelli's *Florentine Histories* VII 5, to describe a partisan consideration. The connection between reason of state and acquisition separates the former from medieval instances of *ratio status* discussed by Post (1964, pp. 250-301).

Rowen, H. A. L'état, c'est moi: Louis XIV and the state. *French Historical Studies,* 1961, *2,* 83-93.

Rubinstein, N. Notes on the word *stato* in Florence before Machiavelli. In J. G. Rowe & W. H. Stockdale (Eds.). *Florilegium Historiale.* Toronto: University of Toronto Press, 1971.

Shennan, J. H. *The origins of the modern European state, 1450-1725.* London: Hutchinson University Library, 1974.

Skinner, Q. *The foundations of modern political thought.* 2 vols. Cambridge: Cambridge University Press, 1978.

Starkey, T. *A dialogue between Reginald Pole and Thomas Lupset* (K. M. Burton, Ed.). London: Chatto & Windus, 1948.

Sternberger, D. *Machiavelli's "Principe" und der Begriff des Politischen.* Wiesbaden: Steiner, 1974.

Strayer, J. R. *On the medieval origins of the modern state.* Princeton, N.J.: Princeton University Press, 1970.

Tarcov, N. Political thought in early modern Europe.

Journal of Modern History, 1982, *54,* 56-65.

Thomas Aquinas, Saint. *In Libros Politicorum Aristotelis Expositio.* (R. M. Spiazzi, Ed.). Rome: Marietti, 1951.

Thomas Aquinas, Saint. *Sententia Libri Politicorum.* In *Opera Omnia,* Leonine ed. vol. 47. Rome: Ad Sanctae Sabinae, 1971.

Tierney, B. The Prince is not bound by the laws; Accursius and the origins of the modern state. In B. Tierney (Ed.). *Church law and constitutional thought in the Middle Ages.* London: Variorum Reprints, 1963, *3,* 378-400.

Tierney, B. *Religion, law, and the growth of constitutional thought, 1150-1650.* Cambridge: Cambridge University Press, 1982.

Ullmann, W. *Law and politics in the Middle Ages.* Ithaca, N.Y.: Cornell University Press, 1975.

Ullmann, W. *Principles of government and politics in the Middle Ages.* New York: Barnes and Noble, 1961.

Whitfield, J. H. *Machiavelli.* Oxford: Blackwell, 1947.

[16]

MACHIAVELLI IN THE LIBERAL COSMOS

J. G. A. POCOCK
The Johns Hopkins University

ACHIAVELLI demands assignation to contexts: to his own, which we must recover if we are to understand him, and to our own, in which we must read him if we are to interpret him. In the language of Wilamowitz, recently quoted by Hugh Lloyd-Jones,[1] we must give our blood to the ghosts if they are to speak to us, but then empty them of it if they are not to speak with our own voices. You put your heart's blood in, you take your heart's blood out. It is not easy, but has to be tried. Two recent interpreters of Machiavelli have trouble with history, as we all must; but the troubles they have are interesting in proportion as their enterprises are intelligently designed. Mark Hulliung's[2] troubles are of his own making; he wants to take Machiavelli out of history and make him a contemporary—he appears to regard history as the creation of a false liberal consensus—but the contemporary he rigorously defines emerges as an oddly archaic figure. Hanna Fenichel Pitkin's[3] problems are far more interesting, because they are not rooted in misunderstanding, but in the nature of her enterprise. She attempts to interpret Machiavelli's thought as containing flaws and ambivalences that may be attributed to inadequacies in his perception of gender; his understanding of humanity is incomplete and his understanding of masculinity insecure, because women are excluded from his perception of life and return to it in distorted and menacing shapes. One wants this enterprise to succeed, because there is obviously a great deal of truth in the proposition; but the difficulties are formidable and have not yet been overcome.

To begin with, the terms in which we explain gender relations are hard to make culturally or historically specific. The analyses of the probable development of infantile sexuality, which Pitkin presents along Freudian and Kleinian lines, are interesting and plausible, but

POLITICAL THEORY, Vol. 13 No. 4, November 1985 559-574
© 1985 Sage Publications, Inc.

would clearly apply about as well to Athens or Boston as to Florence; there are difficulties, consequently, in linking them to the history-specific knowledge that we have of any one of these cultures. The historian is plagued by missing links in the journey from the breast to the polis; this does not mean that the question is *mal posé*, only that we are having major difficulty in giving answers. A radical response is that the two are not linked: that women have been so thoroughly excluded from the public structures created by men, in which the acts and reflections constituting history as we know it have been performed, that they have inhabited a different historical *durée* that must be recovered by different historiographical techniques. But this does not abolish the problems that arise as soon as it is claimed that the male world can be understood, and its history written, by attention to the absence or the distorted presence of women.

This claim is evidently true, and true of Machiavelli; yet to say that it is true does not of itself tell us how to make its truth historically arguable. It is one thing to say that what is present is distorted by what is absent; it is another to show, in any real detail, how this has been happening. And the counter-factual tends to be based on a value judgment: What might have happened but did not will almost certainly turn out to be what we could wish had happened. How else can we imagine it? Pitkin can tell us that Machiavelli's perceptions are flawed by the exclusion of women, but not what they would have been like if they had not been flawed in this way. She has far too good an apprehension of history to try to tell us, but she cannot escape leaving us faced with this unanswerable question: answerable, that is, in terms of our perceptions and what they ought to be like, but never in terms of what a sixteenth-century Florentine's perceptions were not but might have been. Machiavelli, then, becomes a tool for telling us how we do and how we might think. There remains the possibility that the tool may turn in our hand and ask us questions about the question we are using it to ask and answer. When tools are texts, this sometimes happens.

Pitkin aims to prove two contentions: first, that Machiavelli's perception of political manhood is so deeply flawed that it is self-destructive; second, that this is connected with his inability to perceive women as anything but a force alien and menacing to political life—the force typified as the female figure of Fortune, whom the political man of *virtù* must beat and subdue, because she likes it if he does but will unman and destroy him if he doesn't. I shall argue that the two perceptions are severally to be found in Machiavelli, but that the association between them (which I am disposed to accept) ought to be more strongly made out than it is by Pitkin. In the first place, that Machiavelli presents the political man as a being radically flawed by nature is beyond doubt; one has only to consider the implications of identifying him with the centaur. If man is by nature a political animal, and the political animal is half man and half beast, it inexorably follows that man is by nature only half a man, which is contradiction sufficient.[4] Whether Machiavelli is saying this because he is deeply unsure of his own manliness is, however, another question; and where that uncertainty comes from, if it exists, is another. Up to now the accepted reading has been that Machiavelli wrote in this way not because of something he failed to perceive about women, but because of something he did perceive about politics; and whether politics are (if they are) as Machiavelli perceived them in consequence of women being excluded from them by men (as they have been) is the question at the bottom of the barrel.

But Pitkin does not make much use of the centaur image, preferring to rely on another of Machiavelli's beast analogies: the proposition that the prince (or political man) needs to be both lion and fox (they appear, heraldically supporting what seems to be a Tudor rose, on the jacket of Hulliung's book). She is insistent that Machiavelli never succeeds, or believes that he has succeeded, in bringing lion and fox together, and that consequently none of his images of political man really work or convince him. Something is trapping Machiavelli, she tells us—and what can it be but an incomplete and obsessive vision of sexuality?—so that, much as he admires the fox for running to and fro, smelling out the traps before the lion can fall into them, the fox is himself trapped; Machiavelli is trapped in his own foxiness. To make her case, she presents the fox as cunning because he lacks the lion's strength and is therefore dependent on a being less intelligent than he is; the fox is a jackal. There is evidence for this presence in Machiavelli's vision, no doubt; there is Ligurio the con man and go-between in *Mandragola*, content to supply the ideas by which the richer but stupider Callimaco wil get the girl. Machiavelli openly identifies himself with Ligurio. But here we have to do with the figure of the parasite, an ancient figure in Greco-Roman comedy (he has been known to beat the lion to it and get the girl himself). That Ligurio-Machiavelli is a parasite is not enough to make the fox a parasite every time he appears, or to render the lion-fox composite forever unrealizable, as Pitkin seems to be contending. The fox-figure in European literature and mythology is bigger and more complex than this. Certainly, if Machiavelli fails to see this and can never present the fox as more than a jackal, it will go far to prove Pitkin's point; but does he so fail?

In one perspective, the lion stands for *virtù,* the power to dominate contingencies, the fox for *prudenza,* the power to manipulate them. Machiavelli incessantly argued for the primacy of *virtù* over *prudenza* against his friend Guicciardini. I am tempted to contend that Guicciardini was the foxier of the two because he had more standing and clout in politics than Machiavelli, not because he had less. But there is a relationship between *prudenza* and comparative lack of power. Machiavelli emphasized the *virtù* of the armed democratic city, Guicciardini the *prudenza* of the diplomatically savvy few in a *città disarmata.* However, to oppose the two in an either-or choice was only a game unless it was really impossible to combine them; and in Machiavelli's central (and very unpleasing) sexual image they are combined. The prince who is both lion and fox is to attain a sexual ascendancy over Fortune, and the assumption has to be that women enjoy being seduced by superior cunning as much as they enjoy being dominated by superior force. It appears (regrettably) quite as easy to make this assumption as to have doubts of it, and to say that it is a fantasy is not to say that Machiavelli admitted that it was one.

If we extrapolate from Machiavelli's *erotica* to his *politica,* the lion and the fox will prove to stand for something rather important. The city is not self-sufficient; it exists in a geography and history of contingencies and givens, factual and moral, some of which antedate its being and others of which will arise in a future it cannot determine. Fortune stands for this contingent world, especially if we perceive it without God. The city seeks a total determination of its environment, and therefore has to choose between creating that environment and manipulating it; the problem of time—of temporization, about and against which Machiavelli had so much to say—arises because there is no moment of creation in political history, no absolute freedom for the city or its founder to create a new world, but only a series of moments (may I add of Machiavellian moments?) at which some givens can be changed and some cannot, some can be preserved and some cannot. The prince (or the city) is not a god; consequently, he cannot be all lion, neither can lion and fox be combined to form a new kind of creature. The prince must be both lion and fox, but cannot be both at the same time; he must live in a time series, changing from one to the other. The problem of time, stated like this, appears to be independent of the problem of gender. How do the two interact?

Pitkin asks why Machiavelli allows himself to become engrossed with the deeply ambivalent figure of the Founder (Lycurgus, Romulus) who exists at the beginning of a city's life in time, unconstrained by givens or contingencies; why he says of the Founder, first, that he will commit terrible acts—fratricide if he is Romulus, filicide if he is Brutus—and, second, that as there is no moment without antecedents, it is impossible that he should exist at all. Why imagine so dreadful a demiurge, unless forced to it by some inner trauma? The question is good, but can be asked of others besides Machiavelli. Whatever became, one wishes to ask, of the pious Aeneas, who founded Rome in the pieties he brought with him from Troy and erected a city with a better civil religion than most Greek foundations? Why was Augustine as determined as Machiavelli to ignore this dutiful man and think only of the terrible and ambivalent Romulus? And to name Aeneas is to remember Dido, the only woman Founder we hear of in the mythography, who seems to have been doing quite well until the Trojans came and entrapped her in romantic subordination, but whose city survived her to become Rome's great commercial and military rival, the Venice of antiquity. Neither Augustine nor Machiavelli makes anything of Dido; nor does Pitkin. Virgil seems to fail as a creator of political archetypes. But if it should be the point that for a woman there are always antecedents, contingencies, and pieties, Dido and Aeneas are on the same side; they respect the moralities inherent in the given, and their politics are Burkean, not Promethean or Machiavellian. Would Pitkin have us accept this great paradigm of Augustan conservatism?

Lion and fox are now becoming ways of coping with historicity: two ways of acting in time. The woman figure of Fortune is being made to stand for time and its contingencies, never for its pieties, which only males appreciate; and the problem of gender politics in Machiavelli is to see why this happens and what it means. Pitkin makes much, and I would like to make more, of a Machiavellian fragment in which both women and beasts perform exceedingly significant roles. This is the *Asino*, an unfinished poem in which Machiavelli set himself the ambitious program of burlesquing, simultaneously, the Circe episode in the *Odyssey*, the *Golden Ass* of Apuleius, and the *Divine Comedy* of Dante, whom he admired deeply and several times tried to send up. Not surprisingly, he abandoned the enterprise after a few cantos.

As the poem opens, a narrator Machiavelli, lost in a wood like Dante, is accosted by a young woman who is herding the beasts into which Circe has transformed men. We gather that he is to take on an ass's shape like Lucius and undergo a metamorphic journey among the beasts, not unlike Dante's journey among the damned, learning how each was transformed by his dominant appetite, until he himself is ready to renew his humanity. But at this point in what is usually an *ascesis*, the narrator and his guide go to bed together. (What happens sounds more like premature ejaculation than orgasm, but there is a literary joke in charge here, so we let it pass.) Pitkin rather oddly says that the herdswoman "seduces" the hero, and she certainly takes the initiative; but the episode is one of mutual pleasure and friendship, unfortunately rare in erotic literature: the lovers talk together of many things, like friends. However, they do not seem to have talked about politics, because no sooner has she left in the morning for her day's work as a herder than Machiavelli jumps out of bed and begins thinking about politics in sixteenth-century Italy. After this interruption—it seems the right word—the poem is never really resumed. There is a long conversation with a figure other authors called Gryllus, who prefers to be a pig rather than a man; and nothing more. The hero never completes his underground journey or recovers a lost humanity. We never meet Circe or complete our knowledge of her significance. It is as if the politics had destroyed the poem.

Machiavelli has introduced sexuality in a way calculated to challenge his models. Intercourse bestializes Lucius and turns him into the Ass; Beatrice sends Virgil as her agent and is beyond sex herself. The hero of the *Asino* makes love in a way that seems to presage his renewed humanity; but then comes the violent turn from love to politics. It is inescapable that Machiavelli is saying that the two don't mix; immediately after about the only happy sexual encounter in all his writings, he announces that politics is a man's affair, from which erotics is only a distraction. There seems, however, to be a further implication: that there is probably no erotic Beatrice and certainly no political one. *Das ewige Weibliche* may lead to the psychopompic journey, in which the self is lost and transformed; intercourse with a real woman in all probability doesn't. As for politics, it is not transformative at all (Donato Giannotti, who says this noncynically,[5] may have learned it from Machiavelli); its business is not the death and renewal of the self, but the association of (masculine) selves to reinforce and better one another. Perhaps the city is the perfection of the political animal, but a political animal who embarks on a solitary journey toward self-renewal is wasting his time. Machiavelli has started the wrong poem and must break it off.

We can now situate him at a point where he could have constructed a concrete and humane erotics and politics simultaneously, and say that the violent caesura he interposes between the two proves that there was some reason why he couldn't. This is Pitkin's central argument, although we have yet to discover the reason and can never imagine the counter-factual. What a two-gender politics would have looked like in Machiavelli's historical universe is really unthinkable (the Abbey of Theleme is not a polis). But there is a buried politics, which may tell us something about Machiavelli's problems, in an aspect of the *Asino* we have not yet considered.

Although we do not meet Circe, she provides the fragment with its central myth: Men are transformed into beasts by their appetites, and to be human is to master them. The question not asked or answered in the *Asino* is how this is to be done by political association; the poem was the wrong way of asking it. But in the *Odyssey* itself, a prepolitical epic, Circe is overcome by Odysseus. Her magic has the effect of making him more manly and godlike than before, after which sexual intercourse between them is no threat to either, and he resumes a voyage that is not a search for the self. In the *Asino* we do not meet Odysseus, and there seems no way for the Machiavelli narrator to assume his role; the poem is a rejection of another kind of journey. But there are ways of exploiting his encounter with Circe that can tell us a great deal.

When Pitkin tells us that the fox figure in Machiavelli is necessarily that of a jackal, we want to disagree with her (or with him, if we accept her reading). The Fox in literature and mythology is a far more powerful figure. He is the Trickster, the Shapechanger, the Hero with a Thousand Faces, the Man of Many Wiles. Sometimes—as Pitkin points out, quoting one Dr. Anton Ehrenzweig—he appears as one of a pair of male personalities (Thor and Loki, Siegfried and Hagen, Esau and Jacob, Othello and Iago, Callimaco and Ligurio) in whom we see the Lion and Fox as two incomplete halves of a personality that has failed to be both at once; so that Pitkin can assume the Fox to stand for the necessary incompleteness of masculinity self-isolated from femininity. But it is doubtful whether Dr. Ehrenzweig was justified in completing his list of Treacherous Twins with the names of Achilles and Odysseus; far from being incomplete without the other, each is complete enough to have furnished Europe with one of its fundamental epics. One is tragic and the other comedic, but these are not modes of incompleteness; they are different kinds of completeness. In the great Riace bronzes now at Reggio di Calabria it is possible to feel you have met Achilles face to face, and very alarming he is: The heroic body and the heroically unreflective intelligence rush upon you, preferring glory to length of days. But there is no statue of Odysseus that I know of, because he is too many-minded to be caught in the bronze;[6] Dante, Tennyson, and Kazantzakis tried to lead him to some final and self-transcending death, but somewhere he is still travelling on, preferring to know many things

566   POLITICAL THEORY / November 1985

rather than one big thing. He is many-minded, polytropic, because he has seen many cities and known their ways.

This Fox is important, even if unmentioned, in the Machiavellian mythography, for the simple reason that Circe is Fortune. She turns men into beasts—that is, into creatures who are less than political animals—by isolating single and dominant appetites till each replaces the whole man. In philosophy reason, in theology the love of God, become that which in each man controls the appetites and keeps him human; in politics the city associates men so that each checks the bestial element in all the others. But Machiavelli's insistent theme is that in politics the city must act, and that its actions are performed by individual men. In a letter to Piero Soderini (the Florentine Jimmy Carter)[7] he gives an explanation of the power of Fortune over men, which Pitkin mentions but does not exploit fully. It is that each actor's personality is the work of his imagination (*fantasia*) and nature, but that the external circumstances he encounters are the work of Fortune; and as the circumstantial, the contingent, and the political contain more variable elements than are contained in the psyche, Fortune is always able to vary the demands of contingency upon individuals in ways that the personality cannot adapt itself to meet in time.

Now—allowing for the element of time, which is not prominent in the *Odyssey*—this is closely akin to what Circe does. She finds personalities dominated by a single drive, in which she then freezes and entraps the personality; Fortune, who is more a political than a moral force, merely faces them with practical demands that they cannot meet and sentences them to political failure. But Circe fails with Odysseus—his human personality is reinforced by her magic, which should destroy it—not because he is single-minded and selfless, but because he is many-minded and polytropic; he is too adaptable for her. How she would have fared with Achilles we do not know. If he is less than Odysseus she changes him into a lion; but probably his love of glory is as irreversibly human as the many-mindedness of Odysseus. All it can do is kill him and (until he finds himself dead) he doesn't mind.

But the Odyssean solution too is ruled out of the *Asino* by politics. Cities, as Pitkin shows, are made up of Founders and Citizens. The Founders exist before Fortune and need only be a special kind of lion; but once they have passed on they are replaced by Citizens, who are individuals and neither heroes nor archetypes. No individual can be both lion and fox; the usurping Prince must try to be, but although he comes as close to it as Cesare Borgia, yet he will fail. But citizens are many, and among them they have many minds (as Aristotle pointed out). Some of them will be more lionlike, others more foxlike, and it is the strength of the polis that it can combine and recombine these qualities, using its collective judgment to appoint magistrates and commanders who have the qualities that the state of contingency calls for. Scipio the lion can be replaced by Fabius the fox when a fox is needed and, should a wrong choice of general lead to disaster at Cannae, still the republic need not despair. There is nothing servile or parasitical about being a fox in the right relation with Fortune: "Massèna is an old fox," wrote Wellington of his opponent, "and as cautious as I am; he risks nothing." The republic can be both lion and fox because it is an association and not an individual; it can be polytropic because it consists of many minds.

I am therefore not quite convinced by Pitkin's attempt to argue that the Machiavellian idea of the republic falls apart because the archetypes of political manliness on which it is built are contradictory to one another. It is true that Machiavelli shows the personality as constantly under almost intolerable stress imposed by historic contingency; but his remedy for this is the republic, which is adaptable because it contains many individuals with diverse personalities, and the individual is invited to associate with those unlike himself. A republic ought not to be resolved (or dissolved) into archetypes confronted with one another; it is composed of individuals, not of archetypes. In this perspective it is an anticipation of liberal society, in which the association can work even if the individuals composing it are imperfect and incompletely harmonized. On the other hand, the republic can have no basis but the virtue of its citizens, and it has always been the liberal criticism of the republic that this basis is narrow, unstable, and, in the end, too harsh an imposition on the individual, so that virtue is destroyed by the demands of too restrictive a conception of it. Here we approach Pitkin's gender-based critique; it is because Machiavelli's conception of humanity is exclusively masculine that it is harsh, insecure, and unworkable. To deny the full humanity of women is to wreck the humanity of men. No one will wish to deny this proposition; the question is whether Pitkin has produced an adequate account of how it works in the case of Machiavelli.

The two chapters that she devotes to a psychological explanation of how the male infant can come to see the female as an exterior and threatening force seem to me to make a wrong choice of strategy. Protection and sustenance are incomprehensibly given and taken away, the argument runs, and so there arises the image of the unpredictable kindness and cruelty of fortune. But this is to make Fortune overwhelmingly a maternal figure, which is not how she appears in the literature; she does not even particularly resemble the Wicked Stepmother. An explanation so much dominated by the infant's experience of the mother or nursing surrogate surely points, as Pitkin's language suggests, toward quite another figure of menacing femininity: the dark, engulfing Earth Mother who gives death where she gives birth, the womb as the grave. Fortune is not like her at all. The Mother stands for the menacing power of nature and the earth, whereas Machiavelli explicitly makes Fortune stand for the terror of a history radically separated from nature; Gryllus the Pig has gone back to the earth to get away from her. All this may be psychoanalytically explained, but we need to recognize the diversity of the images; and historically speaking, we need an explanation of the widespread Renaissance fear of a mutability identified with femininity.[8] All the imagery of wheels and moons and irregular patterns of recurrence loudly declares that we are dealing with male fear of the menstrual cycle, which one would suppose to be postinfantile in origin, although very likely linked with elements in infantile experience. Pitkin does not seem to me to have conducted the right psychoanalytic inquiry or fully recognized the problem as Machiavelli presents it, which is that the mutability of history (which is female) can be overcome only by many-mindedness in the republic (which is male).

One central problem, however, remains. Does the proposition that Fortune is a woman and that women must be dominated (not seduced or married or worshipped) help to explain Machiavelli's all but unequivocal pronouncement that the republic must commit itself to dominating, conquering, and absorbing its neighbors, and must go on until it dominates the whole world? He opposes the "republic for expansion" to the "republic for preservation," says that the former must dominate its neighbors and the latter isolate itself from them, ignores after mentioning the possibility that in ancient Tuscany or modern Germany a plurality of republics may have existed peaceably together, and declares that although the expansive republic will end by destroying itself, glory is preferable to length of days. Why should the republic, which we have seen aim at being both lion and fox, both Achilles and Odysseus, make so exclusively Achillean a commitment? Both Pitkin and Hulliung consider this question.

Pitkin's answer is gender-based: It is Machiavelli's masculinity, insecure because he cannot recognize women in the full humanity of association, that traps him into conceding, and then glorifying, the presupposition that political, or rather interpolitical, relations must in the last resort be relations of domination. The difficulty about her thesis is, of course—and as she well knows—that it can only be tested by supposing a counter-factual: Would our politics be, or would we imagine them as being, any less "Machiavellian" if they were not based on a distorted view of gender? It could easily be a cheap shot to bring up the names of Jiang Qing, Indira Gandhi, and Margaret Thatcher in order to suggest that women in politics are not very different from men, and there would be plenty of comebacks; but it could remind us that Machiavelli has always been understood to say that politics in human life is an independent variable (like Fortune), and that if this is so women in a gender-sane society might still find themselves "Machiavellian" political actors. Pitkin may mean no more than that a sane view of gender might help both men and women to act more agreeably, and this is plausible. But we call "liberal" the assertion that politics is immersed in a context of many interdependent variables, some factual and others moral; and if Pitkin is repudiating that Machiavellian "autonomy of politics" as a masculine error based on a distorted view of gender, her assertion is of the liberal order. None the worse for that; but it does take us into a world of metapolitics, in which we must make statements that are sometimes difficult to test. This is why I could wish her linkages from psychoanalysis to history to politics were rather more specifically worked out.

A mythographic way of approaching the problem of the Achillean republic is to say that although the epic heroes are prepolitical creatures, there is no theoretical difficulty about making Achilles into a citizen; you have only to teach him military and civic discipline—as Machiavelli says, this will call for some unimaginably stern measures—and his glory will become the glory of the republic. Odysseus will be harder to catch; he is polytropic because he has seen many cities and knows their ways, and will not readily accept the discipline of any one of them. He may spend ten years trying to get home to Ithaca, but he knows he won't stay there. His many-mindedness looks beyond glory, and there is something about it incompatible with civic virtue. He will not regard any polis to which he may belong as the origin and cause of all good, and it is the Machiavellian paradox that this assertion is the origin and cause of all "Machiavellism" in politics. If the good is limited to a single city, there is no moral control over its relations with other cities; it must always be at war, always menaced by Fortune, always in need of the lion and fox, and always constrained to choose the lion's role when the play is cast. Odysseus left town some time ago, walking inland and carrying an oar. He has always preferred the cosmopolitan and comic, Achilles the patriotic and tragic. Machiavelli continues to infuriate us by his inveterate preference for black comedy.

I am not quite persuaded, in the last analysis, that Machiavelli opts for republic seeking conquest, glory, and death because of the inadequacies of his understanding of masculinity; it is plausible that it should have been so, but Pitkin does not quite convince me that I have seen the thing happening. And for over two hundred years there has been available another and more materialist explanation of why Machiavelli made this choice, which Pitkin does not consider but which might have been integrated with hers. Before attempting to do so, however, I have to consider the curious fact that this explanation is not mentioned by Mark Hulliung: curious because, as we shall see, Hulliung knows all about it. *Citizen Machiavelli* is an extraordinarily one-eyed book, devoted to the proposition that the choice of conquest, glory, and death is all there is to be said about Machiavelli and that there has been a series of conspiracies to conceal it. Hulliung places it at the center of every reading of every text, bringing all Machiavelli's theses back to the point at which the pursuit of these goals appears as the sole purpose of the enterprise; this, he seems to say, is all Machiavelli ever cared about, and all that need be considered in interpreting him.

Even Machiavelli's erotics are made the effect of his pursuit of conquest; *Mandragola* is deduced from the *Discorsi* in a way almost the reverse of Pitkin's treatment and lumped in, both with Machiavelli's letters to Vettori about whoring—what would we be reading and writing if he had been as compulsively addicted to the chasing and sodomizing of boys as were many Florentines of his generation?—and with his relationship with the actress Barbera, which Hulliung seems to regard as one more proof of his insatiable sexuality. We, in fact, know little about her, except that she was much with Machiavelli in his later years and that her company is said to have played *Mandragola*, but perhaps she was as gay (meaning joyous) and intelligent as the herdswoman of the *Asino*. Some play, novel, or dialogue might be devoted to imagining Machiavelli with a woman to whom he could talk.

But Hulliung writes of politics, and seeks only to show that Machiavelli valued citizenship for the sake of conquest, the free plebeian republic because it could dominate and destroy its neighbors. This has been noticed before, but as Hulliung isolates it and makes it the absolute presupposition of everything Machiavelli ever wrote, he is in a position to declare that it has never been noticed enough, and that those who have noticed it share with those who have not a disposition to deny its importance. A succession of premodern theorists—Guicciardini, Giannotti, Harrington—attempted to play down the option for conquest and integrate Machiavelli's insights into a vision of politics less extreme. A succession of modern historians—Meinecke, Chabod, the two Gilberts, I believe I may add myself—have attempted to show Machiavelli's thought fitting into ongoing patterns of European discourse to which the option for conquest was sometimes central and sometimes not. All these fall under Hulliung's censure, and he condemns both historians and history as concealing the truth that Machiavelli is our contemporary, and that he is most our contemporary when he exercises the option for conquest. History to Hulliung is a kind of liberal conspiracy, and by the last sentence of his text he is reduced to equating the writing of history with the construction of a "great tradition"—a remark it will be lenient to let pass.

Who is this contemporary Machiavelli, whose immediacy to us history can only obfuscate? He appears to be the author of the proposition that republics of armed citizens are to be admired because they can conquer other republics of armed citizens by the power of armed citizenry; and this is really not very like anything going on in the contemporary world, even in Central Africa or Southeast Asia. Machiavelli was innocent of ideology, and might have understood modern mercenaries but never terrorists. The latter do not use swords to conquer, but bombs in parked cars to delegitimize through a subtle exploitation of political sado-masochism, after which they do not conquer but seize centers of administration and degenerate rapidly into apparatchiks. Machiavelli was not a modern and could not have comprehended them at all. And if there is some way of extrapolating propositions from his writings and then translating them into an idiom that renders them relevant to concerns of ours, this goes as far toward proving that Machiavelli is not a contemporary as toward proving that he is. Wilamowitz was right; you must give the ghosts blood and then drain it from them before they can speak to us as they did to Machiavelli. History is infuriating but inescapable, and Hulliung is wasting his time and ours if he thinks he can dismiss it as a smokescreen thrown up by the heirs of the Enlightenment. (Does he say this? He does.)

That Hulliung should be presenting this essentially archaic Machiavelli as our inseparable contemporary is all the more extraordinary because his earlier book, *Montesquieu and the Old Regime,*[9] was largely an account of how Montesquieu killed, ate, and digested Machiavelli and left him behind in the excretions of history. He did this by developing a perception that took shape rapidly among Dutch, English, and Italian intellectuals following the wars against Louis XIV: that an ancient world based on conquest could be said to have been rendered obsolete by a modern world based on commerce. Because the ancient world had lacked a properly organized world market, its inhabitants had been forced into seizing the lands of others by conquest and appropriating their labor as slaves. The warrior-citizen-farmer had joined the legions rather than stay at home and increase his farm's marketable yield by industry, and on his return had as often not found himself in debt, which he must work off as a tenant laborer on someone else's *latifundium*; the individual had found no outlet for his energies but the harsh politics of the city, and no outlet for his intellectual powers but the harsh metaphysics and rhetoric of the academies. Machiavelli, said Hume, was a great genius, but he understood nothing except the little furious republics of antiquity, and the little republics of Renaissance Italy that had tried to imitate them. Here was the Enlightenment's explanation of why Machiavelli, like the Romans before him, had taken the option for conquest and made the Achillean commitment.

The moderns, it began to be said, could opt instead for a commerical world in which patterns and relations of exchange ran across the borders of kingdoms and republics. Conquest was now unnecessary, as production and commerce brought nations greater wealth and power than the crude appropriations of ancient *virtù*. The citizen of the new cosmopolis, founded on transaction rather than on association, had the opportunity to become as many-minded as Odysseus; he could see many cities and learn their ways, and on his return to Ithaca need not lead out the citizens to seize their neighbors' lands, preferring glory to length of days. Gibbon saw two reasons why modern Europe would stand up better to a barbarian invasion than ancient Rome. One was that, instead of a military empire unified by a single carapace, it was a republic of independent states who traded with one another, became diversified from one another, and learned from one another; the second was that the world commerce of which it was the heartland was reaching out to control the lands of the barbarians and annex them to civilization. Odysseus with his oar on his shoulder had arrived among the people who asked him what it was, and had begun to rule them.

As the many-mindedness of the market sought to replace the single loyalties and the *virtù* of the hero, citizen, or patriot, something happened of peculiar importance to the themes of these two books. We should be hard put to show that the actual condition of women improved, but for nearly the first time what were supposed to be feminine values were recognized as having universal merit by male theorists. It was claimed for the new world commerce that it softened, refined, and polished the manners and led to a more general intercourse among nations. Hume—who must have been reading the *Symposium*—was moved to declare that modern conversation was superior to ancient because women were admitted to it; Montesquieu to the apothegm that "il n'y a qu'une sexe, et nous sommes tous femmes dans l'esprit." The patterns of male dominance were, of course, reasserted in every way you can think of, but something had begun to happen.

It did not last, of course; Rousseau wrote *Emile*, and Mary Wollstonecraft realized that she would have to begin all over again. It was hard to accept that the abandonment of a primitive warrior *virtù* entailed the abandonment of *virtù* altogether; the single-minded political animal resisted absorption by the many-minded commercial animal. The commercial utopia, in which the ethos of exchange led to a recognition of feminization and intercourse, was a short-lived product of the rentier-controlled economies of the *ancien régime*. With the American, French, and Industrial Revolutions, the ethos of production became once more hard, imperious, and masculine; the landscapes of the world were overrun by conquistadors on steam engines, followed at a short interval by conquistadors on revolutionary processes; and women found themselves back at being angels in the house—a considerable improvement, perhaps, on their precommercial image, but a form which they found it hard to escape.

There is, then, a history of how perceptions of gender have been combined with perceptions of political economy, which has never been properly written but which it has been in principle possible to write for over two hundred years. (Nearly every theorist of the Scottish Enlightenment who wrote an account of the four stages of human society included a chapter on the condition of women at each stage; this is quite as remarkable as a dog walking on its hind legs.) The first great paradigm into which this history was organized, in the generation of Montesquieu, was capable of offering an explanation of why Machiavelli and the ancients had made the Achillean choice and feared the power of Fortune, and it was feeling its way toward an explanation of why women should be differently perceived by men—not, indeed, of how women might perceive things—at different stages of human development. To remind ourselves of this we have to restate the thesis of Hulliung's second book in light of his first; but some modernized form of the Enlightenment paradigm might usefully be applied to the far more important problems raised by Pitkin. A problem to which this enquiry would lead would clearly be the extent to which psychoanalytic explanations can, and should, be historicized.

NOTES

1. Hugh Lloyd-Jones, *Blood for the Ghosts: Classical Influences in the Nineteenth and Twentieth Centuries* (Baltimore: Johns Hopkins University Press, 1983).

2. Mark Hulliung, *Citizen Machiavelli* (Princeton, NJ: Princeton University Press, 1985).

3. Hanna Fenichel Pitkin, *Fortune Is a Woman: Gender and Politics in the Thought of Niccolo Machiavelli* (Berkeley: University of California Press, 1984).

4. I owe this syllogism to Gordon J. Schochet, who stated it in a conversation as long ago as 1969.

5. J.G.A. Pocock, *The Machiavellian Moment: Florentine Political Thought and the Atlantic Republican Tradition* (Princeton, NJ: Princeton University Press, 1975), p. 307.

6. He appears as his changeable self in black-figure vases, the animated art of antiquity.

7. Perhaps it was to another Soderini.

8. Ian MacLean, *The Renaissance Idea of Woman* (Cambridge: Cambridge University Press, 1980), makes some interesting suggestions.

9. University of California Press, 1976.

J.G.A. Pocock is Professor of History at Johns Hopkins University. Formerly, he was Professor of History and Political Science at Washington University in St. Louis and Professor of Political Science at the University of Canterbury in New Zealand. He is the author of The Ancient Constitution and the Feudal Law *(1957),* Politics, Language, and Time *(1971),* The Machiavellian Moment *(1975),* The Political Works of James Harrington *(1977), and* Virtue, Commerce and History *(1985).*

[17]

VICTORIA KAHN

Virtù and the Example of Agathocles in Machiavelli's *Prince*

Only at a remove from life can the mental life exist, and truly engage the empirical. While thought relates to facts and moves by criticizing them, its movement depends no less on the maintenance of distance. It expresses exactly what is, precisely because what is is never quite as thought expresses it. Essential to it is an element of exaggeration, of over-shooting the object, of self-detachment from the weight of the factual, so that instead of merely reproducing being it can, at once rigorous and free, determine it.
—Theodor Adorno

What gods will be able to save us from all these ironies?
—Friedrich Schlegel[1]

MACHIAVELLI'S INNOVATION in the history of political thought, it is often argued, lies in his revision not only of scholastic but also of humanist notions of imitation and representation, a revision that is reflected in his own representation of the realm of politics. When humanism and scholasticism alike are seen as proposing an idealist or a priori notion of truth, this case is easily made. As many critics of *The Prince* have remarked, Machiavelli scandalizes his readers not because he advises the prince to act in ways previously unheard of, but because he refuses to cloak his advice in the pieties of scholastic or Christian humanist idealism. Instead, he insists that the prince acts in a world in which there are "no prefigured meanings, no implicit teleology,"[2] in which order and legibility are the products of human action rather than the a priori objects of human cognition. To recognize this, he argues, is to acknowledge the reality or truth of power, over against an idealist notion of truth conceived in terms of representation, as correspondence to some a priori standard of judgment or, more specifically, to some a priori moral ideal. Machiavelli accordingly declares his divergence from the idealist tradition of reflection on political affairs in the famous opening to chapter 15:

Since I intend to write something useful [*utile*] to an understanding reader, it seemed better to go after the real truth [*la verità effettuale*] of the matter than to repeat what people have imagined. A great many men have imagined states and princedoms such as nobody ever saw or knew in the real world, for there's such a difference between the way we really live and the way we ought to live that the man who neglects the real to study the ideal will learn how to accomplish his ruin, not his preservation.[3]

It is important to see, however, that while Machiavelli criticizes the stoic and idealist moral philosophy of some humanists, he borrows from the more flexible pragmatism of others, according to whom truth is governed by an intrinsically ethical standard of decorum and consensus. Only when we recognize Machiavelli's imitation of and final divergence from this humanist tradition of pragmatism (and it is in this sense that the term *humanist* will most often be used in the following pages), will we be able to chart his innovation in political thought with any precision. I will argue that Machiavelli moves beyond the constraints of previous humanist reflection on the pragmatic nature of truth—which from his perspective offers yet another version of a mimetic, correspondence, or idealist theory—to a conception of truth as power, in which the pragmatic humanist version of truth itself becomes one weapon among others in the prince's strategic arsenal.

Imitation and Representation

From the very beginning of *The Prince* it is clear that Machiavelli is drawing on the resources of humanism, in particular its notion of imitation.[4] Like the humanists, he wants to educate his reader's practical judgment, the faculty of deliberation that allows for effective action within the contingent realm of fortune, and like them he recognizes that such education must therefore focus on particular examples rather than on the general precepts appropriate to theoretical reason. Furthermore, Machiavelli is concerned, as the humanists were, to criticize an unreflective relation to past examples that would take the form of slavish imitation, simple re-presentation, or a one-to-one correspondence. In fact, it is precisely in the absence of correspondence, of a mirror reflection of the exemplar, that the humanist prince or poet finds both the room to exercise his own will and the measure of his own achievement. Correct imitation accordingly involves imitating and realizing a flexible principle of prudential judgment or decorum. And this in turn gives rise to texts designed to dramatize and inculcate such judgment, whose rhetoric is, therefore, not ornamental but strategic.

Thus, in the prefatory letter to *The Prince*, Machiavelli justifies his gift of a text to Lorenzo de' Medici by suggesting that the latter will be a more effective ruler if he learns to imitate the double perspective, the reflective distance, offered in *The Prince*: "To know the people well one must be a prince, and to know princes well one must be, oneself, of the people" (3 [14]). And in chapter 14, "Military Duties of the Prince," Machiavelli makes the humanist claim for textual imitation even more forcefully by comparing skill in government to skill in reading, by making the ruler's landscape into a text and the text into a realm of forces. The prince is advised to learn to read the terrain (*imparare la natura de' siti*) and to "read history and reflect on the actions of great men." Here, to imitate great men means to imitate imitation, that is, to "take as a model of [one's] conduct some great historical figure who achieved the highest praise and glory by constantly holding before himself the deeds and achievements of a predecessor" (43 [64]).

Machiavelli's defining truth pragmatically *(la verità effettuale)*, rather than ontologically or epistemologically as correspondence to a fixed or absolute origin, would also seem to be consonant with humanism. And yet, if Machiavelli's notion of imitation appears to be essentially humanist, his own pragmatic definition of truth is not; for Machiavelli preserves the humanists' strategic sense of rhetoric only to separate it from its presumed origin in (the author's) and goal of (the reader's) intrinsically ethical practices of imitation. In rejecting the Ciceronian and humanist equation between *honestas* and *utilitas,* the faith that practical reason or prudence is inseparable from moral virtue, Machiavalli thus turns prudence into what the humanists (and their detractors) always feared it would become— the amoral skill of *versutia* or mere cleverness, which in turn implies the ethically unrestrained use of force—in short, *virtù.* He thus opens up a gap between the political agent and the political actor—or rather he makes the agent an actor who is capable of (mis)representation: the prince must appear to be good, virtuous, and so on in order to satisfy his people and thus to maintain his power (chap. 15).[5]

This redefinition of representation as ruse and thus of mimesis as power is the aim of *The Prince* as a whole,[6] but it finds a particularly forceful articulation in chapter 18. Machiavelli begins this chapter by distinguishing between human law and bestial force, but he then abandons the first pole of his binary opposition and proceeds to locate the range of political invention within the single second term of bestiality. Imitation may be a specifically human quality requiring the exercise of judgment, but the objects of imitation are bestial craft and force. Furthermore, the imitation of (bestial) nature has as its goal not correspondence to some fixed, determinate reality but the appearance of (what is conventionally accepted as) truth.

Here illusion is being turned against itself in order to present a truth to the people that will at the same time be effective for the prince. If, in the age-old debate between rhetoric and philosophy, the humanists want a rhetoric that is grounded in the truth and also effective, Machiavelli takes the further radical step not of subordinating or compromising truth in the interests of power, as he has sometimes been charged with doing, but of mutually implicating representation and force. Representation no longer involves even the correspondence to a practical standard of truth but has instead become theatrical. Correct or successful imitation no longer demands the exercise of self-knowledge and moral discretion but has itself become a rhetorical topic of invention to be manipulated in the interests of power.[7] Conversely, power becomes in part, if not entirely, an effect of the representational illusion of truth.

Machiavelli thus borrows—or imitates—the humanists' rhetorical strategies in order to educate his reader to an antihumanist conception of imitation and practice. The following pages aim to clarify Machiavelli's similarity with and divergence from the humanists by taking a close look at what we might call, for heuristic purposes, the repertoire of figures in Machiavelli's strategic rhetoric. These heuristic figures should also help us to discover how Machiavelli's revision of the humanist notion of practical reason is at one and the same time the condition of *virtù* and the potential obstacle to its realization. As we will see, while Machiavelli's realistic analysis of the realm of politics avoids the ethical domestication of *virtù* on the one hand, it threatens to allegorize, reify, or demonize *virtù* on the other, thus finally undermining the flexible political skill that the strategic rhetoric of *The Prince* was designed to encourage.

Irony and Hyperbole

For hyperbole is a virtue [virtus], *when the magnitude of the facts passes all words, and in such circumstances our language will be more effective if it goes beyond the truth than if it falls short of it.*

—Quintilian[8]

Machiavelli's criticism of the humanist version of pragmatism follows from his recognition of the intrinsic irony of politics, or of action within the contingent realm of human affairs: "If you look at matters carefully, you will see that something resembling virtue, if you follow it, may be your ruin, while something resembling vice will lead, if you follow it, to your security and well-being" (45 [66]).[9] But this formulation also allows us to see that Machiavelli wants to control this irony, or rather that he conceives of the man of *virtù* as someone who can *use* the ironies of political action to achieve political stability. (The refusal to *act* in the face of such ironies Machiavelli called literature; see his *History of Florence*, book 5, chap. 1.)[10] This recognition of the irony of politics leads in turn to a revision of humanist argument *in utramque partem*. The humanists, following Aristotle, believed that it is necessary to be able to argue on both sides of a question, not so that one might actually defend a false position but so that one could anticipate and thereby more effectively rebut an opponent's arguments.[11] Machiavelli, however, argues that the prince will actually have to oppose what may appear to be good at a given moment. In fact, in Machiavelli's view, it is the humanists who are guilty of trying to accommodate at a single moment contrary qualities or arguments (e.g., in chaps. 16 and 17) when they claim that the good and the useful are always compatible. Knowledge *in utramque partem* is necessary according to Machiavelli because "the conditions of human life simply do not allow" one "to have and exercise" only morally good qualities (45 [65]; cf. chap. 18, 50 [73]).

It is precisely this intrinsic irony of politics—the gap or lack of a mimetic relation between intention and result—that both allows for and requires solutions that seem extreme from the perspective of the humanist ideal of *mediocritas*.[12] Hence the place of hyperbole and exaggeration in Machiavelli's rhetoric. On the one hand, the examples of great men will always seem hyperbolic or excessive to—beyond the reach of—the imitator. On the other hand, Machiavelli argues, this hyperbole has a rhetorical and pedagogical function.

> Men almost always prefer to walk in paths marked out by others and pattern their actions through imitation. Even if he cannot follow other people's paths in every respect, or attain to the *virtù* of his originals, a prudent man should always follow the footsteps of the great and imitate those who have been supreme. His own *virtù* may not come up to theirs, but at least it will have a sniff of it. Thus he will resemble skilled archers who, seeing how far away the target lies, and knowing the *virtù* of their bow, aim much higher than the real target, not because they expect the arrow to fly that far, but to accomplish their real end by aiming beyond it. (16 [30])

In this view, hyperbolic examples do not correspond to things as they are but to what they might be; they are figures of action rather than perception, of desire rather than cognition or representation. Hyperbole as a mode of speech or behavior is thus the proper response to the irony of politics: it is predicated on a recognition of one's distance both from the situation as it stands and from the situation one would like to create, but it also involves the recognition that such distance—as in the epigraph from Adorno—is itself a precondition of considered action. Finally, hyperbolic action is often ironic according to the classical definition of irony (Quintilian *Institutio oratoria* 8.6.54; 9.2.44–47) because it involves saying or doing one thing in order to arrive at its opposite. In short, the world of Machiavellian politics is intrinsically ironic, and the most effective mode of behavior in such a world is theatrical and hyperbolic. An analysis of the example of Agathocles in chapter 8 will serve to illustrate this point. At the same time, it should also help us to see how Machiavelli's strategic practice as a writer imitates that of his ideal prince.

Strategic Style:
The Example of Agathocles

In a world where a flexible faculty of judgment is constitutive of *virtù*, it is not surprising that Machiavelli should offer us no substantive definition of his terms. This is not simply a failing of analytical skill, as Sydney Anglo has complained,[13] but a sophisticated rhetorical strategy, the aim of which is to destabilize or dehypostatize our conception of political virtue, for only a destabilized *virtù* can be effective in the destabilized world of political reality.[14] In this context, the most effective critique of an idealist or mimetic notion of truth and of representation will be one that stages or dramatizes this lack of conceptual stability, rather than simply stating it as a fact. This rhetorical indirection would not in itself differentiate Machiavelli from the humanists. What is important to see, however, is that Machiavelli uses humanist rhetoric theatrically for antihumanist purposes. Chapter 8 on Agathocles the Sicilian is an exemplary instance of how the Machiavellian critique of representation implicates the humanists' ethical pragmatism as well.

In chapter 8, Machiavelli presents Agathocles as an example of someone who rises to power not by *virtù* or fortune but by crime. Readers of *The Prince* have tended to interpret this example in one of two ways. In this narrative, some argue, Machiavelli registers his own discomfort with the notion of *virtù* that he has been elaborating: it does violence to his sense of morality as well as to that of the reader. J. H. Whitfield speaks of Machiavelli's condemnation of Agathocles, and Claude Lefort remarks on the "réserve troublante" that qualifies Machiavelli's admiration of this figure.[15] Others see the story as an illustration of a cruel but effective use of violence. The interpreters who fall into this camp then differ as to whether this use of violence is immoral or amoral.[16] But in neither case is Machiavelli's own interpretation of Agathocles as one who rose to power by means of crime subject to scrutiny.[17] Thus, while the proponents of the first interpretation make note of Machiavelli's qualifications of Agathocles' actions ("Non si può ancora chiamare virtù ammazzare li sua cittadini . . ."; 42), they read this qualification as a simple pun ("It certainly cannot be called 'virtue' to murder his fellow citizens"; 26) and so save Machiavelli from the charge of failing to make moral distinctions. The second group of interpreters, in accepting the story of Agathocles as an illustration of the uses of crime rather than of *virtù*, make an analogous moral distinction between the excessive cruelty of Agathocles and the politic restraint of the man of *virtù*. In both cases one would argue that this making of distinctions was precisely Machiavelli's intention. Following from the story of Cesare Borgia in chapter 7, the next chapter would serve, in these readings, to correct the reader who had begun to think *virtù* identical with crime. In chapter 8 Machiavelli would then reassure the reader by acknowledging that there is a difference between the two.

In fact, however, there is hardly a less reassuring experience of reading in *The Prince* than that of chapter 8. And it is a chapter whose disturbing quality increases as we read further in the work: while in chapter 6 Machiavelli describes the relation of *virtù* and *fortuna* as a dialectical one, he goes further in chapter 25 when he claims that *fortuna* and *virtù* divide the world of events between them. How then, we wonder, could crime be a third term in Machiavelli's analysis of the way princes rise to power?

In spite of the title and the first paragraph of chapter 8, Machiavelli's introductory remarks about Agathocles seem to confirm the polar opposition of chapter 25: he tells us that Agathocles "joined to his villainies such *virtù* of mind and body that after enlisting in the army he rose through the ranks to become military governor of Syracuse" (25 [41]). And a little further on he reiterates that

Agathocles' success was due to *virtù:* "Considering the deeds and *virtù* of this man, one finds little or nothing that can be attributed to fortune" (26 [41]). But, then, anticipating his reader's objections, he quickly adds:

Yet it certainly cannot be called *virtù* to murder his fellow citizens, betray his friends, to be devoid of truth, pity, or religion; a man may get power by means like these, but not glory. If we consider simply the *virtù* of Agathocles in facing and escaping from dangers, and the greatness of his soul in sustaining and overcoming adversity, it is hard to see why he should be considered inferior to the greatest of captains. Nonetheless, his fearful cruelty and inhumanity, along with his innumerable crimes, prevent us from placing him among the really excellent men. For we can scarcely attribute to either fortune or *virtù* a conquest [*quello*] which he owed to neither. (26 [42])

How are we to make sense of the vertiginous distinctions in this paragraph? Russell Price has suggested that Machiavelli is differentiating in this passage between the military *virtù* and glory [*gloria*] that apply to captains and the political *virtù* and glory that apply to "the really excellent men."[18] Of the former he writes:

It seems that [Agathocles] . . . deserves credit for his martial spirit and deeds (that is, as a *capitano*) after he became ruler; what blackens his reputation is how he became ruler, because he treacherously slaughtered his friends and fellow citizens. Trickery and violence are to be condemned in a ruler or an aspiring ruler. . . . The stain he incurred by the way he seized power is indelible like original sin. (611)

Apart from the dubious appropriateness of an analogy with original sin for a writer of such rabid anti-Christian sentiment, this analysis fails to take account of the fact that Borgia also used trickery and violence to secure his power but is nevertheless not being offered as an example of one who rose to power by crime. Furthermore, although Borgia is not condemned by Machiavelli, neither is he called one of the really excellent men, a phrase that, as J. G. A. Pocock reminds us, refers to legislators rather than new princes.[19]

A more sophisticated version of Price's analysis is presented by Claude Lefort, who argues that the introduction of the theme of *gloria* in chapter 8 signals a turning point in the argument of *The Prince.* Whereas the earlier chapters were concerned with the necessary exercise of violence in the acquisition of power, the example of Agathocles introduces the necessity of *representing* oneself to the people in a certain way in order to hold on to the power one has acquired. While Machiavelli had previously emphasized the self-sufficiency of the prince, he now places the action of the prince in a social context in which it acquires its real significance (380–81). In this way, *virtù* itself is neither identical with nor exclusive of crime, but it does require glory, and it is this concern for glory that will induce the prince to moderate his violent behavior and take greater interest in the welfare of his people. According to this reading, in the sentence that begins "Yet it certainly cannot be called *virtù* to murder his fellow citizens . . . ," it is *called* that should be stressed: *virtù* is not *equal* to crime, though even a "virtuous" man

(Borgia, for example) may find it necessary on occasion to act criminally. Yet if Lefort is not as reassuring as those readers who claim that Machiavelli is asserting a clear-cut distinction between military and political (moral) *virtù*, he nevertheless claims that there is a distinction between Borgia and Agathocles, one that does not lie in the nature of their deeds, since both were guilty of criminal behavior, but rather in the fact that the deeds of the latter "were committed without justification, or without a pretext [*sans masque*], by a man whom nothing, except his ambition, destined to reign . . . a man—Machiavelli took the trouble to make clear—*di infima e abjetta fortuna*, the simple son of a potter *(nato d'uno figulo)*" (380; my translation).

It is not so much the crimes of Agathocles that constitute his original sin, according to Lefort, as his lowly birth. But this interpretation trivializes both the notion of representation and that of fortune in *The Prince*, neither of which, as Lefort elsewhere recognizes, is a static concept involving a one-to-one correspondence, according to which the bad fortune of lowly birth would forever restrict Agathocles' possibilities for representing himself in a favorable light. In fact, by the end of the chapter Agathocles is offered as an example of someone who used cruelty well rather than badly, and who was consequently "able to reassure people, and win them over to his side with benefits" (28 [44]). It would seem, then, that far from excluding Agathocles from the category of "representative men," Machiavelli goes out of his way to stress his inclusion.

As we have seen, most readings of chapter 8 respond to the pressure to make distinctions that is implicit in the apparently contradictory reiteration of *virtù*. But it is important to see that clear-cut or permanent distinctions are finally what cannot be made. Throughout *The Prince* Machiavelli sets up concepts in polar opposition to each other and then shows how the opposition is contained within each term so that the whole notion of opposition must be redefined.[20] Thus in chapter 25 he begins by telling the reader that "fortune governs one half of our actions, but that even so she leaves the other half more or less in our power to control." Fortune is then presented as a natural force, a torrential stream against which men can take countermeasures "while the weather is still fine." But this opposition is a generalization that undergoes startling revision when we come to "the particulars." For a man's ability to take countermeasures—his *virtù*—turns out to be a fact of (his) nature and thus a potential natural disaster over which he has no control:

If a prince conducts himself with patience and caution, and the times and circumstances are favorable to those qualities, he will flourish; but if times and circumstances change, he will come to ruin unless he changes his method of proceeding. No man, however prudent, can adjust to such radical changes, not only because we cannot go against the inclination of nature, but also because when one has always prospered by following a particular course, he cannot be persuaded to leave it. (71 [100])

In this more particular view, human nature is itself a torrential stream that cannot redirect its course with dikes and restraining dams: the favorable constraints are instead introduced by fortune. The purely formal *virtù* that is the ability to "adjust one's behavior to the temper of the times"—and that is precisely *not* constancy of character—is not a quality that can be attributed once and for all: it is rather a generalization that designates only the fortunate coincidence of "nature's livery and fortune's star." Or, as Machiavelli writes of men of *virtù* in chapter 6: "Without the opportunity their *virtù* of mind would have been in vain, and without that *virtù* the opportunity would have been lost" (17 [31]).

If we now return to chapter 8, we can begin to see why Machiavelli cannot call Agathocles' crimes virtuous. In the light of chapter 25, it seems that we should place an even stronger emphasis on *called:* in the case of neither Borgia nor Agathocles can crime be called *virtù*, because *virtù* cannot be *called* any one thing. In short, once the temporal dimension of circumstance is introduced, the fact that crime cannot necessarily be called *virtù* means also that it can be called *virtù*. The danger of the preceding chapter 7 is not only that we might identify Borgia's murder and treachery with *virtù*, but also that we would identify *virtù* with any particular act—criminal or not. The aim of the passage, in short, is to dehypostatize *virtù*, to empty it of any specific meaning. For *virtù* is not a general rule of behavior that could be applied to a specific situation but rather, like prudence, a faculty of deliberation about particulars.

On one level, then, the conclusion of the paragraph concerning Agathocles' *virtù* ("For we can scarcely attribute to either fortune or *virtù* a conquest which he owed to neither") seems to reinforce the distinctions between *virtù*, fortune, and crime with which the chapter began—perhaps as an ironic concession to the reader's moral sensibility. On another level, it simply points up the incommensurability between the generalizations of *fortuna* and *virtù* and the specific instances that cannot be usefully subordinated to any (conceptual) generalization. How else is it possible to explain the end of chapter 8, where Machiavelli makes a distinction between two sorts of cruelty—between cruelty used well or badly—thereby placing the distinction between *fortuna* and *virtù* within cruelty itself: "Cruelty can be described as well used (if it's permissible to speak well about something that is evil in itself) when it is performed all at once, for reasons of self-preservation" (27–28 [44]). Once again the emphasis is on *chiamare* ("Bene usate si possono chiamare quelle [se del male è licito dire bene]"), but here the temporal dimension is explicit, as is the consequent and necessary making of distinctions within "cruelty." And once again, in the parenthetical remark Machiavelli speaks to the reader's moral sensibility—but he has answered the implied question even before it has been posed. Cruelty *can* be called "well used" because Machiavelli has just done so in the preceding clause. The adverbial *bene* then takes on some of the paronomastic color of the earlier paragraph on *virtù*.

The reader wonders if it is permissible to speak *good words (bene)* about evil, while Machiavelli replies by speaking *well (bene)*.[21]

These lines are important because they contain in little Machiavelli's critique of humanism. The humanist's assumption that *honestas* is compatible with *utilitas*, reflected in the maxim that the good orator is necessarily a good man, is politically useless to Machiavelli, however it is interpreted. When the goodness of the orator is interpreted to mean in conformity with ethical goodness (*honestas;* see Cicero *De officiis* 3.3.11, 3.11.49), then the maxim is a stoic tautology and the question of the orator's effectiveness *(utilitas)* need not enter in. When the orator's goodness is interpreted to mean persuasiveness as well as moral rectitude, then the claim that the orator is a good man is a synthetic judgment that is also idealistic and unfounded. One has only to look to experience to see that many morally good men have been politically ineffective. Here the criterion of correct action is not moral goodness or the intrinsically moral judgment of prudence but the functional excellence or effectiveness of *virtù:* a *virtù* we might say, parodying Aristotle, that demonstrates its own excellence by being effective.[22] In speaking well rather than speaking good words, Machiavelli both dramatizes and thematizes this functional virtuosity. He shows that *virtù* is not a substance but a mode of action (not a noun, but an adverb) by speaking well about acting well.

The linguistic play of this paragraph and the earlier one on *virtù* are thus part of a rhetorical strategy to engage the reader in a critical activity that will allow him to discover not the content of "what should be" but the formality of what in any particular situation "can be."[23] Here, if the reader's "natural" disposition to make moral distinctions ("everyone agrees . . .") may be compared to the natural force of the river in chapter 25, which serves as a metaphor for fortune, Machiavelli's prose is the countermeasure that attempts to channel or redirect this course by introducing the element of reflection. In the rewriting of a metaphor from Quintilian (*Institutio oratoria* 9.4.7), Machiavelli proposes a style that is powerful precisely because it is rough and broken. He thus duplicates on the poetic level the practical problem of judgment that the prince will have to face—that of applying the rule of *virtù* to the particular situation at hand. Or, as Roland Barthes has written of Machiavelli's work, "The structure of the discourse attempts to reproduce the structure of the dilemmas actually faced by the protagonists. In this case reasoned argument predominates and the history [or discourse] is of a reflexive—one might say strategic—style."[24]

Theatricality

The suggestion that Machiavelli's style is strategic means not only that the prince may learn something about strategy by reflecting on Machiavelli's prose (the structure and vocabulary of his examples) but also that the actual strategies he recounts may tell us something about Machiavelli's strategy as a

writer. And this reciprocity in turn allows us to read the example of Agathocles
in the light of Machiavelli's earlier remarks on Borgia. As a number of critics
have remarked, Machiavelli's position as counselor is in some ways analogous to
that of the new prince. Both are "student[s] of delegitimized politics,"[25] and for
both the problem is how to impose a new form not only on matter but on an
already informed matter. But Machiavelli's *virtù* as a writer is not simply, as some
readers have suggested, to dramatize in the writing of *The Prince* the resourcefulness and inventiveness of the effective ruler but also to manipulate his audience in much the same way that the prince must manipulate his subjects. In the
first case, imitation involves the cultivation of a purely formal flexibility of judgment or *disponibilità;* in the second, that judgment is tested by the appearances
of the text itself. Thus in chapter 7 Machiavelli proposes Borgia's behavior in the
Romagna as an example worthy of imitation, and in chapter 8 he imitates it in
order to test whether the reader has learned the lesson of a chapter 7. In
short, there are striking analogies not only between the careers of Borgia and
Agathocles but also between the effect of Borgia's behavior on his subjects in the
Romagna and Machiavelli's effect on the reader in chapter 8.

When Borgia took over the Romagna he discovered that "the whole province
was full of robbers, feuds, and lawlessness of every description" (22 [37]). His
way of "establish[ing] peace and reduc[ing] the land to obedience" was to counter
lawlessness with lawlessness: "He named Messer Remirro De Orco, a cruel and
vigorous man, to whom he gave absolute powers. In short order this man paci-
fied and unified the whole district, winning great renown" (22 [37]). But like
Agathocles, Borgia knew that excessive authority can become odious,

so he set up a civil court in the middle of the province, with an excellent judge and a
representative from each city. And because he knew that the recent harshness had generated some hatred, in order to clear the minds of the people and gain them over to his
cause completely, he determined to make plain that whatever cruelty had occurred had
come, not from him, but from the brutal character of the minister. Taking a proper
occasion, therefore, he had him placed on the public square of Cesena one morning, in
two pieces, with a piece of wood beside him and a bloody knife. The ferocity of this scene
left the people at once stunned and satisfied. (22 [37])

This story provides us with two examples of cruelty well used. The first is
De Orco's, the second Borgia's. The function of the first is primarily destructive
and repressive: to pacify his subjects; the function of the second is theatrical and
cathartic: this too pacifies the subjects but by the theatrical display of violence
rather than its direct application to the audience. The first example reestablishes
justice from the perspective of the ruler; the second stages this reestablishment
from the perspective of and for the ruled. As this theatrical display suggests, the
story also provides us with two examples of representation well used. In the first
case, there is an element of representation insofar as Borgia delegates his power,
but this delegation is ultimately a way of concealing the fact of representation

(i.e., representation has become ruse) so that he can deny responsibility for De Orco's cruelty—as he does so effectively by means of (and this is the second example) his theatrical representation in the public square of Cesena.

The example of Agathocles in chapter 8 is just such a theatrical display on the part of Machiavelli. Like Borgia, Machiavelli is concerned to make a distinction between *virtù* and crime—not because they are mutually exclusive but because they are not identical. And like Borgia, he sets up a court with the reader as judge. "He determined to make plain that whatever cruelty had occurred [in the example of Agathocles] had come, not from him, but from the brutal character of his minister" (i.e., of his example). The reader is morally satisfied or reassured by Machiavelli's supposed condemnation of Agathocles, just as the people of the Romagna were by the dramatic and brutal disavowal of Remirro's brutality. But the reader who is taken in by this excuse is in the position of a subject rather than a prince—for Machiavelli has not presented the example of Agathocles in order to pacify his readers but rather to try them. In short, Agathocles is proposed as an example for the prince who might have need to follow him, and the ability to determine that necessity is also the *virtuous* ability to make discriminations about what constitutes *virtù* with respect to any given situation. The example of Agathocles is a test of *virtù*.

The Avoidance of Tautology

When we turn from the examples of Borgia and Agathocles to the rest of *The Prince*, we see that this work is filled with examples of such extreme, ironic, or hyperbolic situations and actions, the most extreme example of which is perhaps Machiavelli's advice that the best way to keep a city is to destroy it (see chap. 5, 14 [28]; and *Discourses* 2.23, 3.40). Many readers have thought that Machiavelli here and elsewhere could not possibly mean what he says, that he is ironic in the sense of unserious.[26] But the example of Agathocles has shown that what is mere exaggeration from the perspective of the conventional virtues may be simple pragmatic advice for the student of *virtù*. This advice will seem hyperbolic because it is beyond good and evil, because it involves the transgression of the conventional philosophical constraints on knowledge (knowledge as cognition of the truth) in the direction of knowledge defined as power.[27] But here precisely lies the problem. While Machiavelli argues in chapter 15 that *virtù* involves knowledge that is useful or effective, he does not want to claim that *virtù* guarantees success. To make this claim would be to fall into a version of the tautology of *honestas* and *utilitas* that he condemns in this same chapter. If there were such a skill as a *virtù* that always yields success, then there would be no fortune or contingency; but contingency is precisely what makes room for *virtù*—indeed, what makes *virtù* necessary in Machiavelli's eyes. Still, a *virtù* that never resulted in success would be patently absurd. Thus Machiavelli claims early in *The Prince* that if we follow the examples of *virtù* that he presents, success will *usually* or most often result (11 [12]).

These ambiguities concerning the relation of *virtù* to success are reflected in Machiavelli's claim to be guided by the *verità effettuale della cosa*. On the one hand he means that he will approach politics realistically, rather than idealistically, by beginning with things as they are. In this view, as Felix Gilbert has argued, "the measure of worth of a political figure [is] . . . formed by his capacity to use the possibilities inherent in the political situations; politics [has] its own criteria to be derived from existing political opportunities."[28] On the other hand, implicit in the claim to be guided by the *verità effettuale* is the assumption that such an approach will prove to be *effective*: in short, that one does not simply imitate necessity but that one can manipulate it—effect it—to one's own advantage.

Machiavelli's vacillation is apparent throughout *The Prince*. Sometimes he equates *virtù* with successful political action; at other times he insists on distinguishing between the two.[29] In the first case *virtù* becomes the goal of technical deliberation, and Machiavelli sounds like a dispassionate political analyst, subordinating means to ends. (The danger here, of course, is to assume that anyone who succeeds demonstrates *virtù*, when in fact success might be due to chance rather than to the activity of the individual.) In the second case, *virtù* is a practical skill that may be an end in itself, and thus structurally (although not ethically) similar to the classical notion of prudence.[30] In this way Machiavelli's vacillation simply conflates in a single term, *virtù*, an amoral version of the structural problem inherent in the classical and humanist concept of prudence—the problem of the relation of means to ends, of prudential deliberation to virtue or, in Machiavelli's case, to *virtù*.

This ambiguity or uncertainty about the status of deliberative skill and its relation to success is also reflected in the nature and function of examples in Machiavelli's texts. As I have suggested, a teacher who subordinates practical judgment to theoretical reason has only to present the student with general precepts and the logical rules of deduction, but a teacher whose theory of action equates judgment with the exercise of practical reason or of decorum will have to educate such judgment through examples. Such examples will not have the status of mere illustrations of theory, as they would if they were subordinated to or subsumed under universally applicable abstract principles. They will not be expendable but necessary, since every judgment of decorum is a judgment of, and must conform to the exigencies of, a particular situation. On the other hand, if such judgment *merely* conformed to the particular, it would cancel itself out as a judgment, since it would involve no reference to a standard other than faithful re-presentation (imitation) of the particular case. Judgment requires distance, and examples that educate such judgment must contain within themselves or dramatize this distance. Thus, in the case of humanist texts, examples are to a certain extent problematizing since they are designed to provoke reflection. But their pedagogical aim also demands a limit to such problematizing: for if excessive identification with the particular leads to the collapse of judgment, excessive difference (the reflection on and putting in question of all possible standards of judgment—whether the standard of virtue or *virtù*) does as well. While Machiavelli lacked the humanists' faith in the ethical criterion of practical reason, he was not usually skeptical about the possibility of deliberation and action. Indeed, he insisted that such possibility could only be realized in a world purged of idealism. Machiavelli thus shares with the humanists a rhetoric of problematizing examples, and like the humanists he needs also to limit such problematizing.[31]

The dilemma that Machiavelli faces is thus intrinsic to the problematic of imitation, but it is also tinged with a peculiarly Machiavellian irony insofar as the ethical claims for humanist imitation are a rhetorical topic contained within and thus ultimately undermined by the Machiavellian strategy of imitation. In this context, Agathocles' "overshooting" of morality is exemplary because, both in Machiavelli's strategy as author and Agathocles' as agent, it dramatizes and encourages the distanced reflection and thus the reflective imitation necessary to, if not sufficient for, success.

Irony and Allegory

Irony descends from the low mimetic: it begins in realism and dispassionate observation. But as it does so, it moves steadily towards myth, and dim outlines of sacrificial rituals and dying gods begin to reappear in it.
—Northrop Frye[32]

As I have argued in the preceding pages, Machiavelli's reflection on the political uses of representation is tied to his revision of the humanist concept of prudential action. The prince is powerful to the extent that he diverges from a naive or moral concept of prudence, but he also maintains his power by "naively" imitating—or representing himself as faithfully reproducing—the conventional virtues. As in chapter 18, power is in part, if not entirely, the effect of the representational illusion of truth. But, as the case of Agathocles demonstrates, the exigency of representation, if representation is conceived of now as the means or the ability to generate the consensus and support of the people (chap. 8, 24 [44], chap. 18, 51 [74]; *Discourses* 2.23, 3.19–23), also finally proves to be a forceful constraint on the abuse of power. Cruelty will be well used if "it is performed all at once, for reasons of self-preservation; and when the acts are not repeated after that, but rather turned as much as possible to the advantage of the subjects" (8.27–28 [44]). The prince must in the long run please his audience if he is to maintain his rule. In the end, the rhetorical topic of truth proves to involve an ironic version of the ethical constraint that the humanists located in custom and consensus. This constraint also helps us to see how the analysis of power in *The*

Prince logically gives way to that of the *Discourses:* the prince, to be successful in the long run, must found a republic because republics are capable of greater longevity and *virtù* than principalities. The "understanding reader" will see that when representation and force are mutually implicated, when representation becomes a means of power, and thus finally when power is mitigated by the exigencies of persuasion, the short-lived individual self-aggrandizement gives way to communal glory, and the prince must of necessity become a fellow citizen.[33]

This is the optimistic way to read the self-destructing rhetoric of *The Prince*. But, as most readers have noted, there is a more radical way in which the analysis of *virtù* undermines itself and Machiavelli's pedagogy in this text. As Machiavelli tells us over and over again, there are no general rules for virtuous behavior (e.g., chap. 20, 59 [85]), and there is no guarantee that the skill one practices in the interpretation of particular examples will enable one to respond appropriately in the next situation. This is, of course, as it should be. As Machiavelli writes in chapter 21, "No leader should ever suppose he can invariably take the safe course, since all choice involves risks. In the nature of things [*nell'ordine delle cose*], you can never try to escape one danger without encountering another; but prudence consists in knowing how to recognize the nature of the different dangers and in accepting the least bad as good" (65 [92]). But the essential emptiness of the concept of *virtù* receives a rather different and finally devastating articulation in chapter 25, where the role of fortune in the individual's ability to act virtuously finally seems to deprive the individual of any initiative whatsoever. As we saw, Machiavelli begins this chapter by discussing the relation of fortune and *virtù* in general terms. On this level he gives fortune a certain allegorical stability, as though fortune were something external to *virtù* that the latter had only to resist. When he descends to particulars, however, fortune has no stability whatsoever. The irony of politics and human action becomes so great—the possibility of action (as opposed to mere passivity) so compromised—that the distance constitutive of reflection finally collapses altogether. To recognize which situations require which kinds of imitation finally necessitates that the prince imitate the absolute flexibility of fortune itself. But one's ability to learn is itself, finally, a function of the *fortune* of one's natural disposition, and is necessarily limited by it. In thus conflating the realm of necessity or nature with the agent of *virtù*, Machiavelli runs the risk of reducing *virtù* to the mere repetition—that is, the willed acceptance—of necessity: the mimetic representation of nature.[34] In so doing, he finally does substitute for the tautology of *honestas* and *utilitas* the tautology of *virtù* and success. It's not surprising, then, that Machiavelli should at this moment invoke the personified figure of Fortune as a woman in a desperate, inconsequential attempt to redeem the possibility of action by relocating it in an interpersonal context.[35]

A few remarks about the allegorical tendency of *The Prince* may help to clarify this point. According to Angus Fletcher, the allegorical hero confronts a world of contingency, a world in which the individual has very little control over the consequences of his actions, and in which there often seems to be little causal connection between events.[36] Narrative sequence is threatened by parataxis but restored on the level of cosmic, often magical necessity.[37] As a result, the hero also seems to be not simply at the mercy of external events but in the control of some external power. In fact, the allegorical hero could be said to operate in a world of demonic powers, a world in which functions have been compartmentalized, personified. The result is that the hero himself becomes depersonalized, no longer a person but a mere personification of a function as well. In a world of Fortuna, in short, the hero becomes of necessity the embodiment of *Virtù*.

In such a world, then, the virtues no longer seem to be attributes of individual agents; rather, they recover their original sense of powers or forces, of *virtù*. As Fletcher remarks, "Like a Machiavellian prince, the allegorical hero can act free of the usual moral restraints, even when he is acting morally, since he is moral only in the interests of his power over other men" (68). To redefine virtue as *virtù* is thus "to rediscover a sense of the morally ambivalent power in action" (an advance, one might say, in the direction of "realism"), but it is also, ironically, to run the risk of doing away with free will. While the intention behind Machiavelli's various exempla of *virtù* is to help the reader understand the formal, innovative character of this faculty, and the role of free will in determining what constitutes *virtù* in any particular situation, the quasi-allegorical status of the man of *virtù*, or of the prince as a *personification* of *Virtù*, suggests that the individual is not at all in control of his behavior—a suggestion that, as we have seen, becomes explicit in chapter 25. The way Machiavelli chooses to combat this demonization or personification of the person is to repersonalize what was becoming an increasingly abstract and *unmanageable* concept of fortune by introducing the figure of Fortune as a woman. In a kind of parody of humanist rhetoric *in utramque partem*, allegory is used to fight the allegorization or reification of the prince's *virtù*.

In light of these remarks, one can also see how the allegorical tendency of Machiavelli's "realism" is manifest in the sublime rhetoric of his concluding chapter.[38] Fletcher calls our attention to the structural similarity between allegory and the sublime. Simply stated, the experience of the sublime involves the inability of the imagination to comprehend sensuous experience, which leads to an awareness of the higher faculty of reason and to "reflection on man's higher destiny" (249). This discrepancy between sensuous experience and the higher claims of reason is analogous to the separation of sensuous representation and allegorical signified in the allegorical text. Furthermore, as Longinus reminds us, allegory is not only analogous to the sublime but can itself have a sublime effect, an ideological (249) or epideictic force when it "incites to action" (246). But, as the epigraph to this section suggests, the structural incommensurability in the allegorical sublime can also have an ironic effect, by suggesting that the principle of authority or meaning (reason, God) is infinitely removed from the world of sensuous immediacy.[39]

Machiavelli obviously intends the sublime or divine rhetoric of his concluding chapter to function as the best of all hyperboles: to incite the Medici to action. Consider the following claim:

> There is no figure presently in sight in whom she [Italy] can better trust than your illustrious house, which, with its fortune and its *virtù*, favored by God and the Church of which it is now the head, can take the lead in this process of redemption. (73 [102])

In these lines, Machiavelli conflates the fortune of the Medici with divine providence and the Church, and thus simultaneously debases religion and confers a certain grandeur upon the rulers of Florence.[40] In this light necessity, too, takes on a different and more positive appearance: it is no longer the necessity of fortune or of contingency or of (one's own) nature that resists *virtù* (as in chapter 25); rather, necessity is now the "providential necessity" that justifies the actions of the Medici. Describing men of *virtù*, he writes:

> Their cause was no more just than the present one, nor any easier, and God was no more favorable to them than to you. Your cause is just: "for war is justified when it is necessary, and arms are pious when without them there would be no hope at all." (73 [103])

In its divine justification of the Medici as the redeemers of Italy, chapter 26 would be the final, brilliant example of Machiavelli's theatrical overshooting of the mark, of a rhetoric of representation that is neither constrained by logic to represent the truth nor guided by practical reason in its achievement of decorum but that aims rather to produce the effect of truth—or to effect it. Yet the obvious alternative reading of the lines quoted above is that providential justification is conflated with the material realm of necessity. In this way, the collapse of the distance and difference necessary for action in chapter 25 turns out to anticipate the rhetoric of chapter 26, a rhetoric that, paradoxically, seems designed precisely to recoup the losses of the preceding chapter. In the end, exaggeration cannot free itself "from the weight of the factual, so that instead of merely reproducing being it can, at once rigorous and free, determine it" (Adorno; see epigraph). In a final ironic twist, Machiavelli's providential rhetoric can then be seen to suggest (no doubt against the free will he assumes he exercises; see chapter 25), that, to answer Schlegel's question, only (the hyperbolic figure of) God can save us from such ironies.

Notes

1. Theodor Adorno, *Minima Moralia,* trans. E. F. N. Jephcott (London, 1978), 126–27; Friedrich Schlegel, "Über die Unverständlichkeit," *Kritische Schriften* (Munich, 1964), 538 (my translation). I am grateful to Charles Trinkaus for his helpful criticism of an earlier draft of this essay.
2. Sheldon Wolin, *Politics and Vision* (Boston, 1960), 224.
3. Niccolò Machiavelli, *The Prince,* trans. and ed. Robert M. Adams (New York, 1977), 44. Throughout, I have substituted *virtù* for the various English translations Adams provides. References to the Italian text are taken from Machiavelli, *Il Principe e discorsi,* ed. Sergio Bertelli (Milan, 1977), and will be given in the text in brackets following English references, as here: 44 [65].
4. Recent interpretations of *The Prince* in the context of the humanist notion of imitation include Mark Hulliung, *Citizen Machiavelli* (Princeton, N.J., 1983), esp. 130–67; Hannah Pitkin, *Fortune Is a Woman* (Berkeley, 1983), 268ff.; and Thomas M. Greene, "The End of Discourse in Machiavelli's 'Prince,' " in *Concepts of Closure,* ed. David F. Hult, *Yale French Studies* 67 (1984): 57–71. Gennaro Sasso also discusses Machiavelli's notion of imitation in *Niccolò Machiavelli: Storia del suo pensiero politico* (Naples, 1958), 381–89. For earlier treatments of Machiavelli in the context of humanism see Felix Gilbert, *Machiavelli and Guicciardini: Politics and History in Sixteenth-Century Florence* (Princeton, N.J., 1965), and "The Humanist Concept of the Prince and the 'Prince' of Machiavelli," *Journal of Modern History* 11 (1939): 449–83; as well as Allan H. Gilbert, *Machiavelli's Prince and Its Forerunners* (Durham, N.C., 1938). In considering Machiavelli's rhetoric, I have also benefited from Eugene Garver, "Machiavelli's *The Prince:* A Neglected Rhetorical Classic," *Philosophy and Rhetoric* 13 (1980): 99–120; and "Machiavelli and the Politics of Rhetorical Invention," paper given at the third biennial conference of the International Society for the History of Rhetoric, Madison, Wis. (April 1981); as well as from Nancy Struever's unpublished paper, "Machiavelli and the Critique of the Available Languages of Morality in the Sixteenth Century."
5. Machiavelli's division of the political agent from the political actor anticipates Hobbes in chapter 16 of the *Leviathan.* On the distinction between cleverness or *versutia* and prudence, see Aristotle *Nicomachean Ethics* (henceforth *NE*) 1144a.25–1144b.
6. See the discussion by Pierre Manent, *Naissances de la politique moderne: Machiavel, Hobbes, Rousseau* (Paris, 1977), 19: "If ruse is, in Machiavelli's eyes, the principal resource of political action, that is because ruse responds to the essence of the political situation" (my translation).
7. Thomas M. Greene, *The Light in Troy: Imitation and Discovery in Renaissance Poetry* (New Haven, 1982), 142, 172, 184.
8. This slightly altered translation is taken from *The Institutio Oratoria of Quintilian,* trans. H. E. Butler, Loeb Classical Library (Cambridge, Mass., 1976), 8.6.7.
9. Wolin discusses Machiavelli's view of the intrinsic irony of politics in *Politics and Vision,* 227.
10. Cited by Hulliung, *Citizen Machiavelli,* 137.
11. Aristotle *Rhetoric* 1355a.20–1355b.5.
12. As Hulliung (*Citizen Machiavelli,* 158–59) and Sydney Anglo (*Machiavelli* [New York, 1969], 244–49) have remarked, Machiavelli's rejection of *mediocritas* or the middle way is also reflected in his antithetical, either/or style of arguing.

13. Anglo, *Machiavelli*, 209.
14. Nancy Struever has an interesting discussion of the dereification of *virtù* in her unpublished paper, "Machiavelli and the Available Languages of Morality."
15. J. H. Whitfield, *Machiavelli* (Oxford, 1947), 80 and 108; Claude Lefort, *Le Travail de l'oeuvre Machiavel* (Paris, 1972), 376. See below for further discussion of Lefort's position. Another representative of this first position is Jerrold Seigel, "*Virtù* in and Since the Renaissance," in *Dictionary of the History of Ideas*, vol. 4 (New York, 1968), 476–86.
16. See Gennaro Sasso, *Niccolò Machiavelli*, 296ff.; Gabriele Pepe, *La politica dei Borgia* (Naples, 1945), 281–82; and Ugo Dotti, *Niccolò Machiavelli: La fenomenologia del potere* (Milan, 1979), 179ff., for the first position; for the second, see J. G. A. Pocock, *The Machiavellian Moment* (Princeton, N.J., 1975), 152 and 167.
17. Greene, "The End of Discourse in Machiavelli's 'Prince,'" notes the tenuousness of the distinction between Borgia and Agathocles (65), but sees this as evidence of a breakdown in the concept of *virtù* rather than a deliberate strategy on the part of Machiavelli. Manent, *Naissances de la politique*, 16, however, sees the distinction as deliberately false.
18. Russell Price, "The Theme of *Gloria* in Machiavelli," *Renaissance Quarterly* 30 (1977): 588–631.
19. Pocock, *The Machiavellian Moment*, 168.
20. See chapter 12 on the pseudo-distinction between laws and arms, as well as chapter 19 on arms and friends.
21. Struever also discusses the general conflation of the ethical *good* and the amoral *well* in *The Prince;* "Machiavelli and the Available Languages of Morality."
22. Aristotle writes: "It is this kind of deliberation which is good deliberation, a correctness that attains what is good" (*NE* 1141b.20; trans. Martin Ostwald [New York, 1962]). My definition of *virtù* as functional excellence is taken from Hulliung's discussion of the similarity between *virtù* and *aretē:* "Since the Latin word *virtus* meant almost exactly what *aretē* had meant in popular Greek usage, simply to use the Latin language as it had always been used had the effect, whether intended or unintended, of undoing the Platonic and Aristotelian effort of reworking and philosophizing pagan values. Once again, 'excellence' was synonomous with all that is heroic, noble, warlike, great"; *Citizen Machiavelli*, 136–37. See also pp. 195ff., 253, and passim on Machiavelli's critique of stoicism.
23. This phrase is taken from Whitfield, *Machiavelli*, 117.
24. Roland Barthes, "Le Discours de l'histoire," *Social Science Information* 6 (1967), 72. In a book that came to my attention after the completion of this essay, Michael McCanles proposes a reading of chapter 8 similar to the one I am offering here. See "The Discourse of 'Il Principe,'" in *Humana Civilitas*, Studies and Sources Relating to the Middle Ages and Renaissance, vol. 8 (Malibu, Calif., 1983). He tends, however, to maintain a strict opposition between Christian virtue and *virtù* even as he denies any substantive definition of the latter. That is, although he argues throughout his book for the dialectical understanding of *virtù* as necessarily including its opposite, he suggests here that what is evil from a Christian point of view will necessarily be good from a political point of view and vice versa (see p. 63). He also does not discuss Agathocles' conversion to representation at the end of chapter 8 (see pp. 59–65).
25. Pocock, *The Machiavellian Moment*, 163.
26. See Adams's remarks on this example in his edition of *The Prince*, 14. See also Leo Strauss, *Thoughts on Machiavelli* (Chicago, 1958), 82; and Gilbert, *Machiavelli and Guicciardini*, 165–66.

27. On Machiavelli's anticipation of Nietzsche, see Hulliung, *Citizen Machiavelli*, 30.

28. Gilbert, *Machiavelli and Guicciardini*, 120.

29. *Virtù* is equated with success in chaps. 8 (28 [44]), 19 (59 [84]), and perhaps 25 (71 [100]), where Machiavelli equates the good with what is effective; cf. the end of this chapter where failure is equated with inaction. *Virtù* is differentiated from success in chaps. 4 (14 [28]), 6 (16 [30]), and 7 (20 [34–35]). In the *Discourses* (3.35), Machiavelli remarks on the superficiality of judging by the result, as he does in *The History of Florence*, book 4, chap. 7, and book 8, chap. 22. On this problem of the relation of *virtù* to success, see Alkis Kontos, "Success and Knowledge in Machiavelli," in *The Political Calculus: Essays on Machiavelli's Philosophy*, ed. Anthony Parel (Toronto, 1972), 83–100.

30. I borrow the distinction between *technical* and *prudential* from Aristotle *(NE)*, who argues that *technē* is concerned with production (the end results), whereas prudential deliberation is a process, and an end in itself. Those many critics who argue that *virtù* is technical skill are right if they mean that the prince is concerned with results, but wrong if they equate *virtù* with the result rather than deliberative skill and energy in action. *Virtù* is not completely technical because technical skill must result in a product (however much that product may reflect a compromise with one's original conception of the object), while *virtù* does not have to produce something else in order to be *virtù*. Or, as Ostwald observes (*NE*, 154, n. 20), "Practical wisdom is itself a complete virtue or excellence while the excellence of art depends on the goodness or badness of the product." Again, I am arguing only for the *structural* identity or homology of *virtù* and prudence or practical reason.

31. On problematizing examples, see Karlheinz Stierle, "L'Exemple comme histoire, l'histoire comme exemple," *Poétique* 10 (1972): 176–98. While Machiavelli was capable of using the same examples to illustrate different points (e.g., Giacomini's loss of favor in the *Discourses* 1.53 and 3.16; cited in Gilbert, *Machiavelli and Guicciardini*, 167), he needed, if his work was to have any practical effect, to stop short of the radical skepticism of a Montaigne, for whom examples could be used to illustrate almost anything. For if this is the case, then one has departed from the realm of *verità effettuale* and entered the realm of the unconstrained imagination, the realm of fiction.

32. Northrop Frye, *The Anatomy of Criticism* (Princeton, N.J., 1957), 42.

33. Hulliung makes this point in *Citizen Machiavelli*, 56, 82, 231. See also Strauss, *Thoughts on Machiavelli*, 288–89; Manent, *Naissances*, 19–25; and *The Prince*, chap. 19, 53–54 [77–78], for Machiavelli's remarks on the origin of the French parliament. Nancy Struever has some interesting remarks about constraint in *The Prince* in her unpublished essay. She argues that Machiavelli wants to oppose the unproblematic constraints of the humanist tradition (ritual, ceremony, the tautological equation of ethical behavior with good results) to the problematic and problematizing constraints on the prince and the reader of *The Prince*. These latter take the form of 1) a narrow lexicon of political analysis (e.g., *virtù, fortuna*); and 2) difficult and ambiguous examples that force readers to judge and to recognize the moral opacity of the "domain of artifice" in which they act. For Struever, all of this amounts to the greater "realism" of Machiavelli's political analysis, a claim that I address below.

34. See Manent, *Naissances*, 9–10, 35–39, for a more positive reading of the willing of necessity in *The Prince*.

35. Pitkin makes this point in *Fortune Is a Woman*, 292.

36. See Angus Fletcher, *Allegory: The Theory of a Symbolic Mode* (Ithaca, N.Y., 1964). All page references will be given in the body of my text.

37. On parataxis in *The Prince*, see Fredi Chiappelli, *Studi sul linguaggio del Machiavelli* (Florence, 1952), 40–42 (cited by McCanles, *The Discourse of 'Il Principe',* 13). See also McCanles, ibid., 13–15.
38. For some provocative interpretations of this concluding chapter, see Greene, "The End of Discourse in Machiavelli's 'Prince' "; and Sasso, *Niccolò Machiavelli,* 278–80.
39. Fletcher quotes Schiller: "For the sublime, in the strict sense of the word, cannot be contained in any sensuous form, but rather concerns ideas of reason, which, although no adequate representation of them is possible, may be excited and called into the mind by that very inadequacy itself which does admit of sensuous presentation"; *Allegory,* 251–52. See also Immanuel Kant, *Critique of Judgment,* trans. J. H. Bernard (New York, 1951), 88, 101 (paragraphs 25 and 28).
40. Pocock makes a similar point in *The Machiavellian Moment,* 171: "We must not say that divine inspiration is being lowered to the level of *realpolitik* without adding that *realpolitik* is being raised to the level of divine inspiration."

[18]

The Paradoxes of Political Liberty

QUENTIN SKINNER

I

These lectures[1] seek to reconsider two connected claims about political liberty which, from the standpoint of most current debates about the concept, are apt to be dismissed as paradoxical or merely confused.

First a word about what I mean by speaking, as I have just done, about the standpoint of most current debates about liberty. I have in mind the fact that, in recent discussions of the concept among analytical philosophers, one conclusion has been reached which commands a remarkably wide measure of assent. It can best be expressed in the formula originally introduced into the argument by Jeremy Bentham and recently made famous by Isaiah Berlin.[2] The suggestion has been that the idea of political liberty is essentially a negative one. The presence of liberty, that is, is said to be marked by the absence of something else; specifically, by the absence of some element of constraint which inhibits an agent from being able to act in pursuit of his or her chosen ends, from being able to pursue different options, or at least from being able to choose between alternatives.[3]

---

[1] For the printed version I have consolidated the two lectures into a single argument. I am much indebted to those who took part in the staff–student seminar at Harvard where the lectures were discussed on 26 October 1984. As a result of that discussion I have recast some of my claims and removed one section of the opening lecture that met with justified criticism.

[2] See Douglas G. Long, *Bentham on Liberty* (Toronto: Toronto University Press, 1977), p. 74, for Bentham speaking of liberty as 'an idea purely negative.' Berlin uses the formula in his classic essay, 'Two Concepts of Liberty', in *Four Essays on Liberty* (Oxford: Oxford University Press, 1969), at p. 121 and *passim*.

[3] For freedom as the non-restriction of options, see for example S. I. Benn and W. Weinstein, 'Being Free to Act, and Being a Free Man', *Mind* 80 (1971): 194–211. Cf. also John N. Gray, 'On Negative and Positive Liberty', *Political Studies* 28 (1980): 507–26, who argues (esp. p. 519) that this is how Berlin's argument in his 'Two Concepts' essay (cited in note 2 above) is best understood. For the stricter suggestion that we should speak only of freedom to choose between alternatives, see

Hobbes bequeathed a classic statement of this point of view —
one that is still repeatedly invoked—in his chapter 'Of the Liberty
of Subjects' in *Leviathan*. It begins by assuring us, with typical
briskness, that 'liberty or freedom signifieth (properly) the absence of opposition' — and signifies nothing more.[4] Locke makes
the same point in the *Essay*, where he speaks with even greater
confidence. 'Liberty, 'tis plain, consists in a power to do or not to
do; to do or forbear doing as we will. This cannot be denied'.[5]

Among contemporary analytical philosophers, this basic contention has generally been unpacked into two propositions, the
formulation of which appears in many cases to reflect the influence
of Gerald MacCallum's classic paper on negative and positive
freedom.[6] The first states that there is only one coherent way of
thinking about political liberty, that of treating the concept negatively as the absence of impediments to the pursuit of one's chosen
ends.[7] The other proposition states that all such talk about negative liberty can in turn be shown, often despite appearances, to
reduce to the discussion of one particular triadic relationship be-

---

for example Felix Oppenheim, *Political Concepts: A Reconstruction* (Oxford: Basil
Blackwell, 1981), ch. 4, pp. 53–81. For a defence of the even narrower Hobbesian
claim that freedom consists in the mere absence of external impediments, see Hillel
Steiner, 'Individual Liberty', *Proceedings of the Aristotelian Society* 75 (1975): 33–
50. This interpretation of the concept of constraint is partly endorsed by Michael
Taylor, *Community, Anarchy and Liberty* (Cambridge: Cambridge University Press,
1982), pp. 142–50, but is criticised both by Oppenheim and by Benn and Weinstein
in the works cited above.

  [4] Thomas Hobbes, *Leviathan*, ed. C. B. Macpherson (Harmondsworth: Penguin
Books, 1968), bk. II, ch. 21, p. 261. (Here and elsewhere in citing from seventeenth-
century sources I have modernised spelling and punctuation.)

  [5] John Locke, *An Essay Concerning Human Understanding*, ed. Peter H. Nid-
ditch (Oxford: The Clarendon Press, 1975), II.21.56.

  [6] Gerald C. MacCallum, Jr., 'Negative and Positive Freedom', in Peter Laslett,
W. G. Runciman, and Quentin Skinner, eds., *Philosophy, Politics and Society*, 4th
ser. (Oxford: Basil Blackwell, 1972), pp. 174–93.

  [7] This is the main implication of the article by MacCallum cited in note 6 above.
For a recent and explicit statement to this effect, see for example J. P. Day, 'Individual Liberty', in A. Phillips Griffiths, ed., *Of Liberty* (Cambridge: Cambridge
University Press, 1983), who claims (p. 18) 'that "free" is univocal and that the
negative concept is the only concept of liberty'.

tween agents, constraints, and ends. All debates about liberty are thus held to consist in effect of disputes either about who are to count as agents, or what are to count as constraints, or what range of things an agent must be free to do, be, or become (or not be or become) in order to count as being at liberty.[8]

I now turn to the two claims about political liberty which, in the light of these assumptions, are apt to be stigmatised as confused. The first connects freedom with self-government, and in consequence links the idea of personal liberty, in a seemingly paradoxical way, with that of public service. The thesis, as Charles Taylor has recently expressed it, is that we can only be free within 'a society of a certain canonical form, incorporating true self-government'.[9] If we wish to assure our own individual liberty, it follows that we must devote ourselves as wholeheartedly as possible to a life of public service, and thus to the cultivation of the civic virtues required for participating most effectively in political life. The attainment of our fullest liberty, in short, presupposes our recognition of the fact that only certain determinate ends are rational for us to pursue.[10]

The other and related thesis states that we may have to be forced to be free, and thus connects the idea of individual liberty,

---

[8] This formulation derives from the article by MacCallum cited in note 6 above. For recent discussions in which the same approach has been used to analyse the concept of political liberty, see for example Joel Feinberg, *Social Philosophy* (Englewood Cliffs, N.J.: Prentice-Hall, 1973), esp. pp. 12, 16, and J. Roland Pennock, *Democratic Political Theory* (Princeton: Princeton University Press, 1979), esp. pp. 18–24.

[9] Charles Taylor, 'What's Wrong with Negative Liberty', in Alan Ryan, ed., *The Idea of Freedom* (Oxford: Oxford University Press, 1979), pp. 175–93, at p. 181.

[10] For a discussion that moves in this Kantian direction, connecting freedom with rationality and concluding that it cannot therefore 'be identified with absence of impediments,' see for example C. I. Lewis, 'The Meaning of Liberty', in John Lange, ed., *Values and Imperatives* (Stanford: Stanford University Press, 1969), pp. 145–55, at p. 147. (I mention Lewis in particular because, at the request of a Founding Trustee, my lectures at Harvard were dedicated to Lewis's memory.) For a valuable recent exposition of the same Kantian perspective, see the section 'Rationality and Freedom' in Martin Hollis, *Invitation to Philosophy* (Oxford: Basil Blackwell, 1985), pp. 144–51.

in an even more blatantly paradoxical fashion, with the concepts of coercion and constraint. The assumption underlying this further step in the argument is that we may sometimes fail to remember — or may altogether fail to grasp — that the performance of our public duties is indispensable to the maintenance of our own liberty. If it is nevertheless true that freedom depends on service, and hence on our willingness to cultivate the civic virtues, it follows that we may have to be coerced into virtue and thereby constrained into upholding a liberty which, left to ourselves, we would have undermined.

II

Among contemporary theorists of liberty who have criticised these arguments, we need to distinguish two different lines of attack. One of these I shall consider in the present section, the other I shall turn to discuss in section III.

The most unyielding retort has been that, since the negative analysis of liberty is the only coherent one, and since the two contentions I have isolated are incompatible with any such analysis, it follows that they cannot be embodied in any satisfactory account of social freedom at all.

We already find Hobbes taking this view of the alleged relationship between social freedom and public service in his highly influential chapter on liberty in *Leviathan*. There he tells us with scorn about the Lucchese, who have 'written on the turrets of the city of Lucca in great characters, at this day, the word LIBERTAS', in spite of the fact that the constitution of their small-scale city–republic placed heavy demands upon their public-spiritedness.[11] To Hobbes, for whom liberty (as we have seen) simply means absence of interference, it seems obvious that the maximising of our social freedom must depend upon our capacity to maximise the area within which we can claim 'immunity from the service of the commonwealth'.[12] So it seems to him merely absurd of the

[11] Hobbes, *Leviathan*, bk. II, ch. 21, p. 266.
[12] Ibid.

Lucchese to proclaim their liberty in circumstances in which such services are so stringently exacted. Hobbes's modern sympathisers regularly make the same point. As Oppenheim puts it, for example, in his recent book *Political Concepts*, the claim that we can speak of 'freedom of participation in the political process' is simply confused.[13] Freedom presupposes the absence of any such obligations or constraints. So this 'so-called freedom of participation does not relate to freedom in any sense'.[14]

We find the same line of argument advanced even more frequently in the case of the other claim I am considering: that our freedom may have to be the fruit of our being coerced. Consider, for example, how Raphael handles this suggestion in his *Problems of Political Philosophy*. He simply reiterates the contention that 'when we speak of having or not having liberty or freedom in a political context, we are referring to freedom of action or social freedom, i.e., the absence of restraint or compulsion by human agency, including compulsion by the State'.[15] To suggest, therefore, that 'compulsion by the State can make a man more free' is not merely to state a paradoxical conclusion; it is to present an 'extraordinary view' that simply consists of confusing together two polar opposites, freedom and constraint.[16] Again, Oppenheim makes the same point. Since freedom consists in the absence of constraint, to suggest that someone might be 'forced to be free' is no longer to speak of freedom at all but 'its opposite'.[17]

What are we to think of this first line of attack, culminating as it does in the suggestion that, as Oppenheim expresses it, neither of the arguments I have isolated 'relate to freedom in any sense'?

[13] Oppenheim, *Political Concepts*, p. 92.

[14] Ibid., p. 162. For a recent endorsement of the claim that, since liberty requires no action, it can hardly require virtuous or valuable action, see Lincoln Allison, *Right Principles* (Oxford: Basil Blackwell, 1984), pp. 134–35.

[15] D. D. Raphael, *Problems of Political Philosophy*, rev. ed. (London: Macmillan, 1976), p. 139.

[16] Ibid., p. 137.

[17] Oppenheim, *Political Concepts*, p. 164.

It seems to me that this conclusion relies on dismissing, far too readily, a different tradition of thought about social freedom which, at this point in my argument, it becomes important briefly to lay out.

The tradition I have in mind stems from Greek moral thought and is founded on two distinctive and highly influential premises. The first, developed in various subsequent systems of naturalistic ethics, claims that we are moral beings with certain characteristically human purposes. The second, later taken up in particular by scholastic political philosophy, adds that the human animal is *naturale sociale et politicum*, and thus that our purposes must essentially be social in character.[18] The view of human freedom to which these assumptions give rise is thus a 'positive' one. We can only be said to be fully or genuinely at liberty, according to this account, if we actually engage in just those activities which are most conducive to *eudaimonia* or 'human flourishing', and may therefore be said to embody our deepest human purposes.

I have no wish to defend the truth of these premises. I merely wish to underline what the above account already makes clear: that if they are granted, a positive theory of liberty flows from them without the least paradox or incoherence.

This has two important implications for my present argument. One is that the basic claim advanced by the theorists of negative liberty I have so far been considering would appear to be false. They have argued that all coherent theories of liberty must have a certain triadic structure. But the theory of social freedom I have just stated, although perfectly coherent if we grant its premises, has a strongly contrasting shape.[19]

---

[18] See for example Thomas Aquinas, *De Regimine Principum*, bk. I, ch. 1, in A. P. D'Entrèves, ed., *Aquinas: Selected Political Writings* (Oxford: Basil Blackwell, 1959), p. 2.

[19] For a fuller exploration of this point see the important article by Tom Baldwin, 'MacCallum and the Two Concepts of Freedom', *Ratio* 26 (1984): 125–42, esp. at 135–36.

The contrast can be readily spelled out. The structure within which MacCallum and his numerous followers insist on analysing all claims about social freedom is such that they make it a sufficient condition of an agent's being at liberty that he or she should be unconstrained from pursuing some particular option, or at least from choosing between alternatives. Freedom, in the terminology Charles Taylor has recently introduced, becomes a pure opportunity concept.[20] I am already free if I have the opportunity to act, whether or not I happen to make use of that opportunity. By contrast, the positive theory I have just laid out makes it a necessary condition of an agent's being fully or truly at liberty that he or she should actually engage in the pursuit of certain determinate ends. Freedom, to invoke Taylor's terminology once more, is viewed not as an opportunity but as an exercise concept.[21] I am only in the fullest sense in possession of my liberty if I actually exercise the capacities and pursue the goals that serve to realise my most distinctively human purposes.

The other implication of this positive analysis is even more important for my present argument. According to the negative theories I have so far considered, the two paradoxes I began by isolating can safely be dismissed as misunderstandings of the concept of liberty.[22] According to some, indeed, they are far worse than misunderstandings; they are 'patent sophisms' that are really designed, in consequence of sinister ideological commitments, to convert social freedom 'into something very different, if not its opposite'.[23] Once we recognise, however, that the positive view of liberty stemming from the thesis of naturalism is a perfectly

[20] Taylor, 'Negative Liberty', p. 177.

[21] Ibid.

[22] See for example the conclusions in W. Parent, 'Some Recent Work on the Concept of Liberty', *American Philosophical Quarterly* 11 (1974): 149–67, esp. 152, 166.

[23] Anthony Flew, ' "Freedom Is Slavery": A Slogan for Our New Philosopher Kings', in Griffiths, ed., *Of Liberty*, pp. 45–59, esp. at pp. 46, 48, 52.

coherent one, we are bound to view the two paradoxes in a quite different light.

There ceases, in the first place, to be any self-evident reason for impugning the motives of those who have defended them.[24] Belief in the idea of 'human flourishing' and its accompanying vision of social freedom arises at a far deeper level than that of mere ideological debate. It arises as an attempt to answer one of the central questions in moral philosophy, the question whether it is rational to be moral. The suggested answer is that it is in fact rational, the reason being that we have an interest in morality, the reason for this in turn being the fact that we are moral agents committed by our very natures to certain normative ends. We may wish to claim that this theory of human nature is false. But we can hardly claim to know *a priori* that it could never in principle be sincerely held.

We can carry this argument a stage further, moreover, if we revert to the particular brand of Thomist and Aristotelian naturalism I have singled out. Suppose for the sake of argument we accept both its distinctive premises: not only that human nature embodies certain moral purposes, but that these purposes are essentially social in character as well. If we do so, the two paradoxes I began by isolating not only cease to look confused; they both begin to look highly plausible.

Consider first the alleged connection between freedom and public service. We are supposing that human nature has an essence, and that this is social and political in character. But this makes it almost truistic to suggest that we may need to establish one particular form of political association — thereafter devoting ourselves to serving and sustaining it — if we wish to realise our own natures and hence our fullest liberty. For the form of association we shall need to maintain will of course be just that form in

---

[24] At this point I am greatly indebted once more to Baldwin, 'Two Concepts', esp. pp. 139–40.

which our freedom to be our true selves is capable of being realised as completely as possible.

Finally, consider the paradox that connects this idea of freedom with constraint. If we need to serve a certain sort of society
in order to become most fully ourselves, we can certainly imagine
tensions arising between our apparent interests and the duties we
need to discharge if our true natures, and hence our fullest liberty,
are both to be realised. But in those circumstances we can scarcely
call it paradoxical — though we may certainly find it disturbing —
if we are told what Rousseau tells us so forcefully in *The Social
Contract*: that if anyone regards 'what he owes to the common
cause as a gratuitous contribution, the loss of which would be less
painful for others than the payment is onerous for him', then he
must be 'forced to be free', coerced into enjoying a liberty he will
otherwise allow to degenerate into servitude.[25]

III

I now turn to assess the other standpoint from which these
two paradoxes of liberty have commonly been dismissed. The
theorists I now wish to discuss have recognised that there may
well be more than one coherent way of thinking about the idea of
political liberty. Sometimes they have even suggested, in line with
the formula used in Isaiah Berlin's classic essay, that there may be
more than one coherent *concept* of liberty.[26] As a result, they have
sometimes explicitly stated that there may be theories of liberty
within which the paradoxes I have singled out no longer appear
as paradoxical at all. As Berlin himself emphasises, for example,
several 'positive' theories of freedom, religious as well as political, seem readily able to encompass the suggestion that people may

[25] Jean-Jacques Rousseau, *The Social Contract*, trans. Maurice Cranston (Harmondsworth: Penguin Books, 1968), p. 64.

[26] This is how Berlin expresses the point in the title of his essay, although he
shifts in the course of it to speaking instead of the different 'senses' of the term.
See *Four Essays*, esp. p. 121.

236   *The Tanner Lectures on Human Values*

have to act 'in certain self-improving ways, which they could be coerced to do' if there is to be any prospect of realising their fullest or truest liberty.[27]

When such writers express doubts about the two paradoxes I am considering, therefore, their thesis is not that such paradoxes are incapable of being accommodated within any coherent theory of liberty. It is only that such paradoxes are incapable of being accommodated within any coherent theory of negative liberty — any theory in which the idea of liberty itself is equated with the mere absence of impediments to the realisation of one's chosen ends.

This appears, for example, to be Isaiah Berlin's view of the matter in his 'Two Concepts of Liberty'. Citing Cranmer's epigram 'Whose service is perfect freedom', Berlin allows that such an ideal, perhaps even coupled with a demand for coercion in its name, might conceivably form part of a theory of freedom 'without thereby rendering the word "freedom" wholly meaningless'. His objection is merely that, as he adds, 'all this has little to do with' the idea of negative liberty as someone like John Stuart Mill would ordinarily understand it.[28]

Considering the same question from the opposite angle, so to speak, Charles Taylor appears to reach the same conclusion in his essay, 'What's Wrong with Negative Liberty'. It is only because liberty is *not* a mere opportunity concept, he argues, that we need to confront the two paradoxes I have isolated, asking ourselves whether our liberty is 'realisable only within a certain form of society', and whether this commits us 'to justifying the excesses of totalitarian oppression in the name of liberty'.[29] Taylor's final reason, indeed, for treating the strictly negative view of liberty as an impoverished one is that, if we restrict ourselves to such an under-

[27] Ibid., esp. p. 152.

[28] Ibid., pp. 160–62.

[29] Taylor, 'Negative Liberty', p. 193.

standing of the concept, these troubling but unavoidable questions do not arise.[30]

What are we to think of this second line of argument, culminating in the suggestion that the two paradoxes I am considering, whatever else may be said about them, have no place in any ordinary theory of negative liberty?

It seems to me that this conclusion depends on ignoring yet another whole tradition of thought about social freedom, one that it again becomes crucial, at this point in my argument, to try to lay out.

The tradition I have in mind is that of classical republicanism.[31] The view of social freedom to which the republican vision of political life gave rise is one that has largely been overlooked in recent philosophical debate. It seems well worth trying to restore it to view, however, for the effect of doing so will be to show us, I believe, that the two paradoxes I have isolated can in fact be accommodated within an ordinary theory of negative liberty. It is to this task of exposition, accordingly, that I now turn, albeit in an unavoidably promissory and over-schematic style.[32]

Within the classical republican tradition, the discussion of political liberty was generally embedded in an analysis of what it means to speak of living in a 'free state'. This approach was

[30] See Taylor, ibid., insisting (p. 193) that this is 'altogether too quick a way with them'.

[31] I cannot hope to give anything like a complete account of this ideology here, nor even of the recent historical literature devoted to it. Suffice it to mention that, in the case of English republicanism, the pioneering study is Z. S. Fink, *The Classical Republicans*, 2d ed. (Evanston: Northwestern University Press, 1962). On the development of the entire school of thought, the classic study is J. G. A. Pocock, *The Machiavellian Moment* (Princeton: Princeton University Press, 1975), a work to which I am much indebted.

[32] I have tried to give a fuller account in two earlier articles: 'Machiavelli on the Maintenance of Liberty', *Politics* 18 (1983): 3–15, and 'The Idea of Negative Liberty: Philosophical and Historical Perspectives', in Richard Rorty, J. B. Schneewind, and Quentin Skinner, eds., *Philosophy in History* (Cambridge: Cambridge University Press, 1984), pp. 193–221. The present essay may be regarded as an attempt to bring out the implications of those earlier studies, although at the same time I have considerably modified and I hope strengthened my earlier arguments.

largely derived from Roman moral philosophy, and especially from those writers whose greatest admiration had been reserved for the doomed Roman republic: Livy, Sallust, and above all Cicero. Within modern political theory, their line of argument was first taken up in Renaissance Italy as a means of defending the traditional liberties of the city–republics against the rising tyranny of the *signori* and the secular powers of the Church. Many theorists espoused the republican cause at this formative stage in its development, but perhaps the greatest among those who did so was Machiavelli in his *Discorsi* on the first ten books of Livy's History of Rome. Later we find a similar defence of 'free states' being mounted — with acknowledgements to Machiavelli's influence — by James Harrington, John Milton, and other English republicans as a means of challenging the alleged despotism of the Stuarts in the middle years of the seventeenth century. Still later, we find something of the same outlook — again owing much to Machiavelli's inspiration — among the opponents of absolutism in eighteenth-century France, above all in Montesquieu's account of republican virtue in *De L'esprit des Lois*.

By this time, however, the ideals of classical republicanism had largely been swallowed up by the rising tide of contractarian political thought. If we wish to investigate the heyday of classical republicanism, accordingly, we need to turn back to the period before the concept of individual rights attained that hegemony which it has never subsequently lost. This means turning back to the moral and political philosophy of the Renaissance, as well as to the Roman republican writers on whom the Renaissance theorists placed such overwhelming weight. It is from these sources, therefore, that I shall mainly draw my picture of the republican idea of liberty, and it is from Machiavelli's *Discorsi* — perhaps the most compelling presentation of the case—that I shall mainly cite.[33]

---

[33] All citations from the *Discorsi* refer to the version in Niccolò Machiavelli, *Il Principe e Discorsi*, ed. Sergio Bertelli (Milan: Feltrinelli, 1960). All translations are my own.

IV

I have said that the classical republicans were mainly concerned to celebrate what Nedham, in a resounding title, called the
excellency of a free state. It will be best to begin, therefore, by
asking what they had in mind when they predicated liberty of
entire communities. To grasp the answer, we need only recall that
these writers take the metaphor of the body politic as seriously
as possible. A political body, no less than a natural one, is said to
be at liberty if and only if it is not subject to external constraint.
Like a free person, a free state is one that is able to act according
to its own will, in pursuit of its own chosen ends. It is a community, that is, in which the will of the citizens, the general will
of the body-politic, chooses and determines whatever ends are
pursued by the community as a whole. As Machiavelli expresses
the point at the beginning of his *Discorsi*, free states are those
'which are far from all external servitude, and are able to govern
themselves according to their own will'.[34]

There are two principal benefits, according to these theorists,
which we can only hope to enjoy with any degree of assurance if
we live as members of free states. One is civic greatness and
wealth. Sallust had laid it down in his *Catiline* (7.1) that Rome
only became great as a result of throwing off the tyranny of her
kings, and the same sentiment was endlessly echoed by later exponents of classical republican thought. Machiavelli also insists,
for example, that 'it is easy to understand the affection that people
feel for living in liberty, for experience shows that no cities have
ever grown in power or wealth except those which have been
established as free states'.[35]

But there is another and even greater gift that free states are
alone capable of bequeathing with any confidence to their citizens.
This is personal liberty, understood in the ordinary sense to mean

[34] Ibid., I.ii, p. 129.
[35] Ibid., II.ii, p. 280.

that each citizen remains free from any elements of constraint (especially those which arise from personal dependence and servitude) and in consequence remains free to pursue his own chosen ends. As Machiavelli insists in a highly emphatic passage at the start of Book II of the *Discorsi*, it is only 'in lands and provinces which live as free states' that individual citizens can hope 'to live without fear that their patrimony will be taken away from them, knowing not merely that they are born as free citizens and not as slaves, but that they can hope to rise by their abilities to become leaders of their communities'.[36]

It is important to add that, by contrast with the Aristotelian assumptions about *eudaimonia* that pervade scholastic political philosophy, the writers I am considering never suggest that there are certain specific goals we need to realise in order to count as being fully or truly in possession of our liberty. Rather they emphasise that different classes of people will always have varying dispositions, and will in consequence value their liberty as the means to attain varying ends. As Machiavelli explains, some people place a high value on the pursuit of honour, glory, and power: 'they will want their liberty in order to be able to dominate others'.[37] But other people merely want to be left to their own devices, free to pursue their own family and professional lives: 'they want liberty in order to be able to live in security'.[38] To be free, in short, is simply to be unconstrained from pursuing whatever goals we may happen to set ourselves.

How then can we hope to set up and maintain a free state, thereby preventing our own individual liberty from degenerating into servitude? This is clearly the pivotal question, and by way of answering it the writers I am considering advance the distinctive claim that entitles them to be treated as a separate school of thought. A free state, they argue, must constitutionally speaking

[36] Ibid., II.ii, p. 284.
[37] Ibid., I.xvi, p. 176.
[38] Ibid., I.xvi, p. 176; cf. also II.ii, pp. 284–85.

be what Livy and Sallust and Cicero had all described and celebrated as a *res publica*.

We need to exercise some care in assessing what this means,
however, for it would certainly be an oversimplification to suppose
that what they have in mind is necessarily a republic in the modern
sense. When the classical republican theorists speak of a *res
publica*, what they take themselves to be describing is any set of
constitutional arrangements under which it might justifiably be
claimed that the *res* (the government) genuinely reflects the will
and promotes the good of the *publica* (the community as a
whole). Whether a *res publica* has to take the form of a self-
governing republic is not therefore an empty definitional question,
as modern usage suggests, but rather a matter for earnest enquiry
and debate. It is true, however, that most of the writers I have
cited remain sceptical about the possibility that an individual or
even a governing class could ever hope to remain sufficiently disinterested to equate their own will with the general will, and
thereby act to promote the good of the community at all times.
So they generally conclude that, if we wish to set up a *res publica*,
it will be best to set up a republic as opposed to any kind of principality or monarchical rule.

The central contention of the theory I am examining is thus
that a self-governing republic is the only type of regime under
which a community can hope to attain greatness at the same time
as guaranteeing its citizens their individual liberty. This is Machiavelli's usual view, Harrington's consistent view, and the view
that Milton eventually came to accept.[39] But if this is so, we very
much need to know how this particular form of government can
in practice be established and kept in existence. For it turns out
that each one of us has a strong personal interest in understanding
how this can best be done.

[39] See Fink, *Classical Republicans*, esp. pp. 103–7, on Milton and Harrington.
For Machiavelli's equivocations on the point see Marcia Colish, 'The Idea of Liberty
in Machiavelli', *Journal of the History of Ideas* 32 (1971): 323–50.

The writers I am considering all respond, in effect, with a one-word answer. A self-governing republic can only be kept in being, they reply, if its citizens cultivate that crucial quality which Cicero had described as *virtus*, which the Italian theorists later rendered as *virtù*, and which the English republicans translated as civic virtue or public-spiritedness. The term is thus used to denote the range of capacities that each one of us as a citizen most needs to possess: the capacities that enable us willingly to serve the common good, thereby to uphold the freedom of our community, and in consequence to ensure its rise to greatness as well as our own individual liberty.

But what *are* these capacities? First of all, we need to possess the courage and determination to defend our community against the threat of conquest and enslavement by external enemies. A body-politic, no less than a natural body, which entrusts itself to be defended by someone else is exposing itself gratuitously to the loss of its liberty and even its life. For no one else can be expected to care as much for our own life and liberty as we care ourselves. Once we are conquered, moreover, we shall find ourselves serving the ends of our new masters rather than being able to pursue our own purposes. It follows that a willingness to cultivate the martial virtues, and to place them in the service of our community, must be indispensable to the preservation of our own individual liberty as well as the independence of our native land.[40]

We also need to have enough prudence and other civic qualities to play an active and effective role in public life. To allow the political decisions of a body-politic to be determined by the will of anyone other than the entire membership of the body itself is, as in the case of a natural body, to run the gratuitous risk that the behaviour of the body in question will be directed to the attainment not of its own ends, but merely the ends of those who have managed to gain control of it. It follows that, in order to avoid

---

[40] This constitutes a leading theme of Book II of Machiavelli's *Discorsi*.

such servitude, and hence to ensure our own individual liberty, we must all cultivate the political virtues and devote ourselves whole-heartedly to a life of public service.[41]

This strenuous view of citizenship gives rise to a grave difficulty, however, as the classical republican theorists readily admit. Each of us needs courage to help defend our community and prudence to take part in its government. But no one can be relied on consistently to display these cardinal virtues. On the contrary, as Machiavelli repeatedly emphasises, we are generally reluctant to cultivate the qualities that enable us to serve the common good. Rather we tend to be 'corrupt', a term of art the republican theorists habitually use to denote our natural tendency to ignore the claims of our community as soon as they seem to conflict with the pursuit of our own immediate advantage.[42]

To be corrupt, however, is to forget — or fail to grasp — something which it is profoundly in our interests to remember: that if we wish to enjoy as much freedom as we can hope to attain within political society, there is good reason for us to act in the first instance as virtuous citizens, placing the common good above the pursuit of any individual or factional ends. Corruption, in short, is simply a failure of rationality, an inability to recognise that our own liberty depends on committing ourselves to a life of virtue and public service. And the consequence of our habitual tendency to forget or misunderstand this vital piece of practical reasoning is therefore that we regularly tend to defeat our own purposes. As Machiavelli puts it, we often think we are acting to maximize our own liberty when we are really shouting Long live our own ruin.[43]

[41] Book III of Machiavelli's *Discorsi* is much concerned with the role played by great men — defined as those possessing exceptional *virtù* — in Rome's rise to greatness.

[42] For a classic discussion of 'corruption' see Machiavelli, *Discorsi*, I.xvii–xix, pp. 177–85.

[43] Ibid., I.liii, p. 249.

For the republican writers, accordingly, the deepest question of statecraft is one that recent theorists of liberty have supposed it pointless to ask. Contemporary theories of social freedom, analysing the concept of individual liberty in terms of 'background' rights, have come to rely heavily on the doctrine of the invisible hand. If we all pursue our own enlightened self-interest, we are assured, the outcome will in fact be the greatest good of the community as a whole.[44] From the point of view of the republican tradition, however, this is simply another way of describing corruption, the overcoming of which is said to be a necessary condition of maximising our own individual liberty. For the republican writers, accordingly, the deepest and most troubling question still remains: how can naturally self-interested citizens be persuaded to act virtuously, such that they can hope to maximise a freedom which, left to themselves, they will infallibly throw away?

The answer at first sounds familiar: the republican writers place all their faith in the coercive powers of the law. Machiavelli, for example, puts the point graphically in the course of analysing the Roman republican constitution in Book I of his *Discorsi*. 'It is hunger and poverty that make men industrious', he declares, 'and it is the laws that make them good'.[45]

The account the republican writers give, however, of the relationship between law and liberty stands in strong contrast to the more familiar account to be found in contractarian political thought. To Hobbes, for example, or to Locke, the law preserves our liberty essentially by coercing other people. It prevents them from interfering with my acknowledged rights, helps me to draw around myself a circle within which they may not trespass, and prevents me at the same time from interfering with their freedom in just the same way. To a theorist such as Machiavelli, by con-

---

[44] See for example the way in which the concept of 'the common good' is discussed in John Rawls, *A Theory of Justice* (Cambridge: Harvard University Press, 1971), pp. 243, 246.

[45] Machiavelli, *Discorsi*, I.iii, p. 136.

trast, the law preserves our liberty not merely by coercing others, but also by directly coercing each one of us into acting in a particular way. The law is also used, that is, to force us out of our habitual patterns of self-interested behaviour, to force us into discharging the full range of our civic duties, and thereby to ensure that the free state on which our own liberty depends is itself maintained free of servitude.

The justifications offered by the classical republican writers for the coercion that law brings with it also stand in marked contrast to those we find in contractarian or even in classical utilitarian thought. For Hobbes or for Locke, our freedom is a natural possession, a property of ourselves. The law's claim to limit its exercise can only be justified if it can be shown that, were the law to be withdrawn, the effect would not in fact be a greater liberty, but rather a diminution of the security with which our existing liberty is enjoyed. For a writer like Machiavelli, however, the justification of law is nothing to do with the protection of individual rights, a concept that makes no appearance in the *Discorsi* at all. The main justification for its exercise is that, by coercing people into acting in such a way as to uphold the institutions of a free state, the law creates and preserves a degree of individual liberty which, in its absence, would promptly collapse into absolute servitude.

Finally, we might ask what mechanisms the republican writers have in mind when they speak of using the law to coerce naturally self-interested individuals into defending their community with courage and governing it with prudence. This is a question to which Machiavelli devotes much of Book I of his *Discorsi*, and he offers two main suggestions, both derived from Livy's account of republican Rome.

He first considers what induced the Roman people to legislate so prudently for the common good when they might have fallen into factional conflicts.[46] He finds the key in the fact that, under

---

[46] Ibid., I.ii–vi, pp. 129–46.

their republican constitution, they had one assembly controlled by the nobility, another by the common people, with the consent of each being required for any proposal to become law. Each group admittedly tended to produce proposals designed merely to further its own interests. But each was prevented by the other from imposing them as laws. The result was that only such proposals as favoured no faction could ever hope to succeed. The laws relating to the constitution thus served to ensure that the common good was promoted at all times. As a result, the laws duly upheld a liberty that, in the absence of their power to coerce, would soon have been lost to tyranny and servitude.

Machiavelli also considers how the Romans induced their citizen-armies to fight so bravely against enslavement by invading enemies. Here he finds the key in their religious laws.[47] The Romans saw that the only way to make self-interested individuals risk their very lives for the liberty of their community was to make them take an oath binding them to defend the state at all costs. This made them less frightened of fighting than of running away. If they fought they might risk their lives, but if they ran away — thus violating their sacred pledge — they risked the much worse fate of offending the gods. The result was that, even when terrified, they always stood their ground. Hence, once again, their laws forced them to be free, coercing them into defending their liberty when their natural instinct for self-preservation would have led them to defeat and thus servitude.

V

By now, I hope, it will be obvious what conclusions I wish to draw from this examination of the classical republican theory of political liberty. On the one hand, it is evident that the republican writers embrace both the paradoxes I began by singling out. They certainly connect social freedom with self-government, and in con-

---

47 Ibid., I.xi–xv, pp. 160–73.

sequence link the idea of personal liberty with that of virtuous public service. Moreover, they are no less emphatic that we may have to be forced to cultivate the civic virtues, and in consequence insist that the enjoyment of our personal liberty may often have to be the product of coercion and constraint.

On the other hand, they never appeal to a 'positive' view of social freedom. They never argue, that is, that we are moral beings with certain determinate purposes, and thus that we are only in the fullest sense in possession of our liberty when these purposes are realised. As we have seen, they work with a purely negative view of liberty as the absence of impediments to the realisation of our chosen ends. They are absolutely explicit in adding, moreover, that no determinate specification of these ends can be given without violating the inherent variety of human aspirations and goals.

Nor do they defend the idea of forcing people to be free by claiming that we must be prepared to reason about ends. They never suggest, that is, that there must be a certain range of actions which it will be objectively rational for us to perform, whatever the state of our desires. It is true that, on their analysis, there may well be actions of which it makes sense to say that there are good reasons for us to perform them, even if we have no desire — not even a reflectively considered desire — to do so. But this is not because they believe that it makes sense to reason about ends.[48] It is simply because they consider that the chain of practical reasoning we need to follow out in the case of acting to uphold our own liberty is so complex, and so unwelcome to citizens of corrupt disposition, that we find it all too easy to lose our way in the argument. As a result, we often cannot be brought, even in reflection, to recognise the range of actions we have good reason to perform in order to bring about the ends we actually desire.

---

[48] Although those who attack as well as those who defend the Kantian thesis that there may be reasons for action which are unconnected with our desires appear to assume that this must be what is at stake in such cases.

Given this characterisation of the republican theory of free-dom, my principal conclusion is thus that it must be a mistake to suppose that the two paradoxes I have been considering cannot be accommodated within an ordinary negative analysis of political liberty.[49] If the summary characterisation I have just given is cor-rect, however, there is a further implication to be drawn from this latter part of my argument, and this I should like to end by pointing out. It is that our inherited traditions of political theory appear to embody two quite distinct though equally coherent views about the way in which it is most rational for us to act in order to maximise our negative liberty.

Recent emphasis on the importance of taking rights seriously has contrived to leave the impression that there may be only one way of thinking about this issue. We must first seek to erect around ourselves a cordon of rights, treating these as 'trumps' and insisting on their priority over any calls of social duty.[50] We must then seek to expand this cordon as far as possible, our even-tual aim being to achieve what Isaiah Berlin has called 'a maxi-mum degree of non-interference compatible with the minimum demands of social life'.[51] Only in this way — as Hobbes long ago argued — can we hope to maximise the area within which we are free to act as we choose.

If we revert to the republican theorists, however, we encounter a strong challenge to these familiar beliefs. To insist on rights as trumps, on their account, is simply to proclaim our corruption as

[49] I should stress that this seems to me an implication of MacCallum's analysis of the concept of freedom cited in note 6 above. If so, it is an implication that none of those who have made use of his analysis have followed out, and most have ex-plicitly denied. But cf. his discussion at pp. 189–92. I should like to take this opportunity of acknowledging that, although I believe the central thesis of Mac-Callum's article to be mistaken, I am nevertheless greatly indebted to it.

[50] See for example Ronald Dworkin, *Taking Rights Seriously* (Cambridge: Harvard University Press, 1977), p. xi, for the claim that 'individual rights are political trumps held by individuals', and pp. 170–77 for a defence of the priority of rights over duties.

[51] Berlin, *Four Essays*, p. 161.

citizens. It is also to embrace a self-destructive form of irrationality. Rather we must take our duties seriously, and instead of trying to evade anything more than 'the minimum demands of social life' we must seek to discharge our public obligations as wholeheartedly as possible. Political rationality consists in recognising that this constitutes the only means of guaranteeing the very liberty we may seem to be giving up.

VI

My story is at an end; it only remains to point the moral of the tale. Contemporary liberalism, especially in its so-called libertarian form, is in danger of sweeping the public arena bare of any concepts save those of self-interest and individual rights. Moralists who have protested against this impoverishment—such as Hannah Arendt, and more recently Charles Taylor, Alasdair MacIntyre and others[52] — have generally assumed in turn that the only alternative is to adopt an 'exercise' concept of liberty, or else to seek by some unexplained means to slip back into the womb of the polis. I have tried to show that the dichotomy here — either a theory of rights or an 'exercise' theory of liberty — is a false one. The Aristotelian and Thomist assumption that a healthy public life must be founded on a conception of *eudaimonia* is by no means the only alternative tradition available to us if we wish to recapture a vision of politics based not merely on fair procedures but on common meanings and purposes. It is also open to us to meditate on the potential relevance of a theory which tells us that, if we wish to maximise our own individual liberty, we must cease to put our trust in princes, and instead take charge of the public arena ourselves.

[52] For Arendt's views see her essay 'What Is Freedom?' in *Between Past and Future*, rev. ed. (New York: The Viking Press, 1968), pp. 143–71. For Taylor's, see 'Negative Liberty', esp. pp. 180–86. For MacIntyre's, see *After Virtue* (London: Duckworth, 1981), esp. p. 241, for the claim 'that the crucial moral opposition is between liberal individualism in some version or other and the Aristotelian tradition in some version or other'.

It will be objected that this is the merest nostalgic anti-modernism. We have no realistic prospect of taking active control of the political processes in any modern democracy committed to the technical complexities and obsessional secrecies of present-day government. But the objection is too crudely formulated. There are many areas of public life, short of directly controlling the actual executive process, where increased public participation might well serve to improve the accountability of our *soi disant* representatives. Even if the objection is valid, however, it misses the point. The reason for wishing to bring the republican vision of politics back into view is not that it tells us how to construct a genuine democracy, one in which government is for the people as a result of being by the people. That is for us to work out. It is simply because it conveys a warning which, while it may be unduly pessimistic, we can hardly afford to ignore: that unless we place our duties before our rights, we must expect to find our rights themselves undermined.

[19]

Savonarola, Machiavelli and Moses:
a Changing Model

ALISON BROWN

MOSES is all things to all men: holy prophet and warrior chieftain to popes and kings, constitutional head of a mixed government to Thomist theologians, ancient magus to Renaissance philosophers and a contractual sovereign to Hobbes. So chameleon a character must be approached with caution: an unstable model for imitation but a useful index of changing attitudes and values.[1] From this point of view, the Savonarolan period in Florence is important as a moment of change, an unexpected cataract in the slow meanderings of the Mosaic tradition, from which the holy man re-emerges as a tough and all-powerful ruler prepared to murder 'infinite numbers of men' to impose his laws. How did this happen?

Despite the underlying continuity of government in the post-Medicean period,[2] the four years of Savonarola's predominance in Florence from 1494 to 1498 presented the city with a quite new situation: the replacement of the Medici as the guiding influence on politics by a Dominican friar who not only lacked political rights as a foreigner but because of his religious status was excluded from direct participation in government altogether. As he said in 1496: 'I am a friar and I never saw arms; but if I were allowed to, I would show you reasons to prevent you being so afraid . . . I wish I could (I say could, that is, that I were allowed to) put on a *cappuccio* and also a *lucco* [the magistrate's hood and gown]'.[3] In fact, this did not prevent Savonarola from playing a leading political role. He was sent as one of several ambassadors to the king of France in November 1494 and again, on his own, the following year. He was invited into the government palace in January 1495 to advise the citizens on reform. And he preached regularly at Lent and Advent by invitation of the government, sometimes also at times of political crisis.[4] As a preacher he was able to address a far wider audience than he would have been able to as a politician in the council chambers. Because of his charismatic hold over an entirely new group of adherents — not the members of territorially-based clans and *consorterie* who provided the traditional structure of politics but, thanks to his special appeal to women and children, a wide social and geographical cross-section of the community — he has been likened to a modern party leader.[5] Although — as he told his audience, citing St Dominic, Peter Martyr, Cardinal Latini, Catherine of Siena and archbishop Antoninus — there were precedents for religious men intervening in Florentine politics, Savonarola's role was exceptional, as everyone knew, and he drew increasing criticism for 'getting mixed up in affairs of state'.[6]

Underlying this was the more serious problem of filling the political vacuum created by the fall of the Medici — 'our political revolution' as Savonarola called it.[7] Savonarola had been quick to condemn the Medici for behaving as tyrannical heads of a free republic in December 1494 and he continued to hammer the message home: 'You are frightened by no one now, but when you had a head or tyrant, you know that the law of the tyrant is his will . . . that's how the tyrant is: every time he thinks you've done the slightest thing he doesn't like, he doesn't want to see you any more', 'in future no more tyrants can arise in our city, because having been given the Great Council and holding firm to it, be certain of this, there will be no more heads in Florence', 'In the other regime, you didn't have to dare to speak before you were punished', 'you citizens of the other regime, you were subjected to it, and you couldn't have a shop and you had no freedom to marry your daughter'.[8] Yet the achievement of the Medici had been to overcome factionalism by their firm control of the republic and Savonarola was the first to admit after their fall that Florence needed 'a public head being accustomed as it was to living with a private one'. So he found himself in a paradoxical position: needing the arguments developed by the Medici to justify their arbitrary power as platonic 'wise' and 'good' men, yet forced to denounce them on behalf of the popular republicanism he publicly espoused.[9] Trexler has demonstrated how Savonarola solved this problem on an institutional and behavioural level by adopting Medici ceremonies and ritual to 'assume the Lorenzan heritage' while condemning their tyranny.[10] It remained necessary, as Savonarola realised, to resolve it in the more explicit language of politics used 'in the Palace and in the piazzas' where Florentines conducted so much of their busy lives.[11]

Initially Savonarola pre-empted the old Medici basis of authority by claiming power, wisdom and goodness for God, and kingship — or 'captaincy' — for his Son. 'I see you want some one to be your head', he said on 27 December 1494, four days after the Great Council had been created:

> One can't deny that those states that are governed by one head alone are best but he must be perfect . . . So what would you like, Florence, what head, what king can we give you to keep you quiet? I've told you before that it's not better everywhere, nor in every country, for one head to rule, and St Thomas says, too, that in Italy princes become tyrants — come on, Florence,

Savonarola, Machiavelli and Moses　　　59

God wants to satisfy you and give you one head and one king to govern you. And this is Christ. . take Christ for your king and stay under his law and with it he will govern you . . . Let Christ be your Captain . . . be with Christ and don't seek another head'.[12]

Returning to the theme in June, he asked whether the Florentines would not surely trust a great lord who promised to help them, especially if they saw he had the power to do so: 'Everyone knows that God is powerful and wise and good'.[13]

Four months later Savonarola skilfully took over two more Medicean images of authority, the naturalistic image of every 'genus' controlled by one leader — the army by a captain, the city by a single magistrate — and the imperial Golden Age image of Caesar Augustus which the Medici had been increasingly assimilating to themselves. 'Consider the order of the universe, which provides a leader in every 'genus' . . . the army isn't well governed without a captain . . . nor is the city unless it is under one magistrate. You, Florence, have Christ for your king, whom God wanted to demonstrate the fact he was king and dominate right from the moment of his birth . . . and He wanted him to be born at the time when all the world was under a prince, Octavian, to demonstrate that all the world had to be under him'.[14] This subsequently became the image of authority propagated to the children who formed so important a part of Savonarola's following. When Domenico da Pescia printed a letter to 'the children of Florence' in September 1497, he sent it in the name of 'God the lord and Jesus Christ our king', whom he also called 'your emperor' and his mother 'your empress'.[15]

Since neither God nor Christ were heads of state, they were replaced for practical purposes by 'the people' as lord of Florence. In August 1495 the law abolishing *parlamenti*, to prevent anyone daring 'to rise up as Head and make himself dominator and tyrant', declared that such plebiscites were unnecessary now that 'government is in the hands of the people, which is the true and legitimate Lord of our city'.[16] In October 1495 Savonarola asked his audience, in a new political catechism: 'Who is our Lord? Christ is. Who holds the place of Christ? Not the Signoria, but the people are the Lord; and therefore I say to you, keep your eye on the Lord, that is, on the Council'.[17] Piero Parenti relates in his chronicle how Savonarola urged the people, 'since they were lord', to get to their feet if the Signoria refused, when asked, to execute a just law and say: 'we want it', which was something extremely important'.[18] 'The people', as Savonarola said, in effect meant the new Great Council, the sovereign legislature consisting of some three and a half thousand citizens who themselves, or whose parents or grandparents, had held one of the three major offices in the state.[19] This was the body described by Savonarola in February 1496 as 'like a prince and lord . . . this is your king, Florence, this is your lord'. And for this reason, he continued, to attempt to

60   Alison Brown

murder the council would incur the same capital penalty as someone
who murdered a king or prince, the penalty for treason or *lèse-majesté*.[20]
  A council of some three thousand members was an uncharismatic and
unwieldy head of state, however. Moreover, since Savonarola was not a
member of it, he could not even claim to speak on its behalf, as he could
speak for God and Christ as their prophet — or 'ambassador', as he more
diplomatically called himself in 1498.[21] There was one figure of authority
that Savonarola could appropriate for himself to replace the Medicean
philosopher-ruler as head of a free republic and that of course was
Moses. He had to be careful not to make the analogy too explicit because
of the danger of claiming to be a prophet of Moses' stature — 'I am not
worthy to be compared to Moses', he said disarmingly in January 1495[22]
— which is perhaps why it has been largely unnoticed by Savonarolan
scholars. Nor was Moses the only prophet Savonarola used to justify his
authority in Florence. As prophet, legislator and stern leader of a
democratic tribe, however, Moses perfectly, and economically, fitted the
bill.
  Among the many comparisons Savonarola drew between himself and
Moses — he like Moses had broken tablets of stone and the golden calf,
he too experienced popular disillusionment in the desert after crossing
Red Sea, he too recommended 'severe justice' like Moses, who had
someone killed for gathering wood on the Sabbath, in contrast to the
Florentines' 'cruel compassion'[23] — it was Moses' role as legislator and
harsh disciplinarian that assumed greatest importance. As a lawgiver,
Savonarola is better known for his introductory Ten Commandments
— the creation of the Great Council, the law of amnesty and appeal and
the abolition of *parlamenti* — than for what followed; but like Moses he
too followed up his initial reforms with a Levitican programme of civil
as well as moral legislation for his people.[24] In a sermon delivered in the
cathedral before the Signoria and magistrates on the Feast of St Victor
on 28 July 1495 he summarised it as follows: fear of God, the common
good, peace and reform, 'that is, the Council'. Of these, it was reform
that dominated his sermon that day, in which he proposed laws on
sodomy, poetry, prostitutes, games, blasphemers (with St Louis as his
model, for cauterising the lips of a blasphemer), balls, taverns, closed
shops on feast days, clothes, electoral procedure, the creation of peace-
makers, abolition of parties, the need for letters and news to be secret,
the completion of the council chamber to be a priority ('quickly, not
slow, slowly like the ox'), the abolition of *parlamenti*, the appointment of
the Signoria for a year instead of two months in time of plague, silence in
the council chamber, petitions to the council to be stuck up in public a
day in advance so they could be read and understood in advance, and
prayers to be said before deliberations and elections.[25]
  The popular republicanism which underlay these reforms was re-

inforced by a sermon delivered on the day a new Signoria was to be elected in June 1496, when he delivered a long homily on the importance of popular participation in discussion and voting. 'This morning a new Signoria has to be chosen and I'm not sure whether I should preach or not — and whether or not I should embark on our text for the day [Mica 5], which is long'. He then proceeded to advise his popular supporters to let the leading citizens have their say without protesting:

> Don't be bothered by what they say. Hold firm to the Council. Votes count more than fine words. When someone gives his reasons, let him talk away enthusiastically and if you don't like it, go up yourself then, don't complain, don't criticise, but do as those fine fellows do and say: the reasons given are good, but it seems to me there are other reasons to consider — and then give your reasons forcefully, and at the end say: So it seems to me, with due respect to opinions better than mine —. And in this way you will find the truth and what is best for you. Don't believe all they say, however.[26]

He also tried to strengthen popular government by indoctrination: getting parents to teach the new legislation to their children, particularly the phrase from the law against *parlamenti* which they should learn by heart: 'he who wants to summon a *parlamento* wants to take government from the hands of the people'.[27]

For this reason we cannot doubt Savonarola's sincerity as a republican. The problem was, as Rousseau later put it succinctly,[28] the people are willing but uneducated and need a legislator to introduce reforms for them. By identifying himself with the judge and prophet through whom the people of Israel were counselled by God what to do, as he did in an important sermon on Ruth I,1 in May 1496, Savonarola was able to give himself undisputed authority as God's mouthpiece: for 'when I tell you to do justice, He has made me say it and if He errs, I too err. But He cannot err, therefore I do not err either in telling you what God says'.[29] Comparing Florence to the people of Israel, who 'already ruled and governed, as our Florentine people do now, that is, without a king or temporal prince, because they didn't then have a king', Savonarola was also able to appropriate for himself the regal role in Florence's mixed government, as the Medici had done before him:

> Your government then, Florence, is like that of a judge of the Israelites. I have distinguished government into three types [royal, optimate and popular] . . . and I have with reasons shown you that this government of the people is more natural and proper to you than all the others. So I want to tell you that although the government of the Hebrews was popular because the people ruled and the judge didn't command but advised, yet it could be called royal because it depended on the mouth of one person, that is God's, because God was the one who ruled them, because through the mouth of the judge and prophet they were counselled by God what they had to do, and so it was royal, and it was also optimate because God allowed the best to

advance and be elected and govern. So, Florence, your time will come if you
do what I have said. You will find good government and do well. God will
always send someone to enlighten you and you will not be able to do badly.[30]

As the royal figure in Florence's popular government, Savonarola was
thus able to justify his otherwise quite unwarranted intervention in
legislation. To enforce his laws he urged severity upon the clement and
'cruelly compassionate' Florentines in a series of forceful paradoxes.
Emulating Moses, who used the death sentence for civil offences, he said
he wanted to see three fires in the piazza. 'Oh, friar, you are cruel' — 'It's
you who are cruel who, for one pathetic man, put at risk the whole
city'.[31] In two repeated sermons in June 1495 and May 1496, he assumed
the voice of the prophet Micah to preach against forgiveness, telling the
Florentines that the clement Ahab who forgave the tyrant Ben-hadad
had 'changed that "c" and "l" into a "d", for it was dementia and
madness to forgive him'. So too, he warned, the Florentines would have
to pay the penalty of death for their tolerance of sodomites and evil-
doers: 'Yours is not clementia but dementia', not true piety but cruel
piety. 'You people don't want to do it. You must get involved: you are
the Lord'.[32] The Florentines were worse than pagans, for Brutus killed
his sons for the sake of his country, 'and he was a pagan and you are
Christians'.[33] And driving home the paradox, he later told his Christian
audience that, unlike them, the infidel Moslems were stable because they
'defended themselves with the sword'.[34]

It was in July 1496 that Savonarola recounted the story of the
rebellion of Corah as a warning against disobedience. Comparing the
discontented Israelites with the Florentines who wanted Pisa to be
restored to them, he described how Corah and his followers had been
consumed by God because of Moses' anger with them: 'Where is the
Promised Land? Is this the land of milk and honey you told us about?
. . . O brother, where is Pisa that we have to have back?' Telling them
that Moses got the Lord to destroy the rebels, he ordered them to 'stay
and listen to this last word and then I'll send you home'. With the fate of
the Jewish rebels before them, the Florentines were urged yet again to be
severe, to pass good laws with no favouritism and to do justice by
creating a court of appeal or Rota, with a good man invited to be Judge
of Appeals and another Judge of the Mercanzia.[35]

Increasingly under attack and on the defensive, Savonarola also used
Moses as a useful reminder to the 'grumbling' Florentines that not
everything went well, even for Moses, who failed to lead his people to
the Promised Land because of a moment of doubt he suffered when
striking the rock for water. 'He died and did not see his work through to
the end. I am a very great sinner and I have committed worse sins by far,
yet God . . . has not wanted to waste his work . . . You look to yourself,
too, Florence. What have you done to boast about?'[36] The Florentines,

he told them in March 1497, were like those grumbling people, the *mormoratori*, who all day long grumbled against Moses — 'I don't say against me, but against God'.[37]

It was a year later, in March 1498, that Savonarola went furthest in arguing for tough justice and the use of force with the story of Moses killing the Egyptian. Excommunicated and interdicted, he had decided to transfer his Lenten sermons from the cathedral to San Marco on the election of a new, more hostile Signoria at the end of February 1498, and it was there that Machiavelli heard his two sermons on Exodus 1,12: 'But the more they afflicted them, the more they multiplied and grew'; and 2,11–12, with its emotive killing of the Egyptian: 'Take this stab, Egyptian . . . and here's another . . . Do you know what it means to say "interdict, interdict, interdict"? It means "tyrant, tyrant, tyrant"'.[38] Summarising them for the Florentine ambassador in Rome, Machiavelli reported that it was at the end of the first sermon that Savonarola, 'digressing, as is his wont, in order to debilitate his enemies as well as to provide a bridge to his next sermon', threatened that factionalism in Florence would encourage a tyrant to rise up and ruin their homes and destroy the land:

> And the next morning, expounding Exodus and coming to that part where it says that Moses killed an Egyptian, he said that the Egyptian represented the captives and Moses the preacher who killed them by revealing their vices. And he said: 'O Egyptian, I want to give you a thrust of my sword' and at this point he began to ruffle through your books, o priests, and to treat them in such a way that dogs wouldn't have eaten them. And then he added — and this was what he was trying to get at all along — that he wanted to give the Egyptian another greater wound, and he said that God had told him that there was one in Florence who sought to make himself a tyrant and held meetings and plotted to bring this about.

He went on so much about this that people spent the day publicly speculating about whom he could have meant, a man — Machiavelli continued, evidently referring to Francesco Valori — 'who is about as close to becoming a tyrant as you are to reaching heaven'. But having achieved his purpose of unifying his supporters, Savonarola stopped mentioning tyranny and concentrated his energies instead on attacking the pope: 'and so, in my opinion, he keeps changing with the times and colouring his lies to suit them'.[39]

Machiavelli was not alone in understanding Savonarola's self-identification with Moses, which to judge from contemporary comment was well understood by his supporters as well as his critics. In his 1496 *Defence* of Savonarola, the chancellor Bartolomeo Scala had argued that a religious leader was necessary even in a republic — as could be seen from Israel, which divided into twelve tribes, 'as though into a republic' at God's suggestion acting through Moses, 'that very wise and successful

Alison Brown

leader';[40] while the hostile Francesco Altoviti condemned Savonarola
for trying to 'control arms and the government like a dictator, in order
to be able to give his laws to this city and then to the whole world like
Moses'.[41] By the middle of the sixteenth century Savonarola's sermon
about Ahab and Ben-hadad was being used as evidence that Florence
'should have a Head and Ruler — and even as we hope a king, like
Samaria — as the friar mentioned several times'.[42]

But it was the perceptive Machiavelli who understood Savonarola's
political language most clearly. Although he professed not to have heard
a fiery sermon of a Franciscan preacher in Florence, because he had 'no
truck with such affairs',[43] we know he heard at least Savonarola's two
March sermons in 1498 and probably — if only at second hand —
others. It is partly his sensitivity to language that gives this away: the
picking up and reworking of paradoxes like 'cruel piety' or 'wise
madness', and the disjunctive 'peace, peace . . . war, war . . . you say
"peace, peace", and I tell you "there is no peace" '.[44] At a deeper level it
is revealed by the role played by Moses in Machiavelli's political
thought. This was not, I think, due to Machiavelli's religiosity (as I have
recently heard it said) but to his understanding of Moses' importance to
Savonarola and hence his practical relevance to Florentine politics.

The occasions on which Machiavelli refers to Moses and Savonarola
are well-known but need to be quickly rehearsed. Both men enjoyed
extraordinary authority because they talked — or were believed to talk
— with God.[45] They demonstrate that arms are necessary for success; for
whereas Moses and other armed prophets were victorious, Savonarola
failed because he was unarmed and lost control of his followers after they
ceased to believe in him.[46] Moses, we are reminded in *The Discourses*, was
also successful because he was the only one in authority; and since 'to
found a republic it is necessary to be alone', murder and violence to
achieve this is 'excused', as it was with Romulus and 'infinite examples of
other founders, such as Moses'. Moses, we are told elsewhere,
necessarily acted violently in taking over and renaming lands of others.[47]
The lesson of violence and the need for arms is nowhere clearer than in
Discourses III,30, where Moses is again associated with Savonarola:

> And any one who reads the Bible judiciously will see that, in order to get his
> laws and orders adopted, Moses was forced to murder infinite numbers of
> men who opposed his designs, moved by nothing more than envy. Exactly
> the same problem was experienced by fra Girolamo Savonarola . . . [He]
> couldn't overcome it through lack of authority . . . and because he was not
> properly understood by his followers who would have had authority. It was
> not his fault this did not happen, and his sermons are full of accusations and
> invectives against the wise men of the world.[48]

Although Machiavelli attributed his new insights to a 'judicious'
reading of the Bible, we can see how much Savonarola himself must also
have contributed to them, with his talk about arms and severe justice, his

Savonarola, Machiavelli and Moses   65

paradoxes about 'pagan piety' and 'Moslem stability', and his claim to divine sanction as a prophet. Even the hypocrisy and opportunism that Machiavelli condemned in Savonarola — especially for failing to observe the laws he himself introduced — became an essential feature of his successful leader who changes with the times and is prepared to 'do evil' if necessary.[49] Far from it being the constitutional or the reforming, millenarian Savonarola that influenced Machiavelli, as has been suggested [50], it was instead the tough Savonarola with his disturbingly anti-Christian paradoxes that impressed Machiavelli and made his work original and iconoclastic: one has to be prepared to kill in order to establish one's laws, as Moses did and Savonarola was unable to do, such crimes being 'excused' provided the end is good; laws once passed must be executed rigorously, which pagans and heretics are much better at doing than Christians: 'how it is necessary . . . to murder the sons of Brutus', as Savonarola had said;[51] and how, to be effective, laws should be given divine sanction, for 'in truth, there has never been any lawgiver who has not had recourse to God when giving extraordinary laws to the people, because otherwise they would not be accepted'.[52] This early re-statement of the sceptical attitude to law provides perhaps the best evidence of the extent of Savonarola's influence.

Transformed by Savonarola and Machiavelli, Moses begins to look recognisably 'modern' — no longer a holy prophet or magus but a civic lawgiver and popular demogogue, forerunner of Hobbesian Moses, who ruled by popular contract according to a civil decalogue that had to be learnt by children and people alike.[53] Savonarola, too, had realised the importance of publicity and indoctrination — publicising laws in advance, teaching children to learn them by heart, engaging in pamphlet warfare — in order to influence and control a newly-defined public. For Savonarola 'the people' no longer meant a restricted class of eligible citizens but the populace at large, women and children as well as men, whom he harangued in emotive sermons and organised into pressure groups for reform.[54] To judge from the notorious 'burning of vanities' and from the swift rise in anonymous denunciations of the crimes he inveighed against,[55] his impact on what we can begin to call 'public opinion' was impressive — and this, too, clearly impressed Machiavelli, as one of the earliest writers to discuss the political power of popular opinion or 'imagination'.[56] Supporting the Great Council and recognising, as he did, the people as the ultimate judge of successful politics, Machiavelli was as 'republican' as Savonarola and as authoritarian. For both, the populist but autocratic Moses provided an invaluable model for reconciling the apparently contradictory trends of late fifteenth-century Florence.

Royal Holloway and Bedford New College
University of London

66   Alison Brown

Notes

1.   In the apparent absence of a single treatment of the subject, see, *inter alia*, L. D. Ettlinger, *The Sistine Chapel before Michelangelo* (Oxford, 1965), ch. 6, pp. 104–19, summarising changing attitudes to Moses and his renewed importance in the fifteenth century, P. Wormald, 'Lex Scripta and Verbum Regis: Legislation and Germanic Kingship, from Euric to Cnut, *Early Medieval Kingship*, ed. R. H. Sawyer and I. N. Wood (Leeds, 1979), pp. 131–32; B. Tierney, *Religion, law and the growth of constitutional thought, 1150–1650* (Cambridge, 1982), pp. 88–91, 95: 'the Mosaic model of a mixed constitution', quoting Aquinas, *Summa theologiae*, I, 2a, 97.3; I, 2a, 105.1; 2.2a, 183.2, J. Gerson, *De potestate ecclesiastica*, *Oeuvres* (Paris, 1960–73), VI, p. 225; D. P. Walker, *The Ancient Theology* (London, 1972), pp. 1–2, 19, 49–50, etc., quoting P. Crinito, *De honesta disciplina*, III, 2, ed. A. Angeleri (Rome, 1955), pp. 104–5; cf. C. Landino, Praefatio in Virgilio (1462), *Scritti critici e teorici*, ed. R. Cardini (Rome, 1974), I, p. 23, etc., M. Ficino, *De christiana religione*, ch. 26, letter to Braccio Martelli, 'Concordia Mosis et Platonis', *Opera omnia* (Basel, 1576, repr. Turin, 1962), pp. 29 (59), 866 (896), G. Pico della Mirandola, *Heptaplus*, tr. J. B. McGaw (New York, 1977), preface, pp. 15–21); for Hobbes, n. 53 below. Savonarola as the new Moses is mentioned in passing by M. Reeves, *Joachim of Fiore and the Prophetic Future* (London, 1976), p. 88.

2.   See H. Butters, *Governors and Government in early sixteenth century Florence, 1502–1519* (Oxford, 1985), R. Pesman Cooper, 'The Florentine Ruling Group under the "Governo Popolare"', 1494–1512', *Studies in Medieval and Renaissance History*, 7 (1984–85), pp. 71–181: 'The constitutional reforms of December 1494 led to little change in the composition of the Florentine political class or in its inner circles of position and influence' (p. 71).

3.   *Prediche sopra Ruth e Michea*, ed. V. Romano (Rome, 1962), I, p. 436 (26 June 1496): 'Io sono frate, e non vidi mai arme, e, se mi fussi lecito, ti monstrerrei punti, che tu non hai da dubitare tanto . . . Io vorrei così potere (dico potere, cioè che mi fussi lecito) questa mattina mettermi uno cappuccio, e ancora uno lucco: io ti monstrerrei punti e rationi che tu non ai bisogno di avere tanta paura'.

4.   R. Ridolfi, *The Life of Girolamo Savonarola* (London, 1959), pp. 82–83, 123–25, 175; D. Weinstein, *Savonarola and Florence. Prophecy and Patriotism in the Renaissance* (Princeton, N. J., 1970), pp. 115–16, 279, cf. *Prediche sopra i Salmi*, ed. V. Romano (Rome, 1969), II, p. 71 (21 June 1495: 'Io sono stato là in campo', cf. p. 229, 25 October 1495); I, p. 9 (6 January 1495): 'Io fui in Palazzo il dì di santo Silvestro per concludere questa pace universale, e dissiti . . .'; *Prediche sopra Giobbe*, ed. R. Ridolfi (Rome, 1957), II, p. 15 (27 March 1495): 'Dissiti ancora, qui e in palazzo, quando tu mi facesti venire lassù'; *Ruth e Michea*, II, p. 320 (28 October 1496): 'Come ti ho detto, sono venuto questa mattina quassù per ubidire alla Magnifica Signoria, richiesto che io predicasse; e, benché io non sia sottoposto al foro seculare, ho voluto venire e ubidire'.

5.   S. Bertelli, 'Embrioni di partiti alle soglie dell' età moderna', *Per Federigo Chabod (1901–1960)*, ed. S. Bertelli (Annali della Facoltà di Scienze politiche, an. 1980–81, 17), I, pp. 17–35.

6.   *Salmi*, I, pp. 107–8 (20 January 1495); on criticism, Weinstein, pp. 238–9, and the doctoral thesis of Lorenzo Polizzotto, 'The Piagnoni and Religious Reform, 1494–1530', London University, 1975 (to be published), ch. 1, pp. 15–47. Cf. *Salmi*, I, p. 94 (18 January 1495): 'Ma tu dirai: — tu, frate, perché t'impicci tu dello stato?'; *Prediche sopra Amos e Zaccaria*, ed. P. Ghiglieri (Florence, 1971), II, p. 42 (6 March, 1496): 'Tu di' ancora che io mi impaccio dello stato', etc.

Savonarola, Machiavelli and Moses 67

7.   *Giobbe*, II, p. 309 (14 April 1495): 'Tu sai che innanzi alla revoluzione nostra del stato'.

8.   *Prediche italiane ai fiorentini*, ed. F. Cognasso (Perugia and Venice, 1930), I, pp. 195, 215–16, 219 (14 and 16 December 1494), *Amos e Zaccaria*, I, p. 152 (21 February 1496): 'tu non hai ora paura di persona, ma quando el ci fussi capo o tiranno, tu sai che la legge del tiranno è la sua volontà . . . Così fa il tiranno: ogni volta che gli pare che tu gli abbi fatto una minima cosuzza che non gli piacci, non ti vuole più vedere' (cf. esp. pp. 216–31, 24 February 1496, for an extended account of Medicean tyranny); *Salmi* II, p. 191 (11 October 1495); *Ruth e Michea*, I, p. 358 (19 June 1496): 'Tu che stavi subietto all' altro stato, e non potevi fare una bottega, e non avevi libertà di potere maritare la tua figliuola'; cf. R. C. Trexler, *Public Life in Renaissance Florence* (London, 1980), pp. 448–50, nn. 164, 165, 169.

9.   See my article 'Platonism in Fifteenth-Century Florence', *Journal of Modern History* 58 (1986), pp. 403–04, 406; on Savonarola's relationship with Florentine Platonists, see Walker, above, ch. 2, pp. 42–62; and on his republicanism, Weinstein, ch. 9, 'Savonarola, Theorist of Republican Liberty', pp. 289–316; Q. Skinner, *The Foundations of Modern Political Thought* (Cambridge, 1978), I (The Renaissance), pp. 145–48 ('The Survival of Republican Values'); N. Rubinstein, 'Politics and Constitution in Florence at the end of the Fifteenth Century', *Italian Renaissance Studies*, ed. E. F. Jacob (London, 1960), pp. 159–64, and J. H. Whitfield, *Discourses on Machiavelli* (Cambridge, 1969), ch. 6, 'Savonarola and the purpose of the *Prince*', pp. 87–110, all arguing mainly from Savonarola's *Trattato circa il Reggimento e Governo della Citta di Firenze*, 1498 (repr. Turin, 1963).

10.   *Public Life*, pp. 468–69, 482–84, cf. his article, 'Lorenzo de' Medici and Savonarola, Martyrs for Florence', *Renaissance Quarterly*, 31 (1978): 293–308.

11.   Cf. *Salmi*, II, p. 208 (18 October 1495): 'Molti di voi dicano: Io ero in Palazzo, io ero in piazza, io feci, io dissi, io ho liberato questo stato — e quasi dica: Questo stato è mio'.

12.   *Prediche italiane*, I, pp. 362–63 (27 December 1494): 'Non si può negare che quelli governi che si reducano ad uno capo solo non siano ei migliori, ma bisogna che quel capo sia perfetto . . . Orsu, Firenze, che vorresti tu, che capo, che re ti si può dare, che tu stia quieta? Io t'ho detto altra volta che non ad ogni luogo, nè ogni paese, gli è meglio un capo solo che governi, e Santo Tomaso lo dice, che in Italia e principi diventano tiranni . . . Orsu, Firenze, Iddio ti vuol contentare e darti uno capo ed uno re che ti governi. E questo è Cristo . . . piglia Cristo per tuo re e sta sotto la sua legge e con quella ti governa . . . Cristo sia tuo Capitano . . . Sta con Cristo, Firenze, e non cercare altro capo'.

13.   *Salmi*, I, pp. 267–8 (3 June 1495): 'se fussi qua uno gran signore, Firenze, che ti dicesse d'aiutarti, tu ti confideresti in lui, non è vero? E se tu vedessi che lui avessi potenzia d'aiutarti, tu ti confideresti molto in lui . . . Ognuno sa che Dio è potente e savio e buono'; cf. Brown, 'Platonism', pp. 395–98.

14.   *Salmi*, II, pp. 189–90 (11 October 1495): 'Considera l'ordine dello universo, *quod in omni genere est dare unum primum* . . . Lo esercito non è bene ordinato senza capitano . . . Così la città non è bene ordinata, se non si riduce al sommo magistrato. Tu, Firenze, hai Cristo per tuo Re, il quale Iddio volse che si dimonstrassi essere Re e a dominare insino al principio della sua natività . . . e e' volse nascere in quello tempo che tutto il mondo era sotto un principe, Ottaviano, per dimonstrare che tutto il mondo avessi ad essere sotto di lui', cf. *Amos e Zaccaria* I, pp. 215–16 (24 February 1496).

15.   *Epistola. . mandata a' fanciulli fiorentini*, Florence, dated 3 September 1497, fol. a1^r: 'A tucti voi fanciulli . . . Gratia, pace, salute et opportuno adempimento di tucte le presente et future felicità promesse spetialmente a voi da Dio signore et Re nostro Iesu

68   Alison Brown

Christo . . . et per e meriti della passione del suo figliuolo, vostro imperatore, et per le intercessione della gloriosa vostra imperatrice, madre del nostro Salvatore'.

16.   Printed in Florence, 13 August 1495, 'in consilio generali', fol. a1^r: 'essendo venuto el governo in mano del popolo, el quale è vero e legiptimo Signore della nostra Ciptà'.

17.   *Salmi*, II, pp. 217–18 (18 October 1495): 'Quale è il nostro Signore? — Egli è Christo. — Chi tiene il luogo di Christo? — La Signoria no, ma il populo è signore; e però io ti dico: Fa' di avere l'occhio al signore, cioè al Consiglio'.

18.   Ed. J. Schnitzer, *Quellen und Forschungen zur Geschichte Savonarolas*, IV (Leipzig, 1910), p. 124: 'et confortò el popolo poi, da che lui era Signore, che quando con debita reverenza la Signoria rischiesta mettere in opera non volesse la provisione iusta, lui si levasse in pie et dicesse, noi la vogliamo, la qual parola importantissima fu'.

19.   Pesman Cooper, above, pp. 73–79.

20.   *Amos e Zaccaria*, I, p. 151 (21 February 1496): 'Quale è la potestà ordinata a te, populo fiorentino? Ell'è il Consiglio grande, perché quello come principe e signore fa tutti li offiziali. Questo è il tuo re, Firenze; questo è il tuo signore. Or dimmi: che pena merita colui che amazza uno re o uno signore d' una città? — Oh, merita grandissimo punizione, *quia est crimen lesae maiestatis.* — Che meriteria adunque uno che andassi tentando d'amazzare e quastare questo Consiglio? — Certo meriteria quella medesimo pena che merita colui che amazza il re o il principe'.

21.   See his sermon of 11 October 1495 (n. 14 above), in which he goes on to say that God wanted 'uno frate e forastiero, che non se intende niente di stato' to act for Christ as head, 'acciò che la laude sia sola di Dio e non di omo' (p. 191). For the ambassador image, *Salmi*, I, p. 236–67 (28 May 1495) comparing God's use of an angelic messenger to announce his intentions with a king's use of secretaries and ambassadors acting on his commission, which he applied to himself in the last year of his life, *Prediche sopra Esodo*, ed. P. G. Ricci (Rome, 1956), I, p. 309 (7 March 1498): 'io sono imbasciadore, qua, mandato da Dio. Gli imbasciadori possono dire', cf. II, p. 305 (18 March 1498): 'lo imbasciadore può parlare in persona sua e in persona del suo signore che lo mandò'.

22.   *Salmi*, I, p. 123 (25 January 1495): 'Io non sono degno d'essere comparato a Moisè'.

23.   *Giobbe*, I, pp. 289–95 (18 March 1495): 'O Firenze . . . ho spezzato ancora io le tavole come fece Moisè . . . E come Moisè destrusse il vitello dell'oro degl' Israeliti, così io ho destrutta e sbeffata la tua sapienzia humana' (p. 293); *Salmi*, II, pp. 147–8 (12 July 1495): 'Nelli principii della legge bisogna sempre una severa iustizia . . . Vedi Moisè nel principio della legge fece morire uno solamente perche coglieva le legne el sabbato . . . Voi siate pietosi e non vi accorgerete che la vostra è pietà crudele'; cf. *Salmi* I, p. 25 (11 January 1495), *Giobbe* II, pp. 30–35 (28 March 1495, eliding Moses with the prophet Gideon), 'sì come e' fece a Moisè e qui a Gedeone'; *Salmi* I, pp. 202–14 (24 May 1495), II, pp. 64–7 and 195–6 (14 June and 11 October 1495).

24.   Exodus 21–23 and Leviticus; for Savonarola, see U. Mazzone, '*El buon governo*'. *Un progetto di riforma generale nella Firenze savonaroliana* (Florence, 1978), and on his introductory reforms, Weinstein, esp. ch. 8, pp. 247–88, and N. Rubinstein, 'Politics and Constitution', esp. pp. 155–65.

25.   *Salmi*, II, pp. 168–176 (28 July 1495): 'e che vada presto, non come il bue, che va pian, piano'.

26.   *Ruth e Michea*, I, pp. 420, 435–36 (26 June 1496, cf. n. 3 above): 'Questa mattina . . . s'ha a fare la Signoria e per questo io sto in dubitazione, se ho a predicare o no, e se entro nel capitolo del nostro profeta o no. El capitulo è lungo . . . Lascia parlare alli valenti omini quello che vogliono e non mormorare. Non ti dia noia a te quello che si

Savonarola, Machiavelli and Moses 69

parli. Tieni pure saldo el Consiglio; le fave sono poi quelle che hanno a giudicare che ha detto bene omo. Quando uno dice le ragioni sue, lascialo dire arditamente, e se non ti piacciono, va' su poi tu e non mormorare, non biasimare. Ma fa come fanno e valenti omini e di': le ragioni che sono state dette sono buone, ma a me pare che ci sia altre ragioni — e di' le ragioni tue vivamente, e alla fine, di':- Così pare a me, salvo ogni migliore iudicio — E a questo modo tu troverrai la verità e li modi che ti sieno più salute. Non credere però che sieno tante cose quante si dicono'.

27. *Salmi*, II, p. 196 (11 October 1495): 'Dillo a' tua figliuoli, acciò che lo tenghino a mente e insegnali quello verso che "chi vuole fare parlamento, vuole torre delle mane al populo il regimento" '.

28. *The Social Contract*, II, 6 and 7 (Everyman edition, London, 1973), pp. 193, 196: 'Of itself the people wills always the good, but of itself it by no means always sees it . . . This makes a legislator necessary', 'This is what has, in all ages, compelled the fathers of nations to have recourse to divine intervention' (quoting Machiavelli's *Discorsi*, cf. n. 52 below).

29. *Ruth e Michea* I, p. 27 (8 May 1496): 'e' me l'ha fatto dire Lui; e se Lui erra, erro ancora io. Ma Lui non può errare: adunque non erro ancora io a dirti quello che dice Dio'; see the repeated criticism by Francesco Altoviti in his treatise *In defensione de' Magistrati et delle leggi et antiche cerimonie al culto divino della città di Firenze contro alle invettive et offensione di Fra Girolamo*, fol. a6ᵛ: 'tu me l'ai detto tu, se io mento, tu menti', etc.; Piero Vaglienti, *Storie dei suoi tempi, 1492–1514* (Pisa, 1982), p. 31.

30. *Ruth e Michea*, I, pp. 106–08, 121 (18 May 1496): 'El tuo reggimento dunque, Firenze, è simile a quello di uno iudice delli Israelliti. Io ti ho distinto el reggimento in tre parti e dettoti che ogni governo o è di uno e chiamasi regale, o è di più nobili e chiamasi di ottimati, o è universale, e chiamasi populare. E hotti monstro con ragione che questo governo del populo ti è più naturale e più proprio che tutti gli altri. E anche ti voglio dire che questo reggimento e governo delli Ebrei, benché fussi populare, perché il populo reggeva e il giudice non comandava, ma consigliava, *tamen* era ancora e potevasi chiamare governo regale — perché dependeva dalla bocca di uno, cioè di Dio, perché Dio era quello che li reggeva, perché per la bocca del iudice e del profeta erano consigliati da Dio quello che dovevano fare . . . Era adunque quello reggimento regale, e era anche di ottimati, perché Dio permetteva che gli migliori fussino tirati su, e fussino eletti e governassino. Sicchè, Firenze, sarà ancora el tempo tuo, ché se farai quello che ti ho detto, tu troverrai el vado e il governo buono, e farai bene. Dio ti manderà sempre chi ti illuminerà, e non potrai fare male'.

31. *Salmi*, II, p. 147 (12 July 1495): 'Io vorrei pure vedere tre fuochi in piazza. — Oh, tu se' crudele, frate — Crudele sei tu che per uno tristo vuoi pericolare una città'.

32. *Salmi*, I, p. 285 (3 June 1495): 'la tua non è clemenzia ma demenzia', and *Ruth e Michea*, I, p. 29 (8 May 1496): 'In questa clemenza di Acab fu mutato quel "c" e "l" in "d", cioè fu demenzia e pazzia la sua a perdonarli', both sermons expounding 1 Kings 20. For a later account of this sermon, see n. 42 below.

33. *Salmi*, II, pp. 196–97 (11 October 1495): 'Bruto fece ammazzare il proprio figliuolo per la patria e era pagano, e voi siate cristiani'.

34. *Prediche sopra Ezechiele*, ed. R. Ridolfi, Rome, 1955, II, p. 156 (9 March 1497): 'tu dirai che quello [fede] di Macometto sia stabile. Sa' tu perché? Perché la si difende colla spada'.

35. *Ruth e Michea*, II, pp. 66–67 (3 July 1496): 'Dove è la terra di promissione? E questa la terra che tu dicevi, che ci aveva a dare latte e mèle? . . . O frate, dove è Pisa che noi avamo a riavere? . . . Stammi a udire questa ultima parola e manderottene a casa', describing necessary reforms on pp. 67–70.

70   Alison Brown

36. Ibid., II, pp. 408–09 (27 November 1496): 'Morì e non condusse l'opera al fine.
Io sono peccatore grandissimo e ho fatto maggiori peccati, assai senza comparazione,
tamen Dio, per sua misericordia e non guardando alli nostri peccati, non ha voluto
guastare l'opera sua . . . Guarda ancora tu dalla parte tua, Firenze, che hai tu fatto di che
tu t'abbi a gloriare?'; cf. *Ezechiele*, I, p. 58 (11 December 1496).

37. *Ezechiele*, II, p. 265 (16 March 1497): 'Tu, Firenze, sei come quello populo
mormoratore, che tutto el dì mormorava contro a Moyses; non dico io contr'a me, ma
contro a Dio'.

38. *Esodo*, I, pp. 146–203, nos. 6 (2 March 1498) and 7 (3 March): 'Or, togli, Egizio,
questa coltellata . . . Ecco ancora un' altra coltellata . . . Sai tu che vuol dire interdetto,
interdetto, interdetto? Vuol dire tiranno, tiranno, tiranno'.

39. Machiavelli, *Lettere*, 9 March 1498, ed. F. Gaeta (Milan, 1961): 'Dixe di poi,
entrato in vari dischorsi, come è suo costume, per debilitare più gli adversarii, volendosi
fare un ponte alla seguente predicha . . . L'altra mattina poi expondendo pure lo Exodo
et venendo a quella parte, dove dice che Moyses amazò un Egiptio, dixe che lo Egiptio
erono gli huomini captivi, et Moyses il predicatore che gli amazava, scoprendo e' vitii
loro; et dixe: O Egiptio, io ti vo' dare una coltellata; et qui cominciò a squadernare e' libri
vostri, o preti, e tractarvi in modo che non n'harebbono mangiato e cani; dipoi
soggiunse, et qui lui voleva capitare, che volea dare all' Egiptio un' altra ferita et grande,
et dixe che Dio gli haveva detto, ch' egli era uno in Firenze che cercava di farsi tyranno, et
teneva pratiche et modi perché gli riescissi . . . che è tanto presso al tyranno, quanto voi
al cielo . . . et così, secondo il mio iudicio, viene secondando e' tempi et le sua bugie
colorendo' (pp. 32–33).

40. *Apologia contra vituperatores civitatis Florentiae*, 1496, fol. b3ʳ: 'in duodecim tribus
. . . omnis Israelis populus tanquam in unam rempublicam divisus est, auctore etiam
ipso et commonstratore Deo, Moyse autem sapientissimo illo duce atque felicissimo
perficiente' (going on to defend Savonarola's role in suggesting legislation and
prophesying); cf. Bartolomeo Redditi, *Breve Compendio e Sommario della verità predicata e
profetata de R. P. Fra Girolamo da Ferrara*, ed. Schnitzer, *Quellen*, I, p. 38: 'mandò loro un
huomo profeta, come fece di Moise al popolo d'Israel'.

41. *Defensione*, fol. a3ᵛ: 'Così li pare dovere tenere lo stato et l'arme come dictatore
per poter dare le sue leggi a questa città et poi a tutto 'l mondo come Moise'; cf. a5ᵛ:
'nessuno altro giamai più se non solo Moise potè udire la gran voce dell'alto Idio', with
several references to Savonarola's usurpation of the 'cathedra di Moise' (a6ᵛ, a8ᵛ: 'come
perfido Mahometto latrendo nella cathedra di Moise', a9ʳ: 'et nella cathedra di Moise
gridare arme et iustitia, che non voleva altro dire se non sangue et vendetta'). On
Altoviti, Weinstein, pp. 230, 238–39.

42. 'Discorso sopra una figura proposta da Frate Girolamo Savonarola per il
reggimento e stato di Firenze in una Predica da lui fatto il dì viii di maggio sopra Michae',
in a volume dedicated to duke Cosimo de' Medici, 2 August 1562, B.N.F. MS Magl.
25.266, fols. 20ᵛ: 'Et principalmente per la città di Summaria intenderemo Firenze
nostra, dove si vede . . . che Firenze havere doveva in questa sua Repubblica un Capo et
Reggitore, et anche come speriamo Re, come Samaria haveva, il quale Reggitore anche è
stato più volte dal Frate accennato, et infra le altre nella Predica de xii di giugno sopra
l'istesso profeta'. Giovannini also describes how Savonarola inveighed about badly-
executed justice, defining it not (in Aristotelian terms) 'tanto in dar a ciascheduno quello
che si gli conviene quanto defendere e rimovere le ingiurie'(fol. 28ᵛ).

43. *Lettere*, p. 309 (19 December 1493): 'La predica io non la udii, perché non uso
simili pratiche, ma la ho sentita recitare così da tutto Firenze'.

44. *Il Principe*, ch. 17 'De crudelitate et pietate', ed. Bertelli, pp. 68–69: 'Era tenuto
Cesare Borgia crudele, non di manco quella sua crudeltà aveva racconcia la Romagna . . .

Savonarola, Machiavelli and Moses   71

Il che . . . si vedrà quello essere stato molto più pietoso che il populo fiorentino, il quale, per fuggire il nome di crudele, lasciò destruggere Pistoia'; *Discorsi*, I, 58: 'un principe che può fare ciò ch'ei vuole è pazzo; un popolo che può fare ciò che vuole non è savio', for Savonarola's use of these paradoxes, n. 31 above and Brown, 'Platonism', p. 404.; *Ezechiele*, II, pp. 46, 112, 173 (3, 7 and 10 March 1497): 'Voi dite pur *Pax Pax* e io vi dico: non est *pax*, e' non è pace'; 'Tu di' *pax*, *pax*. E la vigna grida guerra, guerra', in Machiavelli's *Lettere*, p. 292 (26 August 1513): 'io credo al frate che diceva *Pax*, *Pax*, *et non erit pax*'. Cf. also 'li uomini sdimenticano più presto la morte del padre che la perdita del patrimonio' (*Il Principe* 17, ed. Bertelli, p. 70), reversing, perhaps, a sermon of fra Mariano da Gennazzano's, 'tu vorresti pi tosto perdere la roba che uno tuo figliuolo e lui [Iddio] vole più tosto torti el figliuolo', ed. Z. Zafarana, 'Per la storia religiosa di Firenze nel Quattrocento', *Studi medievali*, 3rd. ser., 9 (1968), p. 1077 (16 March 1489).

45.   *Il Principe*, ch. 6, p. 31, and *Discorsi*, I, 11, p. 163.

46.   *Il Principe*, ch. 6, p. 32; cf. ch. 19, pp. 83–84, that the 'securità e la fortezza' of the Turks depends on arms, unlike other states, and Savonarola, n. 34 above.

47.   *Discorsi*, I, 9, pp. 154–55; II, 8, pp. 298–99.

48.   Ibid., III, 30, p. 468: 'E chi legge la Bibbia sensatamente vedrà Moisè essere stato forzato, a volere che le sue leggi e che li suoi ordini andassero innanzi, ad ammazzare infiniti uomini, i quali non mossi da altro che dalla invidia si opponevano a' disegni suoi. Questa necessità conosceva benissimo frate Girolamo Savonarola . . . non potette vincerla per non avere autorità a poterlo fare . . . e per non essere inteso bene da coloro che lo seguitavano, che ne arebbero avuto autorità. Nonpertanto per lui non rimase, e le sue prediche sono piene di accuse de' savi del mondo e d'invettive contro a loro'; cf. L. Strauss, *Thoughts on Machiavelli* (Washington, 1969), p. 114.

49.   For Savonarola's hypocrisy, *Discorsi*, I, 45, pp. 233–4, and Machiavelli's letter of 9 March 1498, n. 39 above; cf. *Il Principe*, chs. 18, 25, *Discorsi*, III, 9, etc.

50.   See, for example, Whitfield, 'Savonarola and the purpose of the Prince', n. 9 above (though agreeing with him that 'some of the credit . . . given to Machiavelli as innovator needs to go to Savonarola, who plainly showed the way', p. 96), and D. Weinstein, 'Machiavelli and Savonarola', *Studies on Machiavelli*, ed. M. P. Gilmore (Florence, 1972), pp. 251–64, who uses most of the texts quoted above and provides a very full discussion though with somewhat different conclusions.

51.   *Discorsi*, III, 3 (title), p. 386: 'Come egli è necessario, a volere mantenere una libertà acquistata di nuovo, ammazzare i figliuoli di Bruto', cf. Savonarola's sermon on 11 October 1495, n. 33 above.

52.   *Discorsi*, I, 9, pp. 163, 161: 'E veramente mai fu alcuno ordinatore di leggi straordinarie in uno popolo che non ricorresse a Dio, perché altrimenti non sarebbero accettate'; cf. Hobbes, *Leviathan*, ch. 12, ed. Oakeshott, pp. 75–6; Rousseau, *The Social Contract*, n. 28 above.

53.   *Leviathan*, ed. M. Oakeshott (Oxford, 1946), chs. 20, p. 134 ('This is absolute obedience to Moses'), 26, p. 178 ('he biddeth them to teach it their children, by discoursing of it both at home, and upon the way; at going to bed, and at rising from bed; and to write it upon the posts, and doors of their houses; and to assemble the people, man, woman and child, to hear it read'), 27, p. 188 ('At Mount Sinai Moses only went up to God; the people were forbidden to approach on pain of death; yet they were bound to obey all that Moses declared to them for God's law. Upon what ground, but on this submission of their own . . . '), cf. 40, pp. 308–09, etc.

54.   Trexler, *Public Life*, pp. 474–82, Bertelli, n. 5 above, pp. 28–9, F. W. Kent, 'A Proposal by Savonarola for the Self-Reform of Florentine Women (March 1496)', *Memorie Domenicane*, n. s., 14 (1983), pp. 335–41; Polizzotto, 'The Piagnoni', n. 6 above,

72   Alison Brown

ch. 1, 'The Beginnings of a Movement: The Pamphlet War', pp. 15–47; for his sermons, cf. nn. 38, 39 above.

55.   In anticipation of Michael Rocke's statistical analysis of *tamburazioni*, a very rough count of denunciations in A. S. F., Ufficiali di Notte, 25–27 suggests a seven-fold increase from *c.*100 p. a. in 1489 and 1490 to *c.*766 in 1491–92, when Savonarola began preaching on the Apocalypse. Savonarola's influence can also be detected in the language of the denunciations, which, because they are anonymous, offer the nearest approach to a medieval public opinion poll.

56.   *Discorsi*, I, 11, p. 163. On the importance of the people, *Il Principe*, chs. 18, 19, pp. 74, 83, 'Ghiribizi', *Lettere*, p. 229.

[20]

Reduction and the praise of disunion in Machiavelli's *Discourses*

VICTORIA KAHN, *Princeton University*

> In sharp contrast to the usual ideal of science, the objec-
> tivity of dialectical cognition needs not less subjectivity,
> but more. . . . In philosophy, rhetoric represents that which
> cannot be thought except in language.
> —THEODOR W. ADORNO, *Negative Dialectics.*[1]

I. *Machiavelli's Likeness to Horkheimer and Adorno*

It is a striking fact of Machiavelli scholarship that Machiavelli's own
claims to originality are still being debated.[2] Some intellectual historians insist on his debts to humanism; others tend to stress his radical
departure from traditional humanist thought, but differ on the nature
of this departure. Many scholars attribute to Machiavelli the first fully
articulated divorce of politics from morality and/or the establishment
of politics as a science;[3] while others have claimed that his analysis of
contemporary Florence is not merely descriptive but also prescriptive.
Of the various political theorists who have engaged the work of Machiavelli, Max Horkheimer and Theodor Adorno have made some of
the most interesting comments on Machiavelli's modernity—not least
because they seem to argue on both sides of the question. In *Anfänge
der bürgerlichen Geschichtsphilosophie*, Horkheimer sees Machiavelli

Journal of Medieval and Renaissance Studies 18:1, Spring 1988. Copyright © 1988 by
Duke University Press. CCC 0047-2573/88/$1.50

1. Theodor Adorno, *Negative Dialectics*, trans. E. B. Ashton (New York, 1973),
40 and 55. The research for this essay was supported by a grant from Villa I Tatti, the
Harvard University Center for Italian Renaissance Studies. I would like to thank Elisa-
beth Giansiracusa, Deborah Gordon, and David Quint for their comments on an earlier
draft, and Maurizio Garioli for computer assistance at I Tatti. Helpful suggestions
regarding revision were also made by the anonymous readers for the *JMRS*.
2. See Machiavelli's claims to originality in the preface to book 1 of the *Discourses*,
as well as in the preface to the *Florentine Histories*, where he explicitly criticizes the
historiography of Leonardo Bruni and Poggio Bracciolini. For a summary of the
debate, see Isaiah Berlin, 'The Originality of Machiavelli,' in his *Against the Current*,
ed. H. Hardy (London, 1979), 25-79.
3. See, for example, Ernst Cassirer, *The Myth of the State* (New Haven and
London, 1946); Leo Strauss, *Thoughts on Machiavelli* (Glencoe, Ill., 1958); and Jürgen
Habermas, 'The Classical Doctrine of Politics in Relation to Social Philosophy,' *Theory
and Practice*, trans. John Viertel (Boston, 1973), 41-81.

2   Journal of Medieval and Renaissance Studies, 18 (1988) 1

on the one hand as the proto-political scientist, trying to formulate laws of political behavior similar to the laws of the emerging natural sciences. Paradoxically, this is both an aspect of Machiavelli's modernity and a reason why he is not modern enough, for the search for general laws of political behavior presupposes an ahistorical (or transhistorical) definition of human nature. On the other hand, Machiavelli is not committed simply to an ideal of scientific disinterestedness, since his political analysis is itself in the service of a defense of the emerging, centralized bourgeois state. But this in turn, for Horkheimer, involves an overestimation of the individual human agent and, once again, an ahistorical analysis of individual human nature. Yet, in *Dialectic of Enlightenment* Adorno and Horkheimer refer to "Those somber writers of the bourgeois dawn—Machiavelli, Hobbes, Mandeville . . . —who decried the egotism of the self, acknowledged in so doing that society was the destructive principle, and denounced harmony before it was elevated as the official doctrine by the serene and classical authors."[4] In the following pages I would like to suggest that Machiavelli is more of a kindred spirit than Adorno and Horkheimer recognized, that students of Machiavelli can benefit from reading his texts in the light of Adorno and Horkheimer's own work, and that, far from being anachronistic, this is an approach that Machiavelli's own texts enjoin. In particular, Adorno and Horkheimer's exemplary resistance to the traditional distinction between literary and philosophical or political texts can help us not only to see how literary and political notions of representation and imitation are inextricable in Machiavelli's work but also to recover the rhetoric in his political theory. A rhetorical analysis of the *Discourses*, in particular of the strategies of reduction and disunion, shows that Machiavelli's praise of conflict (what he calls "disunion") in the Roman Republic is analogous in important ways to Adorno and Horkheimer's theory of negative dialectics. The portrait of Machiavelli that finally emerges is of a writer alive to the claims of historicism but resistant to relativism; yet one who is also resistant to the lure of harmony and totality, and thus open to the uses of negation.[5]

4. *Dialectic of Enlightenment*, trans. John Cumming (New York, 1972), 90.
5. For a related attempt to apply a dialectical model to the analysis of political and discursive structures in *The Prince*, see Michael McCanles, *The Discourse of 'Il Principe,'* (Malibu, 1983). For an analysis of the "rhetorical politics" of the *Discourses* in terms of the notion of essentially contested argument, see Eugene Garver, *Machiavelli and the History of Prudence* (Madison, Wis., 1987).

Kahn · *Machiavelli's* Discourses 3

II. *Reduction and Disunion in the Discourses*

Generations of readers have remarked on Machiavelli's reductive, fragmentary, often aphoristic style. Some have seen this style as itself evidence for Machiavelli's break with his predecessors, while others, beginning with Guicciardini, have accused Machiavelli of paradoxically betraying his idealism in the very extremism of his formulations. Felix Gilbert has provided the historical context for any consideration of Machiavelli's rhetoric by showing that his thematic attacks on harmony and consensus are attacks on the dominant rhetoric of the Florentine *pratiche*.[6] But it has not, to my knowledge, been recognized that in addition to reducing a humanist rhetoric of consensus to fragments, Machiavelli explicitly announces his concern with a rhetoric of reduction at the very beginning of the *Discourses*. An examination of the proem and first few chapters of Book 1 can help us see that reduction ("reducere" in its various grammatical forms) describes not only the characteristic rhetorical strategy of the *Discourses*, but also Machiavelli's *return* to the exemplary conflict or disunion of the Roman Republic.

In the proem to Book 1 Machiavelli explains his motives for writing in the following way:

> When, therefore, I consider in what honour antiquity is held, and how—to cite but one instance—a bit of old statue has fetched a high price that someone may have it by him to give honour to his house and that it may be possible for it to be copied by those who are keen on this art; and how the latter then with great industry take pains to reproduce it in all their works; and when, on the other hand, I notice that what history has to say about the highly virtuous actions performed by ancient kingdoms and republics, by their kings, their generals, their citizens, their legislators, and by others who have gone to the trouble of serving their country, is

6. See Felix Gilbert, 'Florentine Political Assumptions in the Period of Savonarola and Soderini,' *Journal of the Warburg and Courtauld Institutes* 20 (1957): 187-214; as well as John M. Najemy, *Corporatism and Consensus in Florentine Electoral Politics, 1280-1400* (Chapel Hill, 1982), especially the Introduction and Epilogue. Najemy's work suggests a Quattrocento analogue for Machiavelli's rhetoric of conflict in the political practice of the Florentine guilds. See also his two articles: ' "Arti" and "Ordini" in Machiavelli's *Istorie*,' in *Essays Presented to Myron P. Gilmore*, ed. Sergio Bertelli and Gloria Ramakus, vol. 1: History (Florence, 1978), 161-91, esp. 167-68; and 'Machiavelli and the Medici: The Lessons of Florentine History,' *Renaissance Quarterly* 35 (1982), 551-76.

rather admired than imitated [più presto ammirate che imitate]; nay, is so shunned by everybody in each little thing they do, that of the virtue of bygone days there remains no trace, it cannot but fill me at once with astonishment and grief.[7]

This passage is usually, and correctly, read as an argument for systematic as opposed to dilettantish or eclectic study of the ancients. But it is important also to note the place of aesthetic admiration in this opposition. While Machiavelli seems at first to be contrasting the active appropriation of antiquity on the part of artists and craftsmen to the neglect of such imitation by statesmen and citizens, there is clearly another way in which the merely aesthetic reproduction of ancient fragments is an activity of limited worth in his eyes. What is striking about this passage from a humanist perspective is the separation of art and politics. There is no sense that such artistic imitation could itself be conducive, as well as analogous, to political action. There is rather an implied contrast between the modern collector of old statues who purchases his honor on the market and the ancient king, general, citizen, or legislator who achieves it through great deeds. The virtuous modern collector, we might extrapolate, would not be the art connoisseur but rather the political counselor whose advice makes it possible for his prince to reproduce in action the achievement of the ancients.

Accordingly, after allying the aesthetic imitation of antiquities to the merely passive admiration of ancient *virtù*, Machiavelli argues that the way to undo the mesmerizing aesthetic effect of ancient authority is to reduce Rome's political achievement to the collection of decisions it originally was—to reduce the history of Rome, that is, to a collection of examples. This reduction is the essential prelude to correct imitation of antiquity:

> For the civil law is nothing but a collection of decisions, made by the jurists of old, which the jurists of today have tabulated in orderly fashion [ridutte in ordine] for our instruction. Nor, again, is medicine anything but a record of experiments, performed by doctors of old, upon which the doctors of our day base their pre-

7. References to the *Discourses* will be given first to the English translation of Leslie J. Walker, S.J., ed. Bernard Crick (Harmondsworth, England, 1979), and then to the Italian text edited by Sergio Bertelli (Milano, 1977), as here: 97–98/123–24. Where appropriate, references to book and chapter will be given prior to page references.

scriptions. In spite of which in constituting republics, in maintaining states, in governing kingdoms, in forming an army or conducting a war, in dealing with subjects, in extending the empire, one finds neither prince nor republic who repairs to antiquity for examples [98/124].[8]

As this passage suggests, the whole proem can be read as an elaborate pun on *reducere* since the reduction of ancient precepts to examples will allow for the reduction of Florentine politics to those of ancient Rome in the etymological sense of leading the Florentines back to the correct principles of political judgment. In thus playing on the double sense of reduction, the proem prepares us for the paradigmatic reduction of the *Discourses*: the ascription of Rome's success to disunion or class conflict rather than to fortune (1.2, 2.1). This is a reduction that is first carried out through Machiavelli's counterpointing of Livy and Polybius. As many readers have noted, Machiavelli invokes the Polybian theory of natural cycles of government only to reduce nature to fortune in the case of Rome. In so doing, he criticizes one strain of classical political theory and thereby makes the active assumption of responsibility possible both in reading and in politics (since not everything is determined by nature, there is room for human deliberation and action). But Machiavelli does not stop with the Livian attribution of Roman success to *fortuna* (interpreted by Machiavelli to mean chance), since in the act of reducing Polybian nature to chance, he also redefines chance as disunion. For, according to Machiavelli, it was the conflict or disunion of different class interests which gave rise to more equitable political representation.[9]

In spite of the fact that Rome had no Lycurgus to give it at the outset such a constitution as would ensure to it a long life of freedom, yet owing to *disunione* between the plebs and the senate, so many things happened that chance effected what had not been

8. For Machiavelli's use of the words *reducere, reducersi,* etc., see also in the Italian edition pages 131, 142, 155, 160, 177, 179, 185, 193, 224, 233, 265, 293, 340, 379, 381, 385, 450; and in a negative sense 215.
9. By this circuitous route Machiavelli ends up subscribing to Polybius' theory of the mixed constitution. On Machiavelli's reading of Polybius, see Harvey C. Mansfield, Jr., *Machiavelli's New Modes and Orders: A Study of the "Discourses on Livy"* (Ithaca and London, 1979), 35ff; Paul Larivaille, *La Pensée politique de Machiavel* (Nancy, 1982), 101ff; Gennaro Sasso, 'La teoria dell'anacyclosis,' *Studi su Machiavelli* (Napoli, 1967), 161–222, esp. 199. On Machiavelli's reading of Livy, and his misunderstanding of Livian *fortuna* as chance, see Mark Hulliung, *Citizen Machiavelli* (Princeton, 1983), 46.

6   *Journal of Medieval and Renaissance Studies*, 18 (1988) 1

provided by a lawgiver. So that, if Rome did not get fortune's
first gift, it got its second. . . . This came about when the Roman
nobility became so overbearing . . . that the populace rose against
them, and they were constrained by the fear that they might lose
all, to grant the populace a share in the government; the senate and
the consuls retaining, however, sufficient authority for them to be
able to maintain their position in the republic [110–111/134–35].[10]

In ascribing Rome's success to class conflict instead of fortune, Machiavelli could be said to effect a reduction in the second sense of the
word—that is, he reduces the indeterminacy of fortune to a dialectical
model of conflict. But what I am concerned with in the following
pages is the way this dialectic is itself contained by Machiavelli's insistence on its inseparability from the faculty of *virtù*. That is, Machiavelli both gives a descriptive account of Roman class conflict and
places constraints on the interpretation of disunion by showing that
this description is inseparable from a prescriptive commitment to certain political values. This argument is played out first in the opposition
between Rome and Sparta; then in Machiavelli's analysis of disunion
in the realm of representation; and finally in what I would like to call

10. I do not believe it has been noticed before that Machiavelli's use of the term
"disunione" in the *Discourses* is remarkably consistent; with a few debatable exceptions, "disunione" is used in a positive sense (e.g. 134, 137ff); while, as has been
noticed, "disordine" (e.g. 223, 229, 239, 242, 255, 258, 265, 330, 369, 370, 379, 383, 434,
441) and "sette" (147–48, 151, 165–66, 210, 217, 227, 234, 242, 266, 271, 292, 452, 482)
are used in a negative sense (but cf. 3.1 where "sette" refers to a religious sect). An
exception regarding disunion may be 2.25.360/357, where Machiavelli writes: "The
Veientes thought that if they attacked the Romans, when disunited, they could overcome them; but their attack caused the Romans to unite and brought about their own
ruin. For discord ["disunione"] in a republic is usually due to idleness and peace,
and unity to fear and war. Had the Veientes been wise, then, the more disunited
they found the Romans to be, the more studiously should they have refrained from
going to war with them, and have striven to get the better of them by the artifices
men use in time of peace." Another place where Machiavelli discusses disunion negatively is 1.12.145/166, where he is describing the negative effect of the Church on
Italy: "The Church, then, has neither been able to occupy the whole of Italy, nor
has it allowed anyone else to occupy it. Consequently, it has been the cause why Italy
has never come under one head, but has been under many princes and *signori*, by
whom such disunion and such weakness has been brought about, that it has now become the prey, not only of barbarian potentates, but of anyone who attacks it. For
which our Italians have to thank the Church, and nobody else." But the use of the
word "disunion," which elsewhere refers to the beneficial balance of forces within
the state, suggests unwitting support for Guicciardini's view that disunion within
Italy is actually positive, i.e. that it creates a situation analogous to disunion within
the city state. See Francesco Guicciardini, *Considerazioni intorno ai Discorsi del
Machiavelli sopra la prima deca di Tito Livio*, in *Francesco Guicciardini, Scritti
politici e Ricordi*, ed. Roberto Palmarrocchi (Bari, 1933) on *Discourses* 1.12 (p. 23).

Kahn · *Machiavelli's* Discourses 7

the discursive disunion of Machiavelli's text—his fragmentation of the narrative into discrete examples (or reduced narratives) by which he aims, both formally and thematically, to reduce the reader to correct political action. As I have already suggested, in the end all of these arguments can be seen as variations on a certain kind of negative dialectic, that is, a dialectic which not only reduces opposition by showing how the antithesis is contained within the thesis but also admits the inevitable role of value and contingent external events in the correct execution of this dialectic. If we now pursue Machiavelli's reflections on disunion, we can see how in its various aspects—in particular, in its relation to reduction in the two senses of leading back and reducing to smaller compass—disunion comes to inform all levels of Machiavelli's text.

III. *Constraints on the Interpretation of Disunion:*
Books 1 and 2

While readers of the *Discourses* agree on Machiavelli's reduction of Roman fortune to disunion, the emphasis on disunion has itself given rise to a conflict of interpretation. To some, beginning (again) with Guicciardini, it looks like yet another example of Machiavelli's dualistic view of the world, his theatrical preference for conflict over consensus. Such readers see the dualistic tendency of Machiavelli's arguments as a symptom of his extremism—his rejection of humanist *mediocritas* or the middle way. Others have construed this dualism as evidence of Machiavelli's pragmatic (proto-political scientist's) concern with securing the state through the almost mechanistic counterpointing of conflicting interests. While neither of these interpretations does justice to the complexity of the *Discourses*, I would like to suggest that it is particularly the second alternative which Machiavelli's reflections on Roman disunion are designed to avoid. For Machiavelli's reduction of fortune to the mixed constitution's balance of power proves to be only the first step—the first reduction—in his argument.[11]

The danger of not advancing beyond this point—of taking the balance of power as a structural model of political reasoning or reading—

11. An early reader of my article objected to the use of the diplomatic term "balance of power" to refer to what is a matter of domestic politics. I hope to have shown by the end of this essay that even these diplomatic connotations are relevant to Machiavelli's analysis of the Roman Republic, since one of the effects of Machiavelli's argument is to collapse the distinction between internal and external affairs.

8   *Journal of Medieval and Renaissance Studies*, 18 (1988) 1

lies in the related assumptions that (i) all simple division is beneficial, and (ii) disunion is to be distinguished from faction by the criterion of success. To accept these pragmatic premises, as Machiavelli knew and as Max Horkheimer has recognized in our century, is to become an apologist for the status quo:

> The pragmatic concept of truth in its exclusive form [i.e., the identification of truth with effectiveness] ... corresponds to limitless trust in the existing world. If the goodness of every idea is given time and opportunity to come to light, if the success of the truth—even if after struggle and resistance—is in the long run certain, if the idea of a dangerous, explosive truth cannot come into the field of vision, then the present social structure is consecrated. ... In pragmatism there lies embedded the belief in the existence and advantages of free competition.[12]

It is precisely to address such a charge that Machiavelli turns in book 1, chapter 5, from the disunion between the plebs and the nobles to the opposition between Rome and Sparta—an opposition which then serves in exemplary fashion to clarify the way we should construe the disunion of class conflict.

In Machiavelli's analysis in this chapter, theoretical reason loses its authority and begins to be implicated in the realm of indeterminacy, since determinations or decisions, it seems, can be made only on the basis of effects. In considering "into whose hands it is best to place the guardianship of liberty" (1.5.115/139)—the people's (as in ancient Rome) or the nobles' (as in ancient Sparta and modern Venice)—Machiavelli writes: "If we appeal to reason arguments may be adduced in support of either thesis; but if we ask what the result was, the answer will favour the nobility, for the freedom of Sparta and of Venice lasted longer than did that of Rome." Yet, though Machiavelli's analysis does not appeal to a conventional notion of theoretical reason (since he reduces "reason" to a "reasonable" response to passion, and tells us elsewhere that such reasons can always be given later [116/139–40]), it also is not pragmatic in the sense of being simply success- or result-oriented. For the definition of success is not a given but must itself be an object of deliberation: "Either you have in mind a republic that looks to founding an empire, as Rome did; or one that is content to

12. Max Horkheimer, 'On the Problem of Truth,' in *The Essential Frankfurt School Reader*, ed. Andrew Arato and Eike Gebhardt (New York, 1982), 425.

maintain the *status quo*. In the first case it is necessary to do in all things as Rome did. In the second case it is possible to imitate Venice and Sparta" (1.5.117/140).

This opposition between Rome and Sparta serves a number of functions, not the least of which is to allow Machiavelli to distinguish between *virtù* and success—for while Sparta lasted longer, Rome demonstrated greater *virtù* (1.6.121/143: "grandezza"). Here we can see the analogy Machiavelli wants to set up between internal and external political affairs. For just as Rome's *virtù* is both manifest in and a consequence of its ability to give representation to conflicting interests within the republic, so *virtù* is both cause and effect of an expansionist foreign policy, which aims not only to conquer but also to integrate and give representation to the conquered within the Roman state. In each case Roman strength is predicated in part on Rome's decision to represent and to arm those who had been previously excluded—whether as plebs or as the conquered people. Furthermore, the alternative between Rome and Sparta is asymmetrical because *all* states eventually will be forced either to expand or to confront internal faction (1.6.123/149; 2.19.335–36/334–35). Those who choose expansion or confrontation will not necessarily be more successful but they will demonstrate greater *virtù* (cf. 1.6.121, 123/149). Accordingly, one implication of this discussion of Rome and Sparta for domestic policy is that one cannot distinguish between faction and disunion in terms of "success" or "effectiveness," since, for example, the Medici certainly were effective in their own way, that is, by promoting faction. Rather, disunion or class conflict must be preferred because it provides a structure or institution which constrains private interest to take the form of public good (1.4.114/137), that is, a structure that generates civic virtue and preserves civic liberty.

Thus, while the reduction of fortune to disunion might at first glance appear to be complicit with a "limitless trust in the existing world," in the end the *Discourses*, like *The Prince*, can be seen to meditate on the problem of defining an exemplary political order simply pragmatically in terms of success.[18] In fact, Machiavelli's critical leverage, his judgment of Florentine faction, depends on his not doing this. As the example of Rome and Sparta shows, disunion (e.g., the

13. I have discussed Machiavelli's meditations on pragmatism in *The Prince* in "*Virtù and the Example of Agathocles in Machiavelli's *Prince*," *Representations* 13 (1986): 63–85.

10   Journal of Medieval and Renaissance Studies, 18 (1988) 1

opposition between Rome and Sparta) must itself be contained by, or reduced to, the value of the common good (republican Rome). Machiavelli could thus be said to use the collapsible distinction between Rome and Sparta as the chief rhetorical paradigm of his text, the paradigm that allows him to avoid the extremes of an idealistic or teleological dialectic of political conflict on the one hand, and a pessimistic surrender to the absolute indeterminacy or factionalism of politics on the other. Accordingly, Machiavelli sets up a variety of oppositions within the *Discourses* (e.g., force/fraud; states that expand/states that do not; *fortuna/virtù*, etc.), only then to show that the opposition is contained within each term. The most important of these is that between Florence and Rome: while Machiavelli begins by distinguishing between the two in terms of the corruption of Florence and the pristine state of Rome, as we read further we see that no state is completely lacking in corruption and that a completely corrupt state would be incapable of regeneration (see 1.16.154/173-74). For even republican Rome required an individual of *virtù* periodically to remind the corrupt citizens of the original principles of government, while in a completely corrupt state no such individual could exist.[14] One effect of this demystification of Rome, as Claude Lefort has argued, is to make Rome a more suitable object of imitation for Florence.[15]

But there are other ways as well in which Machiavelli tries to ensure the possibility of a non-idealistic and still effective imitation of republican Rome. And it is here that we can see how disunion informs his analysis of the realm of appearances as well as of political representation; indeed, it forms the linchpin between the two. For Machiavelli argues that while the good politician will know how to use the absence of correspondence—the disunion—between appearance and reality for his own purposes, he will also eventually be forced to represent the interests of his subjects if he wants to maintain the state. He claims, that is, to uncover a logic of representation by which the self-interested agent will eventually be constrained to move toward a republican form of government. This argument is particularly obvious in Machiavelli's discussion of the tyrant. In 2.2 he tells us that if the tyrant pursues his own interests, he will eventually run counter to the interests not only of the people but also of the city: "Consequently, as

14. See Claude Lefort, *Le Travail de l'œuvre de Machiavel* (Paris, 1972), 501-18.
15. See Lefort, 585.

soon as tyranny replaces self-government the least of the evils which this tyranny brings about are that it ceases to make progress and to grow in power and wealth: more often than not, nay always, what happens is that it declines" (2.2.275–76/280). However, if the tyrant obstructs progress he cannot long remain in power, since the people will eventually rebel. On the other hand, if his goal is maintenance of the state he will in the long run be forced to consider—and to represent—the interests of his subjects. In other words, once the element of time is introduced—both in the sense of time for reflection and in the sense of reflection on the longevity of the state—a transition can be effected between the prince, who is better at founding, and the people, who are better at maintaining, the state (1.58.256/265). Elsewhere Machiavelli articulates this logic in different terms, when he speaks of the need to extend the base of *virtù* for the longevity of the state:

> And because princes are short-lived, it may well happen that when a kingdom loses its prince, it loses also the virtue of its prince. Hence kingdoms which depend on the virtue of one man do not last long, because they lose their virtue when his life is spent, and it seldom happens that it is revived by his successor [1.11.141/162].

Finally, if flexibility is what is required,

> a republic has a fuller life and enjoys good fortune for a longer time than a principality, since it is better able to adapt itself to diverse circumstances owing to the diversity found among its citizens than a prince can do. For a man who is accustomed to act in one particular way, never changes, as we have said. Hence when times change and no longer suit his ways, he is inevitably ruined [3.9.431/417].

Thus, if Machiavelli's chief instance of the way in which fraud or misrepresentation gives way to representation in a primarily uncorrupt state is the shift in Rome from aristocratic to republican government, he now argues that this is a logic which, in a primarily corrupt state, applies to the individual as well.

Yet while Machiavelli argues that the disunion of appearances contains within itself a contingent logic or dialectic which will eventually compel the agent (whether individual or class) who recognizes his own interest to act in the general interest, he also describes the self-conscious manipulation of this disunion as *virtù*. And although he seems to have intended these two strategies (the first dialectical, the second axiomatic or prescriptive) as alternative ways of regenerating the state, in the end they cannot be separated. The analysis of disunion in the realm of appearances is thus strictly analogous to that of the disunion of class conflict. In the first case, where Machiavelli begins with an empirical analysis of conflict or the balance of power, he ends up discussing *virtù*; and where he begins by emphasizing *virtù*, he ends up insisting on the institutional equivalent of a balance of power. Similarly, in the second case, where he begins by discussing the constraints internal to the act of fraud or misrepresentation (constraints that will eventually force the ruler to represent the real interests of his subjects), he ends up arguing that the force of these constraints depends on our recognizing them, and vice versa.[16]

Thus, there are two responses within the text to the initial reduction of Livian fortune to disunion. First, in confronting the charge of a merely pragmatic approach to politics, one which risks confounding "virtue" and the status quo, Machiavelli attempts to develop a dialectical account of representation (construed both as representation in the realm of appearance and as the political representation of different interests), according to which particular interests—whether of an individual or a class—logically give way to the general good. At this point he must confront a charge similar to the first: the charge which can be leveled against a teleological model of dialectic which, if it doesn't involve limitless trust in the existing world, does amount to trust in the future. Secondly, he insists on the necessity of *virtù*—i.e., of right judgment of one's true interests—in the effective execution of this dialectic.

16. In a book that came to my attention after the completion of this essay, *La Pensée politique de Machiavel*, Paul Larivaille makes a related argument about the two strands of argument in the *Discourses*. Larivaille claims that the political situation at the time Machiavelli was writing—specifically, the increasingly autocratic behavior of Lorenzo, Duke of Urbino—gave rise to Machiavelli's concern with the *intention* of princes, a concern he had not expressed in *The Prince*. This in turn led him to try to locate external checks on the prince's behavior: "A ce doute angoissant sur les intentions du prince, caractéristique de l'époque des *Discours*, deux solutions sont successivement proposées: l'une, qui fait fond sur la valeur pédagogique de l'histoire et le ressort psychologique de l'amour de la gloire comme garde-fous contre le césarisme; l'autre, plus typiquement machiavélienne, qui vise à substituer le poids objectif des réalitiés à celui de l'arbitraire individuel, en faisant obligation au (futur) prince, sous peine d'échec, de sacrifier ses aspirations et tentations personnelles aux exigences de la situation politico-sociale ambiante" (161).

Accordingly, there are also two models of reduction at work in the *Discourses*: the first the reduction of fortune (in the sense of indeterminacy) to disunion; the second the double reduction of disunion to *virtù* (as effect and then cause). This second reduction of a binary opposition to a pseudo-alternative is what we would expect of a dialectical form of argument—the antithesis turns out to contain the thesis within it. Dialectic could thus be characterized as an imperialistic or expansive form of argument, and Machiavelli could then be said to enact on the level of his rhetoric the dialectic he ascribes to Roman imperialism. But Machiavelli's is a negative dialectic because it is not idealistic or teleological in the Hegelian sense; that is, because it is informed by *virtù*. Furthermore, it is precisely because *virtù* and the value of the common good are no guarantee of success that Machiavelli's dialectic is negative in another sense as well. For, if the interiorization of the enemy is a source of strength, it is also the eventual cause of failure. Thus Machiavelli writes in 1.6 (118/141), "We have just been discussing the effects produced by the controversies between the populace and the senate. Now, these controversies went on until the time of the Gracchi when they became the causes of the destruction of liberty." Ideally, however—or, in the short run—the reduction of authority is countered by the reduction of (the opposite threat of) disorder. Thus, if it is true that Machiavelli's emphasis on Roman disunion amounts to a privileging of conflict over consensus, it must be recognized that Machiavellian conflict performs its own acts of containment as well. The dualistic model of conflict proves to be, as in the example of Rome and Sparta, asymmetrical.

IV.   *Imitation, Reduction, and Examples: Book 3*

The dialectic we observed in books 1 and 2 of the *Discourses*, between a logic of interest and its institutional equivalent which will constrain an individual or class to act in the service of the common good, and the value of the common good which the individual or class needs to recognize in order finally to be constrained, reappears in book 3, specifically in the contrast between examples of necessity and examples of individuals manipulating necessity. Of course, Machiavelli has been teaching by example all along. But as we move from book 1 to book 3, and Machiavelli's dialectic is revealed to be increasingly contingent or negative, he also uses increasingly many examples to make a single point—thus combining in one instance a kind of reduction which at the same time highlights the element of contingency and the necessity of choice. The result is to fragment the text of Livy, disarticulating the narrative into a storehouse of arguments, making the *Discourses* into a kind of commonplace book.

But the *Discourses* provides the reader with an artificial memory in another way as well. It does not function simply as a repertoire of practical political arguments, but aims to remind the reader (in Machiavelli's phrase "reducersi a mente") of the experience of necessity—the *reduced* circumstances—which he has forgotten (2.19.338/337; 1.2.106–107/131–32). It aims, in other words, to reproduce in reading the experience that led the Romans to form true opinions, the experience that taught them what to praise and blame, what to imitate or avoid. Speaking of Rome's periodic return to its origins, Machiavelli writes:

> the institutions which caused the Roman republic to return to its start were the introduction of plebeian tribunes, of the censorship, and of all the other laws which put a check on human ambition and arrogance; to which institutions life must needs be given by some virtuous citizen who cooperates strenuously in giving them effect despite the power of those who contravene them. Notable among such drastic actions . . . [was] the death of Brutus' sons [for conspiring against the republic] . . . Such events, because of their unwonted severity and their notoriety, brought men back to the mark every time one of them happened; and when they began to occur less frequently, they also began to provide occasion for men to practise corruption, and were attended with more danger than commotion. For between one case of disciplinary action of this type and the next there ought to elapse at most ten years, because by this time men begin to change their habits and to break the laws; and unless something happens ["nasce"] which recalls to their minds the penalty involved and reawakens fear in them, there will soon be so many delinquents that it will be impossible to punish them without danger [3.1.387–88/381].

Obedience to the state requires the forced remembrance of drastic actions. Thus, while urging in humanist fashion the voluntary imitation of antiquity, Machiavelli also proves to be the most coercive proponent of the Renaissance. Accordingly, in the passage just quoted the metaphor of birth ("unless something happens"—"nasce") serves to em-

phasize not only that the renaissance of classical antiquity and of republican principles is a violent process but also that this violence is not
an unfortunate by-product of rebirth, but instrumental to it. Thus, the
distinction is blurred not only between institutional and individual
virtù but also between internal and external affairs, domestic policy
and war.[17] This is, of course, what one expects from Machiavelli by
this point. The violence of war remains an external accident until it
is internalized: until, that is, it is imitated and appropriated by being
used deliberately and theatrically. And it is this act of appropriation
which Machiavelli's own imitation of violent examples from Livy is
designed to exemplify.

This point can be illustrated by turning to the first extended example of an illustrious individual in book 3. Junius Brutus is famous
for having simulated madness not only to protect his property, as
Livy tells us, but also, Machiavelli surmises, to watch out for the interests of the republic: "one can well believe that he practiced [this
dissimulation] . . . in order to escape observation and [so] that he
might get a better opportunity of downing the kings and liberating his
country, whenever they gave him the chance" (3.2.391/384). Madness (a kind of metaphorical violence done to one's identity) proves to
be an effective camouflage of the intention to do violence in the service
of the state. But Brutus is also exemplary because he knows how to
turn the violence done to another into a theatrical event which then
compels the audience to act rather than simply observe:

> [as we see] later, when on the death of Lucretia he was the first to
> pull the dagger out of the wound in the presence of her father, her
> husband and other of her relatives, and to make the bystanders
> swear that they would never tolerate for the future any king
> reigning in Rome [3.2.391/384].

These examples of concealing or staging one's intention to use violence, Machiavelli tells us, illustrate Brutus's prudence. His exemplary
severity, on the other hand, is illustrated by his condemning his own
sons to death for their conspiracy against the republic. Here Brutus's
judgment of his sons brings about a pedagogical act of violence—one
which is intended to instruct not only potential conspirators but also
all other spectators, as we see by Brutus's exemplary presence at the

17. Lefort, 611, makes a related point regarding the example of Brutus, discussed
below.

16   *Journal of Medieval and Renaissance Studies*, 18 (1988) 1

event. A brief digression is necessary to understand the force of this example.

Elsewhere in book 3 Machiavelli takes up the civic consequences of virtuous action, i.e., of glory or reputation in the public realm. On the one hand he has argued that the search for individual aggrandizement will lead to the individual's downfall; on the other hand, he argues for the necessity of constraints supplementary to that logic in the form of laws and, on extraordinary occasions, a dictator. Precisely because reputation may be acquired in the private realm by bestowing favors and creating partisans, an individual of public reputation (i.e., a reputation for serving the common good [3.21–22]) must on occasion intervene. Such an individual, in the logic of Machiavelli's argument, is one who is able to stand for the whole without totalizing the part—without, that is, creating partisans. And he does so by putting distance between himself and his fellow citizens. Machiavelli's chief example here is Manlius as opposed to Valerius. For while both were exemplary men of *virtù*, Valerius was known for his "affability, kindliness, [and] compassion," with the result that the army became devoted to him personally. And, as Machiavelli tells us, "for the army to be devoted to the cause of a private individual is not consistent with his position, since he is bound by the laws and should obey the magistrates" (3.22.470/453). Manlius's behavior, on the other hand, "was entirely in the public interest and was in no way affected by private ambition, for it is impossible to gain partisans if one is harsh in one's dealing with everybody and is wholly devoted to the common good, because by so doing one does not acquire particular friends or—as I have just called them—partisans" (3.22.469/452). If the problem is how to use imitation to contribute to the public good, it turns out that what has to be imitated is not the individual per se but the individual's *relation* to the common good; that is, the individual must not be directly identified with the whole (which would be a form of partisanship) but rather, distance must be built into the relation.

Accordingly, Brutus's murder of his sons is exemplary for Machiavelli not only because it offers yet another instance of the theatrical use of violence in the service of the common good but also because it dramatizes the potential connection between imitation and non-partisanship. This would seem to be underlined particularly by Brutus's presence at the event. While one can easily visualize the attendance of the judge who has passed the sentence or the citizen interested in the

Kahn · Machiavelli's Discourses 17

performance of justice, a father, one imagines, would wish to stay away. In thematic terms what occurs in the example of Brutus is the sacrifice of the part (his sons), and thus of partisanship, for the whole. Brutus's presence thus testifies to what is of importance in formal terms—that the realm of representation can be used to distance oneself from, and thereby in some sense control, the realm of necessity or of fortune—in the case of Brutus, the misfortune of his sons' conspiracy. Violence thus turns out to be a synecdoche for necessity, and the theatrical staging of it a means (by turning effect into cause) of controlling one's fortune. Thus in 2.29 (372/367), Machiavelli writes that "men may second ['secondare'] their fortune but not oppose it"; but this seconding of nature or willing of necessity—which here takes the double form of the theatrical staging of a violent punishment and seconding it with one's presence—is itself *virtù*. "Thus Livy," Machiavelli tells us, "calls necessity 'the last and best of all weapons' " (3.12.443/428). Since necessity can take many forms, "It matters then little to a general along which road he travels, provided he has virtuosity, and his virtue gives him standing with men" (3.21.463/448). As a result, the content and force of the examples in book 3 is less thematic than formal.

If we now return to the question of Machiavelli's style we can see that just as the periodic reduction to a situation of violent conflict was necessary to restore the Roman Republic to its first principles, so a rhetorical reduction is necessary to induce correct imitation in the reader, imitation which involves the internalizing of distance or disunion from the object of imitation. Machiavelli achieves this in part, as Nancy Struever and others have pointed out, by his aphoristic style, his narrow lexicon, and dichotomizing mode of argument.[18] These, along with his use of exemplary anecdote (regardless of specific content), tend to diminish or fragment the narrative component of Machiavelli's argument and place a greater burden of interpretation upon the reader. That is, the reader who finds him- or herself in reduced circumstances is obliged to engage more actively in the process of interpretation. A similar effect is achieved by the occasional references to contemporary Florentine affairs—references which serve to galvanize the text, and encourage the reader to read allegorically.

Finally, both in the case of the individual and in that of the re-

18. Nancy S. Struever, "Machiavelli and the Critique of the Available Languages of Morality in the Sixteenth Century," unpublished paper.

public, what is important for Machiavelli is the the *secondariness* of imitation. For by imitating nature, we willfully take our distance from it and in this distance resides the possibility of determining rather than being determined by nature. But by the end of book 3 Machiavelli has refined our sense of both the agent and the object of imitation (of the "we" and of "nature"). For his reflections on the individual in this book, like those of the individual ruler throughout the *Discourses*, are an attempt to show that the goal of imitation is not the perfecting of one's individual nature, nor the aesthetic composition of the self, but rather the recognition of the limits of such individual powers of transformation. The imitation of nature is not finally an option open to the individual (at least, not for long). The recognition of this—and the seconding of its republican consequences—is the true measure of praise.[19]

In conclusion, what are we to make of Machiavelli's claims to originality? In one way, his attack on the notion of simple disunion (and the "limitless trust in the existing world") can be read as an attack on humanist dialogue, or rhetoric *in utramque partem*, to the extent that this implies that such debate will naturally generate consensus. Machiavelli wants to show that such rhetoric, informed by such assumptions, is potentially complicit with the status quo, that is, with a praise of appearances. And yet, as Guicciardini suggested long ago, there is a way in which Machiavelli remains a humanist—though this allegiance is not, as Guicciardini seemed to imply, the unwitting consequence of Machiavelli's violent desire for change. The interest of Machiavelli, and this is something I think Adorno and Horkheimer noticed, is that the possibility of change is itself tied to the rational analysis of interests and to the ability to distinguish between faction and disunion. For if disunion, in contrast to faction, is a source of *virtù*, it also provides a structural analogue for *virtù* which combines but does not identify knowledge and success or knowledge and power. In thus insisting on the dialectical relation of objective, non-partisan analysis and committed political action, Machiavelli also reveals the critical potential of the humanist tradition. For, even more than the humanists, Machiavelli wants to devise a political ethic that will be capable of respond-

19. Lefort also argues that book 3 does not finally involve an exaltation of the individual (598, 602). In *Niccolò Machiavelli, Storia del suo pensiero politico* (1958, rev. ed., Bologna, 1980) Gennaro Sasso discusses the aporia of Machiavelli's simultaneous attempt to overcome the political "individualism" of Renaissance principalities and his insistence on the necessary intervention of an individual of *virtù* in corrupt republics (508–10).

ing to the particular without losing its critical force. To the pseudo-objectivity of a certain kind of scientific disinterestedness, Machiavelli opposes the objectivity that is available only to the interested. Thus he does not simply invert the humanist equation of the *honestum* and the *utile*, substituting the criterion of efficacy for that of morality. Rather, he displaces the *honestum*/*utile* distinction into the new dialectical relation of disunion and force.[20] The *Discourses* offers one model of this force—one which might be called a critical force because it offers a way of criticizing the existing state of affairs by appealing not to the humanist notion of consensus but to a conflict of interests or disunion.

In the end disunion structures all aspects of Machiavelli's argument. It appears as (i) the disunion of class conflict; (ii) the pseudo-disunion or opposition between Rome and Sparta which both re-enacts in the rhetoric of Machiavelli's examples the imperialism which is his theme and yet shows that imperialism to be a function not of any teleological conception of dialectic, but of a system of values in which conquest is a virtuous deed and in which *virtù* can also take the form of a seconding or willing of necessity (the eventual expansion of all states); (iii) disunion in the realm of representation—the recognition of which allows one to manipulate this disunion to one's advantage; and (iv) more generally, the disunion of imitation, which ideally governs one's relation to the past and thus to the present as well. In all cases the proper attitude toward the object of praise is disunion. Otherwise, imitation appropriate to the present—in Machiavelli's case, the present factional state of Florence—will be impossible. The possibility of change is a function of disunion.

20. I am alluding here to and revising Antonio Gramsci's remarks on Machiavelli in "The Modern Prince," in *Selections from the Prison Notebooks*, ed. and trans. Quintin Hoare and Geoffrey Nowell Smith (New York, 1971), 123–305; especially the section entitled "Prediction and Perspective" (169–72), where Gramsci discusses what the editors call "the dialectical unity of the moments of force and consent in political action" (169, n. 70). On the relation of voluntarism to objectivity in political analysis, see 171.

[21]

5

◁ ══════════════════════════════ ▷

The state

QUENTIN SKINNER

I

In the Preface to *De cive*, his first published work on government, Hobbes describes his own project as that of undertaking "a more curious search into the rights of states and duties of subjects."[1] Since that time, the idea that the confrontation between individuals and states furnishes the central topic of political theory has come to be almost universally accepted. This makes it easy to overlook the fact that, when Hobbes issued his declaration, he was self-consciously setting a new agenda for the discipline he claimed to have invented, the discipline of political science. His suggestion that the duties of subjects are owed to the state, rather than to the person of a ruler, was still a relatively new and highly contentious one. So was his implied assumption that our duties are owed exclusively to the state, rather than to a multiplicity of jurisdictional authorities, local as well as national, ecclesiastical as well as civil in character. So, above all, was his use of the term "state" to denote this highest form of authority in matters of civil government.

Hobbes's declaration can thus be viewed as marking the end of one distinct phase in the history of political theory as well as the beginning of another and more familiar one. It announces the end of an era in which the concept of public power had been treated in far more personal and charismatic terms. It points to a simpler and altogether more abstract vision, one that has remained with us ever since and has come to be embodied in the use of such terms as *état*,

[1] Hobbes (1983: 32). *De cive* was first published in Latin in 1642, in English in 1651. See Warrender (1983: 1). Warrender argues that the translation is at least mainly Hobbes's own work (1983: 4–8). But this is disputed by Tuck (1985: 310–12). Note that, in this as in most other quotations from primary sources, I have modernized spelling and punctuation.

90

stato, *staat*, and state.[2] My aim in what follows will be to sketch the historical circumstances out of which these linguistic and conceptual transformations first arose.

II

As early as the fourteenth century, the Latin term *status* – together with such vernacular equivalents as *estat*, *stato*, and state – can already be found in general use in a variety of political contexts. During this formative period these terms appear to have been employed predominantly to refer to the state or standing of rulers themselves.[3] One important source of this usage was undoubtedly the rubric *De statu hominum* from the opening of Justinian's *Digest*. There the authority of Hermogenianus had been adduced for the fundamental claim that, "since all law is established for the sake of human beings, we first need to consider the *status* of such persons, before we consider anything else."[4] Following the revival of Roman Law studies in twelfth-century Italy, the word *status* came in consequence to designate the legal standing of all sorts and conditions of men, with rulers being described as enjoying a distinctive "estate royal," *estat du roi*, or *status regis*.[5]

When the question of a ruler's *status* was raised, this was generally in order to emphasize that it ought to be viewed as a state of majesty, a high estate, a condition of stateliness. Within the well-established monarchies of France and England, we encounter this formula in chronicles and official documents throughout the latter half of the fourteenth century. Froissart, for example, recalls in book I of his *Chroniques* that when the young king of England held court to entertain visiting dignitaries in 1327, "the queen was to be seen there in an *estat* of great nobility."[6] The same usage recurs poignantly in the speech made by William Thirnyng to Richard II in 1399, in which he reminds his former sovereign "in what presence you renounced and ceased of the state of King, and of lordship and of all the dignity and worship that [be]longed thereto" (Topham *et al.* 1783: 424, col. 1).

[2] On "the state as an abstract entity," and the political transformations that underlay the emergence of the concept, see further in Shennan (1974); and cf. Maravall (1961).
[3] See Hexter (1973: 155) on "the first of its medieval political meanings."
[4] Mommsen (1970, I.5.2: 35): "Cum igitur hominum causa omne ius constitutum sit, primo de personarum statu ac post de ceteris . . . dicemus."
[5] For example, see Post (1964: 333–67, 368–414).
[6] Froissart (1972: 116): "La [sc. the queen] peut on veoir de l'estat grand noblece."

92   QUENTIN SKINNER

Underlying the suggestion that a distinctive quality of stateliness
"belongs" to kings was the prevailing belief that sovereignty is
intimately connected with display, that the presence of majesty
serves in itself as an ordering force. This was to prove the most
enduring of the many features of charismatic leadership eventually
subverted by the emergence of the modern concept of an impersonal state.[7] As late as the end of the seventeenth century, it is
still common to find political writers using the word "state" to point
to a conceptual connection between the stateliness of rulers and the
efficacy of their rule. As one might expect, exponents of divine-right
monarchy such as Bossuet continue to speak of the *état* of *majesté* in
just such terms (Bossuet 1967: 69, 72). But the same assumptions
also survived even among the enemies of kingship. When Milton, for
example, describes in his *History of Britain* the famous scene where
Canute orders the ocean to "come no further upon my land," he
observes that the king sought to give force to his extraordinary
command by speaking "with all the state that royalty could put into
his countenance" (Milton 1971: 365).

By the end of the fourteenth century, the term *status* had also come
to be regularly used to refer to the state or condition of a realm or
commonwealth.[8] This conception of the *status reipublicae* was of
course classical in origin, appearing frequently in the histories of
Livy and Sallust, as well as in Cicero's orations and political works.[9] It
can also be found in the *Digest*, most notably under the rubric *De
iustitia et iure*, where the analysis opens with Ulpian's contention that
law is concerned with two areas, the public and the private, and that
"public law is that which pertains to the *status rei Romanae.*"[10]

With the revival of Roman Law, this further piece of legal
terminology also passed into general currency. It became common
in the fourteenth century, both in France and England, to discuss
"the state of the realm" or *estat du roilme* (Post 1964: 310–22).
Speaking of the year 1389, for example, Froissart remarks that the
king decided at that point "to reform the country *en bon état*, so that

---

[7] For a comparison between those systems of state power in which "the ordering
     force of display" is proclaimed, and those in which (as in the modern West) it is
     deliberately obscured, see Geertz (1980: 121–3), whose formulation I have
     adopted.
[8] See Ercole (1926: 67–8). Hexter (1973: 115) similarly notes that *status* acquired this
     "second political meaning during the middle ages." Cf. Rubinstein (1971: 314–
     15), who begins his analysis by discussing this stage.
[9] See for example Livy (1962, 30.2.8: 372; 1966, 23.24.2: 78); Sallust (1921, 40.2:
     68); Cicero (1913, 2.1.3: 170).
[10] Mommsen (1970, I.1.2: 29): "publicum ius est quod ad statum rei Romani
     spectat." Ercole (1926: 69) emphasizes the importance of this passage.

everyone would be contented."[11] The idea of linking the good state of a king and his kingdom soon became a commonplace. By the middle of the fifteenth century, petitioners to the English parliament regularly ended their pleas by promising the king that they would "tenderly pray God for the good estate and prosperity of your most noble person of this your noble realm."[12]

If we turn from northern Europe to the Italian city-states, we encounter the same terminology at an even earlier date. The first known advice-books addressed to *podestá* and other city-magistrates in the early years of the thirteenth century already indicate that their main concern is with the *status civitatum*, the state or condition of cities as independent political entities.[13] The anonymous *Oculus pastoralis*, perhaps written as early as the 1220s,[14] repeatedly employs the phrase,[15] as does Giovanni da Viterbo in his treatise *De regimine civitatum*,[16] completed around the year 1250.[17] By the early fourteenth century we find the same concept widely expressed in the vernacular, with writers of *Dictamina* such as Filippo Ceffi offering extensive instruction to magistrates, in the form of model speeches, on how to maintain the *stato* of the city given into their charge (Giannardi 1942: 27, 47, 48, etc.).

Discussing the state or standing of such communities, the point these writers generally wish to stress is that chief magistrates have a duty to maintain their cities in a good, happy, or prosperous state.[18] This ideal of aspiring to uphold the *bonus* or even the *optimus status reipublicae* was again Roman in origin, and was largely taken over from Cicero and Seneca by the thirteenth-century writers of advice-books.[19] The author of the *Oculus pastoralis* frequently speaks of the need to uphold the happy, advantageous, honorable and prosperous *status* of one's *civitas*.[20] Giovanni da Viterbo likewise insists on the

[11] Froissart (1824–6, vol. XII: 93): "Le roi . . . réforma le pays en bon etat tant que tous s'en contentèrent."
[12] Petition from the abbey of Syon in Shadwell (1912, vol. I: 64). Cf. also vol. I: 66; I: 82, etc.
[13] For a survey of this literature see Hertter (1910).
[14] Sorbelli (1944) discusses this claim, originally put forward by Muratori; Sorbelli prefers a date in the 1240s.
[15] See Franceschi (1966: 26, 27, 28, etc.).
[16] Giovanni da Viterbo (1901: 230–2, etc.).
[17] For a discussion of the date of composition see Sorbelli (1944).
[18] See Ercole (1926: 67–8) and the similar discussions in Post (1964: 18–24, 310–32, 377–81), Rubinstein (1971: 314–16), and Mansfield (1983: 851–2).
[19] There are references to the *optimus status reipublicae* in Cicero (1914, 5.4.11: 402 and 1927, 2.11.27: 174), and to the *optimus civitatis status* in Seneca (1964, 2.20.2: 92).
[20] See Franceschi (1966: 26) on the need to act "ad . . . comodum ac felicem statum civitatis" and p. 28: "ad honorabilem et prosperum statum huius comunitatis."

desirability of maintaining the *bonus status* of one's community,[21] while Filippo Ceffi writes with equal confidence in the vernacular of the obligation to preserve a city "in a good and peaceful *stato*," in a good *stato* and complete peace" (Giannardi 1942: 28).

These writers also provide the first complete restatement of the classical view of what it means for a *civitas* or *respublica* to attain its best state.[22] This requires, they all agree, that our magistrates should follow the dictates of justice in all their public acts, as a result of which the common good will be promoted, the cause of peace upheld, and the general happiness of the people assured. This line of reasoning was later taken up by Aquinas and his numerous Italian disciples at the end of the thirteenth century. Aquinas himself presents the argument at several points in his *Summa*, as well as in his commentary on Aristotle's *Politics*. A judge or magistrate, he declares, "has charge of the common good, which is justice," and ought therefore to act in such a way "as to exhibit a good aspect from the point of view of the *status* of the community as a whole."[23] But the same line of reasoning can already be found a generation earlier in advice-books for city-magistrates. Giovanni da Viterbo, for example, develops precisely the same theory of the *optimus status* in his treatise *De regimine civitatum*, while Brunetto Latini reiterates and enlarges on Giovanni's arguments in his chapter "Dou gouvernement des cités" at the end of his encyclopedic *Livres dou trésor* of 1266.[24]

This vision of the *optimus status reipublicae* later became central to *quattrocento* humanist accounts of the well-ordered political life. When Giovanni Campano (1427–77)[25] analyzes the dangers of faction in his tract *De regendo magistratu*, he declares that "there is nothing I count more unfavourable than this to the *status* and safety

---

[21] See Giovanni da Viterbo (1901: 230) on the "bonus status totius communis huius civitatis."

[22] Note that they begin to discuss this issue nearly a century earlier than such chroniclers as Giovanni Villani, one of the earliest sources usually cited in this context. See Ercole (1926: 67–8), Hexter (1973: 155), and Rubinstein (1971: 314–16). For Villani on the "buono et pacifico stato" see Villani (1802–3, vol. III: 159; vol. IV: 3, etc.).

[23] Aquinas (1963, I.II.19.10: 104): "Nam iudex habet curam boni communis, quod est iustitia, et ideo vult occisionem latronis, quae habet rationem boni secundum relationem ad statum commune."

[24] See Giovanni da Viterbo (1901: 220–2) on the attributes and policies to be demanded of an elected *rector*, and cf. Latini (1948: 402–5), paraphrasing Giovanni's account.

[25] Note that, in providing dates for the more obscure humanists, I have taken my information from Consenza (1962).

of a *respublica*."[26] If the good *status* of a community is to be preserved, he goes on, all individual or factional advantage must be subordinated to the pursuit of justice and "the common good of the city as a whole" (Campano 1502, fo. xxxxvii^(r-v)). Filippo Beroaldo (1453–1505) endorses the same conclusions in a treatise to which he actually gave the title *De optimo statu*. The best state, he argues, can be attained only if our ruler or leading magistrate "remains oblivious of his own good, and ensures that he acts in everything he does in such a way as to promote the public benefit."[27]

Finally, the Erasmian humanists imported precisely the same values and vocabulary into northern Europe in the early years of the sixteenth century. Erasmus (1974: 162) himself contrasts the *optimus* with the *pessimus reipublicae status* in his *Institutio* of 1516, and argues that "the happiest *status* is reached when there is a prince whom everyone obeys, when the prince obeys the laws and when the laws answer to our ideals of honesty and equity."[28] His younger contemporary Thomas Starkey (1948: 63; also 65, 66–7) offers a very similar account in his *Dialogue* of what constitutes "the most prosperous and perfect state that in any country, city or town, by policy and wisdom may be established and set." And in More's *Utopia* the figure of Hythloday, the traveller to "the new island of Utopia," likewise insists that because the Utopians live in a society where the laws embody the principles of justice, seriously aim at the common good, and in consequence enable the citizens to live "as happily as possible," we are justified in saying that the Utopians have in fact attained the *optimus status reipublicae* – which is of course the title of More's famous book (More 1965: 244).

III

I now turn to consider the process by which the above usages – all of them common throughout late-medieval Europe – eventually gave rise to recognizably modern discussions of the concept of the state. I shall argue that, if we wish to trace both the acquisition of this concept and at the same time its expression by means of such terms

[26] Campano (1502, fo. xxxxvii^r): "nihil existimem a statu et salute reipublicae alienius."

[27] Beroaldo (1508, fo. xv^v): "oblitis suorum ipsius commodorum ad utilitatem publicam quicquid agit debet referre."

[28] Erasmus (1974: 194): "felicissimus est status, cum principi paretur ab omnibus atque ipse princeps paret legibus, leges autem ad archetypum aequi et honesti respondent."

96   QUENTIN SKINNER

as *status*, *stato* or state, we ought not to focus our main attention – as medieval historians have commonly done – on the evolution of legal theories about the *status* of kings in the fourteenth and fifteenth centuries.[29] It was rare even among civil lawyers of that period to use the Latin word *status* without qualification,[30] and virtually unheard of for political writers to employ such a barbarism at all. Even when we find *status* being used in such contexts, moreover, it is almost always evident that what is at issue is simply the state or standing of the king or his kingdom, not in the least the modern idea of the state as a separate apparatus of government.

I shall instead suggest that, in order to investigate the process by which the term *status* and its vernacular equivalents first came to acquire their modern range of reference, we need to keep our main attention fixed on the early histories and advice-books for magistrates I have already singled out, as well as on the later mirror-for-princes literature to which they eventually gave rise. It was within these traditions of practical political reasoning, I shall argue, that the terms *status* and *stato* were first consistently used in new and significantly extended ways.[31]

These genres of political literature were in turn a product of the new and distinctive forms of political organization that arose within late-medieval Italy. Beginning in the early years of the twelfth century, a growing number of cities throughout the *Regnum Italicum* succeeded in acquiring for themselves the status of autonomous and self-governing republics.[32] It is true that these communities later proved unstable, and were widely reorganized in the course of the next century under the stronger and more centralized regimes of hereditary princes (Waley 1978: 128–40). But even in this later period, the great city-republics of Florence and Venice managed to preserve their traditional hostility to the idea of hereditary

---

[29] Cf. Kantorowicz (1957, esp. pp. 207–32, 268–72), Post (1964, esp. pp. 247–53, 302–9), Strayer (1970, esp. pp. 57–9), and Wahl (1977: 80). By contrast, see Ullmann (1968–9, esp. pp. 43–4) on traditional legal concepts as an obstacle to the emergence of the concept of the state.

[30] Note how loftily Hotman still speaks of such usages in his *Francogallia* as late as the 1570s. Writing about the Public Council, he observes that its powers extend "to all those matters which the common people in vulgar parlance nowadays call Affairs of State" ("de iis rebus omnibus, quae vulgus etiam nunc Negotia Statuum populari verbo appellat") (1972: 332).

[31] For the thesis that "*stato*, meaning a State, derives in the main . . . from *lo stato del principe*, meaning the status or estate of an effectively sovereign prince," see Dowdall (1923: 102). Cf. also Skinner (1978, vol. II: 352–8).

[32] On this development see Waley (1978: 83–330).

monarchy, and thereby carried the ideals of participatory republican government into the era of the high Renaissance.[33]

The development of these new political formations posed a new series of questions about the concept of political authority. One of the most pressing concerned the type of regime best suited to ensuring that an independent *civitas* or *respublica* is able to remain in its *optimus status* or best state. Is it wisest to opt for the rule of an hereditary *signore*, or ought one to retain an elective system of government based on a *podestá* or other such magistrate?

Although this question remained in contention throughout the history of Renaissance Italy, it is possible to distinguish two main phases of the debate. The earliest treatises intended for city-magistrates invariably assumed – in line with their Roman authorities – that the best state of a *civitas* can be attained only under an elective form of republican government. After the widespread usurpation of these regimes, however, by the rise of hereditary *signori* in the fourteenth century, this commitment increasingly gave way to the claim that the best means of ensuring the good standing of any political community must be to institute the rule of a wise prince, a *pater patriae*, whose actions will be governed by a desire to foster the common good and hence the general happiness of all his subjects.[34]

Building on this assumption, the writers of mirror-for-princes treatises in the Renaissance generally devoted themselves to considering two related points. Their loftiest aim was to explain how a good ruler can hope to reach the characteristically princely goals of honour and glory for himself while at the same time managing to promote the happiness of his subjects.[35] But their main concern was with a far more basic and urgent question of statecraft: how to advise the new *signori* of Italy, often in highly unsettled circumstances, on how to hold on to their *status principis* or *stato del principe*, their political state or standing as effectively governing rulers of their existing territories.

As a result, the use of the term *stato* to denote the political standing of rulers, together with the discussion of how such rulers should behave if they are to manage *mantenere lo stato*, began to resound through the chronicles and political literature of fourteenth-century

[33] On this "moment" see Pocock (1975: 83–330). Cf. also Skinner (1978, vol. I: 139–89).

[34] On the *pater patriae*, see for example Beroaldo(1508, fos. xiv[r] and xv[r]) and Scala (1940: 256–8, 273).

[35] Petrarch already states these twin ideals (1554: 420–1, 428). They become standard during the *quattrocento*, even recurring in Machiavelli's *Il principe* (1960: 102).

Italy. When Giovanni Villani, for example, speaks in his *Istorie
Fiorentine* of the civic dissensions that marked the city during the
1290s, he observes that they were largely directed against *il popolo in
suo stato e signoria* – against the people in their positions of political
power.[36] When Ranieri Sardo in his *Cronaca Pisana* describes the
accession of Gherardo d'Appiano as leader of the city in 1399, he
remarks that the new *capitano* continued to enjoy the same *stato e
governo* – the same political standing and governmental authority – as
his father had enjoyed before him (Sardo 1845: 240–1). By the time
we reach such late contributions to the mirror-for-princes literature
as Machiavelli's *Il principe* of 1513, the question of what a ruler must
do if he wishes to maintain his political standing had become the
chief topic of debate. Machiavelli's advice is almost entirely directed
at new princes who wish *tenere* or *mantenere lo stato* – who wish to
maintain their positions as rulers over whatever territories they may
have managed to inherit or acquire.[37]

If such a ruler is to prevent the state in which he finds himself from
being altered to his disadvantage, he must clearly be able to fulfil a
number of preconditions of effective government. If we now turn to
consider the ways in which these preconditions were formulated and
discussed in the traditions of thought I am considering, we shall find
the terms *status* and *stato* employed in an increasingly extended
manner to refer to these various aspects of political power.[38] As an
outcome of this process, we shall eventually find these writers
deploying at least some elements of a recognizably modern
conception of the state.

One precondition of maintaining one's standing as a ruler is
obviously that one should be able to preserve the character of one's
existing regime. We accordingly find the terms *status* and *stato* being
used from an early period to refer not merely to the state or
condition of princes, but also to the presence of particular regimes
or systems of government.

This usage in turn appears to have arisen out of the habit of
employing the term *status* to classify the various forms of rule
described by Aristotle. Aquinas has sometimes been credited with
popularizing this development, since there are versions of his
Expositio of Aristotle's *Politics* in which oligarchies are described as
status paucorum and the rule of the people is identified as the *status*

[36] Villani (1802–3, vol. IV: 24). Cf. also vol. IV: 190–4.
[37] For these phrases see Machiavelli (1960: 16, 19, 22, 25–6, 27, 28, 35, etc.).
[38] Rubinstein (1971) similarly analyzes some of these extended usages. While I have
avoided duplicating his examples, I am much indebted to his account.

popularis.[39] Such usages later became widespread in humanist political thought. Filippo Beroaldo begins his *De optimo statu* with a typology of legitimate regimes, speaking of the *status popularis*, the *status paucorum* and even the *status unius* when referring to monarchy (1508, fos. xi^r and xii^v). Francesco Patrizi (1412–94) opens his *De regno* with a similar typology, one in which monarchy, aristocracy, and democracy are all characterized as types of *civilium status* or states of civil society (Patrizi 1594b: 16–17, 19, and esp. 21). Writing in the vernacular at the same period, Vespasiano da Bisticci (1421–98) likewise contrasts the rule of *signori* with the *stato populare*, while Guicciardini later invokes the same distinction in his *Discorsi* on the government of Florence (Vespasiano 1970–6, vol. I: 406; Guicciardini 1932: 274). Finally, Machiavelli used *stato* in just this fashion at a number of places in *Il principe*,[40] most notably in the opening sentence of the entire work, in which he informs us that "All the *stati*, all the dominions that have had or now have power over men either have been or are republics or principalities."[41]

By this stage, the term *stato* was also in widespread use as a way of referring simply to prevailing regimes. When Giovanni Villani, for example, notes that in 1308 "it was the members of the *parte Nera* who held control" in Florence, he speaks of the government they established as *lo stato de'Neri*.[42] When Ranieri Sardo (1845: 125) writes about the fall of the Nove in Siena in 1355, he describes the change of regime as the loss of *lo stato de'Nove*. When Vespasiano (1970–6, vol. II: 171, 173) relates how the enemies of Cosimo de'Medici succeeded in setting up a new government in 1434, he expresses the point by saying that "they were able to change *lo stato*." By the time we reach a theorist such as Machiavelli's friend Francesco Vettori, writing in the early part of the sixteenth century, both these usages of *stato* were firmly established. Vettori employs the term not only to refer to different forms of government, but also to describe the prevailing regime in Florence that he wished to see defended.[43]

[39] See Aquinas (1966: 136–7, 139–40, 310–11, 319–21, 328–30). Rubinstein (1971: 322) credits Aquinas with popularizing these usages. But they were largely the product of the humanist revision of his text issued in 1492. See Mansfield (1983: 851), and cf. Cranz (1978: 169–73) for a full account.
[40] See for example Machiavelli (1960: 28 and 29) on the *stato di pochi*.
[41] Machiavelli (1960: 15): "Tutti li stati, tutti e'dominii che hanno avuto et hanno imperio sopra li uomini sono stati e sono o republiche o principati."
[42] Villani (1802–3, vol. IV: 190–1). Cf. also vol. IV: 25; vol. VIII: 186.
[43] Vettori (1842: 432, 436). Rubinstein (1971: 318) notes that these were already standard usages in late *quattrocento* Florence.

A second precondition of maintaining one's existing state as a ruler is obviously that one should suffer no loss or alteration in the range of territories given into one's charge. As a result of this further preoccupation we find the terms *status* and *stato* pressed into early service as a way of referring to the general area over which a ruler or chief magistrate needs to exercise control. When the author of the *Oculus pastoralis*, for example, wishes to describe the duty of chief magistrates to look after their cities and localities, he already speaks of it as a duty to promote *suos status* (Franceschi 1966: 24). When the authors of the *Gratulatio* sent to the people of Padua in 1310 wish to express the hope that the entire province may be able to live in peace, they say that they are hoping for the *tranquillitas vestri status* (Muratori 1741: 131). Similarly, when Ambrogio Lorenzetti tells us, in the verses that accompany his celebrated frescoes of 1337–9 on the theme of good government, that a *signore* must cultivate the virtues if he is to succeed in levying taxes from the areas under his command, he expresses his point by saying that this is how he must act *per governare lo stato*.[44]

These early and isolated usages first begin to proliferate in the chronicles and political treatises of the high Renaissance. When Sardo (1845: 91), for example, wants to describe how the Pisans made peace throughout their territories in 1290, what he says is that the truce extended throughout *stato suo*. When Guicciardini (1933: 298) remarks in his *Ricordi* that the French revolutionized warfare in Italy after 1494, producing a situation in which the loss of a single campaign brought with it the forfeiture of all one's lands, he describes such defeats as bringing with them the loss of *lo stato*. So too with Machiavelli, who frequently uses the term *stato* in *Il principe* in order to denote the lands or territories of a prince. He clearly has this usage in mind when he talks at length in chapter 3 about the means a wise prince must adopt if he wishes to acquire new *stati*; and he evidently has in mind the same usage when he asks in chapter 24 why so many of the princes of Italy have lost their *stati* during his own lifetime (Machiavelli 1960: 18, 22, 24, 97).

Finally, due in large measure to these Italian influences, the same usage can be found in northern Europe by the early years of the sixteenth century. Guillaume Budé, for example, in his *L'Institution du prince* of 1519, equates the range of *les pays* commanded by Caesar after his victory over Antony with the extent of *son estat*.[45] Similarly,

---

[44] The verses are reproduced in Rowley (1958, vol. I: 127).

[45] Budé (1966: 140). Although Budé's *Institution* was not published until 1547, it was completed by the start of 1519. See Delaruelle (1907: 201).

when Thomas Starkey (1948: 167) argues in his *Dialogue* of the early 1530s that everyone living in England should be represented by a Council, he remarks that such a body "should represent the whole state." And when Lawrence Humphrey warns in his tract *The Nobles* of 1563 that evil conduct on the part of a ruler can easily set a bad example throughout an entire community, he expresses his point by saying that the vices of a ruler can easily "spread the same into the whole state" (1973, sig. Q. 8ᵛ).

As the writers of advice-books always emphasized, however, by far the most important precondition of maintaining one's state as a prince must be to keep one's hold over the existing power structure and institutions of government within one's *regnum* or *civitas*. This in turn gave rise to the most important linguistic innovation that can be traced to the chronicles and political writings of Renaissance Italy. This took the form of an extension of the term *stato* not merely to denote the idea of a prevailing regime, but also, and more specifically, to refer to the institutions of government and means of coercive control that serve to organize and preserve order within political communities.

Vespasiano speaks on several occasions in his *Vite* of *lo stato* as just such an apparatus of political authority. In his life of Alessandro Sforza, for example, he describes how Alessandro conducted himself "in his government of *lo stato*" (Vespasiano 1970–6, vol. I: 426). In his life of Cosimo de'Medici he speaks of "those who hold positions of power in *stati*," and praises Cosimo for recognizing the difficulties of holding on to power in *uno stato* when faced by opposition from influential citizens.[46] Guicciardini in his *Ricordi* similarly asks why the Medici "lost control of *lo stato* in 1527," and later observes that they found it much harder than Cosimo had done "to maintain their hold over *lo stato di Firenze*," the institutions of Florentine government.[47] Finally, Castiglione in *Il cortegiano* likewise makes it clear that he thinks of *lo stato* as a distinct power structure which a prince needs to be able to control and dominate. He begins by remarking that the Italians "have greatly contributed to discussions about the government of *stati*," and later advises courtiers that "when it comes to

---

[46] Vespasiano (1970–6, vol. I: 177, 192). On the latter passage see also Rubinstein (1971: 318).

[47] Guicciardini (1933: 287, 293). Note that Guicciardini – though not Machiavelli – also speaks explicitly of *ragione di stato*. See Maffei (1964, esp. pp. 712–20). For the subsequent history of that concept in *cinquecento* Italy, see Meinecke (1957, esp. pp. 65–145).

questions about *stati*, it is necessary to be prudent and wise" in order to counsel one's rule about the best way to behave.[48]

Of all the writers of advice-books, however, it is Machiavelli in *Il principe* who shows the most consistent willingness to distinguish the institutions of *lo stato* from those who have charge of them. He thinks of *stati* as having their own foundations, and speaks in particular of each *stato* as having its own particular laws, customs, and ordinances (Machiavelli 1960: 53; 76, 84). He is willing in consequence to speak of *lo stato* as an agent, describing it as capable, among other things, of choosing particular courses of action and of calling in times of crisis upon the loyalty of its citizens (Machiavelli 1960: 48, 92). This means, as Machiavelli makes clear at several points, that what he takes himself to be discussing in *Il principe* is not simply how princes ought to behave; he also sees himself as writing more abstractly about statecraft (*dello stato*) and about *cose di stato* or affairs of state (Machiavelli 1960: 21, 25).

IV

It has often been argued that, by the time we reach the usages I have just been examining, we are already dealing with a recognizably modern conception of the state as an apparatus of power whose existence remains independent of those who may happen to have control of it at any given time. Gaines Post and others have even suggested that this conception is already present in a number of allusions to the *status regni* in the fourteenth century.[49] A similar claim has been advanced with even greater confidence about the employment of the term *stato* by Machiavelli and some of his contemporaries. As Chiappelli puts it, for example, "the word bears the meaning of 'State' in its full maturity" in a majority of the places where Machiavelli uses it.[50]

These claims, however, are I think greatly exaggerated. It is usually clear – except in the small number of deeply ambiguous cases I have cited[51] – that even when *status* and *stato* are employed by these writers to denote an apparatus of government, the power structure

---

[48] Castiglione (1960: 10, 117–18). For other *cinquecento* uses see Chabod (1962, esp. pp. 153–73).

[49] See Post (1964, esp. pp. viii, 247–53, 302–9, 494–8 and pp. 269, 333) for alleged "anticipations" of Machiavelli's thought. Cf. also Kantorowicz (1957, esp. pp. 207–32) on "polity-centered kingship."

[50] Chiappelli (1952: 68). Cf. also Cassirer (1946: 133–7), Chabod (1962: 146–55), D'Entrèves (1967: 30–2).

[51] It is important to emphasize, however, that in the cases cited in nn. 46 to 48, as in the case of Machiavelli, it would arguably be no less of an overstatement to insist

in question is not in fact viewed as independent of those who have charge of it. As Post himself concedes, the usual aim in early legal discussions of the *status regni* was to insist on a far more personal view of political power,[52] a view that was later to be revived by the proponents of absolute monarchy in the seventeenth century.[53] According to this argument, the ruler or chief magistrate, so far from being distinguishable from the institutions of the state, is said to possess and even embody those institutions himself. The same point can in most cases be made about Machiavelli's invocations of *lo stato* in *Il principe*. When he uses the term to refer to an apparatus of government, he is usually at pains to emphasize that it needs to remain in the hands of the prince: that *lo stato*, as he often puts it, remains equivalent to *il suo stato*, the prince's own state or condition of rulership.[54]

Even after the reception of humanist ideas about *lo stato* in northern Europe, the belief that the powers of government should be treated as essentially personal in character was to die hard. It is clearly this assumption, for example, which underlies many of the quarrels between kings and parliaments over the issue of taxation in the course of the sixteenth century. The basis of the parliamentary case was generally an assertion of the form that, except in times of dire necessity, kings should be able "to live of their own."[55] They should be able, that is, to ensure that their personal revenues remain sufficient to uphold both their own kingly state and the good state of their government.

that these are all unequivocally traditional usages. In the retreat from the type of overstatements cited in n. 50, this point seems in danger of being lost. Hexter in particular irons out a number of ambiguities that ought to be admitted (1973, esp. pp. 164–7 and cf. the corrective in Gilbert [1965, 329–30]). Mansfield (1983: 853) similarly concludes that we do not find anywhere in Machiavelli's writings "an instance of the impersonal modern state among his uses of *stato*." If by this he means that Machiavelli cannot unambiguously be said to express that concept, this is undoubtedly correct. My only objection is that there are several ambiguous passages; the history of the acquisition of the concept cannot be divided into such watertight compartments.

[52] See Post (1964: 334), on *status* being used to stress that the king "was not only the indispensable ruler but also the essence of the territorial State which he ruled."

[53] For this revival, see below, n. 94. Post claims that the medieval sources he discusses "anticipated the idea" of "l'état, c'est moi" (1964: 269; and cf. also pp. 333–5). But when this remark was uttered in seventeenth-century France (if it ever was) it was by then blankly paradoxical, and this would have been the point of uttering it. On this point see Mansfield (1983: 849) and cf. Rowen (1961) on Louis XIV as "proprietor of the state."

[54] See Machiavelli (1960: 16, 47, 87, 95). Cf. on this point Mansfield (1983: 852).

[55] In England this demand (and this phrase) can be found as late as early-Stuart arguments over royal revenues. See for example the parliamentary debate of 1610 quoted in Tanner (1930: 359).

I conclude that, for all the importance of the writers I have been considering, they cannot in general be said to articulate a recognizable concept of the state with anything like complete self-consciousness. It would not perhaps be too bold to assert, indeed, that in all the discussions about the state and government of princes in the first half of the sixteenth century, there will be found scarcely any instance in which the *état*, *staat* or state in question is unequivocally separated from the status or standing of the prince himself.[56]

This is not to deny, however, that the crystallizing of a recognizable concept of the state was one of the legacies of Renaissance political thought. It is merely to suggest that, if we wish to follow the process by which this development took place, we need to focus not merely on the mirror-for-princes literature on which I have so far concentrated, but also on the other strand of thought about the *optimus status reipublicae* that I began by singling out. We need, that is, to turn our attention to the rival tradition of Renaissance republicanism, the tradition centring on the claim that, if there is to be any prospect of attaining the *optimus status reipublicae*, we must always institute a self-governing form of republican regime.

Among the republican theorists of Renaissance Italy, the main reason given for this basic commitment was that all power is liable to corrupt. All individuals or groups, once granted sovereignty over a community, will tend to promote their own interest at the expense of the community as a whole. It follows that the only way to ensure that the laws promote the common good must be to leave the whole body of citizens in charge of their own public affairs. If their government is instead controlled by an authority external to the community itself, that authority will be sure to subordinate the good of the community to its own purposes, thereby interfering with the liberty of individual citizens to attain their chosen goals. The same outcome will be no less likely under the rule of an hereditary prince. Since he will generally seek his own ends rather than the common good, the community will again forfeit its liberty to act in pursuit of whatever goals it may wish to set itself.

This basic insight was followed up within the republican tradition in two distinct ways. It was used in the first place to justify an

---

[56] Even in France, the country in which, after Italy, traditional assumptions about the *status* of princes first changed, this arguably remains true until the 1570s. On this point see below, section V, and cf. Lloyd (1983: 146–53). In Spain the old assumptions appear to have survived until at least the middle of the seventeenth century, *pace* Maravall (1961). See Elliot (1984: 42–5, 121–2). In Germany a purely patrimonial concept of government appears to have survived even longer. See the comments in Shennan (1974: 113–14).

assertion of civic autonomy and independence, and so to defend the *libertas* of the Italian cities against external interference. This demand was initially directed against the Empire and its claims of feudal suzerainty over the *Regnum Italicum*. It was first developed by such jurists as Azo, and later by Bartolus and his followers,[57] seeking to vindicate what Bartolus described as "the *de facto* refusal of the cities of Tuscany to recognize any superior in temporal affairs."[58] But the same demand for *libertas* was also directed against all potential rivals as sources of coercive jurisdiction within the cities themselves. It was claimed on the one hand against local feudatories, who continued to be viewed, as late as Machiavelli's *Discorsi*, as the most dangerous enemies of free government (Machiavelli 1960, I.55: 254–8). And it was even more vehemently directed against the jurisdictional pretensions of the church. The most radical response, embodied for example in Marsilius's *Defensor pacis* of 1324, took the form of insisting that all coercive power is secular by definition, and thus that the church has no right to exercise civil jurisdictions at all (Marsilius 1956, esp. II.4: 113–26). But even in the more orthodox treatises on city government, such as that of Giovanni da Viterbo, the church is still refused any say in civic affairs. The reason, as Giovanni expresses it, is that the ends of temporal and ecclesiastical authority are completely distinct (Giovanni da Viterbo 1901: 266–7). The implication is that, if the church tries to insist on any jurisdiction in temporal matters, it will simply be "putting its sickle into another man's harvest."[59]

The other way in which the basic insight of the republican tradition was developed was in the form of a positive claim about the precise type of regime we need to institute if we are to retain our *libertas* to pursue our chosen goals. The essence of the republican case was that the only form of government under which a city can hope to remain "in a free state" will be a *res publica* in the strictest sense. The community as a whole must retain the ultimate sovereign authority, assigning its rulers or chief magistrates a status no higher than that of elected officials. Such magistrates must in turn be treated not as rulers in the full sense, but merely as agents of *ministri* of justice, charged with the duty of ensuring that the laws established by the community for the promotion of its own good are properly enforced.

[57] See Calasso (1957: 83–123), and Wahl (1977). For analogous reinterpretations of the Decretals, see Mochi Onory (1951). For a survey see Tierney (1982).

[58] See Bartolus (1562, 47.22: 779) on the "civitates Tusciae, quae non recognoscunt de facto in temporalibus superiorem."

[59] Giovanni da Viterbo (1901: 266): "in alterius messem falcem suam mittere."

This contrast between the freedom of republican regimes and the servitude implied by any form of monarchical government has often been viewed as a distinctive contribution of *quattrocento* Florentine thought.[60] But the underlying assumption that liberty can be guaranteed only within a republic can already be found in many Florentine writers of the previous century.[61] Dante speaks in the *Inferno* of the move from seigneurial to republican rule as a move from tyrany to a *stato franco*, a state or condition of civic liberty (1966, xxvii. 54: 459). Ceffi repeatedly emphasizes in his *Dicerie* that the only means of guaranteeing civic *libertá* is to ensure that one's city remains under the guidance of an elected magistrate (Giannardi 1942: 32, 35, 41, 44). And Villani in his *Istorie Florentine* likewise contrasts the free *stato* of the Florentine republic with the tyranny imposed by the Duke of Athens as *signore* in 1342 (1802–3, vol. VIII: 11).

It is certainly true, however, that the equation between living in a republic and living "in a free state" was worked out with the greatest assurance by the leading republican theorists of Venice and Florence in the course of the high Renaissance. Among the Venetian writers, Gasparo Contarini furnished the classic statement of the argument in his *De republica Venetorum* of 1543. Owing to the city's elective system of government, he declares, in which "a mixture of the *status* of the nobility and of the people" is maintained, "there is nothing less to be feared in the city of Venice than that the head of the republic will interefere with the *libertas* or the activities of any of the citizens."[62] Among Florentine theorists, it was of course Machiavelli in his *Discorsi* who provided the most famous version of the same argument. "It is easy to understand," as he explains at the start of book II, "whence the love of living under a free constitution springs up in peoples. For experience shows that no cities have ever increased in dominion or in riches except when they have been established in liberty."[63] The reason, he goes on, "is easy to perceive, for it is not the pursuit of individual advantage but of the common good that makes cities great, and there is no doubt that it is only

---

[60] This is, for example, the main thesis of Baron (1966).

[61] For this assumption in *trecento* Florentine diplomacy, see Rubinstein (1952).

[62] Contarini (1626: 22 and 56): "temperandam ... ex optimatum et populari statu ... nihil minus urbi Venetae timendum sit, quam principem reipublicae libertati ullum unquam negocium facessere posse." On Contarini see Pocock (1975: 320–8).

[63] Machiavelli (1960, II.2: 280): "E facil cosa è conoscere donde nasca ne' popoli questa affezione del vivere libero: perché si vede per esperienza le cittadi non avere mai ampliato né di dominio né di ricchezza se non mentre sono state in libertà."

under republican regimes that this ideal of the common good is followed out."[64]

From the point of view of my present argument, these commitments can now be seen to be crucial in two different ways. It is within this tradition of thought that we encounter, for the first time, a vindication of the idea that there is a distinct form of "civil" or "political" authority which is wholly autonomous, which exists to regulate the public affairs of an independent community, and which brooks no rivals as a source of coercive power within its own *civitas* or *respublica*. It is here, in short, that we first encounter the familiar understanding of the state as a monopolist of legitimate force.

This view of "civil government" was of course taken up in France and England at an early stage in their constitutional development. It underlies their hostility to the jurisdictional power of the church, culminating in France in the "Gallican" Concordat of 1516, in England in the Marsiglian assumptions underpinning the Act of Appeals in 1533. It also underlies their repudiation of the Holy Roman Empire's claim to exercise any jursidictions within their territories, a repudiation founded on a reworking of Azo's and later Bartolus's theories of *imperium* into the celebrated dictum that *Rex in regno suo est Imperator*.

For the origins of this view of civil government, however, we need to turn back to thirteenth-century Italy, and specifically to the political literature engendered by the self-governing city-republics of that period. Writing in the 1250s, Giovanni da Viterbo already takes his theme to be the analysis of civil power, that form of power which upholds the *civium libertas* or liberty of those who live together as citizens (Giovanni da Viterbo 1901: 218). Writing only a decade later, Brunetto Latini goes on to add that those who study the use of such power in the government of cities are studying "politics," "the noblest and the highest of all the sciences."[65] It is this neoclassical tradition to which later theorists of popular sovereignty are ultimately alluding when they speak of an autonomous area of "civil" or "political" authority, and offer to explicate what Locke (1967: 283) was to call "the true original, extent and end of civil government."

The other way in which the republican tradition contributed to

---

[64] Machiavelli (1960, II.11: 280): "La ragione è facile a intendere: perché non il bene particulare ma il bene comune è quello che fa grandi le città. E sanza dubbio questo bene comune non è osservato se non nelle republiche."

[65] See Latini (1948: 391) on "politique ... la plus noble et la plus haute science."

crystallizing a recognizable concept of the state is of even greater importance. According to the writers I have been considering, a city can never hope to remain in a free state unless it succeeds in imposing strict conditions on its rulers and magistrates. They must always be elected; they must always remain subject to the laws and institutions of the city which elects them; they must always act to promote the common good – and hence the peace and happiness – of the sovereign body of its citizens. As a result, the republican theorists no longer equate the idea of governmental authority with the powers of particular rulers or magistrates. Rather they think of the powers of civil government as embodied in a structure of laws and institutions which our rulers and magistrates are entrusted to administer in the name of the common good. They cease in consequence to speak of rulers "maintaining their state" in the sense of maintaining their personal ascendancy over the apparatus of government. Rather they begin to speak of the *status* or *stato* as the name of that apparatus of government which our rulers may be said to have a duty to maintain.

There are already some hints of this momentous transition in the earliest treatises and *dictamina* intended for chief magistrates of city-republics. Brunetto Latini insists in his *Trésor* of 1266 that cities must always be ruled by elected officials if the *bien commun* is to be promoted. He further insists that these *sires* must follow the laws and customs of the city in all their public acts (Latini 1948, esp. pp. 392, 408, 415; 402, 412). And he concludes that such a system is indispensable not merely to maintaining such officials in a good *estat*, but also to maintaining "the *estat* of the city itself."[66] A similar hint can be found in Giovanni da Vignano's *Flore de parlare* of the 1270s. In one of his model letters, designed for the use of city ambassadors when seeking military help, he describes the government of such communities as their *stato*, and accordingly appeals for support "in order that our good *stato* can remain in wealth, honor, greatness and peace."[67] Finally, the same hint recurs soon afterwards in Matteo dei Libri's *Arringa* on the identical theme. He sets out a very similar model speech for ambassadors to deliver, advising them to appeal for help "in order that our good *stato* may be able to remain in peace."[68]

It is only with the final flowering of Renaissance republicanism,

---

[66] Latini (1948: 403) on "l'estat de vous et de cette ville." Cf. p. 411 on the idea of remaining "en bon estat."

[67] Giovanni da Vignano (1974: 247): "che il nostro bom stato porà remanere in largheça, honore, grandeça e reponso."

[68] Matteo dei Libri (1974: 12): "ke 'l nostro bon stato potrà romanire in reposo."

however, that we find such usages occurring with their unequivocally modern sense. Even here, moreover, this development is largely confined to the vernacular literature. Consider, by contrast, a work such as Alamanno Rinuccini's Latin dialogue of 1479, *De libertate* (1957). This includes a classic statement of the claim that individual as well as civic liberty is possible only under the laws and institutions of a republic. But Rinuccini never stoops to using the barbarous term *status* to describe the laws and institutions involved; he always prefers to speak of the *civitas* or *respublica* itself as the locus of political authority. So too with such classic Venetian writers as Contarini in his *De republica Venetorum*. Although Contarini has a clear conception of the apparatus of government as a set of institutions independent of those who control them, he never uses the term *status* to describe them, but always prefers in a similar way to speak of their authority as embodied in the *respublica* itself.[69]

If we turn, however, to the rather less pure latinity of Francesco Patrizi's *De institutione reipublicae*, we encounter a significant development in his chapter on the duties of magistrates. He lays it down that their basic duty is to act "in such a way as to promote the common good," and argues that this above all requires them to uphold "the established laws" of the community.[70] He then summarizes his advice by saying that this is how magistrates must act "if they are to prevent the *status* of their city from being overturned."[71]

It is in the vernacular writers on republicanism of the next generation, however, that we find the term *stato* being used with something approaching full self-consciousness to express a recognizable concept of the state. Guicciardini's *Discorso* on how the Medici should act to improve their control over Florence provides a suggestive example. He advises them to gather around themselves a group of advisers who are loyal to the *stato* and willing to act on its behalf. The reason is that "every *stato*, every form of sovereign power, needs dependents" who are willing "to serve the *stato* and benefit it in everything."[72] If the Medici can manage to base their regime on such a group, they can hope to establish "the most

---

[69] See Contarini (1626, at pp. 28 and 46), two cases where, in Lewkenor (1969), *respublica* is rendered as "state." On Lewkenor's translation see Fink (1962: 41–2).

[70] Patrizi (1594: 281) on the duty to uphold "veteres leges" and act "pro communi utilitate."

[71] Patrizi (1594a: 292 and 279) on how to act "ne civitatis status evertatur" and "statum reipublicae everterunt."

[72] Guicciardini (1932: 271–2): "ogni stato ed ogni potenzia eminente ha bisogno delle dependenzie . . . che tutti servirebbono a beneficio dello stato." Cf. also pp. 276, 279.

powerful foundation for the defence of the *stato*" that anyone could aspire to set up.[73]

Finally, if we turn to Machiavelli's *Discorsi*, we find the term *stato* being used with even greater confidence to denote the same apparatus of political authority. It is of course true that Machiavelli continues largely to employ the term in the most traditional way to refer to the state or condition of a city and its way of life (Machiavelli 1960: 135, 142, 153, 192, 194, etc.). And even when he mentions *stati* in the context of describing systems of government, these usages are again largely traditional: he is generally speaking either about a species of regime,[74] or about the general area or territory over which a prince or republic holds sway.[75]

There are several occasions, however, especially in the analysis of constitutions at the start of book I, where he appears to go further. The first is when he writes in chapter 2 about the founding of Sparta. He emphasizes that the system of laws promulgated by Lycurgus remained distinct from, and served to control, the kings and magistrates entrusted with upholding the laws themselves. And he characterizes Lycurgus's achievement in creating this system by saying that "he established *uno stato* which then endured for more than eight hundred years."[76] The next instance occurs in chapter 6, where he considers whether the institutions of government in republican Rome could have been set up in such a way as to avoid the "tumults" which marked that city's political life. He puts the question in the form of asking "whether it might have been possible to establish *uno stato* in Rome" without that distinctive weakness.[77] That last and most revealing case occurs in chapter 18, where he considers the difficulty of maintaining *uno stato libero* within a corrupt city. He not only makes an explicit distinction between the authority of the magistrates under the ancient Roman republic and the authority of the laws "by means of which, together with the magistrates, the citizens were kept under control."[78] He adds in the same passage that the latter set of institutions and practices can best be described as "the order of the government or, indeed, of *lo stato*."[79]

---

[73] Guicciardini (1932: 273): "uno barbacane e fondamento potentissimo a difesa dello stato."

[74] See for example Machiavelli (1960, I.2: 130–2, and also pp. 182, 272, 357, etc.).

[75] See in particular Machiavelli (1960, II.24: 351–3).

[76] Machiavelli (1960, I.2: 133): "Licurgo . . . fece uno stato che durò più che ottocento anni."

[77] Machiavelli (1960, I.6: 141): "se in Roma si poteva ordinare uno stato . . ."

[78] Machiavelli (1960, I.18: 180): "le leggi dipoi che con i magistrati frenavano i cittadini."

[79] Ibid.: "l'ordine del governo o vero dello stato."

It has often been noted that, with the reception of Renaissance republicanism in northern Europe, we begin to encounter similar assumptions among Dutch and English protagonists of "free states" in the middle of the seventeenth century.[80] It has less often been recognized that the same assumptions, couched in the same vocabulary, can already be found more than a century earlier among the first writers who attempted to introduce the ideals of civic humanism into English political thought. Thomas Starkey, for example,[81] distinguishes at several points in his *Dialogue* between the state itself and "they which have authority and rule of the state" (Starkey 1948: 61; cf. also 57, 63). It is the "office and duty" of such rulers, he goes on, to "maintain the state established in the country" over which they hold sway, "ever looking to the profit of the whole body" rather than to their own good (Starkey 1948: 64). The only method, he concludes, of "setting forward the very and true commonweal" is for everyone to recognize, rulers and ruled alike, that they are "under the same governance and state" (Starkey 1948: 71).

The same assumptions can be found soon afterwards in John Ponet's *Short Treatise of Politic Power* of 1556. He too speaks of rulers simply as the holders of a particular kind of office, and describes the duty attaching to their office as that of upholding the state. He is thus prompted to contrast the case of "an evil person coming to the government of any state" with a good ruler who will recognize that he has been "to such office called for his virtue, to see the whole state well governed and the people defended from injuries" (Ponet 1942: 98).

Finally, and perhaps most significantly, we find the same phraseology in Tudor translations of the classic Italian treatises on republican government. When Lewes Lewkenor, for example, issued his English version of Contarini's *De republica Venetorum* in 1599, he found himself in need of an English term to render Contarini's basic assumption that the authority of the Venetian government remains inherent at all times in the *civitas* or *respublica* itself, with the Doge and Council serving merely as representatives of the citizen-body as a whole. Following standard humanist usage, he generally expresses this concept by the term "commonwealth." But in speaking of the relationship between a commonwealth and its

---

[80] See Fink (1962: 10–20, 56–68); Raab (1964: 185–217); Pocock (1975: 333–422); Haitsma Mulier (1980: 26–76).

[81] I see no justification for the claim that Starkey merely "dressed up" his *Dialogue* in civic humanist terms. See Mayer (1985: 25) and cf. Skinner (1978, vol. I: 213–42) for an attempt to place Starkey's ideas in a humanist context.

own citizens, he sometimes prefers instead to render *respublica* as "state." When he mentions the possibility of enfranchizing additional citizens in Venice, he explains that this can take place in special circumstances when someone can be shown to have been especially "dutiful towards the state." And when he discusses the Venetian ideal of citizenship, he feels able to allude in even more general terms to "the citizens, by whom the state of the city is maintained" (Lewkenor 1969: 18, 33).

V

For all the undoubted importance of these classical republican theorists, however, it would still be misleading to conclude that their use of the term *stato* and its equivalents may be said to express our modern concept of the state. That concept has come to embody a doubly impersonal character.[82] We distinguish the state's authority from that of the rulers or magistrates entrusted with the exercise of its powers for the time being. But we also distinguish its authority from that of the whole society or community over which its powers are exercised. As Burke (1910: 93) remarks in his *Reflections* – articulating a view already well entrenched by that time – "society is indeed a contract," but "the state ought not to be considered as nothing better than a partnership agreement" of a similar nature. Rather the state must be acknowledged to be an entity with a life of its own; an entity which is at once distinct from both rulers and ruled and is able in consequence to call upon the allegiances of both parties.

The republican theorists embrace only one half of this doubly abstract notion of the state. On the one hand there is, I think, no doubt that they constitute the earliest group of political writers who insist with full self-consciousness on a categorical distinction between the state and those who have control of it, and at the same time express that distinction as a claim about the *status*, *stato* or state. But on the other hand they make no comparable distinction between the powers of the state and those of its citizens. On the contrary, the whole thrust of classical republican theory is directed towards an ultimate equation between the two. Although this undoubtedly yields a recognizable concept of the state – one that many Marxists and exponents of direct democracy continue to

---

[82] A point emphasized by Shennan (1974: 9, 113–14) and Mansfield (1983: 849–50).

espouse – it is far from being the concept we have inherited from the more conservative mainstream of early-modern political thought.

The differences can be traced most clearly in the literature in praise of "free states." Consider again, for example, one of the earliest English works of this character, John Ponet's *Short Treatise of Politic Power*. As we have seen, Ponet makes a firm distinction between the office and person of a ruler, and even uses the term "state" to describe the form of civil authority our rulers have a duty to uphold. But he makes no analogous distinction between the powers of the state and those of the people. Not only does he maintain that "kings, princes and governors have their authority of the people"; he also insists that ultimate political authority continues to reside at all times in "the body or state of the realm or commonwealth" (Ponet 1942: 106, 105). If kings or princes are found to be "abusing their office," it is for the body of the people to remove them, since the ultimate powers of sovereignty must always remain lodged within "the body of every state" (Ponet 1942: 105; cf. also pp. 111, 124).

The same commitment is upheld even by the most sophisticated defenders of "free states" in the seventeenth century. A good example is furnished by Milton's *Ready and Easy Way to Establish a Free Commonwealth*. If we are to maintain "our freedom and flourishing condition," he argues, and establish a government "for preservation of the common peace and liberty," it is indispensable that the sovereignty of the people should never be "transferred." It should be "delegated only" to a governing Council of State (Milton 1980: 432–3, 456). The institutions of the state are thus conceived as nothing more than a means of expressing the powers of the people in an administratively more convenient form. As Milton had earlier emphasized in *The Tenure of Kings and Magistrates*, whatever authority our rulers may possess is merely "committed to them in trust from the people, to the common good of them all, in whom the power yet remains fundamentally" at all times (Milton 1962: 202). As a result, Milton, Harrington, and other defenders of "free states" hardly ever use the term "state" when speaking of the institutions of civil government. Believing as they do that such institutions must remain under the control of the whole community if its members are to preserve their birthright of liberty, they almost always prefer the term "commonwealth" as a means of referring not merely to bodies of citizens, but also to the forms of political authority by which they must be governed if they are to remain "in a free state."[83]

The same is no less true of the "monarchomachs" and other contractarian opponents of early-modern absolutism who first rose to prominence in the later sixteenth century, especially in Holland and France. Deriving their arguments mainly from scholastic rather than classical republican sources, these writers are not generally republican in the strict sense of believing that the common good of a community can never be satisfactorily assured under a monarchical form of government. Usually they are quite explicit in claiming that (to cite Marsilius of Padua's terminology) as long as the ultimate powers of a *legislator humanus* within a *civitas* or *respublica* remain in the hands of the *populus*, there is no reason to doubt that – as Aristotle had taught – a variety of different constitutional forms may be equally capable of promoting the common good, and hence the peace and happiness of the community as a whole. Some writers within this tradition, such as Marsilius himself, in consequence exhibit little interest in whether a republican or a monarchical regime is established, save only for insisting that if the latter type is chosen, the *pars principans* must always be elected.[84] Others, including François Hotman and other French monarchomachs who followed his lead in the 1570s, remain content to assume that the body of the commonwealth will normally have a monarchical head, and similarly concentrate on hedging the institution of monarchy in such a way as to make it compatible with the liberty and ultimate sovereignty of the people.[85] Still others, such as Locke in his attack on Filmer's absolutism in the *Two Treatises of Government*, suppose there to be good reasons for preferring a monarchical form of government with a liberal allowance of personal prerogative, if only to mitigate the rigours of an undiluted theory of distributive justice by allowing a "power to act according to discretion for the public good."[86]

In common with the defenders of "free states," however, these writers still assume that the apparatus of government in a *civitas* or *respublica* amounts to nothing more than a reflection of, and a device

[83] See Harrington (1977: 173) for the claim that "the interest of the commonwealth is in the whole body of the people," and his invariable preference, in the "Preliminaries" to *Oceana*, for speaking of "the city" or "commonwealth" as the locus of political authority. See also pp. 161, 170, 171–2, 182–3.

[84] Marsilius of Padua (1956, I.8 and 9: 27–34). For the special significance of Marsilius within this tradition of thought see Condren (1985: 262–9).

[85] See esp. Hotman (1972: 287–321), where he lays out his view of the French constitution as a mixed monarchy.

[86] Locke (1967: 393). On Locke's *Two Treatises* essentially as an attack on Filmerian absolutism, see Laslett (1967: 50–2, 67–78) and cf. Dunn (1969: 47–57, 58–76, 87–95). On the place of this concept in Locke's theory see Dunn (1969: 148–56).

for upholding, the sovereignty of the people. Even in a theory such as Locke's, government is still viewed simply as a trust established by the members of a community for the more effective promotion of their own good, "the peace, safety and public good of the people" (Locke 1967: 371).

The effect of this commitment, in this tradition no less than in classical republicanism, is that no effective contrast is drawn between the power of the people and the powers of the state.[87] These writers do distinguish, of course, between the apparatus of government and the authority of those who may happen to have control of it at any one time. Just as strongly as the republican theorists, they insist on a complete separation between a ruler's person and his office, and argue that – as Locke puts it – even a supreme magistrate is merely a "public person" who is "vested with the power of the law" and charged with directing the legislative toward the attainment of the common good.[88] They still assume, however, that the range of powers a community establishes over itself when its members consent to become subjects of a civil government must ultimately be identified with its own powers as a community. As Locke (1967: 369, 385) insists, we never "deliver up" our fundamental liberties in establishing a commonwealth, but merely depute or delegate a known and indifferent judge to safeguard them more effectively on our own behalf. Although this means that we commit ourselves to setting up a complex apparatus of government, it also means that the powers of such a government can never amount to anything more than "the joint power of every member of the society." This is how it comes about, as Locke concludes, that "the community perpetually retains a supreme power" over its prince or legislative, "and must, by having deputed him, have still a power to discard him when he fails in his trust" (Locke 1967: 375, 385, 445).

As a result, these writers never find themselves tempted to use the terms *status* or state when describing the powers of civil government. When they envisage the members of a *civitas* or community instituting what Locke (1967: 434) calls a form of umpirage for the settlement of their controversies, they conceive of them not as

---

[87] Howell (1983: 155), while agreeing that this is true of Hotman, argues that two other "monarchomach" theorists – Beza and the author of the *Vindiciae contra tyrannos* – "implied the existence of the secular state as an entity distinct from ruler and people." I cannot see that either writer distinguished the powers of the state from those of the people. Cf. Skinner (1978, vol. II: 318–48).

[88] Locke (1967: 386). Cf. also pp. 301, 360–1, 371, 381 for the idea of rulers as mere trustees. See also Hotman (1972: 154 and 402–4) on kings as magistrates "tied" by the duties of their office.

entering a new state, but simply as setting up a new form of society –a civil or political society within which the wealth or welfare of the community can be better secured. So they continue to invoke the terms *civitas* or *respublica* to refer to the apparatus of civil government, usually translating these terms as "city" or "commonwealth." As Locke (1967: 373) explicitly states, "by commonwealth I must be understood all along" to mean "any independent community which the Latins signified by the word *civitas*, to which the word which best answers in our language is commonwealth."

If we wish, therefore, to trace the process by which the powers of the state finally came to be described as such, and seen at the same time as distinct from both the powers of the people and of their magistrates, we need at this juncture to turn to a strongly contrasting tradition of early-modern political thought. We need to turn to those writers who addressed themselves critically to the thesis of popular sovereignty we have just been considering, whether in its republican guise as a claim about "free states," or in its neoscholastic form as a claim about the inalienable rights of communities. We need to turn, that is, to those theorists whose aspirations included a desire to legitimize the more absolutist forms of government that began to develop in western Europe in the early part of the seventeenth century. It was as a by-product of their arguments, and in particular of their efforts to insist that the powers of government must be something other than a mere expression of the powers of the governed, that the concept of the state as we have inherited it was first articulated with complete self-consciousness.

Some of these counter-revolutionary theorists were mainly concerned with the radical scholastic thesis– associated in particular with Marsilius and his successors – to the effect that the *populus* and the *legislator humanus* can be equated. The repudiation of this doctrine became one of the chief polemical aims of later sixteenth-century Thomism, with Suarez's *De legibus* of 1612 containing the fullest and most influential summary of the alleged counter arguments.[89] Others were more disturbed by the monarchomach theories of popular soveignty thrown up by the religious wars in the latter part of the sixteenth century. Bodin in particular seeks in his *Six livres de la république* of 1576 to refute the arguments of those who were claiming that, as Knolles's translation of 1606 puts it, "princes sent

---

[89] On this school of thought see Hamilton (1963) and Fernandez–Santamaria (1977). On the character of their natural-law (as opposed to divine-right) theories of absolutism see Sommerville (1982 and 1986: 59–80). For a contrast with later theories of popular sovereignty see Tully (1980: 64–8 and 111–16).

by providence to the human race must be thrust out of their kingdoms under a pretence of tyranny."[90] Still others were no less perturbed by the implications of the republican allegation that, as Hobbes (1968: 369) scornfully paraphrases it in *Leviathan*, "the subjects in a popular commonwealth enjoy liberty," while "in a monarchy they are all slaves." Hobbes himself, like Grotius before him, engages with this as well as with the neoscholastic thesis of popular sovereignty, and undoubtedly offers the most systematic attempt to answer the question that preoccupies all these theorists: how to vindicate an account of civil government which at once concedes the original sovereignty of the people and is at the same time absolutist in its political allegiances.

If there is one thesis by which these writers are all especially agitated, it is the suggestion that the powers of civil government constitute nothing more than a reflection of the powers of the people. They concede, of course, that coercive authority must be justified by its capacity to ensure the common good, and in consequence the peace and happiness of the citizen-body as a whole. Hobbes believes no less firmly than Marsilius that, as he repeatedly declares in *Leviathan*, all governments must be judged by their "aptitude to produce the peace and security of the people, for which end they were instituted."[91] What none of these writers can accept, however, is the idea that the form of authority required to produce such benefits can appropriately be envisaged as nothing more than a trustee, a type of official to whom the people delegate the exercise of their own authority purely as a matter of administrative convenience. Political power, they all admit, is originally instituted by the people, but never in the form of a trust. It is instituted by means of what Suarez calls "absolute transfer" of the people's sovereignty, one that takes the form of "a kind of alienation, not a delegation at all."[92] To set up a mere "depository" or "guardian" of sovereign power, as Bodin agrees, is not to set up a genuine "possessor" of sovereignty at all.[93] For the people to perform that particular act, as Hobbes similarly stresses at several points in *Leviathan*, it is essential for them to recognize that they are "renouncing and transferring" their own original sovereignty, with

---

[90] See Bodin (1962: A71). For Bodin's concern to refute the "monarchomachs" see Franklin (1973, esp. pp. vii. 50, 93) and Salmon (1973, esp. pp. 361, 364).
[91] Hobbes (1968: 241). Cf. also pp. 192, 223, 237, etc.
[92] Suarez (1612: 210): "Quocirca translatio huius potestatis a republica in principem non est delegatio, sed quasi alienatio . . . simpliciter illi conceditur."
[93] Bodin (1576: 125) distinguishes between "possesseurs" of sovereignty and those who "ne sont que depositaires et gardes de cette puissance."

the implication that it is totally "abandoned or granted away" to someone else (Hobbes 1968: 190, 192).

Civil government, they insist, cannot therefore be seen as the powers of citizens under another guise. It must be seen as a distinct form of power, for reasons that Hobbes enunciates with complete assurance in *De cive* almost a decade before giving them classic expression in *Leviathan*. "Though a government," he declares, "be constituted by the contracts of particular men with particulars, yet its right depends not on that obligation only" (Hobbes 1983: 105). By constituting such a government, "that right which every man had before to use his faculties to his own advantages is now wholly translated on some certain man or council for the common benefit" (Hobbes 1983: 105). It follows that whatever power is thereby installed in authority must be recognized "as having its own rights and properties, insomuch as neither any one citizen, nor all of them together" can now be accounted its equivalent (Hobbes 1983: 89). This, as he was later to put it, "is the generation of that great Leviathan, or rather (to speak more reverently) of that mortal God, to which we owe, under the immortal God, our peace and defence. For by this authority, given him by every particular man in the commonwealth, he hath the use of so much power and strength conferred on him, that by terror thereof, he is enabled to form the wills of them all to peace at home and mutual aid against their enemies abroad" (Hobbes 1968: 227).

It is important, however, not to conflate this form of absolutism with that of the divine-right theorists who rose to such prominence during the same period. A writer like Bossuet, for example, deliberately sets out to obliterate the distinction between the office and person of a king. Echoing the celebrated remark attributed to Louis XIV, he insists that the figure of a ruler "embodies in himself the whole of the state": *tout l'état est en lui*.[94] By contrast, even Hobbes declares as unambiguously as possible that the powers of a ruler are never personal powers at all. They are owed entirely to his standing as holder of "the office of the sovereign," the principal duty of which, as Hobbes never tires of repeating, "consisteth in the end for which he was trusted with the sovereign power, namely the procuration of the safety of the people" (Hobbes 1968: 376).

With Hobbes no less than with Bodin, Suarez, Grotius, and the whole developing tradition of natural-law absolutism, we accordingly arrive at the view that the ends of civil or political association

---

[94] Bossuet (1967: 177). On this variety of absolutism see Keohane (1980: 241–61) and Sommerville (1986: 9–50).

make it indispensable to establish a single and supreme sovereign authority whose power remains distinct not merely from the people who orginally instituted it, but also from whatever office-holders may be said to have the right to wield its power at any particular time. What, then, is this form of political authority to be called?

Not surprisingly, these writers at first respond by reaching for traditional names. One suggestion, much canvassed by Bodin and later adopted by Hobbes in *De cive*, was that we should think of the authority in question as embodied in the *civitas*, the *ville* or the city as opposed to either its citizens or its magistrates.[95] But the most usual proposal was that we should think of it as that form of authority which inheres in the *respublica*, the *république* or the commonwealth. Suarez and Grotius, writing in Latin, both speak of the *respublica*.[96] Bodin, writing originally in French, speaks analogously of *la république*; translating his treatise into Latin in 1586, he rendered this as *respublica*; and when Knolles issued his English version in 1606, he in turn called the work *The Six Bookes of a Commonweale*.[97] Finally, Hobbes largely comes round to this terminology in *Leviathan*, speaking far less frequently of the city, and instead describing his work on its title-page as an enquiry into "the matter, form and power of a commonwealth" (Hobbes 1968: 73).

As these writers increasingly recognized, however, none of these traditional terms really served to render their meaning adequately. One obvious difficulty with "commonwealth" was the fact that, as Raleigh (1661: 3,8) complains in his *Maxims of State*, it had come to be used "by an usurped nickname" to refer to "the government of the whole multitude." To invoke it was thus to risk confusion with one of the theories of popular sovereignty they were most anxious to repudiate. Nor was it altogether satisfactory to speak instead of the city or *civitas*. It is true that Hobbes (1983: 89) consistently does so in *De cive*, declaring that "a city therefore (that we may define it) is one person whose will, by the compact of many men, is to be received for the will of them all." But the obvious difficulty here – in the face of which even Hobbes's confidence seems to have evaporated – was the need to insist on such a purely stipulative definition so strangely at variance with the ordinary meaning of the term.

It was at this juncture, within this tradition of thought, that a

[95] See Bodin (1576: 9 *et passim*) on the "ville" and "cité." Cf. Hobbes (1983: 89–90 *et passim*) for the concept of "a city or civil society."

[96] See Suarez (1612: 351–60) on the relations between the *princeps*, *leges* and *respublica*, and cf. Grotius (1625: 65) on *civitas* and *respublica* and p. 84 on the *romana respublica*.

[97] Cf. the full titles of Bodin (1576), Bodin (1586), and Bodin (1962).

number of these theorists began to resolve their difficulties by speaking instead of the *state*, while making it clear at the same time that they were consciously using the term to express their master concept of an impersonal form of political authority distinct from both rulers and ruled.

Bodin already hints at this final crystallizing of the concept at several points in his *République*.[98] Although he continues to write in traditional terms about rulers "who maintain their *estats*," he also uses the word *estat* on several occasions as a synonym for *république*.[99] Most significantly of all, he feels able to speak of "the state in itself" (*l'estat en soi*), describing it both as a form of authority independent of particular types of government, and as the locus of "indivisible and incommunicable sovereignty."[100] It is striking, moreover, that when Knolles came to translate these passages in 1606, he not only used the word "state" in all these instances, but also in a number of other places where Bodin himself had continued to speak in a more familiar vein of the authority of the *cité* or *république*.[101]

If we turn to English writers of the next generation, and above all to those "politic" humanists who were critical of classical republicanism, we find the same terminology used with increasing confidence. Raleigh, for example, not only speaks freely of the state in his *Maxims*, but makes it clear that he thinks of the state as an impersonal form of political authority, defining it as "the frame or set order of a commonwealth" (Raleigh 1661: 2). Bacon (1972: 89) writes in the final version of his *Essays* in a way that often suggests a similar understanding of political authority. He describes rulers as well as their councillors as having a duty to consider "the weal and advancement of the state which they serve." And he writes in a

---

[98] See Lloyd (1983: 156–62). Fell (1983, esp. pp. 92–107, 175–205) lays all his emphasis on Bodin's contemporary Corasius, though without investigating the extent to which he used the term *status* to express his concept of "the legislative state." But by the next generation the use of the vernacular term *état* (or *estat*) to express such a concept had become well entrenched in France. See Church (1972: 13–80) and Keohane (1980: 54–82, 119–82). Dowdall (1923: 118) singles out Loyseau's discussion in his *Traité des seigneuries* (1608) of the relationship between "seigneuries souveraines" and "estats" as being of particular importance, and this point has been much developed. See Church (1972: 33–4) and Lloyd (1981 and 1983: 162–8).

[99] Bodin (1576, e.g. at pp. 219, 438).

[100] Bodin (1576: 282–3): "Et combien que le gouvernement d'une Republique soit plus ou moins populaire, ou Aristocratique, ou Royale, si est-que l'estat en soi ne reçoit compairison de plus ni de moins: car toujours la souveraineté indivisible et incommunicable est à un seul." Note also Bodin's use of the phrase 'en matière d'estat" (576: 281, 414).

[101] See Bodin (1962: 184, 250, 451) and cf. pp. 10, 38, 409, 700 for some additional uses of "state."

number of other passages about the state and its rulers, the state and its subjects, the "founders of states" and the "subversion of states and governments" (Bacon 1972: 11, 42, 160, 165).

It is above all in Hobbes, however, and in other theorists of *de facto* sovereignty in the English revolution, that we find this new understanding of the state being articulated with complete assurance. It is true, as we have seen, that if we turn to the body of Hobbes's texts, we still find him exhibiting a preference for the traditional terminology of "city" and "commonwealth." But if we turn instead to his Prefaces, in the course of which he stands back from his own arguments and reviews their structure, we find him self-consciously presenting himself as a theorist of the state.

This transition can already be observed in the Preface to *De cive*, in the course of which he describes his project as that of explaining "what the quality of human nature is, in what matters it is, in what not, fit to make up a civil government, and how men must be agreed among themselves, that intend to grow up into a well-grounded state" (Hobbes 1983: 22). But it is in the Introduction to *Leviathan* that he proclaims most unequivocally that the subject matter of his entire investigation has been "that great Leviathan, called a Commonwealth or State (in Latin Civitas)" (Hobbes 1968: 81). Hobbes's ambition as a political theorist had always been to demonstrate that, if there is to be any prospect of attaining civil peace, the fullest powers of sovereignty must be vested neither in the people nor in their rulers, but always in the figure of an "artificial man."[102] Surveying this final redaction of his political philosophy, he at last felt able to add that, in speaking about the need for such an impersonal form of sovereignty, what he had been speaking about all along could best be described as the state.

VI

As the above account suggests, the idea that the supreme authority within a body politic should be identified as the authority of the state was originally the outcome of one particular theory of politics, a theory at once absolutist and secular-minded in its ideological allegiances. That theory was in turn the product of the earliest major counter-revolutionary movement within modern European history, the movement of reaction against the ideologies of popular sovereignty developed in the course of the French religious wars,

[102] Hobbes (1968: 82) states that the aim of *Leviathan* is "to describe the nature of this artificial man."

and, subsequently, in the English Revolution of the seventeenth century. It is perhaps not surprising, therefore, to find that both the ideology of state power and the new terminology employed to express it provoked a series of doubts and criticisms that have never been altogether stilled.

Some of the initial hostility derived from conservative theorists anxious to uphold the old ideal of *un roi, une foi, une loi*. They wished to repudiate any suggestion that the aims of public authority should be purely civil or political in character, and thereby to reinstate a closer relationship between allegiance in church and state. But much of the hostility stemmed from those who wished to uphold a more radical ideal of popular sovereignty in place of the sovereignty of the state. Contractarian writers sought in consequence to keep alive a preference for speaking about the government of civil or political society,[103] while the so-called commonwealthmen maintained their loyalty to the classical ideal of the self-governing republic throughout much of the eighteenth century.[104]

It is true that, at the end of the century, a renewed counter-revolutionary effort was made to neutralize these various populist doubts. Hegel and his followers in particular argued that the English contractarian theory of popular sovereignty merely reflected a failure to distinguish the powers of civil society from those of the state, and a consequent failure to recognize that the independent authority of the state is indispensable if the purposes of civil society are to be fulfilled. But this hardly proved an adequate reassurance. On the one hand, the anxiety of liberal theorists about the relationship between the powers of states and the sovereignty of their citizens generated confusions which have yet to be resolved. And on the other hand, a deeper criticism developed out of these Hegelian roots, insisting that the state's vaunted independence from its own agents as well as from the members of civil society amounts to nothing more than a fraud. As a result, sceptics in the tradition of Michels and Pareto, no less than socialists in the tradition of Marx, have never ceased to insist that modern states are in truth nothing more than the executive arms of their own ruling class.

Given the importance of these rival ideologies and their distinctive vocabularies, it is all the more remarkable to observe how quickly

---

[103] Benjamin Hoadly, for example, continues to speak about "the civil power," "civil government" and "the power of the civil magistrate" rather than about the state. See "The Original and Institution of Civil Government, Discussed" in Hoadly (1773, vol. II: 189, 191, 201, 203 *et passim*).

[104] See the usages in Robbins (1959: 125, 283) and cf. Kramnick (1968, esp. pp. 236–60) and Pocock (1975, esp. pp. 423–505).

the term "state" and its equivalents nevertheless became established at the heart of political discourse throughout western Europe. By the middle of the eighteenth century the new terminology had become virtually inescapable for all schools of thought. Even so nostalgic an exponent of classical republicanism as Bolingbroke found himself constrained in his pamphleteering of the 1720s to talk about the authority of the state, and about the need for the state to be supported, protected, and above all reformed (1967a: 19, 43, 93, 131). By the time we come to Hume's essays of the 1750s,[105] or Rousseau's *Contrat social* of a decade later,[106] we find the concept of the state and the terms *état* and *state* being put to work in a consistent and completely familiar way.

The immediate outcome of this conceptual revolution was to set up a series of reverberations in the wider political vocabularies of the western European states. Once "state" came to be accepted as the master noun of political argument, a number of other concepts and assumptions bearing on the analysis of sovereignty had to be reorganized or in some cases given up. To complete this survey, we need finally to examine the process of displacement and redefinition that accompanied the entrenchment of the modern idea of the state.

One concept that underwent a process of redefinition was that of political allegiance. A subject or *subditus* had traditionally sworn allegiance to his sovereign as liege lord. But with the acceptance of the idea that sovereignty is lodged not with rulers but with the state, this was replaced by the familiar view that citizens owe their basic loyalty to the state itself.

This is not to say that those who originally advanced this argument had any desire to give up speaking of citizens as *subditi* or subjects. On the contrary, the earliest theorists of the state retained a strong preference for this traditional terminology, using it as a means of countering both the contractarian inclination to speak instead about the sovereignty of the *populus* or people, and the classical republican contention that we ought to speak only of *civitates* and *cives*, of cities and their citizens. Hobbes, for example, with his usual cunning, maintains in the first published version of his political theory that he is writing specifically "about the citizen" – *de cive*. Yet he makes it one of his most important polemical claims that "each

---

[105] Hume's main discussions of state power occur in his essays "Of Commerce" and "That Politics may be Reduced to a Science." See Hume (1875, vol. I: 100, 105 and 289, 294–5).

[106] See Rousseau (1966, "De l'état civil", pp. 55–6). On "état" in the political vocabulary of Rousseau and his contemporaries see Derathé (1950: 380–2) and Keohane (1980, esp. pp. 442–9).

124   QUENTIN SKINNER

citizen, as also every subordinate civil person" ought properly to regard himself as "the subject of him who hath the chief command" (Hobbes 1983: 90).

Hobbes is in complete agreement with his radical opponents, however, when he goes on to argue that citizens ("that is to say, subjects") ought not to pay allegiance to those who exercise these rights of sovereignty, but rather to the sovereignty inherent in the state or commonwealth itself (Hobbes 1983: 151). Hotman and later "monarchomach" theorists had already insisted that even holders of offices under a monarchy must be viewed as councillors of the kingdom, not of the king, and as servants of the crown, not of the person wearing it.[107] Hobbes simply reiterates the same argument when he declares with so much emphasis in *De cive* that the "absolute and universal obedience" owed by each and every subject is due not to the person of their ruler, but rather "to the city, that is to say, to the sovereign power" (Hobbes 1983: 186).

A further and closely connected concept that was comparably transformed was that of treason. As long as the concept of allegiance was connected with that of doing homage, the crime of treason remained that of behaving treacherously towards a sovereign lord. By the end of the sixteenth century, however, this came to seem less and less satisfactory. Even in the case of England, still bound by the Statute of 1350 which defined treason as compassing or imagining the king's death, the judges began to place increasingly wide constructions upon the meaning of the original Act. The aim in almost every case was to establish a view of treason essentially as an offence against the king in virtue of his office as head of state.[108] Meanwhile the political writers of the same period, untrammeled by the need to wrestle with precedents, had already arrived by a more direct route at the familiar view of treason as a crime not against the king but against the state. As always, Hobbes states the new understanding of the concept most unequivocally. As he declares at the end of his analysis of dominion in *De cive*, those who are guilty of treason are those who refuse to perform the duties "without which the State cannot stand"; the crime of treason is the crime of those who act "as enemies to the Government" (Hobbes 1983: 181).

Finally, the acceptance of the state as both a supreme and an impersonal form of authority brought with it a displacement of the more charismatic elements of political leadership which, as I indicated at the outset, had earlier been of central importance to the

[107] See Hotman (1972, e.g. pp. 254, 298, 402).
[108] On this process see Holdsworth (1925: 307–33).

theory and practice of government throughout western Europe.

Among the assumptions that suffered displacement, the most important was the claim I began by stressing: that sovereignty is conceptually connected with display, that majesty serves in itself as an ordering force. Machiavelli, for example, still assumes that a ruler can expect to derive protection from *la maestá dello stato*, from a connection between his own high state of stateliness and his capacity to maintain his state.[109] It proved impossible, however, for such beliefs about the charisma attaching to public authority to survive the transfer of that authority to the purely impersonal agency – the "purely moral person," in Rousseau's phrase[110] – of the modern state. By the start of the eighteenth century, we already find conservative writers lamenting that, as Bolingbroke (1967b: 333) puts it, "the state is become, under ancient and known forms, an undefinable monster," with the result that a monarchy like England finds itself left with "a king without monarchical splendour" as head of state.

It was of course possible to transfer these attributes of majesty to the state's agents, permitting them to conduct state openings of parliament, to be granted state funerals, to lie in state, and so forth. Once it became accepted, however, that even heads of state are simply holders of offices, the attribution of so much pomp and circumstance to mere functionaries came to be seen not merely as inappropriate but even absurd, a case not of genuine pomp but of sheer pomposity. This insight was first elaborated by the defenders of "free commonwealths" in their anxiety to insist that, in Milton's phrase, rulers should never be "elevated above their brethren" but should "walk the streets as other men" (1980: 425). More's *Utopia*, for example, contains an early and devastating portrayal of public magnificence as nothing more than a form of childish vanity (1965: 152–6). Ponet's *Politic Power* includes a more minatory reminder of the punishments God visited upon the Israelites for demanding "a gallant and pompous king" (1942: 87). And Milton in *The Ready and Easy Way* condemns with deep disdain those rulers who aspire "to set a pompous face upon the superficial actings of state" (1980: 426).

One outcome of distinguishing the authority of the state from that of its agents was thus to sever a time-honoured connection

---

[109] Machiavelli (1960: 74, and cf. also pp. 76, 93). The same applies even more strongly to Machiavelli's contemporaries among "mirror-for-princes" writers. See for example Pontano (1952: 1054–6), Sacchi (1608: 68).

[110] Rousseau (1966: 54) on "la personne morale qui constitue l'Etat."

between the presence of majesty and the exercise of majestic powers. Displays of stateliness eventually came to be seen as mere "shows" or "trappings" of power, not as features intrinsic to the workings of power itself.[111] When Contarini concedes, for example, that the Doge of Venice is permitted to uphold the dignity of his office with a certain magnificence, he emphasizes that this is just a matter of appearances, and uses a phrase that Lewkenor translates by saying that the Doge is allowed a "royal appearing show."[112] Speaking with much greater hostility, Milton (1980: 426, 429) agrees that a monarch "sits only like a great cypher," with all his "vanity and ostentation" being completely inessential to the ordering force of public authority.

Finally, for the most self-conscious rejection of the older images of power, as well as the most unambiguous view of the state as a purely impersonal authority, we need to turn once more to Hobbes. Discussing these concepts in chapter 10 of *Leviathan*, Hobbes deploys the idea of an effective power to command in such a way as to absorb every other element traditionally associated with the notions of public honour and dignity. To hold dignities, he declares, is simply to hold "offices of command"; to be held honourable is nothing more than "an argument and sign of power" (Hobbes 1968: 152, 155). Here, as throughout, it is Hobbes who first speaks, systematically and unapologetically, in the abstract and un-modulated tones of the modern theorist of the state.

---

[111] On the distinctiveness of this conception of public power see Geertz (1980: 121–3).
[112] See Lewkenor (1969: 42), translating "specie regia" from Contarini (1626: 56).
For invaluable help with earlier drafts I am greatly indebted to John Dunn and Susan James.

REFERENCES

Aquinas, St. Thomas. 1963. *Summa theologiae*, 3 vols., edited by P. Caramello. Turin: Marietti.
    1966. *In octo libros politicorum Aristotelis expositio*, edited by R. Spiazzi. Turin: Marietti.
Bacon, F. 1972. *Essays*, edited by M. Hawkins. London: Dent.
Baron, H. 1966. *The Crisis of the Early Italian Renaissance*, 2nd edn. Princeton, NJ: Princeton University Press.
Bartolus of Sassoferrato. 1562. *Digestum novum commentaria*. Basel.
Beroaldo, F. 1508. "Libellus de optimo statu." In *Opuscula*. Venice, fos. x–xxxiiii.
Bodin, J. 1576. *Les Six Livres de la république*. Paris.

1586. *De republica libri sex.* Paris.

1962. *The Six Books of a Commonweale*, translated by R. Knolles and edited by K. McRae. Cambridge, MA: Harvard University Press.

Bolingbroke, Lord. 1967a. "A Dissertation upon Parties." In *The Works*, 4 vols., vol II. London: F. Cass, pp. 5–172.

1967b. "Letters on the Study and Use of History." In *The Works*, 4 vols., vol. II. London. F. Cass, pp. 173–334.

Bossuet, J.-B. 1967. *Politique tirée des propres paroles de l'Ecriture Sainte*, edited by J. Le Brun. Geneva: Droz.

Budé, G. 1966. *De l'institution du prince.* Farnborough: Gregg.

Burke, E. 1910. *Reflections on the Revolution in France*, Everyman edn. London: Dent.

Calasso, F. 1957. *I Glossatori e la teoria della sovranità.* Milan: Giuffrè.

Campano, G. 1502. "De regendo magistratu." In *Opera omnia.* Venice, fos. xxxxiii–xxxxviii.

Cassirer, E. 1946. *The Myth of the State.* New Haven, CT: Yale University Press.

Castiglione, B. 1960. *Il libro del cortegiano.* In *Opere*, edited by C. Cordié. Milan: R. Ricciardi, pp. 5–361.

Chabod, F. 1962. *L'idea di nazione*, 2nd edn. Bari: G. Laterza.

Chiappelli, F. 1952. *Studi sul linguaggio del Machiavelli.* Florence: F. Le Monnier.

Church, W. 1972. *Richelieu and Reason of State.* Princeton, NJ: Princeton University Press.

Cicero. 1913. *De officiis*, translated by W. Miller. London: Heinemann.

1914. *De Finibus*, translated by H. Rackham. London: Heinemann.

1927. *Tusculanae Disputationes*, translated by J. King. London: Heinemann.

Condren, C. 1985. *The Status and Appraisal of Classical Texts.* Princeton, NJ: Princeton University Press.

Contarini, G. 1626. *De republica Venetorum.* Lyons.

Cosenza, M. 1962. *Biographical and Bibliographical Dictionary of the Italian Humanists*, vol. V: *Synopsis and Bibliography.* Boston, MA: G.K. Hall.

Cranz, F. 1978. "The Publishing History of the Aristotle Commentaries of Thomas Aquinas." *Traditio* 34: 157–92.

Dante Alighieri. 1966. *Inferno*, edited by G. Petrocchi. Milan: A. Mondadori.

Delaruelle, L. 1907. *Guillaume Budé.* Paris: H. Champion.

D'Entrèves, A. 1967. *The Notion of the State.* Oxford: Oxford University Press.

Derathé, R. 1950. *Jean-Jacques Rousseau et la science politique de son temps.* Paris: Presses Universitaires de France.

Dowdall, H. 1923. "The Word 'State.'" *The Law Quarterly Review* 39: 98–125.

Dunn, J. 1969. *The Political Thought of John Locke.* Cambridge: Cambridge University Press.

Elliott, J. 1984. *Richelieu and Olivares.* Cambridge: Cambridge University Press.

Erasmus, D. 1974. *Institutio christiani principis*, edited by O. Herding. In *Opera omnia*, part IV, vol. I. Amsterdam: North-Holland, pp. 95–219.

Ercole, F. 1926. *La politica di Machiavelli*. Rome: Anonima Romana Editoriale.

Fell, A. 1983. *Origins of Legislative Sovereignty and the Legislative State*, vol. I. Cambridge, MA: Atheneum.

Fernandez-Santamaria, J.A. 1977. *The State, War and Peace*. Cambridge: Cambridge University Press.

Fink, Z. 1962. *The Classical Republicans*, 2nd edn. Evanston, IL: Northwestern University Press.

Franceschi, E. 1966. "Oculus pastoralis." *Memorie dell' accademia delle scienze di Torino* 11: 19–70.

Franklin, J. 1973. *Jean Bodin and the Rise of Absolutist Theory*. Cambridge: Cambridge University Press.

Froissart, J. 1824–6. *Chroniques*, 14 vols., edited by J. Buchon. Paris: Vordière, J. Carez.

    1972. *Chroniques: début du premier libre*, edited by G. Diller. Geneva: Droz.

Geertz, C. 1980. *Negara*. Princeton, NJ: Princeton University Press.

Giannardi, G. 1942. "Le 'Dicerie' di Filippo Ceffi." *Studi di filologia italiana* 6: 27–63.

Gilbert, F. 1965. *Machiavelli and Guicciardini*. Princeton, NJ: Princeton University Press.

Giovanni da Vignano. 1974. *Flore de parlare*. In Matteo dei Libri, *Arringhe*, edited by E. Vincenti. Milan: R. Ricciardi, pp. 229–325.

Giovanni da Viterbo. 1901. *Liber de regimine civitatum*, edited by C. Salvemini. In *Bibliotheca iuridica medii aevi*, 3 vols., edited by A. Gaudenzi, vol. III. Bologna: Società Azzoguidiana, pp. 215–80.

Grotius, H. 1625. *De iure belli ac pacis*. Paris.

Guicciardini, F. 1932. *Dialogo e discorsi del reggimento di Firenze*, edited by R. Palmarocchi. Bari: G. Laterza.

    1933. *Scritti politici e ricordi*, edited by R. Palmarocchi. Bari: G. Laterza.

Haitsma Mulier, E. 1980. *The Myth of Venice and Dutch Republican Thought in the Seventeenth Century*, translated by G. T. Moran. Assen: Van Gorcum.

Hamilton, B. 1963. *Political Thought in Sixteenth-century Spain*. Oxford: Clarendon.

Harrington, J. 1977. *The Political Works of James Harrington*, edited by J. Pocock. Cambridge: Cambridge University Press.

Hertter, F. 1910. *Die Podestalitteratur Italiens im 12. und 13. Jahrhundert*. Leipzig. B.G. Teubner.

Hexter, J. 1973. *The Vision of Politics on the Eve of the Reformation*. New York: Allen Lane.

Hoadly, B. 1772. *The Works*, 3 vols. London: W. Bowyer and J. Nichols.

Hobbes, T. 1968. *Leviathan*, edited by C. Macpherson. Harmondsworth: Penguin.

    1983. *De cive: The English Version*, edited by H. Warrender. Oxford: Clarendon.

Holdsworth, W. 1925. *A History of English Law*, vol. VIII. London: Methuen.

Hotman, F. 1972. *Francogallia*, edited by R. Giesey and J. Salmon. Cambridge: Cambridge University Press.

Hume, D. 1875. *Essays*, 2 vols., edited by T. Green and T. Grose. London: Longmans Green.

Humphrey, L. 1973. *The Nobles, or Of Nobility*. In *The English Experience*, no. 534. New York: Da Capo Press.

Kantorowicz, E. 1957. *The King's Two Bodies*. Princeton, NJ: Princeton University Press.

Keohane, N. 1980. *Philosophy and the State in France*. Princeton, NJ: Princeton Unversity Press.

Kramnick, I. 1968. *Bolingbroke and his Circle*. Cambridge, MA: Harvard University Press.

Laslett, P. 1967. "Introduction." In Locke 1967: 1–120.

Latini, B. 1948. *Li Livres dou trésor*, edited by F. Carmody. Berkeley, CA: University of California Press.

Lewkenor, L. 1969. *The Commonwealth and Government of Venice*. In *The English Experience*, vol. 101. New York: Da Capo Press.

Livy. 1962. *Ab urbe condita*, vol. VIII, translated by F. Moore. London: Heinemann.

1966. *Ab urbe condita*, vol. VI, translated by F. Moore, London: Heinemann.

Lloyd, H. 1981. "The Political Thought of Charles Loyseau (1564–1610)." *European Studies Review* 11: 53–82.

1983. *The State, France and the Sixteenth Centiry*. London: George Allen and Unwin.

Locke, J. 1967. *Two Treatises of Government*, edited by P. Laslett, 2nd edn. Cambridge: Cambridge University Press.

Machiavelli, N. 1960. *Il principe e discorsi*, edited by S. Bertelli. Milan: Feltrinelli.

Maffei, R. de. 1964. "Il problema della 'Ragion di Stato' nei suoi primi affioramenti." *Rivista internazionale di filosofia del diritto* 41: 712–32.

Mansfield, H. 1983. "On the Impersonality of the Modern State: A Comment on Machiavelli's Use of *Stato*." *The American Political Science Review* 77: 849–57.

Maravall, J. 1961. "The Origins of the Modern State." *Journal of World History* 6: 789–808.

Marsilius of Padua. 1956. *The Defender of Peace*, translated by A. Gewirth. New York: Columbia University Press.

Matteo dei Libri. 1974. *Arringhe*, edited by E. Vincenti. Milan: R. Ricciardi.

Mayer, T. 1985. "Faction and Ideology: Thomas Starkey's *Dialogue*." *Historical Journal* 28: 1–25.

Meinecke, F. 1957. *Machiavellism*, translated by D. Scott. London: Routledge and Kegan Paul.

Milton, J. 1962. *The Tenure of Kings and Magistrates*. In *Complete Prose Works*, vol. III, edited by M. Hughes. New Haven, CT: Yale University Press, pp. 190–258.

1971. *History of Britain*. In *Complete Prose Works*, vol. V, edited by F. Fogle. New Haven, CT: Yale University Press.

1980. *The Ready and Easy Way to Establish a Free Commonwealth.* In *Complete Prose Works*, vol. VII, edited by R. Ayers, revised edn. New Haven, CT:Yale University Press, pp. 407–63.

Mochi Onory, S. 1951. *Fonti canonistiche dell' idea moderna dello stato.* Milan: Società Editrice 'Vita e pensiero.'

Mommsen, T. (ed.). 1970. *Digesta*, 21st edn. Zurich: Weidmannes.

More, St. Thomas. 1965. *Utopia.* In *The Complete Works of St. Thomas More*, vol. IV, edited by E. Surtz and J. Hexter. New Haven, CT: Yale University Press.

Muratori, L. (ed.). 1741. "Gratulatio." In *Antiquitates Italicae*, vol. IV. Milan: Arretti, pp. 131–2.

Patrizi, F. 1594a. *De institutione reipublicae.* Strassburg.

1594b. *De regno et regis institutione.* Strassburg.

Petrarch, F. 1554. *Opera quae extant omnia.* Basel.

Pocock, J. 1975. *The Machiavellian Moment.* Princeton, NJ: Princeton University Press.

Ponet, J. 1942. *A Short Treatise of Politic Power.* Reprinted in W. Hudson, *John Ponet.* Chicago, IL: University of Chicago Press, pp. 131–62.

Pontano, G. 1952. "De principe." In *Prosatori latini del quattrocento*, edited by E. Garin. Milan: R. Ricciardi, pp. 1023–63.

Post, G. 1964. *Studies in Medieval Legal Thought.* Princeton, NJ: Princeton University Press.

Raab, F. 1964. *The English Face of Machiavelli.* London: Routledge and Kegan Paul.

Raleigh, W. 1661. "Maxims of State." In *Remains of Sir Walter Raleigh.* London: W. Sheares, pp. 1–65.

Rinuccini, A. 1957. *Dialogus de libertate*, edited by F. Adorno. In *Atti e memorie dell' accademia toscana di scienze e lettere La Colombaria* 22: 265–303.

Robbins, C. 1959. *The Eighteenth-century Commonwealthman.* Cambridge, MA: Harvard University Press.

Rousseau, J.-J. 1966. *Du contrat social*, edited by P. Burgelin. Paris: Garnier-Flammarion.

Rowen, H. 1961. ' "L'état, c'est à moi.' Louis XIV and the State." *French Historical Studies* 2: 83–98.

Rowley, G. 1958. *Ambrogio Lorenzetti*, 2 vols. Princeton, NJ: Princeton University Press.

Rubinstein, N. 1952. "Florence and the Despots. Some Aspects of Florentine Diplomacy in the Fourteenth Century." *Transactions of the Royal Historical Society*, 2: 21–45.

1971. "Notes on the word *stato* in Florence before Machiavelli." In *Florilegium historiale*, edited by J. Rowe and W. Stockdale. Toronto: University of Toronto Press, pp. 313–26.

Sacchi, B. 1608. *De principe viro.* Frankfurt.

Sallust. 1921. *Bellum Catilinae* translated by J. Rolfe. London: Macmillan.

Salmon, J. 1973. "Bodin and the Monarchomachs." In H. Denzer (ed.), *Bodin.* Munich: Beck, pp. 359–78.

Sardo, R. 1845. *Cronaca Pisana.* In *Archivio storico italiano* 6, part II: 73–244.

Scala, B. 1940. *De legibus et iudiciis dialogus*, edited by L. Borghi. In *La Bibliofilia* 42: 256–82.

Seneca. 1964. *De beneficiis*, translated by J. Basore. London: Heinemann.

Shadwell, L. (ed.). 1912. *Enactments in Parliament Specially Concerning the Universities of Oxford and Cambridge*, 4 vols. London: Clarendon.

Shennan, J. 1974. *The Origins of the Modern European State, 1450–1725*. London: Hutchinson.

Skinner, Q. 1978. *The Foundations of Modern Political Thought*, 2 vols. Cambridge: Cambridge University Press.

Sommerville, J. 1982. "From Suarez to Filmer: A Reappraisal." *The Historical Journal* 25: 525–40.

    1986. *Politics and Ideology in England, 1603–1640*. London: Longman.

Sorbelli, A. 1944. "I teorici del reggimento comunale." *Bullettino dell' istituto storico italiano per il medio evo* 59: 31–136.

Starkey, T. 1948. *A Dialogue between Reginald Pole and Thomas Lupset*, edited by K. Burton. London: Chatto and Windus.

Strayer, J. 1970. *On the Medieval Origins of the Modern State*. Princeton, NJ: Princeton University Press.

Suarez, F. 1612. *Tractatus de legibus, ac Deo legislatore*. Coimbra.

Tanner, J. 1930. *Constitutional Documents of the Reign of James I*. Cambridge: Cambridge University Press.

Tierney, B. 1982. *Religion, Law and the Growth of Constitutional Thought, 1150–1650*. Cambridge: Cambridge University Press.

Topham, J. *et al.* (eds.). 1783. *Rotuli Parliamentorum*, vol. III. London.

Tuck, R. 1985. "Warrender's *De cive*." *Political Studies* 33: 308–15.

Tully, J. 1980. *A Discourse on Property*. Cambridge: Cambridge University Press.

Ullmann, W. 1968–9. "Juristic Obstacles to the Emergence of the Concept of the State in the Middle Ages." *Annali di storia del diritto* 12–13: 43–64.

Vespasiano da Bisticci. 1970–6. *Le vite*, 2 vols., edited by A. Greco. Florence: Nella sede dell' istituto nazionale di studi sul rinascimento.

Vettori, F. 1842. *Parero* [On the Government of Florence, 1531–2]. In *Archivio storico italiano* 1: 433–6.

Villani, G. 1802–3. *Istorie fiorentine*, 8 vols. Milan: Società tipografica dei classici italiani.

Wahl, J. 1977. "Baldus de Ubaldis and the Foundations of the Nation-State." *Manuscripta* 21: 80–96.

Waley, D. 1978. *The Italian City-republics*, 2nd edn. London: Longmans.

Warrender, H. 1983. "Editor's Introduction." In Hobbes 1983.

1

◁ ═══════════════════════════════════ ▷

Machiavelli and Florentine republican experience

NICOLAI RUBINSTEIN

Florence, wrote Machiavelli in 1519 or 1520 in his *Discursus* on the reform of the Florentine government, has never been a 'repubblica . . . che abbi avute le debite qualità sue'[1] – an observation which recapitulates the statement made a few years earlier in his *Discorsi sopra la prima deca di Tito Livio* that 'per dugento anni che si ha di vera memoria', Florence had never possessed a 'stato, per il quale la possa veramente essere chiamata republica'.[2] In the *Discorsi*, he attributes this to the fact that before acquiring its independence from the Hohenstaufen Empire, Florence had always lived 'sotto il governo d'altrui'. That it had never been a true republic, he states in the *Discursus*,[3] is borne out by the regime, the *stato*, it had had since 1393, when under Maso degli Albizzi's leadership the city became a 'repubblica governata da ottimati' and thus acquired an oligarchical regime, which lasted until 1434, when it was replaced with the Medici regime. Its 'difetti' were the excessive power, and yet insufficient 'reputazione', of the Signoria, the long intervals between the electoral scrutinies which qualified citizens for office-holding, the influence which private citizens exercised over the decisions of the government through their membership of advisory bodies, the *pratiche*, the lack of institutional safeguards against the formation of factions or *sètte* – 'le quali sono la rovina di uno stato' – by great citizens, 'uomini grandi'. But the worst of these 'disordini', the one 'che importava il tutto', was the virtual exclusion from the regime of the people, 'il popolo', which 'non vi aveva dentro la parte sua'. These criticisms, which reflect Machiavelli's disapproval of government by *ottimati*, as well as his passionate concern for a true 'ordine civile', contrast with the praise his friend Francesco Guicciardini had lavished, about ten years earlier, on the aristocratic regime of the early fifteenth century, of which 'meritamente si dice che . . . è stato el più savio, el più glorioso, el più felice governo che mai per alcuno tempo abbi avuto la città nostra'[4] – a judgement which echoed the nostalgia which that regime had evoked, later in the fifteenth century, among *ottimati*.[5] Florence, it

---

[1] *Discursus florentinarum rerum post mortem iunioris Laurentii Medices*, ed. M. Martelli, Niccolò Machiavelli, *Tutte le opere* (Florence, 1971), p. 24.   [2] *Ibid.* I, 49, p. 131.   [3] *Ibid.*
[4] *Storie fiorentine*, ed. R. Palmarocchi (Bari, 1931), pp. 2–3.
[5] Cf. N. Rubinstein, 'Florentine constitutionalism and Medici ascendancy in the fifteenth century' in N. Rubinstein, ed. *Florentine Studies* (London, 1968), p. 460.

4 *Nicolai Rubinstein*

was said, was then ruled by citizens who 'non dovriano dirsi inferiori a quei più savi Romani cosi celebrati dall' antichità'[6] and who placed the common good before private interest; Niccolò Soderini, one of the leading opponents of Medici ascendancy in 1465–6, declared that 'chi non governò innanzi al 33, non sa governare'.[7]

By way of criticism, as well as of praise, the regime under which Florence was governed in the early fifteenth century was thus considered by later generations the most significant manifestation of republican government the Florentines had experienced before the establishment, in 1494, of the Great Council. In this chapter on republican experience in fifteenth-century Florence, I shall therefore concentrate on the period before 1434, and then briefly discuss the changes which that experience underwent under the Medici, and after their expulsion in 1494.

This is a large subject, and in order to do it a modicum of justice, I propose to distinguish, in what must perforce be very general observations, the following three aspects of that experience: the concept contemporaries formed of Florence's republican institutions; the ways in which the working of these institutions affected Florentine citizens; and the extent to which they actively participated in the government of Florence.

If we want to ask how the Florentines conceptualised their republic, we have to go back to the fourteenth, and even the thirteenth century, when the rise of the Signoria in Northern and Central Italy brought about, in the surviving Italian city republics, the perception of a fundamental antithesis between despotic rule and the 'popoli che vivono in libertà',[8] the 'libertas populi',[9] a term which, in the fifteenth century, the humanists replaced with the classical one for commonwealth, *res publica*. According to Cicero's definition, as explained by St Augustine,[10] 'omnino nullam esse rem publicam, quoniam non esset res populi'; and, in his translation of the *Politics*, Leonardo Bruni rendered Aristotle's term for the third true constitution, *politeia*, with *res publica*.[11] The chief difference between the republican and the despotic regime was to concern the contrast between the absolute and arbitrary exercise of government and its limitation by law and the will of the people.

---

[6] Luca della Robbia, in his life of Bartolomeo Valori composed around 1500, ed. P. Bigazzi, *Archivio Storico Italiano*, 4, 1 (1843), pp. 239–40.

[7] That is before the victory of the Albizzi faction, which, after Cosimo de' Medici's return from exile in 1434, was followed by the establishment of Medici ascendancy. Ed. G. Pampaloni, 'Nuovi tentativi di riforme alla Costituzione Fiorentina attraverso le consulte', *Archivio Storico Italiano*, 120 (1962), p. 572 (*pratica* of 8 July). For a contemporary narrative of the crisis of the Medici regime in 1465–6, see M. Phillips, *The Memoir of Marco Parenti. A Life in Medici Florence* (Princeton, 1987 and London, 1989), chs. 7, 9, 10.

[8] See e.g. Matteo Villani, *Cronica*, IX, 87, ed. F.G. Dragomanni (Milan, 1848) VI, p. 275.

[9] E.g. Ferreto de' Ferreti, *Historia*, ed. C. Cipolla (Rome, 1908–20), II, p. 11.

[10] *De civitate Dei*, II, 21; cf. Cicero, *De re publica*, I, 25.

[11] *Politics*, 1279a: 'Cum autem multitudo gubernet ad communem utilitatem, vocatur communi nomine rerumpublicarum [πολιτειῶν] omnium, respublica [πολιτεία]', Aristoteles, *Libri omnes quibus tota moralis philosophia . . . continetur* (Lyons, 1579), v, p. 571.

Machiavelli and Florentine republican experience   5

Bruni was the first humanist to attempt, in his *Laudatio Florentinae urbis* of 1403,[12] an analysis of the republican constitution of Florence; but, largely owing to the panegyrical nature of this work, his analysis is incomplete and necessarily biased; while his later, more objective account, in his short Greek treatise on the Florentine *politeia*,[13] suffers from his attempt to apply Aristotelian constitutional theory, in the form of the mixed constitution, to Florence. What does, however, stand out in these analyses are a number of basic principles, which are conceived by Bruni as fundamental to an understanding of the Florentine system of government: for the executive, the Signoria, a strict limitation, by a variety of means, of its almost regal authority, and its dependence, in the last resort, on the will of the people, as voiced in the legislative councils of the People and of the Commune; for the citizens, liberty under the law, and an equality which implied, among other things, as Bruni pointed out in 1428 in his funeral oration for Nanni Strozzi, equal opportunity to rise to high office;[14] for the social classes, as he states in his constitutional treatise about ten years later, a balance between the patricians and the people which, while tilted towards the former, took no account of the extremes of private power and of poverty, whose representatives were excluded from government. How far did the political experience of Florentine citizens conform to these principles?

The overriding experience the average Florentine citizen had of his republic must have been the power, and indeed the majesty, of the Signoria, with its eight Priors and the Gonfalonier of Justice, a power which Gregorio Dati described, at the beginning of the century, as 'grande sanza misura'.[15] Decisively reasserted in 1382 after the Ciompi revolt of 1378,[16] it included the authority to initiate legislation, as well as the right to intervene in criminal jurisdiction when the public interest might demand it. But the Signoria, which deliberated jointly with its two Colleges, the Sixteen Gonfalonieri di compagnia and the Twelve Buonuomini, was not the only magistracy which the citizens would regard as the governing body of the republic. The Otto di Guardia, set up after the Ciompi revolt to protect the security of the state, had acquired extensive powers in policing it, the Dieci di Balia were, after 1384, in times of war, in charge of military operations and diplomatic negotiations, the Ufficiali del Monte administered the funded debt and had become the central financial magistracy of the Commune. The increasing range of the powers and competence of the executive branch of government was part of the political experience of the Florentines from the 1380s onwards; it was largely due to the

---

[12] *From Petrarch to Leonardo Bruni*, ed. H. Baron (Chicago and London, 1968), pp. 217–63.
[13] 'Leonard Bruni's Constitution of Florence', ed. A. Moulakis, *Rinascimento*, 2nd series, 26 (1986), pp. 141–90. It was probably composed in 1439 or 1440: *ibid.* pp. 154–5.
[14] *Miscellanea*, ed. E. Baluze and G.D. Mansi, 4, (Lucca, 1764), p. 3.
[15] *Istoria di Firenze*, ed L. Pratesi (Florence, 1904), p. 148.
[16] See N. Rubinstein, 'Il regime politico di Firenze dopo il Tumulto dei Ciompi' in *Il Tumulto dei Ciompi* (Convegno Internazionale di Studi 1979) (Florence, 1981), pp. 105–24.

6   *Nicolai Rubinstein*

traumatic effects of the Ciompi revolt and its aftermath and of the wars against Giangaleazzo Visconti, and to the aggrandisement and reorganisation of the city's territorial dominion. But there were limits to this development. A permanent commission of eighty-one composed almost entirely of members of the executive branch, with full powers to hire mercenaries and levy taxes for this purpose, which had been set up in 1393,[17] was for all practical purposes abolished eleven years later, and a contemporary diarist commented: 'il populo ne fu molto lieto'.[18] It was significant of this reluctance to increase the powers of the executive even further, that when in 1411 a new council, of 200, was created, without whose assent no military action was to be undertaken, it consisted only partly of official members, and its decisions required in their turn the assent of the councils of the People and the Commune.[19] Indeed, these two ancient councils of the republic, whose membership totalled over 500,[20] provided the most important of the checks to the powers of the executive. They could be seen to represent the broad foundation of the republican structure of government. As Bruni puts it in his *Laudatio*, in terms derived from Roman law, 'quod enim ad multos attinet', must be decided by the many.[21]

Bruni points out that another check to the great power of the Signoria was the short term of their office. All public offices were held for short periods, mostly for six months, those of the Signoria for two months only. This, as well as the proliferation of offices since the second half of the fourteenth century, provided the citizens with a wide range of opportunities to hold office, and consequently to participate directly in government and administration. This extensive availability of public office was thus a major aspect of the republican experience of the citizens, and thus of the Florentine *libertas*;[22] another concerned the methods by which this availability was translated into fact, in other words, the methods by which citizens were actually elected to office.

Since early in the fourteenth century, election to public office was based on periodical vetting for eligibility in so-called scrutinies (*squittini*), which were carried out by specially convened commissions consisting of the Signoria, its two Colleges, a number of other ex officio members, and eighty additional members elected by the Signoria and the Colleges, which gave the executive a key role in determining the composition of the commission.[23] Actual

[17] See A. Molho, 'The Florentine oligarchy and the "Balìe" of the late Trecento', *Speculum*, 43 (1968), pp. 31ff.
[18] Giovanni di Pagolo Morelli, *Ricordi*, ed. V. Branca (Florence, 1956), pp. 426–7. Cf. G. Guidi, *Il governo della città-repubblica di Firenze del primo Quattrocento* (Florence, 1981), II, p. 146.
[19] Law establishing the council of 200, *Sulla repubblica fiorentina a tempo di Cosimo il Vecchio*, ed. F.C. Pellegrini (Pisa, 1880), Appendix, pp. ix–xiii.
[20] Cf. Guidi, *Il governo*, II, pp. 140, 142.
[21] *Laudatio*, as above, n. 12, p. 260: *Codex*, 5, 59, 5, 2. Cf. Rubinstein, 'Florentine constitutionalism', p. 446, n. 1.
[22] See N. Rubinstein, 'Florentina libertas', *Rinascimento*, 2nd series, 26 (1986), pp. 13, 15.
[23] On this and the following, see N. Rubinstein, *The Government of Florence under the Medici (1434 to 1494)* (Oxford, 1966), pp. 56ff.; Guidi, *Il governo*, I, pp. 283ff.

appointment to office followed on the extraction of the names of eligible
citizens from the pouches in which they had been placed after the scrutinies.
There were separate pouches for different offices or groups of offices, and of
these the most prestigious contained the names of the citizens who had been
made eligible for the so-called three highest offices, the Signoria, the Sixteen
Gonfalonieri di compagnia, and the Twelve Buonuomini. Scrutinies – that of
the Tre Maggiori Uffici was separate from that of all the other public offices –
were to take place every five years (in fact, the intervals were usually longer),
and votes were cast on nominations by the Gonfaloniers of the ancient militia
companies, who could be assumed to be well acquainted with the citizens of
their sixteen districts;[24] and both the identity of the voters and the results of the
vote were kept strictly secret. This meant that citizens who had been nominated
would not know whether they had been made eligible until their names were
extracted from the pouches prior to the filling of a vacancy. This was a matter of
particular importance for the three most prestigious offices, which included the
Signoria; accordingly, even if a citizen, though eligible to them, was
temporarily barred from being elected (for instance, because he had held the
same office recently), he was now known (*veduto*), as were those who were
actually elected to office (*seduti*), to have been qualified for government. This
gave the group of *veduti* and *seduti* a preferential position not only in subsequent
scrutinies, but also when it came to electing the membership of councils, such as
that of 200, which were endowed with special responsibilities and powers, and
hence affected the participation of citizens in political life.

The secrecy which was an essential feature of the Florentine electoral system
conformed to that which surrounded the working of both the executive and the
legislative organs of the republic; it formed an essential part of the republican
experience of Florentine citizens. Just as the deliberations of the Signoria were
meant to be kept secret – an obligation which was physically reflected in the
separate location of their living quarters on the second floor of their palace – so
the vote in the councils was by secret ballot. This concern with secrecy was
underlined by the lengths to which the government would go in trying to
prevent the formation of caucuses, as in the temporary suppression of religious
confraternities, which were banned, for instance, in 1419, on the grounds that
some of them encouraged factionalism; later in the century citizens who, as
veduti or *seduti*, were known to be eligible to government, were forbidden to
attend meetings of confraternities while electoral scrutinies were in progress.
But there were ways of evading such prohibitions; we know of at least one of
the more prestigious confraternities which, around the middle of the century,

---

[24] D.V. and F.W. Kent, *Neighbours and Neighbourhoods in Renaissance Florence: the District of the Red
Lion in the Fifteenth Century* (Locust Valley, New York, 1982), pp. 17–19.

had special sponsors, *sollecitatori*, to support weaker members in the ongoing scrutiny of 1454.[25]

In fact, while the secrecy of the electoral system was, on the whole, effective, the same did not apply to the independence of the scrutinies from outside influence. It was quite usual for citizens to canvass members of scrutiny commissions to nominate them; there was even a technical term for this, *pregheria*, and family *ricordanze* would record such *pregherie* and the sense of obligation they involved. Gregorio Dati's *Libro segreto* throws a vivid light on this practice, as well as on the ways in which Florentine citizens experienced the intricacies of their electoral system. On 3 May 1412 Dati records that his name had been drawn for the office of Gonfaloniere di compagnia for his district; until then, he says, he had not been sure that his name was in the pouches for the Colleges, but for the sake of his own honour and of that of his descendants, 'pur lo disiderava'; 'onde', he continues, 'per non esser ingrato né volendo usare lo insaziabile appetito, che quanto più ha più disiderano, mi sono proposto e diliberato che da ora inanzi per ufici di Comune che s'abiano a fare o a squittinare mai non debo pregare alcuno, ma lasciare fare a chi fia sopra ciò . . .'.[26]

The desire to hold public office was, in fact, one of the most striking characteristics of the republican experience of Florentine citizens. A number of the offices in the administration of the dominion were sought not only for *onore* but also for *utile*, and could indeed bring considerable financial advantages to their holders; the honour which membership of the Signoria, whose salary was only intended to cover expenses, brought with it, could also mean social advancement and political influence for oneself and one's family. While the holding of public office was extolled by humanists such as Matteo Palmieri as the duty of the citizen who placed the common good above private interest and who knows 'essere commessa in lui la publica degnità et il bene commune essere lasciato nella sua fede',[27] others castigated the 'ambitio officiorum', the 'volere gli ufici', as the cause of 'tutto ciò che di male è stato nella benedetta città di Firenze';[28] while Alberti, in a famous passage, has Giannozzo deride the citizens' scramble for public office, which makes them into nothing better than 'publici servi': it was far preferable to 'vivere a sé, non al comune'.[29] Some

[25] See J. Henderson, 'Le confraternite religiose nella Firenze del tardo Medioevo: patroni spirituali e anche politici?', *Ricerche storiche*, 15 (1985), pp. 77–94, and also Rubinstein, *The Government of Florence*, p. 119.

[26] *Mercanti storici. Ricordi nella Firenze tra Medioevo e Rinascimento*, ed. V. Branca (Milan, 1986), pp. 550–1.   [27] *Vita civile*, ed. G. Belloni (Florence, 1982), p. 132.

[28] Rinaldo degli Albizi in a *pratica* of 1431 (Pellegrini, ed., *Sulla repubblica fiorentina*, p. xxxiii): 'Causa vero [discordiarum] est ambitio officiorum'; Marchionne di Coppo Stefani, *Cronaca fiorentina*, ed. N. Rodolico, *Rer. Ital. Script.*, 30, 1 (Città di Castello, 1903 – Bologna, 1955), rubrica 923, p. 413 (*ad* 1382).

[29] Leon Battista Alberti, *I libri della Famiglia* in *Opere volgari*, C. Grayson, ed. (Bari, 1960–73), 1, pp. 179–82.

Machiavelli and Florentine republican experience 9

citizens would agree, Giovanni Rucellai, for example, during his time in the political wilderness after Cosimo's return from exile and before being accepted, nearly thirty years later, into the Medici regime.[30] For the vast majority, however, high office represented the peak of their republican experience. The memoirs of fifteenth-century Florentines clearly show the role office-holding played in their lives. The 'cursus honorum' might begin with the election to the consulate of one of the guilds; communal offices would follow, until finally successful citizens would reach the plateau of the top offices of government and administration, which included, first of all, the Signoria and their Colleges, but also such powerful and prestigious magistracies as the Dieci di Balia, the Otto di Guardia, and the Ufficiali del Monte.

The citizens who had reached this plateau, after having been made eligible for the government, constituted what the Florentines called the *reggimento*; after the scrutiny of 1411, it amounted to just over 1,000 citizens; by the time the scrutiny of 1433 had completed its business, it had risen to over 2,000.[31] While this shows a remarkable degree of social mobility, it should be added that only a fraction of these men (185 and 327 respectively) belonged to the craft guilds, although these contributed a quarter of the members of most offices: evidently because only a very small section of the lower classes were considered fit for positions in the government. Another significant feature of these figures is the prevalence of single families: of the 1757 citizens of the greater guilds who were made eligible to the three highest offices in 1433, just under 100 were individually successful, the rest belonged to 227 families. Among these a very small group was represented with far greater numbers than the average of 7.3 per family – such as the Capponi with 20 and the Strozzi with no less than 40 members. The *reggimento*, it has been said, has to be seen 'as a constellation of families rather than as an aggregate of individuals'.[32]

Nor was the elitist tendency in the access to high public office, and hence to a high level of political participation, confined to the procedure of qualification for these offices. The methods by which the results of the electoral scrutinies were used in the final stage of the electoral process, that is the extraction from the pouches which had been filled with the names of the successful candidates, included in their turn an element of selection. The Signoria comprised, besides the eight Priors, the most prestigious and influential member of the government, the Gonfalonier of Justice, and, to make appointment to this office exceptionally difficult, there had always been a separate pouch for it. To select

---

[30] See *Giovanni Rucellai ed il suo Zibaldone*, 1: '*Il Zibaldone Quaresimale*', ed. A. Perosa (London, 1960), pp. 39–43; cf. p. 122.

[31] For this and the following, see D. Kent, 'The Florentine reggimento in the fifteenth century', *Renaissance Quarterly*, 28 (1975), 575–638; see also A. Molho, 'Politics and the ruling class in early Renaissance Florence', *Nuova Rivista Storica*, 52 (1968), 401–20.

[32] Kent, 'The Florentine *reggimento* in the fifteenth century', p. 587.

names to be placed in this pouch from among those who were eligible to the Priorate, was the job of the officials who were in charge of the technical aspects of the scrutinies of the Tre Maggiori Uffici; but from 1387 onwards, these officials, the *accoppiatori*, could also place the names of those citizens into a special pouch for the Priorate, the *borsellino*, which, owing to the smaller number of name tickets it contained, provided their owners with greater opportunities for being actually elected to office.[33]

Even so, on the eve of the establishment of the Medici regime, the citizens who were eligible to government represented a sizeable part of the population of Florence, which in 1427 amounted to about 37,000 persons.[34] Of these, well over one half were men (*c.* 20,000); on the other hand, again according to the calculations of Herlihy and Klapisch, 46 per cent were under 20;[35] 25 was the minimum age for office-holding, 30 for the Priorate.

At the same time, one has to bear in mind that the Tre Maggiori Uffici represented only a fraction of the offices that had to be filled recurrently within the city and its territory. Only a few of the most sensitive of these were temporarily filled by way of direct elections, as were many of the minor ones, but here too the normal method was by sortition preceded by scrutiny. These scrutinies of the 'internal and external offices' concerned magistracies such as the Dieci di Balìa and the Otto di Guardia, whose importance could in some respects equal or even surpass that of the Signoria, as well as top offices of the territorial administration, such as those of the Captains of Pisa and of Arezzo, which combined great responsibilities with extensive powers; but the scrutinies also made citizens eligible for a host of minor administrative offices in the city and its territory. If republican experience, in terms of participation in government and administration, was to be based on eligibility to office, its range, despite all the gradations of that eligibility, was remarkably wide.

But if we define republican experience in terms of actual participation in decision-making, the picture is very different. Among the 3,000-odd posts, including membership of the councils, that had to be filled every year,[36] those which belonged to the executive branch of government were, at any given point in time, occupied by a small section of the citizens who were eligible for them. On the other hand, while participation in actual decision-making was restricted to a small group of citizens, this was counterbalanced by the rapid rotation of office. It was further compensated by the regular use, by the Signoria, of advisory committees, which consisted, apart from ex officio members, of citizens who at the time did not belong to the executive branch of government.

---

[33] Cf. *Cronica volgare di Anonimo Fiorentino*, ed. E. Bellondi, *Rer. Ital. Script.*, 27, 2 (Città di Castello, 1915 – Bologna, 1917), pp. 34–35.

[34] D. Herlihy and C. Klapisch-Zuber, *Les Toscans et leurs familles* (Paris, 1978), p. 183.

[35] *Ibid.* pp. 348, 375.

[36] Molho, 'Politics and the ruling class in early Renaissance Florence', p. 407.

Machiavelli and Florentine republican experience   11

Without any status in the constitution, the composition of these meetings, or *pratiche*, was determined by the choice of the Signoria, a choice which in its turn was based on convention. That eminent citizens should be summoned was long-established practice; under the regime established after 1382, the *pratiche* were the most reliable mirror of its aristocratic features. Since the Signoria seldom ignored their advice, they formed an essential, usually decisive, element in the process of decision-making. The new elitist style of politics is borne out by their increasing frequency and also by the shift, noticeable after the turn of the century, from advice being given by speakers on behalf of corporate bodies to being offered independently, or on behalf of other members.[37] The citizens who were regularly summoned to these consultative meetings represented the elite of the *reggimento*; in the early fifteenth century, they amounted to about seventy men.[38] In this inner circle of the regime, Maso degli Albizzi held, from 1393, a dominant position, in which he was succeeded, after his death in 1417, by his son Rinaldo. However, they shared this position with a few other prominent citizens, such as Rinaldo Gianfigliazzi and Niccolò da Uzzano, and their status within the *reggimento*, influential as it was, did not materially detract from its prevalently aristocratic character.

The aristocratic and elitist tendencies in the regime were counterbalanced by the role the legislative councils continued to play in it. Membership of these, and in particular of the council of the People, could be regarded, by way of the assent they had to give to the decisions of the government, as the most democratic feature of political participation within the regime, and hence of republican experience. But for the mass of Florentine citizens there was still another, more restricted sphere in which this experience could make itself felt. Dale and F.W. Kent have recently shown, in a seminal study, the role played in civic life by the *gonfaloni*, that is the sixteen districts into which the city was divided.[39] The *gonfaloni* had their own assemblies which were presided over by the Gonfalonieri di compagnia, who represented their districts in the electoral scrutinies by nominating residents for eligibility to office, and who helped the Commune in the distribution of the tax burden that had been allocated to their districts while the Catasto was not in force, that is, before 1427 and between 1434 and 1458. Meeting periodically in the principal parish church, they elected committees of residents to function as syndics for the tax assessments, and this provided a modicum of civic participation on the local level. Yet here too, appearances can be deceptive: in the district studied by these authors, Lion rosso, over a period of forty-six years about two-thirds of the citizens who attended these assemblies belonged to ten to fifteen families: the 'patrician families who ruled the city also provided leadership in the local world of the *gonfalone*'.[40]

---

[37] G. Brucker, *The Civic World of Early Renaissance Florence* (Princeton, NJ, 1977), pp. 284ff.
[38] *Ibid.* pp. 264ff.   [39] *Neighbours and Neighbourhoods*, pp. 17–19.   [40] *Ibid.*, pp. 77–8.

On an even more general level of republican experience the popular assemblies, or *parlamenti*, of all citizens were, like Marsilius of Padua's *legislator humanus*, considered to possess the ultimate political authority in the republic. However, they were summoned only on rare occasions to approve constitutional reforms or to grant full powers to decide on such reforms to specially elected councils (*balìe*).

Insofar as Florence's political system was based on direct participation, republican experience manifested itself in the membership of the legislative councils and of *pratiche* and in the holding of public office. This participation could, in a generalised fashion, be conceived ideally as representative; 'ogni buono cittadino', writes Palmieri, 'che è posto in magistrato dove rapresenti alcuno principale membro civile, inanzi a ogni altra cosa intenda non essere privata persona, ma rapresentare l'universale persona di tutta la città'.[41] Palmieri here reiterates pleas to set public over private interest, which were particularly frequent and emphatic during the years after 1426, a period which ended with the collapse of the regime by which Florence had been governed since the 1380s. Now the 'ambitio officiorum' became one of the major causes of the formation of two rival factions. Nothing shows better the extent to which the political fabric had been shaken than the creation, in 1429, of the new magistracy of the Conservatori di legge: their function was to exclude unqualified citizens from office-holding and to prosecute citizens who abused their public positions. This led to a flood of denunciations, but did little to restrain the sectarian spirit in the regime and, on the contrary, may have increased it.[42]

Machiavelli, who considered factionalism a deep-rooted disease of the Florentine body politic and a pervasive theme of the city's history, argues in the *Discursus* that one of the causes of the downfall of the aristocratic regime of the early Quattrocento was that 'non si era constituito un timore agli uomini grandi che non potessero far sètte, le quali sono la rovina di uno stato', that is of a regime.[43] But this had been precisely one of the aims the Conservatori di legge were meant to achieve. That the new office proved to be, in this respect, largely counterproductive, may be taken to show that, contrary to Machiavelli's belief, there was no institutional remedy of this problem – as there was none to stop the calumnies, notwithstanding his belief 'che se fusse stato in Firenze ordine d'accusare i cittadini, e punire i calunniatori, non seguivano infiniti scandoli che sono seguiti'.[44] But Machiavelli's overriding critique of that regime was that it

---

[41] *Vita civile*, p. 131.

[42] Cf. D. Kent, *The Rise of the Medici* (Oxford, 1978), pp. 201–2, 244–5; Brucker, *The Civic World*, pp. 490–2.

[43] *Tutte le opere*, p. 24. On the meaning of the word *stato*, see N. Rubinstein, 'Notes on the word *stato* before Machiavelli' in *Florilegium Historiale, Essays presented to Wallace K. Ferguson*, J.G. Rowe and W.H. Stockdale, eds. (Toronto, 1971), pp. 314–26.   [44] *Discorsi*, I, 8; *Tutte le opere*, p. 89.

was a 'repubblica governata da ottimati',[45] a form of government liable to turn
into an oligarchy, which he condemned as corrupt.[46] Whether he gave a
balanced account of it is a different matter. It could be argued that his analysis of
its defects was profoundly influenced by his own experience of the working of a
republican regime in Florence, which was in many respects a very different one
from that of the early fifteenth century.

The new regime had been established after the expulsion in 1494 of the
Medici, under whose dominance Florence had been governed for sixty years.
The Medicean regime, 'lo stato di Cosimo', which replaced the preceding one in
1434, 'pendé', Machiavelli says, 'più verso il principato che verso la repubblica',[47] thus implying, correctly, that however effective and pervasive its
institutional reforms and the dominant influence of Cosimo were, the new
regime had by no means eliminated republican experience. What it did do was
to modify it profoundly. I shall, before concluding this chapter, touch on a few
major changes which that experience underwent after 1434.

The electoral system based on sortition and scrutiny remained in existence,[48]
but scrutinies were held at increasingly long intervals by councils whose
members were expected to be loyal to the regime, and, while the vast majority of
offices continued to be filled as before by the drawing of names from pouches,
the most sensitive and powerful ones, such as the Dieci di Balìa, were
increasingly filled by way of election in Medicean councils. Above all, sortition
was at first temporarily suspended, and then in practice abolished, for the
Signoria. The Signoria was now elected *a mano* – in fact, by a kind of highly
selective sortition – by the *accoppiatori*, who, from having originally been a
technical office in charge of filling the pouches after scrutinies, had become a
key institution of the regime, since they had to see to it that the Signoria, whose
powers were legally undiminished, and who could theoretically overthrow the
regime (as that of September 1434 had done by having Cosimo recalled from
exile) was recruited from responsible supporters of the Medici. The regime
retained, as far as its social structure was concerned, the upward, as well as
downward, mobility of its predecessor. However, that mobility, and hence the
share in political participation, was now increasingly determined from above.
This created a new and expanding network of political patronage. Instead of
pregherie being addressed to members of scrutiny councils, in order to obtain
eligibility to public office, we now find appeals to the leaders of the regime, to
have oneself or one's relative or friend elected to the Signoria, or at least to have
their names drawn from the bags, so that they were, as *veduti*, known to be
eligible, even if they were not appointed to the office (*seduti*). Under Lorenzo,

[45] *Discursus, ibid,* p. 24.
[46] *Discorsi,* I, 2; cf. *Istorie fiorentine,* VII, 3 and 4; *ibid.,* pp. 80, 794.
[47] *Discursus, ibid,* pp. 24–5.
[48] For the following see Rubinstein, *The Government of Florence,* pp. 56ff.

these pleas had reached such proportions that on at least one occasion he asked, in despair, to be left alone: 'de' Priori', he writes in 1485 to his secretary Niccolò Michelozzi, 'non mi advisate cosa nissuna, perché non voglo anchora questo carico. Io harei caro solamente che fusse de' Priori Filippo Carducci . . . Gl'altri faccino chi pare loro [i.e. the *accoppiatori*]. Levatemi le pregherie d'adosso, perché io ho più lettere di Priori che voglono essere, che non sono dì nell'anno . . .'[49] As before, and even more so now, to have been *veduto* or *seduto* for the Tre Maggiori Uffici gave a citizen a privileged position in the *reggimento*, but within that group the men who had been *veduti* or *seduti* for the Gonfalonierate of Justice came to constitute the elite in a regime which was increasingly hierarchical. At the same time, the decline of the political influence and independent authority of the Signoria was bound to change the role it played in the political experience of the members of the *reggimento*. The same applied, to a much greater extent, to the legislative councils of the People and of the Commune, which were replaced, as the chief areas of political participation for the majority of the *reggimento*, first with the Medicean *balie* and, from 1459, with the new council of Cento. Conversely, the consultative *pratiche*, which had been so prominent a feature of the aristocratic regime, gradually declined in importance, together with the Signoria whom they were designed to advise, and were for all practical purposes abolished under Lorenzo, their place being largely taken by informal meetings in the Medici Palace. As Alamanno Rinuccini put it in 1479, in a scathing critique of the regime: while previously 'viri graves de rebus agendis propositis sic in utramque partem libere disputabant, ut facile quid in quaque verum esset inveniretur . . . Nunc . . . cum paucissimos ad maximarum rerum consultationem adhibeant Catones nostri, ea plerunque decerni videmus quae postridie iidem ipsi . . . constituunt'.[50] The Settanta, which was created in the following year as the supreme council of the republic, while reaffirming Lorenzo's dominant position after the end of the war of the Pazzi conspiracy, also responded to such criticisms by being composed of the leading citizens of the regime. Its size bears a striking resemblance to the inner circle of the aristocratic regime of the early Quattrocento, but, unlike the loosely structured elite of the earlier *reggimento*, that of the Medici regime was institutionalised and headed by one man.

If, then, republican experience in terms of participation in government underwent profound changes under the Medici, the same applied to the citizens' perception of republican government itself. The awe with which they had regarded the power and majesty of the Signoria was now shifted to a large extent to the head of the regime who, unlike the Signoria, could dispense a vast amount of political patronage, and who was eulogised by humanists and

[49] Florence, Biblioteca Nazionale, Fondo Ginori Conti, 29, 129,1 (Bagno a Morbo, 17 April).
[50] *Dialogus de libertate*, ed. F. Adorno, in *Atti e Memorie dell' Accademia toscana di scienze e lettere 'La Colombaria'*, 22 (1957), p. 284.

courtiers as a sort of Platonic ruler, although Lorenzo himself insisted on his being a private citizen.[51] There were criticisms in the *reggimento* itself of the controls and restraints the Medici had imposed on the republican constitution, and in particular of the abandonment of the traditional methods of electing the government. These criticisms came to a head under Piero de' Medici in 1465, when elections *a mano* were in fact temporarily abolished. But the same patricians who played a leading role in the abortive republican reaction against Medicean controls would have agreed with Lorenzo that 'a Firenze si può mal vivere senza lo stato', that is without a prominent position in the regime.[52] They would witness, and reluctantly accept, a social mobility which was, owing to the manipulation of the electoral system, less open to free opportunity than it had been in the aristocratic regime at the beginning of the century. As Piero Guicciardini put it at the time of the last Medicean scrutiny, in 1484, 'continovamente viene su gente nuova, onde è necessario, che mettendosi nel reggimento tuttavia de' nuovi, a rincontro se ne cacci de' vecchi; et così si fa'.[53] As for the reaction of the people to the progressive emasculation of their share in the government of the republic, and thus of their republican experience in terms of participation, this is far more difficult to gauge. The violence of the uprising against Lorenzo's son Piero only two and a half years after his death suggests that the regime was not as universally popular as later apologists of it would imply, and the enthusiasm with which the Great Council was embraced after 1494, confirms this impression.

However great the changes which republican experience had undergone under the Medici, the experience still had much in common with that which prevailed in the early fifteenth century. One of these common features was the share in government through eligibility to office being provided by electoral scrutinies, another the elitist concentration of effective participation in decision-making in relatively small groups of citizens; a third the mobility within the social structure of the regime. The constitutional reform of December 1494 changed the forms of political participation, and hence of republican experience, to an extent which can be compared with the establishment of the Priorate in 1282. The 3,000-odd members of the Great Council became a virtually closed class that monopolised office-holding as well as legislation and, through electing to the Signoria and to other high offices, exercised an unprecedented control over the executive.[54] Admission to the Great Council

---

[51] See A. Brown, 'Platonism in fifteenth-century Florence and its contribution to early modern political thought', *The Journal of Modern History*, 58 (1986), 383–413; Rubinstein, *The Government of Florence*, pp. 226–8.

[52] *Ibid.* pp. 140ff.; *Ricordi* of Lorenzo de' Medici, ed. A. Fabroni, *Laurentii Medicis Magnifici vita* (Pisa, 1789), II, p. 42.

[53] Ed. Rubinstein, in *The Government of Florence*, p. 323.

[54] See N. Rubinstein, 'I primi anni del Consiglio Maggiore di Firenze (1494–99)', *Archivio Storico Italiano*, 12 (1954), 103–94, 321–47.

16   *Nicolai Rubinstein*

was based on the group of *veduti* and *seduti* appointed to the Tre Maggiori Uffici
over three generations, although some additional admissions were provided
for. Membership was, for all practical purposes, restricted to the citizens, or
their forbears, who had been made eligible to government under the Medici
regime. This continuity was characteristic of the social structure of politics in
the Florentine republic, which was relatively little affected by the changes in its
regimes.[55] The tensions and conflicts between aristocratic, oligarchical, and
democratic tendencies were now played out within the Great Council in terms
of extending, or restricting, participation in government and decision-making,
and led to changes in the methods by which the Council conducted its elections
and, finally, to the transformation of the Gonfalonierate of Justice into an office
for life.[56]

The Great Council provided the framework for the republican experience of
Machiavelli, who had just reached the minimum age required for office-holding
when the new republican constitution was established. But that experience will
be the subject of another chapter.

[55] See R. Pesman Cooper, 'The Florentine ruling group under the *"governo popolare"*, 1494–1512',
Studies in Medieval and Renaissance History, 7 (1985), 73ff., 92ff.
[56] Cf. Guicciardini, *Storie fiorentine*, pp. 136–7, 178–9, 242.

[23]

Chapter Three

Humanism and Political Thought

RICHARD TUCK

I

For fifteen hundred years, from the fourth century to the nineteenth, schoolchildren in Europe were exposed daily to two books. One was the Bible, and the other was the works of Cicero. The co-existence of these two texts in our culture is a remarkable phenomenon, for on a clear-headed reading of each of them they have very little in common (though their readers' heads have seldom been entirely clear). Cicero and the other comparable Roman authors, such as Seneca, Sallust or Quintilian, remained the writers who instructed the young in correct Latin, the role they have always performed; they thus in a sense controlled access to the Bible itself. And yet the moral messages contained in the pagan writers were not merely superficially at variance with the moral message of the Bible, but were fundamentally in conflict with it. Unravelling this conflict and taming the old, pre-Christian culture was the concern of generations of Christians, and different approaches were popular at different times; the Renaissance itself can be seen as yet another move in this prolonged campaign.

The fundamental challenge to Christian values represented by these authors rested on their implicit or explicit endorsement of the themes of late Hellenistic philosophy, and in particular of both Stoicism and Academic scepticism (the Academy of Plato having by the time of Cicero become a centre of scepticism). In general philosophical matters, indeed, Cicero was avowedly a sceptic, providing in his *Academica* one of the central texts of ancient epistemological scepticism: the sceptics argued that there can be no secure knowledge of the physical world,

43

vitiated as our perceptions are by illusion and uncertainty. But equally avowedly, Cicero did not extend this scepticism fully to moral matters: in this area, the common concern of the Roman writers was the pursuit of a *beata vita*, something conventionally translated as a 'happy life'.

In the Stoic tradition which they all more or less followed, man (like all animals) was taken to be fundamentally self-interested: 'Every living creature loves itself, and from the moment of birth strives to secure its own preservation; because the earliest impulse bestowed on it by nature for its life-long protection is the instinct for self preservation and for the maintenance of itself in the best condition possible to it in accordance with its nature', wrote Cicero in his *De Finibus* (V.24), and similar passages could be cited from his *De Officiis* and from Seneca (particularly his *Epistula Moralis* 121).[1] This view immediately set up a tension in the pursuit of *beatitudo* between what was directly beneficial to oneself – described by the Romans as *utile* – and what was conventionally 'moral' – *honestum*. All the Roman moralists worried about the relationship between these concepts, particularly as they had constantly to look over their shoulders at the Epicureans with their message that all that mattered was what was *utile*. They also had to be concerned about the sceptics, represented above all by the second-century B.C. philosopher Carneades, who denied the possibility of any stable universal principles of morality, but were prepared to accept that men are always motivated by the desire of preserving themselves. There was in fact a strand in Stoicism (far more marked in Seneca than in Cicero) which entirely endorsed this, and which stressed the need for a complete intellectual and emotional detachment in order to preserve oneself psychologically – a condition they termed *apatheia*.

The standard Roman answer to these views was given extensive discussion in Cicero's *De Officiis*: it was that what was *honestum* was what was *utile* to human society. Cicero in fact very often identified the requirements of human society with those of one's own state, eloquently defending the idea that 'there is no social relationship more close, none more dear than that which links each one of us with our country' (I.57). Usually, the requirement of one's *respublica* was that one lived a life defined by the cardinal virtues of prudence, justice, temperance and fortitude, and Cicero in general denied that the interests of the state could lie in any other kind of conduct. 'The occasion cannot arise when it would be to the state's interest to have the wise man do anything immoral' (I.15a). But in certain passages he conceded that political interest could override certain orthodox moral rules; thus promises might be broken for political reasons. 'Suppose that a man

---

1. The quotation from *De Finibus*, like all the quotations from Cicero which I shall cite, is from the Loeb edition.

who has entrusted money to you proposes to make war upon your country, should you restore the deposit? I believe you should not, for you would be acting against the state, which ought to be the dearest thing in the world to you,' (III.95, Loeb translation corrected).

Playing one's appropriate role in the service of the *respublica* was the source of glory among one's fellow-citizens, and all these Roman writers stressed the importance of glory as a goal for action: the public esteem attached to one's conduct was a powerful motive to behave in the way the public good required. Cicero wrote a whole treatise *De Gloria* which was still extant at the beginning of the Renaissance, though it has subsequently disappeared, and the term resonates throughout both his works and those of Seneca. The Roman historians explored the implications of this in the history of Rome: it had been a 'glorious' republic by virtue of its imperial expansion, and both Livy and Sallust inquired into the reasons for this greatness (Sallust, particularly, stressing the importance of free republican institutions).

The idea that your state represented the focus of your moral life might be taken to imply that only political action was truly *honestum* or virtuous. Quintilian was fiercest in arguing this (especially 12.2.7), but neither Cicero nor Seneca were single-mindedly in favour of the life of action. In the *De Officiis* Cicero did say (e.g. at I.153) that political action should be ranked higher than any other virtuous activity, and in particular than the life of *contemplatio* or *cognitio* (that is, philosophy); but even in that work he could say that 'earnest and thoughtful men' might be justified in certain circumstances in retiring to a contemplative life of *otium* or leisure (I.69). Seneca wrote extensively on just this topic, with ambiguous results; in one treatise devoted entirely to it, the *De Otio*, he made the compelling point that both the Epicureans and the Stoics 'consigned us to *otium*' though by different routes: 'Epicurus says, "the wise man will not take part in politics, except upon some special occasion"; Zeno [the founder of Stoicism] says, "the wise man will take part in politics, unless prevented by some special circumstances".'[2]

What these special circumstances were, was rather indeterminate: old age or ill health certainly qualified, but so could disgust at the corrupt state of political life – a circumstance which Seneca enlarged on in his *Epistulae Morales*. Philosophical *otium* could be defended as itself in the interests of the *respublica*, and in *De Otio* and his *Epistulae* Seneca argued both that philosophy could be of greater service to some republics than political action, and that there was a wider human community than the

---

2. *Dialogorum* VIII.3.2; trans. A. Stewart, *Seneca. Minor Dialogues* (1900) p. 242. For an excellent discussion of the whole Roman approach to this issue, see M. T. Griffin, *Seneca. A Philosopher of Politics* (Oxford, 1976) chapter 10.

state whose interests were certainly served more by philosophy than by political action. In a lost work entitled *Hortensius* Cicero himself probably argued the same. Apparently (according to Cicero and Quintilian) the question, 'should a wise man take part in public affairs?' was a regular exercise in the rhetoric schools of the late Republic and the Principate, and it is clear that the Roman orators were not tied by their general theory to any particular answer to this question.

The commitment to serving the republic in some form, even through appropriate *otium*, might also be thought to imply a commitment to what we would call republican forms of government, in which such political participation was widely possible. Cicero is famous for just such a deduction, but again there are qualifications to be made: Seneca in his *De Clementia* provided an eloquent defence of virtuous *princely* rule, arguing that such a prince would be the most effective protector of his state: 'Men love their own safety, when they draw up vast legions in battle on behalf of one man . . . he is the bond which fastens the commonwealth together.'[3]

This Roman moral philosophy was of course avowedly pagan – indeed, virtually atheistical, for though *contemplatio* might include thinking about divine matters, it need not. Cicero in his *De Natura Deorum* gave prominence to a number of sceptical arguments about religious belief, though in the very last sentence he rather lukewarmly sided with Stoic theism against scepticism. But the defence of *contemplatio* in the Roman tradition as something which might serve the *respublica* naturally challenged the primacy of religion, making it something which had in some sense to serve the state. The service which Cicero or Seneca had in mind, no doubt, was of a rather high-minded kind; but there was a persistent belief in antiquity (voiced most eloquently by the Greek historian Polybius) that the Roman governing class used religion in the most cynical way to bolster its own power over the masses.

Accordingly, Roman moral philosophy suffered a direct and often bitter and jeering assault from early Christian Latin writers. Themselves often trained up in the rhetoric schools, the Christians did not merely put an alternative view alongside that of the Romans; they directly disputed the meaning of the key terms which the pagan philosophers used, and sought to give a narrowly Christian connotation to each of them. This process was taken to its extreme in Lactantius's *Divine Institutes* (c. 310–20), which methodically changed the meaning of all the principal classical moral terms such as *honestum*, and which also came close to advocating a kind of cultural revolution, in which the

---

3. *De Clementia* I.4, trans. A. Stewart, *op. cit.* p. 385.

46

pagan texts would be extirpated and replaced by properly Christian ones. 'No one can doubt that false religions will quickly disappear, and philosophy altogether fall, if all shall be persuaded that this alone is religion and the only true wisdom.'[4] This period of attack ended with terms such as *beatitudo* and *contemplatio* having taken on their familiar Christian meaning, and the Roman philosophy having become something which committed Christians found difficult to reproduce sympathetically.

The one element in it which Lactantius at least *could* endorse was the occasional use by the Roman Stoics of the term 'law of nature'. They had used it to refer to the basic natural instincts and capacities of men and animals, though one should not overestimate its centrality within their writings; but Lactantius picked up some passages (now lost) from Book III of Cicero's *De Republica* extolling the importance of the natural law, and remarked 'who that is acquainted with the mystery of God could so significantly relate the law of God, as a man far removed from the knowledge of the truth has set forth that law?'[5] As this illustrates, the *legal* character of the 'law of nature' was crucial to the Christians, for they straightforwardly associated the law of nature with the law of God upon which they relied for their distinctive ethical beliefs.

It is Augustine, above all, whom the Latin West has to thank for preserving the Roman philosophy. If the radical views of men like Lactantius had triumphed, we would no doubt have seen a burning of the books; but Augustine explained to a Christian audience how one might use Roman culture for Christian purposes. He did so in a variety of ways, but the principal one is illustrated by the title of his greatest book, *The City of God*. Within every human *respublica*, he argued, there have been hidden elements of an ancient and much wider *respublica* or *civitas*, the *civitas* of God. This *civitas* is formed of citizens intent on understanding and worshipping God; but once that is allowed for, the standard Roman glorification of the *respublica* can simply be applied to this special *civitas*. It will then be true that our 'state . . . ought to be the dearest thing in the world', though our state will not be the Roman *respublica*. The Roman philosophers can then be read as a kind of general guide to living in cities of all kinds, and the primacy of the Christian religion will be secured by its quasi-political expression in the City of God. (The Greek East, at about the same time, found a different route to the same conclusion: the conversion of Constantine, argued Eusebius of Caesarea, had transformed the Roman Empire itself into

---

4. Lactantius, *Works* trans. A. Roberts and J. Donaldson, *Ante-Nicene Christian Library* (Edinburgh, 1871) p. 302.
5. Ibid., p. 371.

The Impact of Humanism on Western Europe

a *civitas Dei*, and all that the Roman writers said in defence of their state could then be applied directly to the defence of a Christian *civitas*.)

There is a poetic elegance to Augustine's vision, but it rested of course on a *metaphor*. It left the Roman writers unassailed as texts in the Latin schools, and if one was unpersuaded by the metaphor it also left one exposed to the fundamental discrepancy between their views and those of conventional Christianity. There was still plenty of scope for a new account of how these texts fitted into a Christian view of the social world. That new account was provided from the twelfth century onwards by the ethical works of Aristotle: it is, I think, seldom recognised how much Aristotle's ideas (in this area) in fact came as a *relief* to Christians troubled by the Roman writers. Historians have tended to concentrate on the orthodox Christian hostility to Aristotle's works of natural philosophy (which were the works banned at Paris in 1210), and to assume that in some way the hostility would also have been directed towards the ethical works; but read straightforwardly, Aristotle's *Ethics* offers a new and persuasive solution to the dilemma I have outlined. Aristotle argued in the *Ethics* that the virtues necessary to maintain a desirable civic life – the 'moral' virtues in the strict sense, products of 'practical wisdom' – are intrinsically worthwhile, and need no defence in terms of any values beyond themselves; this was an argument very close in spirit to the Roman authors'. But he went on to argue (notably in Books VI and X) that there are other virtues, the 'intellectual' ones, which are also intrinsically worthwhile, and which include above all scientific inquiry and contemplation. Moreover these virtues are *superior* to the moral virtues, in the sense that a life lived in pursuit of philosophic contemplation will be better than one lived in accordance with the needs of one's city, though both ways of life would be intrinsically good. The *Ethics* thus did the Christians' job for them admirably, for it provided an argument which entirely respected, and indeed endorsed, the views of the Romans about civic virtue, but which justified the theologian in believing that the pursuit of religious truth was nevertheless the finest goal of humanity (for religion could effort-lessly be placed into Book X as the highest form of contemplation).

It is, incidentally, interesting that the first bits of the *Ethics* to be translated into Latin (probably early in the twelfth century), the *Ethica vetus*, were Books II and III, which expound the theory of moral virtue – Aristotle seems first to have been treated as an adjunct to the Roman writers, and only at the beginning of the thirteenth century with the appearance of the comprehensive *Ethica nova* did his alternative view become clear.[6] In a sense, the *Ethica vetus* belongs to the so-called

6. B. G. Dod, 'Aristoteles latinus' in *The Cambridge History of Later Medieval Philosophy* ed. N. Kretzmann, A. Kenny and J. Pinborg (Cambridge, 1982) pp. 47–9.

twelfth-century Renaissance, the period in which the study of the
Roman writers reached heights which it was not to scale again for two
hundred years; the coming of the *Ethica nova* symbolises the dominance
for a time of an anti-Roman philosophy.

One of the important implications of the Aristotelian theory was that
the Roman writers should continue to be used as models for the study
of moral virtue, provided that it was continually recognised that they
were *merely* that, and provided that Aristotle was treated as their philosophical master. The subordination of the Romans to the Greek was
symbolised in the widespread organisation of courses in the new
universities which came into being from the twelfth century onwards:
the basic Arts course required students first to master the *Trivium*, in
which grammar, logic and rhetoric were studied, and for which the
Roman texts were basic, and then to proceed to the *Quadrivium*, effectively the study of Aristotle's works. The success and status of the
universities was from the beginning posited upon the supremacy of
science argued for in Aristotle.

But this being acknowledged, the Roman texts could be used as
models in many circumstances where rhetorical effects – persuading
people to action – were crucial; above all, often, in politics. A striking
example of this, and one which is particularly appropriate in a volume
dedicated to Denys Hay, comes from Scotland itself. There in 1320 an
anonymous author drafted the famous 'Declaration of Arbroath', a
letter to the pope in which the independence of Scotland from the
English Crown was asserted. Petrarch himself was only sixteen at the
time, and one would hardly have expected a Scotsman of this date to
have exhibited a Renaissance-like approach to politics; and yet the
Declaration consists in part of a network of paraphrases and direct
quotations from Sallust praising the ideal of 'liberty' – 'that alone,
which no honest man gives up but with life itself.'[7]

What the Declaration of Arbroath illustrates is that in appropriate
circumstances anywhere in medieval Europe, the Roman rhetoric of
republican liberty might be called upon. Such circumstances, however,
arose most often in Northern Italy, for it was there above all that
political entities had self-consciously to defend their 'liberty' from
external attack. From the beginning of the twelfth century, the Italian
cities sought to establish their independence from the jurisdiction of the
emperor, and though at first writers on their behalf exploited the interpretative possibilities of the Roman Law, they also turned automatically
to Cicero or Sallust as models. The best example of this, as Quentin

---

7. G. W. S. Barrow, 'The Idea of Freedom in Late Medieval Scotland', *The Innes
Review*, 30 (1979) p. 28.

Skinner has pointed out[8], is Brunetto Latini who composed his *Li livres dou trésor* in the early 1260s, drawing on a number of earlier works such as the *Oculus pastoralis* of *c.* 1220 and John of Viterbo's *De regimine civitatum* (*c.* 1250). These writers' primary concern was with the methods used by the rulers of the cities to maintain peace and good order within them; they display very little acquaintance with Aristotle, and use the Roman moralists almost exclusively in order to make their point. The *Oculus pastoralis* even asserted that successful rulers will bring *glory* to their city by safeguarding its tranquillity, a clear case of a Roman theme re-appearing in an Italian context, and a noteworthy contrast with the later Christian Aristotelian suspicion towards the ideal of worldly glory.

But writers much more openly conscious of the force of Aristotelian arguments could also utilise the Roman writers in just this way; a notable example of this is Marsiglio of Padua, writing at about the same time as the Declaration of Arbroath was penned, who began his *Defensor pacis* by stating (with a number of direct quotations from both Sallust and Cicero) the evils of discord and the importance of *pax*, before launching off into his examination of the new source of discord unknown in antiquity, the pretensions of the Church. The bulk of the *Defensor pacis* is thoroughly Aristotelian; but the terms in which its theme is first broached are equally thoroughly Roman. Moreover, Marsiglio's conclusion was that, *inter alia*, the peace of the *civitas* will best be secured under a regime where the rulers are *elected* by the people, for such a regime will both secure the common good and will leave the citizen body *free*. Such an argument is of course highly Ciceronian; it is not particularly Aristotelian, though Marsiglio strained every possible passage of Aristotle to try to show that it was.

Because of this conjunction of Aristotle and Rome, it has always proved difficult for historians of political thought satisfactorily to isolate specifically 'humanist' themes. For example, the idea that only what we would call 'republics', of the kind Marsiglio had in mind, could secure a proper and secure life for their citizens – an idea often associated with Quattrocento humanists – was present in many fourteenth-century Italian Aristotelians other than Marsiglio (Ptolemy of Lucca is an obvious example); while a degree of pessimism about republican politics and a stress on the need for a single ruler to master the lawless mob is found in both thirteenth-century Aristotelians and in Petrarch. Nevertheless, the repudiation of Aristotle, or at least of the Aristotelian placing of the Roman writers in a subordinate context,

---

8. Q. R. D. Skinner, 'Ambrogio Lorenzetti: The Artist as Political Philosopher', British Academy Raleigh Lecture on History, forthcoming in *Proceedings of the British Academy*.

which gathered pace during the fifteenth century, did have some
marked effects on political discourse.

II

The emancipation of the Romans from their Greek tutelage is conventionally ascribed to early Quattrocento Florence, and there still seems
little reason to deny this (once due allowance has been made to Petrarch
as a forerunner of the movement). The crucial symbolic move was
made by Leonardo Bruni, who embarked on a daring programme of
translating Aristotle into classical or Ciceronian Latin. Such a
programme carried a clear ideological message: this was because the
existing medieval translations of Aristotle had in many cases quite
deliberately left Aristotle's Greek technical terms in what amounted to
the original. A fine example is the word 'politics' itself, which was of
course by classical Latin standards a peculiar term, supplanting the
study of the *civitas* by the study of the *polis*; but it had the inestimable
advantage of being (for a Latin audience) unconnected with the specifically *civic* themes of the Romans, and therefore applicable to the
concerns of barbarous Northern monarchies. In general, Aristotelianism appeared in the medieval translations as a different and higher
science of ethics and politics, ruling the Romans through greater technical virtuosity.

Bruni disputed this in his new translations, of which the most
famous were the *Ethics* (1416–19) and the *Politics* (1437). As a preface
to his *Ethics* he added an essay explaining what he was doing, and
making explicit his desire to render Aristotle in *Ciceronian* Latin.

> What is commoner among those who write about morals than the
> word *honestum*? For instance the Stoics, of whom Seneca is the
> most important to us, thought that the point of having goods was
> to lead a life of *honestas*; moreover there is frequent debate about
> the difference between what is *utile* and what is *honestum*, while
> we say that the whole life of virtue is contained in *honestum*. But
> for this *honestum* in Greek, the Latin translation of Aristotle always
> has *bonum*, absolutely absurdly . . .[9]

Contemporary Aristotelians were fully aware of what Bruni was up to:
one of them, the Castilian Alonso García de Santa María or Alfonso
de Cartagena (the son of the converted ex-rabbi Solomon ha-Levi)

---

9. A. Birkenmajer, 'Der Streit des Alonzo von Cartagena mit Leonardo Bruni
Aretino' in his *Vermischte Untersuchungen zur Geschichte der Mittelalterlichen Philosophie,
Beiträge zur Geschichte der Philosophie des Mittelalters*, 20 (1922) p. 159.

engaged in a prolonged debate with Bruni over this translation. He pointed out that while Cicero and Seneca were pre-eminent in rhetoric, 'I have never read that they had such a pre-eminence in the scientific distinction of virtues and the subtle investigation of moral instances.'[10]

The debate between García and Bruni is one of the key documents of the Renaissance, for it shows exactly what was at stake in the move by humanists into territory traditionally patrolled by medieval Aristotelians. Bruni's translation made Aristotle a participant in a conversation whose general form was determined by the Roman moralists, and very quickly Aristotle's arguments about, in particular, the superiority of intellectual to practical virtue were assimilated to the Senecan or (partially) Ciceronian arguments for the superiority of philosophical *otium*. The importantly different grounds upon which Aristotle based his case tended to be disregarded. A good example of this, coming from an absolutely representative fifteenth-century Italian humanist, is provided by the Neapolitan Giovanni Pontano's remarks in his *De prudentia* (1499) about the superiority of *contemplatio*. He used both Senecan and Aristotelian phrases, but the overall thrust of his argument was undoubtedly Senecan. (The growth of a kind of humanist Platonism can also be seen in this light – the Platonists used the Roman arguments in support of their own programme of meditative retirement.)

Now the tables had been turned: Aristotelian science was justified as serving the republic, rather than politics being justified according to the principles of Aristotelian science. Once the relationship was put this way round, the humanists were not necessarily opposed to the study even of Aristotle's most technical writings, provided that they were put into an intelligible Roman form; thus Alamanno Rinuccini, the pupil of one of the great humanist translators of Aristotle, Johannes Argyropulos, remarked 'as we are taught by Cicero, the eloquent man we seek cannot be formed without philosophy', and urged his readers to seek a true understanding of Aristotle.[11] One of the greatest Renaissance Aristotelians, Agostino Nifo (1473–1546) ('alter Aristoteles' as he was termed by contemporaries) believed the same: he too produced modern, humanist translations of Aristotle's scientific works, and he defended his scientific activity in the Roman terms of social utility – thus when he wrote a treatise entitled *De iis qui apte posse in solitudine vivere*, the arguments he used in favour of the solitary, contemplative life were far more Senecan than Aristotelian – for example, that the life

---

10. Ibid., p. 173.

11. J. E. Seigel, 'The Teaching of Argyropulos and the Rhetoric of the First Humanists' in *Action and Conviction in Early Modern Europe* ed. T. K. Rabb and J. E. Seigel (Princeton, 1969) p. 252.

of philosophy developed the cardinal virtues in a man just as much as a life of political action.[12]

The lead given by these earlier writers was followed enthusiastically by some humanists in the later sixteenth century, such that a Roman defence of the necessity of philosophical *otium* and even of religion itself came to be a widespread and influential phenomenon. The movement in part took the familiar form of translating Greek philosophy into appropriate Latin: thus in 1535 Mario Nizzoli of Brescia published his *Observationes in Ciceronem* with an appendix listing the chief technical philosophical terms which were un-Ciceronian and suggesting alternatives, while in 1540 Joachim Péron of the university of Paris began a programme of translating the central works of Greek philosophy into absolutely pure Ciceronian Latin. Plato's *Timaeus* appeared in 1540, and two years later Péron started a series of translations of Aristotle which eventually covered all the major texts. He added to his translation an essay, *De optimo genere interpretandi*, which set out the guiding principles of this ultra-Ciceronian school. A few years later the great Cicero scholar Denys Lambin published improved versions of Péron's translation of the *Ethics* and *Politics*.

Such writers and translators sought to allow themselves to be Aristotelians by putting Aristotle into a Ciceronian style, and despite the frequent oddity of their approach others did the same with their Christianity. Two early examples of this were a couple of papal secretaries, Pietro Bembo and Jacopo Sadoleto (both of whom ended as cardinals), about whose devotion to Cicero many anecdotes circulated. It was said that Bembo advised Sadoleto not to read St Paul's letters, as they would corrupt his prose style. Certainly Bembo's history of his native Venice contained many strained examples of Ciceronian diction – the Turks became the Thracians, and the nunneries, temples of vestal virgins. Even in his official correspondence, Bembo referred to the Virgin Mary as *Dea ipsa*. Nevertheless, though Bembo's locutions look pagan to us, and were (as we shall see presently) fiercely attacked by some contemporaries, there is no doubt about his piety, nor about that of Sadoleto (who despite Bembo's alleged advice wrote commentaries on St Paul). Sadoleto was the more philosophically inclined of the pair, writing Ciceronian dialogues *De gloria* and *De laudibus philosophiae* – the latter an attempt to reconstruct the argument of Cicero's *Hortensius* in defence of philosophical *otium* and religious contemplation as a means of serving the republic.[13] Péron is a particularly good example of the same phenomenon from a slightly later period, for alongside his Ciceronianising of Aristotle he published in 1549 a Ciceronian volume entitled

---

12. The treatise is to be found most accessibly in his *Opuscula* (Paris, 1645).
13. *De laudibus philosophiae libri duo* (Lyons, 1538) pp. 201 ff.

Topicorum theologicorum libri duo, quorum in posteriore de iis omnibus agitur, quas hodie ab haereticis defenduntur.

Péron's pressing Cicero into the service of the Roman Catholic Church against the 'modern heretics' was to be prophetic, for as the Jesuit Order organised itself with precisely this intention, it too based itself upon Cicero. At the Roman College of the Society, from its foundation in 1551 onwards, Jesuits worked on a universal plan of education in the schools and colleges which the Society was founding, a programme which culminated in the famous *Ratio Studiorum* of 1599. In all the early drafts of the *Ratio* as well as in the final definitive version, the imitation of Cicero is the principal exercise in the study of the humanities. This corresponded to a widespread adherence among the early Jesuits to the principles of Italian Ciceronianism; so that as early as 1548 one of the first Jesuits, Peter Canisius, could congratulate his fellow Jesuit Adrian Adriani on coming into the Ciceronian camp – 'I am glad to see you have changed your style, brother Adrian, and I hope to see you pre-eminent among the Ciceronians'. Peter John Perpinian, author of a treatise on education in 1565 which was very influential among his fellows, also proclaimed his former error in not being a dedicated Ciceronian.

The imitation of Cicero in the sixteenth-century Society reached its climax, perhaps, in the work of Julius Negrone of Genoa, a teacher in some of the Jesuit colleges of Italy, who published a collection of his lectures in 1608. In them he praised Cicero, 'whom our nascent Society embraced as its own and proposed to us as a model, tacitly warning all not to depart from this master of the spoken and written word.' He even proposed to erect at Padua a votive tablet inscribed M. T. CICERONI M. F. HUMANAE FACUNDIAE PRINCIPI QUAEST. AEDI. PRAET. COS. PROCOS. IMPERATORI P. P. STUDIOSI ELOQ.[14] The fact that Péron and the others had made Aristotle legible for a Ciceronian was a great service to these Jesuits, for it was a combination of Cicero and Aristotle upon which they founded their intellectual machine, and the compatibility between the two authors was a crucial postulate.

Not only Catholics adhered in this way to the insights of the 'pure' Ciceronians. Among Lutherans, there also grew up a tradition of studying Cicero and Aristotle together in this way. This was something which they inherited from the man who pre-eminently inspired the first generation of Lutheran educators, Philip Melanchthon. Melanchthon was the first true humanist to become a Lutheran, and his writings are full of praise for both Cicero and Aristotle, and attempts to reconcile them, not with Catholic, but with Evangelical Christianity. The fore-

---

14. A. P. Farrell, *The Jesuit Code of Liberal Education* (Milwaukee, 1938) pp. 177–80.

word to his edition of Cicero's *De Officiis* (1534) contains the essentials
of his view:

> as it is right for Christians to develop and foster a civil society,
> so this doctrine of civic morals and duties must be studied. For
> it is not godly to live like the Cyclops, without a legal order or
> an ethical doctrine, or the other frameworks to our life which
> classical literature provides. Those who abuse philosophy, are at
> war not only with human nature, but also and more importantly
> with the glory of the Gospel; for it teaches that men should be
> constrained by civic discipline . . .[15]

The *De Officiis*, according to Melanchthon, contained the 'definitions
of virtue' and many suggestions about the moral life, all expressed in
a 'popular' oratorical form which men of common sense could follow;
Aristotle, on the other hand, should only be studied by educated men,
though what he put forward (Melanchthon stressed) was 'not an illib-
eral doctrine', that is, it was compatible with Cicero.

We must be clear about the implications of this position for all these
writers' Christianity. In effect, they were claiming two things. The first
was that Christianity was *speculatively true* – that is, that philosophical
enquiry could establish the truth of the Christian religion (as earlier
Aristotelians had also believed). But the second was that this philosophical and religious enquiry should only be undertaken for *practical*
reasons: knowledge of these truths, and the pursuit of this mode of life,
was to be justified by their utility to the *respublica*. Faith in Christianity
brought social peace and a rightly-ordered way of living. (This was to
be precisely the argument which Jesuit writers such as Possevino were
to use against Machiavelli.) The problem about holding these two
beliefs is of course that they are inconsistent: for if Christianity is true,
then it will also be true that religion is not to be justified by its social
utility. These Christian Ciceronians were unwilling to abandon either
claim; but their position represented precisely the problem which the
Christian Fathers had been troubled by.

III

It was made doubly difficult by the fact that, throughout the period,
other Ciceronians were quite prepared to assert absolutely plainly, for
the first time since antiquity, the straightforward superiority of *action*
over contemplation, and in particular the superiority of a life of political
activity devoted to the common good of a city. The very first statement

---

15. P. Melanchthon, *Werke* III (Gütersloh, 1961) p. 86.

of this case may have been by Pier Paolo Vergerio in a letter purporting to be from Cicero to Petrarch, composed in 1394, but it was put most clearly and influentially by Bruni himself in his famous *Laudatio Florentinae Urbis* of 1403–4. It was there associated with praise for the republican regime of Florence (especially its wide popular base – *governo largo* as it was termed in the vernacular), praise which fourteenth-century proto-humanists had been reluctant to lavish (preferring the rule of virtuous princes), but which as we have seen did have familiar precedents among Italian writers. The distinctiveness of the *Laudatio* lay not so much in its specific constitutional or political views, as in the role which it unequivocally allocated to politics – the role of, in effect, the master-activity of mankind, displacing scientific or religious contemplation from that position.[16]

But a thousand years of effort had gone into taming the Roman moralists on behalf of Christianity, and any suggestion that their cage should now be opened was met with immediate suspicion and hostility. For example, Cino Rinuccini's *Invettiva* against alleged slanderers of Dante, Petrarch and Boccaccio (*c.* 1400) included an attack on contemporary humanists for their paganising tendencies – 'as to the philosophy of things divine, they say that Varro wrote many books on the worship of the pagan gods in a very elegant style, and they praise him most excessively, preferring him in secret to the doctors of our faith . . .'[17] Similar accusations were made (as we shall see presently) against Bembo and his contemporaries: Ciceronianism of the Quattrocento kind always walked along a knife-edge, and might at any moment become an object of suspicion.

That this was entirely justified, is illustrated by the purest and most extreme Ciceronian of them all: Machiavelli. Machiavelli was deeply committed to exploring the Roman ideas on politics, and it can be said that he saw more clearly than any other Renaissance writer the real implications of Cicero's central belief: that the survival and advancement of one's republic had to take precedence over all things, and that the conventional virtues might not in fact always be adequately instrumental to that end. But as Quentin Skinner has stressed, Machiavelli continued to work with many of the same values of the more conventional Ciceronian humanists (for example *glory* was as important to him as it was to any other Italian humanist), and even some of the standard virtues are allowed a place in his writings.[18]

This has always been recognised as basically true for Machiavelli's

---

16. For Vergerio and Bruni, see H. Baron, *The Crisis of the Early Italian Renaissance* (Princeton, 1966) pp. 128, 191–212.

17. Ibid., p. 294.

18. See particularly his *Machiavelli*, Pastmasters (Oxford, 1981).

Discourses on the first ten books of Livy, which he wrote (probably) between 1515 and 1519, and in which he extolled the merit of republican institutions and civic feeling as guarantors of a city's liberty. It is true that even in that work, there are elements which are very different from the compromised Ciceronianism of the Quattrocento; in particular, Machiavelli argues that the two means whereby republican *virtù* can best be sustained in a citizenry are, first, a constitution which encourages competition and conflict between the social groups within a city and, second, the appropriate use of religion to foster civic *virtù*. The first of these arguments has some claim to be Machiavelli's most original idea, for it was very unlike any earlier humanist theory (earlier writers, back to the proto-humanists of the thirteenth century, had stressed the need for civic *concord*). But in a way it was a logical extension of the fundamental ideas of the Roman moralists: they had seen the ideal citizen as one who fought for his own freedom and the freedom of his city, and Machiavelli realised that a political structure which obliged citizens to stand up for their own concerns as well as those of their city could foster just this sort of fighting spirit.

The second of the two arguments was what horrified contemporaries most (though the first did disturb other humanists). And yet Machiavelli here was very plainly speaking the Roman language in an untroubled fashion; his originality lay in being prepared to say clearly what the Roman texts implied, but no earlier humanists had dared to articulate so clearly. Seen in this light, Machiavelli's remarks on religion were precisely the kind of threat which Ciceronianism had always posed, and which the Augustinian or Aristotelian strategies had been designed to counter; its re-emergence in the second decade of the sixteenth century drew attention to the need for a new strategy (though percipient contemporaries had divined this need long before they read the *Discourses*, which were not published until 1531).

Superficially, Machiavelli's *Prince* (which he probably wrote in 1513) seems much more of a challenge to Roman moralism. Seneca, who defended the government of princes, did so on the grounds that a *virtuous* prince would secure the liberty of the *respublica*, but the virtues such a prince should exhibit were such things as clemency and liberality (in addition to the more familiar cardinal virtues appropriate to all men). Cicero was not impressed by princely government, and in his works we can find in general only a defence of true republicanism. But Machiavelli in the *Prince* apparently argued for the merits of princely rule while simultaneously denying that the virtues such a prince should exhibit were the conventional ones – instead, he should if necessary be both devious and cruel. But again, there are qualifications to be made to this view. As we saw earlier, Cicero himself in the *De Officiis* did countenance (for example) breaking one's promise in the interests of one's country, though he also asserted that immoral conduct would in practice never further the interests of the *respublica*. If one's *fundamental* value is the survival of one's city, and of one's life as a free citizen within it (which was undoubtedly the fundamental Roman value), and if as a matter of contingent fact a single ruler can secure those goals more effectively in some circumstances than a free republic, and can secure them by conventionally immoral conduct, then the natural implication of the Roman view is that the prince is to be applauded.

The important qualification here is, 'one's life as a free citizen': there is no point (on the Roman view) in one's city being free from outside domination, if the citizens are made the slaves of a single ruler from within the city. A striking aspect of the *Prince* is that Machiavelli effectively endorses this view: he does so in a famous and difficult chapter of the *Prince*, 'Of those who have attained the position of prince by villainy' (Chapter VIII). Two 'villains' are condemned for their brutality in seizing power – Agathocles, tyrant of Syracuse, and Oliverotto Prince of Fermo. The puzzle about this chapter (on some readings of the *Prince*) is that Agathocles at least was spectacularly successful in establishing the independence and indeed the imperial dominance of Syracuse within Sicily, and retained power until his natural death. Why is he a 'villainous' prince, without *virtù*, as Machiavelli expressly says, when other princes such as Cesare Borgia are praised for their effective brutality? The answer seems to be that the route which both Agathocles and Oliverotto took to power was the mass slaughter of the senatorial class in their respective cities – in other words, they in effect closed down politics within their cities, and removed the vital public and political dimension from the lives of their citizens. Machiavelli clearly disapproved of this, holding that even under a prince there must be genuine *citizenship* (a belief manifested also in his insistence that a *virtuoso* prince would rule through a citizen army and not through mercenaries).

In some ways (surprisingly, from our point of view), *The Prince* may have been seen as somewhat less shocking than the *Discourses* by contemporaries, largely because Machiavelli did not spell out in the earlier work his instrumental view of religion. It is interesting in this context that Agostino Nifo in 1523 unblushingly printed in a work entitled *De regnandi peritia* (and dedicated to Charles V) large chunks of the *Prince*, without apparently thinking that they were anything other than a reasonable example of Ciceronian argument. This was in fact the first appearance of the *Prince* in print – it did not appear in full and under Machiavelli's name until 1532.

IV

Nevertheless, Machiavelli can stand for our purposes as an example of
the dangers (from a Christian standpoint) of over-faithful Ciceronianism. The most effective strategy from within humanism to counter
these dangers came from the North, in the form of a simple but
profoundly influential idea by Desiderius Erasmus – who fully deserved
on this account his astonishing reputation among the humanists of
Northern Europe. In 1528 Erasmus published a dialogue entitled *Ciceronianus*, in which he launched an explicit attack on the Italian
Ciceronians and on one of their recent French followers, accusing them
of endangering Christianity itself by their use of purely Ciceronian
concepts. 'If ever you have visited the libraries of the Ciceronians at
Rome, recall, I pray, whether you saw an image of the crucifix or of
the sacred Trinity or of the apostles. You will find them all full of the
monuments of heathenism . . . We do not dare to profess paganism.
We plead as an excuse Ciceronianism.'[19]

But the important feature of Erasmus's argument was that he did
not attack Cicero himself, and that he remained loyal to the essential
values of the 'old' humanism. Cicero was to remain as the key exemplar whose ideas were to be followed accurately and fully; but as
Erasmus repeatedly said, Cicero was himself a man of his own time
and the modern Ciceronian must also be a man of *his* own time.

> What effrontery then would he have who should insist that we
> speak, on all occasions, as Cicero did? Let him bring back to us
> first that Rome which was; let him give us the Senate and the
> senate house, the Conscript Fathers, the Knights, the people in
> tribes and centuries; . . . Wherever I turn I see things changed,
> I stand on another stage, I see another theatre, yes, another world.
> What shall I do? I, a Christian, must speak to Christians about
> the Christian religion. In order that I may speak fittingly, shall
> I imagine that I am living in the age of Cicero and speaking in
> a crowded senate in the presence of the senators on the Tarpeian
> Rock?[20]

But the general approach of Cicero was still possible The true modern
Ciceronian is

---

19. I. Scott, *Controversies over the Imitation of Cicero* (New York, 1910) p. 75. I prefer
this translation to the more recent one in Erasmus, *Collected Works* VI ed. A. H. T. Levi
(Toronto, 1986) p. 396, though the ancillary scholarship of the later translation is of
course much more up-to-date.

20. Ibid., (Scott) p. 61, (Levi) p. 383.

he who busies himself with the same zeal in the field of the Christian religion as Cicero did in that of secular things; who drinks
in the psalms and prophets with that feeling which Cicero drank
in the books of the poets; who desires to find out the decrees of
the apostles, the rites of the church, the rise, progress and decline
of the Christian Republic with such vigilance as Cicero laboured
to learn thoroughly the rights and laws of the provinces, towns,
and allies of the Roman City . . .[21]

This was the heart of Erasmus's case, and it was (as he repeatedly
insisted) an appeal for a more radical and authentic Ciceronianism than
that of the apparently radical Italians. A proper attention had to be paid
to the governing ideas of Cicero, rather than merely to his language;
and in particular, the fact had to be stressed that Cicero's commitment
had been to understanding and working within and for the norms of
his own society. In our quite different society, the same approach
would lead to different results; above all, a fundamental feature of our
society is its *Christianity*. Anyone who lived in this way in the modern
world was to be praised, and Erasmus even argued that Aquinas and
Scotus, 'though they boast themselves neither eloquent nor Ciceronians, are more Ciceronian than those who demand to be considered not
only Ciceronians but even Ciceros.'[22] The scholastics had after all been
wholly involved in the religion and law of their own time. The Italian
Ciceronians' enterprise of expressing in Ciceronian Latin the central
themes of ancient philosophy thus became a pointless or misleading
enterprise, for a modern Ciceronian might well want to *distance* himself
from (say) Aristotle (as indeed the historic Cicero had done), rather
than assimilate him.

Again, we have to be clear about the implications of *this* strategy.
Whereas the earlier Ciceronians had treated religion as a branch of philosophic contemplation, and had then utilised the only Roman argument
which was available for engaging in such a practice, the Erasmian
Ciceronians treated religion as an aspect of their practical, political life:
Christianity was part of the public life of modern states, and the Bible
was a governing text for man's actual life, comparable (as Erasmus said)
to the law-books of the Romans. Clearly, this strategy put much less
weight on the *truth* of the Christian religion than the earlier one had
done, and Erasmus and his followers, when pressed, would concede
their closeness to ancient scepticism – the wise man will follow the laws
and customs of his country without enquiring into their objective

---

21. Ibid., (Scott) p. 79, (Levi) p. 400.
22. Ibid., (Scott) p. 65, (Levi) p. 387.

Humanism and Political Thought

truth.[23] It also opened up the possibility that the sceptical critique of Aristotle and the other dogmatic ancient philosophers might be repeated in the modern world.

Erasmus's followers in the battles of the 1530s and 1540s against the contemporary Ciceronians perceived this implication very clearly, and in the name of Cicero or of true eloquence they proclaimed the need for a modern and open-minded approach to ancient philosophy. In particular, an open and extensively-argued anti-Aristotelianism became a central feature of their work, going well beyond the stray barbs which many earlier humanists had launched at Aristotle. One of the clearest examples of this process is provided by Erasmus's close associate in the 1520s and 1530s, Juan Luis Vives, the Spanish humanist who (through his long period of residence in England and the Netherlands) became very influential on northern humanism. In 1532 Vives published his major work, *De disciplinis*, in which the maleficent influence of Aristotle in every branch of human knowledge is systematically exposed; he followed it up five years later with an equally explicit *Censura de Aristotelis operibus*. But the most important figure in this tradition was the Frenchman Pierre de la Ramée (Peter Ramus), who worked away at Paris during the 1540s and 1550s to counter the influence of the humanist Ciceronians and Aristotelians there, and whose name later became a byword for aggressive Anti-Aristotelianism. Ramus proudly proclaimed himself an heir to Erasmus, and wrote a *Ciceronianus* of his own; he was also attacked by contemporaries as a new kind of sceptic.[24]

It is against the background of this Erasmian idea that we must read the only work of Renaissance political theory which rivals Machiavelli's works in importance – Thomas More's *Utopia* of 1516. More had been a supporter of Erasmus in his various ideological struggles since 1499, and like his mentor he had also been a close student of Augustine – no doubt because Augustine provided the most plausible non-Aristotelian strategy for coping with the disconcerting implications of the Roman moralists. Much (though, it must be acknowledged, not all) of *Utopia* makes sense in the context of Erasmus's 'modern' reading of Cicero. The book begins with a dialogue set against the background of agrarian crisis and a demand for land reform in contemporary England (a background identical in many ways to the background of Cicero's political career in the twilight of the Roman republic, a republic brought low, Cicero believed, by the socially disruptive demagoguery of men like the Gracchi). The dialogue is focused on the question of *counsel* – should

---

23. See R. H. Popkin, *The History of Scepticism from Erasmus to Spinoza* (Berkeley, 1979) pp. 5–6.

24. Ibid., p. 29. Ramus's *Ciceronianus* was published at Paris in 1557; for a discussion of it, see I. Scott, *op. cit.* pp. 100ff.

a wise man enter politics, and in particular the service of a Northern monarch with its necessary compromises and subterfuges? One of the participants in the dialogue, the imaginary character Raphael Hythloday, argues that he should not, unless the institution of private property which had led to the agrarian crisis is dismantled and replaced by a new social order. More, speaking in his own person as a young man, responds that this is misguided: it is important to keep the present show on the road. 'Don't spoil the entire play just because you happen to think of another one that you'd enjoy rather more.'[25]

More's sentiments here clearly echo those of Cicero, whose primary moral commitment had been to doing just that, and who had criticised Cato for behaving 'as if he lived in the Republic of Plato, rather than in the dregs of the state of Romulus' (*Letters to Atticus* II.1, Loeb pp. 108/9). Cicero had also condemned what he took to be the Platonic notion of communism, remarking about one of the schemes for land reform in the late republic that 'it favoured an equal distribution of property; and what more ruinous policy than that could be conceived? For the chief purpose in the establishment of constitutional state and municipal governments was that individual property rights might be secured' (*De Officiis* II.73). Hythloday is depicted as responding to this Ciceronianism by describing the state of the Utopians in which private property had been abolished, and all worked well. That the Utopians are obtrusively anti-Ciceronian is indeed characteristically hinted at in a passage where Hythloday lists the books he took with him to Utopia – all were in Greek, as 'I didn't think there was anything in Latin that they'd like very much'.[26]

Not only are the Utopians anti-Ciceronian, they are also in effect anti-Christian. Though Hythloday told them about Christ, and though they responded enthusiastically to his account, More goes to some pains to deprive Hythloday of the two things which contemporary Christians (including most definitely More himself) took to be vital for true Christianity – the Bible and the apostolic succession of the priesthood. Hythloday's list of books does not include the Bible, and no priest accompanied him on his voyage.[27] That Utopia is fundamentally at variance with More's idea of religion and the Church is revealed by a

---

25. *Utopia* trans. P. Turner (Harmondsworth, 1965) p. 63. For the most recent study of *Utopia*, which also stresses the Ciceronian aspect, and to which I am greatly indebted (though differing from it in some respects), see Q. Skinner, 'Sir Thomas More's *Utopia* and the language of Renaissance humanism' in A. Pagden ed., *The Languages of Political Theory in Early-Modern Europe* (Cambridge, 1987) pp. 123–58.

26. Ibid., p. 99.

27. Ibid., pp. 100, 118.

marginal note in one of his later works, his polemic against Luther.[28]

So *Utopia* depicts an ideal anti-Ciceronian republic, as Erasmus at least understood Ciceronianism – one in which there are no difficult practical choices to be made, and in which the reality of the modern world (including pre-eminently its Christianity) is kept firmly at bay. The interpretative problem about the book is that *imaginatively* the weight of the work is on the Utopians' side – the minute and concrete description of their state is what has always fascinated readers. Yet how can this be squared with the known position of the Northern humanists on these issues, and with the position which More himself espouses in the dialogue on counsel earlier in the book? We can either suppose that More's imagination here outran himself, or we can conclude that the covert message of *Utopia* is a conservative one – we should not introduce measures such as land reform piecemeal, for we would need a wholly restructured society for them to work at all, and such a radical reconstruction is out of the question in the real world which as true Ciceronians we must inhabit. Which route we take is a question which has occupied all readers of More, and it would, I think, be folly to suppose that it is possible to resolve the question in any wholly persuasive way.

By the middle of the sixteenth century, Ciceronianism (whether of the Italian or the Northern sort) had become the generally accepted language of moral and political discourse, at least outside the circles of technically-minded theologians. The Spanish Empire in particular rested its claims to European domination on the rhetoric of Cicero – either in its more conventional form, as when Sebastian Fox Morcillo portrayed the King of Spain as a Senecan prince in his *De regni, regisque institutione* of 1556, or in a more Machiavellian form, as in the case of Stephen Gardiner's advice to the government of Philip and Mary in England.[29] But by the end of the century the dominance of Cicero was over, and he had been replaced so comprehensively that one is entitled, I think, to talk of a wholly new kind of humanism which differed almost as much from the humanism of the earlier Renaissance as that humanism had differed from Aristotelianism.

V

The central role in this development was played by *Tacitus*. Though a Roman, Tacitus had never been included in the group of writers

---

28. *Responsio ad Lutherum* in More, *Collected Works* V ed. J. M. Headley (New Haven, 1969) pp. 118–19.

29. P. S. Donaldson, *A Machiavellian Treatise by Stephen Gardiner* (Cambridge, 1975).

studied continuously throughout the Middle Ages; his style was utterly unCiceronian, and his sentiments equally alien to the earlier writers, for he viewed politics and ethics with a sceptical detachment, and treated the struggle for liberty as doomed. Princes, on his account, were wholly untrustworthy tyrants, and republican activists noble but foolish. It is thus not surprising that Ciceronian humanists were repelled by him, and it is noteworthy that even Machiavelli was uninterested in his views. One writer in Machiavelli's Florence did express admiration for Tacitus; this was Guicciardini, whose own vision of Italian politics came close to Tacitus's. But Guicciardini's lead was not to be followed until the 1560s, when a group of Italian exiles at the court of Catherine de' Medici in France began to study Tacitus closely, and to link him with Guicciardini and (to an extent) with Machiavelli as key writers for the modern world, who would have no truck with illusory moralities.[30] An associate of this group even attempted the unpromising task of defending the 1572 St Bartholomew's Day Massacre from moral condemnation, employing a clipped Tacitean prose to do so.[31] By the 1590s the study of Tacitus had virtually replaced that of Cicero as the central activity of the humanist moralist, trying to make sense of European politics in an age of confessional war and imperial aggrandisement. Beleagured Ciceronians (particularly among the Jesuits or their sympathisers) bewailed this development; as one of them, an English Catholic exile named Edward Weston, wrote in 1602, the Tacitist 'neoterici'

> entirely despise the graces of Cicero: like heavily-armoured soldiers (as they themselves say), they set no store by the fragrant scents or sweetly flowing smoothness of cultivated language. They would rather march forward with mail and shield, covered from head to foot with steel, and shattering men's ears with their terrifying expressions: in fact they glory in what they acknowledge is an *armoured* style[32].

Weston saw exactly the moral significance of Tacitism as a prose-style: it was the language of the battle-field, carrying military values with it. When he turned to the substance of his attack on the movement, he argued exactly what one would have expected, attacking Machiavelli (and, interestingly, quoting Sallust against him) and remarking that if

---

30. See G. Cardascia, 'Un Lecteur de Machiavel à la Cour de France: Jacopo Corbinelli', *Humanisme et Renaissance* 5 (1938) pp. 446–52; A. Momigliano, 'The First Political Commentary on Tacitus', *Journal of Roman Studies*, 37 (1949) pp. 91–101.

31. [Guy de Pibrac], *Ornatissimi cuisdam viri, De rebus Gallicis* (Paris, 1573).

32. *De triplici hominis officio* (Antwerp, 1602) II sig.d1.

the *politici* were to be accepted, 'then the consequence would be that these politicians could not properly institute a commonwealth, unless they were to set a cunning prince over a pack of fools.'[33] This defence both of orthodox moral values *and* of a more widespread participation by the populace in political and moral life is absolutely characteristic of the liberal Ciceronian humanist's response to Tacitism.

But Tacitism was not to be stopped by such criticisms, and its influence (interwoven with that of scepticism and of a new kind of Stoicism) was pervasive in the late sixteenth and early seventeenth centuries. It is partly against its background, moreover, that we can best read the great seventeenth-century works of political theory such as Grotius's *De Iure Belli ac Pacis* or even Hobbes's *Leviathan*. Tracing its influence is not part of my present purpose; the conventional view that these seventeenth-century writers lie outside the Renaissance proper has, I think, a common-sense justification precisely in the shift from Cicero to Tacitus as the great ancient moralist. What we intuitively think of as Renaissance humanism is not Tacitism, but an exploration of the implications for modern moral and political thought of the true philosophy of the Golden Age of Rome.

33. Ibid., II p. 182.

[24]

The *Principe* and the puzzle of the date of chapter 26

†HANS BARON

[When Hans Baron died on November 26, 1988, among his papers was a completed book manuscript on the *poeta theologus* and two uncompleted book manuscripts, one an intellectual biography of Leonardo Bruni and the other a detailed investigation of the authorship of the *De regimine principum* attributed to Thomas Aquinas and Ptolemy of Lucca. He had intended to complete the Bruni monograph after finishing work on his two-volume *In Search of Florentine Civic Humanism: Essays on the Transition from Medieval to Modern Thought* (Princeton, N.J.: Princeton University Press, 1988), a collection of eighteen essays, some drastically revised and others new, but his last illness prevented him from taking up the study again. Of the shorter manuscripts only the following article remained in completed form.

Hans Baron was unsurpassed in his awareness that the composition of a text has its own history, which must be seen in the context of the biography of its author and the nature of contemporary events. On the basis of this insight he transformed the study of Italian humanism in his lifetime by creating a new interpretative framework for its evolution, the potentialities of which remain today far from exhausted. The present essay, with its analysis of the problematic relationship of chapter 26 of Machiavelli's *Principe* to the other twenty-five chapters of the work, demonstrates this methodology at its best. As always in Baron's work, the philological investigation is merely the means used to solve issues of major historical dimensions. In this case, at stake is the consistency of Machiavelli's conception of the greatest work of political thought in the Renaissance.

Originally read as a paper at the Newberry Library in 1968 and given in a longer version at Villa I Tatti in 1972, this article forms a companion to his essays "Machiavelli the Republican Citizen and Author of the *Prince*" in volume 2 of *In Search of Florentine Civic Humanism*, originally published in 1961, and "The *Principe* and the Puzzle of the Date of the *Discorsi*," published in 1956. While both of these

Journal of Medieval and Renaissance Studies 21:1, Spring 1991. Copyright © 1991 by Duke University Press. CCC 0047-2573/91/$1.50

earlier writings focus on the chronological relationship of the *Discourses* to the *Prince*, the argument relies in part on the sequence in which portions of the latter work itself were written.

Anthony Cashman of Duke University is responsible for annotating the article. He entitled it "The *Principe* and the Puzzle of the Date of Chapter 26" to parallel Baron's title for the 1956 article dealing with the dating of the *Discorsi*. The additions made in 1972 to the original paper are added in the form of an appendix. The original of this work and the remaining papers of Hans Baron have generously been donated to Duke University by his family.—Ronald Witt, Duke University]

I

In my studies of Machiavelli, I have long been wrestling with an important problem, and a few weeks ago I felt I had some bright ideas about it. Or rather, to tell the truth, I think I have solved it.

At this point, I know well, no one in his senses would wish to read a paper about the matter; it would be wiser to let it rest for a while and then return to it and view it from a distance. But I cannot bring myself to let pass the opportunity to put my problem before an audience like this.

It would be such a good thing, if you should feel that I have found an intelligent and convincing answer. On the other hand, if you should think that my answer is not convincing because I have overlooked something essential, it would be even more useful for me to have your opinion.

The problem, though important, is not very original; it is one of the oldest problems of Machiavellian scholarship. But as long as it has not been solved, it will always be with us.

The problem is whether the *Prince* is a homogeneous work; whether the last, climactic chapter was part of it from the beginning, and whether the meaning of the book may therefore be judged in the light of its epilogue. The *Prince* itself—that is, chapters 1–25—is a statement of cold pragmatism, a prescription for the successful building of power; it is not concerned with the values in whose service (or for whose destruction) power is acquired by mild or brutal means. In complete contrast to this, chapter 26 directs an exhortation to some member of the House of Medici to employ the teachings of the book for the furtherance of an ideal: Italy's deliverance from the tyrannical rule of "barbarian" foreign rulers.[1]

Here, suddenly, the fervent request is made that the *casa Medici*[2] should provide leadership in expelling the alien invaders by founding, in accord with the rules established in the book, a strong new state modeled on the one built a decade earlier by Cesare Borgia as a power nucleus on the borders of north and central Italy—a historic enterprise which only misfortune had prevented from becoming the starting point for Italy's liberation.[3] At present, this suggests a second *occasione* was being offered for an Italian uprising against the foreign masters.[4] "What Italian would refuse obedience" to Italy's "redeemer"? "Who would withhold allegiance? This barbarous domination stinks in the nostrils of everyone."[5] The chapter concludes with some passionate verses from the canzone *Italia mia* by Petrarch:

> Virtù contro a furore
> prenderà l'arme; e fia el combatter corto:
> che l'antico valore
> nelli italici cor non è ancor morto.

It was in the light of these claims of the "Exhortatio" that the *Prince* was for the first time defended and morally vindicated during the early and middle nineteenth century. As Ranke put it, the Machiavellian doctrines were meant to be a prescription for a poison appropriate and necessary to the special case of a pitifully divided country under foreign domination and predominance—a drastic requirement for creating a locus of power for national unification.[6]

1. Niccolò Machiavelli, *Il Principe e Discorsi sopra la prima deca di Tito Livio*, ed. Sergio Bertelli (Milan: Feltrinelli, 1960; reprint 1977), 10:-5. All subsequent references to the *Prince* will be from this edition.

2. *Principe*, 102: "Né ci si vede al presente in quale lei possa più sperare che nella illustre vostra"; 103: "E non è maraviglia se alcuno de' prenominati Italiani non ha possuto fare quello che si può sperare facci la illustre casa vostra"; 104: "Volendo dunque la illustre casa vostra seguitare quelli eccelenti uomini che redimirno le provincie loro"; 105: "Pigli, adunque, la illustre casa vostra questo assunto."

3. *Principe*, 102: "E benché fino a qui si sia monstro qualche spiraculo in qualcuno da potere iudicare che fussi ordinato da Dio per sua redenzione; tamen si è visto da poi come, nel più alto corso delle azioni sue, è stato dalla fortuna reprobato."

4. *Principe*, 101: "se ci era materia che dessi occasione a uno prudente e virtuoso"; 105: "Non si debba, adunque, lasciare passare questa occasione, acciò che l'Italia, dopo tanto tempo, vegga uno suo redentore."

5. Principe, 105: "[Q]uali populi li negherebbano la obedienzia? . . . [Q]uale Italiano li negherebbe l'ossequio? A ognuno puzza questo barbaro dominio."

6. Leopold von Ranke, *Zur Kritik neuerer Geschichtschreiber*, Sämtliche Werke, 34 (Leipzig: Duncker und Humblot, 1874), 171-72.

I think one need not admit that this is the only obvious way to interpret the work as long as chapter 26 is accepted as an original part, the
culmination of Machiavelli's conception of the *Prince*. The nineteenth-
century historians, in their reaction to the *Prince*, may have thought
too narrowly of political unification on a national scale in the nineteenth-century sense. Machiavelli does not really talk of unification,
but only of the liberation of the peninsula from the foreign invaders,
and nowhere does he expressly say that any of his rules should be
followed merely in the service of Italian liberation. Nevertheless, if
Machiavelli had in mind a prince who would use his new state to rouse
Italy to struggle for independence from its foreign rulers, the picture
of Machiavelli as understood by nineteenth-century nationalism would
forever retain a large measure of truth. And, indeed, the national-
Italian interpretation did not entirely disappear when its heyday was
over, but was essentially preserved by such distinguished historians as
Federico Chabod in Italy, Friedrich Meinecke in Germany, and Lord
Acton and L. A. Burd in the commentary accompanying the edition
of the *Prince* that for generations was chiefly used in the English-
speaking countries.[7]

In recent years, of course, there has been a tendency to minimize the
significance for Machiavelli of the ideal of Italy's independence because
political students have become more aware that his Italianism contributed little to his basic ideas of politics and the state. It has been
called an emotional element that scarcely entered into his theory. This
is true in general, but in the special case of the importance of chapter
26 for the interpretation of the *Prince* it begs the question. For if
chapter 26 was conceived and composed together with the preceding
chapters, one motive for the writing of the *Prince* would have been
Machiavelli's concern for Italy and for the means needed to bring
about Italian independence.

It is certainly making things too easy if one points to the rhetorical
form of the epilogue and reasons that since chapter 26 is "rhetorical,"
it need not express Machiavelli's genuine convictions, that it may have
no other purpose but to serve as a piece of brilliance to gain favor with
the potential patron, either Giuliano or Lorenzo de' Medici. There is

7. Federico Chabod, "Del *Principe* di Niccolò Machiavelli," in *Scritti su Machia-*
velli (Turin: Giulio Einaudi, 1964), 64–67; Friedrich Meinecke, *Die Idee der Staatsräson*
in der neueren Geschichte, 3d ed. (Munich and Berlin: R. Oldenbourg, 1929), 51–52;
and Niccolò Machiavelli, *Il Principe*, ed. L. Arthur Burd (Oxford: Clarendon Press,
1891), 1, 22–30.

a simple answer to this kind of reasoning; other occasions were to come when Machiavelli would think or dream of Italy's liberation from foreign domination, especially during the latter part of his life. One of these occasions, in particular, produced a very striking counterpart to chapter 26.

In 1526, the year before Machiavelli's death, when most of the states of central and northern Italy, together with France, were for a moment allied in the Holy League of Cognac to expel Spain, the strongest power of that period, from the peninsula, Machiavelli sent Guicciardini, then the papal governor of the Romagna province, a solemn letter saying that another rare *occasione* had come for the deliverance of Italy from foreign rule. He implored Guicciardini not to miss this opportunity, which would never be repeated. "God has brought things back to such a state that the Pope is in time for action, if now it is not let go. You know how many opportunities have been lost; do not lose this one . . . : Free Italy from long anxiety; root out these frightful beasts, which beyond appearance and voice have nothing human."[8] These sentences, so similar in tone to chapter 26 of the *Prince*, are found in a private letter to a friend in which no striving after literary glamour can have falsified Machiavelli's genuine feelings, and where no personal benefit from a patron can have been expected.

Chapter 26 of the *Prince*, therefore, is not an isolated piece, but rather an expression of a tendency that came to the fore more than once in Machiavelli's life; it cannot be reduced to a merely decorative, rhetorical element, but must be taken seriously when it appears in the *Prince*. If we suppose this fervid nationalism to be a foreign element in the *Prince*, and if we cannot believe that the cool, ruthless pragmatism of the work could have developed in the service of such emotional national sentiments, then we must prove that chapter 26 was not part of the original *Prince*; that it was composed at another time, under conditions that provoked Machiavelli's feelings for Italy; in short, that the epilogue was subsequently added. This is a critical and even philological problem, and it must be posed and answered in strictly critical and philological terms.

8. Niccolò Machiavelli, *Lettere*, ed. Franco Gaeta (Milan: Feltrinelli, 1961), 465, May 17, 1526: "Hora Iddio ha ricondotto le cose in termine, che il papa è a tempo a tenerlo, quando questo tempo non si lasci perdere. Voi sapete quante occasioni si sono perdute: non perdete questa . . . : Libertate diuturna cura Italiam, extirpate has immanes belluas, quae hominis, praeter faciem et vocem, nihil habent."

II

But before doing this, one must be sure that the answer to an elementary question that comes to mind will not nip our argument in the bud: if the last chapter was not present in the original draft of the *Prince*, could the preceding chapter have at any time been the conclusion of the work?

Chapter 25 seeks to prove that, however great Fortuna's might, man's success is half his own doing. Boldness and daring, therefore, are the better counsel, especially since Fortuna, "like a woman, is always a friend to the young, because they are less cautious, fiercer, and master her with greater audacity."[9] In Lord Acton's and Burd's nineteenth-century edition, the reader is warned that it is difficult to believe that the *Prince* could ever have ended with this sentence.[10] From an authoritative Italian edition, the work of a scholar who suspects that chapter 26 was added, one learns that the quoted passage could conclude the *Prince* quite "degnamente."[11] So our personal impressions, when unaided by specific observations, are of little use.

There is some merit in Acton's and Burd's hesitation, at least at first sight. For surely Machiavelli would have been able to conclude more effectively a political treatise on which his every future hope depended. But this conclusion is only valid if circumstances did not compel the author to break off his work prematurely and content himself with a makeshift termination. This, however, may have been precisely what happened. After Machiavelli, on December 10, 1513, had told his friend and helper in Rome, Francesco Vettori, that he would like to dedicate his newly written treatise to Giuliano de' Medici but was still "fattening" and polishing his work, we learn from Vettori on January 18 that he liked the chapters sent by Machiavelli in the meantime, but, *before he had seen the rest*, could not make up his mind whether or not to show the work to Giuliano.[12]

9. *Principe*, 99: "[I]udico potere esser vero che la fortuna sia arbitra della metà delle azioni nostre"; 101: "Io iudico bene questo, che sia meglio essere impetuoso che respettivo, perché la fortuna è donna; et è necessario, volendola tenere sotto, batterla et urtarla. E si vede che la si lascia più vincere da questi, che da quelli che freddamente procedono. E però sempre, come donna, è amica de' giovani, perché sono meno respettivi, più feroci, e con più audacia la comandano."

10. Burd, 365–66, n. 19.

11. *Principe*, 10.

12. Vettori's letter, December 24, 1513, acknowledges receipt of part of the manuscript; *Lettere*, 312: "Chome voi m' havete mandato quello tractato, vi dirò se mi pare

Why should Machiavelli have sent Vettori an incomplete manu-script? He knew that Vettori could neither judge nor act for him as long as he was only in possession of a fragment. It is very improbable, therefore, that the reason he sent an incomplete copy was that his scribe worked slowly, and that the remainder followed a few days later. It is much more likely that an unfinished text was sent (a month after the first announcement) because the author even in January was still un-decided how to wind up his work most effectively with a view to a planned dedication.

Was, then, the twenty-sixth chapter added soon after Vettori's letter of January 18? The circumstances of Machiavelli's life during the sub-sequent weeks and months speak strongly against such a possibility. Only two weeks later, on February 4, Machiavelli wrote the first of those letters of despair characteristic of much of his correspondence in 1514 and 1515, in which he no longer shows an interest in the great events of ancient and modern history (as he says), but only talks of his "amori."[13] By May, he made desperate plans to go to Rome and live for a while in Vettori's house in order to find out whether he could convince the Medici of his political usefulness. By June, he had heard from Vettori that such a visit in his house could compromise Vettori, and Machiavelli, by now without hope, toyed with the idea of relieving his family of the burden of his presence by leaving Florence and taking refuge in an obscure position as a schoolteacher or a quartermaster in a mercenary company.[14]

Is it at all possible that the political excitement of the unusual occa-sione to which chapter 26 refers coincided with this period of abandon-ment of all political interest and passion? One cannot try to reconstruct Machiavelli's life after January 18 without conjecturing that Vettori's letter of that date was quickly followed (before February 4) by the dismaying news that there was no hope that Machiavelli would be admitted to the good graces of the Medici.

---

vegnate a presentarlo." His response, January 18, 1514, is found, ibid., 319: "Ho visto e' capitoli dell' opera vostra, e mi piacciono oltre modo; ma se non ho il resto, non voglio fare judicio resoluto."

13. *Lettere*, 320–23, February 4, 1514. Also representative of this type of corre-spondence ibid., 346–47, August 3, 1514.

14. *Lettere*, 343, June 10, 1514: "Ma egli è impossibile che io possa stare molto cosí, perché io mi logoro, et veggo, quando Iddio non mi si mostri piú favorevole, che sarò un dí forzato ad uscirmi di casa, et pormi per ripetitore o cancelliere di un con-nestabole, quando io non possa altro, o ficcarmi in qualche terra deserta ad insegnare leggere a' fanciulli, et lasciar qua la mia brigata, che facci conto che io sia morto."

90   *Journal of Medieval and Renaissance Studies*, 21 (1991) 1

This does not mean that we should try to make this the basis of an attempt to demonstrate that chapter 26 did not yet exist in early 1514; there are safer grounds on which to build this case. But the facts just related do imply the distinct possibility that the concluding section of Machiavelli's work had reached only the twenty-fifth chapter and was interrupted during the second half of January at the casual point represented by the last sentence of that chapter.

III

I am not the only scholar who suspects that chapter 26 could not have been written under the political conditions prevailing in 1513 and early 1514. A number of years ago, the editor of the Italian (Feltrinelli) edition of the *Prince*, Sergio Bertelli, conjectured that the epilogue was composed together with the final dedication of the work to Lorenzo de' Medici, which occurred between September 1515 and September 1516. The reason for Bertelli's hypothesis was that chapter 26 (the epilogue) repeatedly speaks of "vostra casa illustre," that is, takes the dedication of the work to a member of the Medici family for granted. Bertelli adds that the notion that the epilogue is of late origin and was not composed in 1513 is confirmed by the observation (already made by Chabod and other Italian scholars) that the plan of Pope Leo to found a new state for a *nepote* in north-central Italy (the presupposition of chapter 26) had not become known to Machiavelli before January 1515.[15] Felix Gilbert not long ago accepted Bertelli's thesis because, he said, "it seemed to solve every difficulty we have encountered in the discussion of the chronological problem of the last chapter."[16]

These arguments look persuasive but boomerang when examined more closely. Since Machiavelli had thought of employment by the *casa Medici* as early as 1513 and had intended to dedicate the *Prince* to one or another member of the family, there is no reason why he should not have addressed himself to "vostra casa illustre" at a time when he was still uncertain about the specific member of the family to whom he would eventually dedicate the work.

15. *Principe*, 109–10.
16. Felix Gilbert, *Machiavelli e il suo tempo* (Bologna: Il Mulino, 1977), 340. "E sono convinto che l'ultimo capitolo del *Principe* era una storia di secondo pensiero: talche ho notato con grande interesse l'ipotesi di Bertelli . . . che quest'ultimo capitolo, l'*Exhortatio*, si connette strettamente alla *Dedicatio* e deve pertanto essere datato tra il settembre 1515 e il settembre 1516. Questa tesi mi sembra risolvere tutte le difficoltà in discussione."

Baron · *The* Principe 91

But there is more to this observation: it actually cuts the other way. The fact that the epilogue expects the fulfillment of its hopes—a new state after Cesare Borgia's example, and the expulsion from Italy of the foreign powers—not from an individual unnamed addressee, but from the *casa Medici* collectively, excludes the possibility that the epilogue was composed when the work was dedicated to Lorenzo. Machiavelli writes: "There is nothing now Italy can hope for, but that your illustrious house may place itself at the head of this redemption"; "If your illustrious house, therefore, wishes to follow those great men who redeemed their countries"; "May your illustrious house therefore assume this task!"[17] Would this not be the strangest way ever tried to gain the favor of a proud and imperious man?

But besides implying that the dedication to Lorenzo could not yet have been made when these sentences were written because Machiavelli's phrasing would have been offensive to Lorenzo, this phrasing also provides a positive criterion regarding the historical situation in which the epilogue was written. The turning to the *casa Medici* implies that, at the moment of his writing, Machiavelli regarded the head of the Medici family, Pope Leo, as the decisive leader for possible political action. Had such a situation prevailed at any previous time? This brings us back to Bertelli's second argument: that Machiavelli had first learned about the details of Leo's plans for north-central Italy—especially the procurement for Giuliano of a state composed of the former territories of Parma, Piacenza, Modena, and Reggio—in January 1515.[18]

Machiavelli's correspondence indeed shows that he learned about the plans of Leo echoed in the epilogue only in January 1515,[19] but the indispensable next step must be to ask whether the political situation known to Machiavelli in January 1515 continued to exist to the time when the *Prince* was dedicated to Lorenzo. It is the fatal weakness of

17. *Principe*, 102: "Né ci si vede al presente in quale lei possa piú sperare che nella illustre casa vostra"; 104: "Volendo dunque la illustre casa vostra seguitare quelli excellenti uomini che redimirono le provincie loro"; 105: "Pigli, adunque, la illustre casa vostra questo assunto."

18. *Principe*, 109–10.

19. *Lettere*, 374, January 31, 1515: "Pagolo vostro è suto qui con il Magnifico, et intra qualche ragionamento ha havuto meco delle speranze sue, mi ha detto come sua Signoria gli ha promesso farlo governatore di una di quelle terre, delle quali prende hora la signoria. Et havendo io inteso, non da Pagolo, ma da una commune voce, che egli diventa signore di Parma, Piacenza, Modena et Reggio, mi pare de questa signoria fosse bella et forte, et da poterla in ogni evento tenere, quando nel principio la fosse governata bene."

Bertelli's conjectures that this question is never raised. The epilogue, as we have seen, contends that a unique *occasione* was offering itself for the liberation of Italy through the erection of a state fashioned on the model of Cesare Borgia's enterprise, which had offered the first *occasione* for Italy's liberation. But it is clear that nothing of the kind remained possible after August 1515. In mid-September, the French victory over the Swiss at Marignano changed the Italian picture for a long time to come. This victory put a definite end to the two aims that had determined Leo's policies during the preceding twelve months: the building of a state for Giuliano north of the papal territories and the prevention of the capture of Milan by the French king.

From the day of Marignano, Milan was again in French hands, and this subjection of large parts of northern Italy also sounded the death knell to Leo's aspirations for a *nepote*-state. Already a few weeks after Marignano, in October, he was forced to return Parma and Piacenza to the new lord of Milan, the king of France; although he managed to delay the restitution of Modena and Reggio to the Duke of Ferrara, an ally of France, this was only a temporary holding action since France insisted on this restitution as a part of her new system of dominance over northern Italy. In December, papal acquiescence in the position of France in Italy was demonstrated before the world in a solemn reconciliation between Leo and Francis at Bologna. In subsequent treaties, Leo even gave up his veto against possible investiture of the French king with Naples, and Francis on his part promised to support the position of the House of Medici in Florence and Tuscany. Henceforth the policy of the *casa Medici* was to replace the ruling Duke of Urbino, a *nepote* left by Julius II, with Lorenzo, and the struggle between the two *nepoti* for this papal fief—a mere feud of private interests, in the eyes of all Italy—remained the center of Italian affairs throughout the first half of 1516, ending with the expulsion of Francesco della Rovere from Urbino in June and the papal appointment of Lorenzo as the new duke of Urbino on August 18, 1516.

Against this picture of the year following Marignano and the events of September 1515, is it not absolutely impossible that Machiavelli could at that time have claimed that a unique *occasione* was being offered for a new strong state in north-central Italy and for the liberation of Italy from foreign invaders under Medici leadership? Surely, the twenty-sixth chapter must have been written in advance of the changes in the peninsula that began in September 1515.

Baron · *The* Principe   93

There is, moreover, a textual detail in the chapter that suggests the same chronological conclusion. We are told in chapter 26 that twenty years had passed since Italy had become involved in endless wars ("in tante guerre fatte ne' passati venti anni").[20] It was quite usual for Machiavelli and his contemporaries to count the time of misery of war-devastated Italy from the destructions wrought by the invading army of Charles VIII, which hit Tuscany first in the early autumn of 1494. Normally Machiavelli was scrupulously exact in indicating the time between the moment of his writing and certain past events he mentions. Most probably, therefore, if twenty-one or more years had passed since the autumn of 1494, he would have said so. If written half a year (or more) earlier than September 1515, his count of twenty years would be right.

IV

It should now be clear why Bertelli's attempt to reject the customary attribution of chapter 26 to 1513 has boomeranged: instead of proving that the chapter was added at the time of the dedication to Lorenzo after September 1515, the shortcomings of this thesis allow us to recognize that the opposite is the case, that chapter 26 cannot have been composed as late as autumn 1515, to say nothing of a later date. But if it was composed at an earlier time, when, exactly, was it written?

In our reexamination of the recent queries, we have come to compare the propositions of chapter 26 with the concrete situations that may have formed the historical background. This method of correlating thought and events has proved successful in studying the chronology and genesis of many writings of the Italian Renaissance. In the case of chapter 26, the certainty that the conditions of Italy after September 1515 were not compatible with some of the ideas of the chapter leads inevitably to the question whether, instead, some situation between the drafting of the *Prince* in the autumn of 1513 and the political changes of the autumn of 1515 might prove appropriate to the content of that chapter.

The changes in Leo's Italian policies during these two years are as important for the answer as are Machiavelli's reactions to them. From the beginning of his pontificate in March 1513, Leo was assumed to be striving for princely rank for Giuliano, but until late in 1514 the

20. *Principe*, 104.

objective (at least as far as known in public) had not been a new state for a *nepote* in or near the Church territories, but a Medici dynasty on the throne of Naples. For instance, early in 1514 Spain protested against alleged papal aspirations for Naples, and in May and June a papal-French alliance was in the making with the aim that Giuliano would become king of Naples. In return, a French expedition to Italy would have a free hand in overthrowing the duke of Milan.

Not until the latter part of 1514, when French domination became too threatening a possibility, did Leo begin to veer away from France and to reshape his policy. By September he signed a secret understanding with the emperor and Spain to prevent France from conquering Milan. But since France's military superiority, if it invaded, would be formidable, Leo still wavered, delaying the final decision for the rest of the year. Only at the beginning of January 1515, when Louis was succeeded by the young, active Francis I and when a French invasion could be expected soon, did Leo come out with an elaborate plan for Italian resistance that also satisfied the dynastic aspirations of the Medici.

Giuliano, who was appointed *capitano generale* of the Church on January 10, was to be the ruler of a large, composite state: the territories of Parma and Piacenza were to be taken from former Milanese possessions, Modena and Reggio from those of the Este of Ferrara. On this basis, under papal leadership, with the reluctant consent of the duke of Milan, the preliminaries were signed in early February 1515 for a broad coalition that was to prevent France from conquering Milan. This was an international alliance that relied for military power on the Swiss, Spain, and the emperor; but from the Italian point of view its meaning was to forestall a new foreign invasion that would have meant the permanent takeover of Milan and Lombardy by France. It was a totally new and startling event because it gathered nearly all northwestern Italian states into one defensive league. It would include the Milanese duchy as well as the republic of Genoa, the papal territories, and, indirectly through the *casa Medici*, Florence and the newly designed north-central state.

It is impossible to approach these first months of the year 1515 without being struck by the fact that every basic trait of chapter 26 of the *Prince* has a counterpart in this period, whereas none had yet existed during the preceding two years.

It is true that the political designs of January–February 1515 were carried out only in the watered-down fashion typical of cinquecento diplomacy. Genoa, long accustomed to French rule, soon returned to the French side. The duke of Milan resented the concession of Parma and Piacenza to the state being formed by the pope. The papal troops, at the critical time when the French army crossed the Alps during the summer, moved only to defend Parma and Piacenza, though Leo did share substantially in the financial burden for the Swiss and Spanish resistance to the French. Finally, in September, as we have seen, the French victory at Marignano put an end to all of Leo's endeavors to save Milan from foreign rule, as well as to his plans to create a new power center in northern Italy. But the weakening of the league and these frustrations occurred gradually during the spring and summer; during the first quarter of 1515, there had been a definite period when it could appear that an unheard-of *occasione* was offering itself for both the building of a strong new central state and the collaboration of many Italian states against a new threat of invasion.

v

Does the available information allow us to trace in any detail whether Machiavelli was familiar with these changes in the Italian situation and was impressed by them?

There is nothing in Machiavelli's correspondence before the beginning of 1515 or in the first twenty-five chapters of the *Prince* to suggest that he regarded the founding of a strong *nepote*-state by the pope as a demand of the hour or that he dreamed of Italian military self-reliance under Medici leadership. On the contrary, some views expressed in the *Prince* and in the letters of the years 1513 and 1514 practically exclude such ideas. What are we to think when reading in the eleventh chapter of the *Prince* that Pope Julius II "merits greater praise [than Alexander VI] because he did everything to increase the power of the Church and not that of any private person"?[21] Obviously this means that despite his praise for Cesare Borgia's policy in founding a state, Machiavelli, when writing his *Prince*, did not yet think that Alexander's and Cesare's actions should inspire Leo to create a new *nepote*-state. At the end of the same chapter the author makes it clear that he does not expect—or even wish—the new pope and head of the *casa Medici* to become the "redeemer" of Italy by force of arms. Leo's predecessors had already

21. *Principe*, 52: "[E] con tanta piú sua laude, quanto fece ogni cosa per accrescere la Chiesia e non alcuno privato."

made the pontificate very powerful through arms, we are told; Leo therefore would be able to build on these foundations and, one might hope, would add to the veneration and greatness of the papacy "through his kindness and countless other virtues."[22]

In Machiavelli's letters one finds reason why he could not yet dream of Italy's rescue by the strength of her own arms. As he explained to Vettori just before starting work on the *Prince* in August 1513, it was not invasion by the armies of the great Western monarchies that threatened Italy most; he was at that time more deeply impressed by the presumed historical parallel between the infantry of the Swiss and the Roman legions—two nations in arms. The Swiss, he believed, were going to be the modern Romans, and although they might not conquer all Italy, they threatened to become the arbiters of the Italian states unless the immense power of the French monarchy should stop them.[23] If the weak duke of Milan remained on his throne, Machiavelli told Vettori, Lombardy would become the sure victim of the Swiss. "As to a union of the Italians, you make me laugh," he wrote; concord in Italy is impossible, and the arms of Italy are no match to those of the Swiss. One can, therefore, only wish that France will conquer Lombardy. "And if France does not suffice, I see no other resource and am now ready to weep with you over our ruin and servitude, which, if it does not come today or tomorrow, will come in our time."[24] As long as these conditions prevailed, the salvation of Italy depended upon the dominance of France over Lombardy as the only possible dike against

22. *Principe*, 52–53: "Ha trovato adunque la Santità di papa Leone questo pontificato potentissimo: il quale si spera, se quelli lo feciono con le arme, questo con la bontà e infinite altre sue virtú lo farà grandissimo e venerado."

23. On August 10, 1513 (*Lettere*, 280), Machiavelli wrote to Vettori, "Et Pellegrino Lorini mi disse già che quando si vennono con Beumonte a Pisa, spesso havieno ragionamento seco della virtú della militia loro, et che l'era simile a quella de' Romani, et quale era la cagione che non potessino fare un dí come e' Romani." See also his letter of August 26 (ibid., 296) to Vettori: "Io non credo già che faccino uno imperio come e' Romani, ma io credo bene che possino diventare arbitri di Italia per la propinquintà et per li disordini et cattive conditioni nostre."

24. In the letter of August 10, 1513 (*Lettere*, 279), Machiavelli had previously told Vettori, "Vedesi nella pace vostra un altro pericolo gravissimo per la Italia, il quale è che ogni volta chi si lascerà in Milano un duca debole, la Lombardia non fia di quel duca, ma de' Svizeri." Machiavelli continued, "Quanto alla unione delli altri Italiani, voi mi fate ridere: primo, perché non ci fia mai unione veruna a fare ben veruno; et se pure e' fussino uniti e' capi, e' non sono per bastare, sí per non ci essere armi che vogliono un quattrino dagli Spagnuoli in fuora, et quelli per esser pochi non possono esser bastanti; secondo, per non esser le code unite co' capi." *Lettere*, 296, August 26, 1513: "Et se Francia non basta, io non ci veggo altro rimediare, et voglio cominciare hora a piagnere con voi la rovina et servitú nostra, le quale, se non sarà né oggi ne domani, sarà a' nostri dí."

Baron · *The* Principe 97

the Swiss flood—and not, as in the vision of chapter 26, upon the rise of a new nucleus of Italian power in north-central Italy and upon the reemergence of Italian *virtù*, under Medici leadership, against the foreign invaders.

The views expressed in the letter to Vettori remained characteristic of Machiavelli for quite a while after the composition of the *Prince*. Twice during 1514, in April and December, Vettori succeeded in rousing him from his despair and political lethargy;[25] each time Machiavelli reiterated that only the presence of France in northern Italy could stop the Swiss from overrunning the peninsula. It was the Swiss, he said, who threatened to put an end to the "libertas Italiae,"[26] and when Vettori in December requested from him a political memorandum that might be shown to the pope,[27] he still insisted that the best course for Italian policy was to concede Milan to the French king and to rely on the arms of France.[28]

These views of Machiavelli during 1513 and 1514, coming on top of our preceding observation on Leo's early aspiration to acquire Naples while conceding French rule in Milan, virtually exclude that time through December 1514 as a period in which the basic ideas of chapter 26 could have been conceived. And since, at the other end of the period in question, the time after the battle of Marignano in September 1515 must also be excluded, the critical eight months preceding Marignano remain the only possibility for the composition of chapter 26. At their beginning, in January 1515, Leo was trying to build up a strong *nepote*-state on the northern borders of the Church territories and was attempting to prevent a new foreign occupation of Milan; Machiavelli, on the other hand, as we know from his correspondence, had by late January become familiar with the changed direction of Leo's Italian policy, at least as far as the planned fusion of Parma, Piacenza, Modena, and Reggio into a state for Giuliano was concerned.[29] What is still missing is an idea of the concrete circumstances that could have caused Machiavelli at that moment to take his manuscript of the *Prince* out of its drawer and add to it a new chapter.

25. Machiavelli's reply, April 16, 1514, is found in *Lettere*, 332–35; those of December 10 and 20, 1514, ibid., 351–61 and 363–67.

26. He wrote in the letter of December 10, 1514 (*Lettere*, 356), "Come e' ne hanno preso uno [i.e., a state], actum erit de libertate Italia."

27. *Lettere*, 348–49, December 3, 1514.

28. *Lettere*, 351–61.

29. *Lettere*, 374, January 31, 1515: "Et havendo io inteso, non da Pagolo, ma da una commune voce, che egli diventa signore di Parma, Piacenza, Modena et Reggio."

VI

In a measure, the fact that Giuliano was appointed *capitano generale* of the Church on January 10, 1515, and from then on could be regarded the pretender to a *nepote*-state that recalled the aspirations of Cesare Borgia, should have been reason enough for Machiavelli to resume work on the *Prince* and revive the old plan to dedicate it to Giuliano. But Machiavelli had by then been living for a whole year (since early 1514) in complete separation from political life, except for the exchange of a few letters with Vettori. Thus the hypothesis that early in 1515 he added to the *Prince* a section full of passionate involvement in the issues of the day would lack a measure of final credibility unless we had good reason to think that in or around January 1515 the conditions of his life changed: that for a while, before he relapsed into gloom and lethargy until the autumn of 1515, he was once more in contact with political events and was encouraged to hope that Giuliano's attention might yet be drawn to his work. This is precisely what we can reconstruct from a few interrelated pieces of information.

According to Machiavelli's letter to Vettori of January 31, 1515, he had had an interview in Florence with Paolo Vettori, Francesco Vettori's brother, and had learned that Giuliano intended to appoint Paolo Vettori governor over one of the territories that were to make up Giuliano's composite state.[30] Machiavelli immediately jumped into a conversation with Paolo in the true spirit of the *Prince*. He believed, he told Paolo, summarizing some ideas of the *Prince*, that in founding a healthy and permanent state from the fusion of a few formerly unrelated territories, all future unity and strength depended on centralized administration from the start. If a new prince could not immediately take residence in his new state (and Giuliano would obviously stay chiefly in Rome), he ought to appoint one governor responsible for the entire state; such had been the policy of Cesare Borgia, who (Machiavelli adds) should always be imitated. Needless to say, this theory pleased Paolo Vettori. Evidently, Machiavelli was making shrewd use of an incomparable opportunity to advance both a political project near to his heart and his personal hopes to become a political

---

30. *Lettere*, 374, January 31, 1515: "Pagolo vostro è suto qui con il Magnifico, et intra qualche ragionamento ha havuto meco delle speranze sue, mi ha detto come sua signoria gli ha promesso farlo governatore di una di quelle terre, delle quali prende hora la signoria."

Baron · *The* Principe   99

counselor once more. He told Paolo Vettori—and repeated in writing to Francesco Vettori—that if Paolo were given such a comprehensive governorship over the new state, "this would be a step in making Paolo known . . . to all Italy; . . . he could acquire reputation for himself, for you [Francesco Vettori], and for your family. I spoke of it with Paolo; it pleased him, and he will consider making use of it. I have thought it well to write you [Francesco in Rome] about it, so that you will know our discussion and, wherever it is necessary, can pave the way for this thing."[31] This means that Machiavelli was hoping that Francesco Vettori would later recommend his (Machiavelli's) propositions to Giuliano (for only Giuliano could decide about Paolo Vettori's post and, possibly, Machiavelli's employment), while the same plans were being suggested to Giuliano during his stay in Florence by Paolo Vettori.

Even if Machiavelli was too sanguine in these expectations, there did exist in January 1515 a situation in which he tried to arouse Giuliano's attention, to present him with practical advice taken from the *Prince*, and to point out a parallel between Giuliano's situation and the model set by Cesare Borgia—the point made in chapter 26.

As a matter of fact, Machiavelli's hopes did not spring only from his imagination. We know this from a document written in Rome only two weeks after Machiavelli's letter to Francesco. On February 14, the papal secretary Ardinghelli sent a letter to Giuliano, still in Florence, because word had been received in Rome that Giuliano had taken Machiavelli into his service. Ardinghelli was writing at the request of the second-ranking member of the *casa Medici*, Cardinal Giulio (later Pope Clement VII). The cardinal would not believe the rumor; perhaps it was (he said) an invention of Paolo Vettori's. "But since there has been word of it from Florence, write Giuliano on my behalf that I advise him to have nothing to do with Niccolò."[32] Thus, during the fateful months of January–February 1515, there was at least a rumor that Machiavelli would be employed by Giuliano, a rumor sufficiently

---

31. *Lettere*, 375, January 31, 1515: "[S]arebbe questo un grado da farsi conoscere . . . a tutta Italia; . . . potrebbe dare reputazione a sé, a voi et alla casa sua. Io ne parlai seco; piacqueli, et penserà di aiutarsene. Mi è parso scriverne a voi, acciò sappiate i ragionamenti nostri, et possiate, dove bisognasse, lastricare la via a questa cosa."

32. *Archivio Storico Italiano*, ser. 3, vol. 19 (1874): 231: "El Cardinale de' Medici mi domandò hieri molto strectamente, se io sapevo che V. Excellentia havessi preso a' servitii sui Nicolò Machiavelli; et respondendoli io, che non havevo notitia nè lo credevo, Sua Signoria reverendissima mi disse queste formali parole: Anchora io non lo credo. . . . Questa debbe essere inventione di Paulo Vectori. . . . Scriveteli per mia parte, che io lo conforto ad non si impacciare con Nicolò."

100 *Journal of Medieval and Renaissance Studies*, 21 (1991) 1

widespread to reach Rome, even though eventually no effort could change "la sua dolorosa sorte."

We are not told when—or whether at all—Machiavelli was informed that a formal veto had come from Rome. But as far as we know, the letter of January 31 remained the last he wrote to Francesco Vettori or anyone else during almost the entire rest of the year. There is no other sign from his pen during all this time. The writings once attributed to this period prove to have been written at other times. His hopes, therefore, that at last he had made a comeback and would perhaps impress Giuliano with his ideas, can have lasted only weeks rather than months. By late February or early March, Machiavelli probably knew his fate: before that moment of truth, but after the middle of January, chapter 26 of the *Prince* must have been written.

ADDENDUM

How strong and final is the basis of these conclusions? Perhaps this question should wait until I know whether, in the discussion, any doubts will be raised, or any supplementary points suggested. But I would like to summarize the reasons why I hope that the result amounts to full certainty. They are:

1) Our conclusions have not been based on casual observations, but on a systematic method applied to the full exploration of a fixed period of time.

2) This method is one that has yielded many final certainties in recent years. It is simple: a determination of the guiding ideas of a piece of political writing and an analysis of the political and biographical background during the periods when the work may have been written. It is often apparent that certain ideas of the document or text cannot have developed against a certain background; sometimes, on the other hand, ideas and background prove to be clearly compatible.

3) In the case of chapter 26, only a limited period—three years—is in question: after the composition of the *Prince* in late 1513, and before Lorenzo became Duke of Urbino in October 1516. These three years break down immediately into three sections. In the first and last of these, the political background is in strong contradiction to the ideas and expectations expressed in chapter 26: after Marignano (September 1515), Leo could no longer hope for a northern *nepote*-state along the lines of the model set by Cesare Borgia, and the pontiff was by then the public friend and ally of the new foreign invader of Lombardy, France.

Thus, after September 1515, there was no room for a special *occasione* for a *nepote*-state, or for Medici leadership against the invaders. But until the end of 1514, neither of these two aims was as yet in the making: Leo aimed to gain the throne of Naples for Giuliano even if this implied the reoccupation of Milan through an allied France, and Machiavelli himself was theoretically in favor of a new French invasion into northern Italy because this seemed necessary for checking the Swiss.

Thus we may put it down as definitive that both periods—until the end of 1514, and after September 1515—are out of the running. And of the remaining middle period, January to August 1515, the months of April to August can be excluded for biographical reasons: Machiavelli was out of touch with politics and in deep depression.

4) If then, the political and biographical background for January–March 1515 should be in accord with the tenor and the ideas of chapter 26, the proof for the chapter's composition at that moment would be overwhelming. In both respects, the background is in total accord with the assumptions and ideals of chapter 26. Leo's determined policy at that time was to create a northern *nepote*-state and to prevent the French occupation of Milan. Both policies were then new (at least to public knowledge, including Machiavelli's). Thus for a passionate observer such as Machiavelli, there existed an extraordinary *occasione*, such as had not been offered since the days of Cesare Borgia. And the dedication's appeal to "vostra casa illustre" would then have been most fitting: there was a clear Italian policy under the leadership of the head of the *casa Medici*, Pope Leo. Machiavelli's biographical circumstances also accord with a composition date between January and March 1515: Machiavelli at that moment, and only at that moment, had reason to hope for contact with Giuliano; he might even hope to become a secretary-counselor in the service of the new state.

Nothing, therefore, is missing in the argument that Machiavelli wrote chapter 26 between January and March 1515. Even the apparent textual difficulty of the twenty-year duration of the Italian wars is resolved: from autumn 1494 to early 1515 is twenty years and only a few months. In my opinion there seems to be no hidden fallacy: our conclusions appear definitive.

If this is so, and if chapter 26 was written more than a year after the *Prince* and could not yet have been conceived in the political and biographical situation prevailing in 1513, then another incubus of Machiavellian scholarship has been removed; the "national" interpretation of the *Prince* as created by Hegel, Fichte, Ranke, and the Italian historians of the *Risorgimento*, and still maintained by Meinecke and Chabod, will never have the power to make a comeback. We can now grasp, unconcerned, the pragmatic character of the *Prince* and appraise it realistically; we are at liberty to draw the picture of Machiavelli's evolution from the Machiavellianism of the *Prince* to the new historical vision and the republican and moral values of the *Discourses*.

The full historical appraisal of the Italianism of chapter 26 is another story, or rather the beginning of another story. For, as indicated, we find more incidences and a fuller development of Machiavelli's Italian concerns in his later life, especially in that third period of his development which followed the Machiavellianism of the *Prince* and the Florentine city-state republicanism of the *Discourses*.

In making this statement, I have of course not forgotten that traces of Machiavelli's Italianism are also found within the *Discourses* in the accusations of chapter 12 of the first book that the popes had prevented Italy's national unification along the lines of France and Spain—though this prevention ought not to be deplorable in the light of the basic assumption of the *Discourses* that *virtù* will grow best where there are many independent, free small states. But this Italian perspective of the twelfth chapter, I am sure, can be shown to be a later insertion, probably not made until the role of the papacy in preventing the unification of the peninsula had been discovered in detail during Machiavelli's historical studies for his *Istorie fiorentine*.

The history of Machiavelli's Italianism thus becomes most important when we come to his third phase, when his *Florentine History* was at the center of his literary labors. But, of course, even this Italianism was only one ingredient of his thought, and the full perspective rests on the central new theme: Machiavelli as the historian of Florence.

[25]

IX

THE IDEA OF LIBERTY IN MACHIAVELLI*

By Marcia L. Colish

There is a certain class of thinkers who have evoked such perennial interest since their own times that the voluminous literature devoted to them tends to tell us more about the concerns and predispositions of their commentators than it does about the thinkers themselves. Niccolò Machiavelli definitely falls within this class of thinkers. His political writings have frequently been made an arena for the clash of political ideologies that owe their origins to later ages. These debates, carried on over the prostrate bodies of *Il principe* and the *Discorsi*, show no sign of ending. Recently, however, a small number of scholars have called attention to the need for a fresh approach, which seeks to gain an understanding of Machiavelli's ideas through a precise textual and contextual analysis of his use of language.[1] These scholars have stressed, plausibly enough, that the way to avoid a distorted, anachronistic interpretation of Machiavelli is to refrain from applying rigid, preconceived, and technical meanings to his still fluid, pretechnical vocabulary. They point out that such a vocabulary is none the less susceptible of systematic investigation.[2]

The method suggested by this approach has already borne fruit in J. H. Whitfield's study of the idea of *ordini* in Machiavelli's thought[3] and in J. H. Hexter's two articles on Machiavelli's idea of *lo stato* in *Il principe*, articles which destroy the foundations of the *raison d'état*

*This paper is dedicated gratefully to the late Ewart Lewis. I would also like to thank J. H. Hexter, Julius Kirshner, John D. Lewis, and J. H. Whitfield for their helpful criticism and suggestions.

[1]Giorgio Cadoni, "Libertà, repubblica e governo misto in Machiavelli," *Rivista internazionale di filosofia del diritto*, XXIX, ser. 3 (1962), 462; Fredi Chiapelli, *Studi sul linguaggio del Machiavelli* (Florence, 1952); J. H. Hexter, "*Il principe* and *lo stato*," *Studies in the Renaissance*, IV(1957), 114, 137; "The Loom of Language and the Fabric of Imperatives: The Case of *Il Principe* and *Utopia*," *American Historical Review*, LXIX (July 1964), 945-58; Daniel Waley, "The Primitivist Element in Machiavelli's Thought," *JHI*, XXXI (Jan. 1970), 91-98; J. H. Whitfield, *Machiavelli* (Oxford, 1947), 67-70, 75-78, 93-105, 131-33; "On Machiavelli's Use of *Ordini*," *Italian Studies*, X (1955), 19.

[2]Cadoni, *loc. cit.*, 462, n. 2; Chiapelli, 39, 111; Hans Freyer, *Machiavelli* (Leipzig, 1938), 78; Hanna H. Gray, "Machiavelli: The Art of Politics and the Paradox of Power," *The Responsibility of Power: Historical Essays in Honor of Hajo Holborn*, ed. Leonard Krieger and Fritz Stern (Garden City, 1967), 34; Hexter, "*Il principe* and *lo stato*," 113-17, 119-25; G. H. R. Parkinson, "Ethics and Politics in Machiavelli," *Philosophical Quarterly*, V (1955), 37; G. Prezzolini, *Machiavelli Anticristo* (Rome, 1954), 3-4.

[3]Whitfield, "On Machiavelli's Use of *Ordini*," *loc. cit.*, 19-39.

180

school of Machiavellian interpretation in a dazzling syntactical *tour de force*.[4] But despite these important contributions, Eric W. Cochrane's assertion that the linguistic approach to Machiavelli is still in its infancy is as true today as it was in 1961.[5]

Libertà is among the key terms in Machiavelli which both Whitfield and Hexter list as needing close textual study.[6] What I intend to do in this paper is to apply to *libertà* the method already exemplified in the works of these two scholars. This proposal entails four main tasks: (1) the complete works of Machiavelli will be subjected to scrutiny; (2) attention will be paid to the contexts in which the term *libertà* appears, and, where relevant, to the nature of the works in which these references occur; (3) attention will be directed to synonyms of *libertà* and to terms Machiavelli habitually uses in conjunction with it; (4) on the basis of this kind of analysis we will be in a position to consider what *libertà* means in Machiavelli's thought and how it relates to some of his other political ideas.

I. Liberty in the Commonplace Sense. A close reading of Machiavelli's works shows that he has several definitions of liberty, and that the majority of them are quite precise in their content and implications. At the same time, Machiavelli occasionally uses *libertà* and its cognates in a number of contexts where it has no precise meaning or theoretical implications. It may be helpful to dispose of these commonplace uses of liberty in Machiavelli's writings before directing attention to the more important and characteristic meanings of *libertà* in his thought.

The most frequent general use of *libertà* occurs in historical passages where it means freedom from physical captivity.[7] *Libertà* may also mean the freedom of political action enjoyed by a ruler whose country's laws and institutions place him above criticism. The clearest example cited by Machiavelli is the kingdom of France. France, according to Machiavelli, is a "free monarchy" because the *Parlement* serves as a target both for the insolence and ambition of the powerful and for the fear and hatred of the masses, thus neutralizing the impact

[4]Hexter, "*Il principe* and *lo stato*." 113–38; "The Loom of Language." 945–58.

[5]Eric W. Cochrane, "Machiavelli: 1940–1960," *Journal of Modern History*, XXXIII (June 1961), 124.

[6]Hexter, "*Il principe* and *lo stato*," 114; Whitfield, *Machiavelli*, 4.

[7]Machiavelli, *Istorie fiorentine*, I, 24, 25; II, 2, 30; IV, 17; V, 5, 6; VII, 27; VIII, 6, 17, 35, ed. F. Gaeta; *Legazione decima*, a Cesare Borgia in Urbino, 26 June 1502, no. 7, Soderini and Machiavelli to the Signoria; *Legazione ventesima*, seconda presso la Corte di Roma, Cesena, 7 October 1506, no. 50, Machiavelli to the Dieci di Balìa, *Legazioni e commissarie*, I, II, ed. S. Bertelli, *Opere* (8 vols.; Milan, 1960–65), VII, 114, 115, 141, 182, 293, 335, 336, 493, 519, 539, 573; III, 265; IV, 1015. References to the works of Machiavelli will be to this edition.

of political dissent and permitting the king to pursue his policies un-trammelled by the criticism of either group. It is upon this happy in-stitutional arrangement that the liberty and security of the king depend (*depende la libertà e sicurtà del re*).[8] Other general political mean-ings of *libertà* include free surrender, in the sense of unconditional ac-ceptance by the vanquished of the victor's terms[9] and dissociation from or overthrow of a government held to be objectionable for reasons not specified.[10]

Finally, *libertà* occurs in Machiavelli's writings a number of times in a very broad and not necessarily political context. *Libertà* may de-scribe a person's financial position, as in a passage where Machiavelli ironically contrasts the public and private interests of certain indebted Florentine nobles who supported the Duke of Athens' *coup d'état* in 1341–42, hoping to free themselves from debt by betraying their city (*con la servitù della patria dalla servitù de' loro creditori liberarsi*).[11] Machiavelli defines free men (*uomini liberi*) as those who act on their own initiative, as opposed to those who act as other people's agents.[12] "Free from" may be a simple synonym for "lacking in" or "enjoying (or suffering) the absence of," as when Machiavelli states that the Florentines have been fortunate in remaining free from many ills (*liberi di tanti mali*).[13] Freedom is also a mental or psychological state, as in the case of freedom from fear[14] and freedom from distrac-tion.[15] Additional examples might be produced to illustrate further these general usages of *libertà*, but no purpose would be served by multiplying citations. All that they illustrate, in effect, is that there is a level in Machiavelli's thought where *libertà* functions as a general term, without the specific meanings and connotations imposed upon it by a particular political theory.

II. Free Will. In Machiavelli we find a clear conception of free will as an attribute of human nature, an idea which he denotes in a num-ber of ways. He uses the term *elezione* to mean freedom of choice in a general sense.[16] He uses the term *libera occasione* to describe the freedom of choice which permits the egotistical nature of man to mani-fest itself.[17] But when most specific, Machiavelli uses the traditional term *libero arbitrio*; and he uses it in one of the best known passages in his work, the chapter in *Il principe* where he discusses the relation-ship between *virtù* and *fortuna*. Although Machiavelli gives express treatment to the idea of *libero arbitrio* in this one passage alone, its as-

[8]*Il principe*, XIX; *Opere*, I, 77.   [9]*Istor. fior.*, VIII, 33; *Opere*, VII, 569.
[10]*Ibid.*, III, 18; *Opere*, VII, 249.   [11]*Ibid.*, II, 33; *Opere*, VII, 190.
[12]*Discorsi sopra la prima deca di Tito Livio*, I, 1; *Opere*, I, 126–27.
[13]*Istor. fior.*, proemio; *Opere*, VII, 69.   [14]*Ibid.*, II, 13, 30; *Opere*, VII, 157, 183.
[15]*Discorsi*, I, 31; *Opere*, I, 203.   [16]*Ibid.*, I, 3; *Opere*, I, 127, 128, 136.
[17]*Ibid.*, 3; *Opere*, I, 135.

sociation with the important question of *virtù* and *fortuna* makes its
significance impossible to overlook. For it is on the basis of man's free
will that Machiavelli feels compelled to disagree with those who think
that Fortune rules all of human existence. It is precisely because he
wishes to uphold the dignity of man's free will that he counters with
the theory that Fortune rules only half of human life: "Lest our free
will be extinguished (*perchè il nostro libero arbitrio non sia spento*), I
judge it may be true that Fortune is the ruler of half of our actions, but
that she leaves the government of the other half, more or less, to
us."[18] He goes on in this passage to elaborate the idea that man expresses his free will in the face of *fortuna* by the exercise of *virtù*.

Although he does not expound his doctrine of free will in detail,
Machiavelli thus clearly places himself within the tradition of thinkers
who see in man's free will the sign of human independence, the ground
of ethically meaningful choices, and the guarantee that man will not
be reduced to the status of a plaything at the mercy of capricious and
uncaring cosmic forces.[19] At the same time, Machiavelli gives this
tradition a characteristically new twist, a point which has been clarified
by Francesco Ercole.[20] As Ercole observes, Machiavelli adopts the
traditional terminology but he attaches a different meaning to it. He
does not see free will as a mental faculty. Nor does he see it as uncon-
ditioned arbitrary power. Nor does he see it as the agency through
which man acquires virtue by the actualizing of his inner resources,
the subjection of his desires to reason, and the exclusion from the
realm of moral relevance of events in the world outside the moral subject over which he has no jurisdiction. Machiavelli does not conceive
of free will exclusively or primarily in terms of the inner life; he does
not analyze it in the light of its effects upon the spiritual condition of
the subject vis-à-vis God or the universe. Rather, he applies free will to
man as a whole. Machiavelli pits both the mental and the physical en-
dowments of man against a Fortune that is not merely an abstract
cosmic force but one which operates in concrete historical circumstances, political settings, and social configurations. To succeed in the
contest of *virtù* against *fortuna* is to impose one's directive will upon
the realities of the particular historical situation in which one lives.

While this definition of free will as the practical ability to modify
or influence external events can be found in the humanists of the
trecento and *quattrocento*, particularly Leone Battista Alberti,[21]
Machiavelli goes beyond his humanist predecessors. Not merely does

---

[18]*Il principe*, XXV; *Opere*, I, 99.
[19]G. Prezzolini, *Machiavelli* (New York, 1967), 54-55.
[20]F. Ercole. *La politica di Machiavelli* (Rome, 1926), 5-20, 24, 39-40.
[21]*Ibid.*, 11-14.

MARCIA L. COLISH

he de-emphasize the internalizing tendency of classical and Christian free will theories, he also eliminates their transcendental focus. For Machiavelli it is always the whole man who acts in the exercise of *libero arbitrio*. The subject's aim is not only to form his own mind and character but, by forming it in the mode of *virtù*, to impose his will on external events. He is, to be sure, limited, by Fortune, by the *necessità* entailed by the concatenation of certain sets of circumstances, and by the generic vices of human nature. These limitations, however, manifest themselves not in the abstract realm of metaphysical and ethical theory, but in the context of concrete political practice. The goal of Machiavellian free will is not to avoid being a puppet in the hands of an omnipotent God or an inexorable universe; it is to avoid being a puppet in the hands of other men upon the stage of history.

III. Corporate Libertà. In turning to Machiavelli's specifically political meanings of the term *libertà* we may begin by noting that he conceives of liberty on a large number of occasions in the sense of corporate *libertà*. Except for his substitution of the singular *libertà* for the plural *libertates* or its Italian equivalent, his use of this idea is in complete conformity with the corporation theory developed in the Middle Ages on the basis of the Roman legal idea of the corporation. A free corporation for both the Florentine and his medieval forebears may be a community as a whole or a sub-corporation within it, but in either case its freedom consists in its possession of special prerogatives and exemptions which release it from obligations that would otherwise be incumbent upon it. The Church has such privileges for Machiavelli, no less than for the Middle Ages. In discussing the results of the Becket affair in England, he observes that King Henry II was forced to nullify all policies that contravened the liberty of the Church (*libertà ecclesiastica*).[22] But in dealing with corporate liberty it is primarily to secular communities and above all to the free city that he directs his attention.

Machiavelli defines the nature of the free city in the terms that the Middle Ages had borrowed from the Romans. Cities are free when they possess autonomy, when they live under their own laws (*con le loro leggi*) and not under the jurisdiction of foreigners (*servitù*).[23] *Servitù* in this context is Machiavelli's term for rule by foreigners, regardless of the institutions through which they rule and regardless of their harshness or leniency.[24] A city which has autonomy is sovereign over herself (*principe di se stessa*),[25] a definition which, as Franco Gaeta has noted, parallels Bartolus of Sassoferrato's famous formula

[22]*Istor. fior.*, I, 19; *Opere*, VII, 105.
[23]*Ibid.*, I, 25, 39; VIII, 22; *Il principe*, VIII; *Opere*, VII, 114, 134, 550; I, 42.
[24]*Discorsi*, I, 2; II, 2; *Opere*, I, 129, 284.   [25]*Istor. fior.*, II, 26; *Opere*, VII, 177.

for urban sovereignty, *civitas sibi princeps*.[26] Most of Machiavelli's
examples of free cities are drawn from Italy. But he does not fail to
mention the German free cities (*terre franche, città libere*), which,
he observes, also enjoy their liberty (*godersi la sua libertà*).[27] In fact
he reserves for the Germans and the Swiss, along with the ancients,
the accolade of his vocabulary, the superlative of *libertà*. In ancient
times, he states, there were many completely free peoples (*popoli
liberissimi*);[28] among the moderns, the Swiss are perfectly free
(*liberissimi*); so too the imperial cities of Germany are perfectly free
(*liberissime*), obeying the emperor purely at their own discretion.[29]

Since the autonomy of a city-state is what defines it as a political
entity vis-à-vis other powers, it is not surprising to find that Machiavelli
treats corporate *libertà* in very much the same way that he treats *lo
stato* itself. As Hexter has demonstrated, *lo stato*, at least in *Il
principe*, is a passive entity, something to be possessed, gained, lost,
maintained, or taken away by someone. The fact that Machiavelli
regards *lo stato* as an object of political exploitation is signified by the
fact that *lo stato* always functions grammatically as the object of an active verb or the subject of a passive verb in the sentence in which it
appears.[30] Virtually the same may be said of *libertà* when Machiavelli
uses the term to mean corporate freedom. Its syntactical parallels with
lo stato are not exact, since the idea of liberty is often expressed in
terms of the adjectival and verbal cognates of *libertà* as well as in the
form of the noun. Also, *libertà* is less likely to be treated as an entity
capable of action than *lo stato*, in any era. Where the noun *libertà* is
used, however, it invariably functions, as does *lo stato*, as the object of
the sentence. Likewise, it is passive; it is something to be possessed
or lost, gained or regained, granted or seized, defended, maintained,
and preserved. Machiavelli refers to corporate *libertà* dozens of times
throughout his writings, including his histories and his minor political
works, as well as *Il principe* and the *Discorsi*. Among his works, the
Istorie fiorentine contains the largest number of references to corporate *libertà*, partly because of its length but largely as a consequence of
its subject matter.

The four main headings under which Machiavelli discusses corporate liberty, in order of ascending frequency of occurrence, are the
seizing, gaining, regaining, and defense of *libertà*. The seizure of a
city's *liberta* is generally achieved by military aggression.[31] A variety

---

[26]*Ibid.*, n. 5.   [27]*Discorsi*, II, 2, 19; *Opere*, I, 279, 335-36.
[28]*Ibid.*, II, 2; *Opere*, I, 279.   [29]*Il principe*, XIII, X; *Opere*, I, 55, 49.
[30]Hexter, "*Il principe* and *lo stato*," 119-23, 124-25; "The Loom of Language,"
953-54.
[31]*Istor. fior.*, II, 19; IV, 18; V, 8; *Opere*, VII, 165, 296, 399.

186   MARCIA L. COLISH

of circumstances, however, may enable a city to gain its freedom in the
first place.[32] The reacquisition of liberty may also be accomplished in
various ways. Sometimes Machiavelli is imprecise in describing how
this reacquisition of liberty takes place,[33] but in cases where he does
specify the means he cites the force of arms more frequently than any
other agency.[34] Machiavelli's stress on military means of securing
freedom is even more marked in his treatment of the defense, maintenance, and preservation of *libertà*. He does note a few occasions
when liberty has been defended by diplomacy.[35] But it is more usually
the breakdown of diplomacy into a state of war that cities have to
face in defending their liberty.[36] Tenacity in the defense of corporate
liberty is wholly laudable; as Machiavelli observes in a well known
passage in the *Discorsi*, when the independence of the *patria* is at
stake, no considerations, whether of justice or injustice, pity or cruelty,
praise or blame, should hinder the saving of her life and the maintenance of her freedom.[37]

Because corporate freedom must be maintained forcibly in the face
of omnipresent external threats, Machiavelli places a good deal of
stress on the need for a strong military establishment. He states repeatedly that the preservation of liberty depends on good armies, generals, and strategy in the field,[38] all of which are enhanced if the army
is composed of citizens,[39] on military preparedness and energetic
official leadership at home,[40] and on a high level of public morale.[41]
These familiar themes in Machiavelli's writings occur again and again
in this connection because he thinks it highly likely that a free city will
be called upon to defend herself from outside aggressors, and that con-

[32]*Ibid.*, proemio; I, 14, 22, 25, 26; *Opere*, VII, 70, 97, 111, 114, 116.

[33]*Discorsi*, II, 22; *Istor. fior.*, I, 28, 35; II, 30; VI, 13; *Opere*, I, 343; VII, 119, 129,
182, 406.

[34]*Istor. fior.*, II, 26, 36, 38; III, 27; VII, 26; VIII, 8, 23, 34; *Opere*, VII, 178, 198,
200, 204, 266, 492, 521, 552, 571.

[35]*Ibid.*, I, 29; II, 38; V, 9; VIII, 10; *Nature di uomini fiorentini*, ed. F. Gaeta; *Discorso fatto al magistrato dei dieci sopra le cose di Pisa*; *Opere*, VII, 122, 205, 341, 527;
VIII, 217; II, 13.

[36]*Istor. fior.*, III, 11; IV, 11; V, 11, 12; VIII, 19; *Discorsi*, I, 31; II, 1; *Opere*, VII,
234, 296, 343-45, 346, 545; I, 204, 279.

[37]*Discorsi*, III, 41; *Opere*, I, 495.

[38]*Ibid.*, 17, 41; *Arte della guerra*, II; *Istor. fior.*, V, 1; *Opere*, I, 439, 494-95; II,
393-94; VII, 326.

[39]*Il principe*, XII; *Istor. fior.*, VI, 20; *Opere*, I, 55; VII, 418.

[40]*Istor. fior.*, II, 36; IV, 7; VII, 14; *Provvisioni della repubblica di Firenze per
istruire il magistrato de' nove ufficiali dell' Ordinanza e Milizia fiorentina. Provvisione prima per le fanterie*, 6 December 1506; *Provvisione seconda per le milizie a
cavallo*, 30 March 1512, ed. S. Bertelli; *I Decennali: Decennale primo*, 39, ed.
F. Gaeta; *Opere*, VII, 196, 279, 474; II, 111, 116; VIII, 237.

[41]*Discorsi*, II, 21; *Istor. fior.*, II, 29; V, 19; VII, 15; *Opere*, I, 342; VII, 181, 297, 477.

stant vigilance is necessary for the preservation of her corporate *libertà*.

Refracted through the lens of political insecurity, which causes his gaze to focus on the pressing need to defend civic autonomy by the force of arms, Machiavelli's idea of corporate *libertà* is a direct continuation of the medieval idea of corporate *libertates*. His preeminent interest in civic corporations, as contrasted with other kinds of corporations, reflects the urban environment in which he lived and which he wrote about both in his political works and in his histories. Machiavelli's emphasis on military power in connection with the seizure, reconquest, and preservation of *libertà* is likewise a reflection of the events that passed before his eyes. While Machiavelli borrows the idea of a Roman-style citizen army from the civic humanists, he justifies it in the context of corporate *libertà* in practical terms. His reading of history, ancient and modern, leads him to the conclusion that citizen armies are more successful in the field than are mercenaries or troops led by foreign generals. In short, Machiavelli's conception of corporate *libertà* is traditional. It is not a tradition derived primarily from classical antiquity, except in the sense that the idea of the corporation is rooted ultimately in Roman law, but from the Middle Ages. All that Machiavelli adds to this tradition is his own perspective, the treatment of corporate liberty primarily in the context of practical military considerations.

IV. Libertà within the State. While Machiavelli's view of freedom as a commonplace notion, as a moral idea, and as the definition of corporate autonomy is on the whole clear and consistent, his treatment of *libertà* within the state shows a certain lack of univocity and precision. The ambiguity of Machiavelli's ideas on liberty within the state is reflected in the way that his commentators have handled this topic; for it is by far the most controversial aspect of his conception of *libertà*. Most of the scholars who have dealt with this issue have viewed it in the context of the question of whether the "real" Machiavelli is the "republican" Machiavelli of the *Discorsi* or the "despotic" Machiavelli of *Il principe*. It is well known that for centuries there has been a tradition of Machiavellian interpretation promoting the view of Machiavelli as a republican[42] and strenuously opposing the

---

[42]The most recent treatment of the earlier literature on this subject is Mario Rosa, *Dispotismo e libertà nel settecento: Interpretazioni 'repubblicane' di Machiavelli,* Istituto di storia medievale e moderna, saggi, 3 (Bari, 1964). For bibliography on the more recent literature see Hans Baron, "Machiavelli: The Republican Citizen and the Author of 'The Prince'," *English Historical Review,* LXXVI (April 1961), 218–22; Cochrane, "Machiavelli: 1940–1960," *J. of Mod. Hist.,* XXXIII (1961), 132–36; Émile Namer, *Machiavel* (Paris, 1961), 194–225; Luigi Russo, *Machiavelli,* accresciuta, (Bari, 1949³), 210–14.

188   MARCIA L. COLISH

view, stated most forcefully in recent decades by Friedrich Meinecke, of Machiavelli as a proponent of the *Machtstaat*.[43] Many of the scholars who have studied Machiavelli on liberty have aligned themselves with the republican interpretation and have concluded that, for Machiavelli, liberty within the state can be equated with the constitutional and institutional structures characteristic of republics,[44] or at least characteristic of limited governments.[45] There is even some support in this school for the view that Machiavellian republican *libertà* can be equated with democracy,[46] although several of its members have stressed that Machiavelli's republican *libertà* should not be confused with modern liberalism or social democracy since he is concerned neither with the natural rights of the individual in relation to the state[47] nor with economic and social equality.[48] It is certainly true that, in many passages in his works, Machiavelli identifies liberty within the state with republican institutions based on preliberal and presocialist political assumptions. At the same time, a close scrutiny of the texts shows that Machiavelli's conception of liberty within the state is not always identical with either a purely republican or a purely constitutional definition of the idea of *libertà*.

   Libertà within the state is a topic to which Machiavelli adverts with great frequency and interest, although his references to it are confined with only a few exceptions to two works, the *Istorie fiorentine* and the *Discorsi*. There are only two references to this subject in *Il principe*. In one he identifies liberty with aristocracy while enumerat-

[43]F. Meinecke, *Machiavellism: The Doctrine of Raison d'État and Its Place in Modern History*, trans. Douglas Scott (New York, 1965), 1-22, 29-43.

[44]Henry J. Abraham, "Was Machiavelli a 'Machiavellian'?" *Social Science*, XXVIII (1953), 25-29; Rudolf von Albertini, *Das florentinische Staatsbewusstsein im Übergang von der Republik zum Principat* (Bern, 1955), 66; Edward McN. Burns, "The Liberalism of Machiavelli," *Antioch Review*, VIII (1948), 321-30, who, however, associates the idea of liberty in Machiavelli with modern liberalism; Cadoni, "Libertà, repubblica e governo misto," 463-73, 479-82; Eugenio Garin, *Italian Humanism: Philosophy and Civic Life in the Renaissance*, trans. Peter Munz (Oxford, 1965), 79-81.

[45]Augustin Renaudet, *Machiavel: Étude d'histoire des doctrines politiques* (Paris, 1942), 187-93; Gennaro Sasso, *Niccolò Machiavelli: Storia del suo pensiero politico*, Istituto italiano per gli studi storici, 10 (Naples, 1958), 333-34; Antonio Scolari, "Il concetto di libertà in Niccolò Machiavelli," *Atti e memorie della Accademia di agricoltura, scienze e lettere di Verona*, serie V, vol. X, no. 110 (1933), 52-55.

[46]Hans Baron, *The Crisis of the Early Italian Renaissance: Civic Humanism and Republican Liberty in the Age of Classicism and Tyranny* (rev. ed., Princeton, 1966), 428-29.

[47]Prezzolini, *Machiavelli*, 55-57; Renaudet, *loc. cit.*, 187, 188-89, 190-93; Sasso, *loc. cit.*, 333-44.

[48]Renaudet, *loc. cit.*, 190-93.

ing the three forms of government.[49] In the other he observes that peoples ruled by princes are ignorant of free government (*vivere libero*).[50] In the light of the fact that he is perfectly willing in his other works to admit that one-man rule and liberty are compatible, it is noteworthy that he states the case against princes so strongly in *Il principe*. Perhaps this is Machiavelli's way of delivering a backhanded slap either to the civic virtue of the citizens of Florence or to the virtue, wisdom, or potential legislative prudence of Lorenzo de' Medici, the new ruler of Florence to whom the book was ultimately dedicated.

The *Istorie fiorentine* was also written for a Medici, Giulio, later Pope Clement VII, although it was clearly intended for a wide Florentine audience as well. In this work Machiavelli tries to avoid taking a stand on the Medici, whom he sometimes describes as promoters of liberty and sometimes as its destroyers. He circumvents this issue in the *Istorie* for the most part by expressing opinions on the Medici in the words of other people. He does not use the term *libertà*, its adjuncts, or its antonyms, in describing the Florentine government after the accession of Cosimo de' Medici, relating without comment the constitutional inroads into the republican system made by Cosimo and Lorenzo and their manipulation of civic elections. His restraint breaks down only when he comes to the Pazzi conspiracy, at which point he states that the *coup* failed because the rule of the Medici had so deafened the ears of the Florentines to the cry of liberty that they knew it no longer.[51] The theme of the *Istorie fiorentine,* stated in the preface,[52] is that ambition, factionalism, and flaccid public spirit have prevented the Florentines from establishing good and stable institutions and from working for the common good. Since he thinks that Florentine history offers few good examples of institutions promoting freedom, the majority of his references to internal liberty in this work are passages identifying good rulers, good laws, the rule of law, and the end of the common weal with liberty.

The largest single source of references to *libertà* within the state is the *Discorsi*. Most of these references are found in Book I, where Machiavelli discusses republics. Considering the fact that the work is a treatise on political theory clothed as a commentary on Livy, it is not surprising to find that it is the source for almost all of his remarks on liberty in ancient history and on the institutional features of free states. It is also understandable that he should tend to generalize and to analyze problems in the abstract more here than in the *Istorie fiorentine*. At the same time, it is natural for him to devote attention

[49] *Il principe*, IX; *Opere*, I, 45.   [50] *Ibid.*, V; *Opere*, I, 29.
[51] *Istor. fior.*, VIII, 8; *Opere*, VII, 521.   [52] *Ibid.*, proemio: *Opere*, VII, 68-71.

190   MARCIA L. COLISH

in the *Discorsi* to the principles underlying free governments. It is in this work that we find an important statement in which Machiavelli defines the republic in terms of the common good,[53] as well as his initially perplexing assertion that Florence, despite her free institutions, has not been a republic for two hundred years.[54]

Of less importance is Machiavelli's proposal for a Florentine constitution, the *Discursus florentinarum rerum*, another work written for a Medici patron, Pope Leo X. Here he shows a combined interest in principles and institutions, but stresses the institutions and suggests a list of practical justifications for a republican constitution. Although he calls the constitution he projects in the *Discursus* a republic and asserts that it preserves the traditional liberty of Florence, the polity he outlines is oligarchical in structure and subject in its functions to the princely influence of Leo.[55] The *Arte della guerra*, finally, contributes one of the *loci classici* for Machiavelli's association of a citizen army with civic virtue in a free state, along with its practical justifications.[56]

In the numerous passages where he discusses liberty within the state, Machiavelli uses the noun *libertà* and its verbal and adjectival cognates in much the same way as he does in discussing the corporate liberty of the state from outside control. The Italian city-states, likewise, serve as his chief source of examples. Here too, he often contrasts *libertà* with *servitù*, which, from an intra-state point of view, he equates with tyranny.[57] In the internal, as in the corporate context, *libertà* is passive, not active; it always functions grammatically as the object of a verb or a preposition. Within the state *libertà* may be known,[58] loved,[59] desired,[60] acquired,[61] possessed,[62] established,[63] enjoyed,[64] lost,[65] taken,[66] destroyed,[67] regained,[68] reinstalled,[69] and

[53]*Discorsi*, II, 2; *Opere*, I, 280.   [54]*Ibid.*, I, 49; *Opere*, I, 242.
[55]*Discursus florentinarum rerum post mortem junioris Laurentii Medices*, ed. S. Bertelli; *Opere*, I, 267-69.   [56]*Arte della guerra*, I; *Opere*, II, 348.
[57]*Discorsi*, I, 16; III, 7, 8; *Istor. fior.*, II, 13, 25; III, 25; IV, 1, 19; VIII, 29; *Opere*, I, 174, 412, 416; VII, 157, 176, 263, 271, 299, 562.
[58]*Il principe*, V; *Istor. fior.*, VIII, 8; *Opere*, I, 28-29; VII, 521.
[59]*Discorsi*, I, 52; II, 2; *Istor. fior.*, II, 34; III, 20; V, 6; VI, 13; *Opere*, I, 247, 281; VII, 192, 254, 335-36, 406.   [60]*Istor. fior.*, II, 34; *Opere*, VII, 192.
[61]*Discorsi*, I, 29; *Opere*, I, 199.   [62]*Istor. fior.*, III, 13; *Opere*, VII, 237.
[63]*Discorsi*, I, 17, 29, 40; III, 3; *Istor. fior.*, II, 4; *Opere*, I, 117-78, 199, 224, 386; VII, 144.
[64]*Discorsi*, II, 2; *Istor. fior.*, VI, 13; *Opere*, I, 279; VII, 406.
[65]*Discorsi*, I, 57; *Arte della guerra*, I; *Opere*, I, 260; II, 346.
[66]*Discorsi*, I, 16, 28, 35, 47; II, 2; III, 5, 8; *Istor. fior.*, II, 35, 40; VIII, 22; *Opere*, I, 175, 196, 212, 239, 283, 389, 414; VII, 194, 207, 549.
[67]*Discorsi*, I, 52; *Opere*, I, 247.
[68]*Ibid.*, 16, 17, 46; III, 2, 3; *Opere*, I, 175, 177-78, 235, 385, 386.
[69]*Ibid.*, I, 2, 17; *Istor. fior.*, V, 6; *Opere*, I, 134, 177-78; VII, 335-36.

IDEA OF LIBERTY IN MACHIAVELLI   191

preserved and maintained.[70] As in the case of the independence of the
state as a whole, the preserving and maintaining of its internal *libertà*
is discussed by Machiavelli more often than any of the other vicissitudes of freedom.

While Machiavelli's use of *libertà* in connection with internal
affairs thus parallels his use of *libertà* with reference to corporate
autonomy, in the former context he also has recourse to a number of
other terms which he uses interchangeably with *libertà* or in close association with it. Side by side with terms such as *stato libero, comune
libero, popolo libero,* and *città libera*[71] we find terms such as *vivere
politico, vivere civile,* and *vivere libero;*[72] and Machiavelli often refers
to such states as *bene ordinati* or as possessing *buoni ordini* or *buone
leggi.*[73] These cognates of *libertà*, as a number of scholars have noted,
connote not merely certain institutional forms, but also, and pre-
eminently, civic virtues, such as a respect for law and order and a
concern for the common weal.[74] Insofar as Machiavelli identifies
liberty with these ideas, his conception of *libertà* is rooted less in a
consistent and dogmatic constitutionalism than in the principles and
values which institutions may serve in a variety of kinds of states.

While Machiavelli refers to *libertà* within the state on a few rare
occasions in an unspecified sense[75] and on two occasions as an attribute of a class or group within a given community—in particular, as
the power of the lower classes[76] and the *Parte Guelfa*[77] to influence or
control events in Florence--he usually applies the term to communi-

[70]*Discorsi,* I, 4, 5, 7, 16, 17, 18, 23, 29, 40, 49; II, 2; III, 2, 3, 49; *Istor. fior.,* II, 6,
21; VI, 23, 24; *Opere,* I, 137, 138, 139-40, 146, 173-76, 177-78, 179-80, 188-89, 199,
229, 235, 241-42, 283, 385, 386, 504; VII, 146, 168, 423, 425-26.

[71]*Discorsi,* I, 4, 7, 8, 16, 17, 18, 25, 29; III, 3, 12; *De rebus pistoriensibus,* ed.
S. Bertelli; *Istor. fior.,* I, 8; II, 13, 35; III, 5; VII, 19; *Nature di uomini fiorentini;*
Opere, I, 138, 146, 150, 174, 177, 179-80, 192, 200, 387, 426; II, 30; VII, 88, 157, 194,
219, 482; VIII, 220.

[72]*Il principe,* V; *Discorsi,* I, 2, 6, 16, 17, 23, 24, 25, 29, 49, 55; II, 2, 4, 19, 21, 30;
III, 7, 8; *Parole da dirle sopra la provisione del danaio, fatto un poco di proemio e di
scusa,* ed. S. Bertelli; *Istor. fior.,* II, 4, 18, 34; III, 5; V, 6; VI, 13; *Opere,* I, 28-29, 134,
141, 173, 177, 188-89, 191, 192-93, 199, 241, 255, 279-83, 288, 336, 341, 370, 412, 416;
II, 62; VII, 144, 164, 192, 220-23, 335, 406.

[73]*Il principe,* XIX; *Discorsi,* I, 2, 4, 10, 17, 18, 37, 40, 49; II, 2; *Arte della guerra,*
I; *Istor. fior.,* IV, 1; *Opere,* I, 77, 129-30, 133, 134, 137, 157-59, 177-78, 179-80, 218,
224, 241-42, 283; II, 339; VII, 271.

[74]This notion has been analyzed most fully by Whitfield, *Machiavelli,* 131-47;
"On Machiavelli's Use of *Ordini,*" 22-39; Albertini, *loc. cit.,* 53, 60-61, 62-63; Federico
Chabod, *Machiavelli and the Renaissance,* trans. David Moore (London, 1960), 97;
Hexter, "*Il principe* and *lo stato,*" 133-34; Prezzolini, *Machiavelli,* 56; Sasso, *loc. cit.,*
333-34; Scolari, *loc. cit.,* 52-53. A similar point with respect to the idea of power has
recently been made by Gray, "Machiavelli," *The Responsibility of Power,* 39.

[75]*Discorsi,* I, 23, 49; *Istor. fior.,* III, 1; *Opere,* I, 188-89, 241-42; VII, 213.

[76]*Istor. fior.,* III, 13; *Opere,* VII, 237.   [77]*Ibid.,* IV, 19; *Opere,* VII, 299.

ties as a whole, and especially to those possessing definite characteristics. There is a great deal of evidence pointing to an identification
of free communities with republics in Machiavelli's thought. Sometimes he achieves this identification in negative terms, contrasting
libertà with tyranny, monarchy, aristocracy, license, and factionalism by defining liberty simply as the absence of these conditions. At
other times he refers positively to certain institutional features of republics in describing *libertà*.

Tyranny is clearly antithetical to liberty for Machiavelli. He regards the institutions of the city of Genoa, which combine *libertà* and
tirannide, as distinctly anomalous.[78] He describes a group of disgrun-
tled Florentine citizens who urged Veri de' Medici in 1395 to effect a
coup d'état and to free them from the tyrannical rule of the current
government *(prendere lo stato e liberargli dalla tirannide)*.[79] He notes
that Athens returned to *libertà* after the overthrow of the heirs of the
tyrant Pisistratus.[80] In these and many other passages he defines liberty as the absence or elimination of tyranny.[81]

Machiavelli also defines *libertà* as the absence of princely or monarchical rule, treating them on many occasions as clear antitheses.
Thus, he notes, when the Blacks of Florence asked the Pope in 1300
to send a man of royal blood to come and rule the city, the Whites
denounced the ploy as a conspiracy against freedom *(una congiura
contra al vivere libero)*.[82] After the death of the last Visconti, when
the citizens of Milan set up a new government, some wanted a prince;
but the lovers of liberty *(quelli che amavano la libertà)* wanted to live
in freedom *(vivere libero)*.[83] Sometimes Machiavelli simply contrasts
libertà with princely rule without indicating approval or disapproval
of one arrangement or the other. Thus, he sets forth advice to the ruler of a newly conquered state, whether he governs by freedom or by
a principality *(per via di libertà o per via di principato)*.[84] If it is hard
to preserve *uno stato libero*, he observes, it is also hard to preserve *uno
regno*.[85] It was more difficult for Florence to conquer the towns in
Tuscany, he considers, than for Venice to conquer the towns in the
Venetian *contado*, since the Venetian towns were unfree *(non libere)*,
accustomed to living under princes, while Florence's neighbors were
all free cities *(tutte città libere)*.[86]

More usually, Machiavelli is not content to contrast liberty with

---

[78] *Ibid.* VIII. 29; *Opere* VII. 562.   [79] *Ibid.*, III, 25; *Opere.* VII. 262.
[80] *Discorsi*, I, 2, 28; II, 2; *Opere*, I, 134, 196–97, 279.
[81] *Ibid.*, I, 2, 25, 28, 35; II, 2; III, 5, 7, 8; *Istor. fior.*, III, 17, 20; IV, 1, 19, 27, 28;
Opere, I, 132, 192–93, 195–96, 212, 279–83, 389, 412, 416; VII, 248, 254, 271, 299,
312, 313.
[82] *Istor. fior.*, II, 18: *Opere* VII, 164.
[83] *Ibid.*, VI. 13, 24; *Opere* VII. 406. 425-26.   [84] *Discorsi*, I, 16; *Opere*, I, 175.
[85] *Ibid.*, III, 3; *Opere*, I, 387.   [86] *Ibid.*, 12; *Opere*, I. 426.

monarchy, but rather makes a point of stressing that they are basically incompatible. People who are ruled by princes, he states, simply do not know how to live freely (*vivere libero non sanno*).[87] A people ruled by a prince, he argues, loses the habit of liberty, and, if it becomes emancipated, finds it difficult to preserve its newly gained freedom (*Uno popolo uso a vivere sotto uno principe, se per qualche accidente diventa libero, con difficultà mantiene la libertà*).[88] Thus, when Rome became free after overthrowing her kings, she lacked many establishments necessary for freedom (*che era necessario ordinare in favore della libertà*).[89] As in the case of Tuscany in ancient times, the more that a free people has enjoyed its liberty, the more it has hated the name of prince (*e tanto si godeva della sua libertà, e tanto odiava il nome di principe*).[90] The reason Machiavelli usually gives for the view that liberty cannot exist in a monarchy is that the rule of one man tends to be despotic and tyrannical. Thus, he observes, the lovers of Florence's liberty assumed automatically that the rule of the Duke of Athens would lead to an absolute government, a fear to which the Duke showed his sensitivity by stressing in his propaganda that he was not taking away the liberty of Florence but strengthening it.[91] Elsewhere he makes the same point by referring to princes and tyrants in one breath as if there were no difference between them.[92]

Machiavelli also expresses the idea that the rule of one man, even if he is not a prince or king, is incompatible with liberty. He chooses his examples from members of the Medici family and states his case both in the words of persons whose speeches he reports and in his own words. Thus, he notes, Piero Soderini, who had gained a reputation as a lover of liberty, refused to support Medici rule in Florence because he felt it would destroy that liberty; and, in even stronger terms, Giovan Francesco Strozzi described the rule of Piero de' Medici as tyranny.[93] Earlier, Rinaldo degli Albizzi had urged his fellow citizens to free the city (*liberare la patria*) from the threat of Cosimo de' Medici, who, he argued, would reduce Florence to slavery (*servitù*).[94] And Machiavelli himself states that the Pazzi conspiracy of 1478 failed to free Florence from Medici rule because Lorenzo's regime had deafened her ears to the cry of freedom, and it was no longer known there (*la libertà . . . in Firenze non era cognosciuta*).[95]

But Machiavelli is by no means consistent on this point. In discussing the problem of reforming an outmoded government in a free

[87] *Il principe*, V; *Opere*, I, 29.   [88] *Discorsi*, I, 16; *Opere*, I, 173.
[89] *Ibid.*, 2; *Opere*, I, 134.   [90] *Ibid.*, II, 2; *Opere*, I, 279.
[91] *Istor. fior.*, II, 34, 35; *Opere*, VII, 192-93, 194.   [92] *Discorsi*, II, 2; *Opere*, I, 280.
[93] *Ibid.*, I, 52; *Istor. fior.*, VII, 19; *Opere*, I, 247; VII, 482.
[94] *Istor. fior.*, IV, 28; *Opere*, VII, 313.   [95] *Ibid.*, VIII, 8; *Opere*, VII, 521.

194   MARCIA L. COLISH

city, he advises those who want to set up a new and free polity (*uno vivere nuovo e libero*), whether it be a republic or a monarchy (*o per via di republica o di regno*), to preserve some of its ancient customs, in contrast to those who want to set up a despotism (*potestà assoluta*), whom he advises to wipe the slate clean and start afresh.[96] Here he clearly distinguishes between monarchy and absolutism and includes monarchies, along with republics, among those states capable of internal freedom. Likewise, he asserts, Rome enjoyed liberty under monarchical rule, at least until Tarquinius Superbus despoiled her of all the liberty she had possessed under the other kings (*spogliò Roma di tutta quella libertà ch'ella aveva sotto gli altri re mantenuta*).[97] Kings promote liberty primarily by their legislation, according to Machiavelli. Thus, while Rome did not have the advantage of starting out with a Lycurgus whose establishments would guarantee her a long and free life (*che la potesse vivere lungo tempo libera*), Romulus and her other kings still issued ordinances conformable to a free government (*conformi ancora al vivere libero*);[98] and the ancestors of King Tullus and King Metius attempted to organize the city in such a way as to enable her to live freely for a long time and to make her citizens the defenders of their liberty (*per farla vivere lungamente libera e per fare i suoi cittadini difensori dalla loro libertà*).[99] Also, he notes, since most people want freedom in order to live securely (*desiderando la libertà per vivere sicuri*), a prince can satisfy their desires by ruling according to laws that guarantee security.[100]

At the same time, the rule of one man, even if he is not a king, and even if he is a Medici, is by no means necessarily tyrannical. A single ruler may, indeed, foster liberty. He does this in precisely the same way that kings do, by sage and prudent legislation. As Machiavelli notes, "It is true that when . . . by good fortune there arises in the city a wise, good, and powerful citizen who ordains laws whereby the animosities of the nobles and the people are calmed or whereby they are restrained from evil-doing, that city may be called free and that government may be judged stable and firm."[101]

Even when the role of a single ruler as a legislator and peacemaker is not specified, he may act as the liberator of his city from a government seen as tyrannical or oppressive. Thus, in a passage previously cited, Veri de' Medici was urged by a group of Florentine citizens in 1395 to seize the government and free them from tyranny.[102] Also, the Lombard towns substituted dukes for kings between the sixth and

[96]*Discorsi*, I. 25; *Opere*, I, 92–93.
[98]*Ibid.*, I. 2; *Opere*, I, 134.
[100]*Ibid.*, 16; *Opere*, I, 175.
[102]*Ibid.*, III. 25; *Opere*, VII, 262.

[97]*Ibid.*, III, 5; *Opere*, I. 389.
[99]*Ibid.*, 23; *Opere*, I, 188–89.
[101]*Istor. fior.*, IV, 1; *Opere*, VII, 271.

eighth centuries in order to be free states (*per essere stati liberi*),[103] although it is not at all clear that the regimes of Veri de' Medici or the Lombard dukes would be any less inclined to despotism than the governments they were designed to replace.

For Machiavelli, then, the antithesis between *libertà* and monarchies, principalities, and governments characterized by the rule of one man is not as clear cut as the antithesis between *libertà* and tyranny. He frequently describes monarchical government as inconsistent with liberty, and often defines liberty in contrast or opposition to it, on the grounds that monarchy tends to degenerate into arbitrary and absolute rule. On the other hand, he sometimes describes states ruled by one man, be he a citizen, a noble, or a king, as free governments, either because the ruler apparently has popular support or because he establishes wise and good laws that promote the internal harmony, general welfare, and longevity of his state.

Machiavelli also defines *libertà* negatively as the absence or elimination of aristocracy, although here, as in the case of principalities or states ruled by one man, he is extremely ambiguous, for he associates liberty with aristocracy almost as often as he opposes them to each other.[104] At times he criticizes the nobility severely as a menace to freedom. He describes nobles in general as promoters of slavery (*ministri ... della servitù*),[105] and notes that in ancient Corcyra they took away the people's liberty (*togliessono la libertà al popolo*).[106] He praises Giano della Bella, whose Ordinances of Justice in 1293 prevented the Florentine nobles from serving on the *Signoria*, as having freed the city from aristocratic tyranny (*dalla servitù de' potenti*).[107] Not only do the nobles have despotic inclinations themselves, they may also sin against liberty by cooperating with despotic princes. Thus, the aristocracy of ancient Heraclea urged Clearchus to return from exile and seize the people's *libertà*.[108]

On the other hand, Machiavelli sometimes identifies aristocracy with liberty. In a well known passage in the *Discorsi*, he restates the Aristotelian definition of the three major forms of government: the principality which degenerates into tyranny, the aristocracy which degenerates into oligarchy, and the popular government which degenerates into licentiousness.[109] In a less frequently cited passage in *Il*

---

[103] *Ibid.*, I. 8; *Opere*, VII, 88.

[104] A good recent study of Machiavelli's view of aristocracy is by Alfredo Bonadeo, "The Role of the 'Grandi' in the Political World of Machiavelli," *Studies in the Renaissance*, XVI (1969), 12 30.

[105] *Istor. fior.*, IV, 1; *Opere*, VII, 271.

[106] *Discorsi*, II, 2; *Opere*, I, 283.

[107] *Istor. fior.*, II, 13; *Opere*, VII, 157.

[108] *Discorsi*, I. 16; *Opere*, I, 174.

[109] *Ibid.*, I, 2; *Opere*, I, 130 31. The schema of principality, aristocracy, and popular government is also in *Parole da dìrle*, *Opere*, II, 57.

196   MARCIA L. COLISH

principe, he defines the three major forms of government as princely rule, liberty, and licence (*o principato o libertà o licenzia*),[110] thus appearing to assimilate aristocracy to freedom. Further, if nobles, as noted above, are willing to betray the liberty of the people to a despot, they are also capable of acting as the people's liberators (*suoi liberatori*) from tyranny.[111] Thus, while the nobles sometimes try to increase their power at the expense of the people, they can also serve the people's interests, and can act as a mean between the extremes of autocracy and mob rule.

The people themselves have an ambivalent relationship to liberty. Machiavelli asserts that the desires of a free people are seldom injurious to liberty (*I desiderii de' popoli liberi rade volte sono perniziosi alla libertà*).[112] After raising the question of whether the people or the nobles are better guardians of liberty he concludes that the people are; since they wish not to dominate others but merely to be left alone, they have a stronger motivation toward freedom (*maggiore voluntà di vivere liberi*).[113] On the other hand, he observes that the people revere freedom in name only, wishing in reality to submit neither to the rule of law nor to the rule of men (*della libertà solamente il nome . . . è celebrato, desiderando . . . non essere nè alle leggi nè agli uomini sottoposto*).[114] Thus, for Machiavelli, it is not surprising that when the constitutional crisis in Milan brought on by the ending of the Visconti regime led to a *coup d'état* by the masses (*licenza*), the city failed to preserve her liberty, and its seizure by a despot was a foregone conclusion.[115]

Finally, Machiavelli defines *libertà* negatively in opposition to factions. But, in this case also, he points to circumstances in which factions may promote liberty as well as to circumstances in which they impede or destroy it. Freedom and factionalism are incisively contrasted in a speech Machiavelli reports as given in 1372 by a Florentine citizen who charges that the Italian cities of the day have organized themselves not as free but as divided into factions (*non come libere ma come divise in sètte*). The speaker asserts that factionalism is inimical to liberty, since the parties do not seek laws and policies directed to the common good but only the gratification of their own ambitions. He therefore urges the suppression of factions and their replacement by means of laws suited to a free and law abiding community (*vivere libero*).[116] Machiavelli notes that the conflicts between the popular and senatorial parties in Rome led to the destruction of her

---

[110] *Il principe*, IX; *Opere*, I, 45.
[112] *Ibid.*, 4; *Opere*, I, 138.
[114] *Istor. fior.*, IV, 1; *Opere*, VII, 271.
[116] *Istor. fior.*, III, 5; *Opere*, VII, 219, 220 23.

[111] *Discorsi*, I, 2; *Opere*, I, 132
[113] *Ibid.*, 5; *Opere*, I, 138, 139 40
[115] *Ibid.*, VI, 24; *Opere*, VII, 425 26

freedom (*furono cagione della rovina del vivere libero*) at the time of
the Gracchi.[117] He observes that a newly freed state is particularly
liable to partisanship inimical to its liberty, a point he illustrates with
several examples.[118] The main reason why factions undermine liberty,
according to Machiavelli, is that they breed internal weakness and
corruption in the body politic, which render the community too vitiated
to maintain the liberty it already possesses or to enter into a free life
if it is enfranchised.[119]

At the same time, Machiavelli asserts, in states that are healthy
and uncorrupted, factional conflicts not only are harmless, but are
positively beneficial to the freedom and vitality of the community. In
Rome, for example, dissension between the Senate and the people
produced laws favoring liberty,[120] as a consequence of which the
freedom of the state was established more firmly (*per le quali si
stabilisse più la libertà di quello stato*).[121] Thus, when the Roman
people recovered their freedom after the fall of the Decemvirs, many
different parties arose to defend liberty (*difendere la libertà*).[122]
While maintaining that the factional rivalries between the patricians
and the plebeians were one of the reasons why Rome remained free
for so long (*cause del tenere libera Roma*), Machiavelli admits that
such rivalries do create a certain amount of tumult. Nonetheless,
he states categorically that in Rome all the laws made in favor of
liberty arose from this disunity (*tutte le leggi che si fanno in favore della
libertà, nascano dalla disunione loro*). He defends this view in the following terms:

Neither can one rightly call a republic disordered in any way where there are
so many examples of virtue. For good examples arise from good education,
good education arises from good laws, and good laws arise from these
tumults, which many uncritically condemn. For he who examines their outcome well will not find that they led to any exile or violence disadvantageous
to the common good, but to laws and ordinances beneficial to public
freedom.[123]

Machiavelli's distinction between the negative and positive effects
of factionalism on liberty seems to rest on the question of whether
the state in which factions operate is corrupt or uncorrupted. In an
uncorrupted state, factional conflict is productive of freedom and
civic virtue, but elsewhere it leads to corruption which in turn leads to
the erosion of civic virtue and the loss of liberty. While providing a
rationale for the fact that factions may have different effects in differ-

[117]*Discorsi*, I, 6; *Opere*, I, 141.
[118]*Ibid.*, 16; *Opere*, I, 173 76.   [119]*Ibid.*, 17; *Opere*, I, 177 78.
[120]*Ibid.*, 37; *Opere*, I, 218.   [121]*Ibid.*, 40; *Opere*, I, 224.   [122]*Ibid.*, 46; *Opere*, I, 235.
[123]*Ibid.*, 4; *Opere*, I, 136 37.

198   MARCIA L. COLISH

ent historical circumstances, Machiavelli's reasoning on this point still fails to explain how an uncorrupted state, like Rome, could grow corrupt enough so that factionalism, which had earlier been a sign and cause of her political health and freedom, could become the cause of the collapse of her liberty in the era of the Gracchi.

In addition to Machiavelli's various negative definitions of liberty he has a strong tendency to identify it positively with republics. This tendency can be seen in his repeated references to Brutus as the father of liberty and as the liberator of his people.[124] Machiavelli connects *libertà* with specific characteristics of republican constitutions. In particular, he notes, freedom in republics is associated with the ability of the people to make their own laws and to consent to government policy.[125] It is also associated with officials and magistrates who are elected, not appointed,[126] and whose power is delegated by the people through unmanaged elections. Genoa, he observes, when she was free (*quando la vive nella sua libertà*), elected her Doge by free elections (*per suffragi liberi*). A republic cannot be considered free without such means for the expression of the public will.[127] Free republics also need legal mechanisms for enforcing the laws, for penalizing citizens who attempt to contravene the public order and the general good, for calling the rulers to account, and for redressing the grievances of the ruled. Commenting on the popular institutions of Pistoia, Machiavelli observes that if it did not have legal channels for penalizing graft the commune would not be free at all (*il comune ne sia al tutto libero*).[128] He approves of the proscription of immoral officials in Rome by the Censors, and praises this office as one of the provisions which helped keep Rome free (*che aiutarono tenere Roma libera*).[129] He goes into some detail on the need for legally instituted guardians of liberty, concluding, as noted above, that this responsibility is best vested in the people,[130] and he defines the functions of the guardians as the prosecution of any citizen, official, or group that sins in any way against free government (*quando peccassono in alcuna cosa allo stato libero*).[131]

Another institution essential to the maintenance of republican

[124]*Ibid.*, III, 1, 2, 3, 6; *Opere*, I, 384, 385, 386, 389. For other general identifications of liberty and republics: *ibid.*, II, 4, 21; *Istor. fior.*, VI, 13; *Opere*, I, 288, 341; VII, 406.

[125]*Il principe*, V; *Discursus florentinarum rerum*; *Opere*, I, 28 29; II, 261 63.

[126]*Discorsi*, I, 40, 46, 49; *Discursus florentinarum rerum*; *Istor. fior.*, VI, 23, 24; *Opere*, I, 229, 235, 242; II, 263, 267; VII, 423, 425 26.

[127]*Istor. fior.*, V, 6; *Opere*, VII, 335 36. On *suffragi liberi*: *Discorsi*, I, 20, 49; *Opere*, I, 185, 242.   [128]*De rebus pistoriensibus*; *Opere*, II, 30.

[129]*Discorsi*, I, 49; *Opere*, I, 241 42.   [130]*Ibid.*, 4 5; *Opere*, I, 138 40.

[131]*Ibid.*, 7; *Opere*, I, 146.

liberty is a strong citizen army. In this context, Machiavelli defends a citizen army not merely because he thinks it is more effective in the field than mercenaries but also because he thinks it reflects and reinforces civic virtue, and is hence appropriate to a free government.[132] A citizen army conscripted of amateurs, which should characterize a free republic, has more valor and self-respect, according to Machiavelli, than a professional standing army. Thus, he notes, while the Romans sometimes bought off their enemies under the empire, they never pursued this cowardly policy while they lived in freedom (*vissono liberi*).[133] In contrast to foreign mercenaries, who fight languidly and are easily suborned because they have no concern for the well-being of the city, citizen armies fight enthusiastically and have a patriotic *esprit de corps*. They manifest and strengthen civic virtue. Cities keep themselves uncorrupted (*immaculate*) much longer with citizen armies than without them.[134] While, as noted above, Machiavelli's case for a citizen army in the defense of corporate liberty is purely practical, his argument in the context of liberty within the state is based as much on moral as on practical grounds.

In analyzing the characteristics of free republics, Machiavelli does not merely fasten on a few assorted institutions. He also provides two systematic descriptions of free republican constitutions as a whole. Both of them pertain to Florence, one being drawn from her past history and the other being a reform proposal written by Machiavelli himself. In the thirteenth century, he notes, the Florentines united and agreed to form a free state (*pigliare forma di vivere libero*). The constitution they set up provided for an executive and legislative council of twelve citizens, representing equally six electoral districts and holding office for one year. Two non-Florentine judges were appointed, a *Capitano di Popolo* and a *Podestà*, to deal with civil and criminal cases respectively. Military ordinances were established subdividing the state into ninety-six districts for the conscription of a citizen army. The military leaders were changed annually. On this civil and military government, says Machiavelli, the Florentines founded their liberty.[135] Outside of the fact that the council and the army were composed of citizens, it is not too clear why he thinks that this constitution was free, for he does not indicate how the council was elected, by whom the judges were appointed, or whether the populace retained the right to scrutinize the activities and policies of the officials.

Machiavelli is much more detailed and specific in the tentative constitution for Florence which he wrote at the request of Pope Leo

[132]*Parole da dirle*; *Opere*, II, 62.

[133]*Discorsi*, II, 30; *Opere*, I, 370.   [134]*Arte della guerra*, I; *Opere*, II, 348.

[135]*Istor. fior.*, II, 4, 5; *Opere*, VII, 144, 145 46. This point has been noted by Baron, *Crisis*, 386.

X in about 1520. Machiavelli outlines a republic, giving a purely practical justification for it—the argument that it would be easier to establish than a principality, that it would preserve and increase Leo's control over the city, and that it would enable him to secure and honor his friends and to satisfy the people.[136] This argument is possibly attributable to the fact that Leo might plausibly have been expected to support a return to the Medici system. In any event, Machiavelli proposes the elimination of the current institutions in Florence and their replacement by a hierarchy of three councils, a *Signoria*, a Council of Two Hundred, and a Great Council of one thousand, or at least six hundred. The main links among these councils are to be the offices of *Gonfalonieri* and Provosts, who may veto decisions of the *Signoria* and appeal them to the Two Hundred and who in turn may veto decisions of the Two Hundred and appeal them to the Great Council.[137]

Machiavelli offers two justifications in support of this polity, a polity which, he says, lacks nothing necessary to a republic.[138] In the first place, he observes that there are three kinds of citizens, the important, the middle, and the lowest—distinctions, he stresses, which do not prescind from the political egalitarianism characteristic of Florence but which refer to differences in the political ambitions of these three groups. The three councils in his system are designed to accommodate these differences in ambition.[139] He also points out that his provisions for veto and appeal enable the three groups to scrutinize each other's actions, thus preventing the abuse of power by all branches of the government.[140]

Machiavelli's constitution, however, is neither egalitarian nor truly balanced. All governmental power is concentrated in the *Signoria* and the other two councils enjoy only residual functions or those that the *Signoria* chooses to delegate to them. The membership of the two upper councils is dominated by the wealthy upper guilds, and is to be appointed by Leo for life. The membership of the Great Council is also to be controlled by Leo, either by appointment or by electoral management. The electoral procedures outlined for the *Gonfalonieri* and Provosts by no means rule out the possibility of management in these cases as well.[141] An economic and social oligarchy hence commands most of the power, tempered by the princely initiative of the patron, with only a few symbolic gestures in the direction of participatory government and electoral franchise.

The fact that Machiavelli at some points connects the idea of freedom with a republic marked by broad participation in government and

---

[136]*Discursus florentinarum rerum; Opere,* II, 268–69.
[137]*Ibid.,* 268–75.   [138]*Ibid.,* 274.
[139]*Ibid.,* 267–69. Cf. *Parole da dirle; Opere,* II, 57, on Florence as an egalitarian polity.   [140]*Discursus florentinarum rerum; Opere,* II, 268–75.   [141]*Ibid.*

at other points, as in the case of Florentine constitutions both actual
and hypothetical, with a narrow oligarchy of the rich[142] is somewhat
confusing. To a certain extent this confusion may be dispelled by a
closer look at the meaning of *republica* in his thought. Here Machiavelli diverges noticeably from his Florentine predecessors of the
trecento and *quattrocento*. A tradition of republican thinking existed
in Florence throughout the period, its emphasis shifting in response
to internal and external events and cultural interests. Thus, in the
trecento the republican principle could be advocated in terms of
Guelfism; in the early *quattrocento* Leonardo Bruni could justify it in
terms of Aristotelian ethics and on the grounds that it stimulated art
and literature; and at the end of the *quattrocento* Savonarola could
assimilate it to Christian moral reform. Notwithstanding these shifts,
the proponents of republicanism tended to conceive of the Florentine
republic in constitutional terms, identifying it with participatory
government. In some cases they even identified it with political equality and, like Machiavelli, did not hestitate to apply this description to
the Florentine government of their day without worrying too much
about the disparity between description and political fact.[143] While

[142]Machiavelli's oligarchical proclivities have been noted by Cadoni, *loc. cit.*,
466-72; Renaudet, *loc. cit.*, 189.

[143]Generalizations may be foolhardy considering the fact that scholarship on
this controversial subject is currently in a state of flux and revision. Debate centers on
the origins, constituents, and causes of Florentine republican theory in the *trecento*
and *quattrocento* as well as on the types of evidence apposite to these questions. Many
of the primary sources still remain unedited. A detailed consideration of the literature
would require an excursus not entirely germane to this paper. For further discussion:
Albertini, *loc. cit.*, 21-31, 37-45, 53-74; Baron, *Crisis, passim*, which includes references to Baron's other writings; Marvin B. Becker, "Florentine 'Libertas': Political
Independents and 'Novi Cives,' 1372-1378," *Traditio*, XVIII (1962), 393-407; "The
Republican City State in Florence: An Inquiry into Its Origin and Survival (1280-
1434)," *Speculum*, XXXV (Jan. 1960), 48-49; and more recently *Florence in Transi-
tion* (Princeton, 1967-68), I, *passim*; II, 18-22, 60-61, 93-149, 200, 204, 221, 223, 226-29;
Garin, *Italian Humanism*, 37-81; Felix Gilbert, *Machiavelli and Guicciardini:
Politics and History in Sixteenth-Century Florence* (Princeton, 1965), including
references to Gilbert's other writings; Peter Partner, "Florence and the Papacy in the
Earlier Fifteenth Century," *Florentine Studies: Politics and Society in Renaissance
Florence*, ed. Nicolai Rubinstein (London, 1968), 383; N. Rubinstein, "Florence and
the Despots: Some Aspects of Florentine Diplomacy in the Fourteenth Century,"
Transactions of the Royal Historical Society, 5th series, II (1952), 21-45; "Florentine Constitutionalism and Medici Ascendancy in the Fifteenth Century," *Florentine
Studies*, 445-60; "Political Ideas in Sienese Art: The Frescoes by Ambrogio Lorenzetti
and Taddeo di Bartolo in the Palazzo Pubblico," *Journal of the Warburg and Courtauld Institutes*, XXI (1958), 184-85; J. E. Siegel, "'Civic Humanism' or Ciceronian
Rhetoric?" *Past and Present*, XXXIV (1966), 19-23; Donald Weinstein, "The Myth
of Florence," *Florentine Studies*, 24-44. For the Roman background: C. Wirszubski,
Libertas as a Political Idea at Rome during the Late Republic and Early Principate,
Cambridge Classical Studies (Cambridge, 1950), *passim* and esp. 3-4, 7-17, 27-30,
78-87, 95-127.

he is undoubtedly aware of the ideas of his Florentine predecessors, Machiavelli also uses *republica* in the sense derived by the Romans from its generic Latin meaning of *respublica*, the commonwealth or the common weal. Thus, Machiavelli feels free to apply the term *republica* to any kind of commonwealth regardless of its constitutional form. After defining the three major forms of government, he says that the founder of a state (*republica*) may choose from among the three.[144] He does not hesitate to call a monarchy, that of ancient Rome, a *republica*.[145] While any kind of polity can hence be a republic, the best kind of republic, he asserts, is a mixed government. Rome, for example, in developing from a monarchy to a popular government, retained some elements of monarchy and aristocracy, and thus, remaining mixed, formed a perfect republic (*rimanendo mista, fece una republica perfetta*).[146] On the other hand, Florence, which Machiavelli describes as having had mixed government under the Medici,[147] has not been a republic for two hundred years.[148]

Machiavelli provides an explanation for this startling and contradictory judgment. *Republica* is a norm, not merely a description. A republic is defined by its concern for the common weal: "It is not private interest but the common good that makes cities great. And without doubt this common good is observed only in republics, for they carry out everything that advances it."[149] A constitution, even if it embodies the best form of government, cannot make its people desire the common good. Lacking this overriding concern for the common weal, a state, even with all the institutional advantages, would be no republic at all.[150]

Machiavelli's somewhat ambiguous treatment of republics can be resolved to some extent by admitting the principle that the meaning of *republica* transcends specific institutional forms. The ambiguity in his handling of the relationship between *libertà* within the state and various institutional arrangements can be dealt with in the same way. As we noted above, there are circumstances under which Machiavelli thinks that virtually any kind of political arrangement, from tyranny to principality to aristocracy to popular rule to factions, can be detrimental to liberty. At the same time, there are circumstances under which all of these arrangements, with the exception of tyranny, are conducive to liberty. Free governments, thus, may take a variety of forms. Their parity lies not in their constitutional similarity, but in their objectives, their animating principles, their procedures, and the advantages they hold out to their citizens.

To illustrate this idea, Machiavelli often connects *libertà* with cer-

[144]*Discorsi*, I, 2; *Opere*, I, 130-31.   [145]*Ibid.*, 23; *Opere*, I, 188-89.
[146]*Ibid.*, 2; *Opere*, I, 133, 135.   [147]*Discursus florentinarum rerum*; *Opere*, II, 261-63.
[148]*Discorsi*, I, 49; *Opere*, I, 242.   [149]*Ibid.*, II, 2; *Opere*, I, 280.
[150]*Discursus florentinarum rerum*; *Opere*, II, 263-64.

IDEA OF LIBERTY IN MACHIAVELLI   203

tain personal rights and community benefits that characterize free
states regardless of their constitutions. He clearly identifies freedom
with the protection of private rights. One has a right to one's good
name, and in free cities (*nelle città libere*) there is legal recourse
against slander.[151] One also has the right to the freedom and security
of one's person and one's property and to those of one's family: "The
common advantage provided by a free polity . . . is to be able to enjoy
freely one's own possessions without suspicion, not to worry about the
honor of one's women and children, and not to fear for oneself."[152]
Another common advantage enjoyed by free communities is the increase of power and wealth, which, according to Machiavelli, occurs
only in free states (*Si vede per esperienza che le cittadi non avere mai
ampiato nè di dominio nè di richezza se non mentre sono state in
libertà*). Free states tend toward growth and prosperity, he says, because their people are secure. Thus, they have many children, confident that they will be able to make careers for themselves on the basis
of ability, and they work hard, confident that they will be able to enjoy
the fruits of their labor.[153]

This sense of security and confidence is a reflection of the civic
virtue animating free communities. A state cannot long be free if it is
corrupt;[154] and, if uncorrupted, it will be able to benefit even from
factionalism, which otherwise would be a grave menace to liberty.[155]
As noted above, Machiavelli holds that the high level of civic virtue
attained in ancient Rome enabled her to endure for a long time as a
free state; in the present he praises the imperial cities of Germany for
the honesty, goodness, and friendliness of their people, which virtues
explain, he says, why so many of them live freely.[156] A free state
enhances its civic virtue and preserves itself from corruption from
within as well as conquest from without by instituting a citizen
army,[157] by giving appropriate rewards and punishments to its citizens,[158] and above all by subordinating private interests to the well-
being of the whole.[159]

[151]*Discorsi*, I, 8; *Opere*, I, 150.

[152]*Ibid.*, 16; *Opere*, I, 173 74. This point has also been noted by Abraham, *loc.
cit.*, 29; Cadoni, *loc. cit.*, 479 80, although he sees this security as available only in a
republic; Prezzolini, *Machiavelli*, 56; Renaudet, *loc. cit.*, 186, 188 90; Russo, *loc. cit.*,
217-18, although he interprets this security in terms of hedonism; Scolari, *loc. cit.*,
49, 53.

[153]*Discorsi*, II, 2; *Opere*, I, 279 83.   [154]*Ibid.*, I, 16, 29; *Opere*, I, 173, 199 200.

[155]*Ibid.*, 17; *Discursus florentinarum rerum*; *Opere*, I, 178; II, 263 64.

[156]*Discorsi*, I, 55; II, 19; *Opere*, I, 255, 336.

[157]*Ibid.*, II, 30; *Arte della guerra*, I; *Opere*, I, 370; II, 348.

[158]*Discorsi*, I, 16, 24, 29; III, 28; *Opere*, I, 173, 191, 199 200, 463.

[159]*Ibid.*, I, 4, 18; *Istor. fior.*, III, 5. 25; *Opere*, I, 137, 179 80; VII, 220 23, 262.
This point has been noted by Albertini, *loc. cit.*, 62 63; Chabod, *loc. cit.*, 97; Hexter,
"*Il principe* and *lo stato*," 133 34; Whitfield, "On Machiavelli's Use of *Ordini*." 34 35.

In fact the promotion of the common good can be called the norm of *libertà* within the state just as it is the norm of the *republica*. Free states are characterized by good rulers who promote liberty by ordaining just and wise legislation which conduces to the welfare of the community at large.[160] The common weal and the liberty of the community are served not merely by prudent policy. Like the private rights of the individual, they are guaranteed by the law. The law is the means of instituting *libertà*; it is also the bastion of the citizens against arbitrary government, narrow partisan interests, violent breaches of the peace, and internecine strife. Hence the crucial importance for Machiavelli of *buoni ordini* and of the well ordered state, which he so often associates with *libertà*, and which can manifest itself in a wide number of governmental forms.[161] Hence also the importance of the rule of law, the guarantee that known and legally instituted procedures will be followed, that criticism and dissent will respect the needs of public order and the powers of duly constituted authorities, and that the laws will be binding and enforceable on all without distinction.[162] The rule of law may likewise characterize states with a wide variety of constitutional forms, ranging from that of the Roman Empire to the Italian city-state republic. But in all cases it is the security of the individual and the uncorrupted health, growth, and well-being of the whole community, as instituted by good laws lawfully administered by good men, that Machiavelli sees as the principles underlying *liberta* within the state in the broadest sense.

Conclusion. In summarizing Machiavelli's idea of *libertà* it is evident that some aspects of Machiavellian liberty are rather simple and straightforward while one aspect, the question of *libertà* within the state, is quite complex. Machiavelli's nontechnical uses of *libertà* are commonplace and need not detain us. When he deals with *libertà* in connection with free will, however, he adopts a position that is in some respects conventional and in other respects distinctively his own. Along with other commentators on the traditional *topos* of *libero arbitrio* versus determinism, Machiavelli places a high valuation on free will as a manifestation of human independence and as a condition necessary for meaningful moral choices. At the same time, the kinds of choices made possible by *libero arbitrio* are not, for Machiavelli, directed primarily to the perfection of the intellect and the spirit, and are not oriented to transcendent moral goals. Rather, they involve the

[160]*Discorsi.* I, 10; *Istor. fior.*, IV, 1; *Opere*, I, 157-59; VII, 271.

[161]*Il principe*, XIX; *Discorsi*, I, 2, 16, 17, 37, 40; II, 2; *Arte della guerra*, I; *Istor. fior.*, IV, 1; *Opere*, I, 77, 129-30, 133, 134, 175, 177, 218, 224, 280; II, 339; VII, 271. This point has been noted by Whitfield,"On Machiavelli's Use of *Ordini*," *loc. cit.*, 30, 31, 33-35, 38-39.

[162]*Discorsi*, I, 7, 10, 29; *De rebus pistoriensibus; Istor. fior.*, II, 21, 40; III, 5; IV, 1; *Opere*, I, 146, 157-59, 200; II, 30; VII, 168, 207, 220-23, 271.

development of all the capacities possessed by the individual and are oriented to the imposition of his will on the course of history.

On the other hand, Machiavelli's ideas of corporate *libertà* are fully traditional. They are completely consistent with the medieval and *trecento* conception of corporate *libertates* derived ultimately from Roman corporation theory. For Machiavelli, as for his medieval predecessors, the desirability of corporate liberty as a value in itself is a foregone conclusion and does not require any justification. The only noticeable difference between the two is the fact that Machiavelli concentrates almost exclusively on city-state corporations, and emphasizes the numerous threats to their autonomy which, he feels, must be counteracted by strong military institutions. In this connection he stresses the need for citizen armies, a classical and humanistic theme, but he bases this preference here on the purely practical argument that they are more successful in the field than are other kinds of troops.

When he discusses *libertà* within the state, however, Machiavelli shows little dependence on medieval ideas of liberty, but instead reveals a close dependence on the Roman past as well as on his immediate forebears in the Italian *trecento* and *quattrocento*. Machiavelli sometimes defines liberty within the state in institutional terms, both positively in association with republican institutions and negatively in opposition to tyranny, principality, aristocracy, popular rule, and factions. At other times he indicates that all of these political structures, except tyranny, are capable of fostering liberty. To the extent that this inconsistency can be resolved, and there is no point in assuming that Machiavelli is or needs to be completely consistent, it can be done by referring both republics and free states in general to the legal principles and moral ideals which promote internal and external security, order, prosperity, and civic virtue. Thus, Machiavelli lays heavy emphasis on the protection of private legal rights and the promotion of the common weal, which is as close as he gets to proposing an inclusive norm for judging a polity free.

Machiavelli treats liberty within the state principally in his *Discorsi* and *Istorie fiorentine*, and to a lesser extent in *Il principe*, the *Arte della guerra*, and his *Discursus florentinarum rerum*. The character and intention of the works in which passages on liberty within the state occur take on a significance which they do not have in his discussions of free will or corporate liberty, and his handling of the theme of liberty within the state serves in a number of cases as an implicit commentary on the audiences for whom these works were written.

Wherever found in his works, Machiavelli's references to liberty within the state indicate that he regards *libertà* as a positive value and as the norm of the good state, whether defined in institutional or moral

206   MARCIA L. COLISH

terms. Following in the footsteps of the Romans and the civic humanists, he does not view liberty as an end in itself, as an abstract idea, or
as a natural right. His justifications for liberty, like theirs, are fairly
concrete; in all cases liberty is valued because of its beneficial effects
on the individual and the community. Although Machiavelli stands
closer to the *trecento* and *quattrocento* than to ancient Rome in point
of time, his ideas on liberty within the state are much more a
thoroughgoing revival of the Roman point of view than a simple
perpetuation of the views of his immediate predecessors.[163]
    Machiavelli restores the Roman focus on liberty as the enjoyment
of private legal rights, a notion present in both the republican and imperial eras of Roman history.[164] With the Romans, he defines liberty
as the security of the individual and the protection of hearth and home,
and enshrines the law as the greatest guarantee of liberty, a point not
emphasized by previous Florentine political writers. Machiavelli is
also much more flexible than the *quattrocento* humanists in his use of
the term *republica*, although both are capable of stretching the concept of participatory government to accommodate more or less
oligarchical Florentine constitutions both actual and hypothetical.
Fully at home in the recent Italian past, Machiavelli uses Roman history quite freely to support his theories. He shares with his Florentine predecessors the Renaissance taste for a selective and *ad hoc* use
of classical precedents; having, as they do, a civic cause to argue, he
seeks not to exhume Caesar but to blame him. He is well aware, however, of the humanists' reduction of *libertà* to a propaganda slogan,
and reflects this awareness with ironic wit by putting *libertà* into the
mouths of rebels, aggressors, and defenders of the *status quo* regardless of the nature of the regimes they propose to install or perpetuate.[165]
Machiavelli's approach to republican liberty is much broader than
that of the *quattrocento* theorists. While they define the republic in
exclusively institutional terms, Machiavelli, like the Romans, views it
sometimes in institutional terms, in which context he sees it as the
bastion against tyranny, and sometimes, like his *trecento* predecessors, in literal terms as the common weal, in which context he associates it with good rulers, good laws, and lawful procedures, which can
be found in any well ordered state regardless of its constitutional form.
    While Machiavelli's wholesale restoration of Roman justifica-
tions for liberty shows a distinct broadening of his approach in com-

[163]Cf., on the other hand, Albertini, *loc. cit.*, 53–74; Baron, *Crisis, passim*; Gilbert,
Machiavelli and Guicciardini, 28–200; Renaudet, *loc. cit.*, 188–89.
    [164]Fritz Schulz, *Principles of Roman Law* (Oxford, 1936), 140–63, provides a use-
ful summary of this question and a helpful introduction to the literature.
    [165]E.g., *Istor. fior.*, II, 35; III, 25, 27; VII, 19, 26; VIII, 34; *Opere*, VII, 194, 262,
266, 482, 492, 571.

IDEA OF LIBERTY IN MACHIAVELLI   207

parison with that of the *trecento* and *quattrocento* writers, in other respects his point of view is narrower if less doctrinaire than theirs. Although he retains the Aristotelian definition of the forms of government and the Aristotelian norm of the common weal, he omits the Aristotelian moral rationale for the republic adopted by some *quattrocento* humanists. For Machiavelli the moral corollaries of liberty rest in the civic virtue of the whole community expressed in its concern for the common good, not in the moral perfection of the individual achieved through his participation in politics. He retains in this connection only the idea that participation in a citizen army increases the civic virtue of the individual and of the community, but even here offers practical reasons for a citizen army as well. Machiavelli also limits the cultural justification for free government advocated by Leonardo Bruni and his followers. Culture has only the most tenuous connection with liberty for Machiavelli, and only in the limited sense in which a civic religion and an educational system that indoctrinate civic virtue may be called culture. He certainly adduces no artists or men of letters to demonstrate the advantages of republics.

In place of the perfection of the spirit and the immortality of art, Machiavelli offers two more original justifications for free government, which distinguish his idea of liberty from both that of his Florentine predecessors and that of the Romans. One is the idea that a free state is more dynamic economically and politically than an unfree state. The other is the idea that a free, well ordered state where individual ambitions and partisan rivalries are subordinated to the common good is better able to preserve its autonomy in the face of foreign aggression than its opposite. Since it is stable and harmonious within, it will be able to maintain a united front to the world outside. These two justifications he could have found in *trecento* political theory,[166] but he bases them on purely practical and empirical grounds, claiming to have inferred them from experience.[167] But, while the practical, "realistic" Machiavelli is often regarded as having abandoned the idealism of the *quattrocento* and of having submerged the individual in the group, by restoring a fuller appreciation of the Roman idea of liberty he also resurrects the centrality of the legal rights of the individual and reemphasizes the supremacy of the common good as the norms of *libertà* within the state.

Oberlin College.*

[166]Rubinstein, "Political Ideas in Sienese Art," 184.   [167]Sasso, *loc. cit.*, 334-44.

*This paper was delivered at the Sixth Conference on Medieval Studies, The Medieval Institute, Western Michigan University, Kalamazoo, Michigan, 18 May 1971.

[26]

Sallust and Machiavelli: from civic humanism to political prudence

PATRICIA J. OSMOND, *Rome*

Ciascuno ha letto la congiura di Catilina scritta da Sallustio.
—*Discorsi*, 3.6[1]

In a letter to Niccolò Machiavelli of 23 November 1513, the Florentine ambassador to Rome, Francesco Vettori, included Sallust in his reading list of favorite ancient historians.[2] From Machiavelli's celebrated reply of 10 December, we can infer that he too may have turned to Sallust, during the first painful months of his exile, in search of explanations and solace.[3] He may well have read the *Catilina* and *Jugurtha* together with other works in the Sallustian corpus even earlier, for Sallust, like Livy and Caesar, had long been a staple of the humanist curriculum. Whenever it was, however, that Machiavelli first read or reread these texts, he was strongly influenced by the ideas he encountered. His own major writings, the *De principatibus*, *Discorsi*, and *Istorie fiorentine*, testify to their impact. He did not often mention the Roman historian by name; but then he could assume, like his humanist predecessor Leonardo Bruni—who had spoken of Sallust quite simply as (the) *historicus*—that his audience would immediately recognize the references.[4] As he stated in book 3, chapter 6 of his *Discorsi*: "Everyone has read Sallust's account of the conspiracy of Catiline."

Machiavelli was not far from the truth.[5] Nearly everybody, it seems,

Journal of Medieval and Renaissance Studies 23:3, Fall 1993. Copyright © 1993 by Duke University Press. CCC 0047-2573/93/$1.50

1. Niccolò Machiavelli, *Discorsi*, ed. Sergio Bertelli, 5th ed. (Milan: Feltrinelli, 1977), 409.
2. Francesco Vettori to Niccolò Machiavelli, Rome, 23 November 1513 (no. 139, p. 219) and Machiavelli to Vettori, Florence, 10 December 1513 (no. 140, pp. 301-6) in Niccolò Machiavelli, *Lettere*, ed. F. Gaeta (Milan: Feltrinelli, 1961).
3. On Machiavelli's state of mind during this period, see Werner L. Gundersheimer, "San Casciano, 1513: A Machiavellian Moment Reconsidered," *Journal of Medieval and Renaissance Studies* 17 (1987): 41-54.
4. Leonardo Bruni, *Oratio in funere Johannis Strozzae*. ed. Etienne Baluze, in *Miscellanea*, vol. 3 (Paris: F. Muguet, 1681), reprinted by G. D. Mansi in *Stephani Baluzii . . . Miscellanea* (Lucca: V. Junctinius, 1764), 4:2-7.
5. Quentin Skinner notes Sallust's popularity in his "Machiavelli's *Discorsi* and the Pre-Humanist Origins of Republican Ideas," in G. Bock, Q. Skinner, and M. Viroli, eds., *Machiavelli and Republicanism* (Cambridge: Cambridge University Press, 1990), 121-41 (see esp. 123). This is corroborated by the exceptionally rich manuscript tradi-

408   *Journal of Medieval and Renaissance Studies*, 23 (1993) 3

in the early sixteenth century had in fact read Sallust's *Bellum Catilinae*—and, in addition, all or many of the other works by, or attributed to, the historian of the late Republic: the *Bellum Iugurthinum*,
Historiae, *Epistulae ad Caesarem*, and *Invectiva in Ciceronem*. From
the fifteenth well into the early seventeenth century, C. Sallustius
Crispus headed what might be called the bestseller list of ancient historians. The number of Latin editions and commentaries marks him
as a favorite in the schools and universities; translations of his *Opera*
point to a broad, diversified readership.[6] For humanist teachers and
educators, his work served as a basis for teaching Latin grammar and
rhetoric, inculcating principles of public and private morality, and
illustrating aspects of Roman government, religion, and law. Historians
imitated features of his style, paraphrased his speeches and character
portraits, cited his *sententiae* and *exempla*, and appropriated themes
and motifs, ideas and arguments.

Sallust's reception in the Renaissance reflects an unusually broad
range of contemporary attitudes and interests. Whereas the popularity
of most Roman historians, including Livy and Tacitus, tended to rise
or decline in this same period, that of Sallust remained relatively constant.[7] Yet the reasons for his popularity changed and the precise

---

tion of Sallust's works from the ninth through the fifteenth century. Robert W. Ulery,
Jr., who is currently examining the medieval commentaries on Sallust, has found more
than two hundred manuscripts with substantial marginal or interlinear annotations
dating from this period. Italian versions of speeches and letters excerpted from Sallust's
monographs began to appear in the late thirteenth century; complete translations of
these works were made in the early fourteenth century. By Machiavelli's time, we can
add the evidence of printed editions: over 68 Latin editions of his *Opera* were published
between 1470 and 1500 (as opposed to 27 for the next most popular historian, Valerius
Maximus, 15 for Livy, and 13 each for Caesar and Florus). In the first half of the
sixteenth century, Sallust led the field with 94 editions (against 82 for Valerius Maximus, 34 for Caesar and 31 for Livy). See Miroslav Flodr, *Incunabula classicorum*
(Amsterdam: Hakkert, 1973) for the fifteenth century and Franz Ludwig Anton
Schweiger, *Handbuch der classichen Bibliographie*, vol. 2, pt. 2 (Leipzig: F. Fleischer,
1834), for the later editions.

6. Sallust remained at the top of the list of Roman historians, in the number of Latin
editions and commentaries, during the entire period from 1470 to the early 1600s.
During the period 1600 to 1650 he slipped to second place behind Tacitus, but only by
a difference of one edition. For a study of the medieval and Renaissance commentaries,
see the forthcoming article on C. Sallustius Crispus by Robert W. Ulery, Jr., and
Patricia J. Osmond for the *Catalogus Translationum et Commentariorum*.

7. Most studies of the *fortuna* of Roman historians have so far concentrated on
Livy and Tacitus. According to Peter Burke, the "shift from virtue to prudence, from
eloquence to truth" in the course of the sixteenth and seventeenth centuries was best
illustrated by the decline of Livy and the rise of Tacitus: "A Survey of the Popularity
of Ancient Historians, 1450–1700," *History and Theory* 5 (1966):151. Writing from a
similar point of view, J. H. Whitfield graphically entitled his article on changing
classical models of sixteenth-century Italy "Livy > Tacitus" in R. R. Bolgar, ed.,

nature of his reputation varied—responding to new trends in historical writing and political thought, altered priorities in rhetoric and moral philosophy, and different social realities. In the early phases of the Renaissance, Sallust's two monographs, the *Catilina* and *Jugurtha*, along with speeches and letters from his *Historiae*, helped shape the ethic of civic humanism and promote the ideals of political liberty. By the later sixteenth century, other aspects of his thought were discovered in these texts and in the *Epistulae ad Caesarem*, elements that gave support not to civic virtues or participatory ideals of government but to the cause of absolutism and power politics.

In the shift from one mode of reading to the other, Machiavelli's use of Sallust represents the culmination of earlier republican interpretations and at the same time points to the beginning of a more rational, pragmatic approach to his work. If, like his predecessors of the trecento and quattrocento, he found in Sallust an authoritative defense of popular government, he also drew out the more radical implications of his ideas and set them within a new context of political realism. Moreover, if a study of Machiavelli is important for the understanding of Sallust's reception in the Renaissance, the investigation of the latter's *fortuna* also elucidates key terms in Machiavelli's political vocabulary and fundamental elements in his conceptual framework.

I. Sallust: From Politics to History

Between his voluntary or forced retirement from politics in 44 B.C. and his death c. 35 B.C., Gaius Sallustius Crispus composed two monographs—the *Bellum Catilinae*, on the Catilinarian conspiracy of 63 B.C., and the *Bellum Iugurthinum*, on the Roman war in Numidia in 111–105 B.C.—plus a longer work, the *Historiae*, which covered the post-Sullan period from 78 B.C. down to (and perhaps beyond) the end of the Third Mithridatic War, but which survives only in part.[8] Each of

---

Classical Influences on European Culture, A.D. 1500–1700 (Cambridge: Cambridge University Press, 1976), 281–94. In an article analyzing the rhetorical and philosophical trends of sixteenth-century France, J. H. M. Salmon associated Livy and Cicero with the participatory ethic of the early decades, while linking Tacitus and Seneca to the rise of political pragmatism during the wars of religion: "Cicero and Tacitus in Sixteenth-Century France," *American Historical Review* 85 (1980): 307–31. On Sallust's reception in the Middle Ages and Renaissance (a comparatively neglected subject), see the bibliography in note 10 below.

8. Whether the two *Epistulae ad Caesarem* and the *Invectiva* or *Oratio in M. Tullium Ciceronem* were the work of Sallust is still a debated issue. Both formed part of the Sallustian *corpus*, nevertheless, and during most of the Renaissance were accepted as genuine. The two *epistulae*, composed or "set" in the period between the end of

410   *Journal of Medieval and Renaissance Studies*, 23 (1993) 3

the works dealt with what Sallust considered one of the crucial stages in the breakdown of the Roman Republic and contrasted the spreading corruption in private and public life with the simple habits and heroic achievements of earlier centuries. On the surface, he presented a clear and straightforward explanation of a state's rise and decline, emphasizing the relation between moral character and political vicissitudes. *Virtus*, the pursuit of glory through the performance of great deeds, had assured the growth of the city-state from obscure origins to world dominion. Ambition and avarice, ostentation and indolence (the products of prolonged peace and excessive prosperity) had destroyed civic harmony and threatened the very survival of the *res publica*.

There were also contradictions or ambiguities in Sallust's writing, nevertheless—between individual and collective values, idealism and pessimism, or moral versus utilitarian concerns.[9] On the one hand, he painted a utopian picture of the ancient city-state and constructed a moralistic scheme of history; yet he was also capable of subtle analysis and sharp social criticism. He exalted the value of intellectual activity (especially the writing of history), but appealed for vigorous political action and commitment to public service. While ascribing events to the capricious play of Fortune, he yet professed a strong faith in human reason and initiative. As politician turned historian, Sallust brought to his writing not only the traditional assumptions of Roman and Greek historiography but also the disappointed ambitions of his personal career and the ambivalent attitudes of the Late Republic.

II. Civic Humanist Interpretations

Sallust was not a new discovery of the Renaissance. From antiquity onwards, readers had admired and used his work as a model of Latin prose and oratorical eloquence, a repository of moral lessons and

Caesar's proconsulship in Gaul and the beginning of his dictatorship, purported to advise him on the reform and reorganization of the Roman state and the means of establishing a lasting peace. The *Invectiva* or *Oratio in M. Tullium Ciceronem*, allegedly delivered in the Senate about 54 B.C., assailed the former consul as a "mercennarius patronus" and "levissimus transfuga." It was usually accompanied by an equally vitriolic rejoinder attributed to Cicero, the *Invectiva* or *Oratio in C. Sallustium Crispum*.

9. On Sallust's political views, see Donald C. Earl, *The Political Thought of Sallust* (Cambridge: Cambridge University Press, 1961); Antonio La Penna, *Sallustio e la "rivoluzione" romana*, 2nd ed. (Milan: Feltrinelli, 1969); and Sir Ronald Syme, *Sallust* (Berkeley: University of California Press, 1964). Also useful are Patrick McGushin's introduction to his commentary on the *Bellum Catilinae* (Leiden: Brill, 1977) and the articles collected by Agostino Pastorino, ed., *Sallustio: letture critiche* (Milan: Mursia, 1978).

philosophical wisdom, and a trusted source for the history of the Roman Republic.[10] Between the late thirteenth and early fourteenth centuries, he also came into prominence as a political authority, especially in the context of an emerging civic humanist ideology. To exponents of the rhetorical and scholastic traditions, his two monographs, as well as passages in his other works, supported basic arguments in the contemporary defense of liberty: the importance of civic virtues and the common good, the corrupting effects of avarice, the dangers of factionalism, and especially the link between elective government and the growth of a commune in honor, prestige, and prosperity.[11] Most important in this respect was chapter 7 of his *Catilina*, describing the extraordinary growth of Rome once the last king had been expelled and monarchy replaced by a government of freely elected magistrates:

> Sed ea tempestate coepere se quisque magis extollere magisque ingenium in promptu habere. Nam regibus boni quam mali suspectiores sunt semperque iis aliena uirtus formidulosa est. Sed ciuitas incredibile memoratu est adepta libertate quantum breui creuerit: tanta cupido gloriae incesserat.[12]

10. On Sallust's reception in the Middle Ages, see Ezio Bolaffi, *Sallustio e la sua fortuna nei secoli* (Rome: Perrella, 1949); Beryl Smalley, "Sallust in the Middle Ages," in R. R. Bolgar, ed., *Classical Influences on European Culture, A.D. 500–1500* (Cambridge: Cambridge University Press, 1971), 165–75; Robert Stein, "Sallust for His Readers," Ph.D. diss., Columbia University, 1977; and most recently, Quentin Skinner, "Machiavelli's *Discorsi* and the Pre-Humanist Origins of Republican Ideas." On his reception in the Renaissance, see the articles by Antonio La Penna and William McCuaig cited in notes 21 and 33 below, and my forthcoming articles "*Princeps Historiae Romanae,*" a survey of Sallust's *fortuna* from the fifteenth through the seventeenth centuries to appear in *Memoirs of the American Academy in Rome*, and "Jacopo Corbinelli and the Reading of Sallust in Late Renaissance France," to appear in *Medievalia et Humanistica*.

11. Quentin Skinner, *The Foundations of Modern Political Thought*, 2 vols. (Cambridge: Cambridge University Press, 1978), vol. 1, *The Renaissance*, chaps. 1–3; idem, "Machiavelli's *Discorsi* and the Pre-Humanist Origins of Republican Ideas." See also the articles by Charles T. Davis reprinted in *Dante's Italy and Other Essays* (Philadelphia: University of Pennsylvania Press, 1984) and Hans Baron, *The Crisis of the Early Italian Renaissance*, 2nd ed. (Princeton: Princeton University Press, 1966). In chapters 2 and 3 of the first volume of his *Foundations*, Skinner identifies "two distinct traditions of political analysis" in the late Middle Ages: (1) from the study of rhetoric, emphasizing the link between moral character and concern for the common good, as the basis of liberty and (2) from the study of scholastic philosophy, which stressed the importance of the machinery of government and constitutional safeguards. Although both here and in his "Pre-Humanist Origins" he connects the use of Sallust chiefly to the rhetorical tradition, I find evidence of his influence in both currents.

12. *Bellum Catilinae* 7.1–3. Quotations from Sallust's work are taken from L. D. Reynolds's edition for the Oxford Classical Texts: C. Sallustius Crispus, *Catilina, Iugurtha, Historiarum fragmenta selecta, Appendix Sallustiana* (Oxford: Clarendon, 1991). Translations are taken from or, with occasional stylistic modifications, based

412 *Journal of Medieval and Renaissance Studies*, 23 (1993) 3

Now at that time every man began to lift his head higher and to have his talents more in readiness. For kings hold the good in greater suspicion than the wicked, and to them the merit of others is always fraught with danger; still the free state, once liberty was won, waxed incredibly strong and great in a remarkably short time, such was the thirst for glory that had filled men's minds.

Authors of treatises on the *ars dictaminis* and civic government, such as Giovanni da Viterbo and Brunetto Latini, drew upon this passage and other introductory chapters of the two monographs to extol the merits of republican institutions. For Latini, who was especially attracted to the moral and rhetorical features of Sallust's work, the *Catilina* also furnished material for exalting Cicero's role as citizen-orator, illustrating Aristotle's *Nichomachean Ethics*, and translating specimens of classical oratory into the vernacular.[13] In the same years, Thomas Aquinas quoted the lines from *Catilina* 7.2–3 in his *De Regno ad Regem Cypri* to affirm the importance of liberty in the spiritual progress of the individual and underscore the positive purposes of human society.[14] At the Florentine convent of Santa Maria Novella, passages from Sallust's writings were cited by the priors Remigio de' Girolami and Tolomeo da Lucca. Interest in ethical and political philosophy, especially in relation to contemporary civic controversies, encouraged a rereading of classical authors, and scholastic learning could be fruitfully combined with efforts to promote the kind of patriotic spirit and devotion to the *bene comune* exemplified in the ancient Roman republic.[15] It was at Santa Maria Novella, moreover, that the Dominican

---

upon J. C. Rolfe's English version for the Loeb Classical Library (Cambridge: Harvard University Press, 1931; reprint 1985).

13. Brunetto Latini, *Li livres dou tresor*, ed. Francis J. Carmody (Berkeley: University of California Press, 1948). On Brunetto's humanism, see in particular Charles T. Davis, "Brunetto Latini and Dante," *Studi medievali*, 3rd ser., 8 (1967): 421–50, reprinted in *Dante's Italy and Other Essays*. Many collections of speeches and letters from Sallust's two monographs, preserved in dozens of Tuscan and northern Italian manuscripts from the late thirteenth century on, contain Italian versions of Caesar's and Cato's orations from *Catilina*, 51 and 52, as well as other excerpts allegedly translated by Latini.

14. Thomas Aquinas, *De regno* 1.3–4. *Opera omnia*, Commissio Leonina, vol. 42 (Rome: Editori di San Tommaso, 1979) and Gerald B. Phelan's translation, *On Kingship* (Toronto: Pontifical Institute of Mediaeval Studies, 1949).

15. Tolomeo quoted Cato's lines in *Bellum Catilinae* 52.19–21 ("Unde respublica ex parva effecta est magna, quia in illis domi fuit industria, foris iustum imperium, animus in consulendo liber, neque delicto, neque libidini obnoxius") in his continuation of Aquina's *De regno*; see J. Mathis's edition, *De regimine principum* (Turin: Petrus Mariettus, 1924), 2:8. On the author, see Charles T. Davis, "Ptolemy of Lucca and the Roman Republic," *Proceedings of the American Philosophical Society* 118 (1974):

friar Bartolomeo da San Concordio composed the first complete Italian translation of Sallust's monographs, emphasizing the practical relevance of his history and celebrating the role of personal merit and *virtuose opere*.[16]

The nearly chronic factionalism of the Italian communes also prompted historians to search for causes of a republic's breakdown, as well as its success. In a series of treatises composed between about 1313 and 1329, the Paduan historian and poet Albertino Mussato formulated a scheme of constitutional change based partly upon notions of natural biological cycles, partly on ethico-political arguments borrowed from the *Catilina*, 6–10.[17] Sallust's own account of Rome's early expansion had been followed by an analysis of its decline, and Mussato repeated his condemnation of avarice and ambition and deplored the loss of *labor atque iustitia*. In the same period, the Florentine chronicler Giovanni Villani invoked Sallust as *maestro d'istorie* and *grande dottore*.[18] Episodes of the *Catilina* offered *memoria e esemplo* of ancient

30–50, reprinted in *Dante's Italy*, and Emilio Panella, O.P., "Tolomée de Lucques," *Dictionnaire de spiritualité* 15 (1990), 1017–19, and "Livio in Tolomeo da Lucca," *Studi Petrarcheschi* 6 (1989): 43–52. On the uses of Roman republican history in the political writings of leading Dominicans at Santa Maria Novella, see Panella's work on the priors of the convent, "Priori di S. Maria Novella di Firenze," *Memorie domenicane* n.s. 17 (1986): 253–84, and especially his "Dal bene comune al bene del comune. I trattati politici di Remigio dei Girolami nella Firenze dei bianchi-neri," *Politica e vita religiosa a Firenze tra '300 e '500*, Memorie domenicane n.s. 16 (1985): 1–198. Although the convent did not witness at this time any significant humanist activity in the sense of a literary-philological movement, there was a growing propensity to reread such ancient authors as Cicero, Livy, and Sallust in the light of contemporary political issues and an effort to recover, through their writings, the ethico-political ideals of Roman republicanism.

16. Bartolomeo da San Concordio, *Il Catilinario ed il Giugurtino*, ed. Basilio Puoti (Naples: Diogene, 1827). On the author, see C. Segre, "Bartolomeo da San Concordio," *Dizionario biografico degli italiani*, 6:768–70. On the merits of his translation, see Emanuele Cesareo, *Le traduzioni italiane delle monografie di Sallustio* (Palermo: Scuola tip. "Boccone del Povero," 1924). The translation was commissioned by a Nero Cambi, perhaps the merchant banker and leader of the Black faction.

17. Albertino Mussato, *De gestis Italicorum*, in Rerum italicarum scriptores, 10, cols. 573–768; idem, *De lite inter Naturam et Fortunam*, Padua, Biblioteca Civica, Ms. B.P. 2531, fols. 1–46, also Seville, Biblioteca Colombina, Ms. 5.1.5 (cited by Rubinstein [see below], 169, n. 5); *De traditione Patavii ad Canem Grandem anno 1328* is included as book 12 of the *De gestis*. On these works, see Nicolai Rubinstein, "Some Ideas on Municipal Progress and Decline in the Italy of the Communes," in Donald James Gordon, ed., *Fritz Saxl 1890–1948: A Volume of Memorial Essays* (London: T. Nelson, 1957). Rubinstein points to the close similarities in word and thought between *De traditione*, col. 716, and chapter 10 of the *Catilina*; see p. 172 and n. 2.

18. Giovanni Villani, *Cronica*, 8 vols. (Florence: Magheri, 1823). A new edition of books 1–8 has appeared in volume 1 of *Nuova Cronica*, ed. Giuseppe Porta (Parma: Guanda, 1990). On Villani, see Eric Cochrane, *Historians and Historiography in the Italian Renaissance* (Chicago: University of Chicago Press, 1981), 10 and passim; also

414 *Journal of Medieval and Renaissance Studies*, 23 (1993) 3

valor (viz., Cicero's defense of the republic); it also warned readers of the evils of domestic discord and the disasters that could befall a state weakened by internal dissension.

If the experience of communal strife intensified the appeal to justice and civic harmony, the impact of external events stimulated new constitutional arguments justifying Florence's foreign policy. In the latter part of the fourteenth century, the city was entering upon a period of conflict with the papacy and Milan, and from his office in the Florentine chancery, Coluccio Salutati developed the themes of a militant propaganda.[19] Moving beyond the conventional Guelf contrasts between liberty and tyranny and traditional appeals to public order, he identified liberty with elective government and portrayed Florence as the leader of the free Italian communes. Livy's first *Decade* recounted stirring examples of individual patriotism from the early days of the Roman Republic; Sallust's *Catilina* suggested a connection between a popular regime, territorial expansion, and imperial power. Salutati knew the monographs both directly and through his reading of Augustine and Aquinas, and in his letter to the Romans of 6 November 1377, he took up the ideas of *Catilina* 7–9 to explain and assert the city's political ascendancy. The Romans of the ancient Republic, he claimed, had overcome the peoples of Italy, Spain, and Africa by fighting for their own and their allies' liberty. Once they had come under the rule of Caesars, their empire had vanished and Italy had been laid waste. It was only the desire for liberty, in other words, that had allowed the Roman people to acquire their "dominion, glory, and honor."[20]

Achille Tartaro, "La prosa narrativa antica," in *Letteratura italiana*, vol. 3, pt. 2 (Turin: Einaudi, 1984), 646–49.

19. *Epistolario di Coluccio Salutati*, ed. Francesco Novati, 4 vols. (Rome: n.p., 1891–93); Ronald G. Witt, *Coluccio Salutati and His Public Letters* (Geneva: Droz, 1976). On the author's contribution to contemporary political thought, see Ronald G. Witt, "Coluccio Salutati and the Origins of Florence," *Il pensiero politico* 2 (1969): 161–72; idem, "The Rebirth of the Concept of Republican Liberty in Italy," in Anthony Molho and John A. Tedeschi, eds., *Renaissance Studies in Honor of Hans Baron* (Florence: Sansoni, 1971), 175–99; and idem, *Hercules at the Crossroads: The Life, Works, and Thought of Coluccio Salutati* (Durham, NC: Duke University Press, 1983).

20. "Non putetis, excellentissimi domini, quod maiores vestri et nostri, communibus quidem parentibus gloriamur, serviendo domi, tantum tamque memorabile Imperii decus fundaverunt nec dimictendo suam Ytaliam sub externa vel domestica servitute. Illa quidem moles imperii, assistendo sociis et pro eorum libertate pugnando, vobis primo subegit Ytaliam, Yspaniam vicit, Affricam superavit, demum vero in tantam est imperium vestrum sublimatatem evectum quod Romanum nomen cunctis nationibus prefuerit. Sublata autem sub Cesaribus libertate—extollant quicumque volunt laudibus Cesarem et [ceteros imperatores]—in ipsorum manibus certe vastitatem recepit Ytalia et illud imperii culmen effluxit. *Solum itaque libertatis studium et imperium et gloriam*

If Salutati was instrumental in molding the civic humanist ideology of his contemporaries and successors—and there are striking parallels between these lines and certain passages in the work of Leonardo Bruni—it was Sallust in turn, more than any other Roman historian, who contributed the central themes of *libertas, virtus,* and *gloria.* If, in an even broader sense, there was any continuity in the development from the late duecento to the early quattrocento in the rhetorical and scholastic traditions of republican thought, Sallust's work, and particularly the *Catilina,* supplied perhaps the most important of the connecting links. By the time Salutati's pupil and successor in the Florentine chancery, Leonardo Bruni, set out to write his *Historiae Florentini populi* in 1415, Sallust's ideas on political liberty were certainly familiar to Florentine readers. Bruni coupled him with Cicero at the very beginning of his work, citing the two authors admiringly as *praestantissimi auctores.* In his later *Oratio funebris* for Nanni Strozzi, he referred to Sallust quite simply as the *historicus*—an author, he believed, whom everyone would know and recognize.

The introductory chapters of the *Catilina* furnished the key to Bruni's understanding of history: a socio-psychological concept of liberty that explained the intimate connection between republican self-government, strength of character, and political greatness—or, conversely, between tyranny, moral corruption, and decline.[21] Whereas

---

(et) omnem Romanis peperit dignitatem." Quoted in Witt, *Coluccio Salutati and His Public Letters,* 54 (my italics).

Cf. Salutati's letter of 1 July 1376 to the Bolognese: " 'He who possesses virtue, when he begins to be a source of fear to the ruler, always feels the threat of the axe on his neck or is prepared for proscription or exile'." In a second letter of 28 July, he writes: "[Liberty] is the teacher of the virtues since no one hesitates in his own republic which flourishes with liberty to demonstrate how much and what a virtuous man can do" (ibid., 55). I would like to thank Ronald Witt for bringing my attention to this evidence of Sallustian influence. On the use of Sallust to prove the Roman republican foundation and heritage of Florence, see Witt, "Coluccio Salutati and the Origins of Florence."

21. Leonardo Bruni, *Historiarum Florentini populi libri XII,* ed. E. Santini, Rerum italicarum scriptores, n.s. 19:3–288 (Città di Castello: Lapi, 1914). On Bruni's life and work, and for translations of selected texts, see G. Griffiths, J. Hankins, and D. Thompson, eds., *The Humanism of Leonardo Bruni* (Binghamton, NY: Medieval and Renaissance Texts and Studies, 1987). On Bruni's use of Sallust, see Antonio La Penna, "Die Bedeutung Sallusts für die Geschichtsschreibung und die politischen Ideen Leonardo Brunis," *Arcadia* 1 (1966): 255–76, republished in Italian as "Il significato di Sallustio nella storiografia e nel pensiero politico di Leonardo Bruni," in *Sallustio e la "rivoluzione" romana,* 2nd ed. (Milan: Feltrinelli, 1969), "Appendice prima," 409–31. The present discussion is indebted to La Penna's detailed analysis.

With the exception of La Penna, most historians have focused on the role of Tacitus (e.g., Hans Baron, *Crisis*; and Kenneth Schellhase, *Tacitus in Renaissance Political Thought* [Chicago: University of Chicago Press, 1976]). While the works of Tacitus

other authors, including Salutati, had borrowed Sallustian ideas somewhat casually, Bruni was the first to develop the progression of
libertas–virtus–gloria into a coherent and comprehensive explanatory model. A comparison of *Catilina* 7 with the first book of the
Historiae reveals the decisive influence of this chapter on the entire
conceptual framework of his history, from the crisis of the Etruscan
city-states to the rise and fall of the Roman empire and, ultimately, to
the rebirth of the Italian towns and the remarkable achievements of
Florence in his own day. In the evolution of the Roman state, the
turning point had been Caesar's dictatorship. Until then, as Bruni
argued,

> character was the route to honor, and . . . high public offices were
> open to men of *magnitudo animi*, *virtus*, and *industria*. But as soon
> as the republic was entrusted to one man, strength of character and
> magnanimity became suspect in the eyes of the rulers. Only those
> were acceptable to the emperors who lacked the mental vigor to
> care about liberty. The imperial court thus opened its gates to the
> lazy rather than to the strong, to flatterers rather than to hard work-
> ers, and as government fell to the worst men, the empire was grad-
> ually brought to ruin.[22]

Under the weight of imperial rule, Bruni continued, the smaller
cities of Italy gradually lost their vigor; Rome itself eventually fell
prey to the invading barbarians. As soon as the worst of the "dark
ages" had passed, however, those towns that had survived were free
once again to grow and prosper. Capturing the very spirit of Sallust's
words as he described the resurgence of Florence in the late duecento,
Bruni expressed the same sense of enthusiasm. "It is marvelous," he
wrote, "how . . . the strength of the people developed . . . once the

---

were undoubtedly important, it should be pointed out that his views, both in his own
historical writing and in the interpretation given to them by Bruni, were to a considerable extent a development and elaboration of ideas first enunciated by Sallust.

22. The translation, with minor stylistic variations, is taken from that of Renée Neu
Watkins in *Humanism and Liberty: Writings on Freedom from Fifteenth-Century
Florence* (Columbia: University of South Carolina Press, 1976), 46. The passage reads:
"Prius namque per virtutem ad honores via fuit, iisque ad consulatus dictaturasque et
caeteros amplissimos dignitatis gradus facillime patebat iter, qui magnitudine animi,
virtute et industria caeteros anteibant. Mox vero ut respublica in potestatem unius
devenit, virtus et magnitudo animi suspecta dominantibus esse coepit. Hique solum
imperatoribus placebant, quibus non ea vis ingenii esset, quam libertatis cura stimulare
posset. Ita pro fortibus ignavos, pro industriis adulatores imperatoria suscepit aula, et
rerum gubernacula ad peiores delata ruinam paulatim dedere"; *Historiae* 1:13–14.
Cf. La Penna, "Il significato di Sallustio," 412–13.

sweetness of liberty had been tasted and once the people themselves could grant the honors of public office."[23] From this point on, he could thus begin to trace the growing magnificence of the city, the splendid achievements of its artists and writers, its steady annexation of most of Tuscany, and—following the death of Giangaleazzo Visconti and the recent capture of Pisa (which he compared in his preface to Rome's victory over Carthage)—the increasing prestige and power of Florence's own *imperium*.[24]

Like Sallust, Bruni stressed the competitive character of *virtus*: the desire to win renown by vying with fellow citizens in the performance of great deeds. It was not just liberty as equality before the law or as absence of tyranny that made popular government superior to monarchy (and oligarchy), but rather the opportunity for all citizens to

23. "Ab hiis initiis profectum, mirabile dictu est quantum adoleverit populi robur. Homines enim, qui dudum aut principibus aut eorum fautoribus, ut vere dixerim, inservierant, gustata libertatis dulcedine, cum populus iam ipse dominus auctorque honoris esset, totis se viribus attollebant, quo dignitatem inter suos mererentur. Igitur domi consilium et industria, foris autem arma fortitudoque valebant"; ibid., 2:27. Cf. La Penna, "Il significato di Sallustio," 412, who describes this as "lo slancio che anima il popolo . . . liberatosi dal regime monarchico." Cf. also the oration composed for Giovanni de' Ricci for the year 1387 (*Historiae* 9:242–43), which recalls the contrast between liberty and servitude in Memmius's speech against the nobles in *Bellum Iugurthinum* 31.

Like Sallust, Bruni identified nobility with merit, not birth, and denounced the arrogance of nobles who oppressed the people's rights and openly defied the laws, but at the same time—like Sallust too—he distrusted both the "ignorant and fickle" masses and the demagogic tendencies of popular leaders. On Bruni's political conservatism, see La Penna, "Il significato di Sallustio," 426. On Bruni's political philosophy, see also B. L. Ullman, "Leonardo Bruni and Humanist Historiography," *Medievalia et Humanistica* 4 (1946): 45–61, reprinted in idem, *Studies in the Italian Renaissance* (Rome: Edizioni di Storia e letteratura, 1955; reprint 1973).

24. Bruni viewed a state's ability to expand and establish an empire as one of the chief marks of its *grandezza*. At the beginning of his *Historiae*, he explained the early deterrents to Florence's expansion: "Only the nearness of Rome in her grandeur limited the growth of Florence. . . . How then might the city of Florence grow? She could not augment her borders by war under the rule of the empire . . . ; nor could she increase the power of her administrators"; *History of Florence*, 33. At the end of book I, he observed: "The Roman empire was founded and shaped by the Roman people. The later [Germanic] kings never attained such wide domains as to merit the name of empire. . . . The empire was created by the armed conquest of almost all Africa and a great part of Asia. . . . All this was done in four hundred and sixty-five years, by the free people of a single city"; ibid., 60. In his *Laudatio Florentinae urbis*, Bruni had celebrated the victories of Florentine armies over the cities of Volterra, Siena, and Lucca, representing the campaigns as "just wars" fought in defense of her allies. "Panegyric to the City of Florence," trans. Benjamin G. Kohl, in Kohl and Ronald G. Witt, eds., *The Earthly Republic: Italian Humanists on Government and Society* (Philadelphia: University of Pennsylvania Press, 1978), 166. Bruni probably intended to bring the *Historiae* to a climactic close with an account of Florence's expanding dominion in Tuscany and the victory over Pisa in 1406, but the work (left incomplete at his death) extended only as far as 1402; see Griffiths, *Leonardo Bruni*, 178–79.

418 *Journal of Medieval and Renaissance Studies*, 23 (1993) 3

compete for public office and civic honors. Summing up these themes in the *Oratio funebris* of 1428, Bruni repeated Sallust's words in *Catilina* 7 (while evoking as well the speeches of Memmius and Marius against the nobles in chapters 31 and 85 of the *Jugurtha*):

> What king has there ever been who would carry out all acts involved in government for the sake of his people, and desire nothing for his own sake beyond the mere glory of the name? . . . Kings, the historian says, are more suspicious of the good than of the evil man, and are always fearful of another's virtue . . . Thus the only legitimate constitution left is the popular one . . . in which legal equity is the same for all citizens, in which pursuit of the virtues may flourish without suspicion. And when a free people are offered this possibility of attaining offices, it is wonderful how effectively it stimulates the talents of the citizens. When shown a hope of gaining office, men rouse themselves and seek to rise; when it is precluded they sink into idleness.[25]

25. Leonardo Bruni, *Oratio in funere Johannis Strozzae*, 2–7. An introduction and translation of the first half of the oration by G. Griffiths is included in *Leonardo Bruni*, 105–7 and 121–27; the translation above is that of Griffiths (125). It was in this period, as Bruni was entering upon his second appointment as chancellor of Florence, that Filippo Maria Visconti, Giangaleazzo's successor, had resumed Milan's expansionist policy in northern and central Italy, threatening once again the Tuscan cities. Quoting several passages from the panegyric, Hans Baron described them as some of "the most beautiful expressions of the civic ideal in the period when Florence was locked in struggle with the Visconti" (*Crisis*, 419), although—as James Hankins warns—there were undoubtedly elements of rhetorical exaggeration in what was after all an epideictic oration. In any event, as La Penna points out ("Il significato di Sallustio," 415–16), Baron failed to recognize Sallust's influence and to identify him with the *historicus* Bruni cited, even when Bruni was repeating verbatim the words of *Bellum Catilinae* 7.

The original passage of Bruni's oration reads: "Forma reipublicae gubernandae utimur ad libertatem paritatemque civium maxime omnium directa, quae quia aequalissima in omnibus est, popularis nuncupatur. . . . Aequa omnibus libertas, legibus solum obtemperans, soluta hominum metu. Spes vero honoris adipiscendi ac se attollendi omnibus par, modo industria adsit, modo ingenium et vivendi ratio quaedam probata et gravis. Virtutem enim probitatemque in cive suo civitas nostra requirit: cuicumque hoc adsit, eum satis generosum putat ad rem publicam gubernandam. Haec est vera libertas, haec aequitas civitatis, nullius vim, nullius iniuriam vereri, paritatem esse iuris inter se civibus, paritatem reipublicae adeundae. Haec autem nec in unius dominatu nec in paucorum possunt subsistere. . . . Regibus, inquit historicus, boni quam mali suspiciores sunt, semperque his aliena virtus formidulosa est. . . . Ita popularis una relinquitur legitima rei publicae gubernandae forma, in qua libertas vera sit . . . in qua virtutum studia vigere absque suspicione possint. Atque haec honorum adipiscendorum facultas potestasque libero populo, haec assequendi proposita mirabile quantum valet ad ingenia civium excitanda. Ostensa enim honoris spe, erigunt sese homines atque attollunt, praeclusa vero inertes desidunt, ut in civitate nostra cum sit ea spes facultasque proposita, minime sit admirandum et ingenia et industriam plurimum eminere"; *Oratio in funere Johannis Strozzae*, 3–4.

Osmond · *Sallust and Machiavelli* 419

The spread of civic humanism and the immense popularity of Bruni's work assured Sallust's role in republican history and political thought through the mid-1400s. Bruni's protégé Buonaccorso da Montemagno incorporated motifs from Marius's speech in his *Disputatio de nobilitate*, defending the cause of personal merit against patrician claims to noble ancestry.[26] Poggio Bracciolini, Bruni's successor as chancellor of Florence, adopted Sallustian themes to extol the patriotic uses of history.[27] Some years earlier, in a controversy over the merits of Caesar and Scipio, Poggio had vigorously championed the cause of liberty with an appeal to Sallust's *Catilina*.[28] The political climate of mid-quattrocento Florence was considerably different, however, than that in which Bruni had begun his history. As Cosimo de' Medici consolidated his power, humanists such as Poggio grew more circumspect in recounting the former glories of their city-state. If they drew upon Sallust to praise republican values, they quoted him even more frequently on ambition and avarice or the destructive effects of party factionalism.[29] Under Lorenzo de' Medici, there remained little incentive even for this. To the extent that Sallust's work conveyed any political message at all, it taught the benefits of princely rule.[30]

The calamities of late fifteenth- and early sixteenth-century Italy,

26. Buonaccorso da Montemagno, "De nobilitate," in *Prosatori latini del Quattrocento*, ed. and trans. Eugenio Garin (Milan: Ricciardi, 1952); see especially 142 and 156.

27. Poggio Bracciolini, *Historia florentina*, ed. J. Baptista Recanatus (Venice: Hertz, 1715). Summarizing the early history of the city, Poggio linked its growth and vitality to the institutions of a free commune. Cf. Matteo Palmieri, *De captivitate Pisarum liber*, ed. Gino Scaramella, Rerum italicarum scriptores, n.s., 19:2 (Città di Castello, 1904); Palmieri introduced Sallustian character portraits and orations into this work of circa 1448 in order to dramatize the heroic exploits of Florence's "citizen" army and immortalize Florence's victory over Pisa.

28. "Stomachatus sum cum legi verba illius historici [i.e. Dio Cassius] in hac parte delirantis. Ait, ut traducit Guarinus, plura maiora et meliora obvenisse ex Regibus quam ex populis, ut Romanorum gesta testantur. Hic praeponit gesta Regum Romanorum his quae postmodum liberata patria a servitute regia acta sunt. Unum Salustii dictum, qui Regibus bonos quam malos dixit esse suspectiores, universum Dionem confundit"; "Defensiuncula Poggii Florentini contra Guarinum Veronensem ad Franciscum Barbarum," *Opera* (Basel: Henricus Petrus, 1538), 388–89.

29. In his "De avaritia," in *Opera*, 1:21, Poggio commented: "Testis et auctor gravis sit Sallustius."

30. In his apology for the Medici regime, composed soon after the Pazzi conspiracy of 1478, Angelo Poliziano portrayed the rebels with all the criminal passions of Catiline. Like Leon Battista Alberti, who had already compared the Roman rebel Stefano Porcari to Catiline in his *Commentarius* of 1453, composed for his own patron Pope Nicholas V, he was eager to celebrate the blessings of peace and stable government. Angelo Poliziano, *Della congiura dei Pazzi* (*Coniurationis commentarium*), ed. Alessandro Perosa (Padua: Antenore, 1958); Leon Battista Alberti, *Commentarius de coniuratione Porcaria*, ed. L. Mehus, Rerum italicarum scriptores (Milan, 1751), cols. 309-14.

420 *Journal of Medieval and Renaissance Studies*, 23 (1993) 3

precipitated by Charles VIII's invasion, further undermined the humanist ethic of an active life of public service, whatever the specific constitution of a city-state. In the wake of political upheavals and mounting pessimism, historians developed a more detached, critical approach to their subject, as well as a more cynical attitude. What Neapolitan authors such as Giovanni Albino and Giovanni Pontano now responded to in Sallust's writing was his sense of the instability of human affairs, his penetrating analyses of human character, his sharp contrasts between words and facts, appearances and reality.[31] As the "historian of calamities," Sallust unveiled the causes of the spreading turmoil and violence, exposed the self-seeking ambitions of party leaders, and denounced the ruthless struggles for power.[32] At the same time, his rapid, abrupt manner of writing and characteristic use of antithesis helped express their own mood of critical and bitter disillusionment. The Florentine aristocrat Bernardo Rucellai, author of *De bello italico commentarius*, contrasted the opportunism of popular leaders with their lofty professions of public concern, reproducing in his own elegant Latin not only the ideas and words but the very syntax and style of Sallust's prose.[33]

III. Machiavelli and Sallust

Like his humanist predecessors, Machiavelli looked to Sallust for explanations of a republic's growth and prosperity, for examples of patri-

31. Giovanni Albino, *De bello Hetrusco; De bello Hydruntino; De bello intestino; De bello Gallico*, in *Raccolta di tutti i più rinomati scrittori dell'istoria generale del Regno di Napoli*, ed. G. Gravier (Naples: Gravier, 1769), vol. 5. A critical edition of the *De bello Hydruntino* by I. Nuovo is included in Lucia Gualdo Rosa et al., eds., *Gli umanisti e la guerra otrantina* (Bari: Dedalo, 1982). Giovanni Pontano's *Historia belli quod Ferdinandus Rex Neapolitanus senior contra Ioannem Andegaviensem ducem gessit* is also found in volume 5 of Gravier's *Raccolta*.

32. Eric Cochrane calls Sallust "the most obvious ancient model for historians of calamities" (*Historians and Historiography*, 166), a phrase that recalls Sir Ronald Syme's description of Sallust as "the historian of the decline and fall" (*Sallust*, 56). On Neapolitan historiography in the fifteenth century, see Jerry H. Bentley, *Politics and Culture in Renaissance Naples* (Princeton: Princeton University Press, 1987).

33. Bernardo Rucellai, *De bello Italico commentarius* (London: William Bowyer, 1733), 42. See William McCuaig, "Bernardo Rucellai and Sallust," *Rinascimento* 22 (1982): 75–98. McCuaig notes, for example, the close similarities between Rucellai's passage (78–79) and Sallust's *excursus* in the *Catilina*, 38: "Pars, plebe sollicitata, bonum publicum simulantes, direptionem moliri; plerique irae atque iniuriae, pauci principatus libidini, nemo fere saluti patriae obtemperare." Cf. Sallust, *Bellum Catilinae* 38.3: "Namque, uti paucis uerum absoluam, post illa tempora quicumque rem publicam agitauere honestis nominibus, alii sicuti populi iura defenderent, pars quo senatus auctoritas maxuma foret, bonum publicum simulantes pro sua quisque potentia certabant."

otic spirit and public virtues, personal merit and the common good.[34] Like many of his contemporaries, he also shared Sallust's views on the unpredictability of human affairs, the egoism of human nature, and the hypocrisy of politics. Yet Machiavelli did not allow any ideal of republican government to stand in the way of what he considered more politically effective regimes, and he transformed the idea of domestic discord into a dynamic concept of the historical process—inviting, not impeding, human action. In doing this, he also placed Sallust's ideas in a new framework of political realism and moral relativism, drawing out the radical implications of his thought and suggesting fresh, often provocative, interpretations.

Of all Roman historians, C. Sallustius Crispus was closest to Machiavelli in personal experience, intellectual inclinations, and political philosophy.[35] Both men turned to writing in a period of crisis, after the failure of their own political careers and in the impending failure of the political order that they represented. Both brought to their work a natural aptitude for observation and analysis, sharpened by long years of experience in politics and by personal disappointment. The writing of each author also expressed a unique blend of optimism and pessi-

34. On aspects of Machiavelli's political philosophy and approach to ancient history, I note in particular Franco Gaeta, "Sull'idea di Roma nell'Umanesimo e nel Rinascimento," *Studi Romani* 25 (1977): 169–86; Felix Gilbert, *Machiavelli and Guicciardini* (Princeton: Princeton University Press, 1965); Myron Gilmore, "The Renaissance Conception of the Lessons of History," in *Humanists and Jurists* (Cambridge: Harvard University Press, 1963), 26–37; J. G. A. Pocock, *The Machiavellian Moment* (Princeton: Princeton University Press, 1975); Gennaro Sasso, *Niccolò Machiavelli: Storia del suo pensiero politico* (Naples: Istituto italiano per gli studi storici in Napoli, 1958; rev. ed., Bologna: Il mulino, 1980); idem, *Machiavelli e gli antichi* (Milan: Ricciardi, 1987); Quentin Skinner, *Foundations of Modern Political Thought*, vol. 1; idem, *Machiavelli* (New York: Hill and Wang, 1981); John Humphreys Whitfield, *Machiavelli* (Oxford: Blackwell, 1947); and the recent contributions to Gisela Bock, Quentin Skinner, and Maurizio Viroli, eds., *Machiavelli and Republicanism* (Cambridge: Cambridge University Press, 1990).

35. Much has been written about the influence of Livy and Tacitus on Machiavelli, but only a few historians have noted the role of Sallust. Sir Ronald Syme himself, though he sensed the affinities between Sallust and Machiavelli in language, mood, and political discourse, states that Sallust "is mentioned or quoted only three times in all the *Discorsi*" and wonders why Machiavelli did not make more use of him. See his article "Roman Historians and Renaissance Politics," in Ronald Syme, *Roman Papers*, ed. E. Badian (Oxford: Clarendon, 1979), 1:470–76. Among the few historians who do note Sallust's influence are Gilbert, *Machiavelli and Guicciardini*; Sasso, *Machiavelli e gli antichi*; Leslie J. Walker, S.J., *The Discourses of Niccolò Machiavelli*, 2 vols. (New Haven: Yale University Press, 1950), vol. 2, Table XIII; and especially Whitfield, *Machiavelli* and, most recently, Skinner, "Pre-Humanist Origins." Much of what Werner Gundersheimer says about Machiavelli's troubled state of mind in his article "San Casciano, 1513" could also be applied to Sallust's reaction to his own political exile.

mism: a disillusioned, cynical view of contemporary conditions, yet an enduring confidence in the ability of man to control rather than be controlled by the course of events.

What was needed in the contemporary crisis, Machiavelli stated in the "Proemio" to his *Discorsi*, was a "true cognizance of history" aimed at discovering the means to establish, maintain, or increase the power of republics or monarchies, and based on those "judgments" or "remedies" proposed by the ancients. The *Discorsi* were conceived as a commentary on Livy's *History of Rome*, and Sallust was only one of several *antichi* whom he drew upon either here or in his other major works, the *De principatibus* and *Istorie fiorentine*.[36] Yet Sallust's influence was pervasive, and his monographs supplied many of the broad explanatory principles illuminating the causes and consequences of political change—whether in the evolution of a republic from obscurity to greatness and from prosperity to decay, in the transition from popular to autocratic government, or in the conditions inviting revolution or permitting reform.

In the first place, Machiavelli believed, good government did not aim only at promoting *il vivere civile* in the sense of fostering the moral and intellectual capacities of its citizens. Rather, it was a matter of maintaining order and security at home and especially—for those states that had the potential to expand—of achieving "greatness." Salutati and Bruni had already enlarged the prehumanist concept of *grandezza*, with its emphasis on the rule of justice and internal harmony, to include aspirations of territorial aggrandizement and political dominion.[37] In choosing the Roman (as opposed to the Spartan or Venetian)

36. The *Discorsi* were undertaken as a commentary on the first ten books of Livy's *Ab urbe condita*, and Livy indeed furnished Machiavelli not only a format for organizing his discussion and comparing and contrasting Florentine and Roman history, but also a wide range of episodes and idealized character portraits illustrating the patriotic spirit and religious piety of the Roman people, the selfless devotion of the citizen militia, and the spirit of concord which (for a time) had assured cooperation between nobles and plebs. See Whitfield, "Machiavelli's Use of Livy," in his *Machiavelli*. Tacitus, who was just coming into prominence at this time, could be used in the civic humanist tradition of Bruni to defend republican government or, more often, as a historical source for the Empire and as a guide to princes and their subjects. See Kenneth Schellhase, "Tacitus in the Political Thought of Machiavelli," *Il pensiero politico* 4 (1971): 381–91. Polybius, like Sallust, contributed general notions of the historical and political process, particularly the idea of constitutional cycles and mixed government. See Arnaldo Momigliano, "Polybius' Reappearance in Western Europe," in idem, *Essays in Ancient and Modern Historiography* (Oxford: Blackwell, 1977), 79–98.

37. In his letter to the Romans of 6 November 1377 (quoted above in note 20), Salutati refers repeatedly to *imperium* (understood as supreme administrative and military power exercised by a ruling nation over another people, or the resulting

model for his ideal republic, however, Machiavelli focused almost exclusively on the expansionist aims of the state and the role of the citizen army in attaining such greatness. For this reason, perhaps, he was also more sensitive to the tensions between the notion of *virtus* as an aggressive force and the principles of *concordia* and *tranquillitas*.

In book 2, chapter 2 of the *Discorsi*, Machiavelli echoed Sallust's thought and words in *Catilina* 7–9 as he described the extraordinary efforts that Roman soldiers had made in subduing the peoples of Italy:

> E facil cosa è conoscere donde nasca ne' popoli questa affezione del vivere libero: perché si vede per esperienza le cittadi non avere mai ampliato né di dominio né di ricchezza se non mentre sono state in libertà. E veramente maravigliosa cosa è a considerare a quanta grandezza venne Atene per spazio di cento anni, perché la si liberò dalla tirannide di Pisistrato. Ma sopra tutto maravigliosissima è a considerare a quanta grandezza venne Roma poiché la si libero da' suoi Re. La ragione è facile a intendere: perché non il bene particulare ma il bene comune è quello che fa grandi le città. E sanza dubbio questo bene comune non è osservato se non nelle republiche.

And it is easy to understand whence that affection for liberty arose in the people, for they had seen that cities never increased in dominion or wealth unless they were free. And certainly it is wonderful to think of the greatness which Athens attained within the space of a hundred years after having freed herself from the tyranny of Pisistratus; and still more wonderful is it to reflect upon the greatness which Rome achieved after she was rid of her kings. The cause of this is manifest, for it is not individual prosperity, but the general good, that makes cities great; and certainly the general good is regarded nowhere but in republics.[38]

---

dominion or empire), associating it with both the possession of *libertas* and the pursuit of *gloria* and *dignitas*. In the *Laudatio Florentinae urbis* and the *Historiae Florentini populi*, Bruni regularly measures the greatness of a city-state, whether of ancient Rome or of his own Florence, in terms of political dominion (see note 24 above). On this theme in Machiavelli, see especially book 1, chapters 4–6 of the *Discorsi* (and passages quoted below in note 40). Nearly the whole of book 2 focuses on the means of aggrandizing the state through diplomacy and war.

38. *Discorsi* 2.2 (p. 280); translation from *The Discourses*, 282. I have used the following Italian editions: *Il Principe e Discorsi sopra la prima deca di Tito Livio*, ed. Sergio Bertelli, 5th ed. (Milan: Feltrinelli, 1977) and *Istorie fiorentine*, in *Opere di Niccolò Machiavelli*, ed. S. Bertelli, vol. 3 (Milan: Feltrinelli, 1968). The English versions of this and the following passages from Machiavelli's works are taken from L. Russo's translation of the *Prince* and C. E. Detmold's translation of the *Discourses* in the Modern Library edition (New York, 1950).

424   *Journal of Medieval and Renaissance Studies*, 23 (1993) 3

Machiavelli also understood more clearly than any of his humanist predecessors that if liberty generated a spirit of competition and in turn disunion, the latter both promoted and threatened the well-being of a republic.[39] On the one hand, the dissension between the nobility and the people, he observed, was largely responsible for the creation of good laws: the very laws that, by preserving a mixed form of government and preventing the domination of any single social order, guaranteed the liberty of all citizens. Dissension was inevitable too, he argued, in all republics that aimed at *grandezza*. Indeed, without a large population and a strong citizen army, a state could not hope to expand—even though armed men, eager for conquest, would not be docile and easily governed at home.[40] In recognizing the vital, creative nature of *disunione*, Machiavelli thus perceived and expanded upon the historicist elements in Sallust's own notion of *virtus* and *certamen gloriae*.

At the same time, Machiavelli was not blind to the potentially destructive nature of dissension and, like Sallust, distinguished between virtue and ambition and between healthy rivalry and factional struggles: the former inspired by the *bene comune*, the latter by the *bene particulare*. Good examples and good laws could restrain men's selfish impulses but not permanently suppress them, especially in a republic

Skinner sees Sallust's influence here in terms of his "traditional" role in illustrating the connection between free government, civic concord, and pursuit of the common good ("Pre-Humanist Origins," 135–41). I see it chiefly in terms of the nexus *libertas—virtus—gloria* which in turn suggests Sallust's innovative role in supporting, and perhaps even suggesting, what Skinner calls Machiavelli's "defence of the 'tumults'."

39. Sallust never completely explained the relationship between *certamen gloriae* and *concordia*. In the *Catilina*, he attempted to reconcile the competitive energy of *virtus* and the aggressive pursuit of *gloria* and *imperium* with the ideal of *concordia*: "Accordingly, good morals were cultivated at home and in the field; there was the greatest harmony and little or no avarice; justice and probity prevailed among them, thanks not so much to laws as to nature. Quarrels, discord, and strife were reserved for their enemies; citizen vied with citizen only for the prize of merit" (*Bellum Catilinae* 9.1). In the *Jugurtha*, however, he stressed the contradictions. Describing the peaceful state of Rome before the fall of Carthage, he attributed this concord to fear of the enemy (*Bellum Iugurthinum* 41.2).

40. As Machiavelli wrote in *The Discourses* 1.6: "[If] the republic had been more tranquil, it would necessarily have resulted that she would have been more feeble, and . . . lost with her energy also the ability of achieving that high degree of greatness to which she attained; so that to have removed the cause of trouble from Rome would have been to deprive her of her power of expansion" (127). He concluded: "If any one . . . wishes to establish an entirely new republic, he will have to consider whether he wishes to have her expand in power and dominion like Rome, or whether he intends to confine her within narrow limits. In the first case, it will be necessary to organize her as Rome was, and submit to dissensions and troubles as best he may; for without a great number of men, and these well armed, no republic can ever increase" (128).

aiming at dominion. In *Discourses* 1.37, he identified the beginning of the Republic's decline with the conflict occasioned by the Gracchan bill for the distribution of public land to the poor: a turning point or crucial stage in the collapse of the Republic which Sallust himself had singled out in *Bellum Iugurthinum* 41.10. In the *Florentine History* Machiavelli made civic discord, or what he called *naturali inimicizie*, the central theme of his work. Here, as he commented in the preface to book 7, certain divisions—those generated by "sectarian" interests—inevitably harmed the republic; those that were free from partisanship, however, could actually benefit it.[41]

Like Sallust, Machiavelli also divided the citizen body into two opposing parties, the nobility and the people: the one bent on domination, the other straining to preserve its freedom.[42] Sallust had introduced this theme in the speech of Gaius Memmius in *Bellum Iugurthinum* 31. After contrasting the might of the dominant faction with the servitude of the people, the *cura dominationis* of the oligarchs with the *cura libertatis* of the commons, the Roman tribune summed up the basic nature of the opposition: "They wish to lord it over you, you to be free; they desire to inflict injury, you to prevent it."[43] Machiavelli now adopted the same arguments, also tending like Sallust to polarize the terms of the conflict and oversimplify its causes. In *The Prince* he set out the main lines of the antagonism:

> Perché in ogni città si truovano questi dua umori diversi; e nasce da questo, che il populo desidera non essere comandato né oppresso da' grandi, e li grandi desiderano comandare et opprimere el populo: e da questi dua appetiti diversi nasce nelle città uno de' tre effetti, o principato o libertà o licenzia.

> For in every city these two opposite parties are to be found, arising from the desire of the populace to avoid the oppression of the great, and the desire of the great to command and oppress the people. And from these two opposing interests arises in the city one of the three effects: either absolute government, liberty, or licence.[44]

41. On related aspects of this issue, see Victoria Kahn, "Reduction and the Praise of Disunion in Machiavelli's *Discourses*," *Journal of Medieval and Renaissance Studies* 18 (1988): 1–19; also Gisela Bock, "Civil Discord in Machiavelli's *Istorie Fiorentine*," in *Machiavelli and Republicanism*, 181–201.

42. Cf. Whitfield, *Machiavelli*, 139–42.

43. "Dominari illi uolunt, uos liberi esse; facere illi iniurias, uos prohibere" (*Bellum Iugurthinum* 31.23). In the central excursus of the *Jugurtha*, 41.1–5, Sallust divided the whole state into rival parties, but denounced both *optimates* and *populares*.

44. *De principatibus*, 9 (p. 45); trans., *The Prince*, 36.

426 *Journal of Medieval and Renaissance Studies*, 23 (1993) 3

In the *Discourses*, debating whether the "guardianship of liberty" should be entrusted to the nobles or the people, he developed this antithesis a step further:

> E sanza dubbio, se si considerrà il fine de' nobili e degli ignobili, si vedrà in quelli desiderio grande di dominare ed in questi solo desiderio di non essere dominati, e per conseguente maggiore volontà di vivere liberi, potendo meno sperare di usurparla che non possono i grandi; talché essendo i popolari preposti a guardia d'una libertà, è ragionevole ne abbiano piú cura, e non la potendo occupare loro, non permettino che altri la occupi.

> [And] doubtless, if we consider the objects of the nobles and of the people, we must see that the first have a great desire to dominate, whilst the latter have only the wish not to be dominated, and consequently a greater desire to live in the enjoyment of liberty; so that when the people are intrusted with the care of any privilege or liberty, being less disposed to encroach upon it, they will of necessity take better care of it.[45]

Comparing the Romans and Florentines in the preface to book 3 of the *Florentine History*, Machiavelli explained the entire course of their history as the result of this conflict:

> Le gravi e naturali nimicizie che sono intra gli homini popolari e i nobili, causate da il volere questi comandare, e quegli non ubbidire, sono cagione di tutti i mali che nascono nelle città; e perché da queste diversità di umori tutte l'altre cose che perturbano le republiche prendono il nutrimento loro.

> The grave and natural enmities which exist between the people and the nobles, caused by the desire of the latter to command and of the former not to obey are the cause of all the ills that arise in cities; for all the other things which disturb republics derive their nourishment from these differences of disposition.[46]

As to which of the two parties was chiefly to blame for stirring up trouble in the republic, Machiavelli concluded that it was primarily the nobles who, driven by an insatiable desire for riches, had exacerbated tensions and instigated public outbreaks of violence. In part, it was an attitude that recalls the ascetic, Savonarolan tradition of Chris-

---

45. *Discorsi* 1.5 (p. 139); trans., *Discourses*, 121–22. Cf. 1.4 (p. 137) on "dua umori."
46. *Istorie fiorentine* 3 (p. 169); the translation is mine.

tian ethics, in part too the contemporary attacks upon the Florentine aristocracy. But Machiavelli's sympathy for the plight of the commons, oppressed and exploited by the nobles, and the contrast he drew between private and public wealth, point to Livy and Sallust—and especially Sallust—as his principal authorities.[47] The lust for money, they agreed, could overturn the mightiest of empires. In both his monographs, Sallust had identified *avaritia* as the principal cause of the Republic's decline; in his second letter to Caesar (assuming, as Machiavelli did, that Sallust was the author of the two *Epistulae*), he had made it the major target of his ideal reform program.

Accompanying or preceding the spread of avarice, whether in Rome or in Florence, was the disappearance of *virtus*, or rather the perversion of *virtus* into *ambitio*. In the introductory chapters to the *Catilina* Sallust had described the stages through which self-sacrificing patriotism had given way to personal ambition, healthy rivalry to fratricidal wars. In a later passage of the same monograph, he concluded that only two men of outstanding merit were left in the state: Gaius Caesar and Marcus Cato, equal in *magnitudo animi*—if each for different reasons. Comparing the two in the famous *synkrisis* of chapter 54, he remained apparently loyal to his former patron, but betrayed perhaps a more genuine admiration for Cato.[48] Like his great-grandfather the Censor, the younger man did not fear to upbraid his fellow senators and expose the venality of the governing oligarchy. His speech appealed for vigilance and action: at a time of crisis, Sallust believed, the example of a man like Cato could—and temporarily did—save the state.

Machiavelli's concept of *virtù* was rooted, like that of Sallust, in the notion of *vis animi*, a term that signified the intellectual or psychological energy, or force of will, that drives an individual to mold and dominate the world. It was that quality of mind that manifests itself in creative, competitive action and is directed, above all, to building or saving the commonwealth: the civic spirit that animated the soldiers of republican Rome and the citizens of Florence, and that (afterwards) survived in a few outstanding men—reformers or princes—called upon to rescue and regenerate their states. Sallust's political thought, as D. C. Earl has argued, rested "on a concept of *virtus* as the functioning of *ingenium* to achieve *egregia facinora*, and thus to win *gloria*, through

---

47. See *Discorsi* 1.5; 1.37; and 2.16. On Sallust as a source and authority for Machiavelli's aversion to wealth, cf. Gilbert, *Machiavelli and Guicciardini*, 175–76.

48. Syme, *Sallust*, 123; on Sallust's attitude toward Caesar and Cato the Younger, see 110–26.

bonae artes."[49] *Virtus*, though deriving its force from the intellect, was dependent upon *ingenium bonum* and the exercise of *bonae artes*. As Antonio La Penna has pointed out, however, there was also an element of amoralism in Sallust's notion of *virtus*. The same energy that could shape and dominate the world could also be diverted (in the case of a Catiline or even of such men as Marius and Caesar) into the purely selfish pursuit of power.[50] Or it could employ nonlegal means for legitimate ends (as Cato advised in calling for the immediate execution of Catiline's accomplices) if the safety of the state were imperiled.

Machiavelli's preoccupation with action, that is, successful action, also led him to present familiar aspects of Sallust's work in a new and potentially disquieting light. A case in point is his treatment of conspiracies in book 3, chapter 6 of the *Discorsi*, where he drew extensively upon the *Catilina*: the book, he stated, that "everyone had read." His purpose, so he claimed, was to encourage obedience to established authority—even tyrannical princes and corrupt oligarchies—and hence to advise princes and governors of republics how to guard against conspiracies. In the process of describing the measures that a state should take to defend itself, however, Machiavelli also revealed what in effect could make *congiure* successful. Conspiracies against a republic, for example, were easier to organize than those against a prince, for they entailed fewer risks even if the plot were detected. As Sallust could testify:

> Possono adunque i cittadini per molti mezzi e molte vie aspirare al principato, dove e' non portano pericolo di essere oppressi: si perché le republiche sono piú tarde che uno principe, dubitano meno, e per questo sono manco caute; sí perché hanno piú rispetto ai loro cittadini grandi, e per questo quelli sono piú audaci e piú animosi a fare loro contro. Ciascuno ha letto la congiura di Catilina scritta da Sallustio, e sa come, poi che la congiura fu scoperta, Catilina non sola-

---

49. Earl, *The Political Thought of Sallust*, chap. 3. On Machiavelli's concept of *virtus*, see Whitfield, *Machiavelli*, 92–105.

50. Caesar was not Machiavelli's ideal *principe*, however, any more than he may have been (in the final analysis) for Sallust himself. Like Agathocles, he had risen to power by *via scellerata e nefaria*; he had obtained fame but not true glory; see *Principe*, 8 (pp. 40–42). Following the republican tradition, Machiavelli compared him to Catiline and described him as the "primo tiranno in Roma, talché mai fu poi libera quella città"; *Discorsi*, 1.37 (p. 218). Although more disposed than Sallust toward a relativist view of government and ready to advocate monarchy where republic failed, he did not lose sight of the distinction, which Sallust himself had emphasized, between *virtus* and *ambitio*, between exercising power for the public good and mere personal aggrandizement.

mente stette in Roma ma venne in Senato, e disse villania al Senato
ed al Consolo: tanto era il rispetto che quella città aveva ai suoi
cittadini. E partito che fu di Roma e ch'egli era di già in su gli
eserciti, non si sarebbe preso Lentulo e quelli altri se non si fossoro
avute lettere di loro mano che gli accusavano manifestamente.[51]

> Citizens of a republic . . . may by a variety of ways and means aspire
> to sovereign authority without incurring great risks. If republics are
> slower than princes, they are also less suspicious, and . . . less cau-
> tious; and if they show more respect to their great citizens these in
> turn are thereby made more daring and audacious in conspiring
> against them. Everybody has read the account written by Sallust of
> the conspiracy of Catiline, and knows that, after it was discovered,
> Catiline not only stayed in Rome, but actually went to the Senate
> and said insulting things to the Senate and Consul; so great was the
> respect in which Rome held the citizens. And even after his depar-
> ture from Rome, and when he was already with the army, Lentulus
> and the others would not have been seized if letters in their own
> handwriting had not been found, which manifestly convicted them.

Whether or not Machiavelli actually intended to help princes and republics guard *against* conspiracies, the coolly detached, objective manner in which he analyzed the causes of their success or failure could,
and later did, elicit different responses—to the *Catilina* as well, of
course, as to his own writings.[52]

Certainly Machiavelli was prepared to admit the use of force and
deception in the interests of the state far more openly and unequivocally than was Sallust. Contemplating the moral degeneracy of the
people and the breakdown of law, he also turned far more decisively
than Sallust to the individual leader, whether reforming statesman or

51. *Discorsi* 3.6 (pp. 408–9); trans., *Discourses*, 431. On the other hand, Machiavelli
noted, there were usually difficulties in executing such plots. Either the conspirator
needed large armies or he had to rely on deceit, treachery, and foreign aid.

52. On conspiracies in Florence in Machiavelli's own lifetime and among his own
circle of friends in the Orti Oricellari, see Delio Cantimori, "Rhetoric and Politics in
Italian Humanism," *Journal of the Warburg and Courtauld Institutes* 1 (1937): 83–102.
Cantimori mentions that Machiavelli read aloud his chapter on conspiracies to a group
that included certain Florentines later involved in the plot of 1522 to overthrow the
Medici. No suspicion seems to have fallen on Machiavelli himself, however, and I have
found no reference in the correspondence of Zanobi Buondelmonti (one of the conspirators who had been present at these readings) to Sallust's *Catilina* (see A. M. Russo
and C. Guasti, eds., "Documenti della congiura fatta contro il Cardinale Giulio de'
Medici nel 1522," *Giornale storico degli archivi toscani*, Archivio storico italiano n.s.,
9, pt. 1; 10, pt. 1 (1859).

430   *Journal of Medieval and Renaissance Studies*, 23 (1993) 3

prince. If corruption had not spread too far, it might still be possible, he believed, to effect a *rinnovazione*: the personal example of such men as Horatius Cocles, Scaevola, Regulus, and the two Catos might restore the republic to its original principles. But in times of extreme moral decay and social antagonisms, only a *principe* could impose and enforce public order. Whatever his personal sympathies, Machiavelli realized that, when corruption had penetrated the mass of the people or where gross inequalities of wealth were deeply entrenched, it was impossible to maintain a popular government.[53]

In making mental excellence and energy the essential attributes of *virtus*, and in asserting his confidence in the possibility of human action, Machiavelli nevertheless owed more to Sallust than to any other ancient authority. For both authors, man remained the "architect of his own destiny."[54] Human intellect, initiative, and will—the ancient *vis animi* of Sallust's works adapted to Machiavelli's own Renaissance brand of *virtù*—could still make the most of unexpected situations and, at favorable conjunctures of events, even overcome the obstacles of Fortune. Both writers endeavored to explain the decline of their republics, both gave vent to their personal bitterness and pessimism; but neither was prepared to rule out entirely the possibility of intervening in, and shaping, the contemporary course of events. In times of political and social turmoil (and perhaps above all in such times) there was still the need and opportunity, they believed, for individual action.

IV. Prudential Readings of Sallust in the Later Renaissance

Exponents of republicanism in late Renaissance Europe, whether in Venice, the free cities of Germany, or, later, in the newly independent provinces of the Dutch confederation, continued to invoke Sallust's support of liberty and civic patriotism.[55] Even historians who defended

53. See *Discorsi*, 1.9 (pp. 152–55); 1.10 (pp. 156–59); 3.1 (pp. 379–84); cf. Whitfield, *Machiavelli*, 157. When the moral character of the people had deteriorated beyond repair, it was necessary to turn to autocratic government: "Perché altri ordini e modi di vivere si debbe ordinare in uno suggetto cattivo che in uno buono, né può essere la forma simile in una materia al tutto contraria"; *Discorsi*, 2.18 (pp. 181–82); cf. 3.8 (p. 415).

54. "Sed res docuit id uerum esse quod in carminibus Appius ait, fabrum esse suae quemque fortunae, atque in te maxume, qui tantum alios praegressus es ut prius defessi sint homines laudando facta tua quam tu laude digna faciundo"; *Epistula ad Caesarem* [*I*] 1.2.

55. See, for example, in Venice, the edition of Sallust's *Opera* by Paolo Manuzio (1557) and the commentary on the *Oratio Lepidi* by Antonio Zeno (1569), as well as

the *res publica*, however, tended to adopt a more cautious approach to political issues, seeking to reconcile self-government with ideals of peace and concord and shifting the emphasis from the active, creative forces of growth and change to the preservation of the status quo. The Venetian statesman-historian Paolo Paruta, for instance, felt a genuine commitment to his city and, in principle, to an active life; like Machiavelli he also stressed the practical value of ancient history.[56] When it came to applying the lessons of Roman antiquity, however, he disagreed with Machiavelli's reading of Sallust. The greatness of a state, he believed, should not be measured in terms of political power and dominion but of internal stability, the result of a balanced constitution and a precondition for *civile felicità*. If the Roman republic had collapsed amid civil dissension, the cause (as Sallust had demonstrated, if not acknowledged) was its militaristic foreign policy and overly aggressive expansion.

Far more common, nevertheless, was the tendency to enroll Sallust in support of absolute government and reason of state. In the courts, universities, and intellectual circles especially of northern Europe, historians and political theorists turned increasingly to his work to defend authoritarian regimes and justify the use of force and deception in the interests of public order. This shift to a prudential mode of reading took place gradually over the course of the following decades, and several different factors, besides Machiavelli, helped shape the trend: the association of Sallust with Tacitus, *pater prudentiae*; the influence of Lipsius, who ranked Sallust second only to Tacitus; the popularity of Sallust's works, especially in translation, at the French court; the enthusiastic propagation of his *Opera* by the German jurisconsult and philologist Christoph Coler; and Ben Jonson's representation of the *Catilina* on the London stage.[57] The new pragmatic approach also

---

the work of Paolo Paruta; in Germany, see the annotated editions by Johann Rivius and Christoph Coler, and in the Netherlands, the commentary on the *Catilina* by the Dutch jurist and philologist Dirk Graswinckel. William J. Bouwsma examines the surviving republican traditions in Venice in his "Three Types of Historiography in Post-Renaissance Italy," *History and Theory* 4 (1965): 303–14 and in *Venice and the Defense of Republican Liberty* (Berkeley: University of California Press, 1968).

56. *Discorsi politici*, ed. with introduction by G. Candeloro (Bologna: Zanichelli, 1943). See especially 1.7 (pp. 87–88).

57. It is also important to keep in mind the widespread distrust of Machiavelli in many countries or *ambienti*. On his reception in the sixteenth century, see for example, in general, Giuliano Procacci, *Studi sulla fortuna del Machiavelli* (Rome: Istituto storico italiano per l'età moderna e contemporanea, 1965); *Machiavellismo e antimachiavellici nel Cinquecento* in *Atti del Convegno di Perugia* 30, IX - 1, X, 1969 (Florence, 1969); (for England) Felix Raab, *The English Face of Machiavelli* (London: Routledge &

432   *Journal of Medieval and Renaissance Studies*, 23 (1993) 3

reflected, of course, the growing consensus for strong government—
evident in the spread of *politique* theories, Bodinian concepts of sovereignty, and doctrines of divine-right monarchy—at a time when
much of northern Europe was devastated or threatened by civil and
religious strife.[58]

The growing tendency to couple Sallust with Tacitus was particularly symptomatic of the changing attitudes. In the early Renaissance,
Sallust had regularly been linked with Livy and Caesar in a triumvirate
of Roman historians, authors who had embraced the ideology of *virtus*
and *gloria* and who had undertaken (or justified) their task as a form
of public service: a means of preserving the memory of ancient valor,
inculcating civic virtues, inspiring pride in an expanding empire. If in
the later Renaissance Sallust was paired more frequently with Tacitus,
it suggests a growing affinity with the disillusioned, critical spirit
and pragmatic attitudes that characterized (in part) their political
thought.[59] While Tacitus excelled in exposing the *arcana imperii*,
Sallust unmasked the self-seeking aims of party leaders. If Tacitus advocated monarchy where republican government had failed, and acqui-
esced in tyranny rather than encourage futile opposition, Sallust also

Kegan Paul, 1964); and (for France) Antonio D'Andrea, "The Political and Ideological
Context of Innocent Gentillet's *Anti-Machiavel*," in *Renaissance Quarterly* 33 (1970)
and Donald R. Kelley, "Murd'rous Machiavel in France: A Post Mortem," *Political
Science Quarterly* 85 (1970): 545–59.

58. On Tacitism in the Renaissance, see especially Peter Burke, "Tacitism," in T. A.
Dorey, ed., *Tacitus* (London: Routledge & Kegan Paul, 1969), 149–71; Antonio La
Penna, "Vivere sotto i tiranni: un tema tacitiano da Guicciardini a Diderot," in Bolgar,
ed., *Classical Influences on European Culture A.D. 1500–1700*, 295–304; Arnaldo Momig-
liano, "The First Political Commentary on Tacitus," *Journal of Roman Studies* 37
(1947): 91–102, reprinted in *Essays on Ancient and Modern Historiography*, 205–29;
Kenneth C. Schellhase, "Tacitus in the Political Thought of Machiavelli"; idem,
Tacitus in Renaissance Political Thought; J. H. M. Salmon, "Cicero and Tacitus in
Sixteenth-Century France"; idem, "Stoicism and Roman Example: Seneca and Tacitus
in Jacobean England," *Journal of the History of Ideas* 50 (1989): 199–225; André
Stegmann, "Le Tacitisme: Programme pour un nouvel essai de définition," *Il pensiero
politico* 2 (1969): 445–58; and Whitfield, "Livy > Tacitus." The only notable men-
tion of Sallust in association with Tacitus, however, appears in the essays by Morris
W. Croll on the vogue of Atticist rhetoric in the late sixteenth and early seventeenth
centuries; see J. Max Patrick and R. O. Evans, eds., *Style, Rhetoric, and Rhythm*
(Princeton: Princeton University Press, 1966).

59. The growing preference for the *genus humile* reflected a change in literary and
rhetorical taste from the elaborate Asianism of forensic oratory to the simpler, more
sober style of Atticist prose, and in turn a different intellectual atmosphere. The qualities of brevity and conciseness, the figures of wit and thought, were suited to philosophical essays, the confidential correspondence of royal counsellors, and the subtle,
rational analysis of political interest. On corresponding changes in rhetorical tastes and
ancient models, see especially Morris W. Croll's essays in *Style, Rhetoric, and Rhythm*
and Marc Fumaroli, *L'Age de l'éloquence* (Geneva: Droz, 1980).

Osmond · Sallust and Machiavelli   433

sympathized with the need for public order and a strong government to enforce that order.

Certainly Sallust was no proponent of monarchy, let alone autocracy, but his repeated denunciations of factional strife, his aversion to *novae res*, and his appeals for vigorous leadership and decisive action could further the cause of authoritarian regimes, as could many *sententiae* taken (in or out of context) from the speeches in his monographs and *Historiae*. His *Epistulae ad Caesarem* called for lasting peace and offered advice to a leader whose position, at least from the standpoint of the Renaissance, was clearly monarchical. Passages in the *Catilina* appeared to condone the use of extralegal methods in times of emergency. As Cato himself advised:

> Nunc uero non id agitur, bonisne an malis moribus uiuamus, neque quantum aut quam magnificum imperium populi Romani sit, sed haec, quoiuscumque modi uidentur, nostra an nobiscum una hostium futura sint. . . . Sint sane, quoniam ita se mores habent, liberales ex sociorum fortunis, sint misericordes in furibus aerari: ne illi sanguinem nostrum largiantur et, dum paucis sceleratis parcunt, bonos omnis perditum eant. . . . Non uotis neque suppliciis muliebribus auxilia deorum parantur: uigilando, agundo, bene consulendo prospere omnia cedunt.[60]

> Now . . . the question before us is not whether our morals are good or bad, nor how great or glorious the empire of the Roman people is, but whether all that we have, however we regard it, is to be ours, or with ourselves is to belong to the enemy. . . . Let these men by all means, since such is the fashion of the time, be liberal at the expense of our allies, let them be merciful to plunderers of the treasury; but let them not be prodigal of our blood, and in sparing a few scoundrels bring ruin upon all good men. . . . Not by vows nor womanish entreaties is the help of the gods secured; it is always through watchfulness, vigorous action, and wisdom in counsel that success comes.

By elaborating upon Sallust's ideas in terms of political necessity, Machiavelli had helped create the intellectual context for a prudential evaluation of his work. Many of the late Renaissance historians and political thinkers who quoted Sallust on the benefits of strong leadership and the need for public order had indeed read his work in the company of the *Prince* and *Discourses*. The Flemish scholar Justus

---

60. *Bellum Catilinae* 52.10, 12, 29.

434 *Journal of Medieval and Renaissance Studies*, 23 (1993) 3

Lipsius drew frequently on Sallust, whom he considered second in importance as a political authority only to Tacitus, in his *Politicorum sive Civilis Doctrinae Libri Sex* of 1589.[61] The book on *civilis prudentia* cited Lepidus's speech in the *Historiae* on the need for *severitas* and Cato's speech in the *Catilina* on administering strong, preventive punishments. In confronting the moral dilemma posed by the use of fraud and deception in governing a state, Lipsius attempted to reach a compromise. He did not agree (on this occasion) with the remark of Lepidus that any and all means of securing power were honorable.[62] But *diffidentia* and *corruptio*, such as Sallust had described elsewhere, could reasonably be mixed with *prudentia* as long as they were used in moderation and, as Machiavelli had argued, the end justified the means.

In early Stuart England, in an atmosphere of political intrigue and mounting religious tensions, contemporary conspirators were branded as "worse-than-Catilines," while the figure of Cato was exalted as a model of Stoic courage and constancy.[63] Robert Dallington, a skillful courtier and shrewd observer of monarchies, relied upon Sallust, together with Tacitus and Seneca among the ancients and Machiavelli among the moderns, to illustrate his *Aphorismes Civil and Military*, a commentary on Guicciardini's *Storia d'Italia* which he published in 1613.[64] In his chapters on diplomacy and "public relations," he com-

61. *Politicorum sive Civilis Doctrinae Libri Sex* in *Opera Omnia*, 4 vols. (Vesalia: Andreas van Hoogenhuysen, 1675), vol. 4. Sallust, like Tacitus and Seneca, is cited throughout the work, but see especially book 4 on *civilis prudentia* and the *notae* to book 6. Lipsius's preferences among Roman historians were already adumbrated in his Jena oration of 1572. In the preface to his "Notae" on Tacitus's *Opera*, first published in 1574, he clarified his judgment of Sallust and also defined more closely his relationship to Tacitus. Among the historians of the Republic, he concluded, only Sallust possessed all three qualities required of a good historian: *delectatio, fides*, and the ability to speak *ad vitam*. Tacitus himself was then introduced as his *imitator*. For the text of his preface to the first edition of Tacitus, see Robert W. Ulery, Jr., "Tacitus," *Catalogus Translationum et Commentariorum* 6 (Washington, DC: Catholic University of America Press, 1986), 113. On the Jena oration, see Kenneth Schellhase, *Tacitus*, 118.

62. Sallust, "Oratio Lepidi," *Historiarum fragmenta selecta* 1.55.8. L. A. Burd noted this *sententia* in his discussion of Machiavelli's political realism and its classical parallels; see *Il principe*, ed. L. A. Burd (Oxford: Clarendon, 1897), 307.

63. Sallust was often cited in tandem with Tacitus. Yet, while Tacitus served chiefly as "a vehicle of discontent," Sallust could be safely used to bolster the authority of monarchy. On Tacitus in early seventeenth-century England, see J. H. M. Salmon, "Stoicism and Roman Example." On the frequent allusions to Catilinarian conspirators, especially in the theater, see Barbara N. De Luna, *Jonson's Romish Plot: A Study of "Catiline" in Its Historical Context* (Oxford: Clarendon, 1967).

64. Robert Dallington, *Aphorismes Civill and Militarie* (London: Edward Blount, 1613; 2nd ed. London: Robert Allot, 1629). On the author see Salmon, "Stoicism and Roman Example," 215-17.

bined Sallustian aphorisms with Machiavelli's warnings to beware of other rulers' personal interests in seeking alliance, to avoid taking advice from persons one had previously injured, and, in case of popular uprisings, to secure the favor of the masses by punishing only the leaders of the insurrection. In times of emergency, even force and deception were permissible, and here Dallington bolstered Machiavellian precepts and Lipsius's doctrine of *prudentia mixta* with Cato's injunction to his fellow senators: "Let not that gentleness and clemency of yours lead to your own undoing." Security is but justice, he concluded. Otherwise, as Cato had warned: "While you spare the wicked, you allow the good to perish."[65]

Those who read Sallust in association with Machiavelli were often influenced of course more by contemporary perceptions of the Florentine author and his reputation than by anything he had actually said or even implied. Such is the case, for instance, in the reactions (both positive and negative) to his treatment of conspiracies in book 3 of the *Discorsi*. At the court of Henry III, Jérôme de Chomedey attached to his new French version of the *Catilina* a "discours de Machiavel touchant les conjurations."[66] Like his *Histoire de la conjuration de Catilina*, it was meant to defend the principle of strong, authoritarian rule and foster obedience to the French monarchy. As Machiavelli, quoting Tacitus, had exhorted the subjects of a prince to tolerate all rulers, good or bad, "lest rebellion involve them and their country in ruin," so Sallust, Chomedey concluded, had demonstrated the fate of would-be revolutionaries.

In post-Tridentine Italy, where most political thinkers sought to reconcile *ragion di stato* with moral and religious orthodoxy, the proponents of absolute monarchy either substituted Sallust, like Tacitus, for the censored Machiavelli or associated all three writers in the same category of "evil counsellors."[67] The Neapolitan historian of the mid-

---

65. Cf. Sallust: "Ne ista uobis mansuetudo et misericordia, si illi arma ceperint, in miseriam conuortat"; *Bellum Catilinae* 52.27. "Sint sane, quoniam ita se mores habent, liberales ex sociorum fortunis, sint misericordes in furibus aerari: ne illi sanguinem nostrum largiantur et, dum paucis sceleratis parcunt, bonos ominis perditum eant"; ibid. 52.12.

66. Chomedey mentions in his preface "Au Roy" that he has added to his translation of the *Catilina* "un discours de Machiavel touchant les conjurations, pourceque l'a dedans y a une fort bonne instruction, tant pour les Princes que pour les sujets, accompagnée d'une infinité de beaulx exemples, entre lesquels celuy de Catilin n'est oublié." In the same years, Henri III's "lecteur italien," Iacopo Corbinelli, annotated his copy of the *Discorsi* with references to Sallust and Tacitus.

67. Giuseppe Toffanin created the classic definitions of "tacitismo nero," "tacitismo critico," and "tacitismo rosso," in *Machiavelli e il "tacitismo:" la "politica storica" al*

436   *Journal of Medieval and Renaissance Studies*, 23 (1993) 3

sixteenth century Camillo Porzio combined observations from Sallust's *Catilina* with precepts taken from book 3, chapter 6 of the *Discorsi*—though he was careful not to mention Machiavelli by name.[68] On the other hand, Iacopo Bonfadio, author of the *Annales Genuenses* of circa 1548–50, placed the *Catilina* in the same class of dangerously subversive books as "the life of Nero" and the *Prince*. Echoing Bonfadio's words in his own work, *La congiura di Gio. Luigi de' Fieschi* of 1629, Agostino Mascardi warned his readers that, by teaching those wicked "materie di Stato," the *Catilina*—like the works of Machiavelli and Tacitus—might actually incite aspiring rebels.[69] In the suspicious atmosphere of certain Counter-Reformation circles, Sallust's monograph

---

tempo della Controriforma (Padua: Draghi, 1921) to characterize the different reactions to Machiavelli's work. A recent study of Machiavelli's role in sixteenth-century Italy is Robert Bireley's *The Counter-Reformation Prince: Anti-Machiavellianism or Catholic Statecraft in Early Modern Europe* (Chapel Hill: University of North Carolina Press, 1990).

68. Shortly after the abortive coup of Gianluigi Fieschi in Genoa in 1548, the historian Uberto Foglietta contrasted the *concordia civium*, which Genoa (he declared) had enjoyed under the just and benevolent guidance of Andrea Doria, with the factional discord that had fostered the criminal ambitions of the young Fieschi. *Ex universa historia rerum Europae suorum temporum . . . ; Coniuratio Ioannis Ludovici Flisci; Tumultus Neapolitani . . . ; Caedes Petri Ludovici Farnesii Placentiae Ducis* (Naples, Iosephus Cacchius, 1571). Brief notes on the references to or borrowings from Sallust in the conspiracy histories of this period are found in Antonio La Penna's "Appendice seconda," *Sallustio*. Iacopo Maria Campanacci endeavored to make Fieschi appear less wicked than Catiline in his *Genuensis Reipublicae motus a Jo. Aloysio Flisco excitatus eiusdem et L. Sergii Catilinae comparatio* (Bologna: Benacius, 1588), but observed that if studying criminal deeds had any justification at all, it was only for the sake of producing the right "antidote." In the meantime, the Neapolitan historian Camillo Porzio had introduced Sallustian character sketches and speeches into his own account of the uprising in *Storia d'Italia*, while paraphrasing Machiavelli's warnings against potential conspirators: *L'istoria d'Italia nell'anno MDXLVIII e la descrizione del Regno di Napoli*, intro. by A. Gervasio (Naples, 1839) and *La congiura de' baroni del Regno di Napoli contra il Re Ferdinando Primo e gli altri scritti*, ed. E. Pontieri (Naples: Tramater, 1958). It was the "pravi passioni" of the barons, Porzio argued, that had destroyed domestic harmony and paved the way for foreign invasion.

69. Iacopo Bonfadio, *Annales Genuenses* (Genoa: Girolamo Bartoli, 1586); Agostino Mascardi, *La congiura del conte Gio. Luigi de Fieschi* (Antwerp: n.p., 1629). Such judgments were often accompanied by criticisms of Sallust's "unfair" treatment of Cicero, as for example in Mascardi's *Dell'arte istorica* (Florence: Le Monnier, 1859), a tradition that had its Renaissance origins in Costanzo Felici's *De coniuratione L. Catilinae liber unus* (Rome: Iacobus Mazochius, 1518).

Some trace of prudential readings of Sallust might be seen in the conscious or unconscious blending of traits characteristic of Sallust the historian with the attributes of his great-nephew, C. Sallustius Crispus II, of Tacitean fame. See, for instance, the portraits of both Sallusts in Giovanni Botero, *Della ragion di stato*, ed. Luigi Firpo (Turin: Unione Tipografico, 1948) and Traiano Boccalini, *Ragguagli di Parnaso e scritti minori*, ed. G. Rua and L. Firpo, in *Scrittori d'Italia*, vols. 6, 39, and 199 (Bari: Laterza, 1910–48).

might still be admired as a literary work, but it was also becoming a target of anti-Machiavellism and "critical Tacitism." [70]

Neither Machiavelli nor the other Renaissance writers who appropriated Sallust's ideas and language made any conscious attempt to understand his thought in its original framework of meaning.[71] Occasionally a historian or philologist might comment on his factual accuracy and objectivity (or lack thereof), but no one undertook to explain his views (or bias) in light of contemporary Roman politics and intellectual life. For the most part, readers were preoccupied with making ancient history relevant to their own experience and tended, as a result, to treat his work selectively, borrowing, imitating, adapting whatever seemed to suit their aims.[72]

The same readers, however—Machiavelli foremost among them—discovered in Sallust's works a remarkable range of ideas and themes. If they approached his writing from the standpoint of their own political loyalties and prejudices, they also brought to light the rich variety of meanings and associations inherent in it: evidence of his capacity, as a political historian, to elicit new views and suggest new interpretations in an ongoing dialogue with each new generation.[73] The age

70. Sallust's writing was generally admired as a model of language and style, either as an alternative to the "easy, flowing" prose of Livy (as quattrocento humanists had proposed), or as a forerunner of the Silver Age prose represented by Tacitus and Seneca. Some of the more zealous Ciceronians, however, found fault with the literary aspects of his works as well with its content. His chief critic was the Paduan scholar Paolo Beni. See P. B. Diffley, *Paolo Beni: A Biographical and Critical Study* (Oxford: Clarendon, 1988).

71. Quentin Skinner discusses the methodology of understanding a work and uncovering an author's intention in his "Meanings and Understanding in the History of Ideas," *History and Theory* 8 (1969): 3–53. On Renaissance modes of reading classical texts and in particular the question of allegorical or imitative as opposed to historical and critical approaches, see Anthony Grafton's articles, including: "On the Scholarship of Politian and Its Context," *Journal of the Warburg and Courtauld Institutes* 40 (1977): 152–62, and "Renaissance Readers and Ancient Texts: Comments on Some Commentaries," *Renaissance Quarterly* 38 (1985): 615–49. James Hankins sets forth a working typology of reading and interpreting classical texts in the fifteenth century in the Introduction to his *Plato in the Italian Renaissance*, 2 vols. (Leiden: Brill, 1990), 1:18–26.

72. Much of the Renaissance scholarship on Sallust, as seen in the textual and antiquarian commentaries from the mid-sixteenth century on, was likewise undertaken not for the purpose of recovering the original text "for its own sake," or of reconstructing the past "as it really was," but as a means of making the author's work more accessible and, in turn, relevant to contemporary interests and issues.

73. On "Rezeptionsgeschichte" see Hans R. Jauss's contributions to *Theory of Aesthetics Reception and Literary Communication, Proceedings of the IXth Congress of the International Comparative Literature Association*, vol. 2, ed. A. Konstantinovic, M. Naumann, and H. R. Jauss (Innsbruck: Institut für Sprachwissenschaft der Uni-

438   *Journal of Medieval and Renaissance Studies*, 23 (1993) 3

to which Sallust himself belonged was one of the most dramatic periods of change in the ancient world, an era that witnessed the transformation of a republican government into monarchy and the transition from civic and communal ideas to philosophies of individualism and panegyrics of *pax et princeps*. Whether he celebrated the values of *libertas* and *virtus*, denounced the corruption of party politics, or defended the established order, Sallust could express the attitudes and preoccupations of a new age of competing ideologies.

I would like to express my thanks to John H. M. Salmon and James Hankins for their valuable comments on earlier versions of this paper and to the American Philosophical Society for a recent research grant in Italy.

Postscript to pp. 428–29.

A further illustration of Machiavelli's pragmatic approach to the matter of conspiracies and, in turn, to the reading of Sallust, is found in book 7, chapters 33–34 of his *Istorie fiorentine*, where he relates the plot of Girolamo Olgiati and his accomplices against the "tyrant" Galeazzo Sforza of Milan in 1476. On the one hand, Machiavelli described the republican ideas of the Milanese humanist Cola Montano, the alleged instigator of the conspiracy, in phrases echoing Sallust's praises of *libertas* and *virtus* in *Catilina* 7.2-3. In commenting, however, on the outcome of the plot (which ended with the arrest and execution of Olgiati), he analyzed the events purely in terms of success and failure, thus providing political advice for both princes and their republican opponents.

> The deed of these unfortunate young men, although secretly planned and courageously executed, produced no effect, because those upon whom they had relied for defence and support neither defended nor supported them. Therefore let princes live and carry themselves in such a way that they are loved and honoured, then no one can hope in killing them to escape himself, and let conspirators remember that all thoughts of relying upon the multitude are utterly vain, because although the people may be discontented they will never join or support you in danger. (*Florentine History*, trans. W.K. Marriott (New York, rpt, 1976), 313. For other accounts of this conspiracy, with references to Sallust's *Catilina*, and bibliography relating to the question of Catilinarianism, see my "*Princeps Historiae Romanae*: Sallust in Renaissance Political Thought," *Memoirs of the American Academy in Rome* 40 (1996) 101–43 (at 117 and notes).)

---

versität Innsbruck, 1980) and *Toward an Aesthetic of Reception*, trans. T. Bahti, Theory and History of Literature, vol. 2 (Minneapolis: University of Minnesota Press, 1982).

Name Index